LRC - Batavia HS
Batavia, IL 60510

AMERICAN HEROES

MAGILL'S CHOICE

AMERICAN HEROES

Volume 2
Althea Gibson — Martina Navratilova
351-718

from
The Editors of Salem Press

SALEM PRESS, INC.
Pasadena, California   Hackensack, New Jersey

Cover image: © Joseph Helfenberger/Dreamstime.com

Copyright © 2009, by Salem Press, Inc.
All rights in this book are reserved. No part of this work may be used or reproduced in any manner whatsoever or transmitted in any form or by any means, electronic or mechanical, including photocopy, recording, or any information storage and retrieval system, without written permission from the copyright owner except in the case of brief quotations embodied in critical articles and reviews. For information address the publisher, Salem Press, Inc., P.O. Box 50062, Pasadena, California 91115.

∞ The paper used in these volumes conforms to the American National Standard for Permanence of Paper for Printed Library Materials, Z39.48-1992 (R1997)

Some of the essays in this work originally appeared in the following Salem Press sets: *Great Lives from History: The 18th Century* (2006), *The 19th Century* (2006), and *The Twentieth Century* (2008), updated through 2008. New material has been added.

Library of Congress Cataloging-in-Publication Data

American heroes / from the editors of Salem Press.
    p. cm. — (Magill's choice)
    Includes bibliographical references and index.
    ISBN 978-1-58765-457-2 (set : alk. paper) — ISBN 978-1-58765-458-9 (v. 1 : alk. paper) — ISBN 978-1-58765-459-6 (v. 2 : alk. paper) — ISBN 978-1-58765-460-2 (v. 3 : alk. paper) 1. Heroes—United States—Biography. 2. Celebrities—United States—Biography. I. Salem Press.
   CT105.A47 2008
   920.02—dc22

2008017124

First Printing

PRINTED IN CANADA

Contents

Complete List of Contents xxxiii
Key to Pronunciation xxxix

Althea Gibson 351
John Glenn 356
Emma Goldman 361
Al Gore 367
William Crawford Gorgas 371
Billy Graham 376
Nathanael Greene 380
Wayne Gretzky 387

Mary A. Hallaren 390
William F. Halsey 393
Fannie Lou Hamer 398
Alexander Hamilton 402
Learned Hand 408
Barbara Harris 413
Ernest Hemingway 417
Patrick Henry 422
Katharine Hepburn 426
Aileen Clarke Hernandez 432
Wild Bill Hickok 437
Oveta Culp Hobby 441
Bob Hope 446
Grace Murray Hopper 450
Sam Houston 455
Samuel Gridley Howe 460
Dolores Huerta 465
Charles Evans Hughes 471
Cordell Hull 478

Andrew Jackson 483
Jesse Jackson 488
Stonewall Jackson 494
Thomas Jefferson 498
Steve Jobs 503
Bobby Jones 507
John Paul Jones 513
Mother Jones 519

Barbara Jordan	524
Michael Jordan	529
Chief Joseph	533
Kamehameha I	538
Helen Keller	542
John F. Kennedy	546
Robert F. Kennedy	551
Billie Jean King	557
Martin Luther King, Jr.	562
Robert M. La Follette	569
Robert E. Lee	574
John L. Lewis	579
Meriwether Lewis and William Clark	584
Liliuokalani	589
Abraham Lincoln	594
Charles A. Lindbergh	600
Belva A. Lockwood	606
Henry Cabot Lodge	610
Huey Long	616
Joe Louis	621
Juliette Gordon Low	627
Shannon W. Lucid	632
Douglas MacArthur	635
Dolley Madison	642
James Madison	646
Malcolm X	650
Wilma Mankiller	655
Rocky Marciano	660
George C. Marshall	664
John Marshall	669
Thurgood Marshall	675
Golda Meir	680
Thomas Merton	686
John R. Mott	690
John Muir	696
Edward R. Murrow	700
Ralph Nader	705
Carry Nation	709
Martina Navratilova	714

Complete List of Contents

Volume 1

Publisher's Note vii
List of Contributors ix
Complete List of Contents xvii
Key to Pronunciation xxiii

Hank Aaron 1
Ralph Abernathy 4
Abigail Adams 9
John Adams 14
Samuel Adams 19
Jane Addams 26
Muhammad Ali 31
Maya Angelou 38
Susan B. Anthony 43
Neil Armstrong 48

Robert D. Ballard 55
Benjamin Banneker 60
Clara Barton 64
Alexander Graham Bell 70
Mary McLeod Bethune 75
Black Hawk 80
Daniel Boone 84
Omar Nelson Bradley 89
Louis D. Brandeis 94
Joseph Brant 100
William J. Brennan 105
John Brown 109
Olympia Brown 115
Ralph Bunche 119
Richard Byrd 124

Frances Xavier Cabrini 129
Rachel Carson 133
Jimmy Carter 138
George Washington Carver 144

Mary Ann Shadd Cary 149
Carrie Chapman Catt 152
Wilt Chamberlain 158
César Chávez 161
Shirley Chisholm 164
Hillary Rodham Clinton 171
Ty Cobb 175
Bessie Coleman 179
Bill Cosby 183
Crazy Horse 187
David Crockett 194
Walter Cronkite 198

Clarence Darrow 201
Dorothy Day 207
Eugene V. Debs 212
Stephen Decatur 217
Jack Dempsey 221
Joe DiMaggio 227
Walt Disney 231
Dorothea Dix 238
Jimmy Doolittle 243
Helen Gahagan Douglas 247
William O. Douglas 251
Frederick Douglass 254
W. E. B. Du Bois 259

Amelia Earhart 265
Mary Baker Eddy 270
Marian Wright Edelman 277
Thomas Alva Edison 281
Albert Einstein 287
Dwight D. Eisenhower 292
Chris Evert 297

Louis Farrakhan 302
Betty Ford 305
Benjamin Franklin 309
John C. Frémont 315
Betty Friedan 322

William Lloyd Garrison 327
Marcus Garvey 333

Complete List of Contents

Bill Gates	337
Lou Gehrig	341
Geronimo	346

Volume 2

Complete List of Contents	xxxiii
Key to Pronunciation	xxxix

Althea Gibson	351
John Glenn	356
Emma Goldman	361
Al Gore	367
William Crawford Gorgas	371
Billy Graham	376
Nathanael Greene	380
Wayne Gretzky	387
Mary A. Hallaren	390
William F. Halsey	393
Fannie Lou Hamer	398
Alexander Hamilton	402
Learned Hand	408
Barbara Harris	413
Ernest Hemingway	417
Patrick Henry	422
Katharine Hepburn	426
Aileen Clarke Hernandez	432
Wild Bill Hickok	437
Oveta Culp Hobby	441
Bob Hope	446
Grace Murray Hopper	450
Sam Houston	455
Samuel Gridley Howe	460
Dolores Huerta	465
Charles Evans Hughes	471
Cordell Hull	478
Andrew Jackson	483
Jesse Jackson	488
Stonewall Jackson	494
Thomas Jefferson	498
Steve Jobs	503

Bobby Jones	507
John Paul Jones	513
Mother Jones	519
Barbara Jordan	524
Michael Jordan	529
Chief Joseph	533
Kamehameha I	538
Helen Keller	542
John F. Kennedy	546
Robert F. Kennedy	551
Billie Jean King	557
Martin Luther King, Jr.	562
Robert M. La Follette	569
Robert E. Lee	574
John L. Lewis	579
Meriwether Lewis and William Clark	584
Liliuokalani	589
Abraham Lincoln	594
Charles A. Lindbergh	600
Belva A. Lockwood	606
Henry Cabot Lodge	610
Huey Long	616
Joe Louis	621
Juliette Gordon Low	627
Shannon W. Lucid	632
Douglas MacArthur	635
Dolley Madison	642
James Madison	646
Malcolm X	650
Wilma Mankiller	655
Rocky Marciano	660
George C. Marshall	664
John Marshall	669
Thurgood Marshall	675
Golda Meir	680
Thomas Merton	686
John R. Mott	690
John Muir	696
Edward R. Murrow	700

Complete List of Contents

Ralph Nader	705
Carry Nation	709
Martina Navratilova	714

VOLUME 3

Complete List of Contents	xlix
Key to Pronunciation	lv
Jack Nicklaus	719
Chester W. Nimitz	723
Barack Obama	728
Sandra Day O'Connor	733
Osceola	739
Jesse Owens	742
Thomas Paine	747
Rosa Parks	752
George S. Patton	758
Alice Paul	763
Robert Edwin Peary	768
John J. Pershing	774
Colin Powell	779
A. Philip Randolph	785
Jeannette Rankin	793
Ronald Reagan	798
Red Cloud	805
Walter Reed	809
Paul Revere	814
Sally Ride	819
Paul Robeson	824
Jackie Robinson	832
John D. Rockefeller	838
Knute Rockne	844
Eleanor Roosevelt	847
Franklin D. Roosevelt	852
Theodore Roosevelt	859
John Ross	864
Bill Russell	868
Babe Ruth	874

Sacagawea	880
Jonas Salk	885
Pete Sampras	889
Margaret Sanger	893
Junípero Serra	898
Alan Shepard	902
William Tecumseh Sherman	907
Sitting Bull	913
Margaret Chase Smith	917
Elizabeth Cady Stanton	922
Adlai E. Stevenson	928
James Stewart	934
Anne Sullivan	938
Ida Tarbell	942
Zachary Taylor	947
Tecumseh	952
Norman Thomas	956
Jim Thorpe	963
Harry S. Truman	968
Sojourner Truth	974
Harriet Tubman	979
Nat Turner	984
Earl Warren	988
Booker T. Washington	994
George Washington	1000
John Wayne	1005
Ida B. Wells-Barnett	1009
Elie Wiesel	1013
Hazel Wightman	1019
Oprah Winfrey	1023
Tiger Woods	1029
Orville and Wilbur Wright	1034
Chuck Yeager	1040
Babe Didrikson Zaharias	1044
Subjects by Category	1051
Ethnicity Index	1057
Subject and Personages Index	1061

Key to Pronunciation

Vowel Sounds

Symbol	Spelled (Pronounced)
Symbol	*Spelled (Pronounced)*
a	answer (AN-suhr), laugh (laf), sample (SAM-puhl), that (that)
ah	father (FAH-thur), hospital (HAHS-pih-tuhl)
aw	awful (AW-fuhl), caught (kawt)
ay	blaze (blayz), fade (fayd), waiter (WAYT-ur), weigh (way)
eh	bed (behd), head (hehd), said (sehd)
ee	believe (bee-LEEV), cedar (SEE-dur), leader (LEED-ur), liter (LEE-tur)
ew	boot (bewt), lose (lewz)
i	buy (bi), height (hit), lie (li), surprise (sur-PRIZ)
ih	bitter (BIH-tur), pill (pihl)
o	cotton (KO-tuhn), hot (hot)
oh	below (bee-LOH), coat (koht), note (noht), wholesome (HOHL-suhm)
oo	good (good), look (look)
ow	couch (kowch), how (how)
oy	boy (boy), coin (koyn)
uh	about (uh-BOWT), butter (BUH-tuhr), enough (ee-NUHF), other (UH-thur)

Consonant Sounds

Symbol	Spelled (Pronounced)
Symbol	*Spelled (Pronounced)*
ch	beach (beech), chimp (chihmp)
g	beg (behg), disguise (dihs-GIZ), get (geht)
j	digit (DIH-juht), edge (ehj), jet (jeht)
k	cat (kat), kitten (KIH-tuhn), hex (hehks)
s	cellar (SEHL-ur), save (sayv), scent (sehnt)
sh	champagne (sham-PAYN), issue (IH-shew), shop (shop)
ur	birth (burth), disturb (dihs-TURB), earth (urth), letter (LEH-tur)
y	useful (YEWS-fuhl), young (yuhng)
z	business (BIHZ-nehs), zest (zehst)
zh	vision (VIH-zhuhn)

AMERICAN HEROES

ALTHEA GIBSON

" You ... aren't considered a real champion until you have defended your title successfully. Winning it once can be a fluke; winning it twice proves you are the best. "

Tennis player

The first African American to win a Wimbledon singles title and the winner of five major singles championships, Gibson was an important figure in establishing blacks as equal competitors at the highest levels of the tennis world. She overcame the prejudice of the tennis world at a time when racial barriers still operated in the sport. She will be remembered as one of the stellar performers in the history of women's tennis.

Born: August 25, 1927; Silver, South Carolina
Died: September 28, 2003; East Orange, New Jersey
Area of achievement: Sports

EARLY LIFE

Althea Gibson (ahl-THEE-ah GIHB-suhn) was born the eldest of the five children of Daniel Gibson and Anna Washington Gibson. Her parents worked in the South Carolina cotton fields; their families were sharecroppers and poor farmers. When Althea was three, her parents moved to New York City, and she grew up in Harlem during the 1930's. She was a rebellious child who was often absent from school. Her relationship with her father was stormy, and his treatment of her verged on physical abuse at times. She learned to defend herself in the dangerous world of the streets and honed the courage and self-reliance that would carry her to the top of women's tennis.

Her athletic career began on the paddle tennis courts of a Police Athletic League "play street" near her home. While she learned tennis on regular courts, she competed in local tournaments in the New York area. After she won the American Tennis Association girls' singles crown in 1944 and 1945 and was runner-up for the women's title in 1946, she moved to North Carolina with the family of R. W. Johnson. There she attended high school and practiced her game. In 1948, she won the national American Tennis Association's women's title. She won the championship of this African American tennis association for the following nine years.

LIFE'S WORK

Gibson entered Florida A&M University in 1949 on a tennis scholarship. Meanwhile, she pursued her tournament career. She played well in the National Indoor Tennis Championships in 1949, and she won the Eastern Indoor championship of the U.S. Lawn Tennis Association (USLTA) in March of 1950. Nevertheless, she faced an informal racial barrier because of the unwillingness of the USLTA to invite a black player to participate in the U.S. Open at Forest Hills. The USLTA used the excuse that Gibson had not played in enough tournaments to demonstrate her talents on the highest level.

A former women's champion, Alice Marble, provided a decisive boost to Gibson's career at this key moment. In a hard-hitting editorial for *American Lawn Tennis* magazine, Marble urged that Gibson be given a chance to prove herself in genuine competition. "If Althea Gibson represents a challenge to the present crop of women's players, it is only fair that they should meet that challenge on the courts, where tennis is played." The USLTA relented, and Gibson was invited to the U.S. Open in August of 1950, the first African American to participate in the tournament. Her debut was a memorable one. In her second-round match, she was ahead of the noted player Louise Brough in the third set when rain stopped play. She was on the verge of upsetting a Wimbledon and U.S. Open champion. The night's interval and a tense press conference after the match was suspended worked against Gibson's concentration. The next day Brough came back to beat Gibson, 6-1, 3-6, 9-7. Despite the setback, Gibson had proved that she could play at the highest level of tennis. Her tennis talent, however, was still raw and undisciplined. Her performances varied between excellence and mediocrity. The top women players knew that she might crack if they put pressure on her weaker strokes. She had confidence in her own ability but needed to see her game mature.

For the next six years, however, Gibson did not live up to the expectations that her first appearance at the U.S. Open had created. She played in Great Britain at Wimbledon, the pinnacle of the tennis world, in June of 1951, the first African American to do

Althea Gibson.
(International Tennis
Hall of Fame)

so, but lost in the quarter-finals. She rose to a ranking of ninth in the United States in 1952 and moved up to seventh a year later. She then fell back to thirteenth in 1954. In the meantime, to support herself in an era when tennis was still ostensibly an amateur sport, she taught in the physical education department at Lincoln University in Missouri during 1954 and 1955. By now, she had given serious thought to retiring from tennis and pursuing a military career.

Gibson then received an offer to be one of the American tennis players on a goodwill tour of Asia for the State Department in late 1955. Playing tennis on such a sustained basis revitalized Gibson's game, and she found that her talents were still sharp. She went on a run of victories that impressed the doubters in the tennis world. In 1956, she won sixteen of the eighteen tournaments she entered before Wimbledon, including the Asiatic women's singles crown, the Indian national title, and the French indoor doubles championship with Angela Buxton of Great Britain. She did all this while living from week to week on meager financial resources. Tennis in the 1950's was still an "amateur" sport, and an African American player had to struggle to survive without the monetary help that white players enjoyed. Gibson won her first Grand Slam tournament, the French Open, on the red clay of Roland Garros Stadium over Angela Morton, 6-0, 12-10. The American press finally began to take notice of her accomplishments on the court. Her streak of singles victories came to an end when Shirley Fry beat her in the quarter-finals at Wimbledon. The British crowds rooted against her, and their journalists denounced the evident display of racial intolerance that so unnerved Gibson. Nevertheless, she won the doubles title, again teaming with Buxton. Out of this experience came a lifelong friendship with Buxton, a talented British player.

Gibson continued her strong play throughout the remainder of 1956. She won several grass court singles titles and reached the finals of the U.S. Open in September. She lost to Shirley Fry, 6-3, 6-4, in a match in which she did not play her best. The tennis circuit then led her to Australia, where she teamed with Fry to win the doubles crown at the Australian Open. Unfortunately, she lost to Fry in the singles of the tournament several days later.

The rest of 1957 saw Gibson reach the top of the world of women's tennis. Fry had retired, and Gibson now sensed that she could defeat the other players that she faced. She won several warm-up tournaments for Wimbledon and came into the fortnight's competition as the odds-on favorite. She reached the finals and played against Darlene Hard. The match was played in 96-degree heat. Gibson's serve worked well, and she was in command from the early points. When her 6-3, 6-2 victory was secured, she exclaimed, "At last, at last." Queen Elizabeth II presented Gibson with the trophy. Gibson also won the doubles championship with Hard. Her accomplishments vindicated her hard work and resolve to reach the top of the sport.

When Gibson returned to the United States, she received a ticker-tape parade in New York City. It was, she said, the greatest honor she had ever received. She capped her championship year with a victory at the U.S. Open over Louise Brough, 6-3, 6-2. Vice President Richard Nixon presented her with the trophy, and the crowd gave her a sustained round of applause.

The following year brought more victories for Gibson. She took the Wimbledon crown for the second time. She won over Angela Mortimer of Great Britain, 8-6, 6-2.

Gibson, Althea

Gibson went on to win the U.S. Open again with a three-set victory over Hard, 3-6, 6-1, 6-2. She then announced that she was retiring from amateur tennis. The trophies were nice, she said, but she had to make a living. Until 1958, she had never even earned enough money in a single year to require her to file an income tax return.

In her prime, Gibson was an overpowering tennis player. She stood five feet ten inches tall, and her powerful serve reminded many people of the speed and force of the serves of male players. Her volleys and overhead smash were also devastating. She exuded confidence on the court, a quality that sometimes irritated those who competed against her. Billie Jean King has said that Gibson was one of the most underrated champions in women's tennis. Given the obstacles she had to overcome at a time when racial bias permeated the sport, her record becomes even more impressive. Unlike modern women tennis players, Gibson did not blossom as a teenager. She was in her late twenties before her talents came together in championship form.

After her departure from amateur tennis, Gibson played professionally as an attraction with the Harlem Globetrotters during 1959. She competed on the Ladies Professional Golf Association tour for a time and coached tennis in New Jersey. She also served as the State Athletic Commissioner of New Jersey during the mid-1970's. Gibson had a well-acted supporting role in a John Wayne film set during the Civil War, *The Horse Soldiers* (1958). She married William Darben in 1965, but they were divorced, and her second marriage was to Sidney Llewellyn in 1983. Gibson was named to the Lawn Tennis Hall of Fame and Museum in 1971, to the Black Athletes Hall of Fame in 1974, and to the International Women's Sports Hall of Fame in 1980. She continued to teach and to play tennis, although she no longer competed in the professional arena. Her last years were a time of loneliness, personal depression, and persistent poverty as the tennis world had forgotten her and her championships. Her friend Buxton worked with others in the tennis community to make Gibson's life more comfortable than it otherwise would have been. Nonetheless, Gibson did not receive the full recognition that she deserved as a past champion. Only with her death in 2003 did there come a belated sense of what she had meant to her sport and to American society.

SIGNIFICANCE

Gibson earned a reputation as the greatest African American woman tennis player before the advent of Venus Williams and Serena Williams. Despite the prejudice and discrimination that confronted her during a period before the Civil Rights movement of the 1960's, she surmounted the obstacles that were placed in her path to become a dominant player of her era. From 1956 through 1958, she mastered the world of women's tennis, and she could have added more titles to her record if she had so desired. Unfortunately, Gibson's example did not lead to a surge of black women tennis players. The tennis establishment failed to encourage the development of young African Americans with potential to be top-flight players. The next great African American star would be the male player Arthur Ashe, who emerged in the following decade. Gibson was an outstanding champion. Her courage, will to win, and perseverance deserve more attention than they have received from historians of tennis and from scholars of women athletes in the United States.

—Karen Gould

FURTHER READING

Biracree, Tom. *Althea Gibson*. New York: Chelsea House, 1989. As one of the entries in the publisher's American Women of Achievement series for juvenile readers, this biography provides a fine introduction to Gibson's life and career and includes useful information regarding her activities after her retirement from professional competition.

Brown, Gene, ed. *The Complete Book of Tennis*. New York: Arno Press, 1980. This compilation of *The New York Times* coverage of tennis during the twentieth century contains excellent accounts of Gibson's major tournament victories during the 1950's.

Collins, Bud. *My Life with the Pros*. New York: E. P. Dutton, 1989. A longtime reporter of tennis, Collins covers Gibson's emergence as a tennis star, and his book gives a good sense of the obstacles Gibson faced from the white media and tennis establishment.

Davidson, Sue. *Changing the Game: The Stories of Tennis Champions Alice Marble and Althea Gibson*. Seattle: Seal Press, 1997. Looks at the careers of these two women in tennis and how Marble helped Gibson get a chance to play in major tournaments despite the racial prejudice against her.

Gibson, Althea. *I Always Wanted to Be Somebody*. Edited by Ed Fitzgerald. New York: Harper & Brothers, 1958. A vivid account of Gibson's rise to the top of the tennis world. Its depiction of her formative years makes it an important contribution to African American autobiographies.

Gibson, Althea, with Richard Curtis. *So Much to Live For*. New York: G. P. Putnam's Sons, 1968. A second installment of her autobiography.

Gray, Frances Clayton, and Yanick Rice Lamb. *Born to Win: The Authorized Biography of Althea Gibson*. New York: John Wiley, 2004. A full account of Gibson's struggles and triumphs.

King, Billie Jean, and Cynthia Starr. *We Have Come a Long Way: The Story of Women's Tennis*. New York: McGraw-Hill, 1988. The section on Gibson is a perceptive assessment of her career and her effect on women's tennis during the 1950's. It makes the persuasive argument that Gibson has not received the recognition she deserves.

Lumpkin, Angela. *Women's Tennis: A Historical Documentary of the Players and Their Game*. Troy, N.Y.: Whitston, 1981. This survey of writing about women's tennis and the history of the sport provides references to the major published articles regarding Gibson during her years at the top of women's tennis. A valuable source of information about her career.

Schoenfeld, Bruce. *The Match: Althea Gibson and Angela Buxton—How Two Outsiders, One Black, the Other Jewish, Forged a Friendship and Made Sports History*. New York: Amistad, 2004. A perceptive and insightful treatment of Gibson's career and her friendship with her doubles partner from the 1950's. The closest book to a full biography with much fresh information about her life and times.

Wade, Virginia, with Jean Rafferty. *Ladies of the Court: A Century of Women at Wimbledon*. New York: Atheneum, 1984. Has a very informative chapter on Gibson's successes at Wimbledon.

JOHN GLENN

> *" You go with me on Memorial Day coming up, and you stand in Arlington National Cemetery . . . and you watch those waving flags, and you stand there, and you think about this nation, and you tell me that those people didn't have a job. "*

Astronaut and U.S. senator (1974-1999)

On February 20, 1962, Glenn became the first American to orbit Earth in a flight that reduced the Soviet Union's early lead in the space race. Glenn later served as a U.S. senator from Ohio in four consecutive terms from 1974 to 1998, made an unsuccessful bid for the presidency in 1984, and, in 1998, became the oldest human to fly in space during his flight aboard the space shuttle Discovery.

Born: July 18, 1921; Cambridge, Ohio
Also known as: John Herschel Glenn, Jr. (full name)
Area of achievement: Aviation and space exploration

EARLY LIFE

John Glenn was born in Cambridge, Ohio, to John and Clara Glenn. Glenn and his sister Jean grew up in New Concord, Ohio, a largely Presbyterian town of about two thousand inhabitants where their father ran a heating and plumbing business and, at one time, also owned a Chevrolet car dealership. Glenn was an honor student at New Concord High School and played several varsity sports. After graduating from high school in 1939, Glenn enrolled in Muskingum College in New Concord, an institution affiliated with the Presbyterian Church. Glenn served in the choir of the local Presbyterian church and later became a Sunday school teacher. When he was in the Mercury program, Glenn told the press, "I am a Presbyterian and I take my religion very seriously." Glenn played on the Muskingum football team and enrolled in a Navy-sponsored civilian pilot training program.

After the United States' entry into World War II, Glenn joined the Navy in March, 1942. He took advantage of an opportunity to receive his commission in the Marine Corps at Corpus Christi Naval Air Training Center and, in March, 1943, became a Marine lieutenant and Navy aviator. Returning briefly to New Concord, Glenn married Anna Castor (whom he had known since age six) in April, 1943, before being shipped out to the Pacific theater. From February, 1944, to February, 1945, Glenn flew fifty-nine combat missions in F4U Corsairs for VMO-155, based at Roi-Namur and Kwajalein, against Japanese positions in the Marshall Islands campaign. His unit employed napalm bombs as its primary ordnance on the dive bomb missions. For his World War II service, Glenn earned two Distinguished Flying Crosses (DFCs) and ten Air Medals.

Glenn served at several Marine air bases in the United States from February, 1945, to December, 1946, and did patrol duty in northern China and Guam from 1947 to 1949. While in China, Glenn flew Corsairs with VMF-218, based near Beijing. The

Glenns' first child, John David, was born in 1946 and their second, Carolyn, in 1947. Glenn served as flight instructor from 1949 to 1951 at Corpus Christi. He attended Amphibious Warfare School in Quantico, Virginia, in 1951-1952 and a jet training course before requesting combat in the Korean War. Based primarily at P'ohang, Glenn flew for VMF-311 and for a time as an exchange pilot with the Air Force. In his ninety combat missions in Korea from February to September, 1953, Glenn piloted F9F Panther jets and F86 Sabre jets (fighter-interceptors), and he shot down three enemy MIG aircraft in the last nine days of the war. Some of his missions were along the Yalu River. Glenn earned two more DFCs and eight more Air Medals for his Korean War service.

LIFE'S WORK
Glenn rose steadily in the ranks, becoming a captain in 1945, a major in 1952, and a colonel in 1959. He became a test pilot in 1954 and on July 16, 1957, as pilot for Project Bullet, set a record for the first coast-to-coast, nonstop supersonic flight in an F8U-1 Crusader jet (Los Angeles to New York). He received his fifth DFC for this event, and the attention he received from the transcontinental flight got him an invitation to be on the television show *Name That Tune*.

In the following year, he volunteered for the National Aeronautics and Space Administration's (NASA) Project Mercury man-in-space program. On April 9, 1959, he

John Glenn.
(Library of Congress)

was one of seven military test pilots (but the lone Marine) chosen to become the United States' pioneer astronaut corps, a group that became known to the public as the Mercury Seven. Glenn and his Project Mercury colleagues performed a variety of grueling physical and psychological simulations in preparation for the experience of single-person spaceflight. Glenn's technical expertise as a pilot enabled him to aid in the design of the Mercury cockpit and control system. Although he was the oldest of the Mercury astronauts, Glenn initiated a rigorous daily personal training regimen in addition to regular rounds of NASA tests. He visited his family only on weekends. The purpose of Project Mercury was to put astronauts in Earth orbit in short-duration, single-person flights as the preliminary stage toward the anticipated goal of lunar missions and to beat out the Soviet Union in the space race amid a climate of rising Cold War tensions.

Glenn was chosen to pilot the first Mercury orbital flight, originally scheduled for December 20, 1961. The Soviet Vostok program had already placed two cosmonauts in orbit by this time, and NASA, as well as the American public, regarded Project Mercury's first orbital flight as a means to cut the advantage held by the Soviets since their 1957 launch of the satellite *Sputnik*. Glenn's mission, however, had to be canceled ten times over the next two months because of technical problems and inclement weather.

Finally, on February 20, 1962, Glenn blasted off into orbit from Cape Canaveral, Florida, aboard his small, bell-shaped capsule *Friendship 7*. Glenn's three orbits, covering 81,000 miles, lasted 4 hours and 56 minutes. His average altitude ranged between 99 and 162 miles. Flying backward, Glenn narrated his visual experiences through the capsule's small, overhead porthole. He performed a variety of experiments and, with the camera he brought along, also became a pioneer of space photography.

Toward the middle of the mission, Mercury Control's monitoring panels received a signal indicating that the heat shield on Glenn's capsule might have come loose from its securing connections. The flight directors feared that Glenn and his capsule might incinerate upon reentry if he jettisoned his retropack (attached to the outside of the heat shield) as planned. Glenn was instructed not to jettison the retropack and to fly the capsule manually during reentry. He saw pieces of the retropack break free and melt from the intense heat, but the heat shield held in place. There was an atmosphere of exceptional tension at Mercury Control during the 4 minute and 20 second blackout period.

Glenn splashed down south of Bermuda in the Caribbean and was picked up by the USS *Noa*. He was called to the White House, and President John F. Kennedy presented him with a special medal. Glenn was cheered in victory parades by a quarter of a million people in Washington, D.C., and by four million people in New York City. While addressing a special joint session of Congress, Glenn made contacts that would serve him well in his future political career. Although he wished to return to space, it was widely believed that NASA passed him by in the Gemini and Apollo programs because he was considered by the administration as too great of a national asset to risk in future missions.

Glenn retired from the Marine Corps in 1965 and served as an executive with Royal Crown International before being elected as a Democrat to the U.S. Senate from Ohio in 1974. Glenn had previously unsuccessfully run for the Senate twice. In 1964 he was injured in a home accident and had to withdraw, and in 1970 he was defeated in the

Democratic primary by Howard Metzenbaum. He won in 1974 by beating Republican contender Ralph Park, former mayor of Cleveland. He was reelected in 1980, 1986, and 1992, becoming the first senator from Ohio elected to four terms. In the Senate, Glenn served on the Governmental Affairs Committee, the Foreign Relations Committee, the Armed Services Committee, the Select Committee on Intelligence, and the Special Committee on Aging. In 1978, he coauthored the Nonproliferation Act.

Glenn ran for the presidency in 1984 after a major film appeared based on Tom Wolfe's book *The Right Stuff* (1980), an epic about the Mercury program. Glenn, however, lost in the Democratic Party's primary to former Vice President Walter Mondale. Glenn lent his support to fellow Democrat Bill Clinton's victory in the 1992 presidential election and appeared live on television with the president in Ohio during Clinton's journey to the Democratic National Convention in 1996. On the thirty-fifth anniversary of his historic flight (February 20, 1997), Glenn announced that he would retire from the Senate at the end of his fourth term in 1998.

Glenn had been lobbying for a spot on a future space shuttle mission since 1996, and despite some criticism for preferential treatment, NASA announced in January, 1998, that he would serve as a payload specialist on an October, 1998, flight of the shuttle *Discovery* (STS-95). The detailed medical records on Glenn from Project Mercury were used as a yardstick to measure metabolic and bone density changes that occurred in zero-gravity conditions. Glenn noted before the mission that such a study was important because the changes that occur in young astronauts in zero gravity are similar to those experienced by the elderly on Earth.

Glenn's flight on *Discovery* lasted for almost nine days, orbited Earth 134 times, and spanned 3.6 million miles. The seven-person international crew included astronauts from Japan and Spain. Glenn provided blood, urine, and saliva samples on the mission for study. The mission also provided Glenn with yet another record—at seventy-seven years old, he became the oldest human ever to undertake spaceflight.

In addition to performing age-related experiments involving Glenn, the crew deployed a "Spartan" satellite designed to photograph the Sun (specifically the solar corona and solar winds), which orbited for two days until the crew retrieved it. They also deployed the Hubble Space Telescope Orbital Systems Test Platform. The experiments for which Glenn was responsible involved the separation and purification of biological materials. During the flight, Glenn exchanged e-mail with President Clinton. Glenn wrote in his memoirs that his shuttle flight at age seventy-seven should serve as evidence that elderly astronauts can "continue to go into space as active mission participants and research subjects."

On his return, Glenn and his six crewmates were honored in parades in Houston and New York City. He became one of only a few people (including Amelia Earhart) to receive more than one ticker tape parade in New York. Glenn published his memoirs in 1999 and helped found the John Glenn Institute of Public Service and Public Policy at Ohio State University in Columbus. The institute houses Glenn's archives and artifacts of his career. Glenn's boyhood home was restored at its original location and became a historic site. Both Glenn and his wife served on the board of trustees of their alma mater, Muskingum College. They lived in Columbus and maintained another home near Washington, D.C.

Glenn, John

SIGNIFICANCE

Glenn's impressive political and military careers are usually overshadowed by his career as a pioneering astronaut—as a member of the Mercury Seven, as the first American to orbit Earth, and as the oldest human to achieve spaceflight. His February, 1962, orbital flight was without a doubt a crucial moment in the space race between the United States and the Soviet Union and was therefore also an important political moment in the Cold War confrontation between the superpowers. Contemporary Americans tended to regard Glenn's flight as a sign that the United States had caught up with the Soviets and would soon take the lead in the space race, fulfilling President Kennedy's 1961 claim that the United States would put a person on the Moon by the end of the decade. Glenn, however, humbly insisted before his mission, "This is a technological problem, not a space race. Our primary concern is not to beat the Russians but to put a man up and bring him back safely." His February, 1962, mission proved that this goal was indeed attainable. Glenn's October, 1998, spaceflight aboard the shuttle *Discovery* broke another record: He became the oldest person to fly in space. The mission, however, was not intended simply to boost morale in the space program; the scientific data collected from the mission were employed in studies on aging and zero gravity.

—*William E. Watson*

FURTHER READING

Bell, Joseph N. *Seven into Space: The Story of the Mercury Astronauts*. London: Ebury Press, 1960. This account of Project Mercury and the Mercury Seven was written before any of the piloted launches took place but during a time of tremendous public interest in the lives of the astronauts. The book includes a great deal about Glenn's background. It also contains interesting information on the selection process and photos of the tests and simulations undertaken by the astronauts.

Carpenter, M. Scott, et al. *We Seven: By the Astronauts Themselves*. New York: Simon & Schuster, 1962. This is a well-edited collection of autobiographical essays by Glenn and the other Mercury Seven astronauts, with their accounts of the selection and training process and the flights through spring of 1962. The book also contains interesting photos of the astronauts in training and at launch time.

Committee on Aeronautical and Space Sciences, United States Senate. *Project Mercury: Man-in-Space Program of the National Aeronautics and Space Administration*. Washington, D.C.: Government Printing Office, 1959. This report explains NASA's objectives in Project Mercury and the costs of the program.

Glenn, John, with Nick Taylor. *John Glenn: A Memoir*. New York: Bantam Books, 1999. Glenn's memoirs contain insightful first-person narrative about his World War II and Korean War experiences, as well as his Mercury orbital flight and his experiences on the shuttle *Discovery*.

Launius, Roger D. *Frontiers of Space Exploration*. Westport, Conn.: Greenwood Press, 2004. A sweeping overview of the history of space exploration with solid material on Project Mercury and Glenn.

McDougall, Walter A. *The Heavens and the Earth: A Political History of the Space Age*. New York: Basic Books, 1985. McDougall's authoritative and sweeping assessment of the Soviet and American space programs includes reliable information about Glenn and the importance of his 1962 orbital mission.

Shepard, Alan, and Deke Slayton, with Jay Barbree and Howard Benedict. *Moon Shot: The Inside Story of America's Race to the Moon.* Atlanta, Ga.: Turner, 1994. This is an insightful account of the Mercury, Gemini, and Apollo programs by two of the Mercury Seven—Shepard, who was the first American in space (in a 1961 suborbital flight) and who landed on the Moon with Apollo 14 in 1971, and Slayton, whose heart condition grounded him from a Mercury flight but who participated in the Apollo-Soyuz linkup in 1975. They offer an interesting perspective on Glenn and his 1962 flight.

Wolfe, Tom. *The Right Stuff.* New York: Bantam, 1980. This is a popular, highly readable epic about the Mercury program and the test pilot background from which the Mercury Seven emerged. It captures the drama of early piloted spaceflight and also contains some gossipy, insider stories about the astronauts told by their colleagues. It served as the basis of the 1983 Academy Award-winning film of the same title.

EMMA GOLDMAN

> *Idealists are foolish enough to throw caution to the winds. They have advanced mankind and have enriched the world.*

Lithuanian-born American social reformer

A leading member of the anarchic Left in the early twentieth century, Goldman was a critic of both capitalism and socialism and an advocate of women's rights.

Born: June 27, 1869; Kovno, Lithuania, Russian Empire (now Kaunas, Lithuania)
Died: May 14, 1940; Toronto, Ontario, Canada
Also known as: Red Emma; E. G. Smith (pseudonym)
Areas of achievement: Government and politics; social reform; women's rights

EARLY LIFE

Emma Goldman (GOHLD-muhn) was born in Kovno (now Kaunas) in Lithuania, which was then part of the Russian Empire. Her parents, Abraham Goldman and Taube Binowitz Zodikow, were already rearing two daughters, Helena and Lena, from Taube Goldman's first marriage (she was a widow when she entered into an arranged marriage with Goldman). Beaten frequently by her father and denied comfort by her mother, Goldman was unable to find either emotional or financial security in the Goldman household. For a time, she lived with relatives in Königsberg, a city in the northeastern corner of Germany. Her experience in her uncle's household was, if anything, worse, and Goldman returned to her parents, who themselves moved first to Königsberg and then, in 1881, to St. Petersburg in Russia.

Goldman did find some satisfaction in life. She was able to attend school in Königsberg, where a young teacher befriended her and introduced her to music and lit-

Emma Goldman.
(Library of Congress)

erature, both of which became lifelong sources of pleasure. In St. Petersburg, however, the family's economic privation meant that Goldman had to abandon her hopes of continuing her education and becoming a doctor (her father could not understand why a woman needed an education) to work in factories that made gloves and corsets.

Rebelling against her father's authority and the Jewish religious and cultural traditions in which she was raised, Goldman became fascinated with radicalism. An avid reader, she found inspiration in Vera Pavlovna, the heroine of Nikolay Chernyshevsky's radical novel *What Is to Be Done?* (1863), who defied authority and convention. Especially meaningful to Goldman, whose father suggested arranging a marriage for her, was Pavlovna's rejection of that practice as the auctioning of a sex object. Goldman also admired the martyred young women who had been active participants in the 1870's Russian radical movement, the People's Will.

Goldman sought immediate relief from her despair by immigrating to the United States, the land of hope, departing Russia with Helena late in 1885. They intended to live with their sister Lena, who was married and living in Rochester, New York. To Goldman's dismay, she soon seemed trapped in Rochester by the very things she wished to escape: monotonous, low-paying work in a clothing factory; further talk of an arranged marriage; and the presence of her parents, who followed their daughters to the New World.

Again, Goldman found inspiration in the story of martyred radicals: four men executed (a fifth committed suicide) in November, 1887, for the bomb murder of several Chicago police officers during a mass workers' meeting at the Haymarket Square in Chicago the previous year. What especially angered Goldman was that the authorities never ascertained who threw the bomb, making it seem clear that the men who had been arrested were really being tried for their beliefs. If injustices similar to those that occurred in Russia could also take place in the United States, reasoned Goldman, it was time for her to align herself with the opponents of capitalism and its tools, the state and the church.

Later, in Rochester, Goldman fell in love with a fellow worker, the handsome and seemingly intellectual Jacob Kershner, whom she married in February, 1887. The marriage seemed to offer escape from familial pressures but did not succeed. Kershner proved to be impotent and took comfort in gambling with his cronies. For a time, Goldman tried to avoid the stigma of divorce, but at age twenty, she divorced Kershner and moved to New Haven, Connecticut. She briefly returned to Rochester, remarried Kershner, divorced him a second time, and moved to New York City.

Life's Work

Among the new friends Goldman made in the immigrant neighborhoods of New York's Lower East Side, two stood out: Alexander Berkman, who became her lover, and Johann Most, an older man who had made a name for himself in Germany and became a leading figure among anarchists in the United States. Although she was familiar with socialist thought, she regarded it as menacing to individual freedom because it accepted large state-owned industry as positive. Anarchism, in contrast, promised a society based on justice and reason and opposed both the centralization of the corporation and the centralization of the state.

Schooled by Most in both anarchist theory and public speaking, Goldman made her first speaking tour in 1890 and was delighted to realize that she had the power to sway people with the spoken word. She also came to realize, however, that the words she was speaking were not hers but Most's, and she repudiated his mentorship. Converts to anarchism and to the communal living that Goldman and Berkman advocated were disappointingly few, and the two thought of returning to Russia.

In 1892, a pressing new cause kept them in the United States: planning the assassination of tycoon Henry Clay Frick, who had violently suppressed a strike at the Homestead steelworks of Pittsburgh. They decided that Berkman would shoot Frick, while Goldman, who helped him plan the assassination attempt, would explain his actions. The affair went awry. Berkman merely wounded Frick, and other radicals, including Most, distanced themselves from Berkman and from assassination as a political weapon.

Goldman had now come to another turning point in her life. She thought of herself not as an exile from Russia but as a woman who could have a meaningful future fighting for change in the United States. Although she escaped prosecution for her role in Berkman's attack on Frick, she was arrested in 1893 and sentenced to a year in Blackwell's Island prison for her activities at a protest demonstration in New York's Union Square.

On her release, Goldman met a new lover, the Austrian-born anarchist Ed Brady, who wished to marry her. She rejected marriage but did heed his suggestion to find another outlet for her compassion and sympathy for the downtrodden. To support herself, she was already working as a practical nurse (a skill she had learned in the prison hospital), and she went to Vienna to earn certificates in nursing and midwifery. During her year in Vienna (1895-1896) and another year in Paris (1899-1900) she also immersed herself in avant-garde literature and drama.

For some time, Goldman hoped to have two careers: the first as a nurse and midwife among the downtrodden in New York, the second as a radical lecturer. The two careers were not necessarily compatible, however, for as a lecturer she was attracting increasing fame as an opponent of war in 1898, of organized Christianity, and of conventional sexual morality. She became widely known as an advocate of free love, a term that added to her notoriety as "Red Emma." In using the expression "free love," Goldman meant not indiscriminate sexual activity but love without a legally recognized marriage, which she regarded as one of many devices society used to exploit women.

Goldman again faced prison in 1901 when she was arrested following the assassination of President William McKinley. She was not involved in the crime and was not held for trial, but with her characteristic defiance she could not resist asking Americans to show compassion for the condemned assassin, Leon Czolgosz. Public outrage made it impossible for her to book a lecture hall, and she was further embittered when radicals repudiated Czolgosz. For a while she retreated from public view. Using the pseudonym E. G. Smith, she tended to the poor in New York's slums.

By 1903, however, she was ready to resume lecturing. In 1906, she undertook a second commitment, that of publisher of a new periodical that she founded and named *Mother Earth*. She chose the name to suggest that the earth should provide the opportunity for all humankind to lead free and productive lives. *Mother Earth* would serve as a forum not only for anarchism but also for the issues of the Lyrical Left—personal liberation, freedom of artistic expression, and equality in sexual relations.

The journal, however, did not sell well enough to support Goldman—after one year it had two thousand subscribers—so she had to lecture more than ever. Often traveling with her new lover, Ben Reitman the "hobo" doctor, who acted as her booking agent, Goldman gave hundreds of speeches a year, reaching out to the "psychologically stifled middle class" as well as to the impoverished. Small of stature, she impressed listeners with her intensity and with her command of humor and sarcasm. In the question-and-answer sessions that usually followed her talks, she also showed a mastery of many subjects that came from countless hours of reading. English had long since become Goldman's primary language, but although her most publicized lectures were to American audiences, she insisted on making separate lectures in Yiddish.

From 1906 to 1916, Goldman continued to write and lecture on the sins of capitalism and also on art, drama, literature, and women's issues. She addressed the topic of birth control, criticized the institution of marriage, denounced the corset, and dared women to have more sexual experiences. Much of what she said infuriated social conservatives, but for good measure she also condemned suffragists as single-issue reformers. Ethical and social conventions, she maintained, were bigger obstacles to women's emancipation than were suffrage restrictions and other external barriers.

From 1914 on, World War I became an issue she had to address. As long as the

United States remained neutral, Goldman could freely oppose the war, but even when the United States entered the war in 1917 she remained uncompromising in her opposition to it. No pacifist, she regarded war as more capitalist exploitation. The conscription law that the Wilson administration endorsed in 1917 was both repressive and illogical, she asserted, since it meant Prussianizing America in the name of democratizing Germany. Although she did not explicitly advocate resistance to the draft, she and Berkman (who had been released from prison in 1906 and was the editor of *Mother Earth*) were arrested on June 15, speedily tried, and sentenced to prison terms of two years. In a separate action, the government stopped the publication of *Mother Earth*.

In 1919, Goldman, Berkman, and more than two hundred other radicals of foreign birth were deported from the United States to Soviet Russia, but life there proved intolerable for her. Goldman did have an interview with communist leader Vladimir Ilich Lenin, but she soon concluded that a new era of statist repression was dawning.

She left Russia in 1921 and proceeded to relate her observations in lectures and in two books that were condemned by other leftists. At various times she lived in Sweden, England, France, and Canada, writing her memoirs and carrying on a large correspondence with many friends and members of her family with whom she had long before reconciled. In 1934, she was allowed to return to the United States, where she desperately wished to live, just long enough to make a speaking tour. In her last years, she expressed contempt for both Nazism and Stalinism, but when World War II began in September, 1939, she refused to make a choice between the evil of war and the evil of a dictatorship. An individualist to the last, she died in Toronto in 1940.

Significance

During Goldman's lifetime, anarchism never became a mass creed. If anything, it declined in the United States because of government actions against radicalism, the growing appeal of trade unions, and because communism, especially after the Leninists had gained power in Russia, was able to win more converts. Nevertheless, Goldman was of major importance in the history of American radicalism, for her success lay not in contributing to the demise of capitalism or the state but in alerting people to issues involving personal liberation and self-fulfillment.

Unlike most members of the political left, who argued that the advent of the socialist state would emancipate women, Goldman demanded that women's issues be addressed immediately. Jeered, arrested, and threatened on many occasions, she won admirers among many middle-class Americans who might not have become converts to her causes but who believed in her right to advance them. She herself became a major spokesperson for free speech. It is therefore in the cultural history of twentieth century America that Goldman has most significance, for the issues she had raised prior to 1918 were issues that again seemed relevant in the 1960's, when a new generation of American dissenters and feminists rediscovered Goldman and celebrated her as a symbol of defiance and liberation.

—*Lloyd J. Graybar*

Goldman, Emma

FURTHER READING

Chalberg, John. *Emma Goldman, American Individualist.* Edited by Oscar Handlin. New York: HarperCollins, 1991. Written as part of an ongoing series of brief biographies of eminent Americans, this book provides the best introduction to Goldman's life.

Drinnon, Richard. *Rebel in Paradise.* Chicago: University of Chicago Press, 1961. Especially helpful for its explanation of the historical and social context in which Goldman lived. Shows the maturation of Goldman from youthful enthusiast to spokesperson for a cultural revolution.

Fellner, Gene, ed. *Life of an Anarchist: The Alexander Berkman Reader.* 2d ed. New York: Seven Stories Press, 2005. A collection of Berkman's writings, including several letters he and Goldman wrote each other.

Goldman, Emma. *Living My Life.* 2 vols. New York: Alfred A. Knopf, 1931. Written while Goldman was residing in St. Tropez, France, this memoir is inaccurate and misleading in many areas but is still the best source for information about Goldman's childhood.

_____. *Nowhere at Home: Letters from Exile of Emma Goldman and Alexander Berkman.* Edited by Richard Drinnon and Anna Maria Drinnon. New York: Schocken Books, 1975. This topically organized compilation reveals much about Goldman's thoughts on communism and on the approach of World War II. Thoughtful editorial notes are included.

Moritz, Theresa, and Albert Mortiz. *The World's Most Dangerous Woman: A New Biography of Emma Goldman.* Vancouver, B.C.: Subway Books, 2001. This biography focuses on the three periods of Goldman's life when she lived in Canada, 1926-1928, 1933-1935, and 1939-1940, placing her life there within the larger context of Canadian leftist politics.

Shulman, Alix Kates. *To the Barricades: The Anarchist Life of Emma Goldman.* New York: Thomas Y. Crowell, 1971. This book for juvenile readers provides a lucid introduction to Goldman's life and thought.

Solomon, Martha. *Emma Goldman.* Boston: Twayne, 1987. Solomon analyzes Goldman's rhetorical style in both her written and spoken words. Provides insight into Goldman's thought, especially her evaluations of early twentieth century literature and drama.

Wexler, Alice. *Emma Goldman: An Intimate Life.* New York: Pantheon Books, 1984. In this three-hundred-page work, Wexler challenges many views of Goldman and seeks to explain the contradictions between the public Goldman and the private Goldman.

_____. *Emma Goldman in Exile.* Boston: Beacon Press, 1989. Wexler concludes her study of Goldman with this assessment of her last twenty years.

AL GORE

> *Make no mistake, the next generation will ask us one of two questions . . . : 'What were you thinking; why didn't you act?' or they will ask instead: 'How did you find the moral courage to rise and successfully resolve a crisis that so many said was impossible to solve?'*

Vice president of the United States (1993-2001)

Gore, both as politician and activist, underscored the need for public concern, discussion, and debate on issues of technology, consumption, and the environment. In 2007 he was awarded the Nobel Peace Prize for his work on global warming. In 2000, he received a majority of the popular vote for president of the United States but was not permitted to take office after the U.S. Supreme Court decided against a further recounting of damaged ballots in Florida.

Born: March 31, 1948; Washington, D.C.
Also known as: Albert Arnold Gore, Jr. (full name)
Areas of achievement: Government and politics; environmentalism

EARLY LIFE

Al Gore was born and raised in Washington, D.C., where his father was serving as a representative from Tennessee's Fourth Congressional District. When the younger Gore was only four years old, his father had been elected to the Senate. While Gore spent many summers on the family farm near Carthage, Tennessee, he lived and attended private schools in Washington.

Gore graduated from Harvard University with a degree in government in 1969 and entered the U.S. Army, intending to serve in Vietnam despite his opposition to the war. While he had comparatively safer duty as a reporter for a military newspaper, simply being in Vietnam was dangerous. Gore was one of the very few sons of Washington politicians to serve in the war zone. After Vietnam, he attended Vanderbilt University and took graduate courses in religion. Not satisfied with this area of study, he switched to the Vanderbilt law school. He also worked as a reporter for the Nashville *Tennessean* while pursing his graduate education.

LIFE'S WORK

At age twenty-eight, Gore quit law school to run for the congressional seat his father had once held. As a border state Democrat, Gore represented his district's moderately conservative views but sought to establish progressive credentials by developing expertise in arms control and the protection of the environment. He served four terms in the House until Tennessee's senior senator, Republican Howard Baker, retired in 1984. Gore then won his seat in the Senate. He broadened his policy credentials by developing expertise in modern technology, especially the Internet (before the advent of the World Wide Web).

Four years later, in 1988, Gore ran for president. Although he won a number of southern Democratic primaries, he was not able to win the New York primary and real-

Gore, Al

ized he could not win the party's nomination with so many candidates vying that year. His showing was good enough to support a future run for the presidency, although his son's serious car accident kept him from running in 1992. In 1992, Gore published his *Earth in the Balance*, which became the first best seller published by an incumbent senator since John F. Kennedy wrote *Profiles in Courage* in the 1950's.

Bill Clinton, who would become U.S. president in 1993, made an unusual decision by picking Gore, a southern moderate from an adjacent state, as his running mate in 1992. Still, Gore's service in Vietnam mitigated some of the concern over Clinton's lack of service in the same conflict. Upon his election as vice president, he expanded his previous policy expertise into the arena of reorganizing the federal bureaucracy and produced a major report on the subject in 1995. In line with a growing trend to make the vice presidency a more important office, Gore became the most actively involved vice president in the history of that office.

In 2000, Gore was heavily favored for the Democratic presidential nomination, easily overcoming a challenge from former U.S. senator Bill Bradley of New Jersey. He defeated Bradley in every primary. In the general election, Gore ran a strong campaign and showed his policy expertise in each of the three debates with his Republican opponent, George W. Bush. While the experts rated Gore's performance as superior, Bush went into the debates with low expectations but performed well enough to make slight gains in the polls. Bush made additional mistakes, including failing to disclose

Al Gore.
(U.S. Department of Defense)

early in the campaign that he had been arrested in 1976 for drunk driving. This disclosure on the last weekend before the election damaged Bush's candidacy greatly, leading to his loss of the popular vote by more than a half million.

Unfortunately for Gore, the election was not decided by popular vote but by the electoral college, where a majority of the electoral votes—organized by states—selects a president. Normally, the popular and electoral votes produce the same result, but in 2000, Florida's popular vote was very close. Gore led early in the evening, but Bush pulled ahead after midnight. Later, Bush's lead fell to just a few hundred votes, staying there until certification, now in the hands of Florida state officials. Some critics of this election have argued that because the most important of these officials were Republican, they had acted to "protect" Bush's lead.

Gore has the unfortunate distinction of being one of only four former candidates for president—all Democrats—who won the popular vote for office but lost the election in the electoral college. Two candidates—Andrew Jackson and Grover Cleveland—ran for office at a later time and won their respective presidential elections. Another candidate, Samuel Tilden, abandoned electoral politics and became a social critic and activist for progressive causes. Gore's career has resembled that of Tilden.

The fairness of the election was challenged. A recount of all the ballots likely would have produced a narrow victory for Gore, based on a subsequent unofficial recount conducted by a consortium of national news organizations. Soon after the vote, pollsters found that thousands more Floridians had intended to vote for Gore, and not for Bush. Many voters had cast their ballots incorrectly, thereby unknowingly voiding their own ballots or voting for the wrong candidate. A full recount and a complete judicial review of the various challenges in the courts would have helped to determine the outcome of the elections and given credibility to the electoral system.

However, in an unprecedented move, the U.S. Supreme Court intervened in the election controversy and stopped further counting of the votes. After a narrow 5-4 decision, the Court claimed the authority of the equal protection clause of the Fourteenth Amendment and argued that the Florida Supreme Court incorrectly allowed the recounting of some but not all ballots. This decision has been widely criticized by both conservative and liberal legal scholars. In effect, it was the court system, and not the voters (via the electoral college), that selected Bush for the presidency. After the Court decision, Gore gave a gracious concession speech and served the remainder of his term as vice president.

SIGNIFICANCE

Gore remained in the public realm after his work in electoral politics as a college lecturer, writer, and environmental activist. His book on climate change, *An Inconvenient Truth: The Planetary Emergency of Global Warming and What We Can Do About It* (2006), was a best seller and stirred public debate about the rapid changes to Earth's climate patterns. The book was made into an Academy Award-winning documentary film. For his work to raise awareness about global warming and climate change, he was awarded the Nobel Peace Prize in 2007. He shared the award with the United Nations' Intergovernmental Panel on Climate Change.

Also in 2007, Gore published *The Assault on Reason*, which argued against the trend

Gore, Al

in U.S. politics that ignores facts and analyses in policymaking. He further argues in the book that, at the expense of democracy, television threatens public discourse because it is focused on entertainment, and, through powerful gatekeepers that include the corporate-owned news media, it presents a one-sided perspective and interpretation of the world. The Internet (and World Wide Web), he argues, is an interactive medium that could change that threat by keeping public discourse and debate alive.

—*Richard L. Wilson*

FURTHER READING

Dionne, E. J., Jr., and William Kristol, eds. *Bush Versus Gore: The Court Cases and the Commentary.* Washington, D.C.: Brookings Institution, 2001. A collection of editorial-page pieces and newspaper articles written during the events following the November, 2000, election that focus on the legal issues and court cases.

Downie, Leonard, Jr., ed. *Deadlock: The Inside Story of America's Closest Election.* New York: Public Affairs, 2001. More than forty members of the political staff of *The Washington Post* collaborated to produce this highly readable narrative of the 2000 presidential elections.

Gore, Albert A., Jr. *The Assault on Reason.* New York: Penguin, 2007. Gore argues that public discourse has declined in the United States because of the one-sidedness and bias of corporate-controlled media. Also outlines the Bush administration's "assault on reason" with its dismissal of facts and analysis in making policy decisions.

_____. *Common Sense Government: Works Better and Costs Less.* New York: Random House, 1995. As vice president, Gore was in charge of an initiative to reform the U.S. executive branch. He wrote this book based on his experience in this role.

_____. *Earth in the Balance: Ecology and the Human Spirit.* 1992. New ed. Boston: Houghton Mifflin, 2000. Gore's first environmental book made him the first incumbent U.S. senator to write a best seller since the 1950's and John F. Kennedy's *Profiles in Courage.*

_____. *An Inconvenient Truth: The Planetary Emergency of Global Warming and What We Can Do About It.* New York: Rodale Books, 2006. Based on the popular documentary that won the Academy Award for Best Documentary and contributed to his receipt of the Nobel Peace Prize in 2007.

Hosansky, David, ed. *The Environment A to Z.* Washington, D.C.: CQ Press, 2001. An encyclopedic collection of articles focusing on "all things" environmental, including an entry on Gore and his work on climate change and global warming.

Issacharoff, Samuel, Pamela S. Karlan, and Richard H. Pildes. *When Elections Go Bad: The Law of Democracy and the Presidential Election of 2000.* New York: Foundation Press, 2001. A careful academic study of the constitutional law governing election litigation.

Rakove, Jack N. *The Unfinished Election of 2000: Leading Scholars Examine America's Strangest Election.* New York: Basic Books, 2001. In-depth academic articles on the long-term effects of the 2000 presidential election.

Sabato, Larry J. *Overtime: The Election 2000 Thriller.* New York: Longman, 2002. This collection features analytical pieces by journalists that provide a broad view of the issues of the 2000 election.

WILLIAM CRAWFORD GORGAS

> *We realized that the subject of yellow fever was by far the most important phase of sanitation with which we had to deal.*

Surgeon general of the U.S. Army (1914-1918)

Gorgas, a dedicated physician and humanitarian, led the effort that eliminated yellow fever as one of the major epidemic diseases throughout the world. This feat was accomplished through the diligent and practical application of scientific discoveries concerning the disease.

Born: October 3, 1854; Toulminville, Alabama
Died: July 4, 1920; London, England
Also known as: W. C. Gorgas
Areas of achievement: Medicine; public health

EARLY LIFE

William Crawford Gorgas (GOHR-gahs) was born to Josiah Gorgas, an officer in the U.S. Army and a Northerner, and to Amelia (Gayle) Gorgas, a Southerner. The sectional strife in the late 1850's caused Josiah Gorgas considerable anxiety, for both marriage and experience inclined him to the Southern side. Eventually, he resigned his commission and offered his services to the Confederacy. The family was soon living in Richmond, where Josiah was serving as chief of ordnance with the rank of general. His son, known as Willie while a child and W.C. as an adult, spent his early formative years intoxicated with the military romanticism of the rebellion. He never stopped wanting to be a soldier or wishing that the rebels had won.

When the war ended, the family settled in Brierfield, Alabama, where Josiah Gorgas invested his small remaining capital in a blast furnace. Willie got what schooling was available and was in fact fortunate that his father's business quickly failed. When the senior Gorgas obtained a position at the University of the South in Sewanee, Tennessee, his son entered as a preparatory student. In 1870, the young Gorgas went as a volunteer to fight a yellow fever epidemic in New Orleans, an experience that started his lifelong interest in the disease. He still wanted to be a soldier, and when he was graduated, his father, who wanted him to study law, reluctantly and unsuccessfully tried to get him an appointment to West Point. Gorgas decided to get into the Army via the medical corps. In 1876, he entered Bellevue Hospital Medical College in New York. Although he had felt no initial call to the profession, he found that medicine fascinated him. After graduation and a year of internship at Bellevue Hospital, he realized his longtime ambition by becoming in June, 1880, a lieutenant in the U.S. Army.

Gorgas was tested both physically and spiritually during his first two decades in the Army. He was stationed at out-of-the-way posts in Texas, North Dakota, and Florida, where, as the only doctor in the area, he worked long hours serving the local civilian population as well as keeping up with his military duties. His small frame and frail appearance belied his toughness, and his devotion to military life never dimmed. He

Gorgas, William Crawford

charted his own future course when in 1883, while stationed at Fort Brown, Texas, he violated orders by working with victims of a yellow fever epidemic. Having been exposed, he was kept at the task, and he met his future wife, Marie Doughty; she was the sister of the post commander, whom he treated and with whom, after contracting the disease himself, he convalesced. Gorgas and Doughty were married the next year. His illness not only led him to a bride but also deepened his interest in yellow fever, which he continued to study over the next few years. Gorgas was soon recognized as an expert on the disease, though he was not impressed with the mosquito transmission theory that was gaining more and more attention. Little did the hardworking small-post Army doctor know it, but yellow fever was about to become the center of his life.

Life's Work

When, in 1898, the Spanish-American War put large numbers of American soldiers into the Caribbean, the medical corps proved ill-prepared to handle the inevitable outbreaks of tropical disease. Already known for his work with yellow fever, Gorgas was assigned to the yellow fever camp at Siboney, near Havana. His best advice was the burning of everything that might have been in contact with victims—even buildings. Later in 1898, Major Gorgas was appointed sanitary officer of Havana. The city was littered with sewage and filth and was a pool of yellow fever infection, exporting the disease with trade goods to American ports. Gorgas went to work on the needed cleaning only to find that, contrary to expectations, yellow fever became increasingly common. This was, of course, a result of the arrival of more and more nonimmunes. At first the bitterly disappointed Gorgas seemed headed for failure, but the solution to his problem was at hand.

An American medical commission headed by Walter Reed had come to Cuba to study the problem of yellow fever. With Gorgas as fascinated observer, the Reed Commission combined past discoveries with new experiments to answer the question of transmission. A number of investigators—most recently Carlos J. Finlay—had suggested mosquitoes as the carrier, but no one had actually been able to show such a transmission. Henry Rose Carter in Mississippi had, however, established that there was a period of development for the germ in the mosquito's system before it could be passed along. The Reed Commission was able to show conclusively that the mosquito had to bite an infected person within three days of the initial infection and that the mosquito itself was not dangerous for at least ten days. It was also determined that the carrier was the *Stegomyia fasciata* (now called *Aëdes aegypti*). This proved the vital information.

Despite the efforts of the Reed Commission, Gorgas remained dubious. The only real test, he believed, was to rid the city of the mosquito and see what happened. Reed agreed but believed that such an extermination was impossible. Gorgas first tried for a vaccine but soon focused his attack on the insect. Studying its habits, he found that it preferred to live in and around human habitations and lay its eggs in fresh water held in artificial containers. It also had a fairly limited range. Dividing the city into zones, Gorgas assigned teams to eliminate or put a film of kerosene on all open water. Windows were screened, and houses, especially those where a case of yellow fever had occurred, were fumigated. Civilian objections to such intrusions were gently but firmly put aside. October, 1901, would become the first October in the recorded history of

Gorgas, William Crawford

William Crawford Gorgas.
(U.S. Army)

Havana without a case of yellow fever. A happy side effect of the campaign was that malaria cases were reduced by fully three-quarters as well. The surgeon general of the Army recognized Gorgas's efforts by deciding that he should become the Army expert on tropical diseases. In 1902-1903, he was sent to attend the world conference on tropical medicine in Cairo and to have a look at the antimalaria work done at Suez. He was also promoted to colonel.

These assignments were to help prepare him for a job in the planned construction of a canal across the Isthmus of Panama. The American Medical Association (AMA) lobbied for his appointment to the Canal Commission, headed by Admiral John G. Walker, but he was merely appointed chief sanitary officer. Problems caused by disease had played a substantial part in the failure of the French effort to construct a canal in Panama, and Gorgas believed that he could prevent such problems. Admiral Walker and the other commissioners, however, considered the idea of mosquito transmission of disease foolish and were much more concerned with economy and avoidance of even the appearance of graft than with sanitation. Indeed, the sanitary staff was hopelessly inadequate in number, and its requests for supplies were often denied or reduced to a fraction of the amount requested. Pay scales were set so low that qualified medical personnel were uninterested in the positions.

Gorgas protested as strongly as his sense of military hierarchy and his courtly Southern demeanor would allow, but to no avail. During the first yellow fever season, the disease was at low ebb, but Gorgas knew that, as in Havana, the influx of nonimmunes would provide the raw material for an epidemic. In the spring and summer of 1905, the number of cases began to increase rapidly, and official reaction was to blame Gorgas. Fortunately, the AMA sent a physician, Charles A. L. Reed, to investigate and report to Secretary of War William Howard Taft. The report, which was made public, supported Gorgas totally and in addition to other studies led President Theodore Roosevelt to reorganize the Canal Commission. The new chair, however, Theodore P. Shonts, also rejected the mosquito transmission theory and tried to get rid of Gorgas. Although inclined to agree with Shonts and other doubters, the president sought the advice of several prominent physicians, all of whom maintained that Gorgas was the best person for the job and that mosquito transmission had been proved. Roosevelt ordered that Gorgas be given full support.

Gorgas quickly began to apply the lessons learned in Havana. By November, 1905, he had four thousand men, and although earlier his entire budget had been fifty thousand dollars a year, he was able to order ninety thousand dollars' worth of window-screen wire alone. Panama City and Colón were fumigated house by house, piped water was supplied to end the need for open household cisterns, and pools of standing water that could not be drained were regularly sprayed with kerosene. By the end of 1905, yellow fever was under control. Other diseases that had threatened, such as cholera and bubonic plague, were gone, and malaria was much reduced. Health care for workers was very good generally, and death rates would have been acceptable in virtually any American city. The arrival in April, 1907, however, of George Washington Goethals as chief engineer proved a beginning of renewed frustration for Gorgas. Goethals had been given extremely broad powers and used them dictatorially. His efforts at economy, Gorgas feared, would weaken the sanitary effort. The two rarely found common ground personally or professionally, but the sanitary foundation had been laid and morbidity rates did not increase.

Gorgas's success in the Panama Canal Zone led to numerous honors. In 1907, he received the Mary Kingsley Medal and in 1908 was elected president of the AMA. He was also granted many honorary degrees. An invitation came in 1913 to consult on the problem of pneumonia among miners in South Africa, and with the canal nearing completion, he received permission to accept. Although his visit was cut short in February, 1914, by his appointment as surgeon general of the Army—with promotion to the rank of brigadier general—his report proved the basis for a program that improved the miners' situation significantly.

As surgeon general, Gorgas was responsible for reforms that prepared the Army Medical Corps for World War I. He encouraged doctors to join the service and helped develop the Medical Reserve Corps, which supplied many of the physicians needed when the United States entered the war in 1917. Between the beginning of American participation and the armistice, the number of doctors in the military service increased by more than thirty times its original amount. Sanitation in military camps proved a problem, and at times Gorgas faced strong criticism. He was able to defend himself by pointing out failures to follow basic regulations through ignorance or more often through pressure to enlist and train an army before the British and French were overwhelmed. He also became involved in a controversial political struggle over provision of higher rank for American medical officers and eventually saw the necessary legislation through Congress. On October 3, 1918, Gorgas turned sixty-four, and despite protests from friends and admirers, he had to retire from active duty. He spent the rest of his life working on behalf of the Rockefeller Foundation trying to eliminate the remaining pockets of yellow fever in the world. After getting the program started in South America, he died in London on July 4, 1920, while on a journey that had been intended to take him to West Africa, where yellow fever was still often epidemic. British king George V visited the hospital to bestow on Lieutenant General Gorgas, the only son of a Confederate general officer to achieve a similar rank in the Army, the Order of St. Michael and St. George. It was a high and fitting last honor.

Significance

Two quintessentially American qualities are the hallmarks of Gorgas's career: practicality and hard work. Although he made none of the basic scientific discoveries needed to end the scourge of yellow fever, when those discoveries were made he took advantage of them. His dogged and eventually successful struggle to get the necessary support for his sanitation program saved thousands of lives among the workforce that built the Panama Canal and was a key factor in making construction possible. He proved that controlling the mosquitoes that spread the disease would prevent epidemics. These lessons, when applied throughout the world, saved countless thousands more.

Gorgas's work as surgeon general of the Army was also extremely successful. The American Expeditionary Force in World War I suffered almost twice as many combat deaths as deaths from disease. The Army as a whole had fewer than 25 percent more deaths from disease than in battle. While to modern ears the latter may not sound like success, it was unprecedented for its day.

Gentle and soft-spoken, Gorgas was widely admired and often loved. Although a brasher person might have gotten things done in a shorter time, his courtesy made it very difficult to turn him away, and his gentleness masked an iron determination. His achievements helped to establish modern standards of public health, standards that have improved the quality of life in almost every part of the globe.

—*Fred R. van Hartesveldt*

Further Reading

Crosby, Molly Caldwell. *The American Plague: The Untold Story of Yellow Fever, the Epidemic That Shaped Our History*. New York: Berkley Books, 2006. This historical account of yellow fever includes information about Walter Reed's trip to Cuba and Gorgas's efforts to combat the disease.

Duffy, John. *Sword of Pestilence: The New Orleans Yellow Fever Epidemic of 1853*. Baton Rouge: Louisiana State University Press, 1966. Although its subject predates Gorgas's activity, this short book gives an excellent picture of what a yellow fever epidemic meant before modern public health brought the disease under control.

Gibson, John M. *Physician to the World: The Life of General William C. Gorgas*. Durham, N.C.: Duke University Press, 1950. The most recent and scholarly biography of Gorgas, it contains some anecdotes of dubious authenticity and is flawed by racial and ethnic stereotypes.

Gorgas, Marie D., and Burton J. Hendrick. *William Crawford Gorgas: His Life and Work*. Garden City, N.Y.: Doubleday, Page, 1924. Written by Gorgas's daughter, this biography is overly kind to its subject but does contain interesting personal observations.

Gorgas, William Crawford. *Sanitation in Panama*. New York: D. Appleton, 1915. Gorgas's own account of his program in the canal effort. While not the easiest of reading, this book is the best source about Gorgas's ideas while he was working on the canal.

McCullough, David. *The Path Between the Seas: The Creation of the Panama Canal, 1870-1914*. New York: Simon & Schuster, 1977. Well-written study of the canal with a chapter on Gorgas's life and the problems of sanitation woven throughout. Excellent background for anyone interested in Gorgas or the canal.

Martin, Franklin H. *Fifty Years of Medicine and Surgery*. Chicago: Surgical Publications, 1934. A colleague and admirer of Gorgas, Martin supplies the observations of a trained colleague as well as personal commentary.

Pierce, John R., and Jim Writer. *Yellow Jack: How Yellow Fever Ravaged America and Walter Reed Discovered Its Deadly Secrets*. Hoboken, N.J.: Wiley, 2005. A history of yellow fever, including information about Gorgas's efforts to eliminate the disease.

Spielman, Andrew, and Michael D'Antonio. *Mosquito: A Natural History of Our Most Persistent and Deadly Foe*. New York: Hyperion, 2001. A history of the global problems associated with the mosquito, including malaria.

BILLY GRAHAM

" *Believers, look up—take courage. The angels are nearer than you think.* **"**

Evangelist

Graham created the modern citywide crusade, pioneered national and global television and radio broadcasts, and wrote popular books that reached millions around the world with a simple gospel. A consistent feature of his public ministry was his personal contact with world leaders and other famous personages.

Born: November 7, 1918; near Charlotte, North Carolina
Also known as: William Franklin Graham, Jr. (full name)
Areas of achievement: Evangelism; religion and theology; social reform; oratory; philanthropy

EARLY LIFE

Billy Graham (GRAY-uhm), possibly the world's most famous evangelist, was born on a farm outside Charlotte, North Carolina. His father, William Franklin, was a dairy farmer and husband of Morrow (Coffey) Graham. Early years for the young Graham were spent working on the farm with his siblings and attending grade school. Graham had no strong inclinations toward Christianity until he heard the revival preaching of Mordecai Ham, a traveling evangelist, whose multiday revival in the fall of 1934 inspired the sixteen-year-old Graham to confess his sins to God and ask Jesus Christ to be his personal savior.

This conversion experience was to fundamentally shape the remainder of Graham's life and his professional calling. He felt a clear "call" from God to preach the Gospel. He entered Florida Bible Institute (now Trinity College) and gained early preaching experience by setting up a makeshift orange-crate pulpit among the orange groves and preaching to the trees. His fervor did not escape the notice of a local church in the Southern Baptist Convention. He was ordained to the ministry in 1939 and graduated from the institute the following year. He went on to Wheaton College in Illinois to major in anthropology and was known on campus as "the preacher."

At Wheaton, Graham was introduced by friends to a fiercely independent woman, Ruth McCue Bell (1920-2007), the daughter of medical missionaries to China. Bell was determined upon graduation to travel to Tibet as a single woman missionary, but after much struggle in prayer, she believed God intended her to marry the budding evangelist Graham. The ceremony took place in her parents' American base of operations in Montreat, North Carolina, on August 13, 1943. The two had just graduated from Wheaton College. Graham took up his first and what would be his only pastorate at First Baptist Church in Western Springs, Illinois, from 1943 to 1945. He also ventured into radio ministry on WCFL in Chicago, hosting the program *Songs in the Night*.

Life's Work

Graham, in 1945, began working with Youth for Christ, a fledgling evangelical organization established for ministry to youth and servicemen during World War II. As the group's vice president (1945-1948), he was soon the best-known speaker on the circuit, organizing groups in forty-eight states. Northwestern Schools (now Northwestern College) in Minneapolis-St. Paul, Minnesota, needed leadership, and Graham answered the call, serving both Youth for Christ and the evangelical institution as its president from 1947 to 1952. He published his first of many books, *Calling Youth to Christ*, in 1947.

Graham's powerful preaching in large public arenas drew the attention of publisher William Randolph Hearst, who instructed his reporters to "puff Billy Graham" as he launched a series of crusade meetings in Los Angeles in 1949. He liked Graham's communication style and supported his condemnation of communism's blatant atheism. Graham pointed out that communism prohibited preaching the Gospel and argued that communism spelled the end of democracy in the West. Featured on the front page of Hearst-owned newspapers across the United States, Graham quickly became a national figure. Originally scheduled for three weeks, his crusade meetings in Los Angeles extended to eight weeks and drew overflowing crowds and nonstop press attention, attention that continued throughout Graham's career.

The impact of these crusades led Graham to establish, in 1950, the Billy Graham Evangelistic Association (BGEA) in Minneapolis. Also in 1950 he launched *The Hour*

Billy Graham.
(Library of Congress)

of Decision, a weekly radio and television program on both American and Canadian broadcasting networks and heard internationally via shortwave radio. Within two years, he started his syndicated newspaper column, "My Answer," which was carried across the nation and had more than five million readers the first year alone. The best of these early columns would appear collectively in 1960 as a book by the same name. A pioneer of multimedia, Graham founded World Wide Pictures, which has produced and distributed more than one hundred films. He also became founding president of Blue Ridge Broadcasting Corporation, which operated a commercial-free radio station, WFGW, in Black Mountain, North Carolina. Also, he became editor-in-chief of *Decision* magazine, which circulated by the millions to patrons and interested parties worldwide.

Graham's most powerful instrument for change was the large, citywide crusade that became the hallmark of the BGEA. Each crusade proceeded along similar lines: opening crusade choir songs and then corporate singing; testimonies of conversion from notable figures from Hollywood, sports, politics, and the music industry; special music from a guest singer; a crusade solo before the message; a sermon from Graham; and an open invitation for people to leave their seats and come forward to signal their desire to accept Jesus as their savior.

Graham developed a clearly enunciated policy for the crusades, which stated that support for the crusade and active participation should be sought from churches regardless of their denomination or theology. He insisted that the crusades had to be integrated rather than segregated. These two positions caused many churches to refuse to participate in crusades, and it fueled criticism within conservative as well as liberal Christian circles. The crusades themselves were carefully planned: picking venues and times, soliciting and preparing local volunteers by the thousands, raising funds, media blitzes announcing meetings, and a sophisticated follow-up system for every person who registered a decision for Christ or sought additional help from the organization. Graham also pioneered phone banks, personal counseling through mail and in person, and linking people within local churches. The BGEA also engaged in philanthropic work around the globe, work that included disaster relief. The BGEA is now in partnership with Samaritan's Purse, which is led by one of Graham's five children, Franklin Graham.

Graham reported that his salary, unlike that of many other radio and television preachers, was paid directly and was determined by the businesspeople who sat on the BGEA board, maintaining that he never handled crusade or other organizational funds (which totaled more than $300 million annually at the peak of his ministry) and ensured his followers that the organization's accounting records were externally audited each year and made available to anyone upon request. Son Franklin succeeded his father as BGEA president in 2001.

Graham received many honorary degrees and other awards, most notably the Templeton Foundation Prize for Progress in Religion (1982), the nation's highest civilian award (Presidential Medal of Freedom, 1983), and the Congressional Gold Medal (1996). He was made a Knight of the Order of the British Empire in 2001. He was inducted into the Religious Broadcasting Hall of Fame (1981) and the Gospel Music Hall of Fame (1999), and he was ranked consistently in the top ten of the most admired persons in the world in annual Gallup polls.

On the political scene he was a visible and frequent adviser to U.S. presidents, starting with Dwight D. Eisenhower, and often was called to the White House at the darkest periods of the nation's history. His critics, however, have noted that he was politically naïve and was often manipulated to political advantage. He frequently found it difficult to reconcile a president's acceptance of evangelical Christianity with that president's participation in scandals while in office.

Significance

Graham's impact on Christianity in particular and on society in general is difficult to fully calculate. He helped establish the modern American evangelical movement and was instrumental in steering it from its more fundamentalist leanings. Furthermore, Graham likely has preached to more people than any other individual in human history. Millions have heard his sermons in person or on radio or television, have read his newspaper columns or books, and have watched films produced by World Wide Pictures (more than 250 million viewers). Several of his books are best sellers, and many have been translated.

Even though Graham never personally participated in the Civil Rights movement and its freedom marches and rallies, he believed that the Gospel was intended for all humanity. He did criticize the Civil Rights movement, however, for seeking too much, too fast. His message of religious tolerance has garnered awards from many ecumenical and Jewish organizations. He helped establish a number of Christian organizations and periodicals, most notably the magazine *Christianity Today*, which served as a formal and vital voice for the new evangelism.

—*Dennis W. Cheek*

FURTHER READING

Aikman, David. *Billy Graham: His Life and Influence*. Nashville, Tenn.: Thomas Nelson, 2007. An admiring biography of Graham by a former senior correspondent of *Time* magazine who knew him personally.

Gibbs, Nancy, and Michael Duffy. *The Preacher and the Presidents: Billy Graham in the White House*. New York: Center Street, 2007. Two *Time* correspondents carefully examine Graham's complex relationships with American presidents, from Eisenhower to the Bushes, with particular attention to what they see as his overstepping of clerical boundaries in the case of Richard Nixon.

Graham, Billy. *Just as I Am: The Autobiography of Billy Graham*. New York: HarperOne, 2007. A reissued edition of Graham's autobiography, first published in 1997. Discusses his early life and the beginnings of his ministry as well as his relationships with world leaders and dignitaries. A work of close to eight hundred pages.

Lowe, Janet. *Billy Graham Speaks: Insight from the World's Greatest Preacher*. New York: John Wiley & Sons, 1999. A collection of quotations from Graham interspersed with short anecdotes from his life and ministry. Material in this book is organized by topic. A valuable resource for those who want to better understand Graham's views and philosophy.

NATHANAEL GREENE

" *We fight, get beat, rise, and fight again.* **"**

Military leader

Greene was one of George Washington's most trusted military leaders throughout the Revolutionary War, playing significant roles as a field commander and as the Continental army's quartermaster general.

Born: August 7, 1742; Potowomut (now Warwick), Rhode Island
Died: June 19, 1786; Mulberry Grove plantation, Georgia
Area of achievement: Military

EARLY LIFE

Nathanael Greene was one of the numerous descendants of the Quaker John Greene, who followed Roger Williams to Rhode Island in 1636 in search of religious freedom. He was born in Potowomut (modern Warwick), Rhode Island. Because of his father's suspicion of learning, Greene was largely self-educated, his early reading being directed by a chance meeting with Ezra Stiles, later president of Yale College. The young Greene was five feet ten inches tall and well built, with an oval face, blue eyes, a straight nose, a full and determined mouth, a large forehead, and a firm double chin. A stiff right knee gave him a slight limp, but neither this nor periodic bouts of asthma prevented him from engaging in normal physical activity.

Like his brothers, Greene spent most of his youth working in the prosperous family forge and mills. In 1770, his father gave him control of the family forge in Coventry, Rhode Island, where he built his own house, including a library of 250 volumes. From early youth he had shown a fondness for dancing and an interest in things military; some time after his father's death, the Quaker meeting in Coventry dismissed him for attending a military parade.

Greene lived as a typical young man of his class, being elected to the Rhode Island General Assembly in 1770, 1771, 1772, and 1775. On July 20, 1774, he married Catharine Littlefield, and the two had two sons and three daughters. Greene was aware of the growing tensions between the American colonies and the mother country, becoming convinced as early as October, 1775, that a break with Great Britain was necessary to preserve American liberties. He was instrumental in the formation of the Kentish Guards, a militia company organized in response to the Boston Port Act of 1774; he served as a private when some members indicated that a captain who limped would be a blemish on the company.

LIFE'S WORK

Nathanael Greene's military career, which occupied the rest of his life, began when he was commissioned brigadier general of Rhode Island's three regiments on May 8, 1775. He took his troops to Boston, where he first met George Washington and, on June 22, was appointed one of the eight brigadier generals of the Continental army. He commanded in Boston after the British evacuation in March of 1776; by May, he was supervising the building of fortifications on Long Island, though a three-week bout with fever kept him out of the battles there. He was made major general on August 9 and by mid-September was commanding his division during the retreat from New York. At this point, as commander of Forts Lee and Washington, Greene was confident that both could be held, and Washington took his advice. However, on November 16, Fort Washington surrendered, Fort Lee had to be evacuated, and Washington's army retreated through New Jersey.

Greene's division crossed the Delaware River with Washington, and Greene led the left column against Trenton, capturing the Hessian artillery. In early January, he delayed Lieutenant General Cornwallis while Washington made his night march to Princeton. At the Battle of Brandywine on September 10, Greene's division covered four miles in forty-five minutes to aid the right wing, covered the retreat, and saved the artillery. Arriving late at the October 4 dawn attack on Germantown, Greene's left column fought in the two-hour battle and then protected the rear for five miles of the retreat, without losing a gun. On December 19, 1777, the army went into winter quarters at Valley Forge.

On February 25, 1778, Greene reluctantly agreed to become quartermaster general (officially appointed on March 2). A difficult job at best, it was much involved with the

Greene, Nathanael

politicking and intrigue swirling around Washington and in the Continental Congress; the eddies alone could destroy a reputation, and Greene preferred military activity. Yet his realization of the importance of the work and his strong sense of obligation to Washington and the revolutionary cause kept Greene in the position for eighteen months. During this time, he set up a system of supply depots and required monthly reports from his deputies. He was as effective as congressional politics, intercolonial squabbling, and inadequate financing allowed. On the march to Monmouth, for example, he picked good campsites and had them prepared with wood, straw, barrels of vinegar, latrines, and stone-walled springs, while seeing to the repair of equipment and the collection of fodder.

For the Battle of Monmouth on June 28, Greene resumed his line command and led the right wing, pushing back Sir Henry Clinton's line. Sent to Rhode Island to further a projected French-American push, Greene commanded the right wing on August 11, when American troops were defeated while Count d'Estaing refused to disembark his four thousand French soldiers. Greene acted as peacemaker in the subsequent arguments and again as right-wing commander in an unsuccessful engagement on August 29. The ensuing military lull did not extend to the quartermaster department, Greene administering approximately $50 million in 1779; his effectiveness at supply helped to support the Army during winter quarters in Morristown and to keep it mobile during the summer's maneuvering. When Congress adopted a plan to reorganize the department, Greene's resignation (the last of several) was accepted, on August 3. During September, while performing quartermaster duty until his successor took over, Greene also presided over the board of general officers that condemned Major John André to be hanged as a spy.

The war in the North wound down after 1778 as the British shifted their major operations to the South, taking Augusta and Charleston and setting up a chain of interior posts. After General Horatio Gates's defeat at Camden, Washington appointed Greene to the Southern command on October 14, 1780, and Congress ratified this to include control of all troops between Delaware and Georgia. In Philadelphia, Greene arranged for a medical department, engineers, artillery, clothing, horses, and equipment; in Richmond, he established cooperation with Governor Thomas Jefferson; in North Carolina, he ordered the building of boats and established cooperation with the patriot organizations.

On December 2, in Charlotte, he took formal command, which was marked almost immediately by cooperation with the partisan leaders General Andrew Pickens, General Thomas Sumter, and Colonel Francis (Swamp Fox) Marion, and by his use of able subordinates such as General Daniel Morgan, Colonel Otho H. Williams, and Colonel William Washington, with General Henry (Light-Horse Harry) Lee's Legion as his intelligence arm. Throughout his tenure as the commander of the Southern Department, Greene made effective use of these brilliant and independent-minded leaders while maintaining good relations with political leaders in several states and paying his usual careful attention to the logistical details that made his strategy possible. A nationalist, the Rhode Islander felt no constraint in the South; more diplomatic as commander than he was as quartermaster general, he was able to get maximum cooperation from detached and independent forces.

American losses at Charleston and Camden had seriously reduced both numbers and morale, so Greene appointed good quartermaster officers and added to the strength of his forces, having about two thousand Continentals and between five hundred and one thousand partisans. Moving his camp to the Cheraw Hills, South Carolina, on the Pedee River, he once again faced Lieutenant General Cornwallis. Like Greene, Cornwallis did not have enough men to control the South, and his serious supply problems were never solved; although popular with his troops (with whom he shared privation and hardship) and fearless in battle, he did not plan in detail for long campaigns and often blundered.

Greene took the initiative and divided his army, sending off half under Morgan to the victory at Cowpens on January 17, 1781. Cornwallis burned his baggage and set off in pursuit. Both armies raced for the Dan River, but Greene had provided boats and Cornwallis had not. Greene, maneuvering while waiting for reinforcements, took a strong position near Guilford Courthouse on March 15; he used his 4,200 men well, but few were veterans. Cornwallis attacked with 2,000 veterans, but although Greene retreated after three hours of hard fighting, Cornwallis lost a quarter of his force and had to withdraw toward the coast, unable to resume the offensive in the Carolinas.

Greene was physically exhausted after six weeks with little sleep and no change of clothing, but after some rest he planned the best use of his limited resources: He was left with about 1,450 troops and the partisans. Cornwallis's subordinate Lord Francis Rawdon attacked Greene's new position (near Camden) on April 25; because of Colonel John Gunby's injudicious order to fall back, Greene was forced to make a general retreat from Hobkirk's Hill. Rawdon, however, his communications and supply lines threatened, was forced to move off. Greene's detachments took the British posts, Lee's Legion took Augusta; Greene besieged Fort Ninety Six, but Rawdon relieved the garrison on June 19. This was Rawdon's second Pyrrhic victory, for he had to abandon the post. Thus, by July, Greene held nearly the entire lower South, having forced Cornwallis to leave the theater of operations. After the campaign's long marches and short rations, Greene took his army to camp at the High Hills of Santee for six weeks of recuperation, drill, and discipline.

The army moved out on August 23 and on September 8 surprised Lieutenant Colonel Alexander Stuart at Eutaw Springs, fighting a bloody battle against an army of equal size. The militia fought well, British regulars were pushed back in open fighting, and an American bayonet charge was successful. When, however, Lee's Legion and the artillery advanced beyond troops who stayed to enjoy the food and rum in the abandoned British camp, Greene was forced to leave the field. This indecisive battle, at best a draw, marked the end of the fighting in the lower South, as Stuart withdrew to Charleston. Congress later voted Greene thanks for the victory, along with a gold medal and a British standard, and Washington congratulated him in a letter.

With the onset of the cool season, Greene brought his army down from the Santee camp to besiege Charleston on January 2, 1782, holding a superior British force in the city until the end of the war. Supplying his army, aiding the restoration of civil government, and attempting to prevent mistreatment of Loyalists occupied Greene until all troops began to leave in July of 1783. The legislatures of Georgia and of North Carolina and South Carolina had voted to grant him land in gratitude. Greene rode home to Rhode Island in November but in 1784 had to return and sell the South Carolina plantation to settle claims made on him stemming from his arrangements for supplying the army before Charleston. (Congress granted, to his widow, the financial relief for which he had asked, in June, 1796.)

In the autumn of 1785, Greene moved his family to the Mulberry Grove plantation granted him in Georgia. He settled in to the life of a gentleman farmer, but on June 14, 1786, after walking in the afternoon sun, he developed head pains and inflammation, and died five days later. He was buried in the cemetery of Christ Episcopal Church in Savannah and in 1902 was re-interred under the Greene monument in Johnson Square in that city. The Marquis de Lafayette, a longtime friend of Greene, educated his son George Washington Greene in France until 1794; shortly after his return, at the age of nineteen, the boy drowned in the Savannah River. On June 28, 1796, Greene's widow married Phineas Miller; she died in 1814.

Significance

In many respects, Nathanael Greene exemplified the American experience. Descended from early English settlers fleeing religious persecution, he was continuing the economic and educationally upward mobility that characterized colonial society when the Battle of Lexington and Concord in 1775 interrupted an essentially undistinguished life. Appointed a brigadier general despite an almost complete lack of experience, Greene quickly demonstrated his military value to Washington. Throughout the revolution he held important commands, in all of them giving his country unstinting service despite personal and financial hardships.

On many points he was somewhat ahead of general public opinion. Early in the conflict, he urged independence as a goal. He saw the need of a strong central government, and, equally in vain, advocated a large regular army, enlisted for the duration, with central command and adequate supply and financial support. In this he differed from both contemporary and historical opinion, which was that the traditional militia was an effective military force expressing the popular nature of American society without endangering American liberties. Military historians have come to see the revolutionary patriot militias as a cross section of the colonial yeomanry, the "nation-in-arms" proficient with weapons and familiar with its home terrain, fighting well with its own officers and in its own way. For example, its usual casual "desertions," to deal with farm and business needs, produced not only a constantly fluctuating troop strength but also far less pressure on slender resources than a consistently large regular army would have.

Yet a commander and quartermaster general was bound to concentrate on the militia's weaknesses, even when planning them into his tactics, as Greene placed mostly raw militia in his first two lines at Guilford Courthouse: He wanted them to retreat after a few volleys, knowing that militia usually broke and ran in the face of an enemy advance, particularly of a bayonet charge, "grim lines of scarlet-coated men emerging from the mist and heading straight toward . . . them with naked steel," wrote historians Mary Wickwire and Franklin Wickwire. As quartermaster general, Greene was too preoccupied with shortages and inefficiencies to feel grateful that he had to provide for forces that were smaller than they would have been had militiamen been metamorphosed into duration-of-the-war Continentals.

Quartermaster generals, however efficient, are rarely remembered except by the troops whom they contrive somehow to supply. Even secondary commanders, however much relied upon by their chiefs, do not decide strategy: While Washington accepted Greene's assurance that Fort Washington could be held, it was Washington's own decision to attempt to block British operations in New Jersey. As commander of the Southern Department after the Camden debacle, Greene came fully into his own, demonstrating great abilities in tactics and strategy, as well as what in a military leader is called "character": courage, determination, dominating one's opponent, taking the psychological initiative. Greene chose his subordinates well, dealt diplomatically with both political and partisan leaders, and achieved results truly remarkable in the light of his command, which consisted of a small and inadequately supplied army supplemented by independent partisan groups and undisciplined militia.

In the South, Greene lost every major engagement he personally commanded, usually through the failure of troops at crucial points in the battle, when victory seemed imminent. Frustrating as these situations must have been to him—he had an impulsive temperament and was easily angered—he remained a cautious tactician, never risking a desperate continuation that might have won a battle but might as easily have destroyed his force. Like Washington, he realized the necessity of retaining an army able to fight again; he was willing to retreat, even run, but always to return to the conflict.

For despite his defeats, his Southern strategy achieved all the objectives of his campaigns; Cornwallis and Rawdon won battles but lost control of the lower South. By rapid movement, constant pressure on the enemy, the use of a variety of methods (raids, harassing supply lines, sieges, battles), Greene kept Cornwallis off balance, prevented his controlling the lower South and protecting its Loyalists, and possibly contributed to Cornwallis's decision to attempt a Virginia offensive rather than one in the Carolinas. That decision brought Cornwallis finally to Yorktown, where he surrendered in 1781.

—*Marsha Kass Marks*

FURTHER READING
Alden, John R. *A History of the American Revolution*. New York: Alfred A. Knopf, 1969. A basic general history, providing the necessary perspective. Includes a very clear section describing Greene's campaigns in the South.
Golway, Terry. *Washington's General: Nathanael Greene and the Triumph of the American Revolution*. New York: Henry Holt, 2005. Golway maintains that Greene's appointment as the commander of the revolutionary forces in the South was the decisive moment of the Revolutionary War.
Greene, Francis Vinton. *General Greene*. New York: D. Appleton, 1893. Reprint. Port Washington, N.Y.: Kennikat Press, 1970. A biography as slanted as one would expect from a late nineteenth century descendant of Greene. Nevertheless, well written and reasonably objective, with a nice balance of information on Greene's personal life and military career, the political background, and the prominent individuals whose lives intersected with his.

Greene, George Washington. *The Life of Nathanael Greene, Major-General in the Army of the Revolution.* 3 vols. New York: Hurd and Houghton, 1871. The late nineteenth century flavor of this work by Greene's grandson is amply compensated for by the author's intuitive grasp of his subject's character and development. Includes numerous quotations from primary sources. At age seventeen, the author knew Lafayette, was a friend of Henry Wadsworth Longfellow, and spoke at length with Greene's brothers and contemporaries in their old age.

Hairr, John. *Guilford Courthouse: Nathanael Greene's Victory in Defeat, March 15, 1781.* Cambridge, Mass.: Da Capo Press, 2002. One in a series of books about famous American battlefields, this work recounts the military exploits of Greene and Cornwallis at Guilford Courthouse. Chapter 1, "The Man from Rhode Island: Nathanael Greene," provides a brief overview of Greene's life and military career.

Higginbotham, Don. *The War of American Independence.* New York: Macmillan, 1971. A basic work on the Revolutionary War, but with a certain tendency to draw parallels between the revolution and twentieth century warfare, stretching the comparisons slightly. However, the book has an effective presentation of the overall military situation, specific battles, and the general political background of the time.

Ketchum, Richard M. "Men of the Revolution: III." *American Heritage* 23 (December, 1971): 48-49. A brief but comprehensive biographical sketch accompanied by Charles Willson Peale's portrait of Greene.

McCullough, David. *1776.* New York: Simon & Schuster, 2005. McCullough focuses on one year in the American Revolution, 1776, describing the battles between America's ragtag troops and British forces. Using letters, journals, diaries, and other primary sources, he describes the leadership of Nathanael Greene, George Washington, and General William Howe, as well as the heroic struggles of American soldiers.

Miller, John C. *Triumph of Freedom, 1775-1783.* Boston: Little, Brown, 1948. A standard overview of the period, including an effective analysis of both Greene and Cornwallis.

Snow, Richard F. "Battles of the Revolution: Guilford Court House." *American Heritage* 24 (June, 1973): 17. A good summary of the military action at Guilford Courthouse, with color paintings of soldiers of the Delaware Regiment and the Seventy-first Regiment of Foot.

Wickwire, Franklin, and Mary Wickwire. *Cornwallis: The American Adventure.* Boston: Houghton Mifflin, 1970. A major study of Cornwallis, this work presents the war from the British perspective, with attention to the problems of the British political and military systems. Although in style somewhat reminiscent of nineteenth century literature, thus giving a quaint flavor to the eighteenth century narrative coupled with twentieth century psychological insights, it is quite clear, explaining without explaining away Cornwallis's failures.

Wayne Gretzky

" You'll always miss 100 percent of the shots you don't take. "

Hockey player

Immediately after entering professional hockey at age seventeen, Gretzky began breaking single-game, season, and career scoring records. Known as the Great One, he was the major force behind the Edmonton Oilers' winning four championships in five seasons. He also helped build awareness of the sport outside traditional hockey territory and proved that hockey has a place for smaller athletes.

Born: January 26, 1961; Brantford, Ontario, Canada
Also known as: Wayne Douglas Gretzky (full name); the Great One
Area of achievement: Sports

Early Life

Wayne Gretzky (GREHTS-kee) was born to be an athlete. In school, he participated in baseball, soccer, basketball, hockey, lacrosse, golf, track, and cross-country running, doing well in all sports. Hockey, however, was his main sport. At age two he was already skating on the Nith River near his grandparents' farm and in the local park's outdoor rink. When Gretzky was four years old, his father, Walter, flooded the backyard to make an ice "rink" for his son and other neighborhood boys. His father later admitted he made the rink not to help develop his son into a hockey star but because his own feet had gotten too cold from standing around in the park while Wayne skated. His mother, Phyllis, also supported Wayne's skating mania.

Six-year-old Wayne began playing in the major novice league for ten-year-olds, because at that time there was no league for children his age. He scored only one goal in that first year, but the next year he scored 27, then 104, then 196. By the time he reached age ten, he was still just four feet feet four inches tall, but he scored 378 goals in sixty-nine games. The second-place scorer made 140 goals.

It was around this time that a local reporter started to call him the Great Gretzky and the public began besieging him for autographs. Some parents of other Brantford-area boys began to resent his success, and they even threatened him. By the time he was age fourteen, the abuse became so bad that he moved with his family to Toronto and joined the Vaughan Nationals hockey team. Some of his new teammates were twenty years old. Gretzky managed to score two goals in his first game with the new team.

In 1977, Gretzky went to Sault Ste. Marie in northern Ontario, his first time far away from home. He had always worn uniform number 9, honoring his hero Gordie Howe, but a Greyhounds veteran already had that number. Coach Muzz MacPherson suggested that he double it, as Phil Esposito had done when traded to the New York Rangers. Gretzky wore number 99 from then until his retirement in 1999.

In 1978, Gretzky was seventeen years old but too young to play in the National Hockey League (NHL), so he signed an eight-year personal-services contract with Nelson Skalbania, owner of the World Hockey Association's (WHA) Indianapolis

Gretzky, Wayne

Racers. After just eight games, Skalbania sold the contract to former partner Peter Pocklington, owner of the WHA's Edmonton Oilers. That 1978-1979 season was the WHA's last, as the Oilers and three other teams merged into the NHL, bringing with them Gretzky and several other star players.

LIFE'S WORK

One of Gretzky's most cherished records was scoring fifty goals in the first fifty games of a season. Maurice "Rocket" Richard had done so in 1944-1945, and Mike Bossy matched it in 1980-1981. Gretzky aimed for that record during the 1980-1981 season. In the Oilers's thirty-eighth game, he scored four goals to reach forty-five. The next game, he scored five goals to reach fifty in only thirty-nine games, a remarkable feat. He achieved the fifty-in-fifty mark two more times, in 1983-1984 and 1984-1985.

The Oilers and Gretzky did well in the NHL, but they did not win the Stanley Cup—the championship—until 1984, when they beat the reigning New York Islanders in five games. The Oilers won the cup again in 1985, 1987, and 1988.

In the summer of 1988, Gretzky helped engineer a trade that sent him to the Los Angeles Kings, causing an uproar across Canada. Los Angeles had been in the NHL since 1967, but it was the acquisition of Gretzky that made hockey a popular sport there. After he was traded to the Kings, the closest Gretzky ever came to winning the Stanley Cup was in 1993. Los Angeles beat the Montreal Canadiens in the first game of the cup finals, and they led with less than two minutes left in game two. Montreal coach Jacques Demers picked that crucial moment to call for an official measurement of Marty McSorley's stick, whose blade was curved more than the rules allowed. Montreal tied the game on the ensuing power play and went on to win that game and then the series. Gretzky never reached the Stanley Cup finals again. The infamous stick was displayed in a glass case in Gretzky's Toronto restaurant.

Gretzky credits his father for much of his skill. Young Walter played at the junior B level and later served as an amateur hockey coach. He was a finesse player and passed that along to his sons. Not all of Walter's advice was right for his son though. When Gretzky was the stick boy for the team that his father coached, Walter would tell him "never skate behind the net." Many years later, the area behind the net became known as "Gretzky's office" because he was so good at passing to scorers from that location. His low threshold for panic made the spot ideal for Gretzky. In situations where other players would hurriedly get rid of the puck, Gretzky would calmly wait until a player was open or the goalie was out of position. Indeed, his behind-the-net play helped get the goalie out of position, forcing him to look over both shoulders and lose his focus of the game in front of him. With Gretzky behind the net, teammates could get clear on either side of the net, receive his pass, and score as the goalie lost focus.

When Gretzky retired after the 1998-1999 season, the Hockey Hall of Fame selection committee waived the usual three-year waiting period. NHL commissioner Gary Bettman retired Gretzky's number 99 for all teams, the only time that honor has been conferred. In his autobiography, Gretzky said that he dreamed of owning an NHL team some day but definitely did not want to be a coach or a general manager. He became part-owner and managing partner of the Phoenix Coyotes in 2001 and became the team's coach in 2004.

Gretzky, Wayne

Gretzky won the Hart Memorial Trophy as the NHL's most valuable player nine times in his first ten seasons. As the league's leading scorer, he won the Art Ross Trophy ten times, and for his sportsmanship and gentlemanly conduct he was awarded the Lady Byng Memorial Trophy five times. He holds or shares forty regular-season records, fifteen play-off records, and six NHL All-Star Game records. He scored 3,238 points in his career (including the play-offs), far exceeding his closest competitors for individual athletic achievements in hockey.

SIGNIFICANCE
Gretzky's most significant contributions as a player include his ability to anticipate the location of the puck; his behind-the-net play; his great passing ability, coupled with his uncanny awareness of the strengths of his teammates and his ability to complement those strengths; and the exactness of his shooting. Contrary to his father's early instructions, Gretzky found that skating behind the goalie worked for him, and for his team. That the Edmonton Oilers won four championships in five seasons with Gretzky attests to the uniqueness and greatness of his play on the ice.

At five feet eleven inches tall and at 170 pounds, Gretzky was an atypical hockey player. His relatively small stature, however, did not get in the way of his greatness as a player. Even as a child he managed to play against bigger, stronger players. His success has helped aspiring players, even those who are considered "too small" for hockey, work toward their goal of becoming professionals.

—*J. Edmund Rush*

FURTHER READING
Christopher, Matt. *On the Ice with Wayne Gretzky*. Boston: Little, Brown, 1997. Written for a juvenile audience, this biography describes Gretzky's childhood, including the poor treatment he received from parents and neighbors.

Dryden, Steve, ed. *Total Gretzky: The Magic, the Legend, the Numbers*. Toronto, Ont.: McClelland & Stewart, 1999. Based on *The Hockey News*'s commemorative magazine *The Great One*, this collection includes a tribute by Roy MacGregor, a foreword by Peter Gzowski, and articles by former NHL players and *Hockey News* editors and writers. It lists Gretzky's career totals and records, plus lists every game, year by year, of his careers with the NHL, the WHA, as a junior, and in all-star games. Illustrated.

Gretzky, Walter, and Jim Taylor. *Gretzky: From the Back Yard Rink to the Stanley Cup*. Toronto, Ont.: McClelland & Stewart, 1984. Gretzky's father starts with the first successful Stanley Cup drive and other highlights, then describes his famous son's life almost from birth. Illustrated. No index.

Gretzky, Wayne, and Rick Reilly. *Gretzky: An Autobiography*. New York: HarperCollins, 1990. This autobiography, written in the middle of Gretzky's NHL career, covers his life from skating at age two through his trade to the Los Angeles Kings and includes discussion of his marriage. Reilly is a columnist for *Sports Illustrated* magazine. Illustrated. Names index only.

Morrison, Scott. *Wayne Gretzky: The Great Goodbye*. Toronto, Ont.: Key Porter Books, 1999. Written for a juvenile audience, this biography provides photographs

Hallaren, Mary A.

and newspaper accounts from Gretzky's hockey career, along with highlights of his final season.

Raber, Thomas R. *Wayne Gretzky, Hockey Great.* Minneapolis, Minn.: Lerner, 1991. Written for a juvenile audience, this brief biography describes Gretzky's rise from child prodigy to adult superstar.

Mary A. Hallaren

❝ *You don't have to be six feet tall to have a brain that works.* ❞

Military leader

The third director of the Women's Army Corps, Hallaren expanded opportunities for women in the U.S. armed forces during and after World War II. Through her efforts, women moved from auxiliary status to permanent status as regular service members. Furthermore, she was the first woman commissioned an officer in the regular Army.

Born: May 4, 1907; Lowell, Massachusetts
Died: February 13, 2005; McLean, Virginia
Also known as: Mary Agnes Hallaren (full name); Little Colonel
Areas of achievement: Military; women's rights

Early Life

Mary A. Hallaren (HAHL-lah-rehn), director of the Women's Army Corps from 1947 until 1953, was born in Lowell, Massachusetts, to John J. Hallaren and Mary A. (Kenney) Hallaren. Her parents were Irish immigrants who lived in the Pawtucketville section of Lowell. She attended public schools in Lowell, graduating from Lowell High School. She received a teaching degree from Lowell Teachers College in 1927 and taught middle school in Lexington for fifteen years before she entered the military.

Teaching meant that Hallaren had summers free for travel. She hitchhiked and backpacked through the United States and the rest of the world. She started by traveling to national parks in the United States. After seeing most of the country, she toured Canada and Mexico, then traveled through Europe and South America. Hallaren was in Munich, Germany, one summer when she crossed paths with Adolf Hitler. The Nazi leader was virtually unknown in the United States but already was a sensation in Germany. Hallaren remembered that Hitler received a thunderous reception in the Munich town square, but he did not make a strong impression on her. On a hike through Rome, she drew a crowd by wearing pants. (Italians had not seen many women wearing pants.) She was known by her students and her fellow teachers as the Hitchhiking Teacher.

Life's Work

Hallaren's adult life can be divided into her military career and her post-retirement service work. Shortly after the United States entered World War II, the U.S. Army created the Women's Army Auxiliary Corps (WAAC). U.S. Representative Edith Nourse Rogers had introduced a bill in Congress that led to the WAAC's establishment. Oveta Culp Hobby was its first director.

Hallaren followed her brothers into the Army and enlisted in 1942. She had been asked by an Army recruiter about her height. (Hallaren claimed to be five feet tall, but she was likely a few inches shorter.) The recruiter wondered what such a short person could do in the Army, and Hallaren replied, "You don't have to be six feet tall to have a brain that works."

In August, 1942, she was selected to be in the first class of the WAAC Officer Candidate School at Fort Des Moines, Iowa. Hallaren's first job was assistant WAAC commandant at the Second WAAC Training Center in Daytona Beach, Florida, and she trained the First WAAC Separate Battalion. Hallaren's battalion was sent to Europe in July, 1943, the first women's battalion to receive orders to serve overseas in the European theater of World War II. Hallaren began service in Europe as the WAAC staff director attached to the U.S. Eighth and Ninth Air Forces. Upon arrival in England, her unit was divided into companies for service with several Army Air Corps units. The women initially were assigned to jobs as clerks, telephone operators, cooks, and drivers. By the end of the first year, however, they were filling two hundred different jobs, including cryptographer.

Ironically, Hallaren's passion for hiking played a small part in the history of her battalion. At one time during the battalion's tour of duty, the troop ship carrying the WAAC personnel between European ports had been forced to remain docked while Army intelligence officers investigated an alleged tie between one of the WAAC soldiers and the Hitler Youth. Years later, Hallaren learned that she was the one facing investigation. It turns out that she was under suspicion because the German hiking club she had joined earlier eventually folded into the Hitler Youth.

From June, 1945, to June, 1946, Hallaren served as the WAAC staff director for the European theater of operations. Her work and leadership abilities attracted the attention of the Allied supreme commander, Dwight D. Eisenhower. When the fighting ended in Europe, General Eisenhower asked Hallaren to oversee the transition of the Women's Army Auxiliary Corps to the Women's Army Corps (WAC), which was to become a permanent part of the military establishment. Hallaren was promoted to colonel in May, 1947, the first woman commissioned in the regular Army. It also was the highest rank that could be held by a woman at the time. Many under Hallaren's command referred to her as the Little Colonel.

Recalled to Washington, Hallaren worked to encourage Congress to upgrade the official status of women in the military and make them a permanent part of the armed services. Her proposal, which became the Women's Armed Services Integration Act of 1948, first met with strong resistance, especially among members of the House Armed Services Committee. The committee tried to rework the legislation so that it would limit women's status in the service and permit service only in time of national crises (that is, as temporary staff only). Working with former service members, Hallaren indirectly led a lobbying campaign that flooded the offices of members of the Armed Services Committee. The committee eventually agreed that women should become a permanent part of the military, thus forming the Army WACs and the Navy WAVES

Hallaren, Mary A.

(Women Accepted for Volunteer Emergency Service). Colonel Hallaren, the first woman commissioned an officer in the regular Army, served as WAC director from December, 1948, through May, 1953.

Hallaren retired from the Army in 1960. During her years of service, she received numerous citations including the Bronze Star, the Army Commendation Medal, the Legion of Merit, the Croix de Guerre, and the Legion of Honor. Five years after retiring from active military service, Hallaren started a third career. A friend had told her about Women in Community Service (WICS), a national nonprofit organization created by a coalition of five women's groups: American GI Forum Women, Church Women United, National Council of Catholic Women, National Council of Jewish Women, and National Council of Negro Women. WICS had been seeking an executive director, and Hallaren took the job. She led the organization for fourteen years. She also was instrumental in the creation of the Women in Military Service for America Memorial at Arlington National Cemetery in Virginia. Hallaren died on February 13, 2005, of complications from a stroke.

Significance

Hallaren was a pioneer in expanding the role of women in American society. She engaged apparent obstacles with courage, good humor, and a strong sense of curiosity. U.S. representative Barbara A. Mikulski, a Democrat from Maryland, introduced a bill in 1978 to promote Hallaren to brigadier general on the retired list. In her floor statement, Mikulski summed up Hallaren's career, indicating that her military career would not have been limited had Hallaren been a man.

In spite of her many successes, Hallaren maintained a sense of humility. On October 5, 1996, she was inducted into the American Women's Hall of Fame. She accepted the honor with pride and humility, saying that she was a good citizen who had only done a good job in the Women's Army Corps and with WICS.

—*John David Rausch, Jr.*

Further Reading

Brokaw, Tom. *The Greatest Generation*. New York: Random House, 1998. A brief profile of Colonel Hallaren as one of the many Americans who served in the military during World War II. Illustrated.

Dean, Mensah. "Activist's Army of Victories for Women." *Washington Times*, October 10, 1996, p. 8. This profile was written when Hallaren was inducted into the National Women's Hall of Fame. It is an excellent, concise summary of her careers as a schoolteacher, military officer, and social activist.

Morden, Bettie J. *The Women's Army Corps, 1945-1978*. Washington, D.C.: Center of Military History, United States Army, 1990. A detailed examination of the development of the Women's Army Corps from the end of World War II through the end of WAC's existence. Hallaren reviewed the manuscript of the book, and her role as a WAC leader is discussed throughout.

Nathan, Amy. *Count on Us: American Women in the Military*. Washington, D.C.: National Geographic Society, 2004. This book, written for elementary and middle school audiences, examines the role of women in the American military from the

Revolutionary War through the 2003 invasion of Iraq. Colonel Hallaren's career is discussed briefly.

Weiner, Josephine. *The Story of WICS*. Washington, D.C.: Women in Community Service, 1979. A detailed examination of the development of WICS as a nongovernmental organization implementing social policy across the United States.

Witt, Linda. *"A Defense Weapon Known to Be a Value": Servicewomen of the Korean War Era*. Hanover, N.H.: University Press of New England, 2005. This book reviews the role of women in the military during the period immediately before the Korean conflict and during that conflict. A brief sketch of Colonel Hallaren's career appears in the book.

WILLIAM F. HALSEY

" *There are no great men, only great challenges that ordinary men are forced by circumstances to meet.* **"**

Aviator and naval officer

Halsey was a colorful and offensive-minded military fighter who went by the slogan "hit hard, hit fast, hit often." A proponent of naval aviation and an avowed risk taker, he epitomized the aggressive spirit of the U.S. Navy during World War II.

Born: October 30, 1882; Elizabeth, New Jersey
Died: August 16, 1959; Fishers Island, New York
Also known as: William Frederick Halsey, Jr. (full name); Bull Halsey
Area of achievement: Military

EARLY LIFE

William F. Halsey (HAWL-zee) was the son of a former naval captain. Like his father, he attended the U.S. Naval Academy in Annapolis, Maryland, and he graduated as a midshipman in 1904. He served on several ships before joining the battleship *Kansas* as part of President Theodore Roosevelt's Great White Fleet, which steamed around the world from 1907 to 1909. Halsey rose steadily through the ranks and, during World War I, commanded the destroyers *Shaw* and *Benham* while on escort duty in Queenstown, Ireland. Fine seamanship garnered him the Navy Cross in 1918, and he spent the next twenty years holding down various assignments on ship and ashore.

Following several tours in Berlin, Germany; Copenhagen, Denmark; and Stockholm, Sweden, as a naval attaché, Halsey attended the Naval and Army War Colleges before turning his attention to naval aviation. The invention of the aircraft carrier held the potential for revolutionizing naval warfare, and Halsey envisioned opportunities for advancement in this new and untested field. Undeterred by advanced age and poor vision, he received flight training at the Naval Aviator's School at Pensacola, Florida, in 1935 and won his wings at the age of fifty-two. Halsey then transferred to the carrier

Halsey, William F.

service by commanding the *Saratoga* and distinguished himself during various fleet training exercises up through 1937.

In terms of naval tactics, Halsey was no traditionalist and made a name for himself by demanding greater roles for naval aviation. This view was advocated at the expense of the "battleship admirals," who saw airplanes as little more than scouts for the battle fleet. Furthermore, Halsey deliberately cultivated a "fighting sailor" image. When his promotion to vice admiral arrived in June, 1940, Halsey took charge of Carrier Division 2, consisting of the *Enterprise* and the *Yorktown*, and deployed them in the Pacific. War with Japan seemed imminent to Halsey, and on December 1, 1941, while ferrying fighter aircraft to Wake Island, he took the unprecedented measure of placing the ships on a war footing. His premonitions were justified six days later when Japanese carrier aircraft dealt a devastating blow to the U.S. battle fleet at Pearl Harbor, Hawaii.

LIFE'S WORK

Halsey personified aggressive leadership, and he quickly emerged as one of the United States' earliest wartime heroes. In January, 1942, Admiral Chester W. Nimitz ordered him to conduct the Navy's first offensive of World War II by launching air strikes against the Gilbert and Marshall Islands. The following month Halsey also struck Wake and Marcus Islands before embarking on one of the most audacious raids in military history. That April, Halsey commanded a task force that escorted Captain Marc A. Mitscher's carrier *Hornet* to within bombing distance of Japan. On board were sixteen Army Air Force B-25 Mitchell bombers under veteran aviator Colonel James H. Doolittle. Despite a stealthy, northern approach to within 620 miles of the enemy homeland, the Americans were discovered by a Japanese picket vessel the day before the launch was scheduled. With characteristic boldness, Halsey and Doolittle decided to move up the launch date by one day, anticipating that the Japanese now expected a raid by short-range naval aircraft. On April 18, 1942, the bombers were launched against Tokyo and other targets, which completely surprised the defenders. Little material damage was inflicted and all the aircraft subsequently crash-landed in China, but Doolittle's raid provided tremendous lift to American morale.

In Halsey's absence, elements of the U.S. carrier fleet fought a large Japanese task force to a draw at the Battle of Coral Sea in May, 1942. This was the first time in history that two opposing battle fleets traded shots without ever sighting each other. An impending Japanese invasion of Port Moresby, New Guinea, was thwarted, but Japan countered with an ambitious amphibious attack against Midway Island. The intention of Admiral Isoroku Yamamoto was to lure the three remaining U.S. carriers into battle at a numerical disadvantage and destroy them. It was a scenario tailor-made for Halsey's daredevil leadership, but fate intervened when he was sidelined by a skin rash. While he recuperated in Hawaii, the Americans fought and won the decisive victory at Midway Island in June, 1942. Halsey missed the greatest carrier clash in history, but his efficiently trained staff was present and contributed greatly to the battle's successful outcome.

Halsey had no sooner recovered than he was dispatched to the Pacific on an extremely urgent mission. In the wake of Midway Island, the United States had staged its

Halsey, William F.

William F. Halsey.
(Library of Congress)

first amphibious offensive of the war by landing Marines on Guadalcanal in the Solomon Islands in August, 1942. The Japanese responded with a ferocious land, sea, and air offensive intended to drive them out. Over the next few weeks, the U.S. Navy took heavy losses at the hands of the Japanese navy and was withdrawn from the area. This left the Marines stranded on Guadalcanal without support and open to attack from the sea. The Navy Department, dissatisfied by the timid leadership of Admiral Robert L. Ghormley, replaced him in October with the now-recovered Halsey in an attempt to stave off disaster. As commander of the South Pacific Force, he infused all hands with an offensive spirit and issued one standing order: Attack! Halsey then sailed forth to engage the enemy, fighting the Japanese to a draw near the Santa Cruz Islands on October 26-28 and decisively defeating them off Guadalcanal on November 12-15. Victory proved costly in terms of men and ships, but the tide had turned. Within three months the Japanese had abandoned Guadalcanal, and the Allies were free to expand their offensive strategy.

As a reward for his fighting leadership, Halsey received promotion to full admiral and was entrusted with clearing out the Solomon Islands. In this endeavor he was forced to cooperate with another leader of tremendous ability and ego, General Douglas MacArthur. Happily, the two headstrong, aggressive commanders agreed on a number of strategic and tactical priorities. They realized that any advance up the Solomons would eventually encounter the powerful Japanese stronghold on Rabaul at

Halsey, William F.

the northernmost end of the island chain. Rather than risk their few remaining carriers to aerial assault, Halsey and MacArthur decided to seize lightly defended areas around the bastion, construct airfields, and isolate the island with air power. Thus a costly invasion became unnecessary. As the U.S. steamroller continued westward and into the Gilbert and Marshall Islands, Halsey and MacArthur decided that the heavily fortified island of Truk could be bypassed in identical fashion. Consequently, many lives were spared and two sizable enemy garrisons were neutralized without a shot being fired. By March, 1944, the South Pacific region was firmly in Allied hands, and U.S. leaders turned their attention to the bigger objective of recapturing the Philippines.

In October, 1944, Halsey relieved Admiral Raymond A. Spruance as commander of the Third Fleet (Task Force 38) and made preliminary dispositions for cooperating with MacArthur's army. Up to this point, he enjoyed a reputation as the United States' leading naval fighter. However, the impending Philippine campaign was a huge, multifront endeavor combining the resources of many fleets and objectives. The sheer scope of operations, combined with a wily adversary, seems to have gotten the better of Halsey, and his reputation suffered. His initial operations against the original target, the southern island of Mindanao, revealed very weak Japanese air defenses, suggesting that it was also weakly held. Halsey then brilliantly suggested that it be bypassed altogether, an act that would move up the intended invasion of Luzon, the main island, by two months.

Subsequent operations, however, taxed Halsey's abilities to the limit. He was entrusted with the dual responsibility of shielding MacArthur's intricate landings at Leyte Gulf while simultaneously seeking out the remaining Japanese carriers and destroying them. The October, 1944, landings succeeded, but the Japanese countered with a three-pronged naval offensive that confused the U.S. high command. Unaware of the larger picture, Halsey predictably pursued Admiral Jisaburō Ozawa's ships and sank his last four carriers. In doing so, he ignored repeated suggestions from his staff that Ozawa was probably a decoy sent to lure Halsey away from Leyte. In fact, this is exactly what happened. In Halsey's absence, two other Japanese strike forces penetrated the Surigao Strait unopposed and briefly menaced the landing zones. Fortunately, the enemy turned back after meeting heavy resistance from an inferior force of escort carriers and destroyers at Samar Island and disaster was averted. Japanese losses during the Battle of Leyte Gulf were crippling and were achieved at relatively little cost to U.S. forces. Nonetheless, Halsey endured considerable criticism for charging after Ozawa and leaving the beachheads undefended.

In December, 1944, Halsey made another controversial decision by riding out a typhoon that sank three destroyer escorts and damaged his fleet far more than the enemy had. The final months of the war saw Task Force 38 making wide sweeps through the China Sea, Formosa, Okinawa, and the Chinese coast, decimating the remnants of enemy sea and air power. That June he elected to ride out another typhoon, again with appreciable damage to the fleet. By July, 1945, Halsey's aircraft were ranging the Japanese home islands at will, while his ships bombarded installations on shore. Following Japan's capitulation in August, 1945, the official surrender ceremony was concluded aboard Halsey's former flagship, the battleship *Missouri*. In three and one-half years of combat, the old admiral was responsible for sinking more enemy warships than any other naval commander. After the war, Halsey turned over the Third Fleet to Admiral Howard Kingman and returned home to become a five-star fleet admiral. He then performed several months of special duty with the secretary of the Navy before formally retiring in April, 1947. Halsey, one of the most popular sailors in U.S. history, died at the Fishers Island Country Club in New York on August 16, 1959.

Significance

Halsey, dubbed "Bull" by the press for his aggressive swagger, was a proven fighter and a brilliant naval tactician. Given a short-term objective, no matter how daunting, he invariably assembled the means for attacking and proceeded relentlessly until victorious. In this sense, his approach to war reflected the eighteenth century British school epitomized by Lord Horatio Nelson: a single-minded determination to seek out, engage, and destroy the enemy fleet through decisive action. However, his highly individualistic leadership style was more appropriate to this earlier setting and was anachronistic given the mounting complexities of modern naval warfare in which teamwork, analysis, and managerial skills proved paramount.

In truth, Halsey stumbled badly at Leyte and, had the Japanese displayed more aggressive leadership, the ensuing disaster might have compromised MacArthur's invasion. Furthermore, his decision to twice expose the Third Fleet to the ravages of typhoons cost seven hundred lives, several ships, and scores of aircraft, and it called into question his competency as a sailor. Throughout the war, detractors raised legitimate points about his limitations, but Halsey's public popularity and combat record shielded him from recriminations. No other admiral could have made his mistakes and survived. Nevertheless, he enjoyed a lengthy, controversial, and ultimately successful career and is rightly credited with turning the tide of battle in the Pacific. Halsey's efficacy as one of naval warfare's most determined and colorful practitioners is secure and unmatched by any admiral of the twentieth century.

—*John C. Fredriksen*

Further Reading

Adamson, Has C., and George F. Kosco. *Halsey's Typhoons: A Firsthand Account of How Two Typhoons, More Powerful Than the Japanese, Dealt Death and Destruction to Admiral Halsey's Third Fleet*. New York: Crown, 1967. As the title implies, the book provides an eyewitness treatment of the Third Fleet's terrible beating at the hands of nature. The admiral is highly criticized.

Cutler, Thomas J. *The Battle of Leyte Gulf, October 23-26, 1944*. New York: Harper & Row, 1994. Cutler's analysis of the controversial victory credits Halsey with winning the battle. An extensively researched book.

Drury, Bob, and Tom Chavin. *Halsey's Typhoon: The True Story of a Fighting Admiral, an Epic Storm, and an Untold Rescue*. New York: Atlantic Monthly Press, 2007. Describes how the U.S. Third Fleet, under Halsey's command, was struck by a devastating typhoon off the coast of the Philippines in the autumn of 1944.

Halsey, William F., and J. Bryan III. *Admiral Halsey's Story*. New York: McGraw-Hill, 1947. This book contains a journalistic and anecdotal account of high command that suffers from an unabashed lack of objectivity.

Merrill, James M. *A Sailor's Admiral: A Biography of William F. Halsey.* New York: Thomas Y. Crowell, 1976. An exciting and popular account that focuses almost entirely on the war years.

Potter, E. B. *Bull Halsey.* Annapolis, Md.: Naval Institute Press, 1985. This well-researched, engagingly written account is somewhat limited by the author's refusal to criticize Halsey's more questionable decisions.

Thomas, Evan. *Sea of Thunder: Four Commanders and the Last Great Naval Campaign, 1941-1945.* New York: Simon & Schuster, 2006. Recounts the naval battle in the Leyte Gulf from the perspective of four officers, including Halsey and his Japanese counterpart, Takeo Kurita.

FANNIE LOU HAMER

" *I'm sick and tired of being sick and tired.* **"**

Civil rights activist

Born a child of sharecroppers and a descendant of slaves, Hamer rose to prominence as a fearless and eloquent advocate for African American voting rights and as a leader in the larger Civil Rights movement. Her name became symbolic of the movement.

Born: October 6, 1917; Montgomery County, Mississippi
Died: March 14, 1977; Mound Bayou, Mississippi
Also known as: Fannie Lou Townsend (birth name)
Areas of achievement: Civil rights; social reform

EARLY LIFE

Fannie Lou Hamer (HAY-mur) was born Fannie Lou Townsend in Montgomery County, Mississippi. She was the granddaughter of slaves and the last of twenty children born to James Lee Townsend and Lou Ella Bramlett. Her father was a Baptist preacher and bootlegger, her mother a domestic servant, and both were sharecroppers. The family was very poor; meals often consisted of greens and gravy or bread and onions. They lived in a small wooden house without running water or electricity. When Hamer was six years old, she was offered a reward of canned fish and Cracker Jacks candy from the sharecropper boss if she proved how well she could pick cotton. Excited, she passed the test and ended up joining her siblings and working in the fields twelve to fourteen hours a day.

Hamer attended school for several years, but for blacks the school was open for four winter months only, when field-workers could be spared. Still, she learned to read and write, won spelling bees, and sharpened her quick mind. Tragically, she contracted polio as a child and limped with a disabled leg for the rest of her life.

When Hamer was eleven, her family rented their own land, the first step toward independence, and bought three mules, two cows, a plow, and even a car. Two years later, however, someone, most likely a white neighbor who did not want the family to succeed, poisoned the mules, and the family was forced back to sharecropping. In 1939, Hamer's father died, and soon after her mother was injured in an accident that deprived her of sight in one eye.

LIFE'S WORK

Hamer married Perry "Pap" Hamer in 1945, and the couple resettled in nearby Sunflower City. They had their own home, with cold running water. They were able to have children of their own, but they took in and later adopted two girls, whom they raised as daughters. Hamer worked three jobs: picking cotton, supervising other fieldworkers, and cleaning the home of the Marlowes, the plantation owners. The third job showed her how the white population lived, with standard amenities in homes of the day.

Life changed for Hamer in 1962. At a meeting conducted by civil rights workers from the North, she learned that African Americans had the right to vote. When the organizers called for people to register, Hamer raised her hand. This was no small decision. Though the law gave people the right to vote regardless of race, across the South there was much intimidation. African Americans were beaten, fired from their jobs, or killed if they dared to assert their constitutional rights; often, their property was vandalized and their homes burned.

Pap chose not to register, but Hamer, knowing that registering to vote could affect her family and its livelihood, followed through on her pledge. On August 31, 1962, she was one of seventeen African Americans who met activists in the nearby town of Indianola and boarded a bus to take them to register. Voting officials asked the group to copy out a section of the Mississippi state constitution and explain its meaning. Hamer and the others, predictably, failed the test. On the return trip, the bus was stopped by police, ostensibly for being "too yellow," and the driver was arrested and fined thirty dollars.

News of Hamer's attempt to register spread quickly, and Pap's boss threatened to evict the family from the land they worked. The Hamers moved out of their home and stayed with friends in Ruleville. Targeted intimidation ensued, including gunshots in their direction, and the Hamers left the county. Voting rights workers learned of Hamer's courage as well, and they asked her to speak at a meeting of the Student Nonviolent Coordinating Committee (SNCC) in Nashville, Tennessee. Prior to this invitation, Hamer had never left her area of northern Mississippi. In Nashville, she addressed groups and spoke with reporters. When she returned to Ruleville, Pap was fired from his job, and the Hamers lost their home. Hamer took a job with the SNCC, making speeches, recruiting volunteers, and helping to build the organization.

In January of 1963, at the age of forty-five, Hamer finally passed the test and became a registered voter. Her struggle was far from over, however. Six months later, on June 9, she and a group of fellow activists were at a bus station in Winona, Tennessee, traveling home from a meeting. The entire group was arrested and beaten brutally with leather straps in jail. The event left Hamer scarred for life, but it galvanized her resolve. The group sued the officers who had beaten them, but an all-white jury acquitted the defendants on all charges.

Fannie Lou Hamer.
(Library of Congress)

As the 1964 presidential elections approached, civil rights workers felt that the Mississippi Democratic Party did not represent their views, so they formed the Mississippi Freedom Democratic Party (MFDP). As a member, Hamer went to the Democratic National Convention in Atlantic City, New Jersey, that summer. The MFDP sought to replace the Mississippi Democratic Party's all-white delegation. Hamer spoke eloquently, arguing that the state deserved a representatively diverse delegation. The national party rejected the MFDP's request. Hamer, nevertheless, tried to enter the convention, singing what would become her trademark song, "This Little Light of Mine." Though she did not succeed, her attempt was covered on the evening news across the nation. Later that year, Hamer ran for Congress, earning thirty thousand votes, not enough to win the race. In 1968, the MFDP was chosen to represent Mississippi Democrats at the national convention, and Hamer was a delegate.

In 1969, Hamer started the Freedom Farm Cooperative and was invited to the White House for a conference on health and nutrition. She also started a child-care center for children of single and working mothers, bringing the Head Start program to rural Mississippi. She helped build homes for poor families through Young World Developers. She was awarded honorary degrees from Shaw University in Raleigh, North

Carolina, Howard University in Washington, D.C., Morehouse College in Atlanta, and Columbia College in Chicago.

Plagued by her earlier fight with polio and by the injuries she suffered in 1963, Hamer's poor health, which included diabetes, affected her throughout the late 1960's and the 1970's. She was diagnosed with breast cancer in 1976, the same year that her hometown of Ruleville celebrated Fannie Lou Hamer Day. She died in Mound Bayou, Mississippi, on March 14, 1977, at the age of fifty-nine. United Nations ambassador Andrew Young spoke at her funeral, and she was buried in Ruleville. Her gravestone reads, "I'm sick and tired of being sick and tired."

SIGNIFICANCE

Hamer's life provides a stark example of personal accomplishments made through sheer will. Rising from the depths of poverty and living with pain throughout her life, she became a leader of the movement to bring African Americans to the polls. In so doing, she helped to empower a long-oppressed people and to make them a significant and powerful force in the democratic process and in the shaping of twentieth century American history.

—Barry Stewart Mann

FURTHER READING

Donovan, Sandy. *Fannie Lou Hamer*. Chicago: Raintree, 2004. Part of the African American Biographies series for young readers, with short chapters, accessible text, and ample sidebars. Includes generous photographs, a glossary, a simple time line, a short bibliography, and an index.

Haskins, Jim. *One More River to Cross: The Stories of Twelve Black Americans*. New York: Scholastic, 1992. Targeted for adolescents and young adults, this volume includes a sixteen-page chapter on Hamer that is both readable and informative. It sets her among civil rights leaders such as Ralph Bunche, Shirley Chisholm, and Malcolm X. The book includes a bibliography and an index.

Lee, Chana Kai. *For Freedom's Sake: The Life of Fannie Lou Hamer*. Urbana: University of Illinois Press, 1999. A scholarly, comprehensive, and unsentimental rendering of Hamer's life and achievements. Includes several photographs, exhaustive notes, a bibliography, and an index.

Mills, Kay. *This Little Light of Mine: The Life of Fannie Lou Hamer*. New York: Plume, 1994. At 390 pages, a comprehensive and heartfelt account, complete with chronology, a list of individuals important in Hamer's life and work, extensive notes, and an index.

Olson, Lynne. *Freedom's Daughters: The Unsung Heroines of the Civil Rights Movement from 1830-1970*. New York: Scribner, 2001. A fascinating account that includes Hamer in a parade of women, black and white, who kept the Civil Rights movement moving forward. Olson profiles more than sixty women, going beyond prominent figures like Ida B. Wells-Barnett and Rosa Parks to place in context more obscure figures such as Mary Burks, Daisy Bates, and Penny Patch. The book provides plenty of photographs, endnotes, a bibliography, and an index.

Rubel, David. *Fannie Lou Hamer: From Sharecropping to Politics*. Englewood Cliffs,

N.J.: Silver Burdett Press, 1990. A juvenile biography written with lively prose and plenty of background information about life in the South in the mid-twentieth century. The book has photographs, illustrations, and maps. Includes a timetable of events, an index, suggested readings, and an introduction by former U.N. ambassador Andrew Young.

ALEXANDER HAMILTON

> *" . . . the passions of men will not conform to the dictates of reason and justice, without constraint. "*

American politician

Hamilton served as aide-de-camp to Washington during the American Revolution and was a delegate to the Philadelphia Convention of 1787 and signer of the Constitution. An early advocate of a strong national government, he coauthored The Federalist *and was the first secretary of the U.S. treasury.*

Born: January 11, 1755; Nevis, British West Indies
Died: July 12, 1804; New York, New York
Areas of achievement: Government and politics; military

EARLY LIFE

Alexander Hamilton was the illegitimate son of a Scottish ne'er-do-well and a woman previously arrested for adultery. He was born in 1755, although at times he claimed that his birth year was 1757. Hamilton spent his early years in abject poverty on the Caribbean island of his birth, Nevis. After his mother's death, he worked for a merchant family on St. Croix, where he flourished, as his unusual abilities brought him to the attention of his employers. Hamilton quickly rose to be something more than a clerk but less than a partner. By age sixteen, he was giving orders to ship captains, making decisions on when cargoes should be sold, and firing and hiring company lawyers. When not working, he studied on his own.

In 1773, Hamilton's employers, recognizing his precocious genius, sent him to the mainland for his first formal education. From 1773 to 1774, he lived with Elias Boudinot, a future president of the Continental Congress, and studied at a Presbyterian academy in Elizabethtown, New Jersey. In this period, Hamilton socialized with such future patriots and political leaders as William Livingston, Richard Stockton, Philip Schuyler, and Henry Brockholst Livingston. In 1774, Hamilton entered Kings College (now Columbia University) as a sophomore. In 1775, he anonymously published a pamphlet supporting the patriot cause; this was Hamilton's first political activity.

LIFE'S WORK

In March, 1776, Alexander Hamilton dropped out of college to become an artillery captain in the New York militia. He quickly came to the attention of senior officers, and in 1777 he joined George Washington's staff. Hamilton's relationship with the general was complex. The childless Washington often treated Hamilton as the son he never had. Hamilton, whose father was never present in his life, revered Washington, but at the same time he felt stifled working for "The Great Man," as his staff officers called him. As Washington's aide-de-camp, Hamilton had a unique view of the war and the politics of the revolution. It was during this period that he became a committed nationalist, as he saw the states squabbling over issues while the national army went without adequate food and other provisions.

The young Hamilton was short, slim, and not particularly athletic. He was brilliant as an administrator but hardly suited to frontline command. Yet he longed for the opportunity to achieve battlefield glory. This desire strained his relationship with Washington, and in February, 1781, he resigned his position. In July, Hamilton returned with his rank of lieutenant colonel to command a battalion, and at Yorktown he was finally given his opportunity for combat glory. Hamilton led his battalion in a brief and heroic assault on a British position. He was thrilled with his exploit but bitter that Congress never saw fit to award him a medal for his heroism. Shortly after the victory at Yorktown, Hamilton returned to civilian life.

In 1780, Hamilton was married to Elizabeth Schuyler. His father-in-law, General Schuyler, was one of the richest men in America and a powerful politician in New York. This family connection eliminated the taint of his illegitimate birth. In April, 1782, he began preparing for a career as a lawyer, and in July he was admitted to the bar. At first, Hamilton was ambivalent about his new profession, writing to the Marquis de Lafayette that he was "studying the art of fleecing my neighbours." Hamilton quickly threw himself into his law practice and was soon representing many of the wealthiest men in his state. Many of his clients were former Loyalists who sought to regain property taken during the revolution, yet Hamilton had few scruples about representing his former enemies. Between 1783 and 1789, he was involved in massive litigation over huge land claims in upstate New York. He also represented banks, shippers, and merchants. Hamilton's fundamentally conservative nature was reflected by his clients and his law practice.

During this period, Hamilton ventured into politics. The New York legislature chose him as a delegate to the Continental Congress (1782, 1783, 1787, 1788) and to the Annapolis Convention of 1786. Through his political connections, he served a short time as a collector of taxes for the Congress. In 1787, Hamilton was also elected to the New York legislature. With the exception of his election to the convention called to ratify the Constitution, this was the only popular election Hamilton ever won. Although a brilliant political theorist, his personal style prevented him from being a popular candidate.

The Annapolis Convention of 1786 was called to negotiate a trade agreement among the American states under the Articles of Confederation. The convention failed: Most of the states did not bother to send delegates. The meeting at Annapolis led to a call for another convention, however, to be held in Philadelphia the following year. That convention would write the Constitution.

Hamilton was one of three delegates from New York to the Philadelphia Convention of 1787. He received the unanimous support of the state legislature. Even his political enemies (and he had many by this time) believed that Hamilton was one of the ablest men in the state. At the beginning of the convention, a fellow delegate wrote that "Colo. Hamilton is deservedly celebrated for his talents. He is a practitioner of the Law, and reputed to be a finished Scholar.... His manners are tinctured with stiffness, and sometimes with a degree of vanity that is highly disagreeable." While haughty and arrogant, Hamilton was also exceedingly handsome, with auburn hair, deep-blue eyes, and a charming smile.

At Philadelphia, Hamilton was limited in his effectiveness. The other two New York delegates, John Lansing and Robert Yates, were opposed to a strong national government, which Hamilton supported. Thus, Hamilton was able to participate in debates, but his votes on the developing document were canceled by the rest of New York's delegation. In his first major speech, Hamilton argued for an extremely strong central government and a narrow and limited role for the states. Hamilton asserted his belief "that the British Govt. was the best in the world: and that he doubted much whether any thing short of it would do in America." He argued that the "hereditary interest of the King" prevented the dangers of corruption in England and that, for the American chief executive, "the English model was the only good one on this subject." His plan of government, which never received the support of any other delegates, called for a chief executive to serve for life and the appointment of state governors by the national government. This speech has led Hamilton's detractors to conclude that he was a monarchist. While that is perhaps an exaggeration, it is clear that Hamilton did favor a lifetime chief executive and that he leaned toward ruling over the people, rather than the people ruling themselves.

On June 29, Hamilton left the convention, in part because it was not headed in the direction he favored and in part because Yates and Lansing had outvoted him on most issues. Hamilton also wanted to return to his political base in New York and to the Continental Congress. Early in July, however, Yates and Lansing left the convention, and three days later, Hamilton returned. For the rest of the summer, Hamilton moved in and out of the convention. The rules of the convention required that each state have at least two delegates present to vote on the emerging document. Thus, Hamilton could debate but not vote. His most important contributions came in the debates that took place in September and in his work on the committee of style. At the end of the convention, he persuaded his fellow delegates to sign the document, even though New York as a state was not represented under the convention rules.

After the convention, Hamilton actively supported the new Constitution. In collaboration with fellow New Yorker John Jay and with Virginian James Madison, Hamilton planned and wrote a series of essays collectively known as *The Federalist* (1787-1788). All three authors wrote under the pen name Publius. Of the eighty-five separate essays, Hamilton wrote fifty-one and collaborated on another three. Madison's contributions, which included the famous numbers 10, 14, and 51, ended when he left New York in March, 1788, while Jay's writings were limited by illness. Hamilton continued the project without Madison and Jay, producing the last twenty-one essays on his own, including the powerful number 78, which explained the role of the judiciary in the constitutional system. *The Federalist* was written to convince New York voters to support the Constitution, but this goal was not really achieved. The majority of those elected to the New York ratifying convention opposed the Constitution. Neither the essays of Publius nor Hamilton's own speeches at the ratifying convention convinced the delegates to support the Constitution. Ultimately, New York ratified it by a slim three-vote margin, because a number of opponents of the Constitution concluded that with the ratification in Virginia and Massachusetts they had no choice but to ratify. While it was not persuasive in New York, *The Federalist* is generally considered to contain the single most important contemporary analysis of the Constitution and has been cited repeatedly by scholars and courts in the twentieth century.

With the organization of the new government, Hamilton became the nation's first secretary of the treasury. In his first two years in that office, Hamilton organized the nation's finances, established a mint and a system of creating money, and convinced the Congress and the president to support a national bank. He attempted to create a national program to support manufacturing and economic development, but this was defeated.

Hamilton's *Report Relative to a Provision for the Support of Public Credit* (1795), presented to the Congress in January, 1795, laid out a program for putting the nation on a sound financial footing. Hamilton urged that the national government pay off all foreign and domestic debt incurred by the Congress and the states during the revolution and confederation period. Two aspects of this report were particularly controversial. Hamilton recommended that all bondholders receive the face value of their bonds. This meant that speculators who had purchased war bonds at far below their original value would reap great profits, while those who had actually risked their money to support the American Revolution would not even get their original investment back. Hamilton also recommended that the national government pay off all unpaid state war debts. This proposal offended Virginia, which had paid off most of its debts and did not want to have to pay the debts of other states as well. Congressmen from states with small debts, such as Georgia, North Carolina, and Maryland, also opposed this plan. Representatives from states with large debts, including South Carolina, New York, and Massachusetts, naturally supported the plan.

Hamilton's goals in his debt-funding plan were not to aid one section of the nation and harm another. Nor did he seek to enrich speculators at the expense of patriotic investors who were forced, because of a postwar depression, to sell their bonds at low prices. Hamilton simply sought to put the nation on a sound economic footing. Nevertheless, high motives and sound economic policy were not enough to push through his proposal, and Congress adopted it only after much political maneuvering, which included an agreement to move the nation's capital from New York City closer to Virginia. Besides some political advantages, the Virginians hoped that the move would stimulate economic development in the Chesapeake region.

The creation of the Bank of the United States was Hamilton's second major accomplishment as secretary of the treasury. In the cabinet, Secretary of State Thomas Jefferson and Attorney General Edmund Randolph both opposed the bank. Congressional opposition was led by Madison, Hamilton's former collaborator on *The Federalist*. Hamilton's arguments in favor of the bank were more than economic. They were also constitutional. He asserted that the Constitution needed to be read broadly, and he argued that Congress must have the power to go beyond the specific "enumerated powers" in the Constitution through the "necessary and proper clause" of the document. In the cabinet debate, Hamilton prevailed and Washington signed the bank bill into law.

Hamilton's "Report on Manufactures," delivered to the Congress in December, 1791, argued in favor of stimulating manufacturing in the nation through tariff and tax policies. Hamilton's report detailed the types of manufacturing needed, including iron, leather, textiles, sugar, gunpowder, paper, and books. The report anticipated an America in which manufacturing, not agriculture, would be the dominant economic activity. This report was unacceptable, however, to the agrarian America of the 1790's.

In the cabinet, Hamilton proved a tireless and ruthless advocate of expanding national power. He came close to accusing Jefferson of treason when the secretary of state publicly indicated his disagreement with Hamilton. As a cabinet official, Hamilton helped organize the Federalist Party to support his economic and political policies. In 1794, he advocated the use of massive military force against hard-pressed western farmers who opposed his policy of taxing the producers of whiskey. Hamilton's role in the Whiskey Rebellion, was, in the end, almost comical. He led a large army into western Pennsylvania, where a handful of farmers were arrested and then released. Hamilton once again sought military glory, but this time he appeared to be an oppressor of the people; instead of glory, he won contempt.

In 1795, Hamilton left Washington's cabinet for the private practice of law. He quickly became one of the most successful attorneys in New York. In 1798, he became inspector general of the Army when it appeared that a war with France was likely. This was his last public position. Once again, however, military glory eluded Hamilton, and he returned to law after the crisis with France ended.

In his law practice, he was enormously successful, with clients begging for his services. In 1802, Hamilton earned nearly $13,000, an incredibly large sum for the period. Most of his law practice centered on marine insurance, banking law, and other litigation tied to commerce. Hamilton remained involved in politics, but his aggressive personal style and his penchant for intrigue served only to undermine the Federalist Party that he had helped to build in the early 1790's. Hamilton's public and private attacks on John Adams did little except to aid the fortunes of the Democratic-Republicans led by Jefferson and Aaron Burr. In 1804, he vigorously opposed Burr's attempt to gain the governorship of New York, so Burr challenged him to a duel, which took place on July 11. Hamilton once again had an opportunity for glory on the field of "combat." Once again, however, he was unsuccessful. He died, on July 12, of his wounds.

Significance

Alexander Hamilton was one of the great figures of the revolutionary era. He was brilliant, charming, and a first-rate administrator. Yet he was also vain, overly ambitious, arrogant, and insecure over his status and place in the world. Hamilton's influence was undermined by his inability to get along with other leaders of the age. He was also something of a misfit.

Reared in the West Indies, Hamilton was a monarchist when he first came to America. Although he quickly joined the patriot cause, his political views, as expressed in the Constitutional Convention and in Washington's cabinet, were almost always anti-Republican; he had less faith in representative government than any of the other

Founding Fathers. More than most public figures of the period, Hamilton favored a strong chief executive, if not a king. He was similarly out of step with America in his grandiose plans for the nation's economy. Nevertheless, his contributions to American politics, economics, and constitutional theory make him a towering figure of his age.

—Paul Finkelman

FURTHER READING

Bowen, Catherine Dinker. *Miracle at Philadelphia: The Story of the Constitutional Convention, May to September, 1787*. Boston: Little, Brown, 1966. Probably the best narrative history of the convention, and especially appropriate for high school and undergraduate students. Includes good details on convention delegates.

Brookhiser, Richard. *Alexander Hamilton, American*. New York: Free Press 1999. Brookhiser provides an appreciation and assessment of Hamilton, demonstrating why he was one America's most important Founding Fathers.

Chernow, Ron. *Alexander Hamilton*. New York: Penguin Books, 2004. A comprehensive and meticulously detailed biography, offering new information about Hamilton's ancestry, personality, and relationships with George Washington, Thomas Jefferson, John Adams and Aaron Burr. Chernow calls Hamilton "the father of the American government," the Founding Father who set the United States on a course of liberal democracy and capitalist economy.

Cooke, Jacob E. *Alexander Hamilton: A Biography*. New York: Charles Scribner's Sons, 1982. A short, readable biography by one of the nation's leading Hamilton scholars. An excellent place to begin research on Hamilton.

———, ed. *Alexander Hamilton: A Profile*. New York: Hill & Wang, 1967. Contains essays on Hamilton by a wide range of scholars, with articles both favorable and unfavorable to Hamilton.

Emery, Noemie. *Alexander Hamilton: An Intimate Portrait*. New York: G. P. Putnam's Sons, 1982. Much like the James Thomas Flexner biography, although this volume gives more attention to Hamilton's later life.

Flexner, James Thomas. *The Young Hamilton: A Biography*. Boston: Little, Brown, 1978. A superbly written study by the author of a leading biography of George Washington. Focuses on Hamilton's early years and on his psychological development. A fascinating, accessible study.

Hamilton, Alexander. *The Reports of Alexander Hamilton*. Edited by Jacob E. Cooke. New York: Harper & Row, 1964. Contains Hamilton's reports on public credit, the Bank of the United States, and manufacturers. Also contains Hamilton's constitutional arguments in favor of the bank. The reports are models of lucidity and can be read by students, nonspecialists, and scholars.

Hamilton, Alexander, James Madison, and John Jay. *The Federalist*. Edited by Henry B. Dawson. New York: J. and A. McLeon, 1788. Reprint. Cambridge, Mass.: Belknap Press, 1961. Various editions are available in both paperback and clothbound formats, generally including introductions by major scholars. *The Federalist* papers reveal much of Hamilton's political philosophy, although they should be read with care because they were originally written to gain support for the Constitution and not as political theory.

Harper, John Lamberton. *American Machiavelli: Alexander Hamilton and the Origins of U.S. Foreign Policy*. New York: Cambridge University Press, 2004. Focuses on Hamilton's influence on American foreign policy, placing Hamilton's character, personality, and vision in relation to the Renaissance diplomat and thinker Machiavelli.

Mitchell, Broadus. *Alexander Hamilton: A Concise Biography*. New York: Oxford University Press, 1976. An excellent one-volume study by one of Hamilton's major biographers. Mitchell is also the author of a more elaborate two-volume study of Hamilton. This book covers the same ground, but with less detail.

LEARNED HAND

> *Liberty lies in the hearts of men and women; when it dies there, no constitution, no law, no court can save it.*

Jurist

During a career on the federal bench spanning more than half a century, Hand became one of the most respected and honored jurists in the United States. His commitment to tolerance and rigorous thought helped transform and modernize American law in the twentieth century.

Born: January 27, 1872; Albany, New York
Died: August 18, 1961; New York, New York
Also known as: Billings Learned Hand (full name)
Area of achievement: Law and jurisprudence

EARLY LIFE

Learned Hand (LUHR-nehd hand) was the second of two children born to Samuel Hand and Lydia Coit Hand. Learned Hand, who dropped the name "Billings" when he was thirty years old because it sounded too "pompous," came from a distinguished legal family. His paternal grandfather, Augustus Cincinnatus, was a prominent New York attorney, active in the Democratic Party in the late nineteenth century. His older cousin, Augustus, was a lawyer and judge and served for many years on the same federal bench as Hand. Hand's father served a term on the highest state court in New York, the Court of Appeals.

Hand received his early education at a small private school, the Albany Academy, in New York. In 1889, following his cousin Augustus by two years, he enrolled at Harvard College. There he studied philosophy under one of the most distinguished groups of scholars of that time—George Santayana, Josiah Royce, and William James. His intellectual and literary gifts were evidenced by his election to Phi Beta Kappa and by his being chosen commencement orator at his baccalaureate in 1893. He stayed on at Harvard for another year, receiving a master's degree in philosophy.

Though strongly attracted to an academic career in philosophy, Hand again followed his cousin, entering Harvard Law School in 1894. At this time the law school was in the middle of what has been described as its "Golden Age": Teachers such as Christopher Langdell, James Bradley Thayer, and James Barr Ames were revolutionizing the study of law through their casebook approach and in the process were laying the foundation for the transformation of many traditional legal doctrines. In this atmosphere of intellectual ferment, Hand flourished, becoming one of the first editors of the *Harvard Law Review* and being graduated with honors.

Following his admission to the New York bar, Hand practiced law in Albany for the next five years. In 1902 he moved to New York City, where he spent the next seven years in what he described as the "dull and petty" work of a New York law firm. His move to New York City was perhaps also motivated by the fact that he now had a family to support. On December 6, 1902, Hand married Frances Amelia Fincke, a graduate of Bryn Mawr College. They had three daughters: Mary Deshon, Frances Lydia, and Constance.

Hand's lifelong love of the outdoors and hiking (including walking to work every day until his death) was reflected in his looks and physique. Of medium height and stockily built, he had a large, noble head highlighted by rugged features, bushy eyebrows, and dark, piercing eyes. On the bench, he was known for his quick temper, but appropriate apologies were made just as quickly. He did not suffer fools gladly, yet few jurists could be more tolerant. His demeanor was serious but not solemn, and while he craved company and good conversation, he would also have periods of melancholy and brooding. Hand also had a streak of playfulness—he enjoyed dressing up as an Indian chief for his grandchildren's amusement, expertly mimicking William Jennings Bryan, and singing ribald sea chanteys or Gilbert and Sullivan melodies.

Life's Work

Hand began his judicial career in 1909. President William Howard Taft was eager to improve the quality of the federal judiciary, and on the recommendation of Attorney General George W. Wickersham and a number of prominent New York attorneys, Hand was appointed to the federal District Court for Southern District of New York, the lowest level of the court system. Five years later, Hand was joined on this court by his cousin Augustus. During his tenure on the district court, he became a skilled trial judge and an expert on the intricacies of commercial and corporate law.

In 1912, while serving on the federal bench, Hand ran for, and lost, the position of chief judge of the New York Court of Appeals. It was of dubious propriety for a sitting judge to seek an elective office, and Hand compounded this mistake by running as a Progressive (in the election that year, Hand supported Theodore Roosevelt's unsuccessful bid for the presidency on the Progressive, or Bull Moose, Party ticket). In so doing he incurred the wrath of the regular Republicans and their leader, Taft. Taft never forgave Hand his political apostasy, and during the 1920's Taft, as chief justice of the United States, used his considerable influence to prevent Hand's elevation to the High Court.

Hand's judicial accomplishments were, however, at last recognized in 1924, when President Calvin Coolidge appointed him to the U.S. Court of Appeals for the Second Circuit (including New York, Connecticut, and Vermont), replacing Judge Julius M.

Hand, Learned

Mayer. During Hand's tenure on the Second Circuit, he served with some of the most distinguished jurists in the nation. Thomas Walter Swan and Charles Edward Clark were both former deans of Yale Law School, and Jerome Frank headed the Securities and Exchange Commission during the New Deal. Clearly Hand's greatest pleasure, though, was being joined once again by his cousin and closest friend, Augustus, on the same court in 1927.

Over the next twenty years, the Second Circuit Court of Appeals became one of the busiest and most respected federal tribunals in the nation. The measure of Hand's influence was the fact that, by the 1930's, the court was being referred to as "Learned Hand's Court." Unlike the U.S. Supreme Court, which could choose which cases to hear and therefore dealt with far fewer cases, the circuit court would handle an average of some four hundred appeals a year, involving a wide range of public (constitutional) and private-law issues. The latter would involve questions concerning copyright law, patent law, antitrust regulation, admiralty law, contracts, torts, and trusts and estates (among others).

Given the relative obscurity of most of the work done by the federal judiciary below the Supreme Court level, it was not surprising that Hand's leadership and legal influence were recognized mainly by the bar and bench. In May, 1944, however, he was in-

Learned Hand.
(Library of Congress)

vited to give an address at the annual "I Am an American Day" celebration in Central Park. His short speech "The Spirit of Liberty" was greeted with tremendous enthusiasm. Reprints of the work appeared nationwide, and glowing articles in newspapers and magazines introduced Hand's wisdom and style to the general public. During these years, he was also active in a number of professional organizations: He was one of the founders and early leaders of the American Law Institute. The institute was created to simplify segments of the vast body of American law by codifying and restating the thousands of state and federal court rulings, along with relevant legislation, to provide "model" codes of law for future legislative bodies and judges. Hand's specific contributions to the institute included his work on the *Model Penal Code* and the *Restatement of Conflicts of Law, Restatement of Torts*.

Throughout his career, Hand was proposed and considered for elevation to the Supreme Court but never nominated. Why this was so will never be known with absolute certainty. He had the support of the nation's bar, and at least three Supreme Court justices—Oliver Wendell Holmes, Jr., Harlan F. Stone, and Felix Frankfurter—all strongly thought that Hand should join them. Taft's hostility probably accounts for the 1920's. After that it seemed to be a combination of factors—geography, politics, and age—that prevented his appointment. In 1951, Hand officially retired from the Court of Appeals, though in fact he continued to sit on the court off and on for the next ten years. In 1952, a collection of his writings and speeches was published under the title of his 1944 address, *The Spirit of Liberty*. This and the publication of his 1958 Holmes lectures at Harvard University on the Bill of Rights helped spread his fame to the general public even further. Three years later, on August 18, 1961, Judge Hand died of heart failure in New York City.

Significance

It is difficult to assess fully a judicial career that lasted more than half a century. In large part, Hand's achievement was his work: more than two thousand opinions, along with his articles and speeches. His role on the middle level of the federal judicial pyramid gave him the freedom and scope to apply his vast erudition and wisdom but precluded as well any major impact on American constitutional development. However, from his work a number of themes emerge that reflect both the man and the times. Of immense importance was his contribution to the transformation of private law (contracts, torts, and so on) in the twentieth century. Like his friend Justice Holmes, Hand believed that the law did and should reflect changing social and economic conditions. Industrialization in America in the late nineteenth and early twentieth centuries brought with it not only increased business and commercial activity but also expanded governmental authority, as well as a host of social and economic problems. Hand's opinions speak to the necessity of the law to adjust to these changes—for the betterment of society. In this essentially optimistic vision, he shared many of the beliefs common to the Progressive reform movement that appeared during the first part of the twentieth century.

Another element of Hand's legacy was his passion for tolerance and his commitment to the protection of the human liberties embodied in the Bill of Rights. He believed that freedom to express different thoughts and ideas, even unpopular ones, and respect for all persons were both essential to the preservation of democracy. In this, Hand mirrored (and led, to the extent possible for a lower federal court judge) the growing concern by the judiciary for civil liberties and civil rights issues that began in the 1920's and reached its zenith with the landmark decisions of the Supreme Court under Chief Justice Earl Warren in the 1950's and 1960's.

Finally, Hand's opinions and writings reflected the ambivalence within both the legal community and American society concerning the role and function of judges. The dilemma, simply put, was how to balance on one hand the recognition that judges can, and possibly should, actually make law, and on the other hand the necessity for a judiciary that is independent yet responsive to the citizenry. While Hand accepted the necessity and freedom of judges to adapt the law to fit changing times and circumstances, he spoke for the school of thought that first appeared in the early part of the twentieth century (and that became more popular in the 1970's) that urged judicial "restraint," especially when dealing with some legislative action or constitutional interpretation. In so doing, he was embraced by liberals and conservatives, judicial activists and "restraintists" alike. That he could be so many things to so many people is a mark of his greatness.

—*Robert M. Goldman*

FURTHER READING

Blasi, Vincent. *Ideas of the First Amendment*. St. Paul, Minn.: Thomson/West, 2006. Provides information about how leading constitutional thinkers, including Hand, have interpreted the First Amendment.

Carrington, Paul D. *Stewards of Democracy: Law as a Public Profession*. Boulder, Colo.: Westview Press, 1999. Focuses on the role of lawyers, including Hand, in American political history.

Gilmore, Grant. *The Ages of American Law*. New Haven, Conn.: Yale University Press, 1977. A brief and extremely readable survey of the development of American law. A useful introduction to the context of legal thought and practice within which Hand worked.

Griffith, Kathryn P. *Judge Learned Hand and the Role of the Federal Judiciary*. Norman: University of Oklahoma Press, 1973. A detailed and critical analysis of Hand's judicial and legal philosophy. Griffith's early chapters on Hand's life and his world are probably the best introduction to these aspects.

Hand, Learned. *The Bill of Rights*. Cambridge, Mass.: Harvard University Press, 1958. The Oliver Wendell Holmes, Jr., Lectures delivered by Hand at Harvard in 1958. Constitutes Hand's most complete statement of his view of the judicial process and the necessity for judges to exercise restraint in their role as guardians of individual and human rights. One of the classic statements of the "judicial restraint" philosophy.

———. *The Spirit of Liberty*. Edited by Irving Dillard. New York: Alfred A. Knopf, 1952. A collection of Hand's extrajudicial writings and speeches, including his famous speech "The Spirit of Liberty." The introduction by Dillard is indeed a "personal appreciation"—rather uncritical, indeed almost worshipful.

Schick, Marvin. *Learned Hand's Court*. Baltimore: Johns Hopkins University Press,

1970. A detailed and brilliant study of the Court of Appeals for the Second Circuit during the years that Hand sat on the court. Focuses on the work of the court, the relationships among the judges, the impact of the CA2, as it came to be known, other federal courts, and, most important, how Hand's brilliance was able to influence the other judges.

Shanks, Hershel, ed. *The Art and Craft of Judging: The Decisions of Judge Learned Hand.* New York: Macmillan, 1968. A collection of forty-three decisions taken from Hand's almost two thousand opinions written on the bench. Most of the forty-three deal with public law issues. The introduction by Shanks is interesting because it includes details not generally known about Hand (for example, that his close friends called him "B," not for the Billings name that he dropped, but for "Bunny").

White, G. Edward. "Cardozo, Learned Hand, and Frank: The Dialectic of Freedom and Constraint." In *The American Judicial Tradition*. 3d ed. New York: Oxford University Press, 2007. This chapter is part of a larger study of important American judges and is especially interesting in linking Hand with his friend Benjamin Cardozo.

Barbara Harris

> *There seem to be fresh winds blowing across the church.... Things thought to be impossible just a short time ago are coming to be.*

Religious leader

A lifelong advocate for the full inclusion of women and people of color in church life and in society, Harris broke through nearly two millennia of religious tradition when she was consecrated a bishop of the Episcopal Church.

Born: June 12, 1930; Philadelphia, Pennsylvania
Also known as: Barbara Clementine Harris (full name)
Areas of achievement: Religion and theology; social reform; women's rights

Early Life

Barbara Harris (HAR-rihs) was born to Walter Harris and Beatrice Price Harris, lifelong members of the Episcopal Church, in the Philadelphia suburb of Germantown. She was the middle of three children in the family. As a child of the Great Depression, she grew up in a home that emphasized the importance of both work and sharing. Her father supported the family through odd jobs and repair work. He also carefully tended the fruit trees growing in the family's yard. During World War II, he worked in a steel mill. Harris's great-grandmother, who lived with the family when Harris was small, had been a slave, and she told many stories about the hardships of life under slavery. The children's grandmother cleaned the local school and sometimes took young Harris along to help her.

Harris's mother, Beatrice, was an active lay member of St. Barnabas Church, where the family worshiped. St. Barnabas was an all-black Episcopal parish. Located in the same city where Absalom Jones, the first African American to be ordained a priest, had founded his church, St. Barnabas carried on a proud tradition. The church was strongly oriented toward social justice and service, although it also preached values of the Christian gospel in living one's daily life.

As a child and teenager Harris stayed active in church life. She organized a Young Adults Group, which grew to more than fifty members, and regularly played the piano for church-school programs. Her music lessons, practiced on an old Steinway piano, gave her so much pleasure that she thought briefly of making a career of music.

However, Harris's other interests were stronger. While a student at Philadelphia High School for Girls, she got an reporting assignment with the *Pittsburgh Courier*, writing a weekly column about school life. After she graduated in 1948, she enrolled at the Charles Morris Price School of Journalism, aiming for a career with the press.

LIFE'S WORK

With the return of millions of former service members to colleges and their jobs after World War II—and with the swing back to "normality" in American society—it was not the optimum time for a talented young black woman to start a journalistic career. Harris needed a job, and when she heard of an opening for a nurse's aide at a local hospital, she applied and was accepted. Despite her resolve to work hard and do well at anything she tried, she hated the job. When she learned of an opening for a receptionist at a children's hospital, she applied for the job and was hired.

Harris's work at the children's hospital led to a fortunate chance at a bigger job, when the father of one of her friends from high school offered her a job in his firm, Joseph V. Baker Associates. This was a black-owned public relations firm that promoted white-owned products and companies within black communities. The plan was for Harris to learn every aspect of the company's work, from the ground up. She did this so well that within ten years she became the company's president. In all, she was employed at Baker Associates for nineteen years, from 1949 to 1968. During this time she was married briefly, a marriage that ended in divorce. In 1968 she went to work for the Sun Oil Company, where she served as head of the community relations department.

Throughout this time period she continued to be active as an Episcopal laywoman. One of her major projects was the St. Dismas Society, which involved visiting prisons, leading services there, and befriending prisoners. In 1968 she transferred her membership from her home church of St. Barnabas to the Church of the Advocate in North Philadelphia. The latter church and its rector, Paul Washington, were in the vanguard of support for the burgeoning Civil Rights movement, the campaign to empower the poor, and, soon, the push for equality for women within the Episcopal Church.

The cause for women's equality within the Episcopal Church was to soon have its first victory within the church structure—and it was at Harris's Church of the Advocate that this first victory took place. Three retired bishops ordained eleven women to the priesthood there in 1974. The ordination was technically valid at the time but irregular, because the church's general convention had voted against allowing women to be priests in both 1970 and 1973. Nevertheless, a strong current was gathering in favor of women's ordination. The ceremony at Philadelphia was carefully planned, with wide press coverage. Harris, who fully supported women's ordination by this time, volunteered to carry the cross in the opening procession.

When the 1976 general convention authorized women's ordination, Harris began to wonder if the priesthood might be her calling, too. With the diocese of Philadelphia's approval, she entered an alternate course of study leading to the diaconate and then to the priesthood, taking courses at Villanova University and Hobart and William Smith Colleges.

After ordination as a deacon in 1979 and as a priest in 1980, Harris served in parish ministries on an interim basis. She was priest-in-charge at Norristown's St. Augustine of Hippo Church from 1980 to 1984. However, her background in administration and social advocacy soon won her an appointment as executive director of the Episcopal Church Publishing Company and editor of *The Witness*, a progressive periodical focused on the need to confront social issues. Her hard-hitting articles and editorials there drew wide attention within the Episcopal Church, some of it admiring and some quite the opposite.

There were so many admirers of Harris by this time that when the diocese of Massachusetts needed a new suffragan (assistant) bishop, her name was placed in nomination. In the American Episcopal Church, bishops are chosen first by vote of clergy and lay representatives from the diocese and are then confirmed by approval at the triennial general convention. Usually the election process takes several ballots, as it did in Harris's case, She was chosen on the sixth ballot. Although her election was normal in that sense, the issues it raised were not.

The Anglican Communion, like the Roman Catholic and Orthodox branches of Christianity, regards bishops as possessing special authority. They are believed to constitute an unbroken line to Jesus Christ, who charged Simon Peter and his other disciples with leadership of his church. Before the selection of Harris, all such bishops had been men. Coming only thirteen years after the church's acceptance of women priests, Harris's selection shocked the more conservative elements of the Episcopal Church once again. The greatest outrage was that she was a woman. There were also objections to her irregular preparation (not a seminary graduate), her race, and her marital status (divorced), but all these traits had several—or many—precedents within the Episcopal Church's recent history. Women priests and bishops have also been considered roadblocks to ecumenical outreach with the Catholic Church, although some Catholics see the existence of women priests as a hopeful sign that their church also can change.

Many Episcopalians expected that in her new role Harris would serve as the leader of a movement for more radical social change. That did not happen. Although she continued to speak out, most of her work as a suffragan bishop was pastoral. She oversaw churches, sorted out parish disputes and problems, and performed the standard duties such as confirming new members and ordaining clergy.

Almost fourteen years after her consecration as a bishop in 1989, she retired at the mandatory age of seventy-two. A slight, energetic woman with relatively good health and many friends, she worked for several years after retirement as an assisting bishop in the Washington, D.C., diocese.

Harris, Barbara

SIGNIFICANCE

Harris played a pivotal role in the changes that have turned the once-staid Episcopal Church into a body shaken by radical changes. Her removal of the gender barrier to the church's highest rank paved the way for other women bishops. By 2006 there were thirteen female bishops in the Episcopal Church of the United States, with three in Canada's Anglican Church and one in New Zealand. In 2006 another barrier fell when Katharine Jefferts Schori became the twenty-sixth presiding bishop of the Episcopal Church.

Harris's career has been both symbolic of and a spur to further change in the Episcopal Church; to a lesser extent her career has influenced other mainstream Christian churches as well. These changes mirror, and attempt to cope with, events in the larger, secular society and world. The changes are aimed at a more inclusive church, one where social justice goals are viewed as a natural outcome of the work that Jesus himself did. As Harris's story shows, these goals are controversial within the church, but the trend has been toward their realization.

—*Emily Alward*

FURTHER READING

Bozzuti-Jones, Mark Francisco. *The Miter Fits Just Fine! A Story About the Right Reverend Barbara Clementine Harris*. Cambridge, Mass.: Cowley, 2003. A short book written for young readers, and the only book-length biography of Harris. Contains sketches of the world she grew up in, some fictionalized episodes from her childhood, and essential facts.

Harris, Barbara Clementine. *Parting Words: A Farewell Discourse*. Cambridge, Mass.: Cowley, 2003. A one-hundred-page transcript of Harris's final sermon before her retirement.

Nicholson, Aleathia Dolores. "Barbara Harris." In *Epic Lives: One Hundred Black Women Who Made a Difference*, edited by Jessie Carney Smith. Detroit, Mich.: Visible Ink Press, 1993. A brief summary of Harris's accomplishments and an extended discussion of the controversy over her elevation to bishop. Includes a portrait.

Turner, Renee D. "The First Woman Episcopal Bishop: Elevation of Christian Social Activist Barbara C. Harris Causes Religious Stir." *Ebony*, May, 1989, 40. Profile in the foremost African American news magazine, reporting on Harris's prior career and investiture. Original print article contains photographs.

ERNEST HEMINGWAY

❝ *Courage is grace under pressure.* **❞**

Novelist

Hemingway was one of the most influential writers in the twentieth century, both as a much-imitated stylist and as a larger-than-life celebrity.

Born: July 21, 1899; Oak Park, Illinois
Died: July 2, 1961; Ketchum, Idaho
Also known as: Ernest Miller Hemingway (full name)
Area of achievement: Literature

EARLY LIFE

Born into a conservative, upper-middle-class family in Oak Park, Illinois, an affluent suburb of Chicago, Ernest Hemingway (EHR-nehst HEHM-ihng-way) spent much of his life and early literary career trying to break away from the constraints of his youth. Hemingway's father, Clarence Edmonds Hemingway, was a physician who had a great interest in hunting and fishing. The young Hemingway, whose father hoped that his son would eventually join him in his medical practice, became an avid outdoorsman at an early age.

During long holidays spent at the family's summer home on Walloon Lake in northern Michigan, Ernest, who was not healthy as a youth, pushed himself to the limits of his physical endurance, as he did throughout much of his later life. He became an enthusiastic sportsman.

Grace Hall Hemingway, Ernest's mother, was a cultivated woman, much interested in music. She dominated her husband, and Ernest realized early that his father was henpecked. Until her death, Grace Hemingway never had a positive word to say about her son's work. She regarded Ernest's writing as an embarrassment to the family because it dealt with a side of life that Grace considered seamy. Never able to win from his mother the approbation that he wanted, Hemingway was early attracted to older women who appreciated his work and who appreciated him. Three of his four wives were considerably older than he, and his first serious romantic encounter was with Agnes von Kurowsky, a nurse who tended him in Italy and was eight years his senior.

Hemingway completed high school in 1917, just as the United States was being drawn into World War I. He had no wish to go to college and was eager to serve his country. His defective vision kept him from serving in the armed forces, so after a summer at Walloon Lake, Hemingway, drawing on his experience in writing for his high school newspaper in Oak Park, went to Kansas City as a reporter for the *Star*, a celebrated daily newspaper of that era. He was to return to Oak Park only five or six times in his entire life after he made the initial break. In Kansas City, Hemingway served an intense journalistic apprenticeship for seven months before he left for Italy as a Red Cross ambulance driver in May, 1918.

Hemingway had been in Italy for less than six weeks when he was wounded at Fossalta di Piave on Italy's boundary with Austria. Despite his wounds, he dragged an injured soldier from the front line to safety. For this act of heroism, he was decorated.

After spending some time in an Italian hospital near Milan recovering from his wounds, Hemingway was sent home, where he was looked on as a hero. He reveled in his newly won celebrity. After he regained his strength at Lake Walloon, Hemingway went to Chicago, where he held a variety of menial jobs. Soon he married Hadley Richardson, eight years older than he, and sailed with her for France, where he served as a foreign correspondent for the *Toronto Star*. He arrived in Paris just as the city was reaching a postwar zenith of intellectual ferment and literary activity, and there he was to remain for the better part of the next decade, coming to know well such influential literary figures as F. Scott Fitzgerald, Gertrude Stein, Ford Madox Ford, Ezra Pound, and James Joyce.

Hemingway, handsome with his animated eyes, his ready smile, and his dark mustache, was soon the darling of Parisian literary society. His good looks and amiability won for him a legion of friends, many of whom ultimately came to see the darker side of his highly complex and often bewildering personality. Aside from his journalistic commitments, he began in Paris to work assiduously on his short stories and on a novel about the aimless postwar expatriates who lived a somewhat undirected existence in France and Spain. On a personal level, Hemingway was able to give purpose to his own life by writing about the aimlessness that characterized many of the Americans of his generation who lived in Europe at that time. He came to deplore the term he had popularized (borrowed from Gertrude Stein): the "lost generation."

Hemingway's first book, a collection of short stories interspersed with imagistic reflections, *In Our Time* (1924), was recognized by the literati as a work of considerable promise. Although the book was not a resounding commercial success, it was clearly the work of a serious author who had begun to master his craft.

Life's Work

Hemingway's first novel, *The Sun Also Rises* (1926), established him as an author of considerable significance, just as *In Our Time* had established him as an author of considerable promise. *The Sun Also Rises*, a book that was right for its time, depicts dislocated members of the postwar generation. Set in Paris and Pamplona, Spain, it featured Hemingway's first extended treatment of one of his lifelong fascinations: the art of the bullfight. It was not merely the timeliness of *The Sun Also Rises* that established Hemingway as a serious artist; it was also the meticulous control that he exercised over his material and the care and authenticity of his spare descriptions that made both readers and literary critics realize that he was an author of extraordinary stature.

The Sun Also Rises was followed by *A Farewell to Arms* (1929), which was published in the year that Hemingway divorced his first wife, Hadley, who had borne him one son, John. The protagonist of *A Farewell to Arms* is an American disenchanted with a society that could let something such as World War I happen. He finally deserts the Italian army, in which he has been serving and which is in disarray. His disenchantment is intensified by the death of his lover in giving birth to their child.

In the years following *A Farewell to Arms*, Hemingway became an increasingly romantic figure, a rugged outdoorsman who spent much time attending bullfights in Spain, hunting big game in Africa, and fishing the waters off Key West, Florida, where

Ernest Hemingway.
(© The Nobel Foundation)

he bought a home in which he resided when he was not traveling. Out of this period were to come such books as *Death in the Afternoon* (1932), an extended discourse on bullfighting in which Hemingway gives valuable insights into his own creative processes, and *Green Hills of Africa* (1935), which remains one of the most sensitively written books about big game and those who hunt it.

Out of Hemingway's Key West experience came his novel *To Have and Have Not* (1937), a mediocre book whose action takes places in Cuba and Key West during the Great Depression. Hemingway's next book, *For Whom the Bell Tolls* (1940), is an optimistic novel that calls for the unity of humankind. The book is set in Spain during the Spanish Civil War, which Hemingway had seen at first hand as a correspondent with strong Loyalist sympathies. *For Whom the Bell Tolls* was to be Hemingway's last novel for ten years, after which he published *Across the River and into the Trees* (1950), an overly sentimental novel of little distinction.

Meanwhile, in 1940, Hemingway divorced Pauline Pfeiffer, his second wife and the mother of his sons Patrick and Gregory, after thirteen years of marriage. He married Martha Gellhorn, a writer, almost immediately and was married to her until 1945. Then he married Mary Welsh, also a writer, to whom he remained married for the remainder of his life.

Hemingway, Ernest

When Hemingway returned from covering the Spanish Civil War, he bought Finca Vigia, a quite modest estate not far from Havana, Cuba, and this was to be his home until 1959, when the political situation under Fidel Castro forced Hemingway out of the country. He then bought a home in Ketchum, Idaho, where he was to spend the remaining years of his life.

During World War II, Hemingway first served as a correspondent in China, then, from 1944 until the end of the war, as a correspondent in Europe, crossing the English Channel on D Day with the Twenty-second Regiment of the Fourth Infantry Division, with which he saw considerable combat in Normandy and later at the Battle of the Bulge. He also devised the Crook Factory, which, in 1943, undertook some ill-conceived and abortive missions on his boat, *The Pilar*, to try to destroy German submarines in the waters off Cuba.

Hemingway's excursion into drama was with a play about the Spanish Civil War, *The Fifth Column* (1938). It was published in *The Fifth Column and the First Forty-nine Stories* (1938), a collection that includes such celebrated stories as "The Killers," "The Snows of Kilimanjaro," and "The Short Happy Life of Francis Macomber."

Hemingway had a writing slump after World War II that plagued him for the remainder of his life. *Across the River and into the Trees* brought vitriolic reviews, and some critics thought that this book marked the end of Hemingway's literary career. He published *The Old Man and the Sea* (1952) two years later, however, and this short, tightly controlled novel about Santiago, an old fisherman who almost dies during a three-day encounter with a marlin, helped to salvage his deteriorating reputation. In 1953, this book won for Hemingway the Pulitzer Prize and was also instrumental in his being awarded the Nobel Prize in Literature in 1954.

The Old Man and the Sea was Hemingway's last novel, although two earlier, unfinished novels, *Islands in the Stream* (1970) and *The Garden of Eden* (1986), were published posthumously. The last of these was constructed by Scribner's editor Tom Jenks from more than fifteen hundred manuscript pages that Hemingway left on his death. Also published posthumously was *A Moveable Feast* (1964), a memoir that details Hemingway's life in Paris during the 1920's and that has much of the power and grace of his early work.

Hemingway began to suffer increasingly from depression and anxiety after World War II, and he was twice hospitalized at the Mayo Clinic for electric shock therapy. On July 2, 1961, after returning to Ketchum from his second hospitalization, Hemingway ended his life with a shotgun blast.

Significance

At a time when much writing was florid and verbose, Hemingway stripped language to the bare essentials for expressing fundamental thoughts and rendering the most accurate descriptions possible. Although he dealt with complex thoughts and emotions, Hemingway labored to achieve directness and simplicity of expression. From Stein, he learned the effectiveness of verbal repetition as a means of achieving the rhythms of language. From Ezra Pound and from his early experience as a journalist, he learned to write exactingly, using accurate verbs and nouns, depending little on adjectives and adverbs.

Hemingway's best work demonstrates careful control, close observation, accurate depiction, and the highest level of artistic integrity. It glorifies the dignity in life as seen in the works that deal with bullfighting, big-game hunting, fishing, war, drinking, brawling, and camaraderie. Hemingway's concept of courage as grace under pressure underlies his finest writing.

As the fourth American author to be awarded the Nobel Prize in Literature, Hemingway brought renewed attention to his country as a source of fine writing. Often a deeply troubled person, Hemingway went through life trying to demonstrate a courage that perhaps he was not convinced he really possessed. His need to display machismo likely stemmed from deep psychological sources that were intimately connected to his artistry.

—*R. Baird Shuman*

FURTHER READING

Baker, Carlos. *Ernest Hemingway: A Life Story*. New York: Charles Scribner's Sons, 1969. Focuses on the origin, development, and reception of Hemingway's writing. Information drawn largely from primary sources, including more than twenty-five hundred letters. Written at the invitation of Scribner's, Hemingway's publisher since 1926. Deals more with events than with ideas.

_____. *Hemingway: The Writer as Artist*. 4th ed. Princeton, N.J.: Princeton University Press, 1972. A solid consideration of Hemingway's literary technique. Baker is knowledgeable but detached and objective. One of the better books on Hemingway.

Bruccoli, Matthew J., with Judith S. Baughman, eds. *Hemingway and the Mechanism of Fame: Statements, Public Letters, Introductions, Forewords, Prefaces, Blurbs, Reviews, and Endorsements*. Columbia: University of South Carolina Press, 2006. This collection of documents demonstrates how Hemingway carefully crafted and marketed his public image.

Burgess, Anthony. *Ernest Hemingway and His World*. Charles Scribner's Sons, 1978. Although a pictorial biography, this book contains some remarkable literary insights and acute critical analysis. Shows how Hemingway introduced a new standard of language, one of "nerves and muscle."

DeFazio, Albert J., III, ed. *Dear Papa, Dear Hotch: The Correspondence of Ernest Hemingway and A. E. Hotchner*. Columbia: University of Missouri Press, 2005. Hotchner, a Hemingway biographer, first met the author in 1948, and the two remained friends until Hemingway's death. Their correspondence enables readers to trace the gradual decay that led to Hemingway's suicide.

Griffin, Peter. *Along with Youth: Hemingway, The Early Years*. New York: Oxford University Press, 1986. Focuses on Hemingway's life from birth until his marriage to Hadley Richardson and his departure for Paris. Prints for the first time a number of Hemingway's poems and early contributions to his high school newspaper.

Meyers, Jeffrey. *Hemingway: A Biography*. New York: Harper & Row, 1985. Well written and intriguing. Meyers clearly demonstrates that Hemingway's life was as interesting as the lives of any of his protagonists. Presents trenchant insights into Hemingway's view of women, particularly as his view was shaped by his early relationship to his mother.

Rovit, Earl H. *Ernest Hemingway*. New York: Twayne, 1963. A useful overview that is now somewhat dated. Well researched although a bit hampered by the restrictions of length and format imposed by the series of which it is a part.

Wagner, Linda W., ed. *Hemingway: Five Decades of Criticism*. East Lansing: Michigan State University Press, 1974. An intelligent selection of salient criticism from the earliest to the time following Hemingway's death.

Young, Philip. *Ernest Hemingway: A Reconsideration*. 1952. Rev. ed. University Park: Pennsylvania State University Press, 1966. This second edition of Young's superb critical study adds an interesting preface telling of the author's difficulties with Hemingway over the publication of the book. Young hypothesizes that Hemingway's heroes were modeled on himself and that his life in turn was modeled on the heroes of earlier American classics, particularly those of Mark Twain.

PATRICK HENRY

" Is life so dear or peace so sweet as to be purchased at the price of chains and slavery? Forbid it, Almighty God! I know not what course others may take, but as for me, give me liberty, or give me death! "

Attorney and politician

Expressing his libertarian ideas through a uniquely powerful oratory, Henry was a principal architect of the American Revolution. He is especially remembered for his poignant words before the revolutionary convention in Virginia in 1775: "Give me liberty, or give me death!"

Born: May 29, 1736; Studley Plantation, Hanover County, Virginia
Died: June 6, 1799; Red Hill Plantation, Charlotte County, Virginia
Areas of achievement: Law and jurisprudence; oratory; government and politics

EARLY LIFE

Patrick Henry was born in Hanover County, Virginia. The second son of John Henry, a well-educated Scotsman from Aberdeen, and Sarah Winston Syme, the young and charming widow of Colonel John Syme, Patrick Henry's early years were characteristic of a farm boy in colonial Virginia. Hunting and fishing were consuming enthusiasms for him, although he also received a sound education (focused on mathematics and the Latin classics) from local schoolmasters, his uncle Patrick Henry (a minister), and his father.

At the age of fifteen, he was apprenticed as a clerk in a country store. A year later, he joined his older brother as a partner in a similar venture, which, however, failed. Meanwhile, Henry had fallen in love with Sarah Shelton, the daughter of nearby landowner John Shelton, and the two were married in the fall of 1754. The young couple took up residence on a small farm that had been given to them by Sarah's father. For three years they eked out a marginal existence, but worse was to come. In 1757, their house was destroyed by fire. Destitute, they moved into the large tavern owned by Sarah's father at Hanover Courthouse, where Henry for a time supported himself and his family, now including four children, by helping manage the tavern for his father-in-law.

By all accounts, Henry was a charming and convivial taverner, but there is otherwise little in his life to this point (age twenty-three) to foretell the kind of impact he would have on American history. Proximity to a busy provincial courthouse and frequent association with those who came and went there must have inspired his latent abilities, for by the age of twenty-four he had resolved upon becoming a lawyer. The normal course for a young man of such ambitions would have been to apprentice himself to an established lawyer who had attended one of the Inns of Court of London (there were no law schools in the American colonies; the first would be established in 1779 in Virginia at William and Mary College).

Henry, however, attempted his project through a program of self-study and, miraculously, succeeded within a year. His board of examiners was headed by the illustrious brothers, Peyton and John Randolph. Impressed more by the force of natural genius he displayed in his examination than by his spotty knowledge of law, they admitted him to the bar. Their somewhat reluctant confidence was more than justified, for within three years, Henry had become a successful lawyer. Having handled some 1,125 cases, most of which he won, he was, at the age of twenty-seven, poised to enter the arena of history-making events.

Life's Work

The case that catapulted Patrick Henry to widespread recognition as a bold political spirit with a singular gift for oratory was the Parson's Cause of 1763. In colonial America, as in England, the Anglican Church was supported by general taxation, and in Virginia, salaries for the clergy were tied to the price of tobacco. A 1758 act of the Virginia legislature had fixed the nominal price of tobacco for this purpose at two pence per pound. Since this was far less than the actual commodity value of tobacco, the clergy petitioned King George III and his Privy Council to overrule the act. George did indeed overrule the act, thereby allowing the Virginia clergy to sue for back pay.

Henry was engaged to handle the defense in the pivotal case brought by the Reverend Mr. James Maury. The youthful attorney's argument asserted that the 1758 law was just and that in overturning it, the king was acting as a tyrant. The jury of sturdy farmers was so impressed that it awarded the plaintiff Maury only a penny in damages. Henry's fame soon spread throughout Virginia, thereby laying the ground for his entry into the forefront of colonial politics.

In May, 1765, Henry entered the House of Burgesses, only a few weeks after Britain had passed the notorious Stamp Act. On his twenty-ninth birthday, only ten days after taking his seat as a representative, he proposed a number of resolutions against the Stamp Act, based on the assumption that only colonial legislatures had the right to levy colonial taxes. A lean six-footer, with plain angular features and dark, deep-set eyes, the somewhat ungainly and roughly dressed young legislator climaxed his defense of the resolutions with the threatening words (as reported by Thomas Jefferson), "Caesar had his Brutus, Charles the First his Cromwell, and George the Third—"

Henry, Patrick

whereupon, interrupted by cries of "Treason!" Henry concluded, "may profit by their example. If this be treason, make the most of it." His daring speech galvanized the House of Burgesses into adopting his resolutions, and Virginia became an example to the other colonies in the rising resistance to taxation without representation.

Over the next few years, Patrick Henry's fame and authority as a revolutionary leader increased, as from his seat in the House of Burgesses he continued to oppose British encroachment upon the autonomy of the colonies. In September, 1774, he served as a member of the First Continental Congress that met in Philadelphia to deal with new British coercive measures imposed in the aftermath of the Boston Tea Party. Some six months later, he was an organizer of the revolutionary convention convened in Richmond to decide how Virginia should respond to the worsening situation, and it was in this setting, on March 23, 1775, that he made the speech that served as a call to arms for the colonies in the coming struggle. Arguing for the need to raise armed forces immediately, he concluded,

> Is life so dear or peace so sweet as to be purchased at the price of chains and slavery? Forbid it, Almighty God! I know not what course others may take, but as for me, give me liberty, or give me death!

Swayed by the dramatic impact of this speech, the members of the convention authorized the formation of companies of militia, one of which was led by Henry himself in May to demand restoration of the gunpowder seized from the Williamsburg magazine by the Loyalist governor, Lord Dunmore. Although he succeeded, he was not cut out for military leadership. After a short appointment as a regimental commander, and burdened by grief for the death of his wife, he resigned his commission and returned home on February 28, 1776.

His absence from public life was only brief; in May, he took part in drafting the new constitution of Virginia and on June 29 was elected the first governor of the newly constituted commonwealth, a position in which he served for three years (retiring in 1779) and to which he was reelected for two years in 1784. Meanwhile, he had married again, to Dorothea Dandridge, and had taken up residence on a huge tract of land in the mountainous western area of the state. A representative of the Virginia legislature from 1786 to 1790, he declined a nomination to the Constitutional Convention, while from his legislative seat he bitterly opposed Virginia's adoption of the Constitution in 1788, fearing its restrictive effect upon the sovereignty of the states, particularly those of the South. His vehement and sustained opposition was insufficient to prevent adoption, but it did prompt a general recognition of the need for constitutional amendments, leading to the framing of the first ten amendments; the Bill of Rights passed in 1791.

From 1790 to 1795, Henry returned to private law practice. The last years of his life were spent in semiretirement at his Red Hill plantation in Charlotte County. He refused the positions of both secretary of state and chief justice offered to him in 1795 by George Washington, but, increasingly reconciled to the principles of Federalism in his last years, he agreed in 1799 to run for the Virginia legislature once again. Elected, he did not live to serve his term, dying on June 6, 1799.

Significance

The American Revolution was produced by heroic talents and energies that together achieved critical mass; within this process, the oratory of Patrick Henry was catalytic in effect. In an era of great public speakers, it was his voice in particular that provided a rallying cry for the colonial patriots at critical moments, especially in 1765, during the Stamp Act controversy, and, ten years later, on the eve of the battles of Lexington and Concord. His oratory was legendary in its own time. Characterized, according to contemporary accounts, by extraordinary dramatic nuance and force, it stands as an enduring example of the power of an individual speaker to influence large-scale events.

Henry's resistance to the principles of Federalism in later years is also indicative of a deep strain both in his character and in American society. Born in a picturesque but still largely "wild" region of Virginia, his first love was the land—its topography and vegetation, its creatures, and its seasons. The concept of liberty for him was rooted in a deep respect for nature and the individual autonomy nurtured by the frontier environment. His opposition to British rule and to federal authority should be seen as the two sides of a single coin. His anti-Federalist speeches in the Virginia assembly were a main influence behind the passage of the Bill of Rights. Yet the same kinds of sentiments divided the nation half a century later on the issue of states' rights—a controversy that even the Civil War did not eradicate.

In many ways, Henry's achievements are the stuff of which American legends have been forged. Son of colonial Virginia, self-made forensic genius, patriot, and lifelong spokesman for individual rights even at the expense of national unity, his life is part of the national mythology of America, and his famous words "Give me liberty or give me death" have etched themselves on the national psyche.

—*Charles Duncan*

Further Reading

Axelrad, Jacob. *Patrick Henry, the Voice of Freedom.* New York: Random House, 1947. A book for the general reader, somewhat dated in approach but useful for its economical account of Henry's career and its informative commentary on contemporary historical events.

Beeman, Richard R. *Patrick Henry: A Biography.* New York: McGraw-Hill, 1974. A solid, thoroughly researched, academic history. Beeman's vision of Henry is somewhat deconstructionist; he's not the legendary hero but a man more characteristic of his times. Beeman deals especially well with the less celebrated aspects of Henry's career, such as his role as governor and administrator.

Campbell, Norine Dickson. *Patrick Henry, Patriot and Statesman.* New York: Devin-Adair, 1969. The value of this work lies in its sense of the living presence of history as well as in the occasional emphatic detail produced by devoted research.

McCants, David A. *Patrick Henry, the Orator.* New York: Greenwood Press, 1990. An analysis of Henry's oratory within its historical and political contexts.

Mayer, Henry. *A Son of Thunder: Patrick Henry and the American Republic.* New York: Franklin Watts, 1986. A substantial, well-researched, and absorbing biography that places Henry in the context of his time. Emphasizes his roots in the "evangelical revolt" against Virginia's aristocratic establishment.

Hepburn, Katharine

Mayo, Bernard. *Myths and Men: Patrick Henry, George Washington, Thomas Jefferson.* Athens: University of Georgia Press, 1959. A collection of perceptive commentaries on the major leadership of the American Revolution. The essay on Henry is valuable as an economical, balanced overview of the issues of scholarship and historiography surrounding his biography.

Meade, Robert Douthat. *Patrick Henry.* 2 vols. Philadelphia: J. B. Lippincott, 1957-1969. The most comprehensive biography of Henry to appear in the twentieth century; likely to become the standard authoritative reference work. Meade's coverage of his subject is meticulous, based on definitive research into all aspects of Henry's private and public life.

Tyler, Moses Coit. *Patrick Henry.* Boston: Houghton Mifflin, 1887. A masterpiece of nineteenth century historiography, the first modern biography of Henry, and best for the general reader. The worshipful view of Henry, though old-fashioned, is deeply sincere.

Vaughan, David J. *Give Me Liberty: The Uncompromising Statesmanship of Patrick Henry.* Nashville, Tenn.: Cumberland House, 1997. Vaughan's book is divided into three sections. Part 1 provides an overview of Henry's life, part 2 describes his character traits, and part 3 assesses his legacy.

Willison, George F. *Patrick Henry and His World.* Garden City, N.Y.: Doubleday, 1969. Probably the best all-around general study. Willison's title is appropriate; the coverage of background historical material is thorough and illuminating. The book is well-paced, admirably written, and spiced with colorful, often amusing anecdotes.

KATHARINE HEPBURN

" *If you obey all the rules, you miss all of the fun.* "

Actor

With a career spanning most of the twentieth century, Hepburn embodied wit, independence, and charm. She was one of the first actors to break down Hollywood's stereotype of women, facing not only a shocked public but also condemnation from film critics. Nevertheless, she was a model of grit and beauty throughout her career.

Born: May 12, 1907; Hartford, Connecticut
Died: June 29, 2003; Old Saybrook, Connecticut
Also known as: Katharine Houghton Hepburn (full name)
Areas of achievement: Theater and entertainment; film; women's rights

EARLY LIFE
Katharine Hepburn (HEHP-burn) was born the second of six children of Katharine "Kit" Hepburn and Thomas Hepburn. Her mother was part of a well-known New En-

gland family, the Houghtons. Encouraged by her dying mother to acquire an education for herself and her sisters, Kit eventually earned a bachelor's degree from Bryn Mawr College (1899) and a master's degree from Radcliffe (1900). Houghton's upbringing encouraged her to value independence, education, and social responsibility, three qualities that dominated her life. Because of her mother's interests, Hepburn had a childhood that was characterized by her family's deep involvement in many social causes of the day: the suffrage movement, the presence of brothels in their home city of Hartford and the associated spread of sexually transmitted diseases, and the efforts to provide safe birth control to women. The latter cause was led by Margaret Sanger, a friend of the Hepburns.

The Hepburn family's social conscience was not, however, guided solely by Kit. Thomas Hepburn was a young medical student when he first met Kit, and his sense of social awareness was as acute as hers. He chose to specialize in urology, an unmentionable subject in the polite society of that time. His practice led him to understand the horrors of syphilis, which was devastating the populations of all social classes. He chose to speak out about this taboo disease, at one point even paying for the printing and distribution of a play (*Damaged Goods*, by French dramatist Eugène Brieux) on the subject.

Another feature of Hepburn's childhood was her family's emphasis on physical activity. From ice-cold baths to swinging on a homemade trapeze strung from the trees to playing tennis and golf, the family's active life was the result in large part of Thomas's belief that a sluggish body led to a sluggish mind.

This closely knit family did suffer one early tragedy that also shaped Hepburn's growth: the accidental death by hanging of the oldest child, Tom, who was especially close to his sister Katharine. (For some seventy years afterward, she used Tom's birthday as her own, not revealing her true birthday until she published her autobiography in 1991.) Soon after her brother's death, Hepburn and her four siblings formed the Hepburn Players, an assortment of neighborhood children who put on performances with their own staging and direction. Even here, the family's social consciousness dominated: All proceeds from their production of *Beauty and the Beast* went to benefit the children of the Navajo Indians in New Mexico. Hepburn played the beast.

Like her mother and grandmother before her, Hepburn attended Bryn Mawr, where she took part in many of the school theatricals. Her parts ranged from playing a young man in one performance to playing Pandora in *The Woman in the Moone*. These experiences seem to have led to her decision to become an actor; just before the end of her senior year, she approached Edwin H. Knopf, a director of a local theater company, armed with a letter of introduction and asking for work. She graduated from Bryn Mawr with a bachelor's degree in history and philosophy in 1928. The same year she married Ludlow Ogden Smith, a businessman. Although they divorced in 1934, they remained lifelong friends.

LIFE'S WORK

In 1928, just before her graduation from Bryn Mawr, Hepburn's persistence overrode Knopf's objections, and he hired her to play one of six ladies-in-waiting in a production of *The Czarina* (1928). Hepburn's early years on the stage were marked by many struggles and ups and downs. She was, as she later said, "a quick study": She could read a part wonderfully and impress the director. When she was hired, however, she lacked the training and experience to carry through a full performance.

In 1932, Hepburn played the supporting role of Antiope, an Amazon warrior, in the Broadway production of *The Warrior's Husband*. Her entrance staggered Broadway: Wearing a short tunic, a helmet, a breastplate, and leggings, and carrying a dead stag over her shoulder, Hepburn leapt down a steep ramp and onto a platform, where she hurled the stag at Hippolyta's feet. Her stature enhanced the effect: At five feet seven inches, she was tall for actresses of the era. The performance led to an offer of a screen test for Hepburn.

On the basis of this screen test, Hepburn was awarded her first role in Hollywood, playing Hillary Fairfield in the 1932 film *A Bill of Divorcement* with the famous John Barrymore. This role led to her instant fame, although her second film in Hollywood, *Christopher Strong*, was neither a popular nor a critical success. Hepburn's popularity returned after her third picture, *Morning Glory* (1933), for which she was awarded her first Academy Award for Best Actress. Hepburn's next film role, Jo in *Little Women* (1933), was critically acclaimed, but she was not to be part of another popular film until *Stage Door* in 1937.

After she received her Academy Award, Hepburn's appeal was so great that she was offered the lead in the stage production of *The Lake* (1934). The play began disastrously, with a hard director apparently trying to browbeat Hepburn into buying out her contract. In her famous review of the play, critic Dorothy Parker gibed that Hepburn had "run the gamut of emotions from A to B." Hepburn stuck to her work, however, and struggled so hard to improve each performance that, by the time the play closed, she was turning in excellent performances. Soon after this experience, Hepburn returned to Hollywood.

In 1938, Hepburn's second film with the talented Cary Grant, *Bringing up Baby*, was released. Though it was not enormously popular upon first release, *Bringing up Baby* later came to be considered the finest of the "screwball comedies" that were so popular during the 1920's and 1930's. In the meantime, her fiery outspokenness, cutting wit, and unconventional life soured many filmgoers of the times. Like her parents she was a firm liberal, and she was a feminist, advocating then socially unacceptable issues such as birth control. Moreover, her relation with the press was often hostile. Once, asked whether she and her husband had any children, she shot back, "Yes, two white and three colored." In her role in the unsuccessful *Sylvia Scarlet* she dressed as a boy during the majority of scenes, which made audiences uncomfortable. In 1938 she was voted "box office poison" in a film industry poll.

Hepburn persevered nevertheless and enjoyed success in dealing with Hollywood on her own terms and, despite her previous difficulty with *The Lake*, often returned to the stage. One of her most successful theatrical runs was in *The Philadelphia Story* (1939). As well as starring in the play, Hepburn was involved in all aspects of its production, from writing to casting to arranging financing. She was as deeply involved in the writing and production of the film version of *The Philadelphia Story* (1940), in which she repeated her role from the stage version. It did much to erase her reputation as box office poison.

Another Hepburn film, *Woman of the Year*, was released in 1942. This picture marked Hepburn's first screen work with the superb actor Spencer Tracy, and it initiated what became the longest screen partnership in history as well as a legendary Hollywood romance. They went on to make nine films together, including such comedy classics as *Adam's Rib* (1949), *Pat and Mike* (1952), and *Desk Set* (1957). As critics have noted, most of the plots were variations on William Shakespeare's *The Taming of the Shrew*, pitting a sharp-tongued woman against a determined, often exasperated, but loving man. Hepburn and Tracy worked together until 1967, when their ninth and last film together, *Guess Who's Coming to Dinner*, was completed shortly before Tracy's death. Hepburn's work in this film earned for her a second Academy Award, which she believed must have been meant for both Tracy and herself.

The African Queen (1951), made with Humphrey Bogart on location in Africa, saw the transition in Hepburn's career from a young Hollywood actor who the studios had tried to portray as a starlet to the mature Hepburn, who was able to show film audiences the confidence and competence she had possessed all along. As one of her biographers, Sheridan Morley, explained, with the role of the missionary Rose Sayer, Hepburn transcended the "battle-of-the-sexes . . . comedies . . . and the old high-society romps" of her early career to become a great dramatic actor. This picture (for which Bogart won the Academy Award for Best Actor) was a critical and financial success for all concerned. She received Academy Award nominations for her leading roles in *Summertime* (1955), *Rainmaker* (1956), and *Suddenly Last Summer* (1959, adapted from a play by Tennessee Williams).

The film that brought Hepburn the greatest critical acclaim was *Long Day's Journey into Night* (1962), in which she gave a compelling performance of a woman sinking into the depths of drug addiction. According to many critics, this performance was the pinnacle of her career, a review that was a bit premature, since Hepburn continued to work. She won her next two Academy Awards for Best Actress for her portrayal of Eleanor of Aquitaine in *The Lion in Winter* (1968) and for her portrayal of Ethel Thayer in *On Golden Pond* (1981). In the meantime, she continued to take leading parts on stage, in *The Madwoman of Chaillot* (1969), Euripides' *The Trojan Women* (1971), and Edward Albee's *A Delicate Balance* (1973). Also in 1973, she appeared in a television production of Williams's *The Glass Menagerie* and in 1975 earned an Emmy Award for her leading role in *Love Among the Ruins*. Her role as a straitlaced spinster in the cowboy film *Rooster Cogburn* (1975), playing opposite John Wayne, was widely popular with fans, if not with critics. All these performances clearly demonstrated to the studios and critics that the American public would not only pay to see but also relish quality films starring mature, competent actors.

Hepburn continued to act in films, plays, and television adaptations until 1994, when she appeared in the films *One Christmas*, *This Can't Be Love*, and *Love Affair*. In 1999 the American Film Institute placed her above all other women actors of the last one hundred years in its Greatest American Screen Legends list. She continued an active life into her last years, riding her bicycle, gardening, and swimming in the ocean.

On June 29, 2003, at the age of ninety-six, Hepburn died in Fenwick, her house in Old Saybrook, Connecticut. Memorial honors soon followed. The lights of Broadway were dimmed for an hour, and in 2004, New York City redesignated the corner of East

Hepburn, Katharine

4th Street and 2nd Avenue as Katherine Hepburn Way. In 2006, Bryn Mawr College dedicated the Katharine Houghton Hepburn Center and inaugurated the Katharine Hepburn Medal, first awarded to actors Lauren Bacall and Blythe Danner.

SIGNIFICANCE

Throughout her career, Hepburn pushed her own limits and those of the motion picture industry and the medium of film. Her stage work, from her struggles with *The Lake* to her success in *The Philadelphia Story* to her frequent Shakespearean roles, bears testimony to her determination not to rest on her laurels. Her four Academy Awards for Best Actress attest to her talent as an actor and to the admiration of her colleagues.

Although initially audiences did not know what to make of her early performances (which were far from Hollywood stereotypes of women), and despite more than her share of critical attacks, Hepburn would come to epitomize honesty, independence, and intelligence, and she was idolized by millions of filmgoers. Hepburn's biographer, Gary Carey, quoted Richard Watts of the *Herald Tribune* as saying,

> Few actresses have been so relentlessly assailed by critics, wits, columnists, magazine editors, and other professional assailers over so long a period of time, and even if you confess that some of the abuse had a certain amount of justification to it, you must admit she faced it gamely and unflinchingly and fought back with courage and gallantry.

Hepburn also would "fight back" in her films with Tracy. Indeed, she believed that in her films with Tracy, the two actors epitomized a type of American couple that appealed to the nation from the 1940's on: both intelligent and forceful, the woman challenging the man with her wit. The man might be the ultimate boss, but his kingdom, as Hepburn would say, "isn't an easy kingdom for him to maintain."

—*Katherine Socha*

FURTHER READING

Andersen, Christopher. *Young Kate*. New York: Henry Holt, 1988. Based on conversations with Hepburn, this book chronicles her parents' lives, vividly recounts what it was like to grow up in the Hepburn family, and provides a detailed family chronology as well as a bibliography of supplementary references.

Berg, A. Scott. *Kate Remembered*. New York: G. P. Putnam's Sons, 2003. Berg relates anecdotes and opinions that he collected during twenty years of conversations with Hepburn.

Carey, Gary. *Katharine Hepburn: A Hollywood Yankee*. New York: St. Martin's Press, 1983. After a brief discussion of her childhood and college years, this book provides a general survey of Hepburn's career from her first theater job through her work in the early 1980's. Includes a chronology of her films from her first in 1932 to *On Golden Pond* in 1981.

Considine-Meara, Eileen. *At Home with Kate: Growing Up in Katharine Hepburn's Household*. Hoboken, N.J.: John Wiley & Sons, 2007. Written by the daughter of Hepburn's cook of thirty years, this memoir tells intimate inside stories about Hepburn's life at home, complete with the recipes that she loved and numerous photographs, movie stills, and cartoons.

Hepburn, Katharine. *The Making of "The African Queen": Or, How I Went to Africa with Bogart, Bacall, and Huston and Almost Lost My Mind*. New York: Alfred A. Knopf, 1987. This is Hepburn's writing at its best as she recalls the making of *The African Queen*. Discusses her first awareness of the project through the trials of working on location in Africa, the completion of the film in the studio, and Bogart's Academy Award.

———. *Me: Stories of My Life*. New York: Alfred A. Knopf, 1991. This book lives up to its title, providing stories of Hepburn's life from childhood through 1990. Written in a warm, readable, almost telegraphic style, the book discusses her career, her films and plays, and her family. Includes many photographs.

Kanin, Garson. *Tracy and Hepburn*. New York: Viking Press, 1971. This personal chronicle of the work and lives of Hepburn and Tracy is based on the author's long friendship with both and tells many stories of their lives together, both privately and professionally.

Mann, William J. *Kate: The Woman Who Was Hepburn*. New York: Henry Holt & Sons, 2006. Based on interviews with Hepburn's family and friends, Mann traces the evolution of her career as a movie star, the various artistic and ideological influences on her, and her complicated, much misrepresented love affair with Tracy.

Morley, Sheridan. *Katharine Hepburn*. Boston: Little, Brown, 1984. This thorough retrospective of Hepburn's career, written by the son of one of her former colleagues, provides detailed information about the progress of Hepburn's career and each of her pictures. A filmography provides thorough documentation (to 1984) of her films, television work, and her stage work.

AILEEN CLARKE HERNANDEZ

> *If black women did step back to allow their men a relative role of superiority, it would only offer the illusion of progress for the black man and result in retrogression for the black woman.*

Civil rights and feminist leader

As president of the National Organization for Women (NOW), director of the International Ladies' Garment Workers Union, and commissioner of the Equal Employment Opportunity Commission (EEOC), Hernandez represented the interests of women and ethnic minorities in the forefront of social reform. She was the first African American woman to hold a national office as EEOC commissioner, and she became a critic of mainstream, organized feminism for its focus on issues affecting mainly white, middle-class women.

Born: May 23, 1926; Brooklyn, New York
Also known as: Aileen Clarke (birth name)
Areas of achievement: Labor movement; social reform; women's rights

EARLY LIFE

Aileen Clarke Hernandez (hur-NAN-dehz) was born in Brooklyn, New York, to Charles and Ethel Clarke, who had emigrated from Jamaica in the British West Indies and eventually became U.S. citizens. Her mother was a costume maker and seamstress in the New York theater district, and her father worked in the art-supply business. Hernandez and her brothers were taught to cook and sew because her parents believed that no gender distinctions should be made in employment. They also emphasized that people should not be treated differently because of race or gender. This family value left an indelible mark on Hernandez, and it would deeply influence her life and career.

Hernandez graduated from Bay Ridge Public School as valedictorian and in 1943 from Bay Ridge High School as class salutatorian. She received a scholarship to attend Howard University in Washington, D.C.; served as editor and writer for the campus paper, *The Hilltop*; and wrote a column for the *Washington Tribune*. In 1946, she received honors in Kappa Mu Society, Howard's counterpart to Phi Beta Kappa.

Hernandez's political philosophy was molded by her college years in Washington, during the postwar period. She joined the student chapter of the National Association for the Advancement of Colored People (NAACP) and demonstrated against the racial discrimination of the National Theatre, Lisner Auditorium, and the Thompson restaurant chain. Her decision to participate in these early pickets stemmed largely from living as an African American in the United States. Venturing south for her college years at Howard, she experienced even more distinct discrimination as she traveled by train and waited for the segregated taxis in Washington, which were always the last in line. Believing that "democratic government requires full participation by all citizens," she supported equal rights for black World War II veterans returning to an unchanged segregated America.

After graduating magna cum laude from Howard in 1947 with degrees in sociology and political science, Hernandez traveled to Norway as part of the International Student Exchange Program and studied comparative government. Having recovered at home from an attack of tuberculosis, she attended New York University, the University of California, Los Angeles, and the University of Southern California. In 1959, she was awarded a master's degree in government, summa cum laude, from Los Angeles State College. Southern Vermont College would grant her an honorary doctorate in humane letters in 1979.

LIFE'S WORK

While attending New York University for graduate school, Hernandez accepted an internship to the International Ladies' Garment Workers Union (ILGWU) Training Institute. She was hired in 1951 and transferred to the ILGWU Pacific Coast region in California as an organizer. Eventually she served for eleven years in the ILGWU's West Coast office at Los Angeles as education director and public relations director. Her duties ranged from organizing social affairs to mobilizing strikes, pickets, and legislative lobbies. She also was responsible for naturalization classes for foreign-born union employees. In 1957, she married Alfonso Hernandez, a Mexican American garment worker she had met in Los Angeles. They were divorced in 1961.

In 1961, Hernandez's career shifted from union work to politics, managing a victorious campaign for Alan Cranston as California State controller. She was appointed assistant chief of the California Division of the Fair Employment Practice Commission (FEPC) in 1962. In this position she supervised a staff of fifty in four field offices. While serving with the FEPC, she initiated the Technical Advisory Committee (TACT). The TACT report was a comprehensive analysis of industrial testing as it affects the hiring of minorities and later prompted revisions in tests used by employers as a criterion for hiring.

By this time Hernandez had acquired experience and recognition for her work in labor relations and fair employment practices. With the recommendation of California governor Edmund G. "Pat" Brown, U.S. president Lyndon B. Johnson appointed her the first woman to the five-member Equal Employment Opportunity Commission (EEOC). Her duties included coordinating the activities of state and local commissions with the national EEOC. During her term on the commission, commercial airlines overturned their traditional policy of terminating female flight attendants when they married, and she helped focus the commission on racial discrimination in construction unions and the sex discrimination implicit or overt in many labor laws pertaining to women. After eighteen months of service, she resigned from the EEOC because she felt that the commission lacked any power to enforce its own policies. In 1967, she established her own consulting firm in San Francisco, California, Aileen C. Hernandez Associates, to advise businesses, government, labor, and private groups in urban affairs, and to foster the hiring of minorities and women.

Hernandez was present in 1966 at the Third National Conference of the State Commissions on Women in Washington, D.C. Betty Friedan, author of the 1963 best seller *The Feminine Mystique*, also was there, and they spoke of establishing a civil rights movement for women. The National Organization for Women (NOW) was created at this conference, and Friedan was chosen as its first president. Initially declining an offer to become a national vice president, Hernandez accepted a 1967 appointment as vice president of the Western region. In 1970 she succeeded Friedan as president of NOW.

Hernandez's leadership and articulation of the women's movement were major assets. Until 1971 many African American women viewed the women's movement as the elitist preserve of white middle-class women with nothing better to do. Hernandez considered NOW an extension of the Civil Rights movement for all women. In one interview, Hernandez addressed the issue head-on when she said,

> Until women, black as well as others, gain a sense of their own identity and feel that they have a real choice in society, nothing is going to happen in civil rights. It's not going to happen for Blacks; it's not going to happen for Mexican-Americans; it's not going to happen for women.

Hernandez served as NOW president until September, 1971. Also in 1971 she helped organized the National Women's Political Caucus, which encourages women to run for public office and is a forum for women's issues. However, Hernandez's relation with NOW became troubled after her tenure as president. She started the Minority Women's Task Force in 1972, sending out a survey to minority women; the response revealed that only 10 percent of NOW's membership was made up of minorities, and many minority members felt isolated. Hernandez herself criticized NOW for neglect-

Aileen Clarke Hernandez. (Library of Congress)

ing minority issues during its focus on promoting the Equal Rights Amendment. She was also unhappy with the paucity of minority representation among the organization's leadership. In 1979 she severed her connection with NOW, although she later attended its anniversary celebrations.

In 1973, Hernandez chaired the summer meeting in Boston of the International Feminist Planning Conference, bringing together women from thirty countries. At the invitation of the U.S. State Department and the Konrad Adenauer Foundation, in 1975 she attended the International Conference on Minorities and the Metropolis in Bonn, Germany. She traveled to the People's Republic of China with an American rights group in 1978. That same year, with the National Commission, she made a fact-finding tour of South Africa. The 1981 report of that regional study by the commission—*South Africa: Time Running Out*—received praise for its analysis of apartheid and U.S. policy in South Africa.

Hernandez continued to build her consulting business, employing four associates and, depending on the project load, as many as thirty staff employees. Specializing in such critical urban issues as transportation, equal opportunity, health, education, economic development, criminal justice, environment, and housing, Aileen C. Hernandez Associates had among its clients United Parcel Service, Standard Oil of California, the National Catholic Conference on Interracial Justice, the Ford Foundation, the Bay Area Rapid Transit District, and the California Department of Health Services.

Hernandez persevered in volunteering her organizational skills. She was vice chair of the National Urban Coalition and of the National Advisory Council of the American Civil Liberties Union, and was chair of Citizen's Trust, a socially sensitive investment group. She served on the Secretary's Advisory Committee on the Rights and Responsibilities of Women for the U.S. Department of Health and Human Services and worked with the California Women's Agenda. She was coordinator for Black Women Stirring the Waters and was a board member for the Pesticide Education Center, the National Women's Museum, the Wellesley Center for Research on Women, the Garden Project, the Meilejohn Civil Liberties Union, the Center for Women Policy Studies, the Center for the Common Good, and the Citizen's Commission on Civil Rights. She also became a life trustee of the Urban Institute and a member of the Ms. Foundation for Women.

Hernandez continued to travel frequently to attend conferences and teach. In 1993 she was the Tish Sommers lecturer at the Institute for Health and Aging of the University of California, San Francisco, was a Regents Scholar in Residence in 1996 at the University of California, Santa Barbara, and taught at the University of California, Berkeley. In 2000 she was part of a conference encouraging cooperation between women in the United States and China.

The numerous awards in recognition of her public service are impressive. She was chosen as Woman of the Year in 1961 by the Community Relations Conference of Southern California. Howard University honored her in 1968 for Distinguished Postgraduate Achievement in the Fields of Labor and Public Service, and that same year she received the Charter Day Alumni Post Graduate Achievement in Labor and Public Services Award. The *San Francisco Examiner* named her one of the Ten Most Distinguished Women of the San Francisco Bay Area in 1969. The Bicentennial Award was granted to her in 1976 by the Trinity Baptist Church of San Mateo County.

Equal Rights advocates commended Hernandez in 1981 for her service to the women's movement, and in 1984 she was honored by the Friends of the San Francisco Commission on the Status of Women. In 1985, the San Francisco League of Women Voters named her among the Ten Women Who Make a Difference, the National Urban Coalition recognized her service to urban communities, and the San Francisco Black Chamber of Commerce presented her with the Parren J. Mitchell Award for dedicated service to the African American community. The Memorial United Methodist Church commended her services to humanity in 1986, and Gamma Phi Delta Sorority made her an honorary member.

Hernandez also received awards in appreciation from the National Institute for Women of Color in 1987, and the following year from the Western District Conference on the National Association of Negro Business and Professional Women's Clubs. The Northern California American Civil Liberties Foundation presented her with its Earl Warren Civil Liberties Award in 1989. In 1995 the San Francisco Planning and Urban Research Association gave her its Silver Spur Award. She received the Eleanor Roosevelt Award from the Democratic Women's Forum in California in 1996 and the Ella Hill Hutch Award in 1997.

SIGNIFICANCE

Hernandez's contributions to labor relations, the women's movement, equal opportunity, political activism, and community service comprise an extensive list of accomplishments. Her dedication to public service made her both a national and an international figure in the forefront of social reform. She was the first African American woman to hold a national office as EEOC commissioner, and she became one of the first active critics of mainstream, organized feminism for its focus on issues affecting mainly white, middle-class women to the detriment of women of color.

—*Emily Teipe*

FURTHER READING

Banner, Lois W. *Women in Modern America: A Brief History*. 2d ed. San Diego, Calif.: Harcourt Brace Jovanovich, 1984. A survey of the women's rights movement from the 1890's to 1984 that places Hernandez in the context of the formation of NOW.

Barakso, Maryann. *Governing NOW: Grassroots Activism in the National Organization for Women*. Ithaca, N.Y.: Cornell University Press, 2004. This history of NOW's development and strategies includes references to Hernandez and her opinions on some issues that affected NOW's early development.

Baxandall, Rosalyn, and Linda Gordon. "Second-Wave Feminism." In *A Companion to American Women's History*, edited by Nancy A. Hewitt. Malden, Mass.: Blackwell, 2002. A concise overview of the second wave of the women's movement in the United States, with brief mention of Hernandez's work.

Dreyfus, Joel. "Civil Rights and the Women's Movement." *Black Enterprise* 8 (September, 1977): 35-37, 45. Discusses Hernandez as the first African American woman to hold a national office and her vision of the women's movement as part of the larger Civil Rights movement.

Lewis, Ida. "Conversation: Ida Lewis and Aileen Hernandez." *Essence*, February, 1971. An interview with Hernandez in the first issue of *Essence* magazine, during her presidency of NOW, in which she speaks about her role and the issues of the women's movement, civil rights, and equal opportunity.

WILD BILL HICKOK

> " ... while firing my last shot, I will gently breathe the name of my wife ... and with wishes even for my enemies I will make the plunge and try to swim to the other shore. "

Frontier lawman

Hickok's prowess with a pistol made him one of the deadliest gunfighters in the American West and one of the most forceful and accomplished lawmen of the Kansas cattle towns. His exploits as a soldier, scout, gunfighter, and lawman made him one of the most recognized figures from the American frontier.

Born: May 27, 1837; Troy Grove, Illinois
Died: August 2, 1876; Deadwood, Dakota Territory (now South Dakota)
Also known as: James Butler Hickok (birth name)
Area of achievement: Law and jurisprudence

EARLY LIFE

Wild Bill Hickok (HIH-kawk) was born James Butler Hickok, the fourth of six children born to William Alonzo and Polly Hickok. In 1836, the family moved to Troy Grove, Illinois, where Hickok's father opened the community's first general store. Known as the Green Mountain House, the store doubled as a way station on the Underground Railroad. Slavery deeply troubled William, and his boys regularly assisted their father in helping runaway slaves escape. William's business failed during the financial panic of 1837, forcing him to turn to farming.

As a young boy, James Hickok kept to himself, and many considered him a loner. Early in his life, he demonstrated a penchant for weaponry, and he acquired his first gun around the age of twelve. At every opportunity, young Hickok retreated into the woods to practice his marksmanship. When William died in 1852, his boys took over the family farm. Because of his prowess with a gun, James was given the responsibility of supplementing his family's diet. He spent much of his time prowling through the woods and fields, hunting deer and small game. He also earned extra income by killing wolves and collecting bounties on their pelts. By his late teenage years, Hickok was known as one of the best shots in La Salle County. His skill and dexterity with firearms would later serve him well as a frontier lawman and soldier.

Throughout Hickok's life, he had a tendency to never back down from a threat, and he regularly stood up for those who could not defend themselves. His first recorded altercation with another man occurred at the age of eighteen while he was working for the Illinois and Michigan Canal. Charles Hudson, a local camp bully, did not like Hickok, and, after exchanging some heated words, a fight broke out. As the pair exchanged blows and wrestled along the bank of the canal, the edge gave way, sending them into the water. Bystanders jumped into the water and pulled Hickok off Hudson, who lay motionless in the canal. Thinking that he had killed his adversary, the youthful Hickok fled the scene and retreated to the family farm. Shortly thereafter, Hickok, along with his brother Lorenzo, left home and headed west to Kansas.

LIFE'S WORK
Hickok arrived in Kansas in 1856 as a nineteen-year-old teenager and, except for brief trips east, spent his entire adult life in the American West. During his twenty years on the Great Plains, Hickok worked as a frontier scout, spy, soldier, teamster, showman, gunfighter, gambler, and lawman. He witnessed many of the important events associated with the development and settlement of the American West, and he personally participated in the Indian Wars, policed the cattle towns, and saw the decimation of the buffalo.

The man who would become one of the most recognized figures of the frontier era stood more than six feet tall. He had piercing gray-blue eyes that reportedly looked right through people. His long and curled auburn hair tumbled to his shoulders, and a drooping mustache hung over his lip. He sometimes dressed in the buckskin clothing of the plainsmen but later became more elegant, sporting a Prince Albert frock coat. Topping off Hickok's appearance were his ever-present guns, two Navy Colt revolvers tucked butts-forward into a red sash wrapped around his waist.

When the Hickok brothers arrived in Kansas in 1856, the territory was on the verge of civil war. Hickok briefly labored as a plowman in Johnson County, but when hostilities erupted over the issue of slavery along the Kansas-Missouri border, Hickok joined Jim Lane's Free-State Army of Kansas. Whether he saw battle is unknown, but legend claims that he became Lane's personal bodyguard.

After leaving Lane's Kansas militia in late 1857, Hickok took his first job in law enforcement as a constable for Monticello Township in Johnson County. He held this position for less than one year before he went to work for the transportation and freighting outfit of Russell, Majors, and Waddell. For two years he drove wagons and stagecoaches on the Santa Fe Trail. While on one of these trips to Santa Fe, Hickok reportedly met Kit Carson, his boyhood hero. Little did Hickok know that within a few years his own status as a Western hero would equal or surpass that of Carson.

In 1861 Hickok was working at Rock Creek Station in southeastern Nebraska. It was here, on July 12, 1861, that Hickok fought his first gun battle. The incident grew out of an ongoing feud between a local bully named Dave McCanles and the station's manager. When McCanles, his son James Woods, and James Gordon appeared at the station and threatened the manager and his wife, Hickok stepped in and shot elder McCanles, Woods, and Gordon. McCanles died almost instantly. Woods and Gordon, both wounded by Hickok, attempted to escape but were hunted down and dispatched by station employees. Nebraska authorities arrested Hickok and two others, but a jury determined that they had acted in self-defense.

After his acquittal, Hickok drifted into Kansas, where he enlisted as a civilian scout in the Union Army. During the war he served as a wagon master, scout, sharpshooter, and spy. He fought at the battles of Wilson's Creek and Pea Ridge. Hickok also spent time behind enemy lines, scouting enemy positions and intercepting Confederate orders and documents. It was during the Civil War that Hickok first gained notoriety. While in Independence, Missouri, Hickok, with his pistols in his hands, dispersed a mob that was threatening to lynch a man. It was from this incident that Hickok earned the name "Wild Bill." After breaking up the mob, a lady from the crowd yelled out, "Good for you, Wild Bill." The name stuck, and from then on James Butler Hickok went by the name Wild Bill.

Hickok's Civil War service as a scout and an 1865 gunfight in which he killed Dave Tutt in Springfield, Missouri, enhanced the name of Wild Bill around Missouri and Kansas. In 1867, an article about Wild Bill in *Harper's New Monthly Magazine* made Hickok a household name and a national hero. The story, written by George Ward Nichols, greatly exaggerated Hickok's Civil War exploits and claimed that he killed ten men at the Rock Creek gunfight. Nichols's portrayal of Hickok influenced later writers who further embellished Hickok's law enforcement career by claiming that he had killed one hundred men in the line of duty. Hickok did not like his image as a "man-killer," but this portrait of him as a deadly gunman earned him respect, which made policing the rowdy cattle towns easier.

Although Hickok's career in law enforcement lasted only a few years, he gained notoriety as one of the best Western lawmen. From 1867 to 1870 he served as a deputy U.S. marshal, chasing army deserters and stock thieves. In 1869 Ellis County, Kansas, elected Hickok sheriff. Hays City, the county seat, was an end-of-the-line railroad town full of gamblers, brawlers, soldiers, buffalo hunters, prostitutes, and gunmen. In three months of service, he killed two men in gunfights and was largely credited with establishing law and order. After losing his reelection bid to his deputy sheriff, Hickok drifted around from place to place. On July 17, 1870, while back in Hays City, Hickok became involved in a drunken altercation with five soldiers from Fort Hays. In the fracas that ensued, Hickok shot two soldiers, killing one and seriously wounding the other.

Because of Hickok's reputation as a lawman and gunfighter, the Kansas cattle town of Abilene hired him as city marshal in 1871. Hickok largely succeeded in quelling disturbances by prohibiting cowboys from carrying guns and keeping a close eye on the drinking and gambling establishments that they frequented. Hickok was involved in only one shooting during his stint in Abilene. On October 5, 1871, Hickok confronted Phil Coe and a number of Texans who had shot their revolvers at stray dogs. Sensing danger from the gun in Coe's hand, Hickok pulled out his revolvers. The two exchanged shots, but only Hickok's found their mark. In the heat of the conflict, Mike Williams, a friend of Hickok who was a special police officer for the Novelty Theater, came running to Hickok's assistance. Catching a glimpse of the fast-approaching Williams out of the corner of his eye and believing him to be a friend of the wounded Coe, Hickok fired two shots, killing Williams.

The death of Williams had a tremendous impact on Hickok. Shortly thereafter he retired from law enforcement and supposedly never again fired his pistols at anyone.

Hickok, Wild Bill

After 1871 Hickok tried his hand at acting. He performed with several Wild West shows, including that of William Frederick "Buffalo Bill" Cody. Realizing that acting was not for him, Hickok returned to the Great Plains where, in March, 1876, he married Agnes Lake Thatcher, a former circus performer. Legend holds that Hickok also had a relationship with Martha "Calamity Jane" Cannary, but there is no basis for such a claim. In July, 1876, Hickok joined the gold rush to the Black Hills in the Dakota Territory hoping to strike it rich and return to his new wife. Hickok, however, seems to have known that his days were numbered. He regularly told his friends that Deadwood in the Dakota Territory might be his last camp. On August 2, 1876, Hickok's premonitions came true when Jack McCall shot him in the back of the head while he played poker in a local saloon. The cards held by Hickok—aces and eights—have come to be known as the "dead man's hand."

SIGNIFICANCE

The historical life of James Butler Hickok is quite interesting but of little significance. He served his country bravely during the Civil War, scouted during the Plains Indian Wars, killed up to ten men in gunfights, and policed some of the rowdiest cattle towns in the West. Perhaps his role as a lawman made those wild and rollicking towns a safer place to live, but on a larger scale his contributions to history and his impact on American society were minimal.

The legendary Wild Bill Hickok, however, is a much different story. He has had a tremendous impact on American culture. Hickok's life and his exploits—whether fact or fiction—have received attention in films, in dime novels, on television shows, and from serious historians. Places such as Deadwood, South Dakota; Abilene, Kansas; and Hays City, Kansas consider Wild Bill as one of their own and continue to promote his name and his image as a colorful frontier figure. Hickok's life has captured the imagination of thousands of people, and he has gone down as one of the true heroes of the American frontier.

—Mark R. Ellis

FURTHER READING

Dykstra, Robert S. *The Cattle Towns*. 1968. Reprint. Lincoln: University of Nebraska Press, 1983. Analyzes the origins and development of the Kansas cattle towns of Abilene, Ellsworth, Wichita, Dodge City, and Caldwell. Although Hickok is not a central figure, this work is important to understanding the social world in which he worked as a lawman.

Miller, Nyle H., and Joseph W. Snell. *Great Gunfighters of the Kansas Cowtowns, 1867-1886*. Lincoln: University of Nebraska Press, 1967. Formerly published under the title *Why the West Was Wild*, this book provides a documentary history of the violence associated with the Kansas cattle towns. Using excerpts from newspapers, diaries, letters, and public documents, this work examines the gun battles and exploits of twenty-one Western gunfighters, including Hickok.

Rosa, Joseph G. *They Called Him Wild Bill: The Life and Adventures of James Butler Hickok*. Norman: University of Oklahoma Press, 1964. The definitive Hickok biography. Probably the best work on any Western gunfighter and lawman.

_____. *The West of Wild Bill Hickok.* Norman: University of Oklahoma Press, 1982. A pictorial biography of Hickok and the people and places associated with his career. Almost every known photograph, drawing, and painting of him appears in this volume.

_____. *Wild Bill Hickok, Gunfighter: An Account of Hickok's Gunfights.* College Station, Tex.: Creative, 2001. Chronicles Hickok's gunfights, providing detailed descriptions of the guns he used, his legendary abilities as a marksman, and the "dead man's hand" Hickok held in the poker game when he was shot to death.

_____.*Wild Bill Hickok: The Man and His Myth.* Lawrence: University Press of Kansas, 1996. An examination of the many myths and legends surrounding Hickok's exploits in the American West. Addresses his reputation as a "man-killer" among other topics.

OVETA CULP HOBBY

> *Women who stepped up were measured as citizens of the nation, not as women. . . . [World War II] was a people's war, and everyone was in it.*

Military leader and U.S. cabinet member

As a U.S. Army officer, cabinet member, and business leader, Hobby was a pioneer for American women in many areas of public life. In her job as the first secretary of Health, Education, and Welfare, she helped to institutionalize the department so that it became an important and necessary Washington fixture. She also helped develop the Women's Army Auxiliary Corps during World War II and was its first head.

Born: January 19, 1905; Killeen, Texas
Died: August 16, 1995; Houston, Texas
Also known as: Oveta Culp (birth name)
Areas of achievement: Military; public health; government and politics; women's rights; journalism

EARLY LIFE

Oveta Culp Hobby (HAW-bee) was born to Isaac William Culp and Emma Hoover Culp. Her father was an attorney who was first elected to the Texas state legislature in 1919; her mother was a homemaker who was active in the woman suffrage movement. From her earliest childhood, Hobby's father took a personal interest in her training and schooling. Isaac Culp instilled an interest in public life in Hobby and convinced her that her gender did not constitute a barrier to any ambition she might have had. It was still somewhat unusual for a woman of her day, even one of the educated classes, to attend college. Not only did Hobby complete her undergraduate work at Mary Hardin-Baylor College, but she also studied law at the main campus of the University of Texas.

At a very young age and only partly through the influence of her father, Hobby began securing positions in the law, business, and government matrix of Texas. At the age of twenty, she was working as assistant city attorney in Houston. For several years, she served as parliamentarian, or chief clerk, for the lower house of the Texas state legislature, a position that enabled her to make extensive contacts in Texas politics. She made some use of these contacts when she decided to run for the legislature as a Democrat in 1929. Despite her efforts, she was not elected; women in electoral politics were to be more truly a phenomenon of her children's generation. On February 23, 1931, Hobby took a more conventional step when she married William P. Hobby, about thirty years her senior, publisher of the Houston *Post*, and a former governor of Texas.

Life's Work

Marriage, however, did not mean retirement to domesticity and obscurity for Hobby, as it did for many women of the period. Hobby immediately threw herself into both the business and editorial aspects of her husband's newspaper business. Starting out as a research editor, she moved steadily up the hierarchy of the newspaper until 1938, when she was named executive vice president. These were not ceremonial positions; Hobby's husband, busy managing other sectors of his extensive business interests, delegated much of his responsibility for the *Post* to his wife.

Houston during the 1930's was a much smaller city than it became later in the century, and the *Post* was in many ways a small, regional newspaper. Hobby made efforts to modernize the newspaper and bring it to the level of sophistication achieved by dailies on the East Coast. She placed a premium on intelligent coverage of women's issues, adding a woman editor to the staff to cover the activities and interests of women. Aside from her newspaper work and her devotion to her children, Hobby was particularly active within the Texas chapter of the League of Women Voters.

Hobby first attained national prominence with the beginning of American involvement in World War II. The United States government realized immediately after the onset of the war that this conflict would be more "total" than previous ones. It would affect not only soldiers fighting the war but also civilians living and working on the home front. Realizing that women would be more actively involved in the war effort than before, the government sought the assistance of recognized women leaders to help coordinate this involvement. Hobby was recruited to be the head of the women's division of the War Department's Bureau of Public Relations. This mainly involved liaison work between the Army and female family members of servicemen, and therefore fell short of giving women full equality in the war effort. The War Department soon realized the inadequacy of this situation, and, in the spring of 1942, the Women's Army Auxiliary Corps (WAAC) was established to mobilize the talents and energy of women. Because of her work with Army Chief of Staff George C. Marshall to plan the WAAC, Hobby was the natural choice to head this corps and, as such, was given military rank, first as a major, and then, more appropriately considering the status of her role, as a colonel.

World War II was one of the great watersheds in the democratization of American society. Most, if not all, of this democratization was unintentional. The government did not set out to use the war to enfranchise women and African Americans, yet staffing needs compelled the government to make use of their talents to serve the war ef-

Oveta Culp Hobby.
(Library of Congress)

forts. Hobby's tenure at the WAAC saw the most thorough emergence of American women into the public sphere in history. Once it was realized that the contribution of women was indispensable to the war effort, their social marginalization was far less viable. The increasing significance of women was recognized when the "auxiliary" was dropped from the name of the corps in the middle of the war. By 1945, Hobby's efforts with the WAC had become nationally known, and, next to Eleanor Roosevelt, Hobby became the second most important woman in the American war effort.

After the war, Hobby returned to her duties at the Houston *Post*, but her interest in Washington affairs continued. In 1948, she advised the commission headed by former President Herbert Hoover on reducing waste in government bureaucracy. Surprisingly, her continuing interest in politics was no longer centered on the Democratic Party. In the Texas of Hobby's girlhood, it had been culturally mandatory for a Texan to be a Democrat, since Texas, like many southern states, was dominated by a virtual one-party system. During her years in Washington, D.C., however, Hobby was increasingly drawn to the Republican Party, especially after its transformation under the leadership of Thomas E. Dewey. Under Dewey, the Republicans accepted most of Franklin D. Roosevelt's New Deal social policies, while being more friendly to the free market and to capitalist initiative than were the Democrats. Hobby, a businesswoman as well as a liberal, was particularly sympathetic to this point of view. In addition, since they did not depend as heavily on the political influence of southern conservatives and urban party bosses, as did the Democrats, the Republicans could theoretically be more responsive in alleviating the oppression of African Americans. As a result, although she continued to support local Democratic candidates, Hobby actively campaigned on behalf of Republican presidential candidates in 1948 and again in 1952.

Although Dewey suffered an upset loss in his 1948 presidential race against incumbent Harry Truman, the Republicans won in 1952 with the election of former general Dwight D. Eisenhower. By this time, Hobby was solidly in the Republican camp. When it came time for the new president to make his appointments, Eisenhower remembered Hobby's wartime service and asked her to be the director of the Federal Security Agency. This agency coordinated the various government efforts directed at securing the health and comfort of American citizens. Socially concerned Democrats had long wanted to give this agency cabinet-level status, but it was the Eisenhower administration, often attacked for its conservatism, that presided over the agency's elevation as the Department of Health, Education, and Welfare (HEW). After her appointment as secretary of this department was approved in 1953, Hobby became the second woman to serve in the cabinet. (Frances Perkins, secretary of labor in the Roosevelt administration, was the first.)

Hobby had enormous ambitions for the department, not all of which were realized during her tenure. She considered plans for overhauling the nation's medical insurance system, proposing legislation that would have established a federal corporation to provide financial backing for private, low-cost medical plans. Although her proposals were defeated as a result of staunch opposition by the American Medical Association and fiscal conservatives in Congress, many elements of her plan received renewed attention during the 1990's under President Bill Clinton. Hobby also wished to focus more attention on the plight of the disadvantaged and economically subordinated, a highly unpopular cause during the prosperous 1950's. So much of the budget was being spent on Cold War defense projects that funding for the projects Hobby wished to undertake was simply not available.

Despite these difficult challenges, Hobby performed her job with dynamism and diligence. She was particularly instrumental in the widespread distribution of Jonas Salk's polio vaccine. As one of the few highly visible women in public life in the 1950's, she made a decided impression on young women growing up at the time. She seemed responsible, capable, and optimistic, someone equipped for the challenges of the political world. Although she had only been in office for two years when she resigned to take care of her ailing husband on July 13, 1955, Hobby had made important contributions during her tenure at HEW.

Hobby did not rest on her laurels after her retirement from government. Taking over the executive reins at the Houston *Post*, she presided over its development into a large metropolitan daily, acquiring the latest in technological equipment to help the paper keep pace with the exponential growth of Houston itself. She also oversaw the expansion of the *Post* media empire into the new realms of radio and, especially, television. She served as cofounder of the Bank of Texas and was invited to serve on the boards of several corporations, including the Corporation for Public Broadcasting. Hobby also developed more interests in the cultural sphere, accumulating an impres-

Hobby, Oveta Culp

sive collection of modern art, including paintings by Pablo Picasso and Amedeo Modigliani. Although Hobby did not pursue public office herself, she did have the satisfaction of seeing her son, William, Jr., elected as lieutenant governor of Texas in 1972 and serve twelve years in that position. In 1978, she became the first woman to receive the George Catlett Marshall Medal for Public Service from the Association of the United States Army in recognition of her contributions during World War II.

Hobby continued to be a prominent and much-beloved figure on the local Houston scene and nationally, serving on boards of businesses and civic bodies. In the later years of her life, her business success and family fortune made her one of the richest women in the United States. She could look back on a remarkable and unmistakably American life. She died in Houston of a stroke.

SIGNIFICANCE

It is difficult to isolate one specific mark Hobby made on American history, if only because her long life saw her excel in so many pursuits. Her wartime service helped pave the way for the promotion of women to a position of full equality in the military as well as in civilian society. Her business success proved that women not only could direct a large corporate concern but also could transform and expand that concern at an age when many business executives typically settled into retirement.

Nevertheless, it was arguably in her cabinet role as the first secretary of Health, Education, and Welfare that Hobby made her most enduring contribution. Hobby started off her cabinet position on a good footing, helping institutionalize it so that it (and, more important, the concerns it represented) became a Washington fixture. The Eisenhower cabinet of which Hobby was a member was derided at the time as consisting of "eight millionaires and a plumber," but it was in fact composed of many remarkable personalities, four of whom survived well into the 1990's: Attorney General Herbert Brownell, Secretary of Agriculture Ezra Taft Benson, Attorney General William Rogers, and Hobby herself. Perhaps slighted by the Democratic bias of many historians, the Eisenhower cabinet was, especially in terms of domestic policy, a progressive force. Hobby's presence was crucial in shaping this tendency.

Hobby's cabinet service also firmly established the tradition of women being present in the cabinet. Under Roosevelt, the Democratic Party had been most associated with the equality of women. Hobby's presence in a Republican cabinet meant that drawing on the abilities of Americans of either gender became a bipartisan concern. Every future woman cabinet member owed her position, in a way, to Hobby's achievements.

—*Margaret Boe Birns*

FURTHER READING

Beasley, Maurine H., and Sheila J. Gibbons. *Taking Their Place: A Documentary History of Women and Journalism*. Washington, D.C.: American University Press, 1993. This book provides an impression of the history of women in journalism before, during, and after Hobby's newspaper years.

Clark, James Anthony, with Weldon Hart. *The Tactful Texan: A Biography of Governor Will Hobby*. New York: Random House, 1958. This biography of Hobby's hus-

Hope, Bob

band provides information on Hobby's early career.

Eisenhower, Dwight D. *The White House Years: Mandate for Change, 1953-1956*. Garden City, N.Y.: Doubleday, 1963. The first volume of Eisenhower's presidential memoirs makes frequent mention of Hobby in her role as head of the Department of Health, Education, and Welfare.

Howes, Ruth, and Michael Stevenson, eds. *Women and the Use of Military Force*. Boulder, Colo.: Lynne Rienner, 1993. This book considers the theoretical issues accompanying women's service in the military.

Hutchison, Kay Bailey. *American Heroines: The Spirited Women Who Shaped Our Country*. New York: William Morrow, 2004. Hutchison, a U.S. senator, provides profiles of women who made history, including Hobby.

Lyon, Peter. *Eisenhower: Portrait of the Hero*. Boston: Little, Brown, 1974. Emphasizes Hobby's role as the nation's top health care official.

Whisenhunt, Donald W., ed. *The Human Tradition in America Between the Wars, 1920-1945*. Wilmington, Del.: SR Books, 2002. A collection of biographical essays describing how a wide range of Americans coped with the significant changes in American society that occurred from 1920 through 1945. Includes an essay on Hobby.

BOB HOPE

> *I've always been in the right place and time. Of course, I steered myself there.*

Entertainer, actor, and humanitarian

Hope was an entertainment icon of radio, television, and motion pictures, a comedian known for joking about fellow entertainers, politicians, and, in particular, himself. He also gained fame for his charity work, entertaining U.S. troops in several wars spanning more than fifty years.

Born: May 29, 1903; Eltham, England
Died: July 27, 2003; Los Angeles, California
Also known as: Leslie Townes Hope; Packy East
Areas of achievement: Theater and entertainment; film; philanthropy

EARLY LIFE

One of the most famous entertainers in American history, Bob Hope was born Leslie Townes Hope in Eltham, England, a suburb of London. Hope's father, William Henry Hope, was a stonemason of English descent and his mother, Avis Townes Hope, was an aspiring singer of Welsh descent. His family moved to Cleveland, Ohio, in 1907, where Hope found a love for entertaining people at backyard picnics. In his teenage years, while attending East High School, Hope worked a number of jobs, including newspaper boy, stock boy in his brother's meat market, soda jerk, and shoe salesman.

He also began performing for money as a singer at restaurants and boxing under the name Packy East, entering the ring for three fights.

Around the same time that he was beginning his entertainment career in modest fashion, Hope became a U.S. citizen, in 1920. After high school, he began taking dancing lessons and working in vaudeville, a form of entertainment popular at the time, which consisted of a number of separate, unrelated acts performed throughout a show. He worked briefly with his girlfriend, Mildred Rosequist, who became his dance partner during some vaudeville acts. In the mid-1920's, he worked with such partners as Lloyd Durbin in Cleveland and then George Byrne and Louise Troxell. He began using his stage name, Bob, in 1928.

Hope gained success working with Byrne, traveling to New York City and eventually being selected for the Broadway show *Sidewalks in New York*. He followed his success in New York working in a theater in Pennsylvania announcing coming attractions to audiences, eventually developing his own act during this stint. While performing in the Broadway show *Roberta*, Hope met nightclub singer Delores Reade, who he married on February 19, 1934. They eventually adopted four children: Linda, Anthony, Kelly, and Laura.

LIFE'S WORK

Hope continued working on Broadway in the mid- to late 1930's, performing in a number of shows, including *Say When* (1934), the *Ziegfeld Follies* (1936), and *Red, Hot, and Blue* (1936). Hope broke into radio during his time on Broadway, appearing on radio promotions for New York's Capital Theatre. Also featured in some of his radio promotions was Bing Crosby. After an appearance on the *Fleishman Hour* starring Rudy Vallee, Hope worked on the *Woodbury Soap Show* in 1937. He soon was rewarded with his own show on NBC, *The Pepsodent Radio Show Starring Bob Hope* (1938-1953), which quickly gained a number-one ranking. Despite juggling a number of other ventures, Hope continued in radio until 1956.

With his success in vaudeville, Broadway, and radio, Hope began his motion-picture career in 1938 in the film *The Big Broadcast of 1938*. In the film, he teamed with Shirley Ross to sing the Academy Award-winning song "Thanks for the Memory," which later became his theme song. The next year, Hope starred in *The Cat and the Canary*, which began another theme of Hope: playing a coward who uses sarcasm and jokes at his own expense. The next year, he starred with Crosby in *Road to Singapore*, beginning a long-term motion-picture collaboration between the two that lasted twenty-two years. Hope appeared in more than fifty films, spanning from the late 1930's until 1985. His other films included *The Paleface* (1948), *Fancy Pants* (1950), and *The Lemon Drop Kid* (1951). He also produced films such as *Alias Jesse James* (1959) and *The Facts of Life* (1960).

At the beginning of World War II, Hope and some of his colleagues visited American troops in California, performing a radio show as entertainment. The positive feedback received from his visit led to another of his long associations: entertaining the troops with the United Service Organizations, better known as the USO. After the California performance, Hope visited troops on both the European and Pacific fronts, providing them with a brief respite from the strain of war. He also began a tradition of trav-

Hope, Bob

Bob Hope (center) poses with U.S. troops in Korea, 1950. (AP/Wide World Photos)

eling to entertain troops during Christmastime, a tradition he continued until he was no longer able to perform. He also entertained the troops during the Vietnam War and Operation Desert Storm. President John F. Kennedy awarded him the Congressional Gold Medal in 1962 for his work for the nation, and he has been honored by Congress five times. He was made an honorary military veteran in 1997.

Hope's stardom led him to the rising popular medium of television. Although he had made a few commercials and guest appearances in the 1930's and 1940's while television was in its infancy, he officially began his TV career in 1950 with the special *Star Spangled Revue*. As Hope's film career was taking a downturn in the 1960's with some highly criticized films, his TV career was blossoming. Although he was not a TV regular, his specials, which included a number of Hope "traditions" such as introducing the All-Americans of college football, were popular with audiences into the late 1990's.

In addition to being an entertainer and philanthropist, Hope also was an avid golfer, hosting an annual Bob Hope Classic tournament (now called the Bob Hope Chrysler Classic). Hope ended his television career in 1996 and made few appearances after he reached his nineties. His one hundredth birthday was celebrated with a TV special featuring numerous clips from his career. Hope died only a few months later, of pneumonia, on July 7, 2003.

Significance

Hope not only was one of the most famous entertainers of the twentieth century but also was one of the most active, appearing in more than fifty films, producing films, performing on Broadway, hosting a radio show for eighteen years, and hosting TV shows for nearly half a century.

Hope was also an innovator. Some of his comedic tactics have been oft-repeated. His penchant for directing jokes at himself, to take one example, remains a staple of many comedians. He also helped bring entertainment and the military together and is one of the most important figures in USO history. He will be remembered for his philanthropic work as much as for his entertainment. According to some sources, he contributed more than one billion dollars to charity. His accolades range from the more trivial, such as his stars on the Hollywood Walk of Fame, to recognitions reflective of his legacy: the streets, buildings, golf tournament, and airport (the former Burbank Airport) named for him.

—*Brion Sever*

Further Reading

Faith, William. *Bob Hope: A Life in Comedy*. Cambridge, Mass.: Da Capo Press, 2003. This book provides an elaborated view of Hope's life in comedy, including his early life.

Hope, Bob, and Linda Hope. *Bob Hope: My Life in Jokes*. New York: Hyperion Books, 2003. A biography that touches on Hope's life, from his childhood years to his beginnings in the entertainment industry, and from his work with the USO to films with Bing Crosby and his television career. Hope also shares his humor with readers.

Hope, Bob, and Pete Martin. *Have Tux, Will Travel: Bob Hope's Own Story*. New York: Simon & Schuster, 2003. This book highlights Hope's early career, focusing on his young adulthood. Includes his early experiences as a prizefighter and as an aspiring entertainer in vaudeville. Also discusses early experiences with entertaining the troops.

McCaffrey, Donald. *The Road to Comedy: The Films of Bob Hope*. Westport, Conn.: Praeger, 2004. This book focuses on Hope's film career and the characters he developed in the process of making the films. Particular attention to how Hope used his characters to reflect on the mood of the time in the United States.

Quirk, Lawrence. *Bob Hope: The Road Well Traveled*. New York: Applause Books, 2000. The author describes some of the difficulties that Hope encountered in making his way to the top of the entertainment industry. The author also provides a critical assessment of Hope's career and life, focusing on his personal life and government-funded work with the USO.

GRACE MURRAY HOPPER

> *" If it's a good idea, go ahead and do it. It's much easier to apologize than it is to get permission. "*

Navy admiral and computer scientist

A pioneer in programming languages, Hopper developed FLOW-MATIC, the foundation of the computer language known as COBOL, and then standardized all U.S. Navy versions. Her work was instrumental to the beginnings of the information age.

Born: December 9, 1906; New York, New York
Died: January 1, 1992; Arlington, Virginia
Also known as: Grace Brewster Murray (birth name); Grand Old Lady of Software; Amazing Grace
Areas of achievement: Computer science; military; mathematics; physics

EARLY LIFE

Grace Murray Hopper (HAWP-pur) was the eldest of three children born to Walter Murray, an insurance broker, and Mary Campbell Van Horne Murray. In reflecting on her childhood, Hopper later said, "I was born with curiosity." When she was seven years old, she wandered into the bedrooms of the family's large summer cottage and, out of curiosity, deconstructed seven alarm clocks. Her hobbies included reading and playing the piano. She eventually became expert at knitting, a pastime she would continue all of her life.

Hopper attended the Graham School and later Schoonmakers School, two private schools in New York City where she played basketball, field hockey, and water polo. When she flunked a crucial Latin exam, Vassar College told her she would have to wait a year to enter. For remediation, Hopper became a boarding student at Hartridge School in Plainfield, New Jersey, and continued her record of active participation. The quotation selected to describe her in the yearbook proclaimed, "In action faithful and in honor clear."

During all of her schooling, Hopper loved mathematics, especially geometry. She remembered, "I used to draw pretty pictures with it." When she entered Vassar College in 1924, her interests in mathematics combined with those in physics and engineering. A gifted student, Hopper also audited all the beginning courses in botany, physiology, and geology. She continued to play basketball and sought out adventure, once flying in a barnstorming biplane over the campus.

A Phi Beta Kappa graduate from Vassar in 1928 with a bachelor of arts degree in mathematics and physics, Hopper undertook graduate studies at Yale University, where she was invited to join Sigma Xi, an honor society that recognizes scientists for their outstanding research achievements. After receiving her master's degree from Yale in 1930, Hopper was married to Vincent Foster Hopper on June 15, 1930.

Because jobs were scarce during the Great Depression, Hopper seized the opportunity to teach at Vassar in 1931 at a salary of $800 a year. As an assistant professor in mathematics, she taught algebra, trigonometry, and calculus. The Hoppers built a house in Poughkeepsie, New York, near the Vassar campus, and Vincent commuted to his teaching position in New York City until they were divorced in 1945. Hopper earned her Ph.D. in mathematics and mathematical physics from Yale in 1934, a significant accomplishment for that era. Her doctoral thesis was entitled "A New Criterion for Reduceability of Algebraic Equations."

Highly patriotic, Hopper yearned to serve her country during World War II. After threatening to quit her post at Vassar, she obtained a leave of absence to enter the United States Naval Reserve. Her admission to the reserve was nearly denied because she weighed only 105 pounds, not the requisite 121 pounds. After obtaining a waiver, in 1943 Hopper entered the USNR Midshipman's School for Women in Northampton, Massachusetts. Despite early errors in identifying carriers and submarines, Hopper graduated first in her class and was commissioned lieutenant, junior grade, on June 27, 1944. She was immediately assigned to the Bureau of Ships Computation Project in Cruft Laboratory at Harvard University with Howard Aiken as director. This assignment, unique because there were fewer than six computer projects under way in the United States, would change the course of her career.

Grace Murray Hopper.
(Naval Historical Center)

Hopper, Grace Murray

LIFE'S WORK

When Hopper reported to work on July 2, 1944, Commander Aiken waved his hand at the Mark I installation and introduced her to this "computing engine," the first programmable digital computer in the United States. He gave her a codebook and asked to have the coefficients for the interpolation of the arc tangent ready by the following Thursday.

Mark I, also known as the Automatic Sequence Controlled Calculator, could do three additions every second—important because rapid computations were needed for the new weapons systems. Mark I was a monster of a machine: fifty-one feet long, eight feet deep, eight feet high, and approximately five tons in weight. It had 800,000 parts and contained more than five hundred miles of wire. Mark I was fed instructions and data punched out on four long paper tapes: one control tape for instructions and three tapes for data input.

To program the Mark I, instructions had to be written in a machine code that told the computer exactly what operations to perform and their precise sequence. The instructions detailed which switches were to be set at either the on or off position, and a new program representing a different pattern of codes had to be written for each task or problem. Because it was easy to make errors, Hopper and her colleagues collected correct programs in a notebook with a routine for the sine, cosine, and the arc tangent. As one of her first challenging tasks, Hopper wrote an operating manual for the computer that eventually became one of the most famous documents in the literature of computers. In this manner, Hopper became the third programmer on the first large-scale digital computer in the United States.

The U.S. Navy leased the Mark I for the remainder of the war to quickly perform the complex calculations necessary to aim new Navy guns with precision. Hopper and her staff of three other officers and four enlisted men operated around the clock, providing critical information about ballistic trajectories. She later said, "I slept nights on a desk to see if my program was going to get running."

Hopper stayed on at Harvard after the war and joined the faculty as a research fellow in 1946. The Mark II, a multiprocessor, had been designed, built, and tested for the Navy Bureau of Ordnance since Hopper's arrival at Harvard and was five times faster than the Mark I. In the summer of 1947, a moth was found in the computer, beaten by a relay that then stopped functioning well, causing erroneous information. The two-inch moth was taped into a notebook and described as "first actual bug found." Later, when little work was being accomplished, Hopper and others would use the handy excuse that they were "debugging" the machine.

In 1949, she joined the Eckert-Mauchly Corporation, a Philadelphia firm run by John W. Mauchly and J. Presper Eckert, coinventors and developers of the world's first electronic computer known as ENIAC (Electronic Numerical Integrator and Calculator). The company had also built EDVAC and BINAC, binary automatic computers, and was building UNIVAC I (Universal Automatic Computer), the first commercial electronic computer. This new smaller computer had many memory devices, including storage tubes and a magnetic core, and was one thousand times faster than the Mark I. Hopper joined the company as senior mathematician.

Hopper reasoned that if computers could be used to write their own programs, they would be used for business purposes. Accordingly, she developed a compiler to alleviate the problem of mistakes in code writing that developed when programs had to be written in octal code (base 8 instead of 10). The compiler translated the programmer's mathematical notations into the machine's binary language and performed the calculations. Her first compiler in 1952 was the A-0 System, standing for algebraic codes starting with routines at zero. By 1955, she had developed A-2, the first compiler to use mathematical computations extensively.

Next, Hopper developed the B-0 compiler for business, the first computer language employing English words rather than mathematical symbols. Earlier called MATH-MATIC, B-0 or FLOW-MATIC was an enormous advance in the development of programming languages. To create FLOW-MATIC, Hopper wrote five hundred typical programs and identified thirty verbs common to all programs, including words such as "count," "divide," "subtract," "move," "replace," and "multiply." She later claimed that she wrote this language because she was lazy: While other programmers wanted to play with the bits, she wanted to get the job done.

By 1959, there were three major computer languages, each requiring one specific computer. That year, a committee was authorized to develop a common business-oriented language to be used with any kind of computer. Heavily influenced by Hopper's FLOW-MATIC, the resulting product, COBOL, uses syntax and terms close to natural English, is easy to understand, and is efficient at processing large quantities of information. Because the Defense Department urged businesses to adopt COBOL if they wanted to continue selling their products to the government, COBOL eventually became the most widely used business computer language.

Hopper retired from the Naval Reserve when she reached the age of sixty in 1966 with the rank of commander. Much to her delight, however, the Navy discovered that it could not get along without her. Its payroll program had to be rewritten 823 times. Several months later, on August 1, 1967, she was called out of retirement to standardize the high-level languages and get the entire Navy to use them. Specifically, Hopper was asked to develop a COBOL certifier, a set of programs that would tell the user whether a compiler labeled COBOL was legitimate for use. Hopper was initially recalled for six months, but the orders were changed to "indefinite"—allowing her to work for nearly twenty additional years. During the years she served as director of the Navy Programming Languages Group, Hopper developed a manual called *Fundamentals of COBOL* to train people on its use as well as a catalog with user hints and an index of sample statements.

In a ceremony held in August of 1986, on *Old Ironsides*, the oldest commissioned warship, Hopper retired from the Navy at the age of seventy-nine with the rank of rear admiral. As the oldest commissioned naval officer on active duty, she said, "I love this ship. We belong together." The only woman admiral in the history of the Navy, Hopper telephoned her friends in Philadelphia to watch the grave of her great-grandfather Russell, who had also been a rear admiral, humorously warning them that he might rise from the dead. Never one to rest, Hopper immediately began working as a senior consultant for Digital Equipment Corporation.

Hopper received many prestigious honors, among them the Man of the Year award from the Data Processing Management Association (1969) and induction into the En-

Hopper, Grace Murray

gineering and Science Hall of Fame in Dayton, Ohio (1984). In recognition of her extraordinary contributions, the Navy dedicated the Grace Murray Hopper Service Center of the Navy Regional Data Automation Center in San Diego, California, in 1985. In 1991, President George H. W. Bush awarded Hopper the National Medal of Technology, and she became the first woman to receive it individually.

Hopper was witty, unorthodox, and sometimes combative—a self-described "boat rocker." She died at age eighty-five of natural causes.

SIGNIFICANCE

Known as the Grand Old Lady of Software, Hopper is considered a primary leader in developing compilers and standardizing computer languages. Cynics scoffed at the idea that computer programs could be written in English, but Hopper confidently proved otherwise.

An innovator, she accomplished many things: She helped to lift computing out of the mechanical age and into the era of electronics, contributed to modernizing the Navy by standardizing its use of the computer, and played a major role in building COBOL, thus making computers accessible to nonmathematicians.

Later in her life, not satisfied to rest on her laurels, Hopper became an ardent spokesperson for education and a public relations asset for the Navy. Amazing Grace, as her associates called her, traveled all over the country, encouraging risk taking and innovation. She spoke as many as two hundred times a year, especially to young audiences. A lover of possibilities, she shared her philosophy with them: "Go ahead and do it. You can always apologize later."

As an educator, she worried that computers might create a new kind of gender discrimination: Men would be "thinkists," women "typists." Hopper insisted that females must study computer science, engineering, and business and gain confidence in their abilities as individuals. She believed women are as capable as men of doing programming and that computing is a good field for career mobility. "Women turn out to be very good programmers for one very good reason: They tend to finish up things, and men don't very often," she stated. Despite her obvious support of women, Hopper once called the women's movement "tommyrot and nonsense." She firmly believed that skilled, ambitious women would not be held back.

The inventor of COBOL, Hopper was a pioneer in developing computer technology. This technology led the country into the information age.

—*Deborah Elwell Arfken*

FURTHER READING

Billings, Charlene W. *Grace Hopper: Navy Admiral and Computer Pioneer*. Hillside, N.J.: Enslow, 1989. A biography for adolescents with a thorough assessment of Hopper's life. Clear explanations of Hopper's groundbreaking work with compilers. Excellent photographs.

Gilbert, Lynn, and Gaylen Moore. "Grace Murray Hopper." In *Particular Passions: Talks with Women Who Have Shaped Our Times*. New York: Clarkson N. Potter, 1981. Lively interviews with thirty-nine celebrated women. Hopper was seventy-three years old at the time of her firsthand account.

Hopper, Grace Murray, and Steven L. Mandell. "Man the Thinkist, Woman the Typist?" In *Understanding Computers*. 2d ed. St. Paul, Minn.: West, 1987. A provocative essay in Hopper's now-classic textbook.

Slater, Robert. "Grace Murray Hopper: Bugs, Compilers, and COBOL." In *Portraits in Silicon*. Cambridge, Mass.: MIT Press, 1987. A portrait focusing on Hopper as a software specialist.

Smith, William D. "Pioneer in Computers: Navy Officer Likes to Rock Boat." *The New York Times*, September 5, 1971, Sec. III, p. 5. A frank interview with Hopper regarding her scientific career.

Tropp, Henry S. "Grace Murray Hopper." In *Encyclopedia on Computer Science*, edited by Anthony Ralston and Edwin D. Reilly. 3d ed. New York: Van Nostrand Reinhold, 1993. A chronological listing of Hopper's achievements as a computer professional.

Williams, Kathleen Broome. *Grace Hopper: Admiral of the Cyber Sea*. Annapolis, Md.: Naval Institute Press, 2004. A thorough account of Hopper's life and career, describing how she brought the Navy into the computer age.

_____. *Improbable Warriors: Women Scientists and the U.S. Navy in World War II*. Annapolis, Md.: Naval Institute Press, 2001. Recounts how Hopper and four other women overcame discrimination to make significant contributions to naval science.

SAM HOUSTON

" *A leader is someone who helps improve the lives of other people or improve the system they live under.* "

Military leader and politician

Houston had one of the most diverse political careers in U.S. history. He served as governor of two different states, commanded the Texan army during Texas's revolt against Mexico, was elected president of the independent Republic of Texas, and served in the U.S. Senate.

Born: March 2, 1793; Rockbridge County, Virginia
Died: July 26, 1863; Huntsville, Texas
Also known as: Samuel Houston, Jr. (full name); Raven
Areas of achievement: Government and politics; military

EARLY LIFE

Sam Houston (HEWS-tuhn)—the name he always used, both formally and informally—was the son of Samuel Houston, Sr., a farmer and veteran of the American Revolution. His mother, née Elizabeth Paxton, came from pioneer stock. Young Sam was the fifth of six sons in a family that also included three daughters. He attended school intermittently until his father's death in 1807, when his formal education ended. The widow Houston moved her family to Marysville, Tennessee, where Sam spent the remainder of his youth. For a time, he worked in the village store, although this was not to his liking. In his teenage years, he sought escape and left home on several occasions to live with the Cherokee Indians. In total, he spent almost four years with them, mastering their language, customs, and culture. The Indians accepted him as one of their own, giving him the name "Raven." He eventually returned home to live with his family.

Houston joined the Army during the War of 1812, serving with distinction at the Battle of Horseshoe Bend. His personal exploits attracted the attention of General Andrew Jackson, who promoted him to the rank of lieutenant. After leaving the military in 1818, Houston studied law and became a practicing attorney at Lebanon, Tennessee. A physically large man of greater than average height, he had a powerful build graced by curly dark hair and a pleasing countenance. Known for his gregarious personality and public speaking ability, he had a dramatic air about him that made him the center of attention and an individual of great personal popularity.

Life's Work

Houston's neighbors in Tennessee elected him a state militia officer in 1819. During 1823, he gave up the practice of law and entered politics, securing in that year election to the U.S. Congress as a representative. Houston quickly became a leader in the Tennessee Democratic Party. He also forged a lifelong personal friendship with Andrew Jackson. Houston became the governor of Tennessee in 1827 and looked forward to a promising career in that state. He married Eliza H. Allen, daughter of a prominent Tennessee family, on January 1, 1829. Within months, Houston's success turned to bitter failure because of problems with his bride. Although historians have never agreed on the specific causes, the marriage to Eliza lasted only a short time. She returned home to her parents (eventually securing a divorce) while Houston, with some despondency, resigned the governorship in the spring of 1829 and moved to Indian territory to start life anew. The Tennessee years became a closed chapter in his life.

Houston spent the following years among his boyhood friends, the Cherokee. He adopted Indian dress and customs, became a citizen of the Indian nation, and took a wife according to the dictates of Cherokee law. His Indian wife, Tiana, assisted him in operating a small trading post. In addition, he served as an advocate for the Cherokee in various matters before the U.S. government. By 1832, the wanderlust had again struck Houston, and he began visiting Texas, although he maintained residence in the Indian nation for a time. He first arrived in the Anglo areas of Mexican Texas as an Indian agent and a representative of investors who sought land in the province. The exact date that he moved to Texas is lost in obscurity, but, by late 1833, he was taking an active part in Texas affairs as a resident. In the process, he left his life with the Cherokee, including Tiana, forever in the past.

Houston's removal to Texas came in the midst of growing revolutionary fervor on the part of Anglo residents unhappy with Mexican rule. Houston played an important role in events that resulted in the eventual break with Mexico. He served as presiding officer of the Convention of 1833, which wrote a proposed constitution for Texas, and attended the Consultation of 1835, which marked the start of the revolution. He signed the Texas Declaration of Independence from Mexico while serving as a delegate to the Convention of 1836. The revolutionary government of Texas appointed him commander in chief of the army with the rank of major general on March 4, 1836. Forever after, in spite of the other high offices he would hold in his career, Sam Houston preferred the title "general."

Taking command of the army at Gonzales shortly after the Alamo fell to Mexican troops commanded by Antonio López de Santa Anna, General Houston led his forces eastward across Texas in a retreat known as the Runaway Scrape. Potential disaster for the Texans turned to stunning victory when Houston and his men met Santa Anna's army, which had pursued them, at the Battle of San Jacinto on April 21, 1836. Santa Anna was captured, his army soundly defeated, and General Houston became the hero of the day.

With independence secured, Houston won election as president of the Republic of Texas on September 5, 1836. His term saw Texas's failure to enter the Union because of opposition in the U.S. Congress, attempts to deal with the Comanche Indians, and growing political factionalism in the republic. While president of the republic, Houston married Margaret M. Lea on May 8, 1840. They eventually had eight children, including Andrew Jackson Houston, who served a short period as United States senator from Texas during the 1930's.

Because the republic's constitution forbade a president from succeeding himself, Houston left office after one term. Mirabeau B. Lamar, with whom Houston had political differences, replaced him. Houston, however, won election to the republic's congress, where pro-Houston and anti-Houston parties soon became the active political factions of the fledgling nation. Houston's opponents objected to several of his policies, including his attempts to keep Austin from becoming the capital city; others believed that he had failed to work hard enough for statehood. Other critics no doubt found the general's large ego and some of his personal habits objectionable, especially his frequent and heavy drinking of whiskey. Whatever the reasons for controversy, Houston would be at the center of politically motivated strife and criticism for the rest of his public career.

Houston's reelection to the presidency of the republic in 1841 came after a heated campaign with the Lamar faction. Houston attempted to undo some of the programs of his predecessor and was faced with additional problems, including a minor, abortive Mexican invasion of Texas in 1842. He was able to deal with all of these efficiently, although not always with complete success. By the end of his second term, in 1844, the annexation of Texas by the United States had become a distinct possibility. Houston, however, wavered in the face of statehood for Texas, sometimes giving the impression that he favored continuing the republic. It fell to his successor, Anson Jones, to have the distinction of serving as the last president of the Republic of Texas.

Along with Thomas J. Rusk, Houston became one of the United States senators representing Texas once statehood had been secured in 1845. He would continue to serve in that body until the eve of the Civil War. Houston continued his pre-Texas affiliation with the Democratic Party during his days in the Senate. He played a role in the debates over the Compromise of 1850, siding with southern delegates while he lobbied for an acceptable settlement to the Texas boundary controversy. He had aspirations for the Democratic Party presidential nomination in 1848 and in 1852, but in both instances he failed to attract enough delegate votes to make a showing at the convention.

Houston's role as a leader in the southern bloc of the Senate came to an end with his vote on the Kansas-Nebraska Bill of 1854. A strong advocate of the Union, he voted with Free-Soilers and Whigs against the bill. This placed him at odds with his southern colleages and many slaveholders in Texas, all of whom wanted the bill passed. By the mid-1850's, Houston became increasingly distanced from the Democratic Party when he embraced the Know-Nothing movement because of his strong commitment to the preservation of the Union. He attended Know-Nothing meetings and conventions. Texas Democrats denounced him for these activities. Houston ran for the governorship of Texas in 1857 but was defeated by Hardin Runnels. He remained in the Senate until the end of his term, in 1859, whereupon he returned to Texas. He ran once more against Runnels for governor in 1859, this time winning by a small margin.

Houston's term as governor, which began in December of 1859, proved to be a time of turmoil for Texas and a period of deep personal anguish for Houston. The election of Abraham Lincoln triggered the secession crisis and the formation of the Confederate States of America. Texas was a slave state, largely settled by persons of southern heritage, and most Texans favored secession although some preferred to remain with the Union. Houston fell into the latter camp. His commitment to the Constitution and the Union was stronger than his desire to secede.

As governor, Houston thus found himself out of step with most Texans and their political leaders. Houston refused to cooperate with the State Secession Convention that met in Austin. When the convention adopted a secession ordinance, the governor took the position that Texas had returned legally to her former status as an independent republic. He therefore refused as governor to take an oath of allegiance to the Confederacy. The Secession Convention therefore declared the office of governor vacant and named Edward Clark to the position. Houston, refusing an offer of federal troops from President Lincoln, decided to accede to the convention's decision and relinquished his office. He retired to Huntsville, Texas, where he died on July 26, 1863.

SIGNIFICANCE

Sam Houston played an important role in the westward movement of the United States during the nineteenth century. As a frontiersman, military figure, and political leader, he assisted in the development of two states (Tennessee and Texas) from frontier outposts into settled areas. His greatest contributions came in Texas, where he led an army to victory, helped to organize a republic, and participated in its transition into a part of the United States. As a senator during the 1850's, he was one of the few southern leaders to foresee the consequences of national political policies that would lead to the Civil War. Once the war came, he stood alone as the most prominent Texas Unionist willing to sacrifice his career for the preservation of the Union. It is fitting that the largest, most industrial city in Texas bears his name.

—*Light Townsend Cummins*

Further Reading

Bishop, Curtis Kent. *Lone Star: Sam Houston*. New York: Julian Messner, 1961. Written for young readers, the book provides a clear assessment of Houston's career and relates the major facts of his life in an easy-to-read narrative.

Campbell, Randolph B. *Sam Houston and the American Southwest*. Edited by Oscar Handlin. 2d ed. New York: Longman, 2002. Biography relating Houston's life and ideas to the development of Texas and other areas of the Southwest during the nineteenth century.

Friend, Llerena B. *Sam Houston: The Great Designer*. Austin: University of Texas Press, 1954. Excellent scholarly biography. Treats Houston's entire career with an emphasis on his impact on national events. It is based on extensive archival research and is a good starting place for a full-scale study of Houston and his time.

Gregory, Jack, and Rennard Strickland. *Sam Houston with the Cherokees, 1829-1833*. Austin: University of Texas Press, 1967. Develops in detail the story of Houston's Indian marriage to Tiana and his role as Cherokee advocate. It is based on solid research previously unconsidered by historians, thereby providing an exhaustive analysis of Houston's years among the Indians.

Haley, James L. *Sam Houston*. Norman: University of Oklahoma Press, 2002. A more personal view of Houston, in which the author seeks to discover what "made him tick" by examining topics of importance to Houston, such as Native American relations. Houston emerges as a deeply troubled man. Well researched, accessible biography.

Houston, Samuel. *Autobiography of Sam Houston*. Edited by Donald Day and Harry Herbert Ullom. Norman: University of Oklahoma Press, 1954. Houston paints himself in the best possible light, but this edited version provides insight into the man and his era.

———. *The Writings of Sam Houston, 1813-1863*. Edited by Amelia Williams and Eugene C. Barker. 8 vols. Austin: University of Texas Press, 1938-1943. A comprehensive collection of the most important letters and papers dealing with Houston's career. Contains most of the extant Houston letters.

James, Marquis. *The Raven: A Biography of Sam Houston*. Indianapolis: Bobbs-Merrill, 1929. Provides a readable narrative with a colorful style. Highlights Houston's role as friend and political associate of Andrew Jackson. Until the appearance of the above-noted study by Friend, this biography ranked as the most complete analysis of Houston.

Wisehart, Marion K. *Sam Houston: American Giant*. Washington, D.C.: R. B. Luce, 1962. A laudatory, popular biography, full of detail. Although not scholarly in nature, it is useful because it is based on the important biographies noted above. An excellent study for readers at the high school level.

SAMUEL GRIDLEY HOWE

> **"** *The strong should help the weak, so that the whole should advance as a band of brethren* **"**

Educator and social reformer

Howe was a universal reformer who made his greatest contributions to the education of the blind, the deaf-blind, and the mentally disabled. His monumental efforts significantly enhanced social concern for persons with disabilities in the United States.

Born: November 10, 1801; Boston, Massachusetts
Died: January 9, 1876; Boston, Massachusetts
Areas of achievement: Social reform; education; social reform; philanthropy

EARLY LIFE

Samuel Gridley Howe was the son of Joseph Howe and Patty Gridley Howe, both of old New England stock. His father was a cordage manufacturer and steadfast Jeffersonian Republican. A man of principle, as his son was to be, he accepted government bonds in payment for purchases during the War of 1812 and suffered serious financial losses. Samuel attended Boston Latin School and was frequently harassed for his father's politics. The only one of three brothers to attend college, Samuel entered Brown, rather than Federalist-dominated Harvard, in 1817. Young Howe excelled at campus pranks, but his academic performance was mediocre. As a Unitarian among Baptists, Howe once again learned to appreciate the position of the underdog—a useful trait for a future philanthropist.

Graduating in 1821, Howe enrolled at Harvard Medical School and began to apply himself, enjoying especially anatomy and dissection. After commencement, however, he decided against a traditional practice. Stirred by the Greek War of Independence, a popular cause of the time, Howe left for the Peloponnisos, arriving in early 1827. In Greece he played many roles with distinction. As a physician, he served Greek forces on land and sea. As the agent of American relief committees, he distributed emergency rations, briefly returning to the United States to raise additional funds. Once back in Greece, he developed and ran sizable work relief programs. For his exertions, Howe was knighted by the Greek king as a Chevalier of the Order of the Holy Savior. With the war all but over, Chev, as his friends now called him, returned to Boston in April, 1831. Tall, dark, and handsome, not yet sporting the beard of later years, Howe was a knight-errant seeking a new cause to uplift humanity.

LIFE'S WORK

As luck would have it, the projected New England School for the Blind, incorporated in 1829, needed a director in order to become a reality; the trustees of the school offered Howe the job. Excited by the challenge, he accepted immediately and sailed for Europe to study current techniques for educating the blind. Howe soon became convinced that European efforts were either too intellectual or too mechanical. A more balanced curriculum, he believed, including physical education and greater encouragement of self-reliance, was required. After imprisonment in Prussia for assisting Polish refugees, Howe returned to Boston in July, 1832. During the following August, the first school for the blind in the nation opened its doors with seven students and three staff members.

As director, Howe tried to tailor the curriculum—reading, writing, mathematics, geography, music, physical education, and manual training—to the needs and abilities of the individual student. He fashioned letters of twine and glued them to cards for reading instruction; he invented an improved method of raised printing that significantly lowered costs of manufacture. (Braille was not yet in use.) Howe trooped his students before legislative committees and popular audiences to secure funds, went out into the country to recruit students, and traveled to other states to promote more schools for the blind. As a result of his strenuous activity, the school, renamed Perkins Institution, soon required larger quarters.

In 1837, Howe heard of Laura Bridgman, an eight-year-old who, at the age of two, had lost her sight and hearing through scarlet fever. Howe, who believed in phrenology and innate mental dispositions, was confident that the child could be taught, despite near-universal opinion that the deaf-blind were completely uneducable. He induced her parents to enroll Laura at Perkins.

For several tedious months, Howe tried to get Laura to match raised words with physical objects and make words of letters. Suddenly one day, Laura understood that here was a way to communicate her thoughts to other minds; her face "lighted up with a human expression." This was the greatest single moment in Howe's career. John Greenleaf Whittier proclaimed that Howe was "the Cadmus of the blind." Charles Dickens, who met Laura Bridgman in 1842, lionized Howe's accomplishment in *American Notes* (1842). Howe soon became a world-renowned figure.

Howe's international stature certainly aided his election as a Whig to the Massachusetts house of representatives in November, 1842. Though only a freshman legislator, he chaired the committee on public charities. Working closely with Dorothea Lynde Dix, Howe personally wrote the bill reforming care of the mentally ill, which passed by overwhelming margins in March, 1843.

In April, 1843, Howe married Julia Ward, who was of a prominent New York family. Their marriage was frequently tempestuous; their personalities did not mesh well. Prideful, demanding, and eighteen years her senior, Howe never approved of Julia's literary aspirations. He normally placed his many reform interests ahead of his wife and his eventual family of six children.

After returning to work in September, 1844, after a European honeymoon, Howe immediately joined his friend Horace Mann, secretary of the state Board of Education, in a battle to reform the Boston grammar schools. In 1845, Howe turned to education of those with mental impairments, undertaking an extensive, two-year training program that he followed up with a comprehensive report to the legislature. Once again, the lawmakers followed his bidding and established in 1848 the Massachusetts School for the Idiotic and Feeble-Minded Youth, another first in American history. Howe served as superintendent of that institution as well as of Perkins until his death in 1876.

Although Howe disapproved of slavery, he remained aloof from agitation until the admission of Texas drew him into the fray. During the Mexican War, Howe became a Conscience Whig, running unsuccessfully for Congress in 1846; in 1851, he helped orchestrate the election of his close friend Charles Sumner to the U.S. Senate. In response to the Kansas-Nebraska Act, Howe moved toward radical abolitionism.

In 1854, Howe was an organizer of both the New England Emigrant Aid Company and the Massachusetts Kansas Aid Committee, the latter formed to obtain guns for antislavery settlers. In January, 1857, John Brown visited Howe and other Boston supporters (the "Secret Six"), obtaining money from the committee and several token guns from Howe personally. In March, 1858, the group gave Brown additional funding to liberate slaves, a plan that culminated in the Harpers Ferry raid of October, 1859. When authorities uncovered Brown's correspondence, Howe fled, panic-stricken, to Canada on the flimsy pretext that he was promoting education of the blind. Involvement of the nation's foremost humanitarian in Brown's scheme further unnerved the South and increased sectional tensions.

During the Civil War, Howe returned to less violent philanthropy. He helped to establish the United States Sanitary Commission in June, 1861, serving on its board for the duration. The commission made important recommendations for "preserving and restoring the health of the troops," which doubtless reduced fatalities. Howe was also a member of the three-man American Freedmen's Inquiry Commission set up in 1863 to investigate the condition of free blacks and make proposals for their future welfare. The commission laid the foundations for the later Freedmen's Bureau.

In 1863, Massachusetts governor John Andrew named Howe chairman of the new Massachusetts Board of State Charities, created to coordinate eleemosynary institutions and programs. After the war, Howe, who strongly disagreed with the sign language system used at the American Asylum in Hartford, sought a charter for a school for the deaf that would teach finger spelling and articulation. The legislature again complied, incorporating Clarke Institution at Northampton in 1867.

Although in declining health after the war, Howe embarked in 1871 on his last crusade. President Ulysses S. Grant, manipulated by speculators, favored annexing Santo Domingo. The Senate rejected the treaty, in part because of Charles Sumner's virulent opposition, but Grant named an investigative commission in hopes of recouping support. Despite his long friendship with Sumner, Howe agreed to serve and after a visit to the island became converted to annexation. Howe apparently had hopes of concluding his career as a territorial governor who in philosopher-king fashion would reform Santo Domingo into a tropical paradise. Such dreams were doomed by continuing Senate opposition.

After the disappointing conclusion of the Dominican affair, Howe's health steadily deteriorated. In constant pain and severely depressed, he collapsed on January 4, 1876, and died five days later. Several hours before the end, Laura Bridgman (symbolically on behalf of all those who had or would benefit from his tireless philanthropy) kissed the unconscious Howe farewell.

SIGNIFICANCE

Samuel Gridley Howe lived in an optimistic age, in a city and state seething with the ferment of reform. He not only was in harmony with the spirit of his times; he was a symbol of the age as well. In those heady days, true heroism was seen by many as victory over social evil and human suffering. As the foremost philanthropist in the nation, Howe was, in the words of John Greenleaf Whittier, "The Hero."

A Whig in politics and a Unitarian in religion, Howe was a Yankee elitist who accepted the essential goodness of God and humanity and the inevitability of progress. A nineteenth century romantic, Howe rejected John Locke's concept of knowledge drawn solely from the five senses for belief in innate mental dispositions. This thinking as well as Howe's emphasis on self-reliance were clearly in line with that of his friend Theodore Parker and other Transcendentalists. Like many other Americans of the era, Howe was also strongly influenced by phrenology. This pseudoscience (which posited a body-mind unity) maintained that a balanced education, both intellectual and physical, could influence cerebral growth and skull dimensions. Howe's phrenological and vaguely Transcendentalist assumptions frequently guided his reform endeavors. His temporary obsession with the abolitionist movement during the 1850's was typical of most antebellum reformers.

Howe was involved in many causes, but his major impact on American society was in his efforts for the education of people with disabilities. He firmly believed that most people with physical and mental disabilities could become independent and productive citizens. His refusal to accept traditional prejudices concerning the capabilities of the blind, the deaf-blind, the deaf, and the mentally impaired led him to found institutions and develop instructional strategies still important today. Howe's most enduring legacy may be his creation of a continuing public consciousness that disabilities can be surmounted, that, in the words of his life motto, Obstacles Are Things to Be Overcome.

—*Parker Bradley Nutting*

FURTHER READING

Brooks, Van Wyck. *Flowering of New England, 1815-1865*. New York: E. P. Dutton, 1936. A scholarly, readable description of the intellectual environment in which Howe thrived. Howe is not discussed in detail, but many of his acquaintances, including Theodore Parker, are.

Clifford, Deborah P. *Mine Eyes Have Seen the Glory: A Biography of Julia Ward Howe*. Boston: Little, Brown, 1979. A well-researched biography quite favorable to Mrs. Howe. It illuminates Howe's stormy marriage and the more disagreeable aspects of his personality. For Howe, reform did not include the liberation of married women.

Dickens, Charles. *American Notes for General Circulation*. London: Chapman and Hall, 1842. Reprint. London: Oxford University Press, 1966. Though frequently critical of things American, Dickens was extremely impressed by Howe's work. He quotes extensively from Howe's annual *Reports* to the Perkins trustees concerning the education of Laura Bridgman, a source not readily available to the interested reader.

Freeberg, Ernest. *The Education of Laura Bridgman: First Deaf and Blind Person to Learn Language*. Cambridge, Mass.: Harvard University Press, 2001. One of two recent books about Howe's relationship with Bridgman. Although Gitter (see below) provides more biographical information, Freeberg focuses on Howe's specific methods for educating Bridgman, describing how he was influenced by Unitarianism and phrenology. Howe, Freeberg maintains, sought to make Bridgman's education a model of "moral discipline" so he could gain greater insight into human nature.

Gitter, Elisabeth. *The Imprisoned Guest: Samuel Howe and Laura Bridgman, the Original Deaf-Blind Girl.* New York: Farrar, Straus and Giroux, 2001. Describes how and why Howe educated Bridgman, explaining the social, intellectual, and cultural context in which Howe and Bridgman transformed public perception of people with multiple disabilities.

Lamson, Mary Swift. *Life and Education of Laura Dewey Bridgman, the Deaf, Dumb, and Blind Girl.* Boston: New England Publishing, 1878. Lamson was one of Laura's teachers. She quotes extensively from her own journal, those of other teachers, and from Howe's *Reports*. A very personal account, it reveals the difficulties of working with Howe.

Richard, Laura E. *Laura Bridgman: The Story of an Opened Door.* New York: D. Appleton, 1928. A full-length biography, written by Howe's daughter, who was Laura Bridgman's namesake. Strong on the relationship between Howe and Bridgman. Includes source materials not readily available.

———, ed. *Letters and Journals of Samuel Gridley Howe.* 2 vols. Boston: Dana Estes, 1906. Collection contains excerpts from Howe's letters, journals, and annual *Reports*, connected by a running commentary. The period to 1832 is accorded the same weight as the rest of Howe's life. Despite such unevenness, this is the closest thing to a printed collection of Howe's papers.

Sanborn, Franklin Benjamin. *Dr. S. G. Howe: The Philanthropist.* New York: Funk & Wagnalls, 1891. The first scholarly biography, still worth consulting. The author, one of the Secret Six, is laudatory, but the book contains extensive, frequently revealing quotations from original sources. Strong on the antislavery days.

Schwartz, Harold. *Samuel Gridley Howe: Social Reformer, 1801-1876.* Cambridge, Mass.: Harvard University Press, 1956. Based on extensive research in the Howe manuscripts in Houghton Library at Harvard. Places Howe solidly in his intellectual and social milieu. Notes influence of phrenology. A very balanced work.

Dolores Huerta

> *" Don't be a marshmallow. Walk the street with us into history. Get off the sidewalk. "*

Labor leader

Cofounder of the United Farm Workers Association with César Chávez, Huerta earned renown through contract negotiations with California growers during the Delano grape strike—the crowning achievement of one of the greatest victories in the history of American workers. Her role as a Chicana labor leader in the male-dominated culture of farmworkers made her a champion of the women's movement as well.

Born: April 10, 1930; Dawson, New Mexico
Also known as: Dolores Fernández (birth name)
Area of achievement: Labor movement

Early Life

Dolores Huerta (doh-LAHR-rehz WEHR-tah) was born Dolores Fernández in the mining community of Dawson, New Mexico. Her mother, Alicia Chávez, was a second-generation New Mexican, and her father, Juan Fernández, was of American Indian and Mexican heritage. Her father later became a union activist and served in the state legislature. Huerta's parents were divorced while she was quite young, and she was reared by her mother and grandfather in Stockton, California. Her mother worked in a cannery and saved enough money to buy two small hotels and a restaurant while establishing her household in an integrated working-class community. (Her mother often housed farmworker families for free in the hotels.) Dolores, along with her two brothers, grew up assuming that women and men were equal, drawing on the example of her mother, who never favored her sons above her daughter and who became a business entrepreneur on her own.

Huerta grew up in a racially mixed neighborhood of farmworkers and other laborers of Chinese, Latino, American Indian, Filipino, African American, Japanese, and Italian descent. As a result, she learned to appreciate the rich diversity of a range of ethnic cultures at a young age. This absence of cultural or sex discrimination, in combination with her egalitarian family background, contributed to Dolores's leadership style in later life. Because she suffered no sense of inferiority at home and subsequently no acceptance of a secondary role in life or in her later career, Dolores came to maturity convinced that she was not required to accept the traditional feminine role of women as submissive domestic partners. Instead, she rebelled against conventional restraints on women and competed directly with her male colleagues.

Dolores was a dedicated Girl Scout in a multiethnic troop, participating in fundraising campaigns to support the USO and its entertainment programs for the armed forces during World War II; she was one of two winners in a national essay contest held by the Scouts. After graduating from an integrated high school in Stockton in 1947, Dolores married her high school sweetheart, Ralph Head, in 1950. The marriage

Huerta, Dolores

ended in divorce after the birth of their daughters Celeste and Lori. Dolores's mother took care of the children while Dolores studied for a teaching degree at Stockton College. Although she eventually received a provisional teaching credential, she became dissatisfied with a career as a teacher. A dawning awareness of the pervasiveness of social injustice confronting the Mexican American community and other ethnic minorities led Dolores in a new direction in 1955.

In that year, Dolores met Fred Ross, an organizer for Saul Alinsky's Industrial Areas Foundation who was trying to encourage the growing political consciousness of members of Mexican American communities throughout California. Ross started the Community Service Organization (CSO), a self-help association that led voter-registration drives, pushed for more Chicanos on police forces, lobbied for Spanish-speaking staff at hospitals and government offices, and campaigned for sewers and community centers in the barrios. Because of her newfound civic activism and devotion to the work of the CSO, Dolores's marriage to her second husband, Ventura Huerta, also ended in divorce.

Dolores Huerta.
(National Archives)

LIFE'S WORK

It was through her activities with the CSO that Dolores Huerta eventually became active as a labor organizer among migrant workers in California's San Joaquin Valley. She first came in contact with César Chávez when she was introduced to him by Ross in 1955 while both were working for the CSO. In 1960 she founded the Agricultural Workers Association. By that time, Huerta was a full-time lobbyist for the CSO in Sacramento and sometimes in Washington, D.C., pressuring politicians to support disability insurance, unemployment insurance, and minimum wage bills for farmworkers. She was instrumental in securing the passage of bills that extended social insurance and welfare benefits to farmworkers and immigrant workers, such as a bill for a Spanish version of the California driver license test in 1960, the repeal of the Bracero program in 1962, and, in 1963, legislation to include California farmworkers in Aid to Families with Dependent Children. Nevertheless, she was convinced that these workers could never escape poverty through the CSO strategy of pressure-group politics. What they needed was a union.

At approximately the same time, Chávez was reaching the same conclusion. By 1962, Chávez had presented the CSO with a program outlining a strategy for the unionization of farmworkers. When this program was rejected, he left the organization. While his wife, Helen Chávez, worked in the fields to support their family of eight children, Chávez organized small meetings of workers sympathetic to the idea of a union of agricultural laborers. The Farm Workers Association (FWA), a precursor of the United Farm Workers (UFW) union, was founded in Fresno, California, in September, 1962, at a convention attended by about three hundred delegates—practically the entire membership. It was organized primarily by Chávez, but the first person he called upon to work with him organizing the Mexican American farmworkers into a union was Huerta, who promptly left her post with the CSO to work with Chávez.

When Huerta began her labor-organizing efforts, she was pregnant with the seventh of her eleven children (she had two by her first husband, five by her second, and four by her live-in lover, Richard Chávez, the brother of César). Because of the demands of her work, Huerta was frequently absent from home, and her children spent much of their childhood in the care of her friends or family. Her union work was always her first priority, to the consternation and outrage of the more traditional adherents to Latin culture. Huerta clearly loved her children and was loved by them in return, but she refused to allow motherhood to deter her from her work. Even her colleague Chávez disapproved of her divorces, her decision to live with his brother, and her seemingly chaotic way of raising her children. Nevertheless, he understood that the union was the center of her life—just as it was for him.

The foundation of the UFW union was laid during the bitter Delano grape strike of 1965-1970. The farmworkers of the 1960's often lived in mind-numbing poverty and toiled under inhumane conditions. The bulk of the workforce spoke little English, was often of illegal residency status, could not vote, and was poorly educated. As a result, the workers were easily exploited by the powerful growers in the agribusiness industry of California. The growers often used deadly pesticides, primarily DDT, in the fields, ignoring the devastating health effects these chemicals had on both the workers and their unborn children. Pickers were paid by the bushel or basket rather than the hour. A field overstaffed with pickers, therefore, could result in a day's labor with little or no pay for the worker. There were no health and welfare benefits, no medical insurance, and no low-cost housing for the mainly transient workforce. Workers were forced to live in cars, shacks, and tents; many workers had no other place to sleep than the chemical-laden fields in which they had worked earlier in the day.

The grape-growing industry was perhaps the worst offender in terms of working conditions and pesticide use in all of California. Because of this, it became the logical site of the 1965 labor battle known as the Delano grape strike with Huerta and Chávez at the forefront. The strike began at dawn, when the workers moved out into the fields around Delano. The pickets met them carrying National Farm Workers Association (NFWA) banners with the union's symbol of a black Aztec eagle on a red flag with the single Spanish word "Huelga" (strike). The pickets led the workers off the fields of Delano, and the five-year battle began. In 1966, Huerta became the first person to negotiate a farmworkers' contract when, as NFWA's representative, she concluded a deal with the Schenley Wine Company. The strike continued on other fronts, and before it ended in 1970, Huerta had been arrested twenty-two times for strike-related efforts.

As quickly as the UFW pickets pulled work crews out, these laborers were replaced by scabs, or strikebreakers, trucked in from Mexico and Texas by the growers. The union's pickets and organizers were harassed and arrested continually by local police, under the influence of the powerful growers. Support for the farmworkers was growing, both within the labor movement and on a national level. Senator Robert Kennedy embraced their cause and became their champion. Powerful unions, including the United Auto Workers (UAW), the Amalgamated Clothing Workers, and the Packinghouse Workers rallied behind the striking grape pickers and provided relief in the form of fresh pickets, food, and money. It was against this backdrop of national labor and political support that Chávez and Huerta made the decision to escalate the strike to a nationwide struggle by declaring a universal consumer boycott. This boycott initially targeted individual growers and products but eventually led to the boycott of all California-grown grapes. Hundreds of workers were delegated throughout the country to promote and organize the boycott, while Huerta organized in New York City. She was an eloquent and powerful public speaker, and her speeches expressed the deep desires and struggles of all poor and dispossessed peoples, not just those who worked the fields.

The UFW boycott was successful. Trade unionists across the country joined forces with the farmworkers, and a new consciousness of the Chicano in the United States was born as a result of the Huelga. On May 30, 1970, the first table grapes bearing a union label—a black eagle on a red flag—were shipped to market. The grapes came from seven growers who, unable to withstand the effects of the boycott, had signed contracts with the UFW. On July 29, twenty-six Delano growers filed into the UFW union hall to sign the contracts that ended the bitter five-year battle. As negotiated by Huerta, the workers received an hourly wage of $1.76, a guaranteed yearly increase of fifteen cents per hour, and a twenty-five-cent bonus per box picked. In addition, the growers were required to contribute to a health and welfare plan and to low-cost housing for their workers. Most important, the growers agreed not to use certain pesticides, and DDT was banned forever from California vineyards. Huerta's efforts also fostered the California Agricultural Labor Relations Act of 1975.

While championing amnesty for undocumented immigrant farmworkers and fighting the federal guest worker programs of the 1980's, Huerta continued to serve in the UFW as negotiator and vice president into the 1990's. She became notorious in the union for her fervor and tenacity; stories are told of growers begging to face anyone at the negotiating table except Huerta. Huerta and Chávez continued their aggressive style of Chicano trade unionism through periodic use of the consumer boycott, most notably against Gallo Wine, the Dole Company, and California table grapes. They worked together to create the Robert Kennedy Medical Plan, Juan De La Cruz Farm Workers Pension Fund, Farm Workers Credit Union, and National Farm Workers Service Center. In the wake of Chávez's death in 1993, Huerta, in her seventies, continued as an eloquent and frequent speaker and organizer on behalf of workers, Mexican Americans, and women. Her fervor elicited both praise and criticism. In 2006, for example, in a graduation address before Tucson High School in Arizona, she denounced programs against illegal immigration, leading to outrage among state and local officials.

In 2002, Huerta received $100,000 as part of the Puffin Foundation/National Institute Award for Creative Citizenship. With this money she founded the Dolores Huerta Foundation, of which she is president. The nonprofit foundation offers aid in community organizing, research in private and public policies affecting workers and immigrants, and educational programs.

Huerta became a board member of People for the American Way and for the Feminist Majority Foundation, took an active role in supporting political candidates, and became secretary-treasurer emeritus of the UFW. In 2003 she held a short-term appointment as a regent for the University of California.

Huerta's leadership in labor issues and humanitarian causes was widely honored. In 1993 she was inducted into the National Women's Hall of Fame. She has won many awards, including the Outstanding Labor Leader Award from the California State senate, the American Civil Liberties Union's Roger Baldwin Medal of Liberty, the Ellis Island Medal of Freedom, the Eugene V. Debs Foundation Outstanding American Award, the Consumers' Union Trumpeter's Award, the Community of Christ International Peace Award, and the Eleanor Roosevelt Human Rights Award, presented by U.S. president Bill Clinton in 1998. In 1993, *Ms.* magazine named her its Woman of the Year, and *Ladies Home Journal* placed her on its list of 100 Most Important Women of the 20th Century. She received honorary doctorates from six universities, including Princeton (2006), and had five grade schools and one high school named for her.

SIGNIFICANCE

Huerta's dedicated and focused work with the Chicano trade union movement was based on four philosophical axioms: to establish a strong sense of identity, to develop a sense of pride, to maintain always the value of services to others, and to be effective and true to oneself. She was convinced of the need to lead through persuasion and personal example rather than through intimidation. She agreed in the vitality of ideas and the necessity of criticism, but for Huerta, action through responsible commitment and moral choice was the key to creating a just society.

Huerta, Dolores

More than a liberal, ethnic unionist, Huerta also was proud of her work as a feminist, a Chicano activist, and, above all, a humanist. Her cause transcended the narrow scope of unionism. As Huerta stated at an organizing rally at Santa Clara University in 1990,

> I would like to be remembered as a woman who cares for all fellow humans. We must use our lives to make the world a better and just place to live, not just a world to acquire things. That is what we are put on the earth for.

Also, Huerta's skills as a negotiator were entirely self-taught. In fact, before the Delano grape strike she had never read a union contract. In addition to negotiating the UFW's first contracts, she had organized for the strike in the fields, in boycott offices, and in union election halls as well as served as a picket herself. In retrospect, however, it was her skill, tenacity, combativeness, and cunning as a negotiator that truly separated Huerta from her peers in the labor movement. Her contract negotiations with the California growers marked the crowning achievement of one of the greatest victories ever in the history of American workers.

—*Derrick Harper West*

FURTHER READING

Acuña, Rodolfo. *Occupied America: A History of Chicanos.* 5th ed. New York: Pearson Longman, 2004. A general history of Chicanos, now a classic. Detailed sections on Chicano agricultural labor organizing, tracing Chicano labor struggles to the turn of the century. Also details labor struggles in other sectors of the economy. Well referenced, with an excellent index.

Coburn, Judith. "Dolores Huerta: La Passionaria of the Farmworkers." *Ms.* 5 (November, 1976): 10-16. An interview with Huerta during a union election dispute in Sacramento, California, in 1975.

Foner, Philip S. *Women and the American Labor Movement: From World War I to the Present.* New York: Free Press, 1980. A historical overview, though dated, of the American labor movement since World War I with an emphasis on the roles of women, both as labor leaders and as workers.

Garcia, Richard A. "Dolores Huerta: Woman, Organizer, and Symbol." *California History* 71 (Spring, 1993): 57-71. This article, appearing in the journal of the California Historical Society, explores the philosophical and ethical underpinnings of Huerta's labor activism.

Hatch, Robert, and William Hatch. *The Hero Project.* New York: McGraw-Hill, 2006. Written for high school readers, this book has an informative biographical sketch of Huerta, followed by a question-and-answer interview about her interests and participation in social reform, especially her activism on behalf of farmworkers.

Hayden, Tom. "Prize for Dolores Huerta." *Nation*, December 23, 2002. In an editorial, Hayden, a former California state senator and supporter of Huerta, explains why she received the Puffin Prize from the Nation Institute for her participation in the Community Service Organization and the United Farm Workers.

Meier, Matt S. *Mexican American Biographies: A Historical Dictionary, 1836-1987.* New York: Greenwood Press, 1988. Meier, an expert on Mexican American history, includes a profile on Huerta in this biographical dictionary. Although brief, the sketch on Huerta does provide a fine summary of her activities on behalf of "la causa."

Schiff, Karenna Gore. *Lighting the Way: Nine Women Who Changed Modern America*. New York: Hyperion Books, 2005. Among Schiff's nine profiles is Huerta, and the long biographical sketch in this book discusses her background and her support of farmworkers, Mexican immigrants, the Community Service Organization, César Chávez, various important strikes and boycotts, feminism, and her concern about pesticides. Includes photographs.

CHARLES EVANS HUGHES

❝ When we lose the right to be different, we lose the privilege to be free. ❞

Chief justice of the United States (1930-1941)

As chief justice of the United States, Hughes supported legal decisions that provided constitutional protection for suffrage (voting rights), the freedom of speech, the freedom of religion, the freedom of the press, and the right to political dissent. As secretary of state he focused on four areas: disarmament, reparations and war debts, and U.S. relationships with the Soviets and with Latin America.

Born: April 11, 1862; Glens Falls, New York
Died: August 27, 1948; Osterville, Massachusetts
Area of achievement: Law and jurisprudence

EARLY LIFE

Charles Evans Hughes was the only child of David Charles Hughes, an evangelical Baptist minister, and Mary Catherine Connelly, a woman who combined intelligence with pious discipline. When Charles was six years old, he convinced his parents that he should be educated at home because he was impatient with his slower classmates at school. By the time he was ten, however, he was back in public school, and in 1876 he entered Madison University (Colgate). Two years later, finding Madison too provincial for his interests, he transferred to Brown University, from which he was graduated at the top of the class in 1881. In 1884, he was graduated from Columbia University Law School. He married Antoinette Carter in 1888. She was the daughter of one of the partners in a New York law firm for which Hughes worked after leaving Columbia. The couple had four children; the eldest was the only boy.

After graduation from law school, Hughes devoted himself to the practice of law for twenty years. He became a law partner by the time he was twenty-five, and within a few years he had made himself financially secure. During this period he gave no thought to public life, but in 1905 he came to the public's attention when he accepted a position as special counsel to the New York legislature investigating the unfair rates of gas and electricity and insurance fraud. Hughes's investigative reports brought him almost unanimous praise from New York City newspapers. Indeed, he became so popular that, in an attempt to shore up the popularity of the Republican Party, President Theodore Roosevelt pushed party members to nominate Hughes for mayor of New York City. Hughes declined the nomination, thereby causing a rift between himself and Roosevelt that would last the rest of Roosevelt's life. However, as a result he was established as a prominent, albeit reluctant, public figure. In his early forties, Hughes was launched on a career of public service that would occupy the rest of his life.

LIFE'S WORK

In 1906, the Republican Party desperately needed a popular figure to run for governor of New York against the powerful, ambitious journalist William Randolph Hearst. The Republicans sought a candidate who, in contrast to the ruthless Hearst, would be perceived as committed to principled government. They chose Hughes, and this time he accepted—and by the narrowest of margins defeated Hearst. He proved to be an effective, popular governor. He was responsible for reform legislation that was to have a long-term effect on the state of New York. He established, for example, public service commissions that regulated utilities and railroads. As a result, service became better and more impartial and rates fairer, while employees for the first time were able to secure safety provisions in their contracts. The eight-hour workday gained acceptance, and the first workers' compensation laws were established.

Again, with this progressive record as governor, Hughes had attracted the attention of the national Republicans, particularly that of the Republican president, William Howard Taft. Taft nominated Hughes for a seat on the Supreme Court of the United States, and Hughes accepted and was confirmed as a justice on the Court in 1910.

He came to the bench when the country was struggling with the issue of constitutional centralization, and he was to play a significant role in settling that issue. Centralization meant placing more power in the hands of the federal government while taking it from the states. Among other factors, the increased complexity of commerce made centralization a necessity, and Hughes's legal decisions were decisive in establishing the limits of state and federal control. Ostensibly, he used the federal authority of interstate commerce to defend decisions that produced Progressive policies. He wrote and supported opinions that regulated working hours, equal accommodations on railroads for black citizens, nonwhite representation on trial juries, equal access to employment for nonnative citizens, trials in locations free from community passions, and numerous other liberal opinions.

Hughes remained on the Court for six years. While on small matters he might render a conservative opinion, on large issues he supported the expansion of federal powers in defense of individual liberties. He did not hesitate in striking down state statutes that he perceived to be in conflict with the Bill of Rights. By 1916, Hughes's brilliant reputation on the Supreme Court had become so distinguished that the Republican Party once again prevailed on him to run for office, this time for president of the United States. He resigned from the bench and ran against the popular incumbent, Woodrow Wilson. Hughes lost. It is fair to say that this was the least satisfactory episode in a distinguished career; Hughes was not a good campaigner, lacking the intense partisan-

Charles Evans Hughes. (Library of Congress)

ship necessary to run for the presidency. He had no success in moving masses of people to follow him. He had a weak and internally feuding political organization. Most important, the Progressive wing of the Republican Party under Theodore Roosevelt's leadership was only lukewarm in its support.

Four years later, the nation elected Republican Warren G. Harding as president. Hughes became Harding's secretary of state. The stolid, provincial Harding had no coherent foreign policy of his own; as a result, responsibility for such decisions fell squarely on Hughes. Clearly, he was up to the task. Few secretaries of state in the history of the United States can be called his equal. None was more intelligent. Few possessed his imagination, his administrative skills, or his genuine idealism. Indeed, many diplomatic scholars consider Hughes to be one of the three top secretaries of state the nation has ever had. His influence was indelible, even though lesser individuals were left to implement his goals.

Hughes's long-term influence was most noteworthy in four areas: disarmament, reparations and war debts, and the United States' relationships with the Soviets and with Latin America. In November of 1921, Hughes invited representatives of the world's nations to Washington, D.C., to consider ways of reducing national tension in the Western Pacific. The conference became known as the Washington Conference on Naval Disarmament. It was Hughes's plan to reduce tensions around the world, particularly in the Western Pacific, by getting the governments of Great Britain, Japan, and the United States to reduce the size of their naval forces. In an opening speech that both astonished and pleased the delegates to the conference, the secretary of state presented a specific plan for this reduction. In addition to setting limits on tonnage levels for the navies of the world (the French proved the most reluctant to concede on this score), Hughes sought to reduce the militarization of various islands in the Pacific controlled by the national powers. He also pushed for the sovereignty and integrity of China, its right to commercial equity, and Japan's abandonment of expansionism on the Asian mainland. Within fifteen years, all the treaties that resulted from the Washington Conference were either being ignored or abrogated, but for a brief moment in history Hughes's "noble experiment" had influenced international relations.

The matter of reparations and war debts, which was closely related to disarmament in Hughes's mind, also required his attention. After the close of World War I, the victorious Allies (and in particular the French) were seeking huge financial reparations from Germany for losses suffered in the war. Hughes convinced the European Allies that they neither would, nor could, get Germany to pay such reparations and that continued insistence on these payments would only exacerbate the volatile and unstable condition of postwar Europe. To balance the various claims against the German government, Hughes proposed a more realistic payment schedule and the acquisition of an international loan for Germany that would enable it to stabilize its currency and generate the money necessary to meet reparation payments. At the same time, he convinced Congress that it was necessary to extend the payment schedule and reduce the interest requirements on debts owed the United States by its Allies. These reparation and refunding policies lasted for only a few years between World War I and World War II, but they did bring a more rational, tranquil policy to an otherwise chaotic situation.

In Russia, the Communists came to power in 1917, but the United States refused to recognize the Soviet government as a legitimate regime. Many in the United States Senate, however, argued that it was in the United States' interest to resume diplomatic relations with Moscow. It was, they argued, the de facto regime, and as such should be recognized; moreover, recognition would encourage the resumption of trade and promote the United States' commercial interests. Hughes held fast against recognition, arguing that the Soviet revolution was on prima facie grounds both illegal and immoral, because its coming to power abrogated international bona fide agreements between legally established governments. What is more, he held, any assumed economic advantage would be problematic, and at best hazardous. As long as the Communists made and encouraged worldwide revolution among legally constituted governments, he argued, the United States had a responsibility not to participate in policies that could legitimate the revolution. As long as Bolsheviks refused to recognize international legal obligation, recognition of this regime could only be a disservice to legitimate democratic governments that continued to meet their international responsibilities.

The last, and in many ways the most important, policy in Hughes's tenure as secretary of state was initiated when he first entered office and lasted throughout his term as secretary. Working together with Sumner Welles, he forged an American policy toward Latin America that was much less interventionist than the policies of administrations that had preceded him. This policy was the beginning of what was later to be called the Good Neighbor Policy. Essentially, the Good Neighbor Policy meant fewer American marines controlling United States interests in Latin America. Hughes believed that U.S. intrusion into the affairs of "our sister republics" was unwarranted and rejected any impulse "to assert an overlordship, to consider the spread of our authority beyond our domain as the aim of our policy and to make our power the test of right in this hemisphere.... [Such assertions] belie our sincere friendship, ... they stimulate a distrust... [and] have no sanction whatever in the Monroe Doctrine." In reality, however, such non-intervention was only partially implemented under Hughes's leadership. The marines were withdrawn from Nicaragua and the Dominican Republic, but not from Haiti and Panama, where the secretary argued that in the latter two countries it was premature and contrary to the United States' "special interests."

Hughes stepped down from his position as secretary of state in 1925; three years later he was a judge on the Court of International Justice, and in 1930 he accepted his last important public position as chief justice of the United States under Herbert Hoover's presidency.

Constitutional scholars are almost unanimous in assessing Hughes as one of the greatest chief justices in Supreme Court history. He served for eleven years, and during that time his legal leadership was dynamic and progressive, never static and protective. Some of his opinions on economic matters were conservative, but on matters of citizens' welfare his positions represented progressive activism. He argued in support of the government's right to determine an equitable balance between the interests of business and the interests of labor. Expressly, he defended the right of Congress to regulate collective bargaining agreements in interstate commerce. The benchmark decision on this issue was the Wagner Labor Relations Act, which paved the way for supporting legislation on the matter of minimum wages and the hours of work required per day. In addition, Hughes led a unanimous court in declaring President Roosevelt's National Recovery Act of 1933 (NRA) unconstitutional (the Court argued that the act allowed code-fixing; that is, it allowed independent nongovernmental agencies to set wages, prices, and working hours). In other words, Roosevelt's NRA appointments from business and industry were prevented from setting codes of competitive commerce between the states, and Congress could not turn over its legislative responsibility to the executive branch of government in this area, Hughes argued.

As a general rule, Hughes supported the expansion of federal power as an instrument for the protection of personal liberty. He upheld, for example, the right of states to fix prices (*Nebbia v. New York*, 1934), the right of the federal government to regulate radio frequencies (*Federal Radio Commission v. Nelson Bros.*, 1933), the right of women to the same minimum wage afforded men (*Morehead v. Tipaldo*, 1936), and the right of citizens to set aside private contracts under certain hardship constraints.

In the arena of civil liberties, the chief justice was no less supportive of the government's constitutional right to intrude where it can be shown that the Bill of Rights has been abrogated. He argued that the state of Alabama had denied due process to a black man because he had been denied an attorney (*Powell v. Alabama*, 1932). He supported the reversal of the notorious *Scottsboro* decision (a case of rape against a group of young black men) by declaring that blacks cannot be excluded from jury service merely by virtue of their color (*Norris v. Alabama*, 1935, and *Patterson v. Alabama*, 1935). He maintained that such exclusion denied "equal protection of the laws" as provided in the Fourteenth Amendment. In a case anticipating by sixteen years the famous

Hughes, Charles Evans

Brown v. Board of Education (1954) school desegregation case, he held that qualified black students must be granted admission to an all-white law school (*Missouri ex rel. Gaines v. Canada*, 1938). As in *Brown*, the Hughes Court declared that separate facilities for blacks was not equal; that is, separate is not equal, and the plaintiff Gaines had not received "equal protection of the laws."

Over the course of Chief Justice Hughes's term on the bench, he supported legal decisions that provided constitutional protection for suffrage (voting rights), the freedom of speech, the freedom of religion, the freedom of the press, and the right to political dissent. Hughes's record on civil liberties can only lead one to agree with Samuel Hendel's observation that he had a "greater fondness for the Bill of Rights than any other Chief Justice."

Significance

The magnitude of Hughes's service to the country was so widespread and pervasive that it is difficult to know just where the emphasis should be placed. In fact, the wise course is to avoid placing undue emphasis on any specific aspect of his numerous accomplishments but rather to review the traits of character that he brought to every public position he held. His strong sense of social interest led him throughout his life to fight institutional dishonesty in all of its forms. He was never reluctant to employ the legal leverage of the judiciary against what he perceived to be the injustices of institutional forms of government, business, and industry. On the bench he was always reluctant to impede social reform with a "judicial veto." His conception of a justice's role was as a principled libertarian; in particular, a member of the judiciary must be prepared to employ the law in defense of the citizen's individual rights against the inevitably unfair advantages of powerful national institutions. Understandably, corporations, industry, and government will exercise the initiative necessary to make their efforts worthwhile and successful. In return, individual citizens have the right, through their legislative representatives, to see to it that they do not fall victim to the aspirations of these powerful organizations. It is the role of the judiciary to establish a balanced fairness between collective interests and public liberties.

Hughes not only had the role of jurist; he also represented the most powerful of all institutions, the government itself. In this role, however, he acted with restraint and with an eye to the common good. Because he was an individual with a scrupulous moral sense, an unshakable commitment to fidelity and honor, and the intellectual powers to match, he was never willing to sacrifice long-term ideals for short-term expediencies. Thus, it seems proper to argue that Hughes was a "futurist" and as such endures as one of America's most gifted and distinguished secretaries of state.

—*Donald Burrill*

Further Reading

Glad, Betty. *Charles Evans Hughes and the Illusions of Innocence: A Study in American Diplomacy*. Urbana: University of Illinois Press, 1966. In this study of U.S. diplomacy between the two world wars, Hughes is the centerpiece. Schooled in mainstream nineteenth century American culture, Hughes formulated U.S. foreign policy throughout the era. It is Glad's contention that Hughes's moral puritanism often led to optimistic illusions. Glad's ideological generalizations are not always convincing.

Hendel, Samuel. *Charles Evans Hughes and the Supreme Court*. New York: King's Crown Press, 1951. This is a case-by-case study of Hughes's judicial career, a careful, detailed assessment and evaluation that has become a sourcebook for much legal scholarship on Hughes's Supreme Court opinions.

Hughes, Charles Evans. *The Autobiographical Notes of Charles Evans Hughes*. Edited by David J. Danelske and Joseph S. Tulchin. Cambridge, Mass.: Harvard University Press, 1973. It is difficult for writers not to sketch Hughes as larger than life. Reading his own notes affords an opportunity to assess his own words; this work reveals the man both directly and indirectly.

_____. *Our Relations to the Nations of the Western Hemisphere*. Princeton, N.J.: Princeton University Press, 1928. Hughes's analysis of the United States' relationship to Canada and Latin America: his assessment of the Monroe Doctrine, the recognition of governments, and the United States' role in honoring Central American treaties and supplying military arms and financial loans to foreign powers. Particularly interesting is the section in which he sets forth the conditions that he believes justify intervention in Latin American affairs.

_____. *The Supreme Court of the United States*. New York: Columbia University Press, 1928. A historical account of the role of the Supreme Court. Ostensibly, the Court's task as the "supreme tribunal" is to interpret the intentions of the nation's legislatures. Hughes argues that it is the Court's role to balance state and national priorities and to determine the rights of citizens against common social interests.

Louria, Margot. *Triumph and Downfall: America's Pursuit of Peace and Prosperity, 1921-1933*. Westport, Conn.: Greenwood Press, 2001. Examines the activities of the three secretaries of state during the presidential administrations of Warren G. Harding, Calvin Coolidge, and Herbert Hoover, describing their efforts to preserve world peace and security. The second part of the book focuses on Hughes.

Perkins, Dexter. *Charles Evans Hughes and American Democratic Statesmanship*. Boston: Little, Brown, 1956. A smoothly written account of Hughes's political and legal career from his start in New York City to his retirement from the post of chief justice of the United States. Throughout, Perkins attempts to portray Hughes as a brilliant, principled individual striving to balance the ideals of liberalism and conservatism in the art of statesmanship.

Pusey, Merlo J. *Charles Evans Hughes*. 2 vols. New York: Macmillan, 1951. One of the best and most exhaustive works on Hughes. Beginning with his childhood in Glens Falls, New York, and ending with his fight against Franklin D. Roosevelt's attempt to "pack the Supreme Court" in 1938, it is a standard text on Hughes. Especially valuable for its interviews with Hughes at the end of his illustrious career: Pusey had the good fortune to interview him many hours a week over a two-and-one-half-year period.

Ross, William G. *The Chief Justiceship of Charles Evans Hughes, 1930-1941*. Columbia: University of South Carolina Press, 2007. Describes the political, economic, and cultural forces that transformed American society and the Supreme Court during Hughes's tenure as chief justice.

CORDELL HULL

> *" There is no greater responsibility resting upon peoples and governments everywhere than to make sure that enduring peace will . . . be established and maintained.* **"**

U.S. senator (1931-1933) and secretary of state (1933-1944)

Serving as secretary of state longer than any person in American history, Hull shaped the world of diplomacy along the lines of his Jeffersonian and Wilsonian principles. His commitment to President Woodrow Wilson's dream of a world organization helped make the United Nations a reality.

Born: October 2, 1871; near Byrdstown, Overton (now Pickett) County, Tennessee
Died: July 23, 1955; Bethesda, Maryland
Areas of achievement: Diplomacy; government and politics

EARLY LIFE

Cordell Hull spent his boyhood in the lovely Cumberland Mountains of Tennessee. Born at the dawn of the industrial era, he absorbed the values of individualism and entrepreneurial activity. His father, William Hull, made a sizable fortune as a merchandiser and a supplier of logs. His mother, the former Elizabeth Riley, imbued him with strong religious (Baptist) and humanitarian sentiments.

Both parents encouraged Cordell and his two older brothers to obtain a formal education. A combination of private tutoring and local schooling eventually led him to normal schools at Bowling Green, Kentucky, and the National Normal University at Lebanon, Ohio. In 1889, illness ended his general education. He did, however, read law on his own, and he became an attorney after completing a ten-month course (in five months) at Cumberland Law School. His next step was into politics.

Before his twentieth birthday, Hull had already become the Democratic Party chair of his county, entering the Tennessee state legislature two years later. His debating skills served him well. Hull enlisted in the Army when the Spanish-American War began in 1898, although the war ended before he saw battle. By 1903, the young lawyer had been appointed to a Tennessee judicial seat (he would be called Judge for the remainder of his life), and he moved to Congress three years later.

By age thirty-six, when he moved to Washington, Hull had exhibited his ambition, his devotion to law and public life, and his principled approach to politics. Even his critics recognized his abilities. He possessed a fine intelligence and a courtly appearance, both of which served as important political assets. He was more reserved than most of his colleagues appreciated, and he combined a strong ethical sense with the moralistic outlook typical of the Progressive period. He was one of the best lawyers in Congress by the time he arrived in 1906, but he was also legalistic in ways that would later inhibit his political effectiveness.

LIFE'S WORK

Hull spent a quarter of a century in Congress. He served in the House of Representatives from 1907 until 1930 (except for a two-year period from 1921 to 1923), and then in the Senate until President-elect Franklin D. Roosevelt offered him the post of secretary of state. As a congressman, he sat on the Ways and Means Committee, where he specialized in tax and tariff matters during a period when federal spending soared. Hull fought for an income tax even before the ratification of the Sixteenth Amendment to the Constitution, and he became one of President Woodrow Wilson's chief congressional allies in the pursuit of a low tariff.

Indeed, the horrors of World War I helped to fix Hull's attention on low tariffs for the remainder of his public career. Like many others in his Progressive generation, Hull believed that the chief cause of war was economic injustice, which he ascribed to tariff barriers that inhibited international commerce. Combined with his faith in the sanctity of law and respect for written agreements and treaties, Hull's approach to international affairs had largely crystallized by the time Germany surrendered in 1918.

It was Hull's tenure as secretary of state, though, that secured his place in history. Hull was a compromise candidate for that post following Roosevelt's victory in 1932. He had already earned Roosevelt's gratitude following his outspoken support for United States' entry into the League of Nations when Roosevelt ran for the office of vice president in 1920, and he ably chaired the Democratic National Committee for the next three years while serving on that body during most of the decade. Hull had few enemies. After 1930, his articulate opposition to the Smoot-Hawley Tariff Act, which disastrously raised rates to the highest levels in American history, guaranteed him national prominence.

Hull's long service as secretary of state obscures the degree to which his record was decidedly mixed. He came to his post with many assets, including an excellent relationship with Congress, a conscientious attitude toward his work, and genuine respect for the professionals in the State Department and the Foreign Service. However, he was handicapped by his moralistic rigidity in a field that placed a premium on compromise, by his limited experience in foreign policy, and by his somewhat formal and distant relationship with the president. Consequently, Hull never achieved the influence in the foreign policy area that he desired. Roosevelt often relied on friends and personal envoys rather than on his secretary of state. The president even bypassed the department entirely at certain critical moments, leaving Hull uninformed and embarrassed. This sort of thing plagued Hull as early as 1933, when Roosevelt undermined his efforts at international cooperation at the London Economic Conference, and as late as 1944, when the secretary of the treasury, but not the secretary of state, joined Roosevelt and Winston Churchill at the Second Quebec Conference to formulate the famous Morgenthau Plan. Bitterly opposed by Hull, the plan aimed to turn post-World War II Germany into an agricultural society.

Indeed, Hull's chief assistants in the State Department were Roosevelt loyalists, who had been appointed largely without consulting the new secretary in 1933, and Roosevelt often relied on Secretary of the Treasury Henry Morgenthau, Jr., or Undersecretary of State Sumner Welles in formulating foreign policy. Hull's memoirs occasionally reflect his dismay at these arrangements. The fact of the matter is that Roosevelt devalued Hull's contributions. Like his cousin Theodore before him, Roosevelt insisted on being his own secretary of state, particularly during the period after 1939, when the line between diplomatic and military affairs was blurred.

Hull, Cordell

Cordell Hull.
(© The Nobel Foundation)

Nevertheless, Hull rarely considered resignation from an administration for which, in fact, he had only limited ideological sympathy. His optimism, loyalty, congeniality, and fascination with power kept him in the cabinet. He often lamented the influence of those whom he considered radicals and extreme New Dealers. His Jeffersonian suspicion of large government kept him something of an outsider in the administration. Despite this fact, he continued to have a cordial, if not close, relationship with the president, and he had an excellent working relationship with conservative cabinet members such as Henry Stimson in the War Department and Frank Knox in the Navy Department.

Hull may have had limited influence within the Roosevelt administration, but his long tenure in the State Department resulted in some notable successes. Perhaps most important was his sponsorship of the Reciprocal Trade Agreements Act, which Congress passed in 1934. Hull's support for this measure—which permitted the president to negotiate lower tariffs on a bilateral basis—stemmed from his belief that lower rates would contribute to both international peace and economic recovery. Based on this act, the secretary helped to negotiate twenty-one agreements that moderated rates from the high Smoot-Hawley levels of the Hoover years. Moreover, the measure shifted tariff authority from Congress to the executive branch, a change congenial to Hull, who was very much influenced by the Progressive movement of the early twentieth century.

Hull's two other chief accomplishments centered on improving relations with Latin America and strengthening the framework of international organizations. He was a prime mover behind Roosevelt's Good Neighbor Policy, which sought to reverse years of American bullying in Central and South America. Hull continued the policy enunciated in the Clark Memorandum of 1930, which renounced the use of military intervention in Latin America. Much of Hull's work was formalized at a series of conferences, the most dramatic of which was held in Montevideo, Uruguay, in 1933. Hull eventually strengthened the relationship of the United States with all Latin American nations except Argentina. He relaxed the heavy hand of American economic imperialism in the hemisphere, and he built a basis for military cooperation during World War II.

Hull was in every sense a Wilsonian in supporting international cooperation through a world organization. He strongly supported the United States' entry into the International Labor Organization in 1934, and he deeply regretted the Senate's rejection of World Court membership for the United States the following year. His most gratifying work as secretary of state was his effort to create a successor organization to the League of Nations. He helped to author the Charter of the United Nations, and he was instrumental in sidetracking regional agreements as a substitute for a genuine world organization. Moreover, Hull's political skills helped to prevent the Republicans from making the United Nations into a partisan issue during the presidential campaign of 1944. He had learned the lessons of 1919.

These successes must be balanced against his most significant failure, for Hull and Roosevelt did little to prevent the drift toward war in 1939. Partly handcuffed by the degree to which most Americans were preoccupied with the economic crisis, Hull maintained a policy toward the future Axis powers that relied excessively on a rigid repetition of moral principles that he assumed to be the universal basis for international conduct. He never understood the degree to which Axis leaders held his principles in contempt, nor the degree to which American interests in distant areas might justifiably be compromised to prevent war.

Significance

For all of Hull's success in such areas as trade, international organization, and good-neighbor relations, his service as secretary of state was marked more by failure than success. His approach to world affairs had been shaped excessively by the moralistic attitudes of the Progressives. Adolf Hitler and Benito Mussolini were unimpressed by his moral pronouncements. Hull's genuine fear of war contributed to lukewarm support for the pre-1939 appeasement policy of Great Britain and France. Hull was more assertive toward Japan, but without the support of the Allied powers he was unwilling to take any action of a decisive nature before 1940, and neither was Roosevelt. American policy was neither courageous nor distinguished before World War II.

Once the Japanese attacked Pearl Harbor, Hull's influence further declined. Roosevelt utilized personal envoys such as Harry Hopkins to sidestep the State Department

Hull, Cordell

during the war. The president cultivated a personal relationship with Allied heads of state such as Joseph Stalin and Churchill, therefore diluting the contributions of his secretary of state. By the time that Hull left office for health reasons in November, 1944, the center of foreign policy decision was no longer in the State Department. Cordell Hull must accept his share of responsibility for this development.

Nevertheless, Hull's achievements cannot be disminished by the circumstances of history. Roosevelt called him the father of the United Nations, and in 1945 the Nobel Foundation saw fit to award him the Nobel Peace Prize for devoting his entire life to the stabilization of international relations. Regardless of his ultimate success, his tenacity in that effort makes him an American hero.

—*Gary B. Ostrower*

FURTHER READING

Drummond, Donald F. "Cordell Hull." In *An Uncertain Tradition: American Secretaries of State in the Twentieth Century*, edited by Norman Graebner. New York: McGraw-Hill, 1961. This is the most skillful short study of Hull. The author admires Hull's opposition to fascism but believes that his rigid emphasis on principle often rendered his diplomacy ineffective.

Hull, Cordell. *The Memoirs of Cordell Hull*. 2 vols. New York: Macmillan, 1948. Hull's own highly detailed and somewhat dull account of his public life. These volumes gloss over the rivalry for influence within the Roosevelt administration, but they nevertheless offer a wealth of valuable information.

Jablon, Howard. "Cordell Hull, His 'Associates,' and Relations with Japan, 1933-1936." *Mid-America* 56 (1974): 160-174. The author argues that Hull's policy toward Japan was merely an extension of Henry L. Stimson's Non-Recognition Policy. Hull, says Jablon, relied excessively on his advisers and an approach that elevated principle over any serious assessment of Japanese interests.

Pratt, Julius. *Cordell Hull: 1933-44*. New York: Cooper Square, 1964. The best and most comprehensive study of Hull as secretary of state. Pratt is often uncritical of Hull, but, like most other historians, he faults Hull's excessive moralism. The book is organized topically.

Rofe, J. Simon. *Franklin Roosevelt's Foreign Policy and the Welles Mission*. New York: Palgrave Macmillan, 2007. Examines Sumner Welles's efforts in early 1940 to forestall a European war, and how his failed attempt widened his disagreements with Hull and other State Department officials.

ANDREW JACKSON

> *" Americans are not a perfect people, but we are called to a perfect mission. "*

President of the United States (1829-1837)

Possessing the characteristics of the roughly hewn Western frontiersman—in contrast to the aristocratic propensities of the eastern and Virginia "establishment"—Jackson came to symbolize the common person in the United States and the rise of democracy.

Born: March 15, 1767; Waxhaw settlement, South Carolina
Died: June 8, 1845; the Hermitage, near Nashville, Tennessee
Also known as: Old Hickory
Areas of achievement: Government and politics; military

EARLY LIFE

Andrew Jackson was born into a family that had come from County Antrim, Ireland. His father, also named Andrew, arrived in America in 1765 and died shortly before his son, the future president, was born. The younger Jackson's teenage years were "rough and tumble." Acquiring little formal education, Jackson made his way through early life by hand-to-mouth jobs, helping his two older brothers support their widowed mother.

During the Revolutionary War, the British invaded Waxhaw, an event that shaped much of Jackson's subsequent life and career. His two brothers were killed, and his mother died of cholera while caring for prisoners of war. Jackson, taken prisoner by the British, was orphaned at the age of fourteen, a situation that taught him independence, both in action and in thought. In 1784, Jackson went to Salisbury, North Carolina, apprenticed to the law firm of Spruce McKay. Within three years, he was admitted to the bar, and in 1788, Jackson made the decision to go west, to Nashville, Tennessee, to seek his fortune.

While Jackson pursued a legal career as a practicing attorney, superior court solicitor, and judge, he also ventured into other activities. He became an avid horse breeder and racer, as well as a plantation owner. Jackson had no formal military training, but he quickly earned a reputation as an Indian fighter, and it was undoubtedly his experience in this area that led to his election in 1802 as major general of the western Tennessee militia. In 1791, Jackson married Rachel Donelson Robards, who had, she thought, been recently divorced from Lewis Robards. The divorce decree had not been issued in Virginia at the time Andrew and Rachel were wed in Natchez, Mississippi. Three years later, when Jackson learned of the error, he and Rachel remarried, but this action did not stop enemies from slandering his wife in subsequent political campaigns.

Jackson was one of few serious duelists in American history (Aaron Burr was another), and his most famous confrontation was with Charles Dickinson, essentially over a problem that started with racehorses. On the occasion, Jackson wore a borrowed coat that was too large for him. When Dickinson fired, he aimed for the heart, located,

Jackson, Andrew

he thought, at the top of Jackson's coat pocket. Because the coat was too big, the top of the pocket was below Jackson's heart. Dickinson hit the target, but Jackson still stood. Dickinson exclaimed, "Great God, have I missed?" Jackson then fired at Dickinson, mortally wounding him. Dickinson lived for a time after being shot, and it was characteristic of Jackson not to allow anyone to tell Dickinson that he really had hit his opponent; he died thinking that he had missed. Jackson was seriously wounded in the duel, and he convalesced for several weeks.

Jackson was a tall, thin man, six feet one inch in height, usually weighing 150 pounds. His nose was straight and prominent, and his blue eyes blazed fiercely whenever he lost his temper, which was often. During the early years, his hair was reddish-brown; in old age, it was white. He had a firmly set chin and a high forehead. Paintings and daguerreotypes suggest a man accustomed to giving orders and having them obeyed.

Life's Work

Jackson became a nationally known figure during the War of 1812. Though he had been elected to his rank rather than earning it by training and experience, he soon proved to be a capable leader. He endeavored to neutralize the Creek Indians in Alabama, who periodically attacked white settlers. He accomplished this objective at the Battle of Horseshoe Bend. So tough and unremitting was he at this engagement that his soldiers began to call him Old Hickory. His greatest battle was against the British at New Orleans. Amazingly, there were some two thousand British casualties, and less than a dozen for the army of westerners, black people, and pirates that Jackson had put together. Although the war was essentially over before the battle took place—news traveled slowly before the advent of modern communications—Jackson became a national military hero, and there was talk in some quarters of running him for president of the United States.

After the war, in 1818, President James Monroe ordered Jackson and his army to Florida, to deal with Indian problems. While there, Jackson torched Pensacola and hanged two Englishmen whom he thought were in collusion with the Indians as they attacked settlers across the border in Alabama. Jackson's deeds in Florida caused diplomatic rifts with Spain and England, and he clearly had exceeded his orders, but his actions appealed to a pragmatic American public, and the general's popularity soared.

When Jackson became a presidential candidate in 1824, some believed that it was the office to which all of his previous activities pointed. If ever there was a "natural" for the presidency, his supporters argued, it was Andrew Jackson. His opponents feared that if Jackson were elected, there would be too much popular government; Jackson, they argued, might turn the republic into a "Mobocracy." Worse yet, he had little experience with foreign policy, and his confrontational style might create one diplomatic crisis after another.

Jackson lost the presidency in 1824, although he received more electoral votes than anyone else. It was necessary to get a majority of electoral votes—more than all the other candidates combined. Because there was no majority in 1824, the election was decided by the House of Representatives, which selected John Quincy Adams; Jackson protested that Adams's victory was engineered by a "corrupt bargain" with Henry Clay, whom Adams appointed as secretary of state after Clay's supporters in the

House ensured Adams's election. In 1828, however, there was no doubt that Jackson would defeat Adams. A political "revolution" had occurred in the four-year term. In 1824, four candidates amassed altogether less than a half million popular votes. In 1828, however, two candidates, Jackson and Adams, collected about 1,200,000, meaning that in four years 800,000 voters had been added to the polls—in large part the result of liberalized voting qualifications—and most of them voted for Jackson.

Jackson's great objective while in office was "executive supremacy." He reasoned: Who was the only government official universally elected to office? The answer was the president. Was it not reasonable, then, that the president was the chief symbol of the American people? Further, if he were the chief symbol, should not the executive branch be as powerful, or more so, than the Congress or the Supreme Court? This concept of executive supremacy displeased numerous congressional leaders. Congress had dominated the federal government since the Revolution, out of a general distrust of administrative centralization. After all, Britain's King George III was a "typical" administrator.

Jackson pursued executive supremacy in a number of ways. One was the patronage system, by which he appointed friends to office. His enemies referred to this policy as the "spoils system"; Jackson called it "rotation in office." The number of those displaced, however (about 10 percent of the government workforce), was no greater than previous or future executive terms. Another procedure that strengthened Jackson's presidency, perhaps the most important, was the "county agent" system that Martin Van Buren created for the Democratic Party. The forerunners of what became known as "county chairmen," these agents enabled the Democrats to practice politics on a grassroots level, going door-to-door, as it were, to collect votes and support for the president.

An important part of Jackson's drive for executive supremacy was the presidential veto. He used this constitutional device twelve times, more than all of his predecessors put together. Moreover, he made good use of the "pocket veto." (If a bill comes to the president less than ten days before Congress adjourns, he can "put it in his pocket" and not have to tell Congress why he disapproves of it. A pocket veto enhances presidential power by preventing Congress from reconsidering the bill, an action that caused presidential critics to call Jackson "King Andrew I.") Though he was not the first president to use the pocket veto—James Madison was first—Jackson made more extensive use of it than any of his predecessors.

Perhaps the most significant presidential veto in American history was Jackson's rejection, in 1832, of the recharter bill, a bill that would have rechartered the Bank of the United States. Among other things, Jackson argued that the executive had the power to judge the constitutionality of a bill brought before him. According to Jacksonian scholar Robert Remini, Jackson's veto on this bill caused an ascendancy of presidential power that did not abate until Richard M. Nixon's resignation in 1974.

In foreign affairs, Jackson conducted a lively policy that gained new respect for the United States from major European powers. He nurtured good relations with England by a conciliatory attitude on the Maine-Canada boundary question and by promising to exempt many English goods from the harsh tariff of 1828 (the Tariff of Abominations). He even held out the prospect of lowering the tariff against the British through a

Jackson, Andrew

treaty. His positive stance on boundary lines and the tariff helped reopen full West Indies trade with the British. Although Jackson may have been an Anglophobe most of his life, it is nevertheless true that he gained concessions from the English that had been denied to his predecessor, the so-called Anglophile, Adams.

The United States almost went to war with its oldest and most loyal ally while Jackson was president. The United States presented France with a "spoliation" bill, going back to the depredations of American shipping during the Napoleonic Wars. When, for various reasons, the French government refused payments, Jackson's tone became strident. In a message to Congress, he said that a "collision" was possible between the two governments if the French remained obstinate. Ultimately, Britain intervened and urged the French to settle the "American matter," because of mutual problems developing with Russia.

Though Jackson personally believed that Texas would one day be a part of the American Union, he did not push its annexation while in office, for he feared that the slavery question that Texas would engender would embarrass his chosen presidential successor, Van Buren. After Van Buren was safely elected, Jackson publicly supported the annexation of Texas, which took place in 1845, the year Jackson died.

While Jackson was president, reforms occurred on state levels. Numerous state constitutions were revised or rewritten, all with liberal trends. Women found it easier to prosecute abusive husbands, and increasingly they could purchase property and dispose of it as they chose, without getting permission from their nearest male kin. Prison reforms began in some states, and insane people were treated for their illnesses rather than being thought to be possessed by the Devil. Public education systems started in several states, notably Massachusetts and New York. In all these reforms, suffrage ever widened, exemplifying the belief that political participation should be based on white manhood rather than property qualifications. Noted scholar Clinton Rossiter has shown that the Jacksonian presidency changed the base of American government from aristocracy to democracy without fundamentally altering its republican character.

After serving as president from 1829 to 1837, Jackson happily returned to the Hermitage. There, he continued as the father figure of his country, receiving dignitaries from around the world, and giving advice to those who followed him in the presidential office. He was especially pleased to see his protégé, James K. Polk, win the office in 1844 and become widely known as "Young Hickory." Jackson died at the Hermitage on June 8, 1845.

Significance

It is fair to say that Andrew Jackson was first and foremost a beneficiary of rising democratic spirits in America. When he attained power, he put his stamp upon events and promulgated additional steps toward democracy. He suggested some reforms, many of which were ultimately enacted. He wanted senators to be popularly elected, as were members of the House of Representatives. He wanted additional judges to take the heavy burden off the judicial system. He believed that the United States Post Office should be reshaped into a semiprivate organization. He suggested some reforms that were not enacted but were widely discussed. He believed that a president should serve for six years and then be ineligible for further election. He thought that the electoral college should either be abandoned or drastically reformed, because, in his opinion, it did not always reflect the will of the electorate.

It is widely held that Jacksonian America heralded the "positive state," where government dominates the private sector. Jackson's presidency is frequently cited as starting the trend toward federal centralization. Jackson's legacy is most visible in his personification of the common American man, even though he, himself, was hardly a "common" man. His was an age of entrepreneurship in which it was believed that government should not grant privileges to one group that it withholds from another. This thought has motivated many reform philosophies in the twentieth century, not the least of which was the Civil Rights movement. In this and other significant ways, Andrew Jackson has spoken to Americans of subsequent generations.

—*Carlton Jackson*

FURTHER READING

Burstein, Andrew. *The Passions of Andrew Jackson*. New York: Alfred A. Knopf, 2003. Comprehensive biography painting a negative portrait of Jackson as a frontier bully, who was, in the author's words, "implacable," "humorless," "self-righteous," and a "rage-filled zealot."

Ellis, Richard E. *Andrew Jackson*. Washington, D.C.: CQ Press, 2003. Jackson's life, career, policies, and the impact of his presidency are examined in short chapters. Also includes pertinent documents relating and appendixes listing the major acts of Congress and U.S. Supreme Court decisions during his presidency. Part of *Congressional Quarterly*'s American Presidents Reference Series.

Gatell, Frank Otto, and John M. McFaul, eds. *Jacksonian America, 1815-1840: New Society, Changing Politics*. Englewood Cliffs, N.J.: Prentice-Hall, 1970. This collection of essays ranges from politics to societal judgments and lifestyles. The essays vary in quality, but the overall result is a lucid explanation of the Jacksonian era.

Pessen, Edward. *Jacksonian America: Society, Personality, and Politics*. Rev. ed. Urbana: University of Illinois Press, 1985. The best summary of the Jacksonian experience is to be found in this book. With an emphasis on social and economic affairs, the author clearly ties up all the various threads of the period.

Remini, Robert V. *Andrew Jackson*. 3 vols. Baltimore: Johns Hopkins University Press, 1998. This is the paperback edition of Remini's three-volume definitive biography. Volume 1 discusses Jackson's role in territorial expansion; volume 2 describes his first presidential campaign and his first term as president; and volume 3 explores his reelection and second presidential administration.

_____. *Andrew Jackson and the Bank War: A Study in the Growth of Presidential Power*. New York: W. W. Norton, 1967. In this book, Remini refers to the bank veto as the most significant presidential rejection in United States history, a culmination of Jackson's drive for executive supremacy. After the veto, presidential power grew considerably.

_____. *The Election of Andrew Jackson*. Philadelphia: J. B. Lippincott, 1963. Discusses the change in the number of eligible voters between 1824 and 1828 and how this change benefited Andrew Jackson.

_____. *Martin Van Buren and the Making of the Democratic Party.* New York: Columbia University Press, 1959. Explains in detail how Martin Van Buren founded the Democratic Party. Van Buren was a politician par excellence, who always seemed to thrive while he held lower offices. His presidency (1837-1841), however, was not successful.

Rossiter, Clinton L. *The American Presidency.* New York: Harcourt, Brace & World, 1956. A work that explains the age-old practice of ranking the presidents and of trying to determine what constitutes greatness in presidential terms. Jackson's presidency was a time of transition in American society, and the way he benefited from it, and then helped to propel it, gave his tenure the label of "great."

JESSE JACKSON

> *Leaders must be tough enough to fight, tender enough to cry, human enough to make mistakes, humble enough to admit them, strong enough to absorb the pain, and resilient enough to bounce back and keep on moving.*

Civil rights leader

Jesse Jackson became one of the most influential, eloquent, and widely known African American political leaders in the United States during the decades after the death of Martin Luther King, Jr.

Born: October 8, 1941; Greenville, South Carolina
Also known as: Jesse Louis Burns (birth name); Jesse Louis Jackson (full name)
Areas of achievement: Civil rights; social reform; government and politics; oratory

EARLY LIFE

Jesse Louis Jackson was born in a six-room house in the textile-mill town of Greenville, South Carolina. His mother, Helen Burns, was a student at Greenville's Sterling High School when she became pregnant with Jesse. His father, Noah Robinson, was married to another woman. The Robinsons lived next door to the Burns family. Two years after Jesse's birth, on October 2, 1943, his mother married Charles Henry Jackson, who bestowed his last name on the boy and formally adopted him in 1957.

The young Jesse Jackson apparently learned the circumstances of his birth sometime during elementary school. Other children who had heard rumors of the small-town scandal taunted him. When Jesse was nine, Noah Robinson began seeing the boy standing in the Robinsons' backyard, peering through a window. The hardships and insecurities did not, however, discourage Jesse. At any early age, he became a high achiever, determined to prove his own worth.

When he was nine, Jesse, whose mother and stepfather were devout Baptists, won election to the National Sunday School Convention in Charlotte, South Carolina. By the time he reached high school, his teachers knew him as a hardworking student, and he excelled at athletics. After he was graduated from Sterling High School in Greenville in 1959, Jackson won a football scholarship to the University of Illinois.

In Jackson's freshman year, however, a white coach told him that blacks were not allowed to play quarterback for the University of Illinois team. Stung by this example of segregation outside the South, the young man transferred the next year to a black college, the North Carolina Agricultural and Technical College in Greensboro, North Carolina. The decision to return to the South was fateful, since Greensboro was a center of the student sit-in movement to integrate lunch counters and other public facilities. Jackson threw himself into the movement and became known as an energetic and outspoken young civil rights activist.

LIFE'S WORK

From his Greensboro years onward, Jackson's life revolved around political struggles for civil rights. On June 6, 1963, he was arrested for the first time, on charges of inciting a riot while leading a demonstration in front of a municipal building. At one sit-in, he met his future wife, Jacqueline Lavinia Davis, whom he married after his graduation in 1964. He became active in the Congress of Racial Equality (CORE), and during his last year at North Carolina Agricultural and Technical College, he was appointed field director of CORE's southeastern operations.

At the same time that Jackson was deeply involved in protests and civil disobedience, he was also displaying an interest in mainstream politics. For a short time during his student days in Greensboro, he worked for North Carolina governor Terry Sanford. Sanford, recognizing the young man's promise, sponsored him as one of the first African American delegates to the Young Democrats National Convention in Las Vegas. Electoral politics absorbed Jackson to the point that he almost entered law school at Duke University, with the goal of using legal qualifications as a political springboard. Instead, however, he decided to enter the ministry.

After receiving a bachelor's degree in sociology, Jackson enrolled in the Chicago Theological Seminary. His stay in Chicago was brief, as the call to struggle for civil rights proved to be more compelling. In 1965, he left the seminary to return south. During the celebrated march in Selma, Alabama, Jackson came to know the Reverend Martin Luther King, Jr. Most of Jackson's biographers have concluded that King became a revered father figure for the young man who had looked longingly through his natural father's window. King, in turn, was impressed with his follower's abilities.

Jackson quickly became a part of the inner circle of the organization headed by King, the Southern Christian Leadership Conference (SCLC). In 1966, King asked him to take over the Chicago operations of Operation Breadbasket, an SCLC-sponsored organization designed to pressure businesses into hiring African Americans. A year later, King appointed him Operation Breadbasket's national director. Jackson was with King in Memphis, on April 4, 1968, the day that King was assassinated.

On June 30, 1968, still without a theological degree, Jackson was ordained as a minister by two famous pastors, the Reverend Clay Evans and the Reverend C. L. Franklin. Instead of taking over a church, however, he continued to head Operation Breadbasket, although his independence brought him into conflict with the leaders of the SCLC. In particular, tensions emerged between Jackson and Ralph D. Abernathy, King's successor as head of the SCLC.

On December 12, 1971, Jackson submitted a formal resignation from the SCLC and from Operation Breadbasket. At the same time, he used the personal following he had built in Operation Breadbasket to form Operation People United to Save Humanity (PUSH). PUSH was a personal power base for Jackson, but he used it to agitate for greater black employment in American businesses and to promote the economic interests of African Americans. At the same time, PUSH operated self-esteem programs for disadvantaged young blacks and encouraged them to excel academically. During the years that Jackson led PUSH, the slogan he urged young people to adopt, "I am somebody," became a well-known motto of self-reliance.

As early as 1980, Jackson was announcing the need for an African American presidential candidate. As the nation approached the 1984 election, Jackson announced on the television program *Sixty Minutes* that he would run for the office. African Americans continued to be his electoral base, but he attempted to broaden his political program to include other Americans who had little power or representation in the American political system. He appealed to what he called a Rainbow Coalition that included poor people, small family farmers, gays, and others who might be sympathetic to a progressive agenda. He advocated government programs for full employment and a freeze on military spending, as well as a renewed commitment to civil rights. Thus, while conservatism had become a dominant force in American political life as President Ronald Reagan approached his second term, Jackson became a major spokesperson for liberal causes. In 1997, Operation PUSH and the National Rainbow Coalition merged to form the RainbowPUSH Coalition, dedicated to promoting civil rights and to seeking greater educational and economic equality in American society.

Jackson's reputation, and his campaign, received a boost at the end of 1983 and the beginning of 1984. Robert Goodman, an African American military pilot, was shot down over the Syrian-controlled area of Lebanon. In December, Jackson flew to Damascus, Syria, to meet with Syrian president Hafez al-Assad. The Syrian leader arranged for Goodman's release, and in early January, Jackson and the freed hostage flew home together.

In January, 1984, Jackson also made one of the most serious blunders of his political career. His support for the Palestine Liberation Organization and his connections to Arab nations had aroused the suspicions of some Jewish Americans. Jackson also had ties to Nation of Islam leader Louis Farrakhan, whom many people accused of being anti-Semitic. During a conversation with reporters at the beginning of 1984, Jackson referred to New York City as "Hymietown," a slang reference to the city's large Jewish population that was widely viewed as offensive. Although he apologized for the remark, the incident contributed to tensions between Jews and African Americans, and many observers speculated that Jackson's comments indicated an unspoken prejudice against Jews.

Although Jackson did not win the Democratic nomination, his strong showing demonstrated that an African American could compete at the highest levels of Ameri-

Jesse Jackson.
(Library of Congress)

can politics. His showing in his second presidential campaign, in 1988, was stronger still. By this time, his Rainbow Coalition had become well organized. Jackson himself had also refined his positions and developed a comprehensive and consistent platform. He advocated a national health care program, an increase in the tax rate on the highest incomes, and the adoption of comparable-worth policies to combat gender inequalities in pay. Although he again failed to win the Democratic nomination, he did receive approximately 7 million—out of 23 million—votes cast in primaries. His strong showing helped to establish him as a national leader, not simply among African Americans but among all Americans. In the 1992 presidential election, Democratic candidate Bill Clinton actively sought Jackson's endorsement, which Jackson withheld until the final weeks of the campaign.

Despite this delay in an endorsement, Jackson allied himself with President Clinton. In 1997, Jackson traveled to Kenya as the president's special envoy to meet with Kenyan President Daniel arap Moi in order to promote free and fair elections in that country. Jackson met with the Clinton family and offered support and advice during the scandal over the president's affair with Monica Lewinsky in 1998. The relationship between Jackson and Clinton became somewhat more difficult in 1999, when Jackson went on his own to Yugoslavia to negotiate the release of three U.S. servicemen who had been captured during the U.S. involvement in fighting in Kosovo. A meeting between Jackson and then Yugoslav president Slobodan Milošević was particularly embarrassing for the Clinton administration. Nevertheless, Jackson continued to have links to President Clinton, who honored the activist with the Presidential Medal of Freedom.

Jackson's relations with Clinton's successor, President George W. Bush, were far less cordial. In the 2000 election, Jackson was highly critical of Republican candidate Bush. After Bush won the presidency in a narrow and controversial election, Jackson joined with others in maintaining that Bush had stolen the election and led rallies and demonstrations against the new Republican administration.

In an echo of the Lewinsky affair, Jackson became embroiled in a personal scandal of his own in 2001. He was reported to have fathered a child in the 1990's with a woman working on his staff and to have used Rainbow Coalition funds to provide payments to the mother. For a short time after this affair was revealed, Jackson limited his public activities. However, following the invasion of Iraq by the United States in 2003, Jackson became an outspoken and widely recognized opponent of the war, speaking at a mass rally against the war in Hyde Park in England.

During the 2004 election, opposition to the war intensified Jackson's efforts to defeat President Bush. At the Democratic National Convention that year, Jackson denounced the war as a moral disgrace. After President Bush was reelected, Jackson became involved in investigating allegations that election procedures in Ohio were biased against mainly Democratic African Americans.

In addition to his efforts in electoral politics, Jackson continued to speak out on highly publicized racial issues. In 2006, he expressed sympathy for an African American woman who accused several Duke University lacrosse players of raping her, and even said that he would pay the woman's college tuition. All charges against the players were later dropped. Jackson accepted an apology from comedian Michael Richards after Richards became infamous at the end of 2006 for using racial insults. In 2007, Jackson was prominent among the African American public figures who criticized radio personality Don Imus after Imus made racially offensive remarks about the women's basketball team of Rutgers University.

Significance

The Civil Rights movement of the 1960's helped secure legislation to ensure and protect basic freedoms for African Americans. Among the most important of these was the right to vote. Jackson played a large part in consolidating this achievement by acting as a voice for African American political aspirations. Both Operation Breadbasket and Operation PUSH resulted in jobs and economic opportunities. As the country moved to the right politically in the 1980's, he continued to use his powerful oratory in the service of liberal causes, broadening and deepening the American political dialogue.

Jackson became a symbol of black political power, perhaps the most widely recognized African American leader since Martin Luther King, Jr. Numerous politicians, including President Clinton, sought his support, providing testimony to the importance of African Americans in the American political process. After the election of President George W. Bush in 2000, Jackson was outspoken in opposition to the Bush administration. Following the American invasion of Iraq, Jackson took a strong antiwar position.

Jackson will perhaps be best remembered for his moral energy and for instilling self-esteem and hope in many disadvantaged people—particularly young people. While working to expand the opportunities available to them, he has exhorted them to make the most of the opportunities they had. In compelling speeches, he has urged young people to avoid drugs and to devote themselves to academic excellence. As a result of his efforts, many have been able to avoid being dragged down by the social and economic forces plaguing the inner cities.

—Carl L. Bankston III

FURTHER READING

Barker, Lucius J., and Ronald W. Walters, eds. *Jesse Jackson's 1984 Presidential Campaign: Challenge and Change in American Politics*. Champaign: University of Illinois Press, 1989. Contains eleven articles that offer an in-depth look at Jackson's first presidential campaign. Describes the political context of the campaign, the mobilization of the black community behind Jackson, his appeal to voters in general, the convention, and the campaign's political and social impact.

Bruns, Roger. *Jesse Jackson: A Biography*. Westport, Conn.: Greenwood, 2005. Illustrated by numerous photographs, this general biography of Jackson presents both positive and negative aspects of the activist's life and career.

Colton, Elizabeth O. *The Jackson Phenomenon: The Man, the Power, the Message*. New York: Doubleday, 1989. A detailed but readable examination of Jackson's second run for the presidency in 1988. Also examines earlier events in his life as background for his role in the election.

Frady, Marshall. *Jesse: The Life and Pilgrimage of Jesse Jackson*. New York: Random House, 1996. A thorough and perceptive biography of Jackson that presents its subject as both an ambitious opportunist and a morally courageous visionary. Frady argues that Jackson's accomplishments have been driven by a loner's need to reinvent himself and that Jackson's slogan, "I am somebody," has always been directed at himself as much as at others.

Haskins, James. *I Am Somebody! A Biography of Jesse Jackson*. Springfield, N.J.: Enslow, 1992. Written primarily for older children and young adults, this biography presents an account of Jackson's life, accomplishments, and goals. Treats the flaws in Jackson's character as well as his strengths. Contains an extensive bibliography.

Hertzke, Allen D. *Echoes of Discontent: Jesse Jackson, Pat Robertson, and the Resurgence of Populism*. Washington, D.C.: Congressional Quarterly Press, 1993. Discusses the role of religion in American politics by comparing the 1988 presidential campaigns of Jesse Jackson and Pat Robertson. Describes the importance of the churches associated with these two candidates and examines how the two brought different types of religious activism into electoral politics. Includes an examination of Jackson's move from leadership of Operation PUSH to political campaigning.

Reynolds, Barbara A. *Jesse Jackson: The Man, the Movement, the Myth.* Chicago: Nelson-Hall, 1975. An early biography of Jackson, covering the period from his childhood to his work as leader of PUSH. Particularly informative on the goals and achievements of PUSH. Also contains an essay by Jackson on how people in low-income minority communities can achieve control over their own economic resources.

Timmerman, Kenneth R. *Shakedown: Exposing the Real Jesse Jackson.* Washington, D.C.: Regnery, 2002. Written by an investigative reporter, this is a highly critical treatment of Jackson's political career. The author claims to provide evidence of Jackson's corruption and ambition. Timmerman maintains that Jackson uses allegations of racism for his personal gain.

Stonewall Jackson

" *Duty is ours; the consequences are God's.* **"**

Military leader

The ablest and most renowned of Robert E. Lee's lieutenants, Jackson led daring marches and employed do-or-die battle tactics that resulted in key victories that helped to sustain the Confederacy through the first two years of the Civil War.

Born: January 21, 1824; Clarksburg, Virginia (now in West Virginia)
Died: May 10, 1863; Guiney's Station, Virginia
Also known as: Thomas Jonathan Jackson (birth name)
Area of achievement: Military

Early Life

Thomas Jonathan Jackson was born in a hilly, heavily forested region of what later became West Virginia that was sparsely populated by the Scotch-Irish settlers who were his forebears. Self-reliance was thrust upon the boy at an early age; the third of four children, he was orphaned by the age of seven. Taken in by an uncle, Cummins Jackson, he grew up in a farm environment in which he acquired numerous practical skills but little schooling. Even as a teenager, however, Jackson clearly demonstrated the traits of physical courage, uncompromising moral integrity, and high ambition serviced by an iron will. Resolved to improve his lot by education, Jackson obtained an appointment to the United States Military Academy at West Point. The shambling young man from the hills cut a poor figure among the generally more sophisticated and better-educated cadets. Yet, impervious to taunts, he earned the respect of his classmates by perseverance and phenomenal concentration, finishing seventeenth in a class of fifty-nine.

Shortly after he was graduated in 1846, Jackson was ordered to Mexico as a second lieutenant of artillery. He took part in the siege of Vera Cruz and distinguished himself in several battles during the advance on Mexico City in the summer of 1847. Jackson's courage and effectiveness brought admiration from his superiors and a rapid succession of promotions; by the end of the war, at the age of twenty-two, he had attained the rank of brevet major. A photograph taken of him at that time shows a man with a trim figure (Jackson stood about five feet ten inches, and weighed about 150 pounds) and a pleasant, earnest face characterized chiefly by the firm set of the mouth and clear, deep-set eyes that gaze out solemnly beneath a prominent brow. (The flowing beard that would give Jackson the appearance of an Old Testament prophet was to come later.)

Assigned to Fort Hamilton, New York, in 1848, Jackson entered the routine existence of a peacetime Army garrison for the next two years. During this time, however, he became more and more deeply involved in religious pursuits. Jackson came to think of his rather frail health, with its persistent digestive disorders, as a visitation of Providence to lead him into more righteous ways. He was baptized, unsure whether he had been as a child, and from that time on, the course of his life was inseparable from his sense of consecration to the will of the Almighty.

Life's Work

In the spring of 1851, an instructor's position at the Virginia Military Institute, founded twelve years earlier on the model of West Point, became available. Jackson was nominated for it, and, bored with his work as a peacetime Army officer, he resigned his commission and reported to Lexington in July, 1851, to take up the duties of a professor of natural philosophy (or, in modern terminology, general science) and artillery tactics for the next nine years.

Not by any account an inspiring teacher, Jackson nevertheless mastered topics in which he had no formal credentials, thereby earning at least the grudging respect of his students. Jackson also came to be regarded as something of an eccentric for his rigid ways and odd personal mannerisms—for example, his habit of frequently raising his left arm, ostensibly to improve circulation, and his silent grimace serving in place of a laugh—which would be remarked on by his troops during the Civil War and give color and distinction to the legend of "Old Jack."

Settled in his new life, Jackson turned his thoughts to marriage. Seeking a wife from the religious community of Lexington, in 1853 he married Eleanor Junkin, the daughter of the Reverend Dr. George Junkin. The union was tragically brief; Eleanor died the next year in childbirth. Two years later and after a summer tour of Europe that restored him from the lethargy of mourning, Jackson courted and married Mary Anna Morrison, the daughter of another clergyman, who would remain his devoted wife until his death and would eventually bear him a daughter.

Life for the Jacksons during the next three years was characterized by affection, tranquillity, and a mutual sense of religious purpose (Jackson was by now a deacon of the Presbyterian Church and maintained a Sunday school for black slaves). The impending events of the Civil War were to bring all that to an end. Although not a champion of either slavery or secession, Jackson felt loyalty deeply rooted to his native soil, and when Virginia seceded from the Union, his course was clear.

In April, 1861, Jackson was commissioned a colonel in the newly formed Confed-

Jackson, Stonewall

erate army and took command at Harpers Ferry. Within three weeks, he distinguished himself by establishing strict military order for the rather undisciplined garrison of raw, untrained soldiers and by capturing a large number of northern locomotives and freight cars for use by the Confederate army.

Some three months later, Jackson earned the sobriquet of "Stonewall" at the Battle of First Manassas (or Bull Run). In this opening major conflict of the war, an army of some thirty-five thousand federal troops under General Irvin McDowell marched south from Washington to crush the rebellion. On July 21, after some preliminary fighting, McDowell made his main attack near Manassas Junction. As the defending Confederates fell back toward Jackson's brigade, which was holding the ridge above Bull Run, General Barnard E. Bee rallied his troops with the cry "Look yonder! There is Jackson and his brigade standing like a stone wall!" Later in the day, it was Jackson's brigade that broke the Union line with a furious bayonet charge, thus halting General McDowell's offensive and forcing a rethinking of strategy in Washington.

With a huge increase in the Union army, the new strategy called for a seaborne assault upon Richmond via the Jamestown Peninsula, led by George McClellan (a classmate of Jackson at West Point) and supported by a secondary force coming down the Shenandoah Valley under the command of Nathaniel Banks. Jackson, now a major general, correctly surmised that a diversion up the Shenandoah Valley would not only neutralize Banks but also threaten Washington and thus divert troops from McClellan's peninsular offensive. Beginning in March, 1862, Jackson led his troops in a succession of battles renowned in military history as the Valley Campaign. Utilizing the tactics of deception, rapid forced marches, and hit-and-run assaults and retreats, Jackson blunted the federal advance down the Shenandoah Valley, alarmed Washington, and consequently stalled McClellan's attack upon Richmond.

Jackson's victories continued to inspire the South and dismay the North during the year 1862. In August, Jackson played the pivotal role in defeating the new Union offensive led by General John Pope at the Second Battle of Manassas. In December, at the Battle of Fredericksburg, he and James Longstreet shared the responsibility for the Confederate victory over the forces of General Ambrose Burnside.

In the spring of 1863, the Union forces, under yet another commander, Joseph "Fighting Joe" Hooker, gathered for a massive offensive upon Richmond. Robert E. Lee, outnumbered two to one, decided to risk his defense on a hazardous division of his forces, with a corps led by Jackson, now a lieutenant general, tasked with flanking Hooker's army. On the evening of May 2, 1863, the unsuspecting Union Eleventh Corps was routed by Jackson's attack some four miles west of Chancellorsville. Darkness brought a lull to the fighting, during which Jackson and a small staff reconnoitered the battlefield to determine a route for a further Confederate advance. Returning to its own lines, however, Jackson's scouting party, in one of the great ironic moments of history, was mistaken for a Union cavalry patrol and fired upon. Hit by several musket balls, Jackson fell, his left arm shattered. Amputation failed to save his life, and on May 10, 1863, he succumbed to pneumonia. His last words uttered in a final, sublime moment of lucidity were, "Let us cross over the river and rest under the shade of the trees."

Jackson, Stonewall

Significance

Jackson's death was a mortal blow to the Confederacy. In subsequent battles in the eastern theater, the absence of his leadership was sorely missed; Lee was to remark later that if he had had Jackson at Gettysburg, he would have won that crucial battle. Beyond such speculation, however, there is no doubt that the loss of such an inspiring leader—by far the most popular commander on either side—seriously undermined Confederate morale.

Jackson's charismatic popularity was the product of both his brilliant generalship and his singular force of character. Merciless in driving his own troops and ruthless in pursuit of his enemy, he nevertheless was admired by both for his legendary courage, integrity, and lack of egotistical motive. Lee venerated his memory, referring to him as "the great and good Jackson."

Jackson's battles (in particular, the Valley Campaign) have been studied as models by successive generations of military students in the United States and Europe. Jackson understood and applied the principles of mass and maneuver as well as any commander in history, concentrating his forces at decisive points against numerically superior but more dispersed opponents. Beyond his significance as a tactical genius, however, "Stonewall" passed early into the realm of national epic, defining an ideal of valor for generations of American youths.

—*Charles Duncan*

Further Reading

Chambers, Lenoir. *Stonewall Jackson.* 2 vols. New York: William Morrow, 1959. Comprehensive, detailed biography. A lucid, graceful writer, Chambers brings admirable clarity and insight to his subject.

Churchill, Winston L. S. *The American Civil War.* New York: Fairfax Press, 1985. A reprint of the chapters on the American Civil War in Churchill's four-volume *A History of the English Speaking Peoples* (1956-1958). In any edition, Churchill's brief history of the Civil War is a masterpiece and focuses especially well on the significance of Jackson's role.

Clark, Champ. *Decoying the Yanks: Jackson's Valley Campaign.* Alexandria, Va.: Time-Life Books, 1984. As the title suggests, primarily a history of Jackson's Shenandoah Valley Campaign in the spring of 1862. Contains, however, a good short biography of Jackson in his early years as well. Lavishly illustrated with contemporary photographs, paintings, and drawings, the book gives a vivid account of the most spectacular achievement of Jackson's generalship.

Farwell, Byron. *Stonewall: A Biography of General Thomas J. Jackson.* New York: W. W. Norton, 1992. Thorough, balanced, and well-written account of Jackson's life.

Henderson, G. F. R. *Stonewall Jackson and the American Civil War.* 2 vols. New York: Longmans, Green, 1898. A classic biography of Jackson. Henderson's thoughtful, elegant study has gone through numerous editions and is still, after more than three-quarters of a century, a valuable resource cited in virtually every work on Jackson that has appeared since its publication.

Robertson, James I., Jr. *Stonewall Jackson: The Man, the Soldier, the Legend.* New

York: Macmillan, 1997. Robertson, a Civil War historian, recounts the details of Jackson's life and military career, depicting his subject as a great military strategist and a man of strong religious faith.

Tate, Allen. *Stonewall Jackson, the Good Soldier.* New York: Minton, Balch, 1928. Reprint. Ann Arbor: University of Michigan Press, 1957. Short biography for the general reader by a leading southern man of letters. Tate's Confederate sympathies date the book but also provide an interesting partisan slant; he excoriates Jefferson Davis for not unleashing Jackson at decisive points that might have turned the tide for the Confederacy.

Vandiver, Frank. *Mighty Stonewall.* New York: McGraw-Hill, 1957. Comprehensive, well-balanced one-volume biography of Jackson by a respected Civil War historian. Vandiver's research is thorough, while his lively, anecdotal presentation brings to life the historical events for the reader.

Wheeler, Richard. *We Knew Stonewall Jackson.* New York: Thomas Y. Crowell, 1977. Extremely useful, well-conceived book of excerpts from contemporary accounts of Jackson linked by the author's commentary. In effect, an economical, accurate, short biography in which the author's sources speak for themselves.

THOMAS JEFFERSON

" *When the people fear their government, there is tyranny; when the government fears the people, there is liberty.* **"**

President of the United States (1801-1809)

A genuine revolutionary, Thomas Jefferson was one of the early and effective leaders of the movement to overthrow British rule in North America. After laboring to create a free, prosperous, enlightened, and agrarian republic, Jefferson served as the third president of the United States.

Born: April 13, 1743; Shadwell, Goochland (now Albemarle) County, Virginia
Died: July 4, 1826; Monticello, Albemarle County, Virginia
Areas of achievement: Government and politics; invention and technology

EARLY LIFE

The man generally considered the first thoroughgoing democrat in U.S. history began life as a Virginia aristocrat. His father, Peter Jefferson, had indeed come from yeoman stock but commended himself to the upper class as an expert surveyor, reliable county officer, and energetic planter. The elder Jefferson then joined that upper class by marrying Jane Randolph. From his parents, Thomas Jefferson inherited wealth, status, and a tradition of public service.

Educated at first in private schools kept by Anglican clergymen William Douglas and James Maury, Jefferson descended to Williamsburg in 1760 to study at the College of William and Mary. A proficient student, he completed the requirements for his degree within two years but stayed on to read law with George Wythe, an uncommonly learned and humane jurist. In his student years, Jefferson was frequently a guest, along with his favorite professor, William Small, and Wythe, in the governor's palace. Admitted to the bar in 1767, the young bachelor attorney became acquainted with all of Virginia by the strenuous but interesting practice of attending the quarter sessions of county courts. Jefferson soon stood among the leaders of his profession.

Entering the House of Burgesses in 1769, Jefferson already owned more than 2,500 acres inherited from his father, who had died in 1757. His marriage to the young widow Martha Wayles Skelton doubled his property in 1772, and the death of Martha's father in 1774 doubled it again, while increasing his slaves to more than two hundred. The Wayles inheritance also brought a large indebtedness, but in 1774, Jefferson might count himself the most fortunate of men, with a lovely wife and a robust baby daughter, a personal fortune, and a position near the top of Virginia's society and politics. He was imposing in appearance, standing more than six feet tall, with plentiful red hair, strong features, and an attitude of vitality and interest. Yet he was also shy and avoided public appearances whenever he could; he was at his very best in the cordial intimacy of the drawing room or the dining table.

Life's Work

In 1774, Virginia chose to support Massachusetts against the assaults of the Coercive (or Intolerable) Acts. To that support, Jefferson contributed the first of his major political writings, *A Summary View of the Rights of British America* (1774). In 1775, he was a delegate of Virginia in the Continental Congress in Philadelphia, supporting George Washington's newly formed Continental army in the defense of Massachusetts. Here, for a few months, Jefferson's sentiments were too radical for the majority, but when independence seemed all but inevitable in June, 1776, Congress placed him (with Benjamin Franklin and John Adams) on the special committee to draft a declaration of independence. Though slightly amended in committee and again on the floor of Congress, the Declaration of Independence is largely Jefferson's work.

For the next several years, Jefferson avoided continental service, preferring the considerable scene of action near his growing family and estate. With Wythe and Edmund Pendleton he drew up a new legal code for the state. He also prepared a plan for the gradual ending of slavery but declined to bring it before the House of Delegates. He also postponed his plans for a general scheme of education and for the separation of church and state. Elected governor in 1779, he found that office an ordeal. To the minor confusion of moving government from Williamsburg to Richmond was added the major trauma of a full-scale British military invasion of his state. Just before Jefferson's second term ended in June, 1781, he had to flee into the Blue Ridge Mountains to escape a raiding party sent to Monticello expressly to capture him.

Already discouraged by his last months as governor, Jefferson was cast into the deepest depression of his life by his wife's death in 1782. He never remarried, but he did accept reappointment to Congress, where, in 1783 and 1784, he worked on the monetary system of the United States, basing it on the plentiful Spanish dollar and applying the rational decimal system to fractional coins. He also drafted a comprehensive scheme for organizing the western territories of the United States. He introduced the idea of rectangular surveys and proposed local self-government from the start. His division of the terrain into eighteen jurisdictions, while convenient for the participatory democracy he had in view, would have long delayed statehood for any of them. A provision barring the introduction of slavery after 1800 failed to win the support of the nine states required under the Articles of Confederation, but Congress did adopt Jefferson's plan, replacing it instead with the Land Ordinance of 1785 and the Northwest Ordinance of 1787. Meanwhile, Jefferson had accepted a diplomatic mission to France; in 1785, he replaced the aged Benjamin Franklin as minister.

The five years in Europe were busy and happy. A tour of France and northern Italy confirmed Jefferson's architectural taste and enlarged his knowledge of agriculture. He flirted with an artistic Englishwoman, Maria Cosway, and enjoyed visiting John Adams in England, though he did not care for English society in general. By mail he kept up with the movement to disestablish religion in Virginia, where his own bill was finally passed under the expert guidance of James Madison. He also encouraged Madison and other correspondents in their drive toward a new federal constitution. In France, he sought help against the Barbary pirates and urged France to remove prohibitions or costly restrictions on such American commodities as tobacco and whale oil. His closest friends were liberal aristocrats such as the Marquis de Lafayette, whose leading role in the early stages of the French Revolution Jefferson followed with interest and encouragement.

Intending a brief visit only, Jefferson returned to the United States at the end of 1789, but he promptly accepted the post of secretary of state from President Washington. After settling his two daughters in Virginia, he took up his duties in the temporary capital, New York City. There he helped bring about the trade of votes that made possible Alexander Hamilton's federal assumption of state Revolutionary War debts and the permanent location of the Federal District on the Potomac River. The government then moved, temporarily, to Philadelphia.

In 1791, Jefferson and Madison began to organize the first opposition party under the new Constitution. Their avowed object was to overturn not Washington but his secretary of the treasury, Hamilton. Washington almost always sided with Hamilton against his rivals, however, so it was really a case of going against a popular president by forcing him to fire a considerably less popular minister and change his policies. Vigorously protesting Hamilton's Bank of the United States and his avowed intention to reach a friendly understanding with Great Britain, Jefferson and his growing party accused Hamilton of secret designs to reestablish aristocracy, monarchy, and even return the United States to the British Empire.

In the spring of 1793, Jefferson opposed Washington's Neutrality Proclamation and initially supported the representative of the new French republic, Edmond Charles Genet. Genet, however, far overreached Jefferson's idea of propriety by licensing privateers to prey on British shipping, setting up prize courts in American seaports and raising an army based in Kentucky to attack Spanish Louisiana. Jefferson had the unpleasant task of opposing all this, while trying to contain the zeal of the many new democratic societies that were supporting Genet. This crisis passed when Genet's group fell from power in France, and, after a harrowing yellow fever epidemic paralyzed the American government in the late summer, Jefferson returned to present Congress with his report

Jefferson, Thomas

on the foreign commerce of the United States. He then resigned and spent three years improving his estate and carrying on a lively exchange of letters with his political friends.

The odd workings of the original electoral system made Jefferson vice president in 1797, after he had finished a close second behind his now-estranged rival, John Adams, in the contest for president. Discreet in public, he acted behind the scenes to stiffen resistance to Adams and his Federalist majorities in Congress during the undeclared naval war with France. Jefferson wrote the Kentucky Resolutions against the partisan Alien and Sedition Acts of 1798; his friend John Breckinridge steered them through the Kentucky legislature. The resolutions contained the extreme doctrine that a state might nullify an act of Congress; the effect, however, was to let off steam until the Federalists and their acts passed from the scene.

Fearful that Adams might sneak in for a second term, every Jeffersonian elector cast one ballot for Jefferson and another for Aaron Burr of New York in the election of 1800. This produced a tie, unintended by the mass of voters, and threw the election into the lame-duck Congress that had been elected in 1798. Enough Federalist congressmen preferred Burr to Jefferson to produce a stalemate for several weeks, but Jefferson finally prevailed; Burr, as vice president, found Jefferson depriving him of federal patronage and Governor George Clinton depriving him of influence in New York. Burr thus began on the course that led to his seeking Federalist support for his political comeback, which in turn produced the famous duel, fatal to Alexander Hamilton, and finally the adventures in the West that led Jefferson to arrest Burr and try him for treason.

Jefferson's first term in office was one of the most popular and successful in the history of the presidency. After many a bad turn, Washington and Adams had secured peace with all the major foreign powers and all the American Indian tribes capable of threatening America's frontiers. By cordially maintaining these arrangements—even with Britain—Jefferson presided over four years of peaceful and prosperous expansion. Yet he proved to be different from his predecessors. With the expert help of Albert Gallatin, secretary of the treasury, and James Madison, secretary of state, he greatly reduced the army, the navy, and the foreign diplomatic corps. His congressional majorities reduced the federal judiciary and repealed the unpopular excises, including the tax on distillations that had set off the Whiskey Rebellion in 1794. The Twelfth Amendment to the Constitution ended forever the confusion of presidential and vice presidential votes.

Jefferson did incur the expense of sending several ships to the Mediterranean, where various North African states were holding American sailors for ransom and demanding tribute that Federalist presidents, and various European governments, had customarily paid. Even in this, Jefferson hoped to save money in the long run, by putting a stop to criminal behavior that, he believed, civilized nations should never have tolerated in the first place.

In private life several years later, but hardly in retirement, Jefferson maintained an extensive political and philosophical correspondence, especially with John Adams, the two now fully reconciled. He also labored long and finally successfully to establish the University of Virginia in nearby Charlottesville. Jefferson and Adams both died on July 4, 1826, while their fellow citizens were celebrating the fiftieth anniversary of the Declaration of Independence.

Jefferson, Thomas

Significance

Thomas Jefferson was brilliant, versatile, energetic, and creative, but he was neither original nor systematic. He contributed no great books to the American tradition, but rather a number of ringing phrases about natural rights, the impositions of tyrants, the virtue of the people, and the beneficence of free inquiry. With Abraham Lincoln, he is the most quotable American public figure, and every conceivable political view has been bolstered by his maxims. Jefferson further helped this trend by being inconsistent in such important areas as the power of the national government, the proper treatment of dissenters, and the crucial question of slavery.

Yet he was perfectly consistent on many points. A true son of the Enlightenment, he believed that scientific study and education would cure the ills of humankind, and he rejected as superstitious all those parts of religion that dwelt on mysterious or miraculous interventions in human affairs. He detested the very idea of inherited power or status and believed that differences among races and national groups were the result of environment. He always believed that government should be kept to a minimum, that standing armies were not republican, and that the true strength of a people resided in the widest possible distribution of virtue, learning, and property, not in armies, national treasuries, or government agencies.

Early in life, he had supposed that the United States might not extend beyond the Appalachians, for he still shared the classical view that republics must be small. By the time he had retired from the presidency, however, he had conceived that all North America might be "an Empire for Liberty."

—*Robert McColley*

Further Reading

Boorstin, Daniel J. *The Lost World of Thomas Jefferson.* New York: Henry Holt, 1948. This is still the best introduction to the place of Thomas Jefferson in the American Enlightenment, written by a well-known American historian.

Ellis, Joseph J. *American Sphinx: The Character of Thomas Jefferson.* New York: Alfred A. Knopf, 1996. Ellis focuses on Jefferson's character to find the "real man" beneath the American icon. He portrays Jefferson as complex and sometimes devious.

Ferling, John E. *Adams vs. Jefferson: The Tumultuous Election of 1800.* New York: Oxford University Press, 2004. Ferling describes how the "contest of titans" between Jefferson and Adams marked a turning point in American history, with Adams's Federalists and Jefferson's Republicans battling over two different ideas of how the new nation should be governed.

Jefferson, Thomas. *The Papers of Thomas Jefferson.* Edited by Julian P. Boyd. 31 vols. Princeton, N.J.: Princeton University Press, 1950-2004. A splendid edition of Jefferson's writings.

Levy, Leonard. *Jefferson and Civil Liberties: The Darker Side.* Cambridge, Mass.: Belknap Press, 1963. Levy maintains that, despite his advanced preaching about civil liberties, Jefferson acted very much the same as his contemporaries.

McCoy, Drew R. *The Elusive Republic.* Chapel Hill: University of North Carolina Press, 1980. An introduction to Jefferson's republican ideology and his special

concern with economic policy as an expression of republicanism.
Malone, Dumas. *Jefferson and His Time*. 6 vols. Boston: Little, Brown, 1948-1981. Malone's work, by a considerable margin, is the longest and richest of the biographies.
Miller, John Chester. *The Wolf by the Ears*. New York: Oxford University Press, 1977. A balanced and thorough review of Jefferson's thoughts and actions regarding African American slavery.
Sheldon, Garrett Ward. *The Political Philosophy of Thomas Jefferson*. Baltimore: Johns Hopkins University Press, 1991. Sheldon describes Jefferson's views on democracy, federalism, freedom, slavery, and other political issues, placing these ideas within the context of his Virginia gentry class.
Wills, Garry. *Inventing America: Jefferson's Declaration of Independence*. Boston: Houghton Mifflin, 2002. Wills contrasts Jefferson's original draft of the declaration with the final accepted version. Wills argues that, contrary to conventional assumptions, Jefferson was not a champion of individual rights but a believer in the interdependence of individuals within society.

STEVE JOBS

" *Be a yardstick of quality. Some people aren't used to an environment where excellence is expected.* "

Computer developer and entrepreneur

As cofounder of Apple Computer, Jobs was critical to the development of the personal computer industry. Apple has had a profound impact on the consumer electronics industry and on culture itself with the introduction of the iPod, iTunes, and iPhone in the early years of the twenty-first century.

Born: February 24, 1955; San Francisco, California
Also known as: Steven Paul Jobs (full name)
Areas of achievement: Computer science; business; invention and technology; telecommunications

EARLY LIFE

Steve Jobs (jawbz) was born to an unwed mother and, in accordance with the mores of the 1950's, was adopted shortly after his birth. Paul and Clara Jobs, a middle-class couple who had tried unsuccessfully for a decade to have children, brought him into their home. Although Jobs would later search for his birth mother and discover that he had a sister, novelist Mona Simpson, he always sharply chastised people who sought to diminish the role of his adoptive parents, insisting that *they were* his parents.

When Jobs was ten years old, his family moved to Mountain View, one of the new so-called bedroom communities flourishing as a result of the manufacturing boom for semiconductors in the Santa Clara Valley in Northern California. The boom was ignited

Jobs, Steve

by the success of the company Fairchild Semiconductor. In Mountain View, Jobs played with the children of engineers and other technology-oriented people. However, he did not immediately show a technical bent. His formidable energies and intellect seemed mostly directed toward mischief until his fourth-grade teacher managed to kindle a love of learning in a boy who had previously been spinning his wheels mentally.

Jobs exercised his strong will when his middle school turned out to be inadequate as a school, simply refusing to return to it the next term. Rather than watch their son become a juvenile delinquent, his parents moved so that Jobs could enroll in a different school district. His new next-door neighbor was Steve Wozniak, another brilliant youth who often turned his skills to annoying adult authority with irreverent pranks. Jobs and Wozniak also became involved in selling blue boxes, devices used to spoof telephone switching systems and gain free calls. Wozniak did the technical work while Jobs handled sales. However, when one deal went wrong and they were nearly killed, they decided the old adage about no honor among thieves was true, and that it was best to get out of the illegal business.

Shortly after finishing college, Jobs went to India seeking spiritual enlightenment. He exchanged his Western clothes for the clothes of a pilgrim and traveled as a mendicant in search of various sages. By the end of his quest, however, he decided that Thomas Edison had done more to help humanity than all the spiritual leaders put together. However, he never repudiated his trip to India as the foolishness of youth and later said that Microsoft founder Bill Gates probably would have been a "broader" person had he, too, spent time in an ashram, or religious retreat.

LIFE'S WORK

On his return from India, Jobs went to work for Atari and picked up his old friendship with Wozniak. Atari was interested in developing a new video game, and Jobs got Wozniak to do the programming. *Breakout* became an enormous hit and spawned thousands of variants. At this time the two were also active in the Homebrew Computer Club, a hobbyist group in the Silicon Valley (the Santa Clara Valley). Recognizing the success of console gaming systems, Jobs decided the market might be ready for a true personal computer.

At the time, computers were either giant mainframes owned by corporations or hobbyist kits such as the Altair, of interest primarily to computer buffs. Jobs, however, imagined a small computer that ordinary people could use for practical things. To succeed, the computer would have to get around common fears of high technology. Hence, Jobs chose the name Apple, a word evoking nature and approachability rather than machinery and technical savvy, as the name of his new computer.

The original Apple, dubbed Apple I, was first sold in 1976 as a kit through the Byte Shop, a Silicon Valley hangout for the "geek" crowd. Although only a few hundred of these first Apples were made, they provided the seed money for Apple to produce a true personal computer. They would later become collectors' items. The Apple II, introduced in 1977, was encased in a warm, tan-colored "box" with rounded lines. At a time when Commodore and other competitors in the new computer industry still relied upon cassette tapes to store data, the Apple had a floppy disk drive. The video circuitry and monitor could support color graphics, another unique feature.

Jobs, Steve

The Apple and its various successors made the young Jobs-Wozniak company, Apple Computer, a leader in personal computer technology, and it made the two entrepreneurs unimaginably wealthy. Jobs, though, refused to stop innovating, particularly after International Business Machines (IBM) entered the personal computer (PC) market in 1981. IBM PC's, however, still required the memorization of arcane user commands, and one mistyped letter could destroy hours of work. For the computer to become a part of everyday life, Jobs believed, the computer would have to become an appliance of sorts, requiring no more understanding of its inner workings than the common knowledge of the inner working of, say, a refrigerator.

Jobs recalled his visit to Xerox Corporation's Palo Alto Research Center (Xerox PARC), where he had seen a computer that used pictures to represent files and a movable pointing device called a mouse. Xerox did not know how to market such a computer, but Jobs believed he could make one inexpensively enough for anyone to afford.

In 1984, an extraordinary television advertisement announced the coming of the Apple Macintosh. On January 24 the Macintosh was unveiled at Apple's annual meeting. After initial consumer enthusiasm for this friendly new computer, sales began to slump because of the system's high price and because of a lack of available software. Furthermore, interpersonal conflicts were damaging Jobs's position at the company he had helped create. His charisma simply could not overcome his stormy temperament, which put him at odds with John Sculley, the person Jobs had brought from Pepsico to

Steve Jobs and the Apple iPhone, 2007. (AP/Wide World Photos)

run his business. By the middle of 1985, Jobs was eased out of his own company.

After some initial floundering, Jobs went on to found a new company, NeXT. However, the market for high-end graphics workstations simply was not sufficiently developed for his hardware to succeed, and after years of struggling he finally had to close down the hardware side and concentrate on Nextstep, his UNIX-based operating system (OS).

Jobs had more success with Pixar, a graphics company set up to do computer animation for companies such as Disney. Pixar, which Jobs bought in 1986, came very close to failing when Disney executives disliked the first version of the animated film *Toy Story* (1995). Only careful rewriting to make the protagonist more sympathetic saved the project, and Pixar.

By the middle of the 1990's, Jobs was finally enjoying real success. Pixar had established itself as a leader in computer animation, and Nextstep had become a serious competitor for Windows and other server and workstation OS's. However, Apple was in trouble as a company. A series of uninspired company chief executive officers (CEOs) had left Apple with an ever-dwindling market share of what had been diehard loyalists, and more than a few pundits speculated that Apple could close its doors altogether, leaving the PC industry to Gates and Microsoft.

In 1997, Apple rehired Jobs as CEO through a complex deal that involved buying NeXT to gain access to the Nextstep OS. Apple wanted to use this OS as the foundation of a modern OS for its Macs, one that would replace the increasingly antiquated classic Mac OS. Jobs immediately made major changes at Apple, terminating a number of floundering products and simplifying Apple's product line. He also worked out a joint venture with Gates that saved Apple and protected Microsoft from allegations of monopolistic business practices. Jobs then introduced the iMac, causing a furor among users because of its lack of compatibility with older hardware.

Jobs introduced a product in 2001 that turned Apple from a struggling computer company to a multimedia powerhouse. That product was the iPod, with its various versions. In 2003, Apple launched the Apple iTunes Music Store, which sold individual songs for download on the World Wide Web. Apple believed that most people were honest and would pay for their digital music if they had a means to do so. The unveiling of a new product line by Jobs led to Apple Computer changing its name in 2007 to Apple Inc. to reflect its expanded focus on the consumer electronics market. Also in 2007, Apple introduced the widely anticipated iPhone and iTouch.

In 2004, Jobs had faced a serious health crisis when he was diagnosed with pancreatic cancer. Fortunately, it was a relatively rare and nonaggressive form that responded to surgery. He resumed his duties as Apple CEO shortly after surgery.

SIGNIFICANCE

Jobs has had a profound and transforming influence upon the computer and consumer electronics industries. The Apple was the first true personal computer, a desktop machine with which ordinary people could do useful, everyday work. The Macintosh introduced what came to be called the graphical user interface (GUI), although Microsoft's Windows OS, also using a GUI, would capture most of the PC market.

—Leigh Husband Kimmel

Further Reading

Carlton, Jim. *Apple: The Inside Story of Intrigue, Egomania, and Business Blunders.* New York: Random House, 1997. A corporate history of Apple, from its foundation by Jobs and Wozniak to Jobs's return in the late 1990's.

Malone, Michael S. *Infinite Loop: How Apple, the World's Most Insanely Great Computer Company, Went Insane.* New York: Doubleday, 1999. A company history that includes a great deal of information on the corporate politics that surrounded Jobs during the time shortly before he was pushed out of the company. Also discusses his return.

Yost, Jeffrey R. *The Computer Industry.* Westport, Conn.: Greenwood Press, 2005. An account of how computer use spread from small groups of elite scientists, engineers, and hobbyists into widespread application in the United States. Explores the ways in which computers have transformed corporate environments and entire industries and examines the role of computer pioneers in a wider social context.

Young, Jeffrey S., and William L. Simon. *iCon: Steve Jobs, the Greatest Second Act in the History of Business.* Hoboken, N.J.: Wiley, 2005. A detailed biography of Jobs, sharply critical of his more outrageous exploits. This book, and all others by Wiley, is banned from Apple stores.

Bobby Jones

" Competitive golf is played mainly on a five-and-a-half-inch course . . . the space between your ears. "

Golfer and businessman

Jones climaxed his career in amateur golf in 1930 by winning in a single year the Grand Slam, the four major American and British open and amateur championships, an achievement still unmatched by the early twenty-first century. He went on to found the Augusta National Golf Club and the Masters Tournament.

Born: March 17, 1902; Atlanta, Georgia
Died: December 18, 1971; Atlanta, Georgia
Also known as: Robert Tyre Jones, Jr. (full name)
Area of achievement: Sports

Early Life

Bobby Jones, who was named for his grandfather, was the son of Robert Purmetus and Clara Thomas Jones. He received his early education at Woodbury School and Tech High School in Atlanta. He later took a degree in mechanical engineering at the Georgia Institute of Technology in 1922 and one in English literature at Harvard in 1924. He also attended Emory University Law School between 1926 and 1927 and was admitted to the Georgia bar in 1928.

Jones's golfing career began at the age of five, when he played with clubs (which

Jones, Bobby

Bobby Jones.
(Library of Congress)

had been cut down for his size) over a five-hole "course" that he and a neighbor boy had laid out in his front yard. Jones's father decided at that time to move from the city to the town of East Lake, where the Jones family lived on the fringes of the East Lake Country Club. Young Jones was not a robust youngster, because of a digestive problem that kept him from eating properly, and it was thought that living in the suburbs would be good for his health.

Jones learned the game by imitating the swing of Stewart Maiden, who came to the job of head professional at East Lake from Carnoustie, Scotland. Jones was six years old at the time. Maiden was never to give Jones a formal lesson, but in the years ahead he would coach him informally; he was the only teacher Jones would ever have.

At the age of seven, Jones was given permission to play at East Lake on any day but Saturday or Sunday. He did so after school in the afternoon, often taking a capful of balls to practice at the thirteenth green, which was located just behind his house. Jones's first tournament victory came at the age of nine, in 1911, when he won the junior championship cup of the Atlanta Athletic Club. At the age of thirteen, Jones won, among other titles, the club championships of both East Lake and the Druid Hills Country Club.

LIFE'S WORK

In 1916, then the Georgia Amateur tournament champion, Jones played in his first national championship, the United States Amateur, in which he was a quarterfinalist. Thus began a fourteen-year career on a national and international level that was to end in 1930 with the Grand Slam, a sweep of the four major American and British open and amateur championships.

Jones was an amateur golfer who achieved his success mostly during the years when he was a university student. For most of the years in which he played competitively, he was in school. Jones experienced a limited tournament schedule, an average of less than four tournaments per year. The greatest number of tournaments he ever played in a single year was eight, in 1920, when he was eighteen. Later, as a young attorney and father (following his marriage in 1924 to Mary Malone and the subsequent births of their three children), his family and his law practice would take precedence.

Although Jones came immediately into the public eye as a fourteen-year-old at his first United States Amateur, he was not an immediate winner on the national scene. For seven years, Jones was without a national title, although he won such tournaments as the Southern Amateur and other regional events. During that time, he was the runner-up in the United States Amateur (1919) at the age of seventeen, and semifinalist in that event in both 1920 and 1922. In 1920, Jones had his initial experience in a national open championship when he played in the United States Open; his first British Open followed in 1921. In his first United States Open at the Inverness Club in Toledo, Ohio, he tied for eighth place. His first tournaments in England were not happy ones. After being eliminated in the fourth round of the British Amateur at the Royal Liverpool Golf Club at Hoylake, Jones entered the British Open at the Old Course of St. Andrews in Scotland. For years, Jones had had a violent temper that led him to throw clubs following errant shots. In time, he curbed that tendency, but at St. Andrews, he withdrew after the eleventh hole after having played the first nine in forty-six shots, taking a double-bogey six at the tenth and missing his first putt after being in a sand bunker at the eleventh. Jones hated St. Andrews, even though it is conceded to be the founding place of the game, but later came to regard the Old Course as his favorite.

Jones's period of dominance in the game finally began two years later, in 1923, when he won the United States Open at the age of twenty-one. Jones and Bobby Cruickshank tied over the seventy-two holes of the championship with a score of 296. Jones won the play-off with a score of seventy-six to Cruickshank's seventy-eight.

Starting in that year, Jones held one or more major titles every year for eight years, for a total of thirteen. His championships included the United States Amateur title in 1924, 1925, 1927, 1928, and 1930; the United States Open title in 1923, 1926, 1929, and 1930; the British Open title in 1926, 1927, and 1930; and the British Amateur title in 1930.

Jones's dominance from 1923 to 1930 was such that he either won or tied for the lead in six of eight United States Opens, finishing second and eleventh in his other two tries. In the United States Amateur, Jones won five of the seven he entered, losing once in the finals and once in the first round. He won all three British Opens in which he played during those years, having failed to win only in his first one, from which he withdrew. The British Amateur was the most difficult, as he was victorious in only one of three. During those eight years, Jones won seventeen of the twenty-eight tournaments he entered and was second six times. In addition, Jones played in the Walker Cup competition, held between the leading amateurs of the United States and Great Britain, a total of five times. The American side was victorious in each instance, and Jones was a hero.

Jones was not an imposing physical specimen, standing only five feet eight inches tall and weighing about 165 pounds at the time he was accomplishing his greatest golfing feats. His clean-cut, boyish appearance had much to do with his almost unparalleled popularity as a 1920's sports figure.

In 1930, Jones finished second in his first tournament of the year, the Savannah Open. He won the other six in which he played, the Southeastern Open, the *Golf Illustrated* Gold Vase, the British Amateur, the British Open, the United States Open, and the United States Amateur. Ironically, he won the British Amateur title on the same St. Andrews course on which he had withdrawn in disgust. (He had also set the British Open record at St. Andrews, where he won that tournament with a seven-under-par 285 in 1927.) Jones's victim in the final match of the British Amateur in 1930 was Roger Wethered, the 1923 British Amateur champion, who was closed out on the thirtieth hole, seven and six. In the British Open at Hoylake, Jones's four-round score of 70-72-74-75-291 was two strokes better than that of Leo Diegel and Macdonald Smith, who shared second place. In the United States Open at Interlachen Country Club in Minneapolis, Smith was again second as Jones won with 71-73-68-75-287, one under par. Jones thus became the first man in history to break par in the United States Open. In the United States Amateur at Merion Cricket Club in Philadelphia, Jones never had to play the last four holes in any of his matches, and he defeated Eugene V. Homans, eight and seven, in the championship finale.

It was fitting that Jones should win what was to be his final tournament of serious competition at Merion, the same club where he had begun his national championship career at the age of fourteen. He also won his first United States Amateur title on that course.

On November 18, 1930, Jones announced his retirement from tournament golf with a letter to the United States Golf Association, surrendering at the same time his amateur status so that he could earn money from the fame he had won on the golf course. Not mentioned by Jones in the letter was the fact that tournament golf was taking its toll on him. Although his demeanor before tournament galleries was outwardly calm, inside he was extremely nervous. He would be sick to the point of vomiting on occasion and would lose as much as eighteen pounds during a tournament.

After retirement, Jones made a series of instructional films seen by an estimated twenty-five million people. He designed the first set of iron golf clubs to be numbered and sold as a matched set for A. G. Spalding and Brothers. Jones wrote newspaper and magazine articles and narrated an instructional series for radio. He also worked for his father's law firm, concentrating on business contracts.

In July, 1931, Jones and Clifford Roberts, a New York City investment broker, announced plans to build the Augusta National Golf Club at Augusta, Georgia. The club opened in the spring of 1933. Building the course was the culmination of Jones's desire to design a course of his own, which he did, with the help of golf architect Alister Mackenzie.

Also in that spring, it was suggested that the Augusta National be the site of the United States Open. When it was decided not to offer the course for the open, Roberts suggested that the club hold its own invitational tournament. Roberts, from the beginning, thought that the event should be called the Masters Tournament. Jones disagreed, believing such a title presumptuous. Instead, the event was officially called the Augusta National Invitation Tournament. By 1938, even Jones had agreed, long after the press, that the tournament was the Masters.

Jones was prevailed on by Roberts to play in the new Masters Tournament, but Jones was never a threat to win it. His best finish, in fact, was in the inaugural 1934 event, when he played the four rounds in 76-74-72-72-294, good enough to tie for thirteenth place.

From that beginning, the Augusta National Golf Club grew in reputation, while the Masters became one of the four tournaments considered the modern Grand Slam, along with the United States and British opens and the American Professional Golfers Association Championship.

Jones continued to play in the Masters through the 1948 tournament. After a back operation, undertaken that same year to correct an injury thought to have occurred in his youth, Jones announced in advance of the 1949 tournament that he would no longer take part.

For a time, it was rumored that the increasing deterioration of Jones's health was because either the 1948 operation or another in 1950 was not a complete success. It was not until 1956 that it was discovered that Jones was suffering from an extremely rare disease called syringomyelia, which attacked Jones's central nervous system and damaged it to such an extent that he could no longer turn the pages of a book. He died of an aneurysm, on December 18, 1971.

SIGNIFICANCE

Perhaps the most striking aspect of Jones's unparalleled success as a golfer was the fact that he accomplished it with apparent ease. Jones spent an average of only three months a year playing golf, for he regarded his family and his legal profession as having greater priority in his life than golf. Yet his technique was exceptional: Jones's golf swing was smooth and effortless, and he could drive a golf ball farther than the great majority of his opponents; his secret was his superb timing. As a result, he was able to distinguish himself with the record of having won four major tournaments in a single year, in 1930.

Jones may also serve as an inspiration to young golfers for his character. Although he had his struggle with a great temper early in his career, Jones overcame it and never appeared unnerved during a tournament. Jones was consistently considerate of both his opponents and the onlookers. Yet his inward turmoil, perhaps a result of the fierce concentration needed to perform as a golfer, took its toll and was a major contributing factor in his retirement from competition at the age of twenty-eight.

Jones contributed to golf and American sports with works other than his exquisite swing. He wrote four books on golf: *Down the Fairway* (1927), *Golf Is My Game* (1960), *Bobby Jones on Golf* (1966), and *Bobby Jones on the Basic Golf Swing* (1969). The last two had to be authored by dictation because of his ailment.

Jones, Bobby

Sometime before his death, it was made known to Jones that some individuals were considering the erection of a monument to him on the grounds of the Augusta National Golf Club. Ever modest, he immediately vetoed the idea; he said that the club itself would be monument enough. Indeed, the Augusta National Golf Club has become perhaps the best-known modern course in the world, and its tournament, the Masters, one of the four most important events in the life of professional golfers every year. The Augusta National is truly a fitting and lasting tribute to Jones.

—*Al Ludwick*

FURTHER READING

Frost, Mark. *The Grand Slam: Bobby Jones, America, and the Story of Golf.* New York: Hyperion, 2005. One of the better books published in honor of the seventy-fifth anniversary of Jones's Grand Slam victories in 1930. Focuses on the Grand Slam, while providing other details of Jones's life and career.

Keeler, Oscar Bane. *The Bobby Jones Story.* Edited by Grantland Rice. Atlanta, Ga.: Tupper and Love, 1953. A complete account of Jones's golfing career.

Matthew, Sidney L. *Bobby: The Life and Times of Bobby Jones.* Reprint. Ann Arbor, Mich.: Sports Media, 2005. A biography of Jones, placing him in the context of his times. Author Matthew has written several books on Jones.

Price, Charles. *A Golf Story: Bobby Jones, Augusta National, and the Masters Tournament.* New York: Atheneum, 1986. The story of Jones's golfing career and his involvement in the founding of the Augusta National Golf Club and the Masters Tournament.

Rapoport, Ron. *The Immortal Bobby: Bobby Jones and the Golden Age of Golf.* Hoboken, N.J.: J. Wiley and Sons, 2005. A critically well-received, exhaustively researched, and comprehensive biography written by a sports columnist for the *Chicago Sun Times.*

Roberts, Clifford. *The Story of the Augusta National Golf Club.* Garden City, N.Y.: Doubleday, 1976. A history of the Augusta National Golf Club, Jones's involvement with the club, the club's members, and President Dwight D. Eisenhower's connections with the club.

Taylor, Dawson. *The Masters.* Cranbury, N.J.: A. S. Barnes, 1973. A concise history of the Masters Tournament and its founding, with a year-to-year listing of the top twenty-four finishers and ties in the event, including a brief account of each tournament.

Wind, Herbert Warren. *The Story of American Golf: Its Champions and Its Championships.* New York: Farrar, Straus, 1948. A comprehensive history of golf in the United States with chapters devoted to Jones's career and the atmosphere in which his feats were accomplished.

JOHN PAUL JONES

> *I can take no delight in the effusion of human blood; but, if this war should continue, I wish to have the most active part in it.*

Admiral and military leader

Known in his own time for his daring raids on British territory and spectacular engagements with British vessels during the American Revolutionary War, Jones is now widely regarded as the founder of the U.S. Navy.

Born: July 6, 1747; Arbigland Estate, Kirkbean, Kirkcudbrightshire, Scotland
Died: July 18, 1792; Paris, France
Also known as: John Paul (birth name)
Area of achievement: Military

EARLY LIFE

John Paul Jones, born John Paul, took the surname "Jones" as an adult. He was the fifth child of an estate gardener and a housekeeper. Growing up in Galloway, near Solway Firth, he evinced an early interest in the sea. At a very early age, he was apprenticed as ship's boy for merchant trading in the West Indies and the American colonies. Over the next several years, he learned navigation, improved his speech and writing, and learned gentleman's manners. On stopovers in Virginia, he stayed with his elder brother William, a tailor in Fredericksburg, and developed an abiding attachment to America. At age seventeen, he shipped for a time on slavers, but, by 1768, he was master of a merchant brig. Two years later, he became a Freemason in Kirkcudbright, and, in 1772, he was commander and part owner of a large merchant vessel sailing from London (where he then lived) to the West Indies. By the time he was twenty-five, he had made £2,500 and wrote often of his desire to become a gentleman farmer in Virginia.

Jones was somewhat below average height (five feet five inches), had hazel eyes, sandy brown hair, high cheekbones, a sharp nose, and a cleft chin. He dressed well, read good literature, and developed a fairly elaborate writing style, also composing poetry; from an early age, he showed a determination to rise both economically and socially. Without money or family connections in an age when both were usually necessary for advancement, he achieved much, despite obstacles and opposition, by dint of hard work and ability. Yet his own character was also sometimes a handicap: He had a violent temper; he took offense easily, incessantly bombarded others with complaints and unsolicited advice; and he was a perfectionist and an egotist.

In Tobago in October, 1773, during an altercation with his crew, John Paul (apparently accidentally) killed the ringleader; fearing a trial by a jury of the crew's friends, he fled with only £50. About the following twenty months, there is little real information available about him; by late 1775, he was in America, had used the name John Jones, and had met some influential North Carolina and Virginia politicians. He was unemployed, and the battles at Lexington and Concord made it impossible for him to access his funds in Tobago. So, on December 7, 1775, John Paul Jones was commissioned a first lieutenant in the Continental navy and assigned to the ship *Alfred.*

LIFE'S WORK

The *Alfred* was part of the Continental navy's five-ship fleet, which, on its first cruise, captured some cannon and powder at Nassau in the Bahamas, and damaged HMS *Glasgow.* On August 8, 1776, John Paul Jones was commissioned a captain and given command of the sloop of war *Providence,* taking sixteen prizes and destroying fisheries on the Nova Scotia coast. A second cruise in October, in command of the *Alfred,* also yielded several prizes.

From its beginnings, the Continental navy was plagued with serious difficulties. Not only did it suffer, as did the Continental army, from inadequate financing, but also it usually came off second best in competition with privateers, which offered crews less danger, looser discipline, and larger shares of prize money. Furthermore, advancement went to those with powerful friends and local connections, as Jones discovered when Congress, on October 10, 1776, placed him number eighteen on the seniority list and gave him command of the *Providence* rather than one of the thirteen new frigates then being built. As most of these frigates never got to sea, that was fortunate for Jones. He had no success, however, in getting Congress to listen to his ideas on naval strategy: drawing off the superior British fleet from American coasts by attacking undefended British areas, rather than using American warships as commerce destroyers.

Amid the confusion, political intrigue, and charges and countercharges that usually enveloped Congress's naval arrangements, Jones was given command of the 110-foot, square-rigged sloop of war *Ranger,* on June 14, 1777 (the same day that Congress adopted the stars and stripes as the United States flag). It was November 1 before the *Ranger* could be fitted out to sail, during which time Jones had a coat of arms made and met, in Boston, the poet Phillis Wheatley. Having taken some prizes with the *Ranger,* Jones was in Paris in early December, where he met the American commissioners and became involved in the convoluted Euro-American diplomacy of the revolutionary period.

Having rerigged the *Ranger* completely (as he always did with his ships) to obtain greater speed and maneuverability, Jones left Brest on April 10, 1778. At dawn on April 23, Jones raided his old home port of Whitehaven, doing little material damage but considerably boosting morale. Later that morning, he landed near his old home in an attempt to capture the earl of Selkirk as a hostage, to force Britain to exchange naval prisoners (whom, unlike army captives, the British considered pirates and refused to exchange). As the earl was not home, some of the men prevailed on Jones to let them go to the mansion and take the family silver from the countess. The next day, as Jones remained in the same waters, there occurred a spectacular battle with the sloop of war HMS *Drake.* Using a tactic frequent with him, Jones moved close to the enemy vessels while his ship was disguised by covered gun ports and because the uniforms of officers and crew were similar to those of the British navy. The raid and the victory over HMS *Drake* provoked a general popular panic in British coastal areas, drove up shipping insurance rates, infuriated Britain, and made Jones well known from then on.

France, however, was not as enthusiastic about Jones's cruise as he had hoped, and for the next nine months he could get no new command, while experiencing major problems concerning the disposition of the prizes and the disinclination of the crew and some of the officers to accept naval discipline and naval, rather than financial, goals for future operations. Jones's own personality made things no smoother, and his irritation was increased by the lack of any official recognition of his exploits and by the fact that the French navy kept most of the British fleet in home waters while the remainder operated freely in American waters while Jones remained idle. Finally, in February, 1779, the French government gave Jones command of a refitted forty-gun East Indiaman, which, after six months of diplomacy and hard work, was finished and named the *Bonhomme Richard* (after Jones's friend Benjamin Franklin's "Poor Richard"). Jones had a squadron as well: the American frigate *Alliance* (commanded by Captain Pierre Landais) and three French ships (the frigate *Pallas*, the brig *Vengeance*, and the cutter *Le Cerf*). He was to make a diversion in northern England while a combined Franco-Spanish invasion fleet descended on southern England. As the projected invasion petered out without even a battle, Jones's exploits were to receive great attention.

Jones's cruise around the British Isles began in August with the taking of several prizes, an abortive attempt (because of a contrary wind in the Firth of Forth) to demand ransom from Leith (the defenseless port of Edinburgh), and a general alarm of the coastal population. The other captains refused to attack Newcastle; such general insubordination and lack of cooperation were common in fleets of the time, especially if the commander, like Jones, was unconventional. The *Richard*'s officers and crew, however, were enthusiastic and loyal. On September 23, off Flamborough Head on the Yorkshire coast, a forty-four-ship British merchant fleet from the Baltic was sighted, convoyed by the sloop of war *Countess of Scarborough* and the fifty-gun copper-bottomed frigate *Serapis*. By the time that a nearly full harvest moon rose, the *Richard* and the *Serapis* had engaged with broadsides; when the *Richard*'s bowsprit plowed into the *Serapis*'s stern, its captain, Sir Richard Pearson, asked, "Has your ship struck?" to which Jones replied, "I have not yet begun to fight." The *Richard* finally grappled the *Serapis*, which could not break loose to bring its superior firepower to bear; the two-hour battle was watched from Flamborough Head by many who had come from nearby towns. The *Serapis* continued firing its below-deck eighteen-pounders into the topsides of the *Richard*, which (in the words of historian Samuel Eliot Morison) became "little more than a battered raft."

In the meantime, the *Pallas* successfully engaged the *Countess of Scarborough*, but Landais, in the *Alliance*, sailed around the battle and deliberately fired into the *Richard* several times, doing major damage. By 10:30 that night, the *Richard* was in desperate shape, but Jones was determined to fight on, serving one of the three nine-pounders himself; with the *Serapis* mainmast about to go, Captain Pearson struck. Jones, the better captain in a worse ship, won; he transferred to the *Serapis* the next day, and, on the following day, the *Bonhomme Richard* sank. It had been a bloody battle: Half of the *Richard*'s crew and a third of the crew of the *Serapis* had been killed.

When the American task force came into port in Holland, Jones became a hero in France. The British press was angry, calling him a pirate and printing much misinformation about him, but simultaneously he became a hero in British popular opinion, with several ballads produced about him. His position in neutral Holland, however, complete with his squadron, prisoners, and prizes, presented diplomatic difficulties and compli-

Jones, John Paul

cated the matter of prize money even more than usual. (The *Richard*'s share later came to $26,583, of which Jones got $2,658.) A brief cruise on the *Alliance* (from January 16 to February 10, 1780) was both unprofitable and unhappy. In mid-April, Jones spent six weeks in Paris, trying unsuccessfully to settle the problems of the prizes. During that brief period, he was generally lionized, presented to Louis XVI (who gave him the Order of Military Merit and a sword), had a new coat of arms made, mixed happily in sophisticated Paris society, was the subject of a mezzotint by Jean Michel Moreau and a bust by Jean-Antoine Houdon, and conducted at least one major love affair.

Jones's return to the port of Lorient opened a confused time in which Landais took command of the *Alliance* by a coup and took it to America and a court-martial conviction. Jones took over the sloop of war *Ariel* on June 20, rerigged it completely, and, by December 18, sailed, with two merchant brigs, carrying military supplies for the Continental army. (Jones was later repaid $4,249.23 by Congress for his expenses since 1777.) Off the West Indies, he surprised and took a faster and stronger British privateer, the *Triumph*, but it managed to escape; this was to be Jones's last battle under the American flag. He arrived in Philadelphia on February 18, 1781, in time for his cargo to be used at Yorktown. Congress passed several complimentary resolutions, and Charles Willson Peale painted his portrait.

The *Ariel*, on loan from the French navy, was sent back. Jones was given command of the ship-of-the-line *America*, being built at Portsmouth, but when a French ship ran aground nearby, Congress voted to replace it with the *America*. Congress also reimbursed Jones for his pay and expenses since 1775 (in the sum of $20,705.27), but the jealousy of the other captains blocked his promotion to rear admiral. A brief cruise as guest and pilot with a French fleet in the West Indies at the end of 1782 enabled him to study fleet evolutions and naval tactics, but the Revolutionary War ended in April of 1783.

Back in Philadelphia, Jones became one of the original members of the Society of the Cincinnati, and, in November, Congress sent him back to Paris to recover the prize money still due (of which Jones got his $22,435 share in July, 1786). During his three years in Paris, Jones invested in unsuccessful merchant ventures, had a love affair with a widow (by whom he probably had a son), and, in 1786, presented to King Louis XVI his *John Paul Jones' Memoir of the American Revolution Presented to King Louis XVI of France* (published in manuscript form in 1979), a brief autobiography, which did not, however, get him a post in the French navy. On his brief visit to the United States in 1787 (still trying to clear up the prize money account), Congress voted to award him a gold medal; the next year, he spent some time in Copenhagen on the same business.

In April of 1788, Jones accepted the post of kontradmiral (rear admiral) in the imperial Russian navy from Empress Catherine the Great (r. 1762-1796), then involved in the Russo-Turkish War. He commanded a squadron, comprising a flagship, eight frigates, and four armed vessels, in two battles of the Liman, in the Black Sea, in June. His successes there, however, went largely unrecognized. His short-lived Russian naval career, marked throughout by confusion, dissension, and intrigues, ended with him writing an angry letter to Grigori Aleksandrovich Potemkin in October. In August, 1789, in the wake of a St. Petersburg scandal probably arranged by his rivals, he left Russia, stopping at various cities until he reached Paris in May of 1790.

In revolutionary France, Jones, short of funds and with nothing to do, irritated busy people such as the Marquis de Lafayette and the American minister Gouverneur Morris, and wrote letters, especially to Catherine and to his two married sisters in Scotland. Documents appointing Jones consul to Algeria, to negotiate for the ransom of United States captives, did not reach Paris until the end of July. On July 18, 1792, Jones died, of nephritis and bronchial pneumonia. City officials organized a funeral procession and burial in the Protestant cemetery outside the walls. In 1905, President Theodore Roosevelt became interested in the exhumation of Jones's body (which had been preserved in alcohol in a lead coffin) and had it brought back to the United States. On January 26, 1913, it was placed in an elaborate tomb in the chapel at Annapolis.

Significance

John Paul Jones had a complex and often contradictory character. From unimpressive beginnings, he educated himself, to a great degree, and developed sophistication and elegant manners, although he was rough and loud on shipboard. He never found a bride who could aid his social ambitions but engaged in numerous affairs, rarely having difficulty attracting women at any level of society. He frequently disavowed any interest in rank, wealth, or fame yet insisted on every penny of prize money and expenses due him and his crews, was sensitive to public opinion about himself, and had ambitions of entering high society, signing himself "le Chevalier Paul Jones" after receiving the Order of Military Merit.

A complete egotist, he saw the world in terms of the scope it afforded for his talents and ideas. He had few friends and only a few patrons (such as Robert Morris, Benjamin Franklin, and Thomas Jefferson). Assertive, vain, and insecure, he was also courageous and considerate of inferiors and captives; his constant concern for his men, overbalanced by his temper and demands for perfection, did not gain for him their loyalty.

He had an eighteenth century attachment to concepts of liberty and asserted that he was a citizen of the world; he also claimed the title of an American patriot and found no inconsistency in serving under the despot Catherine the Great and spending the last years of his life in Europe. He began to be a legend even in his lifetime yet was always blocked and frustrated by lack of recognition for his achievements. Never a democrat, he found the insistence of American ex-merchant crews on majority voting for naval decisions infuriating. Little attention was paid to his long-range concepts, whether that of the destiny of the United States as the world's major sea power, the organization of naval command and administration, or the overall strategy that would benefit the Revolutionary War effort.

A fighting sailor, he was never given full fleet command and so could function only as a naval tactician; in this area he excelled. Although all revolutionary naval captains had problems similar to those of Jones, not surprising in a new and difficult service plagued by localism, politics, and competition for prize money, there was none who could match Jones's record in actual ship-to-ship combat. His abilities and ideas were often discounted during his lifetime; only later, as the importance of the Navy began to increase for the United States, did Jones begin to receive the recognition denied him in life, as the real founder of the U.S. Navy.

—Marsha Kass Marks

Jones, John Paul

FURTHER READING

Bowen-Hassell, E. Gordon, Dennis M. Conrad, and Mark L. Hayes. *Sea Raiders of the American Revolution: The Continental Navy in European Waters.* Washington, D.C.: Naval Historical Center, Department of the Navy, 2003. A brief (seventy-three-page) account of the naval campaigns waged by Jones and other sailors and admirals.

Chapelle, Howard I. *The History of the American Sailing Navy.* New York: W. W. Norton, 1949. Chapter 2, "The Continental Navy," is especially good. Much illuminating detail about the general naval situation and the ships themselves, with several detailed sketches of the ships.

Halliday, Mark. "An Agreeable Voyage." *American Heritage* 21 (June, 1970): 8-11, 70-76. A good account of the Whitehaven raid and the Selkirk affair. Includes contemporary drawings.

Jones, John Paul. *Memoir of the American Revolution.* Translated and edited by Gerard W. Gawalt. Washington, D.C.: Library of Congress, 1979. Jones's autobiography, presented to Louis XVI of France, is a valuable text, as it shows Jones's style, ideas, and perspective on the events of his life.

Lorenz, Lincoln. *John Paul Jones.* Annapolis, Md.: United States Naval Institute, 1944. Despite the style and nebulous speculations and commentary, this 700-page work is apparently the first reliable biography of Jones written in the twentieth century.

MacKay, James. *"I Have Not Yet Begun to Fight:" A Life of John Paul Jones.* New York: Atlantic Monthly Press, 1999. MacKay portrays Jones as a "bit of a bore," a self-absorbed man who was obsessed by rank.

Morison, Samuel Eliot. *John Paul Jones: A Sailor's Biography.* Boston: Little, Brown, 1960. Almost every aspect of Jones's life—because of malice or misunderstanding—is accompanied by numerous false stories and outright fictions. Morison, in this work, provides a text based on meticulous research and in-depth knowledge of maritime matters. As an expert sailor himself, the author includes detailed passages on ship handling and other naval esoterica. The best biography of Jones, completely reliable, clear, and well written.

Morris, Richard B. "The Revolution's 'Caine Mutiny.'" *American Heritage* 11 (April, 1960): 10-13, 88-91. An effective account of Pierre Landais, the paranoid martinet who fired on the *Bonhomme Richard* during the battle off Flamborough Head, took over the *Alliance,* and became so irrational on the voyage to the United States that the officers took over the ship. A 1780 court martial convicted Landais and dismissed him from the Navy.

Snow, Richard P. "Battles of the Revolution: Flamborough Head." *American Heritage* 25 (October, 1974): 53-56. Points out that the grappling of the *Serapis* was a result of Jones's deliberate intention and superb seamanship. Includes excerpts from Nathaniel Fanning's account; Midshipman Fanning was hostile to Jones, and much of what he wrote was biased and inaccurate, but this part of his story is reliable.

Thomas, Evan. *John Paul Jones: A Sailor, Hero, Father of the American Navy.* New York: Simon & Schuster, 2003. Thomas portrays Jones as a tortured warrior and self-made man and argues for a renewed appreciation of Jones's role in the American Revolution.

Warner, Oliver. "The Action off Flamborough Head." *American Heritage* 14 (August, 1963): 43-47, 105. A chapter from Warner's *Great Sea Battles* (1963), it is a very good, succinct summary of Jones's life and an account of the battle. Includes excerpts from some eyewitness accounts and an illustration of a 1780 painting by a French artist.

MOTHER JONES

" *You don't need a vote to raise hell! You need convictions and a voice!* "

Labor organizer

As a labor organizer and fiery and captivating orator, Jones inspired workers and breathed life into union organizing efforts in the early twentieth century.

Born: May 1, 1830; Cork, Ireland
Died: November 30, 1930; Silver Spring, Maryland
Also known as: Mary Harris (birth name); Mary Harris Jones; Miners' Angel
Areas of achievement: Labor movement; social reform; oratory

EARLY LIFE

The birth date of Mother Jones is in dispute, as are other critical facts about her early life. This uncertainty is not unusual for poor and working-class people whose lives are often not recorded in traditional ways. Even births, deaths, marriages, and work history may not be documented.

In her autobiography, Jones herself gave 1830 as her birth year, but she gave other dates in interviews throughout her life. Most historians agree on 1830, although one cites 1839 and another 1843. Her father immigrated to the United States from Ireland and worked as a laborer building canals and railroads. The family followed and settled initially in Toronto, Canada, where young Jones went to school, graduating in 1858 or 1859. Little is known of her father and mother or her siblings.

Jones taught school in Michigan in 1859, worked as a dressmaker in Chicago in 1860, and again taught school in Memphis, Tennessee. In Memphis, she met George Jones, a member of the Iron Workers' Union, and in 1861 they were married. George Jones and all the couple's children died in the yellow fever epidemic of 1867. In her autobiography, Mother Jones claims to have had four children, but some evidence exists to suggest it may have been one or three. No one disputes the fact that Jones was alone after 1867 with no family and no permanent home.

Jones left Memphis in 1867 to return to Chicago, where she resumed working as a dressmaker for the wealthy. In 1871, she was burned out of her home and lost all of her possessions in the great Chicago Fire. Following the fire, she began attending nightly lectures at the Knights of Labor building, which was located near the place where many homeless refugees from the fire were camping out. Records of these years of her life are

Jones, Mother

Mother Jones.
(Library of Congress)

scarce, but it is known that Mother Jones traveled during the 1870's and 1880's from one industrial area to another speaking and organizing, usually in connection with the Knights of Labor. In 1877, she was in Pittsburgh for the first nationwide industrial strike, that of the railroad workers. In 1886, she was in Chicago, active in organizing for the eight-hour workday. In 1890, when the Knights of Labor District 135 and the National Union of Miners and Mine Laborers merged to form the United Mine Workers of America (UMWA), Jones became a paid organizer for the union. She was approximately sixty years old and about to enter the national stage. She was thought of as "the Miners' Angel," the most dangerous woman in the country, or America's most patriotic citizen, depending on the point of view of the different people who encountered her.

LIFE'S WORK

Until her health failed in the late 1920's, Jones traveled the nation speaking and organizing not only for coal miners but also for workers in the textile, railway, and steel industries. She figured in most major strikes in the United States in the early 1900's but was repeatedly drawn to the coalfields of Pennsylvania, Colorado, and West Virginia. For a time, she was active in Socialist Party politics, particularly in the campaigns of Eugene V. Debs. She supported Mexican revolutionary Pancho Villa in his fight for better wages and living conditions for Mexican workers, who were often used as strikebreakers, particularly in Western mines. She did not support woman suffrage or other social reform efforts of her era that were not founded solely on working-class rights.

Her speeches reveal that Jones saw herself as an agitator and educator charged with the tasks of teaching the American working class about the nature of capitalism and mobilizing an international working-class movement. In 1909, she told the national convention of the UMWA that she was there to "wake you up." At a UMWA district convention in 1914 she explained, "I hold no office only that of disturbing." In 1920, near the end of her public speaking career, she summarized her mission: "I am busy getting this working man to understand what belongs to him, and his power to take possession of it."

Jones was so effective at "disturbing" workers that corporate and government officials often went to great extremes to keep her from speaking. She was arrested many times, imprisoned, and forcefully escorted out of strike zones where she had been called to help organize. Her success as an educator is less easily documented, but her speeches and audience responses reveal a talented, tireless woman who was able to move people to action while instructing them about the nature of their conflicts and their place in history.

Conditions in mines and mining communities in the early 1900's were stark. Wages were low, mines were unsafe, rates of deaths and disabling injuries were very high, and children were often employed. Miners lived in company-owned housing and were often paid in scrip, a substitute currency that could be redeemed only at company stores. If miners tried to improve their conditions through union organizing, they and their families were evicted from houses, and armed guards (often from the Baldwin-Felts detective agency) were hired by the companies to fight the organizing efforts.

In the face of these conditions Jones devised a wide array of organizing strategies, as the 1897 UMWA strike at Turtle Creek near Pittsburgh illustrates. She spoke to ten thousand miners and sympathizers urging them to fight. Then she organized farmers in the region to provide food to strikers and escorted the farmers and their wagons to strike headquarters where the food was distributed. She called on neighborhood women to donate a "pound" of something to the cause and urged factory workers to come to miners' meetings and donate. As in many other strikes, Jones made certain that women and children were actively involved and featured in national news coverage of the conflicts. At Turtle Creek, she organized wives of miners into groups of pickets and demonstrators and positioned the children of miners at the front of parades. In one parade fifty little girls marched with homemade banners, one of which read "Our Papas Aren't Scared."

Jones was often in West Virginia in these early years of the twentieth century. In 1902, she worked in the southern coalfields, but she was successful in organizing only in the Paint Creek and Cabin Creek areas near Charleston, the state capital. While trying to organize the northern part of the state, she was arrested and briefly imprisoned. For several years she traveled across the country to protest child labor, organize miners in the West, and support striking brewery workers, textile workers, copper miners, and smelter workers. Then in 1912 and 1913, once again working as a UMWA organizer, Mother Jones returned to West Virginia's southern coalfields. She faced down armed mine guards to allow union meetings and threatened to encourage West Virginia miners to arm themselves and fight back. She was imprisoned again, tried by a state military militia court, convicted of a charge of conspiracy to commit murder, and sentenced to prison for twenty years. She served eighty-five days, passing her eighty-fourth birthday in jail, before national public outcry and the promise of a congressional investigation prompted that state's newly elected governor to free her.

In her final organizing effort with West Virginia miners, Jones attempted to halt the spontaneous 1921 march of thousands of miners on Logan. It was an unusual role for the aging firebrand, and she was not able to stop the march, later known as the "Battle of Blair Mountain." That bloody confrontation left many dead and injured. The determined coal miners proved powerless in the face of armed Baldwin-Felts detectives, the state militia, and the six thousand federal troops and twenty military airplanes sent by President Warren G. Harding to support the coal operators and prevent the union men from marching into nonunion territory. The battle halted organizing efforts in West Virginia until national legislation authorized collective bargaining in 1932.

Organizing miners in Colorado was as difficult as in West Virginia. Jones made her first visits there in 1903 soon after John D. Rockefeller, Sr., bought control of Colorado Iron and Fuel Company and the Victor Fuel Company. These early organizing efforts were not successful and led to a split between Jones and the UMWA leadership over organizing strategy. She did not return to the UMWA payroll until 1911.

In 1913, miners in southern Colorado went on strike for higher wages; an eight-hour day; coal weighing to be monitored by miners; free choice of stores, schools, doctors, and boardinghouses; enforcement of Colorado laws; and abolition of the mine guard system. Although most of these provisions were already law in Colorado, the state did not implement them in the southern fields. When the miners went on strike, they were evicted and lived in tent cities through the bitter cold Colorado winter.

Jones joined the striking miners there in the fall of 1913 and returned in December and again in January. Between January and March of 1914, Jones, then in her early eighties, was arrested many times and spent more than a month in basement jail cells in Colorado. Refusing to be silenced, she smuggled out an open letter to the American people that was read and published across the country. She was not in Colorado in April when the state militia attacked the family tent camp, killing thirty-two, including many women and children. Subsequent state and national investigations into this incident, known as the Ludlow Massacre, were extremely critical of the actions of the governor, the state militia, and Colorado Iron and Fuel Company.

When Jones wrote about her life she always identified her cause with the miners. After her death on November 30, 1930, she was buried as she had requested at the Miners Cemetery in Mount Olive, Illinois. A choir of coal miners sang her final tribute.

SIGNIFICANCE

Jones is remembered as a great labor agitator and a tremendously effective public speaker. Stories of her visits to coal camps, leadership at rallies and demonstrations, and confrontations with company and government officials are part of a living oral history of resistance in mining communities. Her memory continues to inspire the labor movement. When women mobilized in a 1989 UMWA strike against the Pittston Coal

Group, they identified themselves as the "Daughters of Mother Jones" as they carried out actions in her name, such as occupying company headquarters and holding vigils outside jails where union officials were imprisoned.

The message of Jones's life is that ordinary people, indeed unlikely people, can make important contributions to improving workers' lives. She was homeless and alone; she was poor and sometimes in prison; yet Jones used the resources she had—mind, voice, wit, spirit, and energy—to influence conditions for workers in America.

—*Sally Ward Maggard*

FURTHER READING

Fetherling, Dale. *Mother Jones, the Miners' Angel: A Portrait*. Carbondale: Southern Illinois University Press, 1974. This first full-scale biography on Jones presents a sympathetic yet balanced portrait.

Gorn, Elliott J. *Mother Jones: The Most Dangerous Woman in America*. New York: Hill and Wang, 2001. Chronicles Jones's life and work, placing her accomplishments within a wider political and cultural context.

Jones, Mother. *The Autobiography of Mother Jones*. Edited by Mary Field Parton. Chicago: Charles Kerr, 1974. First published in 1925; later editions (1972, 1974) add useful introductions. Insights into coal strikes, early twentieth century labor leadership, and Jones's spirit and personality. Unfortunately marred by inaccuracies and serious omissions.

———. *The Correspondence of Mother Jones*. Edited by Edward M. Steel. Pittsburgh: University of Pittsburgh Press, 1985. A collection of all known letters, notes, and telegrams (eight communications are added in Steel's 1988 collection of Jones's speeches and writings). Illustrates development of her political views over the course of her life.

———. *Mother Jones Speaks: Collected Writings and Speeches*. Edited by Philip S. Foner. New York: Monad Press, 1983. The most comprehensive work and best reference source in conveying the full range of Jones's intellect and activities. Includes speeches, testimony before congressional committees, articles, interviews, letters, an extensive bibliography, and historical background information.

———. *The Speeches and Writings of Mother Jones*. Edited by Edward M. Steel. Pittsburgh: University of Pittsburgh Press, 1988. Collection of thirty-one speeches believed to have been accurately recorded and transcribed in their entirety. Also includes seventeen articles Jones penned for newspapers and socialist periodicals. A helpful "Biographical Notes" section identifies people in her speeches. A good introduction to her life with historical context for her speeches and activities.

Long, Priscilla. *Mother Jones: Woman Organizer—and Her Relations with Miners' Wives, Working Women, and the Suffrage Movement*. Boston: South End Press, 1976. Examines Jones's position as a female leader in the labor movement and her relationships with working-class women and with women's rights organizations of her era.

Schiff, Karenna Gore. *Lighting the Way: Nine Women Who Changed Modern America*. New York: Miramax Books/Hyperion, 2005. Mother Jones is one of the nine women profiled in this book about women who were social reformers.

Jordan, Barbara

BARBARA JORDAN

> *Do not call for black power or green power. Call for brain power.*

U.S. congresswoman (1973-1979)

The first African American elected to the Texas senate since Reconstruction, Jordan went on to become a member of the U.S. House of Representatives. She mesmerized the nation during televised coverage of the House Judiciary Committee's investigation considering the impeachment of President Richard M. Nixon.

Born: February 21, 1936; Houston, Texas
Died: January 17, 1996; Austin, Texas
Also known as: Barbara Charline Jordan (full name)
Areas of achievement: Government and politics; oratory

EARLY LIFE

Barbara Jordan (JOHR-duhn) was born to Benjamin Jordan, a warehouse clerk and part-time clergyman, and Arlyne Patten Jordan. Barbara was raised in a time of segregation and Jim Crow laws. She lived with her parents, her two older sisters, Bennie and Rose Marie, and her grandfathers, John Ed Patten and Charles Jordan.

Jordan's outlook on life as well as her strength and determination can be attributed to the influence of her maternal grandfather, John Ed Patten, a former minister who was also a businessman. While assisting him in his junk business, Jordan learned to be self-sufficient, strong-willed, and independent, and she was encouraged not to settle for mediocrity. Her determination to achieve superiority was quickly demonstrated in her early years.

Jordan spent most of her free time with her grandfather Patten, who served as her mentor. They would converse about all kinds of subjects. His advice was followed and appreciated by the young girl, who adoringly followed him every Sunday as he conducted his business. He instilled in her a belief in the importance of education. Every action, every aspect of life, he stated, was to be learned from and experienced.

With her grandfather's advice in mind, Jordan embraced life and education. She showed herself to be an exemplary student while attending Phillis Wheatley High School in Houston. A typical teenager, Jordan was active in school clubs and other extracurricular activities. She also led an active social life during her years at Phillis Wheatley. It was during her high school years that Jordan was inspired to become a lawyer. She was drawn to the legal profession during a career-day presentation by the prominent African American attorney Edith Sampson. Moved by Sampson's speech, Jordan became determined to investigate law as a possible area of study.

Jordan received many awards during her high school years, particularly for her talent as an orator. Her skill in this area was rewarded in 1952, when she won first place in the Texas State Ushers Oratorical Contest. As part of her victory package, she was sent to Illinois to compete in the national championships. She won the national oration contest in Chicago that same year.

The year 1952 began a new stage in Jordan's education. She was admitted to Texas Southern University after her graduation from high school. It was here that she truly excelled in oration. She joined the Texas Southern debate team and won many tournaments under the guidance and tutelage of her debate coach, Tom Freeman. He was also influential in urging her to attend Boston University Law School. At law school, she was one of two African American women in the graduating class of 1959; they were the only women to be graduated that year. Before 1960, Jordan managed to pass the Massachusetts and Texas Bar examinations. Such a feat was an enviable one. She was offered a law position in the state of Massachusetts, but she declined the offer.

Jordan's impoverished background seemed far behind her. With the continued support of her parents and grandfathers, she opened a private law practice in Houston in 1960. She volunteered her services to the Kennedy-Johnson presidential campaign. She organized the African American constituents in the black precincts of her county. Her efforts were successful. The voter turnout was the largest Harris County had ever experienced. Jordan's participation in such a history-making event demonstrated her talents for persuasion and organization. These skills, coupled with her education and intellect, were to become her assets in all her future endeavors. Jordan's political career was born as a result of the Kennedy-Johnson victory of 1960.

Life's Work

The decade of the 1960's witnessed Jordan's emergence in the political arena. The 1960's was a period of transition and hope in American history. With the election of the first Roman Catholic president and the epic changes brought on by the Civil Rights movement, it was a time of change. Jordan was determined to be part of that change. After becoming the speaker for the Harris County Democratic Party, she ran for the Texas House of Representatives in 1962 and 1964. She lost on both occasions. Undeterred, Jordan ran for a third time in the newly reapportioned Harris County. She became one of two African Americans elected to the newly reapportioned eleventh district. Jordan was elected to the Texas state senate. She became the first African American since 1883 and the first woman ever to hold the position.

Jordan impressed the state senate members with her intelligence, oration, and ability to fit in with the old boys' club. She remained in the state senate for six years, until 1972. During her tenure, she worked on legislation dealing with the environment, establishing minimum wage standards, and eliminating discrimination in business contracts. She was encouraged to run for a congressional seat. She waged a campaign in 1971 for the U.S. Congress. While completing her term of office on the state level, Jordan achieved another first: In 1972, she was elected to the U.S. House of Representatives. Jordan served briefly as acting governor of Texas on June 10, 1972, when both the governor and lieutenant governor were out of the state. As president pro tem of the Texas senate, it was one of her duties to act as governor when the situation warranted. Despite his being present for all of her earlier achievements, Jordan's father did not live to see her take office as a member of the House. He died on June 11, 1972, in Austin, Texas. His demise spurred Jordan to continue her work.

Having already caught the attention of Lyndon B. Johnson while a member of the Texas state senate, Jordan sought his advice on the type of committees to join. She be-

Jordan, Barbara

Barbara Jordan. (Library of Congress)

came a member of the Judiciary and the Ways and Means committees. Little did she know that the Judiciary Committee would evolve into a major undertaking. Jordan's membership in the House was to be one of the many highlights of her political career.

The 1974 Watergate scandal gave Jordan national prominence. Her speech in favor of President Richard M. Nixon's impeachment was nothing short of oratorical brilliance. Her eloquence was considered memorable and thought-provoking. Her expertise as an attorney was demonstrated in 1974 when she spoke about the duty of elected officials to their constituents and the United States Constitution. Despite her personal distaste for an impeachment, Jordan insisted that Nixon be held accountable for the Watergate fiasco. A Senate investigation, she believed, was warranted. Her televised speech was the center of media attention and critique for days to come. She sustained her reputation for eloquence during the 1976 Democratic National Convention. During her tenure in the House, she introduced bills dealing with civil rights, crime, business, and free competition as well as an unprecedented plan of payment to housewives for the labor and services they provide. Jordan's popularity was at its zenith when talk of her running for the vice presidency was rampant among her supporters. She shrugged off the suggestion, stating that the time was not right.

It was discovered in 1976 that Jordan suffered from knee problems. The ailment was visible during her keynote address when she was helped to the podium to give her speech. She admitted that she was having problems with her patella. The damaged cartilage in one knee made it difficult and painful for her to walk or stand for long. Her brilliant oration was not hampered by her muscle weakness during the delivery of her speech in 1976. She opted not to run for reelection in 1978 and entered the educational field.

During his presidency, Jimmy Carter offered Jordan a post in his cabinet. Political rumor persists that she would have preferred the position of attorney general to Carter's suggestion of the post of secretary of the Department of Health, Education, and Welfare. Since Carter was firm in his offer, Jordan opted to refuse the offer rather than settle for something she did not want. Such an attitude is indicative of her childhood training and upbringing.

Jordan was offered and took a teaching post at the University of Texas in Austin. She taught at the Lyndon Baines Johnson School of Public Affairs. In addition to her instructional duties, she also held the positions of faculty adviser and recruiter for minority students. She continued to hold these positions into the early 1990's. In addition, Governor Ann Richards of Texas appointed her to serve as an adviser on ethics in government.

Jordan received innumerable honorary degrees. Universities such as Princeton and Harvard bestowed honorary doctorates on her. She received awards touting her as the best living orator. She was one of the most influential women in the world as well as one of the most admired. She was a member of the Texas Women's Hall of Fame and hosted her own television show. At the 1988 Democratic National Convention, Jordan gave a speech nominating Senator Lloyd Bentsen as the party's vice presidential candidate. She delivered the speech from the wheelchair she used as a result of her battle with multiple sclerosis. In 1992, she received the prized Spingarn Medal, which is awarded by the National Association for the Advancement of Colored People (NAACP) for service to the African American community.

SIGNIFICANCE

Jordan's rise from poverty to prominence through diligence and perseverance in the fields of law, politics, and education is a model for others to follow. During an interview with the Black Entertainment Television channel in February of 1993, Jordan maintained that circumstances of birth, race, or creed should not inhibit an individual from succeeding if he or she wishes to achieve greatness. As an individual who was born poor, African American, and female, Jordan demonstrated the truth of her assertion, and her life is a portrait of success highlighted by a series of significant "firsts" and breakthroughs.

Jordan's honorary doctorates from Princeton and Harvard substantiate her dedication to education and excellence. As an African American woman from the South, Jordan broke one barrier after the other. She maintained her integrity and dignity while in political office. Her defense of the Constitution during the Watergate era as well as her dedication to the field of education continue to be examples to those entering the fields of law and education.

Jordan denied that her life's achievements were extraordinary. Her modesty was part of her upbringing. She endeavored to live a life that she believed would benefit the country. One of the reasons she refused to run for reelection in 1978 was her need to serve more than a "few" constituents in her district. She wished to serve them in addition to the masses. As she stated in her resignation, "I feel more of a responsibility to the country as a whole, as contrasted with the duty of representing the half-million in the Eighteenth Congressional District." She maintained that anyone may succeed with the proper attitude. In 1978, Jordan believed that her legislative role and effectiveness had ceased and that her most effective role in the global community was in the field of instruction. A new challenge presented itself, and Jordan was eager to confront it.

Despite the effects of her long illness, Jordan demonstrated that race, socioeconomic status, and societal barriers may be overcome and dispelled as roadblocks to success. She gave interviews, lectures, and commencement addresses almost up to the time of her death in 1996.

—*Annette Marks-Ellis*

Further Reading

Browne, Ray B. *Contemporary Heroes and Heroines*. Detroit, Mich.: Gale Research, 1990. A collection of biographical profiles on men and women who have made major contributions to American life. Includes a fine piece on Jordan and her career.

Famous Blacks Give Secrets of Success. Vol. 2 in *Ebony Success Library*. Chicago: Johnson, 1973. A collection documenting the lives and achievements of black luminaries. The excerpt on Jordan traces her political achievements through 1973.

Fenno, Richard F. *Going Home: Black Representatives and Their Constituents*. Chicago: University of Chicago Press, 2003. Follows the careers of Jordan and three other African American members of the U.S. House of Representatives to examine their visions of constituent representation.

Holmes, Barbara A. *A Private Woman in Public Spaces: Barbara Jordan's Speeches on Ethics, Public Religion, and Law*. Harrisburg, Pa.: Trinity Press International, 2000. Comprehensive analysis of Jordan's speeches, focusing on how her private moral views informed her public career.

Jordan, Barbara, and Shelby Hearn. *Barbara Jordan: A Self-Portrait*. Garden City, N.Y.: Doubleday, 1979. Jordan's autobiography traces her life from childhood to her political career in the House of Representatives.

Ries, Paula, and Anne J. Stone, eds. *The American Woman: 1992-93*. New York: W. W. Norton, 1992. This book is one in a series of reports documenting the social, economic, and political status of American women. Includes profiles and articles on Jordan as well as female political contemporaries such as Governor Ann Richards of Texas and Senator Nancy Kassebaum of Kansas.

Sherman, Max, ed. *Barbara Jordan: Speaking the Truth with Eloquent Thunder*. Austin: University of Texas Press, 2007. Includes several of Jordan's major political addresses, including one on the erosion of civil liberties and another on the constitutional basis of impeachment. The enclosed DVD contains footage of her delivering some of these addresses.

United States House of Representatives. Commission on the Bicentenary. *Women in Congress, 1917-1990*. Washington, D.C.: Government Printing Office, 1991. Compiled to honor the bicentennial of the House of Representatives, this work provides biographical sketches of the various women who have served in Congress, beginning with Jeannette Rankin in 1917 and continuing through the women serving in 1990.

MICHAEL JORDAN

❝ *I've failed over and over and over again in my life. And that is why I succeed.* **❞**

Basketball player

Jordan, a pure shooter, prolific scorer, and soaring jumper, is considered to be the greatest professional basketball player of the twentieth century. In addition, his charisma and good looks made him one of the most marketable professional athletes, earning him millions of dollars in product endorsements. He not only is credited with having popularized the game around the globe but also has the name that is synonymous with American basketball.

Born: February 17, 1963; Brooklyn, New York
Also known as: Michael Jeffery Jordan (full name); Rabbit (nickname); Air Jordan (nickname); His Airness (nickname)
Area of achievement: Sports

EARLY LIFE

Michael Jordan (JOHR-duhn) was born in Brooklyn, New York, to James Jordan, a mechanic for General Electric and Deloris Jordan, a customer-service supervisor at a bank. Jordan's family moved to Wilmington, North Carolina, a few months after his birth. He had two brothers, Ronald and Larry, and two sisters, Roslyn and Deloris. As a child, Jordan was likable and got along well with others; many even considered him to be happy-go-lucky.

Jordan's close-knit family instilled in him a strong work ethic and encouraged him to avoid alcohol, drugs, and street gangs. His family felt that by avoiding these vices, Jordan would develop his full potential. He played a variety of sports, including basketball, baseball, and football, and he ran track. He began his sports career in Little League baseball and once pitched two games without allowing hits. In his early years he was shorter than his brothers, and his family felt that he would excel in baseball. Regardless of the sport he played, Jordan was a determined athlete, leading his brothers to give him the nickname Rabbit.

Jordan, interestingly, was not a "natural" basketball player. He did not make the basketball team at Laney High School his freshman year, in part because of his height, or lack thereof. He was only five feet eleven inches tall as a freshman—an exceptional height in his family. He barely made the basketball team at the beginning of his sophomore year and began to believe that baseball would be his true calling. However, Jordan grew three inches by his junior year and then added three more inches by his senior year, reaching his final height of six feet six inches soon thereafter. This growth spurt enabled him to excel in basketball. He had the legs of a high jumper and the shoulders of a football linebacker.

Jordan's high school basketball coach, Clifton Herring, picked up the young athlete each morning at 6:00 to practice the game before school. During the summer of his junior year at Laney, Jordan's coach persuaded Howie Garfinkel to allow Jordan to par-

Jordan, Michael

ticipate in his summer Five-Star Basketball Camp in Pittsburgh, Pennsylvania, a camp designed for college basketball prospects. It was at this camp that Jordan came to believe that he was destined to do great things in the sport.

Following the summer camp, in which he excelled, Jordan became one of the most sought after high school basketball players in the United States. At the beginning of his senior year in 1981, he accepted a basketball scholarship to play for legendary coach Dean Smith at the University of North Carolina at Chapel Hill (UNC). Jordan's career at UNC began erratically, and he averaged 13.5 points and four rebounds per game. It was not until the 1982 National Collegiate Athletic Association (NCAA) championship game against Georgetown University that Jordan showed his greatness. In the final seconds of game, with cool composure, Jordan made a fifteen-foot basket that put UNC ahead of Georgetown by one point, enough to win the championship for UNC. Jordan was selected the Atlantic Coast Conference Rookie of the Year.

After his junior year (1984), in which he was named College Player of the Year by *Sporting News*, Jordan left UNC and entered the National Basketball Association (NBA) draft. Before the NBA season, however, he starred during the 1984 Olympic Games in Los Angeles, leading the men's basketball team to a gold medal.

Jordan married Juanita Vanoy in 1989, and the couple had two sons, Jeffrey Michael and Marcus James, and one daughter, Jasmine. The couple, however, divorced in 2007.

LIFE'S WORK

The Chicago Bulls selected Jordan in the third round of the draft of 1984. Upon signing a lucrative contract, he was encouraged by his parents to further develop frugal habits by living on $1,800 each month. After about a month with the Bulls, he was the featured on the cover of *Sports Illustrated* magazine with the headline "A Star Is Born," and he would be on the cover of that magazine fifty times more during his two-decade career. Jordan also was voted the NBA's 1984-1985 Rookie of the Year.

Jordan missed sixty-four consecutive games due to a broken foot during the 1984-1985 season. He made a dramatic comeback during the play-offs by scoring 63 points in one game against the Boston Celtics and averaging 43.7 points per game during the three-game series. His greatest season in the NBA was 1986-1987, in which he scored 3,041 points, becoming only the second player to have reached that milestone, behind Wilt Chamberlain. Jordan also had a shooting percentage of 48.2 and averaged 37.1 points per game. That same season the Bulls advanced to the play-offs for the third year in a row. Also in 1986, Jordan returned to school at UNC and completed his undergraduate degree in cultural geography. He received his first Most Valuable Player (MVP) award, given by the NBA, in 1988. He also was named Defensive Player of the Year in 1988.

Jordan led the NBA in scoring once more in 1987-1988, shooting 53.8 percent and averaging 32.5 points per game. Although the Bulls lost to the Detroit Pistons for a third consecutive year in the 1990 league championship, Jordan scored 33.6 points per game and shot 52.6 percent for the season. He won consecutive MVP Awards in 1991 and 1992 and helped the team win its first NBA championship in 1991. At the 1992

Jordan, Michael

Olympic Games in Barcelona, Spain, he was a member of the U.S. Olympic basketball team—known as the Dream Team because it featured many outstanding NBA players—and helped the team win a gold medal for the United States.

With his contagious smile, good looks, and charismatic personality, Jordan became a natural at endorsing many name-brand products early in his career. The Nike Air Jordan basketball shoe, which he began endorsing in 1985, was a popular seller, and by 1988 he was earning four times his NBA annual salary of $800,000 with product endorsements for McDonald's, Chevrolet, and Nike.

Following the death of his father, who was murdered at a rest stop on Interstate 95 in North Carolina just before the 1993-1994 season, Jordan announced his retirement from the NBA. He honored his father's memory by returning to professional sports as a baseball player. In 1994 he signed a minor-league contract with the Chicago White Sox and was assigned to the Birmingham Barons, but his baseball career was dismal. He rejoined the Bulls in March, 1995, and was back in form by the following season, leading the NBA in scoring with a 30.4 points-per-game average. The Bulls, with Jordan's help, won the NBA championship title in 1996 and again in 1998. Also, Jordan won his sixth and final MVP Award from the NBA.

Jordan retired as a player for a second time on January 13, 1999, but returned to the NBA as president of operations and as co-owner of the Washington Wizards. Not surprisingly, Jordan could not keep from playing. On September 25, 2001, at the age of thirty-eight, he returned once again to the NBA to play for the Wizards, but his return was cut short because of injuries. His final game as a player came in 2003 at the NBA All-Star game, and it was a game for the history books: Jordan passed the legendary center Kareem Abdul-Jabbar as the top All-Star-game scorer.

In May, 2003, Jordan was released as a player from the Wizards, but he continued his ties to the league by signing on as the operations manager for the Charlotte Bobcats. He also participated in many charitable events for the NBA.

SIGNIFICANCE

Jordan is considered to be not only one of the greatest professional basketball players of the twentieth century, with a career that spanned two decades, but also one of the most marketable athletes in professional sports history. During his first decade in the league, he had a net worth of $100 million. The products he endorsed created more than $2 billion in profits for the companies he represented.

Jordan was instrumental in the six NBA championships for the Chicago Bulls. He won the finals MVP Award for each of those championship series; he was named the NBA's Most Valuable Player five times during his career, named to the All-NBA First Team ten times, and named to the NBA All-Defensive First Team nine times. In the end, Jordan amassed more than 30,000 total points over his career and ranks as one of the game's top all-time scorers.

—*Lloyd Johnson*

FURTHER READING

Halberstam, David. *Playing for Keeps: Michael Jordan and the World He Made*. New York: Random House, 1999. A definitive biography of Jordan's career with the

Jordan, Michael

NBA and the significance of his career to the rise of the NBA's popularity both in the United States and around the world.

Jordan, Deloris, Roslyn Jordan, and Kadir Nelson. *Salt in His Shoes: Michael Jordan in Pursuit of a Dream.* London: Aladdin, 2003. Jordan's mother and sister tell the story of his early years in this book written for grade-school students. Interesting for readers at all levels.

Jordan, Michael, and Mark Vancil. *Driven From Within.* New York: Atria, 2006. Jordan discusses his drive to succeed and how that drive was influenced by his family and his own personal will.

———. *For the Love of the Game: My Story.* New York: Crown, 1998. Jordan describes his intense "love of the game" of basketball as one major reason for his success as a basketball player.

Lafeber, Walter. *Michael Jordan and the New Global Capitalism.* New York: W. W. Norton, 2002. Explains how Jordan's likable personality and career success were ideal for his attaining many lucrative product endorsements. Also looks at how the marketing of professional athletes has affected global capitalism in general.

Leahy, Michael. *When Nothing Else Matters: Michael Jordan's Last Comeback.* New York: Simon & Schuster, 2005. Biography of Jordan, beginning with his management of the Washington Wizards and concluding with his return to the NBA at the age of thirty-eight.

Lovitt, Chip. *Michael Jordan.* Fendale, Wash.: Apple, 1999. A biography of Jordan written for ages nine through twelve. Part of the Scholastic Biography series.

Porter, David. *Michael Jordan: A Biography.* Westport, Conn.: Greenwood Press, 2007. A biography of one of the wealthiest and best-known athletes of the world. Also examines how Jordan became the most effectively marketed athlete of his generation.

Williams, Pat. *Quotable Michael Jordan: Words of Wit, Wisdom, and Inspiration by and About Michael Jordan.* Nashville, Tenn.: TowleHouse, 2004. Contains dozens of anecdotes that have been inspirational to Jordan.

CHIEF JOSEPH

> *" Hear me, my chiefs! I am tired. My heart is sick and sad. From where the sun now stands, I will fight no more forever.* "

Native American leader

The leader of his people in the Nez Perce War of 1877, Chief Joseph attempted to retain for his people the freedoms enjoyed prior to white American interest in their lands. Although he ultimately failed to preserve his people's independence, he became an enduring symbol of the fortitude and resilience of Native Americans.

Born: c. 1840; Lapwai Preserve, Wallowa Valley, northeastern Oregon
Died: September 21, 1904; Colville Indian Reservation, Washington
Also known as: Joseph the Younger; Heinmot Tooyalakekt (birth name)
Area of achievement: Native American affairs

EARLY LIFE

Chief Joseph was known as Heinmot Tooyalakekt in his native tongue, which translates as Thunder-Rolling-in-the-Mountains. He was born to Old Joseph (Tuekakas) and Asenoth. His exact birthdate is unknown, but he was baptized Ephraim on April 12, 1840, by the Reverend Mr. Henry H. Spalding, who maintained a Presbyterian mission at Lapwai in the heart of Nez Perce country. This area, which comprises parts of Idaho, Oregon, and Washington, contains some of the most desirable land in the United States. As such, white Americans desired the land upon which the Nez Perce and other bands of Indians lived.

In 1855, the U.S. government greatly reduced the holdings of all tribes and bands in the northwestern United States in a series of treaties at the Council of Walla Walla, called by the governor of the Washington Territory, Isaac Stevens. In those treaties, the Neemeepoo ("the people") or Nez Perce (pronounced "nehz purs") agreed to what amounted to a 50 percent reduction of their territory. The Nez Perce were able to keep this much of their land because the whites were not yet interested in the wild and remote country of west-central Idaho and northwestern Oregon. The Nez Perce had been exposed to Christianity as early as 1820. The existence of Christian names indicates that many practiced that religion. Chief Joseph was, or was generally believed to have been, baptized and named Ephraim. It would fall to him, a kind and gentle man, to deal with the problems—initially encroachment and then expropriation—which threatened the lands of his fathers.

The troubles of the Nez Perce began in 1861, when gold in quantity was discovered along the Orofino Creek, a tributary of the Clearwater. Old Joseph attempted to keep the prospectors from the land but finally accepted the inevitable and sought to supervise rather than prohibit the activity. This plan failed. Once the area had been opened, many whites entered. In violation of the agreements, and of the treaties of 1855, which prohibited such white encroachments, some whites turned to farming.

The results were surprising. The government, rather than forcing the whites to leave, proposed an additional reduction of the Nez Perce lands. The federal government indicated that as much as 75 percent of the holdings should be made available for white settlement. Old Joseph refused; his refusal apparently split the Nez Perce peoples. Some of them agreed to the reduction. Aleiya, called Lawyer by the whites, signed the agreement that the Joseph faction of the Nez Perce would refer to as the thief treaty. Hereafter, the Nez Perce were divided into the treaty and nontreaty bands. Old Joseph refused to leave the Wallowa Valley, where his nontreaty Nez Perce bred and raised the Appaloosa horse.

Old Joseph died in 1871, and, at his parting, he reminded his eldest son, Heinmot Tooyalakekt, or Young Joseph, always to "remember that your father never sold his country. You must stop your ears whenever you are asked to sign a treaty selling your home.... This country holds your father's bones. Never sell the bones of your father and your mother." Chief Joseph was as adamant in his refusal to sell or part with the land as had been his father, but he realized the power and inconstancy of the U.S. government. In 1873, President Ulysses S. Grant issued an executive order dividing the area that the whites were settling between the whites and the Nez Perce. In 1875, however, Grant opened the entire region to white settlement. In 1876, he sent a commission to see Chief Joseph. The decision had been made to offer Joseph's band of nontreaty Nez Perce land in the Oklahoma Indian Territory for all of their Idaho holdings.

What transpired as a result of this decision has been termed by Jacob P. Dunn, Jr., in *Massacres of the Mountains* (1886), "the meanest, most contemptible, least justifiable thing that the United States was ever guilty of...." Chief Joseph refused the offer to move to Oklahoma. General Oliver Otis Howard arrived with orders to enforce the presidential decision. General Howard proposed a swift compliance with those orders. Joseph realized that his Nez Perce could not long stand against a government and an army determined to take their land and move them. Accordingly, a council of chiefs, including Joseph's younger brother Ollokot (a fine warrior), White Bird, Looking Glass, and the Wallowa prophet, Toohoolhoolzote, reached the decision to go to Canada rather than to Oklahoma. General Howard, however, declared that "the soldiers will be there to drive you onto the reservation...."

Life's Work

The Nez Perce War of 1877 is misnamed. It would be more appropriate to label it a chase. It is the story of Chief Joseph's attempt to lead his people to the safety of Canada, where the geography and the climate were more similar to the traditional lands than were those of Oklahoma. The United States Army, under orders to deliver the Nez Perce to the Indian Territory, would pursue Chief Joseph's band during the 111-day war/chase that eventually found Joseph winding over fourteen hundred miles through the mountains. His attempt to elude the military would fail because of nineteenth century technology rather than his lack of ability.

Hostilities began when a member of White Bird's band of Nez Perce, Wahlitits, wanting to avenge the death of his father at the hands of white men, and two other youths, killed four white men. Apparently, some whites were of the opinion that only a war would guarantee the removal of the Nez Perce from the land, and some of them

Joseph, Chief

Chief Joseph.
(Library of Congress)

had been trying for some time to provoke that war. The men killed by Wahlitits had been the first white men killed by Nez Perce in a generation.

Joseph's reaction to the killings was one of regret and the realization that only flight would preserve his people. General Howard's reaction was to move immediately not only against White Bird's people but also against all the nontreaty Nez Perce. The initial engagement on June 17, 1877, was between two troops of the First Cavalry (about ninety men) under Captains David Perry and Joel Trimble. The cavalry was accompanied by eleven civilian volunteers. One of those civilian volunteers fired at the Nez Perce truce team. This action led to a short, unplanned, disorganized fight during which the Nez Perce, under Ollokot, killed thirty-four cavalry. (Important also was the capture of sixty-three rifles and many pistols.)

This initial defeat led Howard, fearing a general uprising of all Nez Perce—treaty and nontreaty alike—to call for reinforcements. Troops from all over the United States were quickly dispatched, including an infantry unit from Atlanta, Georgia, to the Washington Territory. Joseph's strategy was to seek protection from the Bitterroot

Joseph, Chief

Mountain range, where traditional cavalry tactics would be neutralized. Leading his approximately 500 women and children and 250 warriors, he moved over the Lolo Trail, crossed the Bitterroots, and then, hoping to avoid detection, moved southward to the vicinity of the Yellowstone National Park, which he crossed in August, 1877. Joseph then swung northward into present-day Montana, hoping to reach Canada undetected. Seeking the security of the Bearpaw Mountains, Joseph moved his people as quickly as the women and young could travel. They were not quick enough: The Bearpaws would be the location of the final encounter with the military.

Joseph was not a military strategist; Ollokot was. Joseph urged that they try to reach Canada. Ollokot, Toohoolhoolzote, Looking Glass, and other chiefs preferred to fight. Battles had been joined several times along the route. At the Clearwater (July 11), at Big Hole (August 9-10), at Camas Meadows (August 16), at Canyon Creek (September 13), and at Cows Creek (September 23), sharp engagements were fought. Each resulted in Joseph's band eluding capture but with irreplaceable losses. The military, meanwhile, was receiving reinforcements in large numbers. Especially important was the arrival of Colonel Nelson Miles with nearly six hundred men, including elements of the Second and Seventh cavalries.

About thirty miles from the Canadian border, the Nez Perce halted, believing that they had succeeded in eluding the army and had the time to rest. Joseph was wrong: The telegraph and the railroad had outflanked him. Colonel Miles caught the Nez Perce unprepared on September 30, on the rolling plains of the Bearpaw Mountains. Joseph's band, hopelessly outnumbered, held out until October 4. After a hastily convened makeshift council, Joseph decided to surrender. On October 5, he rode to the headquarters of Miles and General Howard, who had arrived in force the day before, and handed his rifle to Howard, who, in turn, passed it to Colonel Miles—still in command of the operation.

Joseph's surrender was apparently based on an assumption that his people could return to the Lapwai. This was not to be. The Nez Perce were loaded onto boxcars and transported to the Oklahoma Indian Territory. In this new climate and country, many of the remaining Nez Perce died. Joseph repeatedly begged for permission to return to the northwestern hunting grounds. Partial success came in 1885, when Joseph was allowed to return with his people to the Colville Reservation in Washington. Thereafter, every attempt on Joseph's part to effect a return to the Lapwai was unsuccessful. Joseph died on September 21, 1904, on the Colville Indian Reservation.

SIGNIFICANCE

Chief Joseph of the Nez Perce was a dignified leader of his people. A man who loved the land of his ancestors, he attempted to retain it. His defiance of the U.S. government was a gallant, almost successful, effort. His failure marked the end of the wars of the Northwest and was the last important Indian resistance except for the Battle at Wounded Knee Creek. The removal of the Nez Perce to reservations marked the end of freedom as the American Indians had known it. As Joseph said, "You might as well expect the rivers to run backward as that any man who was born free should be content when penned up and denied liberty."

—Richard J. Amundson

Further Reading

Allard, William Albert. "Chief Joseph." *National Geographic* 151 (March, 1977): 408-434. A well-illustrated, concise, balanced, readily available source.

Andrist, Ralph K. *The Long Death: The Last Days of the Plains Indians*. New York: Macmillan, 1964. Includes a well-written, sympathetic chapter on the Nez Perce. Especially valuable for detailing the reasons for the decision to go to Canada.

Beal, Merrill D. *"I Will Fight No More Forever": Chief Joseph and the Nez Perce War*. Seattle: University of Washington Press, 1963. A carefully written, well-illustrated account that gives special attention to the hostilities.

Brown, Dee. *Bury My Heart at Wounded Knee: An Indian History of the American West*. New York: Holt, Rinehart and Winston, 1970. A classic study of white-Indian relationships that must be read by the serious student. It contains an excellent account of Chief Joseph and his attempted flight to Canada. White motivation in the contest is perhaps overstated.

Chalmers, Harvey, II. *The Last Stand of the Nez Perce: Destruction of a People*. New York: Twayne, 1962. Contains a valuable glossary of characters and a balanced account of the war.

Dunn, Jacob P., Jr. *Massacres of the Mountains: A History of the Indian Wars of the Far West*. New York: Harper & Brothers, 1886. A chapter devoted to what Dunn argues was an injustice committed by the U.S. government. Many later sources rely upon his analysis.

Josephy, Alvin M., Jr. *The Patriot Chiefs: A Chronicle of American Indian Leadership*. Harmondsworth, England: Penguin Books, 1958. One of the few sources that deals with Chief Joseph as an individual. The account of the war is excellent.

Miles, Nelson A. *Personal Recollections and Observances*. Chicago: Werner, 1896. The final days of the Nez Perce recounted by the officer in the field commanding the United States military. Unsympathetic toward Joseph's motivation.

Moeller, Bill, and Jan Moeller. *Chief Joseph and the Nez Perces: A Photographic History*. Missoula, Mont.: Mountain Press, 1995. Color photos and text depict the places in Idaho and Montana where the Nez Perce Indians camped, followed trials, and sought refuge from government troops between June and October, 1877.

Moulton, Candy. *American Heroes: Chief Joseph, Guardian of the People*. New York: Forge Books, 2005. Well-documented biography, recounting Chief Joseph's attempt to lead his people to safety in Canada and his subsequent diplomatic initiatives to regain his people's homeland.

Park, Edwards. "Big Hole: Still a Gaping Wound to the Nez Perce." *Smithsonian* 9 (May, 1978): 92-99. Deals with a serious setback during the great chase of 1877.

KAMEHAMEHA I

" *E nai wale no oukou i kuu pono, aole e pau.
(The good I have done will always remain.)* "

King of the Hawaiian Islands (r. 1804-1819)

Through his prowess, astute leadership in battle, and adroit use of European advisers, ships, and weapons, Kamehameha overcame his rival and united the Hawaiian Islands for the first time in their history. In the process, he made himself their king and founded a dynasty that helped the islands preserve their independence from European and American rule through most of the nineteenth century.

Born: c. 1758; Halawa, North Kohala, island of Hawaii, Hawaiian Islands
Died: May 8, 1819; Kailua, Hawaii
Also known as: Paiea (birth name); Kamehameha the Great
Areas of achievement: Native American affairs; government and politics

EARLY LIFE

Because Kamehameha (kah-MAY-hah-MAY-hah)—whose Hawaiian name means the "lonely one" or the "silent one" was born before the European arrival in the Hawaiian Islands, and therefore before there were any written records, scholars must rely on native tradition for information about his birth. Estimates of his birth year vary from 1736 to 1758, but the modern consensus favors 1758. Kamehameha's mother was Kekuiapoiwa, and his father was Keoua, although there is a story that his real father was Kahekili, king of Maui.

Kamehameha was described by European contemporaries as being well over six feet tall, athletically built, and savage in appearance. He was a member of the chiefly caste, the *alii*, who ruled despotically over the common people. The *alii* were considered to have descended directly from the gods and possessed varying degrees of divinity. The highest *alii* were those who were born to a high-ranking chief and his sister—a system reminiscent of ancient Egypt. Hawaiians worshiped a number of gods, including Kane, the god of creation; Ku, the war god; and Lono, the fertility god. Life was governed by many prohibitions and strict rules for behavior known as the *kapu* (taboo). A priestly caste had charge of worship in the *heiau*, or open stone temples.

Kamehameha's father, Keoua, died young, and from then on Kamehameha was reared at the court of his uncle, Kalaniopuu, the king of Hawaii. It was during this period that Captain James Cook happened upon the Hawaiian Islands, which he called the Sandwich Islands in honor of John Montagu, fourth earl of Sandwich. Cook came first to Kauai and Niihau in 1778, and in 1779 entered Kealakekua Bay near Kailua on the lee side of Hawaii. The Hawaiians at first considered Cook to be the god Lono, but an unfortunate series of events disillusioned them, and he was killed in a skirmish on the shore of Kealakekua Bay. Kamehameha accompanied Kalaniopuu during a visit to one of Cook's ships and even spent the night there, but he seems not to have been present when Cook died.

Life's Work

When Kalaniopuu died, he left the kingship to his son Kiwalao, who undertook a system of land distribution unfavorable to Kamehameha and the other chiefs of Kona. After a bloody battle at Mokuohai in 1782 in which Kiwalao was killed, and with the assistance of an eruption of the volcano Kilauea that wreaked havoc with other opposing forces and showed them that Pele (the goddess of volcanoes) was against them, Kamehameha gained control over all of Hawaii.

When King Kahekili died in 1794, he controlled all the islands of the Hawaiian chain except Hawaii, Kauai, and Niihau. With the assistance of foreign ships and weapons, Kamehameha soon conquered Maui, Molokai, Lanai, and Kahoolawe. In 1795 he proceeded to Oahu—which now had Kalanikupule, Kahekili's brother, as its king—and landed his forces at Waikiki and Waialae. They drove Kalanikupule's forces up the Nuuanu Valley and forced the bulk of them to fall to their deaths from cliffs. Kalanikupule escaped but was later captured and sacrificed to the war god Kukailimoku.

Kamehameha now ruled all the Hawaiian Islands except for Kauai. He soon started preparations for an invasion of Kauai, and in the spring of 1796, he headed toward the island with a large flotilla of canoes. However, rough seas forced him to turn back and postpone his invasion. Hearing that a rebellion was taking place in Hawaii, he returned there to squelch it. He spent the next six years in Hawaii, during which time he assembled a formidable fleet of double canoes and a number of small schooners constructed by European carpenters. With these ships and a large supply of European weapons, he sailed to Oahu in 1804. However, his invasion plans were frustrated again, this time by a terrible plague (probably cholera) that was brought by foreign ships. The population of Oahu was devastated, and large numbers of Kamehameha's army also succumbed. Kamehameha himself was stricken but managed to survive.

Kamehameha continued to plan his invasion of Kauai and even acquired a large ship, the *Lelia Byrd*, to lead the assault. He also entered into negotiations with the island's king, Kaumualii, to solve the problem without battle. An American captain, Nathan Winship, persuaded the two kings to meet on board his ship, the *O'Cain*, and Kaumualii submitted to Kamehameha's sovereignty on the condition that he could retain his position until death.

Now Kamehameha reigned over all the islands, apparently the first to do so. He was an absolute dictator but used his power wisely. He divided up the lands in such a way that no chief had enough power to be tempted to rebel and appointed governors to administer each island. He issued decrees that made life safer and often worked at menial tasks to set an example for his people to follow. He appointed a Hawaiian named Kalanimoku (known as Billy Pitt after the British prime minister William Pitt) as chief executive officer.

During Kamehameha's lifetime, foreign visitors to the Hawaiian Islands became increasingly numerous. The first ships to appear after Cook's unfortunate visit were those captained by George Vancouver, who had been a member of Cook's crew. Vancouver visited the islands in 1792, 1793, and 1794. He brought cattle and goats and other commodities to the islands but refused to provide any arms. He persuaded Kamehameha to cede the Hawaiian Islands to Britain, although Kamehameha apparently believed that he was entering into a defensive alliance in the hope that he would get help against his enemies. In any event, Britain made no effort to follow through, but a close connection between Britain and the Sandwich Islands continued. This is symbolized by the Hawaiian flag, which bears the Union Jack in the upper left corner.

Although most of the ships that visited Hawaii during this period were traders searching to replenish their ships, there were occasional visits of a different stripe. Anton Schäffer, a German surgeon in the employ of the Russian-American Company, was sent to Hawaii to recover or receive compensation for a Russian cargo lost from a ship wrecked off Kauai. Schäffer got grandiose ideas and attempted, with the help of Kaumualii, to establish Russian outposts in Kauai and Oahu. He was repulsed by the Hawaiians with the assistance of the Americans in Honolulu and was forced to make his escape by hiding on a ship to Canton.

When the Europeans first visited the Hawaiian Islands, they were able to obtain valuable goods from the native Hawaiians for baubles or for small pieces of iron, which were especially prized because they could be made into fishhooks or daggers. Fresh water, hogs, and other food items were needed. As time went by, the Hawaiians became aware of the value of their commodities, and prices went up accordingly. Kamehameha himself secured great amounts of goods in barter and even large amounts of hard money, which he retained in storehouses in Kailua, Lahaina, and Honolulu.

Kamehameha had a total of twenty-one wives, but his favorite was Kaahumanu, by whom he had no children. Kamehameha married Keopuolani for dynastic purposes when she was about thirteen years old. Keopuolani and Kamehameha had three children who survived, one of whom, Liholiho, was designated as the heir to the kingdom. Kamehameha spent most of his last years in Kailua, although he occasionally traveled to the other parts of his realm. In 1819, he contracted a malady that no one could cure, and on May 8, he died. His body was treated in the usual way for *alii:* His bones were stripped of their flesh and hidden somewhere in a cave by one of his faithful retainers.

SIGNIFICANCE

Only a few monarchs in world history have received the appellation "great." Kamehameha, by uniting all of the Hawaiian Islands under his sway and keeping his land independent of foreign dominance, probably deserves such a title. He was flexible enough to adapt to the changing times but still retained his way of life under the taboo system. If he was sometimes harsh and cruel by contemporary standards, he was also kind and generous. During his brief reign as Kamehameha II, his son Liholiho, upon the urging of Kaahumana (a *kuhina nui,* or prime minister), put a dramatic end to the taboo system by publicly eating with the women, which had been strictly forbidden. After Liholiho's death (by measles during a trip to England), Kaahumanu remained as regent until Liholiho's brother came of age, and she saw to it that the remnants of the taboo system were destroyed. In 1819, the same year that Kamehameha died, the missionaries came to Hawaii and transformed Hawaiian life forever.

—Henry Kratz

Further Reading

Daws, Gavan. *Shoal of Time: A History of the Hawaiian Islands*. New York: Macmillan, 1968. Reprint. Honolulu: University of Hawai'i Press, 1974. Daws's book, the best one-volume history of Hawaii, contains an excellent section on Kamehameha and his times, starting with Cook's discovery of the islands. It is very readable, with copious endnotes and an excellent bibliography.

Desha, Stephen. *Kamehameha and His Warrior Kek-uhaupi'o*. Translated by Frances N. Frazier. Honolulu: Kamehameha Schools Press, 2000. Originally published as a magazine serial in the Hawaiian language during the early 1920's, this book recounts the epic tale of King Kamehameha and a warrior named Kek-uhaupi'o. An engaging saga for younger readers that includes a great deal of information about Hawaiian history and culture. Glossary and detailed index.

Kuykendall, Ralph S. *The Hawaiian Kingdom, 1778-1854: Foundation and Transformation*. Honolulu: University of Hawai'i Press, 1938. This first volume of Kuykendall's monumental history of Hawaii contains an extensive account of Kamehameha's life and the history of Hawaii since Cook's appearance there. The book also includes an appendix discussing Kamehameha's controversial birth year.

Malo, David. *Hawaiian Antiquities*. Translated by Nathaniel B. Emerson. 2d ed. Honolulu: Bishop Museum Press, 1951. This volume, written by a native Hawaiian in the Hawaiian language, was translated in 1898 by one of the great experts on Hawaiian culture. It contains a wealth of information about virtually every aspect of Hawaiian life before the European discovery, including old Hawaiian folktales and chants.

Mellen, Kathleen Dickenson. *The Lonely Warrior: The Life and Times of Kamehameha the Great of Hawaii*. New York: Hastings House, 1949. This is a well-researched and readable biography. Mellen used oral sources of Hawaiian traditions along with written sources and was aided in her work by Kawena Pukui, a distinguished scholar of Hawaiian culture and language employed by the Bishop Museum. The book contains several useful maps, including one denoting the battle on Oahu that ended at Nuuanu Pali.

Morrison, Susan. *Kamehameha: The Warrior King of Hawai'i*. Honolulu: University of Hawai'i Press, 2003. Brief biography written for younger readers.

Mrantz, Maxine. *Hawaiian Monarchy: The Romantic Years*. Honolulu: Aloha Graphics, 1973. This forty-seven-page booklet gives a quick summary of the monarchy by providing short biographies of all the monarchs from Kamehameha I to Liliuokalani. It also contains portraits of all the monarchs, as well as other interesting photographs.

Tregaskis, Richard. *The Warrior King: Hawaii's Kamehameha the Great*. New York: Macmillan, 1973. Tregaskis relies heavily on unauthenticated sources and his own imagination to write what amounts to a fictionalized biography. Nevertheless, the main facts are there, and the book contains genealogical tables, a map of the Hawaiian Islands, sixteen pages of reproductions of contemporary paintings, and a useful bibliography.

Keller, Helen

HELEN KELLER

> **"** *I am only one, but still I am one. I cannot do everything, but still I can do something.* **"**

Social reformer and writer

Blind and deaf since early childhood, Keller exemplified by her life of activism the full empowerment potential of disabled persons who receive appropriate adaptive education. She served as a spokesperson and fund-raiser for the benefit of those who are unable to see or hear.

Born: June 27, 1880; Tuscumbia, Alabama
Died: June 1, 1968; Westport, Connecticut
Also known as: Helen Adams Keller (full name)
Areas of achievement: Social reform; education; philanthropy

EARLY LIFE

Helen Keller (KEHL-lur) was born in a small town in northern Alabama to Kate Adams Keller and Captain Arthur Keller, a Confederate Civil War veteran. At nineteen months, Helen suffered an illness that left her unable to see, hear, or, eventually, speak (in Keller's time, these disabilities were termed "blind," "deaf," and "mute"). She remained locked in this lonely state of sensory deprivation until she reached the age of six, when her family employed Anne Sullivan, the twenty-year-old daughter of working-class Irish immigrants, as her tutor. Sullivan herself was visually impaired.

With Sullivan's devoted, creative, and stubborn help, Keller soon rediscovered the concept that concrete things are associated with linguistic symbols—in her case, the letters of the manual alphabet spelled into her hand. Once that breakthrough was made and communication was reestablished, the young girl worked quickly to master manual lip-reading, handwriting, typewriting, Braille, and basic vocal speech. Helen's recovery of communication was aided by the residue of language skills that had developed before she went deaf, by a stimulus-rich home environment, by the early age at which her adaptive education began, and by her own remarkable intelligence and perseverance. Accompanied and assisted by her tutor, Helen attended the Perkins Institution for the Blind (Boston), the Horace Mann School of the Deaf (New York), the Wright-Humason School for the Deaf (New York), and, eventually, Gilman's preparatory Cambridge School for Young Ladies and Radcliffe College (both in Cambridge, Massachusetts), from which she was graduated with honors.

While she was still a schoolgirl, Keller began her lifelong career of philanthropic fund-raising, collecting contributions for the education of a destitute blind and deaf boy when she was eleven, giving a tea to benefit the kindergarten for the blind when she was twelve, and campaigning for money to start a public library in Tuscumbia when she was thirteen.

She also began her career as a writer early. In her childhood, she published several short pieces, but those early successes were also accompanied by what she later referred to as "the one cloud in my childhood's bright sky." In 1892, she wrote a short story called "The Frost King," which she sent as a birthday present to Michael Anagnos at the Perkins Institution for the Blind, who published it in one of the institution's reports. The story was discovered to be remarkably similar to Margaret T. Canby's "The Frost Fairies." The twelve-year-old child was accused of willful plagiarism and was interrogated for many hours. The experience traumatized her so deeply that, although she loved stories, she never wrote fiction again, remaining anxious and uncertain about which were her own ideas and which were impressions she had gathered from other writers. Helen's literary creativity turned toward autobiography.

When she was a sophomore at Radcliffe, she was asked by the editors of *Ladies' Home Journal* to write her life story in monthly installments. With the help of John Macy, a Harvard English instructor, and Sullivan (who eventually married Macy), Keller completed the project, which was later published in 1902 as *The Story of My Life*.

LIFE'S WORK

After her 1904 graduation from Radcliffe with honors in German and English, Keller continued to write. *The World I Live In* was published in 1908; *The Song of the Stone Wall*, in 1910; and *Out of the Dark: Essays, Letters, and Addresses on Physical and Social Vision*, in 1913. She also wrote a number of magazine articles, primarily inspirational pieces. Some critics objected to the visual and auditory imagery in her work, criticizing it as mere "hearsay" or even offering it as evidence of outright fraud. As time went by, however, the disbelief with which some people greeted Keller's accomplishments gradually faded. This widening public estimation of what was possible for the deaf and blind significantly enlarged the field of opportunities available to all people with disabilities after Keller.

Sullivan married Macy soon after Keller's graduation, but the partnership between the two women continued into Keller's adulthood. (Keller never married; her engagement at age thirty-six to Peter Fagan was thwarted by her family.) The two women began to lecture together. Keller would speak her lectures and, because Keller's voice was still very difficult for strangers to understand, Sullivan would interpret. Their lectures served to increase public comprehension of the life of the perceptually impaired.

As Keller gained experience, moving through the world on Sullivan's arm, her scope of interest enlarged from human limitations caused by visual and auditory impairment to include human limitations caused by gender, by class, and by nationalism. She began to see the welfare of all people as being interdependent. She worked for woman suffrage. A pacifist to the core, she spoke against the vast amount of money her country poured into military expenditures. She read Marx and Engels, and in 1909 she joined the Socialist Party, of which John Macy was also a member. At the advent of World War I, she became a member of the Industrial Workers of the World. She wrote and lectured in defense of socialism, supported the union movement, and opposed the United States' entry into World War I. She remained sympathetic toward socialist causes all of her life, but in 1921 she decided to focus her energies on raising money for the American Foundation for the Blind.

Around the time of World War I, the advent of modernism in literature caused Keller's sentimental, rather flowery prose to seem less fashionable. An assertive and political single woman in her middle years, Keller was less comprehensible to the

American public than she had been as a child. Her income from her writing diminished, and, after years of refusing it, she finally accepted a yearly stipend from capitalist Andrew Carnegie. Financial issues became more and more important as Sullivan's health deteriorated and as Macy descended into alcoholism.

Financial pressure prompted Keller and Sullivan to venture into vaudeville. Between 1920 and 1924, their lectures were a great success on Harry and Herman Weber's variety circuit. Besides further deepening public understanding of blindness and deafness, their years of vaudeville gave them the opportunity to meet and develop friendships with many of the famous people of the day, including Sophie Tucker, Enrico Caruso, Jascha Heifetz, and Harpo Marx. Throughout her life, Keller's extensive acquaintance with influential people was part of the power she wielded in the world. (She was received in the White House by every U.S. president from Grover Cleveland to John F. Kennedy.)

During the 1920's, Keller and Sullivan also traveled frequently on fund-raising tours for the American Foundation for the Blind, an agency that Keller supported until her death. She also continued to write. In 1927, she published *My Religion*, an explanation of her understanding of the alternative reality described by the eighteenth century visionary Emanuel Swedenborg. In 1930, *Midstream: My Later Life* appeared as well.

The 1930's saw more of Keller's books produced: *Peace at Eventide* was brought out in 1932, and *Helen Keller's Journal, 1936-1937* was published in 1938. Keller de-

Helen Keller.
(Library of Congress)

plored the rise of the Nazis and supported John L. Lewis's union strikes. Sullivan died in 1936. After the death of her primary life-partner, Keller relied mainly on Polly Thompson, a Scots immigrant who had been assisting her since 1915. They remained together until Thompson's death in 1960.

In 1955, Keller published *Teacher, Anne Sullivan Macy: A Tribute by the Foster-Child of Her Mind*, a biography of Sullivan. She continued to be active on behalf of the blind and deaf until around 1962. In 1964, Keller was awarded the Presidential Medal of Freedom, the country's highest civilian honor. She died quietly in her sleep at the age of eighty-seven.

Keller's life was filled with activity: writing, lecturing, studying, and traveling. Her significance was not simply based on her untiring work on behalf of the constituency that a childhood misfortune and her own choice selected for her. By all accounts, she was a woman of great spiritual authority. Religious faith, the self-mastery needed to overcome tragedy, and a powerful and loving teacher produced in Keller one of the spiritually radiant figures of her time, whose power was based not only on what she did or who she knew but also on who she was and the direct effect of her presence on those whose lives she touched.

SIGNIFICANCE

Keller worked her entire life for the betterment of the disabled. She wrote. She lectured. She exerted her considerable influence over public institutions and powerful people. She raised funds for a number of agencies serving the disabled. She acted as a catalyst for the organization of state commissions for the blind. She helped to educate the American public about the prevention of gonorrheal blindness in newborn babies. The work that she did earned for her numerous humanitarian awards and citations.

The fruits of Keller's work were important, but what is even more important is that she did that work at all. She came into a world that had extremely limiting ideas about what was possible for a deaf and blind woman to accomplish. The disabled were seen as less than fully human; deaf and blind people were still being locked away in mental institutions in the world into which Keller was born. In that world, the mere existence of a powerful, educated, assertive figure such as Keller was profoundly significant. Each lecture she gave, each article she wrote defied stereotypes and served to change the attitudes and expectations of her society. Her public life as an active woman who could not see or hear in the "normal" sense truly altered the intellectual horizons around her. When she died, she left a world that had been radically changed by her life.

—*Donna Glee Williams*

FURTHER READING

Gibson, William. *The Miracle Worker*. New York: Bantam, 1965. The original play that examined the early years of the relationship between Helen Keller and Anne Sullivan.

Houston, Jean. *Public Like a Frog: Entering the Lives of Three Great Americans*. Wheaton, Ill.: Theosophical Publishing, 1993. Concise biographical sketches of Emily Dickinson, Thomas Jefferson, and Helen Keller, highlighting their spirituality. This work is unique in that the biographies are interspersed with personal-

Keller, Helen. *Midstream: My Later Life*. 1930. Reprint. New York: Greenwood, 1968. The story of Keller's life from around 1904 until 1927. Describes her work for the blind, her lecturing and writing career, her experiences in Hollywood, and her relationships with some well-known public figures, including Mark Twain, Alexander Graham Bell, and the Carnegie family.

_____. *The Story of My Life*. New York: Collier Macmillan International, 1972. The best known of Keller's autobiographical works, this book tells the story of her first two decades and includes a selection of letters that illustrate the development of her language skills from the age of seven to adulthood. Contains a useful short introduction by Lou Ann Walker.

_____. *Teacher, Anne Sullivan Macy: A Tribute by the Foster-Child of Her Mind*. Garden City, N.Y.: Doubleday, 1955. Keller's respectful and loving account of Sullivan's life. Seeks to redress what Keller saw as an imbalance between excessive public attention on herself and neglect of Sullivan's accomplishments.

Lash, Joseph P. *Helen and Teacher: The Story of Helen Keller and Anne Sullivan Macy*. New York: Delacorte, 1980. This long dual biography, part of the Radcliffe Biography series, acknowledges the long, fruitful relationship between Keller and Sullivan.

Nielsen, Kim E. *The Radical Lives of Helen Keller*. New York: New York University Press, 2004. Biography focusing on Keller's political views, describing her radicalism and anticapitalist activism.

_____, ed. *Helen Keller: Selected Writings*. New York: New York University Press, 2005. Collection of Keller's letters, excerpts of manuscripts, and other writings that provide insight into her life and ideas.

JOHN F. KENNEDY

" *... ask not what your country can do for you; ask what you can do for your country.* **"**

President of the United States (1961-1963)

Combining intelligence with personal charm, Kennedy became a model to millions around the globe, inspiring them to seek new goals and to work toward those goals with self-confidence. His assassination is still studied and debated.

Born: May 29, 1917; Brookline, Massachusetts
Died: November 22, 1963; Dallas, Texas
Also known as: John Fitzgerald Kennedy (full name)
Areas of achievement: Government and politics; diplomacy

EARLY LIFE

John F. Kennedy (KEH-nuh-dee) was born in Brookline, Massachusetts, an inner suburb of Boston. He was the second son of Joseph P. Kennedy, a businessman rapidly growing wealthy, and Rose Fitzgerald Kennedy, daughter of former Boston mayor John F. "Honey Fitz" Fitzgerald. He was educated at Choate School in Connecticut and was graduated from Harvard in 1940. While his earlier years were plagued by illness and his grades were often mediocre, he revealed himself to be an original thinker. His senior thesis was published as *Why England Slept* (1940), largely by the efforts of Joseph Kennedy's friends. John Kennedy was able to travel widely in Europe in 1937 and 1938 and to spend the spring of 1939 in Britain, where his father was United States ambassador. Still there when World War II began in September, he assisted in caring for American survivors of the first torpedoed passenger ship, gaining a sense of realism about war.

As U.S. entrance into the war became likely, he entered the U.S. Navy as an ensign, September, 1941, six feet tall but extremely thin and looking younger than his years. A thatch of often rumpled, sandy hair added to his boyish appearance. He was sent to the South Pacific where he commanded PT 109, a patrol torpedo boat. The boat was sunk in action on August 2, 1943, and Kennedy not only rescued survivors but also swam for help though badly injured. Awarded the Navy and U.S. Marine Corps Medal, he briefly commanded another boat but soon went on sick leave and was discharged for disability as a full lieutenant in December, 1944. Because of his injury, coming in the wake of earlier illnesses, he was often sick.

Life's Work

Kennedy had thought of writing as a career and covered the United Nations Conference at San Francisco, April-July, 1945, and the 1945 British elections for the New York *Journal-American*. His older brother, Joseph, Jr., slated to be the family's political success, had been killed in the war in Europe, and John took up that task. In 1946, he ran for the House of Representatives from the Eleventh District of Massachusetts, narrowly gaining the Democratic nomination but winning the November election with 72.6 percent of the vote. The district sent him to Washington for three terms, during which time his record was mixed. In favor of public housing and an opponent of the then reactionary leadership of the American Legion, he was friendly with Senator Joseph McCarthy of Wisconsin, whose "red-baiting" began in 1950. Plagued by a painful back, he was diagnosed in 1947 as also having Addison's disease, then usually fatal, and was often absent from the House. He showed more interest in national issues than local ones and became deeply interested in foreign policy. He rejected his father's isolationism, supported the Truman Doctrine and the Marshall Plan, but joined right-wing critics of the so-called loss of China to Mao Zedong. In 1951, he toured Europe and Asia for several weeks and returned better balanced regarding a Soviet threat to Western Europe and the significance of Asian anticolonialism.

Unwilling to spend many years gaining seniority in the House, in 1952 Kennedy ran against Henry Cabot Lodge for the United States Senate. Despite illness, explained to the public as wartime injuries or malaria, he campaigned effectively, helped by family money and friends, building his own political organization. He won 51.5 percent of the vote and would be easily reelected in 1958.

He married Jacqueline Lee Bouvier on September 12, 1953, and they had two children, Caroline, born November 27, 1957, and John, Jr., born November 26, 1960. A

Kennedy, John F.

John F. Kennedy.
(John Fitzgerald
Kennedy Library)

third child, Patrick Bouvier Kennedy, born in August, 1963, lived only a few hours. Jacqueline Kennedy's beauty, charm, and linguistic skills helped the future president on countless occasions.

As a senator, Kennedy gained national publicity by working to cure the economic ills of all of New England. He continued to speak out on foreign policy, often against French colonialism in Indochina or Algeria. He finally turned away from McCarthy as the Senate censured the latter. During one long illness, he put together another book, *Profiles in Courage* (1956), based heavily on others' research, winning a Pulitzer Prize and good publicity. One result of Kennedy's growing national reputation was his almost becoming Adlai E. Stevenson's running mate in the 1956 presidential election. While older politicians often regarded him as a rich young man with no serious intentions, his popularity was growing among voters.

Kennedy began, in 1956, to work for the 1960 Democratic presidential nomination. His brother Robert observed the Stevenson campaign, and afterward, the brothers began building a national organization. Finding his health improving, thanks to the use of cortisone, Kennedy made speeches throughout the country and created a "brain trust" of academic and other specialists who could advise him on policy. To win the nomination and then the 1960 election, Kennedy had to overcome anti-Catholicism and his own image as too young and inexperienced. Campaigning hard both times, he convinced millions of voters that he was intelligent and prepared for the office as well as a believer in the separation of church and state. He named as his running mate Lyndon B. Johnson of Texas, Democratic majority leader in the Senate, who was strong where Kennedy was weak, especially in the South. In televised debates with his opponent, Vice President Richard M. Nixon, Kennedy appeared competent and vigorous; Nixon, exhausted from campaigning, did poorly. Kennedy won the election by 303 electoral votes to 219, with a popular vote margin of only 119,450 out of 68,836,385, so narrow a victory that it limited his political strength. He named a cabinet representing all factions of the Democratic Party and including two Republicans. Despite the administration's New Frontier label, it was balanced between liberals and conservatives.

As president, Kennedy sought a constant flow of ideas of all shades of opinion. He held few cabinet meetings, preferring the informality of task forces on various problems. To reach the public, he used "live" televised press conferences. A handsome face, no longer gaunt and pained, the thatch of hair, plus Kennedy's spontaneity and wit, captivated millions. His inaugural address had promised boldness, especially in the Cold War, and he acted on that in agreeing to a Central Intelligence Agency (CIA) plan for an invasion of Cuba to overthrow Fidel Castro. When the CIA fumbled and the Cuban exile invaders were killed or captured at the Bay of Pigs, Kennedy publicly took the blame and found his popularity rising. He went to Europe to meet French president Charles de Gaulle, who warned against American involvement in Vietnam, and also Nikita S. Khrushchev of the Soviet Union, finding the Communist leader tough, belligerent, and unwilling to help solve any problems.

In domestic matters, Kennedy accomplished little during his thousand days in office. He sought and obtained minor increases in the minimum wage and Social Security coverage, plus money for public housing, and forced a temporary rollback in steel prices. Jacqueline Kennedy supervised a notable redecoration of the White House in Early American style. Only late in his brief term did Kennedy take up the issue of civil rights, because of increasing violence in some southern states. He took executive action where he could and proposed an anti-poll-tax amendment to the Constitution, which passed the Congress while he was still president. He also called for increased federal power to enforce voting rights and a major civil rights act to include the opening of public accommodations and an end to job discrimination.

Kennedy was more active in foreign affairs. Concerned about Soviet moves in the developing world, he founded the Peace Corps and the Alliance for Progress. After the Bay of Pigs and his encounter with Khrushchev, he became "hard line," appointing such militant anticommunists as John McCone as CIA director and General Curtis LeMay as commander of the Air Force. He also vowed that the Western powers would remain in West Berlin.

The major event of Kennedy's foreign policy was the crisis that arose when Khrushchev tried to establish nuclear missiles in Cuba in 1962. Using all of the information and ideas he could get from another task force and forcing his advisers to debate their ideas in his presence, he chose to blockade Cuba and threaten Khrushchev, keeping in reserve an air attack on the missile sites. Khrushchev withdrew the missiles, and countless millions around the world were relieved that no nuclear war took place.

Kennedy learned from the missile crisis. Afterward he was interested in "peace as a

Kennedy, John F.

process," as he put it in the spring of 1963; the United States and the Soviet Union had to find ways to end the nuclear threat. Kennedy established a "hot line" for communication between the White House and the Kremlin and negotiated a treaty that stopped American and Russian outdoor nuclear tests, reducing radioactivity in the atmosphere. It is this, Kennedy's admirers say, that indicates how he would have acted in a second term. Yet Kennedy also listened to advisers who insisted that the United States send troops to Vietnam to go into combat and show the South Vietnamese army how to fight. Skeptical, Kennedy agreed, saying that if this did not work he could change his mind and withdraw the American forces.

Tragically, he did not live to follow that plan. In Dallas on a trip to heal a split among the Texas Democrats, he was assassinated on November 22, 1963.

Significance

Kennedy represented a new generation in American politics, for whom World War II and the Cold War were the major events, rather than the 1920's and the Depression of the 1930's. He brought with him a style different from that of Presidents Harry S. Truman and Dwight D. Eisenhower, a contemporary style without formality and with wry, self-deprecatory humor. While his actual accomplishments were limited largely to proposing domestic legislation and to steps toward détente in foreign policy, he inspired millions in the United States and abroad to reach toward new goals in a spirit of confidence that they could make a difference. As did another assassinated president, Abraham Lincoln, he left a legacy of legend, in this case of Camelot or a new King Arthur's court of brave men and beautiful ladies engaged in serving good ends.

—*Robert W. Sellen*

Further Reading

Dallek, Robert. *An Unfinished Life: John F. Kennedy, 1917-1963*. Boston: Little Brown, 2003. A well-received, comprehensive, and meticulously documented political biography, providing new information about Kennedy's life and career. Dallek conjectures that had he lived, Kennedy might have pulled the United States out of Vietnam.

Dallek, Robert, and Terry Golway. *Let Every Nation Know: John F. Kennedy in His Own Words*. Naperville, Ill.: Sourcebooks MediaFusion, 2006. Contains a compact disc with thirty-two of Kennedy's major speeches and a book placing each speech within its proper historical context.

Frankel, Max. *High Noon in the Cold War: Kennedy, Khrushchev, and the Cuban Missile Crisis*. New York: Ballantine Books, 2004. Frankel, a former reporter for *The New York Times*, reconstructs the incidents of the crisis.

Manchester, William. *One Brief Shining Moment*. Boston: Little, Brown, 1983. The best of the memorials to Kennedy, with superb pictures and a moving text.

Matthews, Christopher. *Kennedy and Nixon: The Rivalry That Shaped Postwar America*. New York: Simon & Schuster, 1996. Describes the parallels between the political careers of Kennedy and Nixon, including their desire for power, and places their careers within a parallel historical context.

Parmet, Herbert S. *Jack: The Struggles of John F. Kennedy*. New York: Dial Press,

1980. The closest there is to a definitive biography, well balanced and based on exhaustive research. Discusses Kennedy's story to 1960.
_____. *JFK: The Presidency of John F. Kennedy*. New York: Dial Press, 1983. The second volume of the best biography is also the best-balanced view of Kennedy as president.
Rorabough, W. J. *Kennedy and the Promise of the Sixties*. New York: Cambridge University Press, 2002. A social history of the early 1960's as viewed through the perspective of the Kennedy presidency. Rorabough describes Kennedy as both "a unique figure and a true representative of his time."
Schlesinger, Arthur M., Jr. *A Thousand Days*. Boston: Houghton Mifflin, 1965. An admiring tale of Kennedy's presidency by a friend and aide.
Talbot, David. *Brothers: The Hidden History of the Kennedy Years*. New York: Free Press, 2007. Examines the inner life of the Kennedy presidency, focusing on the roles of both John and his brother Robert within the administration. Includes information on John's efforts to avoid war and Robert's quest to find his brother's assassin.

ROBERT F. KENNEDY

> *There are those who look at things the way they are, and ask, Why? . . . I dream of things that never were, and ask, Why not?*

U.S. attorney general (1961-1964) and senator (1965-1968)

Kennedy served his brother U.S. president John F. Kennedy as an able and active attorney general. He passionately advocated justice and equality for minorities and the poor in the United States. Like his brother nearly five years earlier, Kennedy was assassinated during his campaign for the presidency.

Born: November 20, 1925; Brookline, Massachusetts
Died: June 6, 1968; Los Angeles, California
Also known as: Robert Francis Kennedy (full name); Bobby Kennedy
Areas of achievement: Government and politics; law and jurisprudence; civil rights

EARLY LIFE

Robert F. Kennedy (KEH-nuh-dee) was born on 131 Naples Road in Brookline, Massachusetts. He was the seventh of nine children born to Joseph Patrick Kennedy and Rose Fitzgerald Kennedy; both of Robert's parents came from distinguished Irish Roman Catholic families of Boston. Rose's father had been the mayor of Boston, and Joseph Kennedy himself was an able financier who earned millions of dollars while still young.

When Robert was four, the family moved to the New York City area, where Joseph,

Kennedy, Robert F.

Sr., believed that he could be more in touch with financial dealings than he was in Boston. Robert first attended school in Bronxville, New York, where he was remembered as a nice boy but not an outstanding student. A constant admonition from his mother in his youth was to read more good books—a suggestion he followed. From his father's advice and guidance in Robert's boyhood, the youngster learned values to which he would firmly adhere all of his life. Joseph, Sr.'s goal was for his children always to try their hardest at whatever they were doing. The father could abide a loser, but he could not abide a slacker.

Robert's position as the seventh child in his family also affected the development of his personality. His older brothers, Joseph P. Kennedy, Jr., and John F. Kennedy, were ten and eight, respectively, when Robert was born. After these oldest boys' births, the Kennedys had had four daughters. Robert, although friendly and playful with his sisters, sought the attention and approval of Joe, Jr., and John. To this end, the little boy developed himself as an athlete, mostly by determination, because he was of small stature. Even as a grown man, Robert was considerably shorter than his brothers. Robert attained a height of five feet ten inches, but his slightly stooped carriage sometimes made him look even smaller. He also appeared somewhat frail, although he was muscular and physically active all of his life. Robert had also inherited the Kennedy good looks; he had deep-blue eyes, sandy-brown hair, and handsome, angular facial bones. He was also shy as a boy.

The Kennedys reared their children as Roman Catholics; of all the boys, Robert was the most religious as a youth and as an adult. He served as an altar boy in St. Joseph's Church, Bronxville.

In 1936, Joseph, Sr., was named by President Franklin D. Roosevelt as ambassador to the Court of St. James (London, England), and the family moved abroad. The number and physical beauty of the Kennedy children caused them to be public favorites in England. They all received press coverage, were presented to royalty, and attended British schools.

When World War II began in 1939, Joseph, Sr., sent his family home for their safety. Robert then attended preparatory schools, including Milton Academy, to gain admission to Harvard; although his grades were not extremely high, he was admitted in 1944. Robert distinguished himself most at Harvard on the football squad. He was too small to be an outstanding football player, but by hard practice and a will to succeed, he did make the varsity team. Among his teammates, he found friends, several of whom he kept throughout his life. These men attest that Robert was always deeply loyal to his friends.

With the United States' entry into World War II, Robert joined the U.S. Navy but did not see battle because of the combat death of his brother, Joe, Jr., a pilot. When he was discharged from the service, Robert finished his interrupted Harvard education and entered the University of Virginia Law School.

While in law school, Robert was introduced to his sister Jean's college roommate, Ethel Skakel. Ethel came from a wealthy Catholic family and was also a vibrant, athletic young woman. She and Robert were married in June of 1950, while he was still a law student. The marriage would produce eleven children, the last of whom was born after Robert's death at the hands of an assassin in 1968.

Kennedy, Robert F.

Robert F. Kennedy.
(Library of Congress)

LIFE'S WORK
Kennedy's political career dates from 1946, when he helped manage his brother John's congressional campaign in Massachusetts. In 1952, when John ran for the Senate, his younger brother was his campaign manager. Between these campaigns, Robert also worked in the federal government. He served as a legal assistant to Senator Joseph McCarthy in 1953, when congressional inquiries were being made into un-American activities. McCarthy's investigations focused on subversive, communist activities in the United States. Robert also served, in 1954, on the John McClellan Committee of the United States Senate, which was investigating organized crime in the United States. Among the groups under the committee's scrutiny was the powerful Teamsters Union, headed by Jimmy Hoffa. Robert displayed relentlessness in questioning Hoffa and in his determination to uncover the corruption in the Teamsters Union. Some of the press viewing the committee's hearings believed Robert to be too rude and harsh in his persistent examination of witnesses, especially Hoffa. The term "ruthless" became attached to Robert's name; it was, his closest friends and advisers believed, a misnomer. Robert's aggressiveness in the Senate hearings demonstrated his strong desire for success and meaningful achievements in public service.

Kennedy, Robert F.

    Robert achieved more national recognition when he managed his brother John's campaign for the presidency in 1960. Robert worked feverishly on John's behalf; he passionately believed in John's ideas for the United States. When the campaign ended after a long night of waiting for election returns, Robert was exhausted but exuberant. He was thirty-five years old, and his brother had just been elected the first Catholic president of the United States.
    In announcing his cabinet members in the weeks following his election, John Kennedy wished to include his brother Robert as the attorney general. In private discussions, Robert showed reluctance; he feared that people would charge John with nepotism. Finally, John and Joe, Sr., convinced Robert to accept the cabinet position.
    Robert proved himself to be a good choice for attorney general. He was John's close adviser in many critical instances. The two worked on controlling the volatile civil rights demonstrations that came close to tearing the United States apart in the early 1960's. Some lives were lost in the blacks' battle for freedom of education, public accommodations, and voting rights in the South, but more may have been sacrificed if the Kennedy administration had not intervened with negotiations (and sometimes with federal troops) at critical junctures.
    Another tension-fraught moment during which Robert aided his brother was the Cuban Missile Crisis. In October of 1962, United States surveillance had determined that Soviet nuclear missiles were being established on secret bases in Cuba. For thirteen days, President Kennedy, his cabinet, and his advisers met to discuss their possible reactions to these missiles, for they could not let them be fully installed. While some cabinet members and military leaders advocated an invasion of Cuba, a bombing of the island, or both, John Kennedy was determined not to begin a war that could easily lead to a nuclear confrontation. During these thirteen days, Robert Kennedy was one of the leading proponents of a naval quarantine of Cuba. This was the method of protest that John did follow. The result of the quarantine was that Soviet ships, bringing in more missiles and installation equipment, turned back. The United States also removed some of its own missiles from Turkey to appease the Soviets. President Kennedy was greatly relieved that his advisers advocating war had not convinced him.
    Tragedy then entered the Kennedy presidency: John was assassinated on November 22, 1963, in Dallas, Texas. Many Americans suffered and mourned, but none so deeply as Robert. His associates in the Justice Department noted his sullenness and depression in the months following John's death. Robert had spent almost all of his political career working on John's campaigns and projects; Robert had never held an elective office at this point in his life. He was spiritually allied to John's plans for the United States, and he was lost without his brother.
    At first, Robert remained attorney general under President Lyndon B. Johnson, to ease the transition of administrations. In 1964, however, when a Senate seat was vacant in New York, Robert decided to seek that office. His running was welcomed by people who believed that he would continue John's work. Yet some New Yorkers were upset that Robert was a Massachusetts native seeking office in their state. To those people opposed to Robert's campaign, his supporters reviewed his life as a boy in New York. The campaign was a success; Robert Kennedy became a U.S. senator when he defeated the Republican Kenneth Keating. When Robert took the oath of of-

fice to begin his work as a senator, his younger brother, Edward, was present as a senator from Massachusetts.

Robert proved to be an energetic and outspoken senator (a role not usually assumed by a freshman). He worked hard to see that his late brother John's civil rights legislation was passed. Robert also toured in many nations during the first years after John's death. Robert was always greeted with great enthusiasm and admiration wherever he went. In these travels abroad, as well as in his extensive touring throughout the United States, Robert was astonished at the deep poverty and endless discrimination under which many people suffered. He began to advocate more strongly legislation providing government aid and training for such groups as rural blacks, inner-city blacks, migrant farmworkers, and American Indians. Some people who disliked Robert Kennedy accused him of visiting the poor for his own publicity, but many of those who traveled with him said that he was genuinely moved by and truly sympathetic to the plight of the lower classes in the United States. He often said that he knew he had been born into the privileges of a wealthy family, and he felt a real obligation to help those so much less fortunate than he.

In 1966, American opinion of the expanding conflict in Vietnam supported President Johnson's policy to fight hard and subdue the Communists. Robert Kennedy, however, began to advocate negotiations and political compromises as the only sensible way of bringing the war to an end. He more openly opposed President Johnson's policies in the months that followed, when American forces heavily bombed North Vietnam. The years 1966 to 1968 (and beyond) were marked by intense domestic debate, particularly centering on opposition to the increasingly bloody and costly war in Vietnam. Robert Kennedy became involved in the effort to negotiate quickly an honest and just settlement of the war. To this end, he struggled for several months with the decision of whether to run for the presidency. Kennedy believed that President Johnson's military escalation to defeat North Vietnam was a doomed and tragically wrong policy. Roundly criticized both by political opponents and by large numbers of citizens, Johnson decided not to run for reelection; he announced this decision to the American people on March 31, 1968. Kennedy had declared that he would seek the Democratic Party's nomination to run for president earlier that same month.

With Johnson out of the race, Kennedy began to campaign intensely for an office that he believed he could win. His one formidable opponent was the Democratic senator Eugene McCarthy of Minnesota, also an antiwar activist. McCarthy defeated Kennedy in an Oregon primary for Democratic voters in late May. Kennedy, however, surged back with a win in the California primary, held the next week. As Kennedy left a platform at the Ambassador Hotel in Los Angeles after thanking his campaign workers for his California success, he was assassinated. He died in a Los Angeles hospital on June 6, 1968, at age forty-two.

SIGNIFICANCE

Kennedy's untimely and tragic death robbed the United States of one of its most dedicated and compassionate public officials. In office or not, Kennedy was always passionately advocating equal rights, a decent education, adequate housing, and freedom from hunger for all Americans. He particularly befriended migrant farmworkers and

Kennedy, Robert F.

American Indians at a time when few national leaders were speaking on behalf of these minorities. Kennedy showed deep personal sympathy for the poor people he visited across the nation and vowed to end their degradation and suffering.

Kennedy did not live to see an end to suffering among America's poor or to see an end to the tragic war in Vietnam. Yet he left behind him many scores of admirers who believed in his social policies and who advocated justice and decent lives for all Americans. Kennedy's greatness lies not only in the struggles he entered during his lifetime but also in the inspiration he gave people to help their fellow Americans in need.

—*Patricia E. Sweeney*

FURTHER READING

Halberstam, David. *The Unfinished Odyssey of Robert Kennedy*. New York: Random House, 1969. A very detailed account of Robert Kennedy's pursuit of the Democratic Party's nomination for the presidency. Halberstam begins with Kennedy's opposition to Johnson's war policies and proceeds to the night of his assassination, ending rather abruptly and inconclusively.

Kennedy, Rose F. *Times to Remember*. Garden City, N.Y.: Doubleday, 1974. A mother's clear and detailed remembrances of her married life and her nine children. Rose Kennedy is candid on the childhood faults of Robert, as well as his admirable traits. She also deals openly with the assassinations, how she learned of them, and their effect on her family.

Palermo, Joseph A. *In His Own Right: The Political Odyssey of Robert F. Kennedy*. New York: Columbia University Press, 2001. Describes Kennedy's political and personal transformation during his years in the U.S. Senate, from 1964 until his death in 1968. Palermo explains how in these years, Kennedy became a more passionate, compassionate, and effective leader who attracted a growing legion of admirers.

Plimpton, George, ed. *American Journey: The Times of Robert Kennedy*. New York: Harcourt Brace Jovanovich, 1970. A fascinating book of candid interviews on Kennedy's personal life and political career. Plimpton and Jean Stein interviewed the mourners aboard Kennedy's funeral train. Included are recollections by relatives and political allies, as well as spectators watching the train pass by.

Schlesinger, Arthur M. *Robert Kennedy and His Times*. Boston: Houghton Mifflin, 1978. An extensive account of Kennedy's life, filled with countless details of his work and recreation. Emphasizes Kennedy's work with Senate committees in the 1950's and his tenure as attorney general in the early 1960's. Schlesinger especially wishes to refute critics of Kennedy's methods and policies.

Sorensen, Theodore C. *The Kennedy Legacy*. New York: Macmillan, 1969. Sorensen, a leading American historian and Kennedy adviser, thoroughly outlines Kennedy's political stances and plans for action, most of which he supports. The author also compares John and Robert Kennedy, analyzing their similarities and differences.

Talbot, David. *Brothers: The Hidden History of the Kennedy Years*. New York: Free Press, 2007. Examines the inner life of the Kennedy presidency, focusing on the roles of both Robert and John within the administration. Includes information on John's efforts to avoid war and Robert's quest to find his brother's assassin.

Thomas, Evan. *Robert Kennedy: His Life*. New York: Simon & Schuster, 2000. Thomas, a *Newsweek* magazine editor, presents a thorough biography containing a great deal of new information based on his access to Kennedy's colleagues, oral histories, and newly declassified documents.

Vanden Heuvel, William, and Milton Gwirtzman. *On His Own: Robert F. Kennedy, 1964-1968*. Garden City, N.Y.: Doubleday, 1970. Both authors were close friends of their subject, and theirs is a powerful, forceful study. They also show much of the inner workings of American politics. They fully present Kennedy as an unselfish proponent of justice for all Americans.

Witcover, Jules. *Eighty-five Days: The Last Campaign of Robert Kennedy*. New York: G. P. Putnam's Sons, 1969. Like Halberstam, Witcover describes Kennedy's last run for public office—the presidency. Unlike Halberstam, however, Witcover continues through the assassination and the funeral (perhaps because he was at both events). The author tries to maintain a balance between Kennedy's strong points and his shortcomings.

BILLIE JEAN KING

> *A champion is afraid of losing. Everyone else is afraid of winning.*

Tennis player

In addition to being a superb tennis player, King was a driving force for the recognition and improvement of women's tennis. Her sensational tennis victory over Bobby Riggs in 1973 established her as the preeminent advocate of equity for women in tennis, and in sports in general. She was the first prominent athlete in the United States to come out as lesbian.

Born: November 22, 1943; Long Beach, California
Also known as: Billie Jean Moffitt (birth name); Mother Freedom (nickname)
Area of achievement: Sports

EARLY LIFE

Billie Jean King was born in Long Beach, California. Her father, Willard J. Moffitt, was an engineer with the city's fire department, and her mother, Betty Moffitt, was a housewife and receptionist at a medical center. Her parents were not affluent, but they encouraged King and her younger brother, Randy Moffitt, to take part in sports. Randy became a major-league pitcher with the San Francisco Giants and other baseball teams.

King's tennis career began at the age of eleven, when her father allowed her to take tennis lessons. She immediately displayed an aptitude for the game and a burning desire to excel. She told her parents that she wanted to compete in the famous Wimbledon tournament in England and that one day she would become the number-one player in the world. She worked at odd jobs to buy a tennis racquet and devoted long hours daily to exercise and practice.

When Billie Jean was fifteen, Alice Marble, the great women's player of the 1930's and early 1940's, became her coach. Billie Jean stood only five feet three inches tall at that stage of her life, and Marble remembered that her student was "short, fat, and aggressive." It was also evident that Billie Jean had the clear makings of a champion because of her positive attitude toward the sport.

Billie Jean's first tournament victory came in the Southern California championship, when she was fourteen years old, and she made steady progress in junior girls' tournaments for the next several years. By the time she was eighteen years old in 1961, she and Karen Hantze won the women's doubles title at Wimbledon, the youngest pair ever to do so. In 1962, she and Hantze won again. In the singles, Billie Jean defeated top-seeded Margaret Smith of Australia, 1-6, 6-3, 7-5, in one of the most stunning upsets in the history of the British grass-court classic. Billie Jean lost in the quarterfinals, but the victory over Smith signaled that she was on her way to the top of women's tennis. During these years, she also attended Los Angeles State College (now California State University, Los Angeles).

King returned to Wimbledon in 1963 and reached the finals before losing to Smith. Her game improved during 1964 and 1965, but she was not successful in the Grand Slam tournaments that she entered. In 1964, she became engaged to Larry King, and they were married on September 17, 1965. Her liberal husband was another force in raising her social awareness of the inequitable treatment of women in athletics. By the end of the year, she was the number-one-ranked women's player in the United States. Her breakthrough to the top of women's tennis would come in 1966.

LIFE'S WORK

King achieved impressive international triumphs in 1966, when she led the Americans to victory over the British in the Wightman Cup competition and three weeks later defeated Maria Bueno in the Wimbledon final, 6-3, 3-6, 6-1. She faltered at the U.S. Open later in the summer but came back in 1967 to win Wimbledon for the second time. She beat Ann Jones of Great Britain, 6-3, 6-4, in the final, and she also captured the women's doubles and mixed doubles crowns. She triumphed at the U.S. Open without losing a single set in the competition. She bested Jones, 11-9, 6-4, in an exciting final.

For the next sixteen years, King was a major star in women's tennis. She became a professional in 1968 and won seventy-one tournaments during her career. She was the first woman to win more than $100,000 in a single year of competition, at the time a landmark for women in professional sports. Her prize money over her storied career totaled $1,966,487. She won the Australian and French opens each on one occasion, but won the U.S. Open singles title four times and the Wimbledon singles title six times. She won twenty Wimbledon titles in singles, doubles, and mixed doubles to hold the all-time record for players in that prestigious tournament. She was named Sportsman of the Year in 1972 by *Sports Illustrated* magazine, the first time a woman, or a tennis player, was selected for that honor.

The grass courts of Wimbledon were the scene for many of Billie Jean's most memorable matches. She lost in the final in 1970 to Margaret Court, 14-12, 11-9, in a con-

Billie Jean King. (Courtesy, Volvo Women's Tennis Cup)

test that both players called one of their all-time best. In 1973, she beat Chris Evert, 6-0, 7-5, for her fifth title. Two years later, King won her last Wimbledon singles crown with a 6-0, 6-1, victory over Evonne Goolagong Cawley. King played her final match at Wimbledon in 1983, when she lost in the semifinals to Andrea Jaeger. The British crowds adored King for her tenacity and fighting spirit.

King's success as a tennis player rested on her absolute unwillingness to lose. Standing five feet four inches tall, with knees that often ached and several times required surgery, she drove herself around the court. She talked to herself during matches, exhorting her body to the athletic extremes that she demanded of herself. She would say, "Oh, Billie, think!" or "You've got the touch of an ox." She resented those who wanted to keep tennis a clubby sport, and she sought to "get it off the society pages and onto the sports pages." She attacked the ball, the net, and her opponents with relentless energy and a shrewd brain for the fine points of the game. Spectators and foes never knew what King might do on the court, but her energy and fiery spirit made her fascinating to watch.

King's outrage at the obvious unfairness in her sport made her a leader for the cause of women's tennis during the 1960's and 1970's. After open tennis came along in 1968, King could not understand why men should receive more prize money and attention than did their female counterparts. She was instrumental in organizing women players to start their own tour and to challenge the supremacy of the United States Lawn Tennis Association. She helped to found the Women's Tennis Association, and she served as its president from 1973 to 1975 and from 1980 to 1981. Women's tennis in its modern form owes a great deal to King's pioneering work.

The event that made King an international celebrity and forever identified her with the cause of rights for women athletes was her match with tennis player Bobby Riggs in 1973. Riggs had been an excellent tennis star during the 1930's and 1940's who gained the Wimbledon championship in 1939 and won a large sum of money betting on himself with London bookmakers. By the 1970's, he had a well-deserved reputation as a "hustler" on the court who could win even when giving his opponents an advantage in advance. In 1973, Riggs loudly claimed in the media and to anyone who would listen that he could easily defeat any of the star women players of that day, even though he was fifty-five years old. He challenged King and other women to televised matches on that basis. At first, King ignored his sexist taunts lest she give him free publicity.

In May of 1973, however, Riggs defeated Margaret Court in a nationally televised match that was labeled the Mother's Day massacre. The feisty Riggs renewed his challenge to King and said that he wanted to play the "women's libber leader." King agreed to meet Riggs, whom she called a "creep" who "runs down women." The buildup to the event, dubbed the Battle of the Sexes, reflected the ambiguity that Americans felt about women's issues in the early 1970's. The match was held at the Houston Astrodome in Texas on September 20. The event drew a crowd of almost 31,000 spectators, and the television audience was estimated to be more than 30 million. ABC Sports had paid $750,000 for exclusive broadcast rights to the event, and Monday Night Football analyst, the legendary and abrasive Howard Cosell, was there to call the match. The event was seen in thirty-six foreign countries via satellite. A circuslike atmosphere prevailed. King came into the stadium on a gold litter carried by four athletic men. Riggs entered the stadium on a shimmering red carriage with gold wheels, surrounded by several beautiful women. Tickets for courtside seats sold for what was then the exorbitant price of $100.

The match was a total victory for King and something of an anticlimax after all the media hype. She outplayed Riggs in every phase of the game on her way to a three-set victory, 6-4, 6-3, 6-3. Rather than rely on her usual attacking game, King kept the ball in play, mixed up the speed of her strokes, and relied on her accuracy and stamina to wear down the older and slower Riggs. After the first set, she was in total command of the match, and in the end the match became no contest at all. For all his bravado, Riggs did not have the shots or the talent to keep up with King at the top of her form. After the match and in the years that followed, however, King and Riggs became close friends who recognized what a turning point their match in the Astrodome had been.

After her retirement from competitive tennis in 1984, King was active as a tennis coach, television commentator, and organizer of World Team Tennis. She wrote her autobiography as well as an engrossing history of women's tennis. She and her husband were divorced in 1987. He had been an important force in promoting her tennis career.

King came out as lesbian and became active in gay and lesbian issues after her retirement. She and her longtime partner, Ilana Kloss, a former professional tennis star who was born in South Africa, appeared in public as a recognized couple. Beginning in the early 1990's, she was active in charitable events that raised money for AIDS research. Controversy, however, has followed King in some aspects of her life. She faced a highly publicized "palimony" suit in 1981 over her several-year relationship with Marilyn Barnett, who had been King's secretary. King won the case. Also, her identification with Virginia Slims cigarettes as a sponsor of the women's tennis tour she founded also raised questions about her financial links to the tobacco industry. King denied that her support of Virginia Slims had been inappropriate.

King's popularity as a major sports celebrity prevailed, however, into the twenty-first century. In 2006, the renowned USTA (U.S. Tennis Association) National Tennis Center in Flushing, New York, site of the U.S. Open, was renamed the USTA Billie Jean King National Tennis Center in her honor. Also in 2006, she was named to the California Hall of Fame. The Sports Museum of America in New York City, to which King was named a member of its board of honorary trustees, also houses the Billie Jean King International Women's Sport's Center. This center also includes the first women's sports hall of fame.

Significance

King was a great champion on the tennis court, especially at Wimbledon, where she dominated for so many years. Her aggressive, attacking style helped popularize women's tennis in the 1960's and 1970's. Off the court, she established the structure of women's tennis, bringing the sport to great heights of popularity and international appeal. Without her energy and resourcefulness, it would have taken much longer for women's tennis to have reached success as a respected sport.

King's match with Riggs, although it was a media event rather than a serious athletic contest, had great symbolic and cultural importance in providing credibility for women's athletics at a time when restrictive male attitudes predominated, especially in professional sports. As a result of that match, King became more than a famous athlete. Her admirers called her Mother Freedom. She emerged as one of the leaders in the movement for equal rights for women that transformed American society during the last quarter of the twentieth century. She also was the first prominent athlete in the United States to come out as lesbian, gay, or bisexual. Indeed, her name has become synonymous in popular culture with not only women athletes but also lesbian athletes and even feminists in general.

—*Karen Gould*

Further Reading

Amdur, Neil. "Mrs. King Defeats Bobby Riggs, 6-4, 6-3, 6-3, Amid a Circus Atmosphere." *The New York Times*, September 21, 1973. This front-page account of the Battle of the Sexes and the results of the match between King and Riggs shows the importance of the event at the time. A good primary source.

Brown, Gene, ed. *The Complete Book of Tennis*. Indianapolis, Ind.: Bobbs-Merrill, 1980. A compilation of stories from *The New York Times*, this book contains accounts of most of the significant matches of King's career.

Danzig, Allison, and Peter Schwed, eds. *The Fireside Book of Tennis*. New York: Simon & Schuster, 1972. This compilation of newspaper and magazine accounts of important tennis players and matches has several important essays that deal with King's rise to prominence in tennis during the 1960's.

King, Billie Jean, and Cynthia Starr. *We Have Come a Long Way: The Story of Women's Tennis*. New York: McGraw-Hill, 1988. A history of the sport, which contains King's own comments about her career and the players with whom she competed. An essential book for understanding her impact on the game.

King, Billie Jean, with Frank Deford. *Billie Jean*. New York: Viking Press, 1982. A candid autobiography in which King discusses the controversial aspects of her career as an athlete and public figure.

Marble, Alice, with Dale Leatherman. *Courting Danger*. New York: St. Martin's Press, 1991. Marble, King's coach, discusses the impression King made on her.

Roberts, Selena. *A Necessary Spectacle: Billie Jean King, Bobby Riggs, and the Tennis Match That Leveled the Game*. New York: Crown, 2005. A detailed examination of the celebrated 1973 encounter between King and Riggs that also serves as a good biographical introduction to King's career and influence on tennis.

Schwabacher, Martin. *Superstars of Women's Tennis*. Philadelphia: Chelsea House, 1997. A work that explores the world of women's tennis, with a chapter on King's career and her tennis legacy. Part of the Chelsea House's Female Sports Stars series.

Wade, Virginia, with Jean Rafferty. *Ladies of the Court: A Century of Women at Wimbledon*. New York: Atheneum, 1984. One chapter deals with King's outstanding record as a champion at Wimbledon and her important impact on the tournament.

MARTIN LUTHER KING, JR.

> *I have a dream that my four little children will one day live in a nation where they will not be judged by the color of their skin but by the content of their character.*

Civil rights leader

As founding president of the Southern Christian Leadership Conference, King spearheaded the nonviolent movement that led to the 1964 Civil Rights Act and the 1965 Voting Rights Act. His work was so profound that his name and messages have become synonymous with civil rights in the United States.

Born: January 15, 1929; Atlanta, Georgia
Died: April 4, 1968; Memphis, Tennessee
Also known as: Michael Luther King, Jr. (birth name)
Areas of achievement: Civil rights; social reform

EARLY LIFE

Martin Luther King, Jr., was the second child of the Reverend Michael Luther and Alberta Williams King. He was originally named Michael Luther King, Jr., but after the death of his paternal grandfather in 1933, King's father changed their first name to

King, Martin Luther, Jr.

Martin to honor the grandfather's insistence that he had originally given that name to his son in the days when birth certificates were rare for blacks. Nevertheless, King was known as M. L. or Mike throughout his childhood. In 1931, King's father became pastor of the Ebenezer Baptist Church on Auburn Avenue, only a block away from the house where King was born.

King's father was both a minister and a bold advocate of racial equality. His mother was the daughter of the Reverend Adam Daniel Williams, who had preceded King's father as pastor of Ebenezer and had established it as one of Atlanta's most influential black churches. Both of King's parents believed in nonviolent resistance to racial discrimination. He grew up under the strong influence of the church and this family tradition of independence.

King was a small boy, but vigorously athletic and intellectually curious. He enjoyed competitive games as well as words and ideas. Intrigued by the influence of his father and other ministers over their congregations, young King dreamed of being a great speaker. Lerone Bennett noted:

> To form words into sentences, to fling them out on the waves of air in a crescendo of sound, to watch people weep, shout, *respond*: this fascinated young Martin.... The idea of using words as weapons of defense and offense was thus early implanted and seems to have grown in King as naturally as a flower.

King excelled as a student and was able to skip two grades at Booker T. Washington High School and to enter Morehouse College in 1944 at age fifteen. At first he intended to study medicine, but religion and philosophy increasingly appealed to him as the influence of Morehouse president Benjamin E. Mays and George D. Kelsey of the religion department grew. Mays, a strong advocate of Christian nonviolence, sensed in King a profound talent in this area. In 1947, King was ordained a Baptist minister, and after graduation the following year he entered theological studies at Crozer Theological Seminary in Pennsylvania.

During his studies at Crozer and later in a doctoral program at Boston University (1951-1954), King deepened his knowledge of the great ideas of the past. Especially influential on his formative mind were the Social Gospel concept of Walter Rauschenbusch, the realist theology of Reinhold Niebuhr, and above all, the nonviolent reformism of Mahatma Gandhi. In Gandhi, King found the key to synthesizing his Christian faith, his passion for helping oppressed people, and his sense of realism sharpened by Niebuhrian theology. King later wrote:

> Gandhi was probably the first person in history to lift the love ethic of Jesus above mere interaction between individuals to a powerful and effective social force on a large scale.... It was in this Gandhian emphasis on love and nonviolence that I discovered the method for social reform.

King realized that nonviolence could not be applied in the United States exactly the way Gandhi had used it in India, but throughout his career King was devoted to the nonviolent method. In his mind, Gandhi's concept of *satyagraha* (force of

King, Martin Luther, Jr.

truth) and *ahimsa* (active love) were similar to the Christian idea of agape, or unselfish love.

In Boston, King experienced love of another kind. In 1952, he met Coretta Scott, a student at the New England Conservatory of Music. They were married at her home in Marion, Alabama, by King's father the following year. Neither wanted to return to the segregated South, but in 1954, while King was finishing his doctoral dissertation on the concepts of God in the thinking of Paul Tillich and Henry Nelson Wieman, he received a call to pastor the Dexter Avenue Baptist Church in Montgomery, Alabama. Their acceptance marked a major turning point in their own lives, as well as in American history.

By then King was twenty-five years old and still rather small at five feet seven inches. With brown skin, a strong build, large pensive eyes, and a slow, articulate speaking style, he was an unusually well-educated young minister anxious to begin his first pastorate. As the Kings moved to the city that had once been the capital of the Confederacy, they believed that God was leading them into an important future.

Martin Luther King, Jr.
(© The Nobel Foundation)

King, Martin Luther, Jr.

LIFE'S WORK

King quickly established himself as a hardworking pastor who guided his middle-class congregation into public service. He encouraged his parishioners to help the needy and to be active in organizations such as the National Association for the Advancement of Colored People (NAACP). Montgomery was a rigidly segregated city with thousands of blacks living on mere subsistence wages and barred from mainstream social life. The United States Supreme Court decision of 1954, requiring integration of public schools, had hardly touched the city, and most blacks apparently had little hope that their lives would ever improve.

An unexpected event in late 1955, however, changed the situation and drew King into his first significant civil rights activism. On December 1, Rosa Parks, a local black seamstress, was ordered by a bus driver to yield her seat to a white man. She refused, and her arrest triggered a 381-day bus boycott that led to a U.S. Supreme Court decision declaring the segregated transit system unconstitutional. King became the principal leader of the Montgomery Improvement Association, which administered the boycott, as thousands of local blacks cooperated in an effective nonviolent response to legally sanctioned segregation.

Quickly, the "Montgomery way" became a model for other southern cities: Tallahassee, Mobile, Nashville, Birmingham, and others. In January, 1957, King, his close friend Ralph Abernathy, and about two dozen other black ministers and laypersons met at the Ebenezer Baptist Church to form a movement across the South. Subsequent meetings in New Orleans and Montgomery led to the formal creation of the Southern Christian Leadership Conference (SCLC), which King used as the organizational arm of his movement.

From this point onward, King's life was bound with the southern nonviolent movement. Its driving force was the heightened confidence of thousands of blacks and their white supporters, but King was its symbol and spokesperson. He suffered greatly in the process. In 1958, while promoting his first book, *Stride Toward Freedom* (1958), an account of the Montgomery boycott, he was stabbed by a black woman. He was frequently arrested and berated by detractors as an "outside agitator" as he led various campaigns across the South. By early 1960, he had left his pastorate in Montgomery to become copastor (with his father) of the Ebenezer Baptist Church and to give his time more fully to the SCLC.

Not all of King's efforts were successful. A campaign in Albany, Georgia, in 1961 and 1962 failed to desegregate that city. At times there were overt tensions between King's SCLC and the more militant young people of the Student Nonviolent Coordinating Committee (SNCC), which was created in the wake of the first significant sit-in, in Greensboro, North Carolina, in February, 1960. King supported the sit-in and freedom ride movements of the early 1960's and was the overarching hero and spiritual mentor of the young activists, but his style was more patient and gradualist than theirs.

King's greatest successes occurred from 1963 to 1965. To offset the image of failure in Albany, the SCLC carefully planned a nonviolent confrontation in Birmingham, Alabama, in the spring of 1963. As the industrial hub of the South, Birmingham was viewed as the key to desegregating the entire region. The campaign there was launched during the Easter shopping season to maximize its economic effects. As the so-called battle of Birmingham unfolded, King was arrested and wrote his famous *Letter from Birmingham City Jail* (1963), in which he articulated the principles of nonviolent resistance and countered the argument that he was an "outside agitator" with the affirmation that all people are bound "in an inextricable network of mutuality" and that "injustice anywhere is a threat to justice everywhere."

The Birmingham campaign was an important victory. Nationally televised scenes of police chief Eugene "Bull" Connor's forces using fire hoses and trained dogs to attack nonviolent demonstrators stirred the public conscience. The Kennedy administration was moved to take an overt stand on behalf of civil rights. President Kennedy strongly urged Congress to pass his comprehensive civil rights bill. That bill was still pending in August, 1963, when King and many others led a march by more than 200,000 people to Washington, D.C. At the Lincoln Memorial on August 28, King delivered his most important speech, "I Have a Dream," calling on the nation to "rise up and live out the true meaning of its creed 'that all men are created equal.'"

After the March on Washington, King reached the height of his influence. Violence returned to Birmingham in September when four black girls were killed at the Sixteenth Street Baptist Church. In November, Kennedy was assassinated. However, in July, 1964, President Lyndon B. Johnson signed into law the Civil Rights Act that ended most legally sanctioned segregation in the United States. Later in 1964, King was awarded the Nobel Peace Prize. Increasingly, he turned his attention to world peace and economic advancement.

In 1965, King led a major campaign in Selma, Alabama, to underscore the need for stronger voting rights provisions than those of the 1964 Civil Rights Act. The result was the 1965 Voting Rights Act, which gave the federal government more power to enforce blacks' right to vote. Ironically, as these important laws went into effect, the ghettos of northern and western cities were erupting in violent riots. At the same time, the United States was becoming more deeply involved in the Vietnam War, and King was distressed by both of these trends. In 1966 and beyond, he attempted nonviolent campaigns in Chicago and other northern cities, but with less dramatic successes than those of Birmingham and Selma.

King's opposition to the Vietnam War alienated him from some of his black associates and many white supporters. Furthermore, it damaged his relationship with the Federal Bureau of Investigation (FBI) and the Johnson administration. Many observers have seen his last two years as a period of waning influence. Nevertheless, King continued to believe in nonviolent reform. In 1968, he was planning another march on Washington, this time to accentuate the plight of the poor of all races. In April he traveled to Memphis, Tennessee, to support a local sanitation workers' strike. On the balcony of the Lorraine Motel on April 4, he was shot to death by James Earl Ray. King's successor, Ralph Abernathy, carried through with the Poor People's March on Washington in June. King was survived by Coretta and their four children: Yolanda Denise (Yoki), Martin Luther III (Marty), Dexter, and Bernice Albertine (Bunny). Soon, Coretta established the Martin Luther King, Jr., Center for Nonviolent Social Change in Atlanta to carry on, like the SCLC, his work.

King, Martin Luther, Jr.

SIGNIFICANCE
King embodied a number of historical trends to which he added his own unique contributions. He was the author of five major books and hundreds of articles and speeches. His principal accomplishment was to raise the hopes of black Americans and to bind them in effective direct-action campaigns. Although he was the major spokesperson of the black movement, he was modest about his contributions. Just before his death, he declared in a sermon that he wanted to be remembered as a "drum major for justice." Essentially, he is. The campaigns he led paved the way for legal changes that ended more than a century of racial segregation.

Above all, King espoused nonviolence. That theme runs through his career and historical legacy. He left a decisive mark on American and world history. His dream of a peaceful world has inspired many individuals and movements. In 1983, Congress passed a law designating the third Monday in January a national holiday in his honor.

—Thomas R. Peake

FURTHER READING
Abernathy, Donzaleigh. *Partners to History: Martin Luther King, Jr., Ralph David Abernathy, and the Civil Rights Movement.* New York: Crown, 2003. Ralph David Abernathy's youngest daughter recounts how her father and King worked together in the Civil Rights movement, chronicling the Montgomery bus boycott, the March on Washington, and other movement activities.

Ansbro, John J. *Martin Luther King, Jr.: The Making of a Mind.* Maryknoll, N.Y.: Orbis Books, 1982. The best study of King's intellectual and spiritual development, based on extensive primary material from King's student days as well as later writings. Ansbro sees King in positive terms, focusing on the pivotal role of nonviolence based on agape in his social theology. Moral premises of nonviolence are skillfully analyzed.

Bennett, Lerone, Jr. *What Manner of Man: A Biography of Martin Luther King, Jr.* 1964. Rev. ed. New York: Johnson, 1976. This well-written volume captures the meaning of King's personality and faith. Bennett, a fellow graduate of Morehouse College and a distinguished black historian and editor of *Ebony*, shares many details of King's childhood and intellectual development. Although less thoroughly documented than some later biographies, Bennett's account is stronger than some in presenting King as a man driven by ideals and willingness to sacrifice.

Branch, Taylor. *At Canaan's Edge: America in the King Years, 1965-1968.* New York: Simon & Schuster, 2006. Branch's critically acclaimed three-volume history of King and the Civil Rights movement (*Parting the Waters: America in the King Years, 1954-1963*, vol. 1; and *Pillar of Fire: America in the King Years, 1963-1965*, vol. 2) traces King's political activities from the Montgomery bus boycott until his final campaign in Memphis in 1968.

Brauer, Carl M. *John F. Kennedy and the Second Reconstruction.* New York: Columbia University Press, 1977. Indispensable reading for understanding King's political impact and the setting within which the Civil Rights movement developed. Brauer traces in detail, and with thorough documentation, the development of Kennedy's civil rights advocacy and the role of King in shaping the political culture of the 1960's.

Garrow, David J. *Bearing the Cross: Martin Luther King, Jr., and the Southern Christian Leadership Conference, a Personal Portrait.* New York: William Morrow, 1986. The most thorough recounting of the life of King, with extensive material on the SCLC as well. Garrow carefully documents King's personal life, the origins and progress of his movement, and does so with specific attention to the famous leader's internal struggles. In particular, King's struggle with sexual temptations and his sometimes agonizing awareness that his life was at risk come through powerfully in this well-researched account. In places, brief on interpretation and perspective, but a highly valuable source on King, the movement, and the FBI's probing of them.

_____. *The FBI and Martin Luther King, Jr.: From "Solo" to Memphis.* New York: W. W. Norton, 1981. Garrow has established impressive authority in analyzing King's public career. This work examines the roots and nature of the FBI's opposition to King and the SCLC and demonstrates that serious efforts were made to discredit King as a national leader. Well documented, although to some degree limited by lack of access to the FBI tapes on King's personal life.

King, Coretta Scott. *My Life with Martin Luther King, Jr.* New York: Holt, Rinehart and Winston, 1969. Written shortly after King's death, this book is a valuable personal account of the King family, the Montgomery bus boycott, and several later SCLC campaigns. Its chief value lies in what it shares about the author's own thinking, her husband's personal trials and accomplishments, and the human reality of the civil rights story. Needs to be balanced by scholarly accounts of the campaigns and King's biography.

King, Martin Luther, Jr. *Stride Toward Freedom: The Montgomery Story.* New York: Harper & Row, 1958. Not only King's first book but also the best as a source of his intellectual pilgrimage. Shares many internal details of his own development as well as the origins and nature of the boycott. The last part is a comprehensive analysis of the church's role in race relations.

Peake, Thomas R. *Keeping the Dream Alive: A History of the Southern Christian Leadership Conference from King to the 1980s.* New York: Peter Lang, 1986. The first comprehensive history of the SCLC, with considerable biographical information on King. Based on a wide variety of sources, including many interviews. Analyzes the SCLC's organizational history, the nature of King's social dream, and the continuity of King's ideas and influence after 1968.

ROBERT M. LA FOLLETTE

> " ... *our Government, above all others, is founded on the right of the people freely to discuss all matters pertaining to their Government, in war not less than in peace.* "

Governor of Wisconsin (1901-1905) and U.S. senator (1906-1925)

As governor of Wisconsin and a U.S. senator, La Follette combined a strong sense of social justice with an intense commitment to principles as a leader of the reform movement in politics from 1900 to 1925.

Born: June 14, 1855; Primrose, Wisconsin
Died: June 18, 1925; Washington, D.C.
Also known as: Robert Marion La Follette (full name); Fighting Bob La Follette (nickname)
Area of achievement: Government and politics

EARLY LIFE

Robert M. La Follette (lah-FAW-leht) was born in Primrose township, Dane County, Wisconsin, a few miles from Madison. His father, Josiah, died before Robert was a year old; in 1862 his mother, née Mary Ferguson, married John Z. Saxton of Argyle, a prosperous merchant and Baptist deacon. La Follette attended school in Argyle until 1870, when he returned with his family to the La Follette family farm in Primrose, where he assumed much of the responsibility for operating the farm. In 1873, a year after his stepfather's death, he began preparatory courses at the Wisconsin Academy in Madison and entered the University of Wisconsin in 1875. He did not distinguish himself in academics but built a reputation as a brilliant speaker and a popular student who financed his education by purchasing and publishing the student newspaper, the *University Press*. Following graduation, he took law courses at the University, read in a Madison attorney's office, and courted his University of Wisconsin classmate Belle Case, whom he married in December, 1881.

La Follette established a legal practice in Madison in 1880; he entered politics the same year with his election to the office of district attorney for Dane County. His warm personality and speaking ability made him popular, and he was easily reelected in 1882. He was elected to the first of three consecutive terms in the United States House of Representatives in 1884, even though he did not have the backing of Republican state bosses. The youngest member of Congress when he entered the House in 1885, La Follette was a fairly regular Republican during his three terms there. He strengthened his political hold on his congressional district by supporting legislation he saw as beneficial to farmers, including assiduous support of the McKinley Tariff of 1890. In spite of his strong political base, he was the victim of an imbroglio over a law requiring English-language instruction in Wisconsin schools. While La Follette had nothing to do with the state law, he was caught in a backlash against Republicans and was defeated in 1890.

La Follette returned to his legal practice in Madison. The clean-shaven, square-jawed lawyer with piercing eyes and upswept, bushy dark hair (which added inches to his five

La Follette, Robert M.

foot five inch frame) built a reputation for dynamism in jury trials. At the same time, he strove to fulfill his political ambitions by establishing, within the Republican Party in Wisconsin, an organization to challenge the control of state bosses, notably U.S. senators John C. Spooner and Philetus Sawyer. By 1897, the La Follette organization had adopted a popular program that grew out of the economic depression that began in 1893: corporate regulation, equity in taxation, and the democratization of the political system through direct primary elections. Refused the gubernatorial nomination by state Republican conventions in 1896 and 1898, La Follette persevered in winning support; in 1900 he was elected governor of Wisconsin and assumed office in January, 1901.

Life's Work

As governor for two full terms and part of a third, La Follette successfully converted Wisconsin into a so-called laboratory of democracy. The transformation, however, did not take place immediately. When he entered office with the intention of redeeming his campaign pledges of a direct primary law and railroad tax legislation, he encountered persistent opposition from the state legislature. The lack of reform accomplishments in his first term led to a sweeping campaign in 1902 not only for his own reelection but also for the election of state legislators who would follow his program. In subsequent sessions, the legislature passed the primary election and railroad tax laws and set up a railroad rate commission. Moreover, La Follette so firmly established the direction of reform politics in Wisconsin that his followers would control state offices for years after he left the governorship. A few weeks after the legislature convened in January, 1905, La Follette was elected to the United States Senate. He left Wisconsin at the end of the year, after securing passage of the railroad rate commission law, and was sworn into the Senate on January 4, 1906.

La Follette made an immediate impact on the Senate. Although unsuccessful in promoting major reform legislation in early sessions, he received widespread attention for pressing for more stringent regulation of railroads and for his attack on the "Money Trust" while filibustering against a monetary bill proposed by Senate Republican leader Nelson W. Aldrich. His national reputation was further enhanced by his frequent Chautauqua speaking tours around the country (which began while he was governor of Wisconsin) and by the attention accorded him by reform journalists such as David Graham Phillips and Lincoln Steffens; the latter proposed a La Follette presidential campaign in 1908 on an independent ticket. While eschewing such a campaign, La Follette successfully assisted Progressive candidates in several states in their congressional races, thus establishing a solid core of reform-minded colleagues for the ensuing Congress. To publicize his causes (and with the hope of a solid financial return), he initiated *La Follette's Weekly Magazine* in January, 1909; he would continue the venture until his death, although it was more a financial liability than a success and was reorganized as a monthly in 1914.

La Follette and his new Senate allies challenged the Taft administration on several important issues and effectively established themselves as an insurgent wing of the Republican Party. By leading Senate Progressives in opposition to the 1909 Payne-Aldrich Tariff and in pressing for conservation measures and a program of direct democracy, La Follette earned the hostile attention of President William Howard Taft,

La Follette, Robert M.

Robert M. La Follette.
(Library of Congress)

who worked hard to unseat the Wisconsin senator in his 1910 bid for reelection. La Follette won easily and returned to Washington in 1911 determined to reconstruct the Republican Party along liberal lines. As much as any individual, he was responsible for the ideological split in the GOP that led to the formation of the Progressive Party in 1912. He was not the presidential nominee, however, as most of his supporters in the National Progressive Republican League (which he had founded in January, 1911) deserted him to support the popular former president Theodore Roosevelt; his candidacy was further impaired by a temporary breakdown he suffered while delivering a speech in February, 1912, before the annual banquet of the Periodical Publishers' Association in Philadelphia. He refused to endorse any candidate in 1912, but his speeches and magazine articles were generally supportive of the Democrat Woodrow Wilson.

La Follette's influence declined in the Democratic-controlled Senate of the early Wilson administration. While he supported some Wilson labor measures and managed to steer his La Follette Seamen's Act through Congress in 1915, he was critical of the president's blueprint for the Federal Reserve System, appointments to the Federal Trade Commission, and policy on racial segregation in the federal government. His greatest opposition to Wilson came in the area of foreign policy. Sharply critical of Wilson's increased military spending in 1915-1916, La Follette argued that such expenditures increased the profits of corporations at the expense of taxpayers and, ultimately, American security interests. Using the same argument, he voted against American entry into World War I and remained a leading antiwar spokesperson throughout. He also led fights for free speech and against censorship laws and proposed new taxes on war profits to pay for the prosecution of the war. He voted against the Versailles Treaty in the Senate, characterizing it as reactionary in its treatment of the Soviet Union and in reinforcing colonialism in Ireland, India, and Egypt.

In the conservative Republican era that followed the war, La Follette fashioned a new political constituency among the farm and labor groups that emerged in political affairs in the early 1920's. Reacting to an agricultural depression and what many saw as an antilabor atmosphere, groups such as the American Federation of Labor, the railroad brotherhoods, the Nonpartisan League, and the American Farm Bureau Federation formed an alliance that resulted in the Conference for Progressive Political Action in 1922 and the Progressive Party in 1924. In a zealous campaign against Republican "normalcy," La Follette and Burton K. Wheeler, Progressive candidates for president and vice president, respectively, polled 4.8 million votes, approximately one in every six cast. La Follette's health was poor during this campaign, which was his last. He died of a heart attack on June 18, 1925, and was buried at Forest Hill Cemetery in Madison four days later.

Significance

La Follette's campaigns, full of vitriol directed against "the interests" as opposed to "the people," largely reflected the populist roots of midwestern Progressivism. In La Follette's view, the most obvious villain was large-scale corporate capitalism; his ideal was an open, competitive economic system—he consistently championed the cause of individuals as voters, consumers, and small-business persons. His political solutions included a roster of Populist planks: the direct election of U.S. senators, direct primary elections, the graduated income tax, and public ownership of railroads, among others.

In opposing corporate growth, La Follette fought a losing battle against modernization; he was also responsible, however, for labor and agricultural programs that eased the adjustment of some groups to modern conditions. In addition, an important facet of the "Wisconsin Idea" he initiated as governor was the modern use of expert panels and commissions to make recommendations on legislation and regulatory activities. His reliance on faculty members of the University of Wisconsin (such as economists John Commons and Richard Ely) not only enhanced the university's reputation but also served as an example to reformers in other states.

Nicknamed Fighting Bob La Follette, the senator possessed notable personal characteristics that made him a symbol of the movement he led. His dynamic, aggressive style was complemented by a fearless quality that enabled him to challenge the leadership of his own party and to risk his career in opposing World War I. When engaged in a cause, his intensity was so great that he suffered several physical breakdowns during his political career. This combination of qualities contributed to a remarkable Senate career; in 1957, the Senate voted to recognize La Follette as one of the five outstanding members in Senate history.

—*Richard G. Frederick*

La Follette, Robert M.

FURTHER READING

Burgchardt, Carl R. *Robert M. La Follette, Sr.: The Voice of Conscience*. Foreword by Bernard K. Duffy. New York: Greenwood Press, 1992. Describes the political views of La Follette.

Conant, James K. *Wisconsin Politics and Government: America's Laboratory of Democracy*. Lincoln: University of Nebraska Press, 2006. Conant provides a history of the state's Progressivism, including the policies implemented during La Follette's gubernatorial administration.

La Follette, Belle Case, and Fola La Follette. *Robert M. La Follette*. 2 vols. New York: Macmillan, 1953. Written by La Follette's wife and daughter. As an insiders' account, the book naturally tends to lack objectivity, but it is strengthened by the authors' intimate understanding of the subject. In addition, the book is meticulously researched and ably written with a wealth of detail.

La Follette, Robert M. *La Follette's Autobiography: A Personal Narrative of Political Experiences*. 1913. Reprint. Madison: University of Wisconsin Press, 1963. Originally published by La Follette as a campaign document for the 1912 presidential election. La Follette provides a detailed narrative of his political thought and activities, as well as his antagonism toward Theodore Roosevelt.

Margulies, Herbert F. *The Decline of the Progressive Movement in Wisconsin: 1890-1920*. Madison: State Historical Society of Wisconsin, 1968. Margulies finds that the Progressive movement in Wisconsin was well into decline before World War I. He details how internal divisions among the Progressives (largely over La Follette's political tactics) led to their defeat by conservatives.

Thelen, David P. *The Early Life of Robert M. La Follette, 1855-1884*. Chicago: Loyola University Press, 1966. A brief examination of La Follette's formative years in Wisconsin to his 1884 election to Congress.

———. *The New Citizenship: Origins of Progressivism in Wisconsin, 1885-1900*. Columbia: University of Missouri Press, 1972. Demonstrates how La Follette came into a movement already under way in Wisconsin in the late 1890's. The book is particularly good in its treatment of the social and political milieu in which reform ideas grew, largely out of issues of the 1893-1897 depression; these issues caused a "new civic consciousness" to develop among politicians and voters of diverse backgrounds.

———. *Robert M. La Follette and the Insurgent Spirit*. Boston: Little, Brown, 1976. Incisively relates La Follette's career to the course of Progressive insurgency in the Republican Party from the late 1890's to the 1920's. Thelen clearly delineates La Follette's positions and contrasts them with those of regular Republicans and Wilsonian Democrats.

Unger, Nancy C. *Fighting Bob La Follette: The Righteous Reformer*. Chapel Hill: University of North Carolina Press, 2000. Biography in which Unger weaves the story of La Follette's family life with his career accomplishments.

Weisberger, Bernard A. *The La Follettes of Wisconsin: Love and Politics in Progressive America*. Madison: University of Wisconsin Press, 1994. A description of the La Follette family and their political views.

Lee, Robert E.

ROBERT E. LEE

> *So far from engaging in a war to perpetuate slavery, I am rejoiced that slavery is abolished. I believe it will be greatly for the interest of the South.*

Military leader

Perhaps the finest military tactician of his generation, Lee commanded the Army of Northern Virginia so brilliantly during the American Civil War that he helped to prolong the life of the Confederacy.

Born: January 19, 1807; Stratford Hall, Westmoreland County, Virginia
Died: October 12, 1870; Lexington, Virginia
Also known as: Robert Edward Lee (full name)
Area of achievement: Military

EARLY LIFE

Last in the long line of the famous Lees of Virginia and fifth of seven children, Robert Edward Lee was born at the family estate of Stratford. His father, Colonel Henry "Light Horse" Harry Lee, had served with distinction as a cavalryman in the Revolutionary War and later as governor of Virginia, although he was financially insecure. His mother, Anne Hill Carter Lee, belonged to another aristocratic Virginia family. The family moved to Alexandria in Robert's fourth year, and he attended the local schools there. Because of the long absences and then the death of his father, Robert gradually took over the major care of his invalid mother. This intimate relationship shaped young Lee's character as one of quiet dignity, high moral integrity, and personal strength.

Desiring to emulate his father and to obtain a free education, Lee attended the United States Military Academy at West Point, where he performed as an outstanding cadet and was graduated second in a class of forty-six in 1829. Entering the engineer corps, he built and maintained coastal fortifications and river works. In June, 1831, he married his childhood friend Mary Anne Randolph Custis, the great-granddaughter of the wife of George Washington, at the opulent Custis estate at Arlington. Their marriage strengthened Lee's deep roots in his native state, though his devotion to his country enabled him to resist the temptation to settle down to the life of a country squire at Arlington, which he managed even while posted elsewhere, and where his seven children were reared. He ably performed the mundane tasks of a peacetime army engineer and held the rank of captain at the outbreak of the Mexican War in 1846.

LIFE'S WORK

Lee's genius as a field officer emerged during the Mexican War and placed him in the public eye. He received the brevet rank of major for his performance as a staff officer in the early campaigns, after which he transferred to the staff of General Winfield Scott for the major invasion of central Mexico. Lee contributed materially to the capture of Vera Cruz in April, 1847; through his ability and bravery in placing artillery and reconnoitering in several battles, he was promoted to brevet lieutenant colonel. After the attack on Chapultepec, in which he was wounded, he became brevet colonel.

Soon, however, Lee returned to routine duties, constructing fortifications near Baltimore and then, during 1852-1855, improving the course of study at West Point as superintendent. His reward was a transfer out of engineering to the Second Cavalry Regiment, with the rank of lieutenant colonel, policing the Indians in west Texas. In July, 1857, he assumed the colonelcy of the regiment. Home on leave during the fall of 1859, Lee was ordered to subdue John Brown's force, which had occupied the armory at Harpers Ferry (then part of Virginia) in Brown's stillborn attempt to incite a slave uprising in the South. After accomplishing the task, Lee returned to his regiment and, in 1860, assumed command of the Department of Texas.

A mild-mannered, even gentle officer with an excellent physique and devoted to the army and the flag, Lee dutifully obeyed his orders to return to Washington upon the secession of Texas from the Union in February, 1861. The next month, he was made colonel of the First Cavalry. By any measure the most able officer in the army, he was the logical choice to command the forces necessary to subdue the southern rebellion, a command offered him by the Lincoln administration upon the outbreak of the Civil

Robert E. Lee.
(Library of Congress)

Lee, Robert E.

War in mid-April, 1861. Following the secession of Virginia and considerable soul searching, however, Lee decided that his loyalty rested with his home state, whereupon he resigned his commission on April 23. He was given command of the Virginia militia and was soon appointed brigadier general in the new Confederate army. Within months, his normal dark hair and mustache would be replaced by a full beard and hair completely grayed, the result no doubt of his awesome responsibilities.

Promoted to the full rank of general during the summer, one of five initially appointed, Lee first advised President Jefferson Davis in organizing the Confederate army. He took command of the forces attempting to hold West Virginia in the Confederacy in August but was soundly defeated the next month at Cheat Mountain. Early in November, he assumed command of the coastal defenses of South Carolina, Georgia, and eastern Florida. Shortages of troops there led him to establish a strong defense against potential Union naval and amphibious penetrations. His strategy was faulty, however, because the Union had no intention of invading the interior in that quarter and instead attacked and successfully occupied key coastal positions merely for use as blockading stations for the navy.

Lee was recalled early in March, 1862, to help Davis organize the defenses of Richmond against the advance of General George B. McClellan's army in the Peninsular Campaign. When the commander of the defending army, General Joseph E. Johnston, was wounded at Fair Oaks, Lee was given command on June 1, and he quickly reorganized his forces into the Army of Northern Virginia, a name he created. He masterfully countered McClellan's forces in the Seven Days' Battles, concluded on July 1, then swung north to defeat the army of General John Pope at the Second Battle of Bull Run in late August. Crossing the Potomac, Lee attempted to gain the support of Marylanders but was stopped by McClellan in the Antietam campaign in September. He concluded the year by repulsing the bloody Union assaults on his well-placed army at Fredericksburg in December.

Lee's true genius in tactics lay in erecting field fortifications and in his remarkable ability to operate from the interior position—that is, to shift his forces between different points in his lines that were threatened by the larger numbers of the opposing Union armies. This tactic was best demonstrated in his stunning victory at Chancellorsville in May, 1863, when his army was half the size of that of the enemy. His greatest gamble occurred when he invaded Pennsylvania a month later. Frustrated from trying to turn the Union flanks at Gettysburg in July, he tried a frontal assault—"Pickett's charge"—that was virtually annihilated by the Army of the Potomac under General George G. Meade. As a result of this defeat, Lee was thereafter confined to the strategic defensive.

Lee fought a steadily losing battle against the vastly greater numbers and better-equipped troops of General Ulysses S. Grant's armies in the Wilderness Campaign during the spring of 1864. Lee's men, inspired largely by his towering leadership, stopped every bloody assault, but Lee was obliged to retreat each time, lest the larger Union forces turn his flank and cut him off from Richmond. As a result, Lee withdrew into the defenses of that city and adjacent Petersburg, to withstand what turned out to be a nine-month-long siege. Near its end, in February, 1865, he was finally made general in chief of all Confederate armies. It was, by this time, too late. He placed Johnston

Lee, Robert E.

in command of the only other remaining major army, in the Carolinas. Then, in April, he attempted to escape a fresh Union offensive at Petersburg to link up with Johnston. Grant cut him off at Appomattox Court House in Virginia, where Lee surrendered on April 9, effectively ending the Civil War. His three sons were with him, two of them major generals, one a captain.

Having lost his home at Arlington, which became the national cemetery, Lee assumed the presidency of Washington College at Lexington, Virginia, in October, 1865. For the next five years, in weakened health, he served effectively not only as a college administrator but also as a quiet symbol of reunion and restoration, burying the passions of the wartime bitterness and thereby setting an example for the defeated South. Following his death, the college was renamed Washington and Lee in his honor.

SIGNIFICANCE

Robert E. Lee became a legend in his own time, first to the embattled peoples of the South and, eventually, to the nation at large. He symbolized the plain fact that, rather than treason, the cause of the Confederacy had represented the playing out of the final contradiction of the American nation. North and South, geographically, economically, and socially distinct, could no longer coexist within the fabric of the Constitution. The southern plantation aristocracy, agrarian and founded upon slavery, had become an anachronism in the modern, industrialized Western world, as Lee himself would acknowledge. Its ultimate survival could be obtained only by arms, in which contest Lee had been the supreme champion. His stately character, bearing, and professionalism represented the ideal of southern society. Though he had opposed slavery, secession, and even war as a final political solution, like so many of his generation, he had had to make the tragic, fateful decision to stand by his neighbors in defense of the only way of life they knew. In defeat, he accepted the course of history without rancor.

The contrast between Lee's conduct and that of his Union counterparts reflected the great shift in social values marked by the Civil War. He ordered his troops to abstain from plundering civilian property, failing to understand—unlike Grant, William T. Sherman, and Philip H. Sheridan—that the modern war that they were all waging was a harbinger of a new age of mass conflict, aimed at breaking civilian resistance with the use of modern industrialized machine weapons, thus destroying the socioeconomic institutions of an enemy. No better example of the adage that the Civil War was the last great war between gentlemen could be found than in the person of Robert E. Lee himself, the perfect gentleman of the long-past Age of Reason that had spawned his noble family.

Lee's achievements on the field of battle, however, established him as one of the greatest army commanders in history. Not merely an inspiring leader, he made correct, informed judgments about his enemy, then struck decisively. As a theater strategist defending his beloved Virginia, he became a master of the mobile feint, thanks largely to several able lieutenants. Stonewall Jackson's fast-moving so-called foot cavalry thrust into the Shenandoah Valley to draw away troops from McClellan during the Peninsular Campaign. J. E. B. Stuart's cavalry rode circles around the Union armies in every campaign. However, both these commanders were killed, in 1863 and 1864, respec-

Lee, Robert E.

tively. Jubal A. Early's drive up the valley the latter year might have succeeded but for the determined riposte of Grant and Sheridan. In grand strategy, however, Lee was not adept, having misjudged Union intentions along the south Atlantic coast early in the war and never having the authority to mastermind Confederate fortunes until near the end of the struggle. He did not attempt to influence Davis beyond the Virginia theater.

Had Lee not been outnumbered most of the time, one can only conjecture what might have been the outcome of the war: As a tactician, he had no match in the Union army. The fatal flaw lay in the nature of the Confederacy itself, a politically loose grouping of rebelling states, devoid of effective central leadership. After Gettysburg, observed one of Lee's generals on the eve of Appomattox, the men had been fighting simply for him.

—*Clark G. Reynolds*

FURTHER READING

Blount, Roy, Jr. *Robert E. Lee: A Penguin Life.* New York: Lipper/Viking, 2003. Concise biography, written from the perspective of a southerner. Particularly strong in detailing Lee's life after the Civil War.

Connelly, Thomas L. *The Marble Man: Robert E. Lee and His Image in American Society.* New York: Alfred A. Knopf, 1977. An excellent interpretative analysis of Lee's reputation as a southern and national hero during and since the Civil War.

Dowdey, Clifford. *Lee.* Boston: Little, Brown, 1965. An excellent one-volume treatment of Lee's career, adding new materials and interpretations of Lee's performance at Gettysburg.

Fellman, Michael. *The Making of Robert E. Lee.* New York: Random House, 2000. Intellectual biography, focusing on Lee's psychology and ideas on race, slavery, and other issues. Describes how Lee struggled to reconcile his Christian virtue, humility, and sense of duty with his desire for success and fame.

Flood, Charles Bracelen. *Lee: The Last Years.* Boston: Houghton Mifflin, 1981. The best analysis of Lee's actions and achievements during the last five years of his life, including his reactions to the late war.

Freeman, Douglas Southall. *R. E. Lee.* 4 vols. New York: Charles Scribner's Sons, 1934-1935. The definitive biography, which dissects Lee's career with such detail and careful interpretation as to become the standard work for all students of Lee.

Johnson, Robert Underwood, and Clarence Clough Buel, eds. *Battles and Leaders of the Civil War.* 4 vols. New York: Century, 1887. The most comprehensive and reliable source of reminiscences of key Civil War leaders, including many of Lee's subordinates and opponents, with complete lists of the opposing armies and navies, down to the regimental and ship level. Excellent maps and illustrations.

Lee, Robert E. *Recollections and Letters of General Robert E. Lee by His Son Capt. Robert E. Lee.* 2d ed. Garden City, N.Y.: Doubleday, Page, 1924. An invaluable memoir, especially useful for insights into Lee's family relationships.

———. *The Wartime Papers of R. E. Lee.* Edited by Clifford Dowdey and Louis Manarin. Boston: Little, Brown, 1961. Primary source material, drawn from official records and private sources, that offers insights into Lee's character and abilities as a commander.

Sanborn, Margaret. *Robert E. Lee.* 2 vols. Philadelphia: J. B. Lippincott, 1966-1967. A sound popular history based on the usual abundant primary and secondary sources.

Thomas, Emory M. *Robert E. Lee: A Biography.* New York: W. W. Norton, 1995. Comprehensive, analytical biography by a prominent Civil War historian. Thomas focuses on Lee as a person, portraying him as a man of many paradoxes.

JOHN L. LEWIS

" Let the workers organize. Let the toilers assemble. Let their crystallized voice proclaim their injustices and demand their privileges. Let all thoughtful citizens sustain them, for the future of Labor is the future of America. "

Labor leader

As president of the United Mine Workers union and founder of the Congress of Industrial Organizations, Lewis dominated the progress of organized labor in the United States from the 1920's through the 1960's.

Born: February 12, 1880; Lucas, Iowa
Died: June 11, 1969; Washington, D.C.
Also known as: John Llewellyn Lewis (full name)
Area of achievement: Labor movement

EARLY LIFE

John Llewellyn Lewis (lew-EHL-lehn LEW-ihs) was the son of Thomas Lewis and Louisa (née Watkins) Lewis, who had been born in Wales and had migrated to the United States in the 1870's. John was the eldest of six sons and two daughters. Thomas worked as a coal miner whenever he could find work, but, having been placed on an employer blacklist for leading a miners' strike in 1882, he often had to fill in with other jobs, such as working as a night watchman.

Young John only went as far as the eighth grade before leaving school to supplement his father's meager and irregular income. He sold newspapers in Des Moines, Iowa, for a few years until the abolition of the blacklist in 1897 allowed his father to return to Lucas, where John, then age seventeen, joined him in the coal mines. John worked there until 1901 and then set off on a working tour of Western mining communities, toiling in copper, silver, gold, and coal mines in Montana, Utah, Arizona, and Colorado. Soon after returning to Lucas in 1906, he married Myrta Edith Bell, the daughter of a local doctor. They would have three children: Margaret Mary (who died in childhood), Florence Kathryn, and John Llewellyn II.

Shortly before Lewis's marriage, the Lucas miners elected him as a delegate to the national convention of the United Mine Workers of America (UMW), the largest union affiliated with the American Federation of Labor (AFL). A few years later, in 1909, he moved his family to Panama, Illinois, and continued his union activity. He

Lewis, John L.

was selected president of the Panama miners' local union and soon thereafter was appointed state legislative agent for District 12 of the UMW. It was in this capacity that he convinced the Illinois legislature to pass a comprehensive package of mine safety and workmen's compensation laws by exploiting the Cherry, Illinois, mine disaster of 1911 that killed 160 men.

Samuel Gompers (founder and president of the AFL), impressed by Lewis's obvious leadership talents, took the young labor activist under his wing and made him a national legislative representative for the AFL in late 1911. This job took Lewis to Washington, D.C., where he was able to learn valuable lessons regarding the politics and management of labor organization. He also continued his rise through the ranks of the UMW. In 1916, he served as temporary chair of the UMW's national convention and, in 1917, he was elected vice president of the union.

Lewis had his first taste of national-level labor confrontation when, in 1919, he became acting president of the union for Frank J. Hayes, who had become too debilitated by alcoholism to carry out his duties. Several months after assuming this position, Lewis called for a strike when mine operators rejected the union's demand for a 60 percent wage hike, a six-hour workday, and a five-day workweek. A federal court issued an injunction against the strike, but, in November, 1919, Lewis defied the injunction, ordering 425,000 men out of the mines. The strike lasted two months and, after a face-to-face meeting with President Woodrow Wilson, Lewis was forced to call the miners back to work. They did gain a wage increase of approximately 30 percent, but their other demands went unsatisfied. The rough, bulky, bushy-eyebrowed Lewis did gain a reputation for toughness during the strike, however, and he parlayed this into an official UMW presidency in 1920. He would hold this position until he retired in 1960.

Life's Work

Lewis assumed the presidency of the UMW at a time when the coal industry had begun to experience serious difficulties. Coal output had skyrocketed between 1916 and 1919 to meet wartime needs but, once World War I was over, demand dropped back to more normal levels, causing a glut of coal on the market. In addition, mine owners with union workers faced rising competition from nonunion mines in the South and from "captive" mines owned by steel companies and railroads. In an effort to meet these threats, unionized producers began to lower both prices and miners' wages. Lewis refused to agree to this wage-reduction strategy, and in 1922 he called a strike. Miners did win a wage increase to $7.50 a day as a result of this strike, but many only worked irregularly as the crisis persisted.

In the years that followed, the situation in the coal industry continued to deteriorate. More than three thousand mines shut down during the 1920's, and UMW membership dropped from a high of 500,000 in 1922 to 150,000 by 1930. Lewis responded by urging coal operators to increase their productivity and thereby halt the precipitous decline in regular miner employment. He opposed pay cuts that were made to keep unprofitable operations in business and instead favored the closing of these marginal mines and the introduction of increased mechanization in remaining ones to make them more efficient and competitive—and thus a stable source of employment for his members. Factions within the UMW opposed Lewis's proposals and organized a series of wildcat strikes to protest his emphasis on mechanization (which they believed would cost even more jobs). This struggle within the UMW, which also contributed to the decline in membership, culminated at the national convention of 1930, where his opponents made a concerted effort to unseat him. Lewis still had enough support within the UMW, however, to resist these attempts and to purge the leaders of this opposition from the union.

As the Depression tightened its grip on the United States after 1930, it also aggravated the problems within the coal industry. Coal sales continued to slump, and thousands of miners lost their jobs. The UMW, in an increasingly weakened position, could do little to resist employer attempts to reduce the wages of miners who managed to keep their jobs. It was at this point that Lewis turned to the national government for help. Although he had been a Republican throughout the 1920's and had even supported Herbert Hoover in 1932, Lewis recognized that the Democrat who defeated his man in that election, Franklin D. Roosevelt, was sympathetic to labor's plight and might come to its aid. Accordingly, Lewis swung to Roosevelt and the Democratic Party and participated actively in the New Deal. He became a labor adviser to the president, a member of the Labor Advisory Board, and a member of the National Labor Board. This close relationship between the UMW and the Roosevelt administration benefited both parties. Because of the passage of the Guffey Act of 1935, National Labor Relations Act (or Wagner Act) of 1935, and section 7A of the National Industrial Recovery Act of 1933, miners received a substantial daily pay raise, a shortened workday, and the right to bargain collectively through their own representatives. The UMW recovered as a result, and, by 1935, its membership was approaching one-half million again. Roosevelt, on the other hand, received the grateful votes of coal miners, relative labor peace in the mines, and large contributions from the UMW to his campaign treasury.

Meanwhile, trouble was brewing in the AFL, and Lewis, as usual, was at the center of it. Lewis had decided that "industrial unionism" (where all workers in a given industry, regardless of their particular trade, would be part of a single union that represented them all) was the best way for workers to fight for their rights, and he tried to convince the AFL, which represented workers by their trade, to adopt this policy. At the AFL national convention of 1935, however, his proposal was soundly rejected. In response, Lewis resigned as vice president of the AFL in November, 1935, and formed a new omnibus labor organization based on industrial unionism, one that eventually became the Congress of Industrial Organizations (CIO). Lewis's UMW led the way in affiliating with this new organization, and it was soon joined by many others. By 1938, the CIO included forty-four unions and more than four million members.

As president of the CIO, Lewis also began the hard struggle to organize automobile and steelworkers and affiliate them with his organization. Employing such tactics as the sit-down strike, he did force the automobile industry to recognize the CIO in 1937. He then convinced the nation's largest steel manufacturer, United States Steel, to accept the CIO (also in 1937). The smaller steel companies, however, such as Bethlehem and Republic Steel, put up strong resistance to Lewis's organizing efforts, forcing him to call a strike against them in May, 1937. Marred by violence, the strike dragged on until late summer of that year, and Lewis ultimately accepted a compromise settlement that fell short of his initial goals.

Lewis, John L.

The strike also provoked a break between Lewis and Roosevelt. Lewis became disappointed and frustrated at the president's lack of support for the so-called Little Steel strike and tried to rally labor behind his Republican opponent, Wendell Willkie, in the election of 1940. Roosevelt nevertheless won easily, but he never forgave Lewis for his defection. Temporarily defeated, Lewis resigned as president of the CIO and devoted his full attention to his UMW.

Lewis opposed American involvement in World War II and stuck to this position right up to the Japanese attack on Pearl Harbor on December 7, 1941. Although he declared his support for the American war effort after this attack, his "noninvolvement" stand up to Pearl Harbor had alienated many of his former allies among the leadership of the CIO. In 1942, therefore, he pulled the UMW out of the CIO and purged CIO sympathizers from his union.

Lewis did not allow the war to stop him from fighting for the coal miners. In 1943, he declared that the wage increase authorized by the War Labor Board was inadequate and called a strike. The conflict lasted nearly a year, and, during its course, the government temporarily took over the nation's mines, and Roosevelt even appealed directly to the miners to return to work. In the end, though, Lewis won a two-dollars-per-day pay increase for his men. He called another strike in 1945 and won again, gaining an increase in overtime pay, the establishment of one-hour travel pay to and from work, and paid vacations for miners. Lewis authorized still another strike in March, 1946, which resulted in a small pay increase and, more important, the establishment of a pension and welfare fund for miners, financed by a five cents per ton royalty on all coal produced.

In October, 1946, Lewis called his third strike in fourteen months in an attempt to reduce the miners' workweek to less than fifty-four hours. A federal court judge issued a restraining order against this work stoppage. When Lewis ignored the order, the judge found him to be in criminal and civil contempt and fined him $10,000 and the UMW $3.5 million. The Supreme Court upheld the judge's order, and Lewis had no choice but to call off the strike.

In between the two strikes in 1946, Lewis had reaffiliated the UMW with the AFL. This reconciliation lasted only a year before Lewis, after a disagreement with other AFL leaders over the organization's position regarding the new Taft-Hartley Act, withdrew the UMW again. It would remain unaffiliated with both the AFL and CIO during the rest of his presidency.

Lewis authorized more coal strikes in 1948 and 1949 and, despite court injunctions, fines, and the strict provisions of the Taft-Hartley law, he won further wage increases, a seven-hour workday, and increases in employer contributions to the pension and welfare fund. At the time of Lewis's retirement from the UMW presidency, a post he had held for forty years, miners earned $24.24 a day and possessed a pension fund of $1.3 billion. Lewis also devoted much of his efforts during the 1950's to improving safety in coal mines and played a major role in obtaining the passage of the Federal Mine Safety Law of 1952.

Following his retirement, Lewis served as a trustee for the union's pension and welfare fund; in 1964, he received the Presidential Medal of Freedom from President Lyndon B. Johnson. Lewis died in Washington, D.C., on June 11, 1969, at the age of eighty-nine.

Lewis, John L.

Significance

Lewis transformed the coal industry and the American labor movement. When he became president of the UMW in 1920, miners were paid seven dollars a day, had no travel-time pay, no paid vacations, and no welfare and pension fund. They had to supply their own tools, and they received no state compensation for mine accidents. In 1960, after forty years of Lewis's leadership, they made more than twenty-four dollars a day, had one hour's paid travel-time per day, a week's paid vacation, a huge pension and welfare fund, and used tools supplied by their employers. All states paid compensation for miners killed or injured in work-related accidents, and, moreover, Lewis had persuaded the federal government to enact rules regarding mine safety that were enforced by a joint operator-miner committee. Lewis not only had greatly improved the material condition of coal miners in the United States but also had made them partners with their employers in determining conditions inside the mines.

Lewis's influence spread far beyond the coalfields. His partnership with Franklin Roosevelt from 1932 to 1940 played a large role in determining the prolabor stance of the early New Deal and helped forge the alliance with organized labor that served the Democratic Party so well in future decades. Through his founding of the CIO in 1935 and his organizing efforts on its behalf, Lewis not only established industrial unionism on a solid and permanent foundation in the United States but also helped create the powerful United Automobile Workers and United Steel Workers unions. In addition, Lewis shaped the nature of modern collective bargaining between unions and management. By employing such tactics as the sit-down strike and through his willingness to call strikes whenever the interests of his men were threatened, regardless of the powers lined up against him, Lewis made organized labor a force to be reckoned with in the United States, one that insisted that it share in the decisions that affected it.

Lewis could be stubborn, vain, autocratic, and even abusive, given to labeling his opponents as "communists." Yet the organized labor movement in the United States made gigantic gains under his uncompromising leadership, and the American worker, not just the coal miner, is much better off because of him.

—*Christopher E. Guthrie*

Further Reading

Alinsky, Saul. *John L. Lewis: An Unauthorized Biography.* New York: G. P. Putnam's Sons, 1949. The author was a formidable organizer himself and appreciates Lewis's talents in this regard. Yet he is also at pains to point out what he sees as weaknesses in Lewis's character, abilities, and tactics. This book is a good, balanced portrait of Lewis the man and Lewis the organizer.

Carnes, Cecil. *John L. Lewis.* New York: Robert Speller, 1936. Published shortly after Lewis founded the CIO in 1935, this book provides a rather colorless account of his career up to that point.

Dubofsky, Melvyn, and Warren Van Tine. *John L. Lewis: A Biography.* Urbana: University of Illinois Press, 1977. This book is not only the most comprehensive and well-written study of Lewis but also an often brilliant analytical survey of the American labor movement from 1920 to 1960.

Kurland, Gerald. *John L. Lewis: Labor's Strong-Willed Organizer.* Charlotteville, N.Y.:

SamHar Press, 1973. A short general examination of Lewis's life and work. It will provide the interested reader with the highlights of Lewis's career but little else.
McFarland, C. K. *Roosevelt, Lewis, and the New Deal, 1933-1940.* Fort Worth: Texas Christian University Press, 1970. A good and concise investigation of the relationship between Lewis and Roosevelt up until their official split during the presidential election in 1940, this book falls a little short in explaining the long-range repercussions of this seven-year partnership.
Preis, Art. *Labor's Giant Step: Twenty Years of the CIO.* New York: Pathfinder Press, 1972. In the course of tracing the first two decades of the CIO, the author also presents a fairly objective portrait of Lewis's role in creating and then almost destroying the organization.
Wechsler, James A. *Labor Baron: A Portrait of John L. Lewis.* New York: William Morrow, 1944. Reprint. Westport, Conn.: Greenwood Press, 1972. Emphasizes Lewis's negative side and downplays his positive achievements.
Zieger, Robert H., and Gilbert J. Gall. *American Workers, American Unions: The Twentieth Century.* 3d ed. Baltimore: Johns Hopkins University Press, 2002. This history of the American labor movement includes information about Lewis.

MERIWETHER LEWIS AND WILLIAM CLARK

" *Great joy in Camp—we are in view of the Ocean, this great Pacific Ocean which we been so long anxious to see....* " *(Clark)*

Explorers

The Lewis and Clark expedition was the first organized exploratory expedition to cross the North American continent from the Atlantic to the Pacific coast within the geographical limits of the present United States. After serving as coleader of the expedition, Clark was for three decades one of the most important administrators of Indian affairs in the nation's history.

MERIWETHER LEWIS

Born: August 18, 1774; Albemarle County, Virginia
Died: October 11, 1809; Grinder's Stand, Tennessee

WILLIAM CLARK

Born: August 1, 1770; Caroline County, Virginia
Died: September 1, 1838; St. Louis, Missouri

Area of achievement: Exploration

EARLY LIVES

Meriwether Lewis was born on a Virginia plantation. His father was William Lewis, who married Lucy Meriwether, after whom the future explorer was named. Meriwether had an older sister and a younger brother. The first Lewises in America, who were Welsh, migrated to Virginia during the mid-seventeenth century, where the family became planters. Meriwether's father was a lieutenant during the Revolutionary War, but he drowned while on leave in 1779. Six months later, Lucy married Captain John Marks. After the war, the Marks family moved to Georgia, but Meriwether soon went back to Virginia to live with his relatives. There he attended several small schools taught by parsons and received some tutoring, but his chief interest and delight was in rambling in the woods, hunting, and observing nature. Although rather stiff and awkward as a child, Meriwether grew up to be a handsome young man.

When John Marks died in 1791, his widow returned to Virginia. She brought with her, besides Meriwether's brother and sister, a son and daughter she had borne her second husband.

A short time after his mother's return, Lewis became a soldier, as he was to remain most of his life. In 1794, he enlisted in the Virginia militia to help suppress the Whiskey Rebellion in western Pennsylvania. Liking this taste of military life, Lewis stayed in the militia until May, 1795, when he became an ensign in the United States Army. A few months thereafter, he was assigned to the "Chosen Rifle Company" that William Clark commanded, and during the short time that the two men were together, they became fast friends. Later that year, Lewis joined the First Infantry Regiment and for the next four years was engaged in a number of noncombatant duties, mainly on the Western frontier. In December, 1800, he was promoted to captain and became regimental paymaster.

It was while he was thus occupied that, in February, 1801, President-elect Thomas Jefferson wrote to invite Lewis to become his private secretary, probably with a view to naming him to command a transcontinental exploring expedition. Jefferson had thought about, and even planned for, such an undertaking since the United States had won its independence in 1783. In 1792, Lewis, then only eighteen years old, had volunteered for the assignment. Jefferson chose someone else, however, who failed to go.

Soon after coming to Washington, Lewis, under the president's direction, began to plan and prepare for the expedition. He obtained scientific and technical training from members of the faculty of the University of Pennsylvania; collected, with their advice, various kinds of equipment and supplies; and gathered information on his proposed route. Following congressional approval and funding of the mission and his formal designation as its commander, Lewis, early in 1803, with Jefferson's concurrence, invited his friend William Clark, with whom he had maintained contact since they served together in the Army, to be its coleader.

Clark was also born on his family's plantation in Virginia. He was the youngest of six sons and the ninth of ten children of John and Ann (Rogers) Clark. The Clarks had emigrated from England some time in the seventeenth century and, like the Lewises, had become planters. When the revolution came, the Clarks were staunch patriots, and all of William's older brothers fought as officers in the War for Independence. The most famous was Brigadier General George Rogers Clark, who was the conqueror of the Illinois Country. William, who was too young to fight, stayed home. He received a little formal schooling and acquired the rudiments of learning, but mainly he developed the skills of a frontiersman: the ability to ride, hunt, and shoot.

When he was fourteen years old, Clark moved with his family to a new plantation near the Falls of the Ohio at Louisville. As a young Kentucky frontiersman, Clark, a big, bluff redhead, served with the militia in several campaigns against the hostile Indian tribes living north of the Ohio River. In March, 1792, he was commissioned a lieutenant in the United States Army and two years later fought under General Anthony Wayne in the famous Battle of Fallen Timbers. In July, 1796, however, Clark resigned his commission and returned home, where for the next seven years he managed his aged parents' plantation. It was there that, in July, 1803, he received Lewis's invitation to join him in leading a transcontinental exploring expedition and quickly accepted it.

Lives' Work

About the time Clark received his letter, Lewis, in the East, completed his preparations for the expedition and received final detailed directions from the president. The mission's purpose, as stated by Jefferson, was to explore the Missouri River up to its source in the Rocky Mountains and descend the nearest westward-flowing stream to the Pacific in order to extend the American fur trade to the tribes inhabiting that vast area and to increase geographical knowledge of the continent. With these instructions, Lewis left Washington for Pittsburgh. Descending the Ohio River by boat, he picked up Clark at Louisville, in late summer 1803. Together with a few recruits for the expedition, the two men proceeded to Wood River, Illinois, opposite the mouth of the Missouri, where they encamped early in December. During the next five months, Lewis and Clark recruited and trained their party and finished their preparations for the journey.

With everything in readiness, the expedition set out on May 14, 1804, for the Pacific. Lewis, still a captain in the First Infantry, was the expedition's official commander. Although commissioned only a second lieutenant of artillerists, on the expedition Clark was called "captain" and was treated in every way as Lewis's equal. During the journey, Lewis, a rather intense, moody introvert, spent much of his time alone, walking on shore, hunting, and examining the country. Because Lewis was better-trained scientifically and the more literate of the two officers, he wrote most of the scientific information recorded in the expedition's journals. Clark, a friendly, gregarious individual, spent most of his time with the men in the boats. He was the expedition's principal waterman and mapmaker, and he was better able to negotiate with the Indians. Together, the two officers' dispositions, talents, and experience complemented each other superbly. Despite the differences in their personalities, they seem always to have enjoyed the best of personal relations.

In its first season's travel, the expedition advanced some sixteen hundred miles up the Missouri and went into winter quarters in a small fort, named Mandan for the nearest Indian tribe, situated in modern North Dakota. The following spring the expedition proceeded to the headwaters of the Missouri, made a portage of the Rocky Mountains, and descended the nearest westward-flowing tributaries of the Columbia as well as the Columbia itself. Lewis and Clark reached the Pacific by mid-November, 1805. After wintering a few miles from the ocean, in a post they called Fort Clatsop, for a nearby tribe, in March, 1806, the explorers set out for home and arrived in St. Louis in September, having long since been given up for lost by virtually everyone but Jefferson.

As rewards for their great achievement, the president appointed Lewis governor of Louisiana Territory and Clark its principal Indian agent and brigadier general of the territorial militia. Detained in the East by business related to the expedition and other matters, Lewis did not actually assume the governorship of the territory until March, 1808. He soon proved to be unsuited for the office by temperament and experience and quickly ran into trouble. He quarreled with Frederick Bates, the territorial secretary, and became unpopular with many of the people of the territory. He seldom reported to his superiors in Washington and failed to consult them on his policies and plans. As a result, he fell under their severe criticism, and he probably would not have been appointed to a second term of office had he survived the first.

In September, 1809, after only about a year and a half in office, Lewis left St. Louis for Washington, in order to try to straighten out his affairs with the government and to renew his efforts to get the expedition's journals published. On the way, while stopping at a tavern on the Natchez Trace, he was either murdered or committed suicide. Although the evidence is inconclusive, there is reason to believe, as did Clark and Jefferson, that Lewis died by his own hand. Thus, on October 11, 1809, at the age of thirty-five, the life of this great pathfinder ended.

Clark, in the meantime, was mainly concerned with improving relations and promoting trading activities with the Indian tribes of the territory and protecting the white settlers against the tribes of the Upper Mississippi who were allied with the British in Canada. Following Lewis's death, he was offered the governorship of Louisiana, but he declined it because he felt he lacked political experience. In June, 1813, however, the governorship of the Territory of Missouri, as the Louisiana Purchase was called after 1812, again became available, and this time Clark accepted it. During the War of 1812, which was then raging, Clark's chief responsibility was to defend the territory against the hostile Indians of the Upper Mississippi. After the war, Indian relations and the economic and political needs of the white settlers pouring into Missouri absorbed his time and interest.

Following Missouri's admission to the Union in 1821, Clark (an unsuccessful candidate to be the state's first governor) was appointed superintendent of Indian affairs at St. Louis and retained responsibility for the tribes of the Missouri and Upper Mississippi. Clark held this office until his death on September 1, 1838. As superintendent of Indian affairs, he played a major role in effecting the removal of Indians living east of the Mississippi and in Missouri to new lands in modern eastern Kansas.

Unlike Lewis, who never married, Clark was an affectionate family man. In 1808, he married Julia Hancock, with whom he had five children. Following Julia's death, in 1821 he married her cousin Harriet Kennerly Radford, a widow, who bore him two sons. Four of his sons lived to adulthood.

Significance

Lewis and Clark's fame rests almost entirely on the success of their great expedition, one of the most extensive explorations undertaken in their time. They and their companions were the first American citizens to cross the continent and the first white men to traverse it within the area of the modern United States. During a journey that lasted a little more than twenty-eight months, the expedition traveled more than eight thousand miles. On the entire trip, only one man, Sergeant Charles Floyd, lost his life, and he died from a cause almost certainly unrelated to his exploring activities.

In their contacts with thousands of Indians, Lewis and Clark had only one minor violent encounter, which cost the lives of two Indians. The total expense of the undertaking was a little less than forty thousand dollars. Although Lewis and Clark did not find a commercially feasible route across the continent, as Jefferson hoped they would, they did make a significant contribution to the existing knowledge of the geography of a great part of North America. They also took a historic step toward opening the Trans-Mississippi West to American trade and subsequently to American settlement, thus providing the basis for one of the strongest U.S. claims to the Oregon Country. Their great achievement stimulated the pride of the American people and served to make Americans aware of the vastness of the continent on which they lived.

Although Lewis's career after the expedition was short and hardly noteworthy, Clark's was long and eminently successful. In three decades of dealing with the tribes of the Upper Mississippi and the Trans-Mississippi West, he carried out the policies of the federal government faithfully and effectively, helping to adjust relations peacefully between the Native Americans and the whites. In doing so, by the standards of his own time, he treated the Indians fairly and sympathetically and, in return, had their respect and confidence.

—*John L. Loos*

FURTHER READING

Ambrose, Stephen E. *Undaunted Courage: Meriwether Lewis, Thomas Jefferson, and the Opening of the American West*. New York: Simon & Schuster, 1996. Best-selling account of the expedition by a prominent historian. Ambrose traveled along the expedition's route to the Pacific and painstakingly re-creates the activities and discoveries of the journey. The book also chronicles Lewis's tragic life in the years following the expedition.

Cutright, Paul Russell. *Lewis and Clark: Pioneering Naturalists*. Urbana: University of Illinois Press, 1969. This volume contains a wealth of detailed information on the scientific and technical aspects of the expedition, including fauna and flora discovered, topographic features discovered or named, and Indian tribes encountered.

Dillon, Richard. *Meriwether Lewis: A Biography*. New York: Coward-McCann, 1965. A noteworthy biography of Lewis, this somewhat sentimental and romantic work provides a relatively comprehensive treatment of the subject with emphasis on the expedition.

Jackson, Donald D., ed. *Letters of the Lewis and Clark Expedition, with Related Documents: 1783-1854*. Urbana: University of Illinois Press, 1962. A comprehensive collection of meticulously edited letters, memoranda, and other documents dealing with all aspects of the expedition gathered from widely scattered sources.

Jones, Landon Y. *William Clark and the Shaping of the West*. New York: Hill & Wang, 2004. Focuses on Clark's private life and public career in the thirty years following his expedition with Lewis. Includes discussions of Clark's duties in the Kentucky militia, his service as governor of the Missouri Territory, and his role as Superintendent of Indian Affairs at St. Louis.

Lewis, Meriwether, and William Clark. *The Journals of Lewis and Clark.* Edited by Bernard De Voto. Boston: Houghton Mifflin, 1953. Based on the eight-volume Thwaites edition of *The Original Journals of the Lewis and Clark Expedition.* Edited by Rubengold Thwaites. 8 vols. New York: Dodd, Mead, 1904-1905. This single volume provides a good, readable narrative of that great enterprise that retains its flavor.

Ronda, James P. *Lewis and Clark Among the Indians.* Lincoln: University of Nebraska Press, 1984. An important, sophisticated, and engaging ethnohistorical study, this work chronicles the daily contact between the explorers and Indians and shows that the expedition initiated important economic and diplomatic relations with them.

Slaughter, Thomas P. *Exploring Lewis and Clark: Reflections on Men and Wilderness.* New York: Random House, 2003. A revisionist view of the expedition, with Slaughter attempting to correct the myths and legends that he believes have surrounded it.

Steffen, James O. *William Clark: Jeffersonian Man on the Frontier.* Norman: University of Oklahoma Press, 1977. Steffen sketches selectively and briefly Clark's life, making an occasional reference to the intellectual framework that he believes explains it.

LILIUOKALANI

> *The people to whom your fathers told of the living God, and taught to call Father, and whom the sons now seek to despoil and destroy, are crying aloud to Him in their time of trouble; and He will keep His promise, and will listen to the voices of His Hawaiian children lamenting for their homes.*

Queen of Hawaii (r. 1891-1892)

The last monarch of the Hawaiian kingdom, Liliuokalani struggled futilely to preserve her people's independence against the pressures of American annexation.

Born: September 2, 1838; Honolulu, Hawaii
Died: November 11, 1917; Honolulu, Hawaii
Also known as: Mrs. John O. Dominis; Lydia Kamakaeha Paki; Lydia Kamakaeha (birth name)
Areas of achievement: Government and politics; Native American affairs

EARLY LIFE

Born into Hawaii's royal family, Liliuokalani (lih-LEE-uh-woh-kah-LAH-nee) was the daughter of a chief named Kapaakea and his wife Keohokalole, who was one of the fifteen counselors of the king, Kamehameha III. Immediately after her birth, she was adopted into another family. A woman named Konia was her foster mother, and her

Liliuokalani

Liliuokalani.
(Hawaii State Archives)

foster father was a chief named Paki. This practice of adoption was the custom among the leading families of Hawaii; it was a way to cement alliances among the chiefs, who were the nobility of Hawaii. All of Liliuokalani's ten brothers and sisters were also adopted into and reared by other families.

When Liliuokalani was four years old, she was enrolled in the Royal School, a boarding school run by American missionaries. The students of this school were all members of the royal extended family, which was made up of the families of the king and chiefs. In this school, Liliuokalani learned English and was taken to church every Sunday, but she said that she never got enough to eat. The school closed in 1848, when Liliuokalani was ten years old, and after that she attended a day school also run by American missionaries. Learning was important to Liliuokalani throughout her life.

After Paki's death in 1855, Liliuokalani continued to live in his home, along with her sister Bernice and Bernice's husband, Charles R. Bishop. The Bishops were to be a major influence on Liliuokalani's life.

Liliuokalani

Although at one time she was engaged to be married to Lunalilo (also known as Prince William), who would become king in 1873, she ultimately was married to the son of an Italian-born sea captain and a New England woman. The man was named John O. Dominis, and the marriage took place on September 16, 1862. The couple began their married life at Washington Place, the estate built by the groom's father for his family. This was to remain Liliuokalani's private residence throughout her life.

Much of Liliuokalani's adulthood before her accession as queen was spent on benevolent work for native Hawaiians. She was also a composer of music, and she wrote more than one hundred songs, including several Christian hymns, but is best known for the famous Hawaiian song "Aloha Oe." In 1887, she attended Queen Victoria of England's Jubilee celebration as an honored guest. She never had any children.

Life's Work

A year after Liliuokalani's marriage, King Kamehameha IV died, on November 30, 1863. Because the young king had recently lost his only son to illness, there was no direct heir to the throne. According to the Hawaiian Constitution of 1852, the king's brother was elected as the new monarch by the cabinet, the privy council, and the *kuhina nui* (the queen, who served as coruler with the Hawaiian king). He became known as Kamehameha V. When he died in 1872, a new constitution had been passed (in 1864) that gave the king the right to choose his own successor. The successor he had named, however, his sister Princess Victoria, had died in 1866, and he had named no one else.

Now it was up to the Hawaiian legislature to elect a new king from among the nobility. This was when Liliuokalani's former fiancé, Lunalilo, ascended the throne. He lived only a year longer, however, and also died without naming an heir. This time, Liliuokalani's brother Kalakaua was elected, and in 1877 she was chosen as heir to the throne. She served as regent from January to October of 1881 while the king was making a trip around the world, which gave her a taste of what it would later be like to be queen. She took this role again in 1890 and 1891 while the king was in California on a trip meant to restore his failing health. He died in January of 1891, however, leaving his sister Liliuokalani as queen.

Liliuokalani was proclaimed queen on January 29, 1891, at the age of fifty-two. She inherited a government that had been, throughout the nineteenth century, a mixture of Hawaiian tradition, British constitutional ideals, Victorian influence, and American interference brought by missionaries, adventurers, and politicians. Symbolic of this mixture were the combinations of names held by the Hawaiian nobility. (Liliuokalani was also known as Lydia Kamakaeha Paki and Mrs. John O. Dominis.) This mixture was strengthened by the frequency of intermarriage between Hawaiians and people of European American extraction, of which Liliuokalani's own marriage was an example.

Liliuokalani's brother, influenced by American businesspeople, had led Hawaii on a course toward ruin by trying to return to a more despotic form of government. This led to revolution in 1887 and to increased American influence, because in the new constitution of that year members of the nobility were to be elected by voters of large income and property, which in practice meant large numbers of Americans and others of

Liliuokalani

foreign birth or ancestry. Hawaii was also under the grip of an economic depression as a result of the McKinley Tariff Act, which removed tariffs on other importers of sugar to the United States. Because sugar had become the center of Hawaii's economy, this act devastated the island nation.

This was the situation the new queen faced: political turmoil and economic difficulty. Her solution was to strengthen the monarchy. Liliuokalani was firmly opposed to the Constitution of 1887, which was far more democratic than previous constitutions had been. At the same time, the political strife and economic difficulties in the islands made the idea of annexation by the United States look rather appealing to some Hawaiians, and by 1892 there were secret organizations working toward that end.

After an attempt by the queen to promulgate a new constitution giving the monarchy more power, in January, 1892, a revolutionary committee took over the government and ended the monarchy, setting up a provisional government until a union with the United States could be worked out. The queen assented against her will, in order to avoid bloodshed, and retired to Washington Place. A treaty of annexation by the United States was drawn up and signed by the provisional government on February 14, 1893. It had not been acted upon, however, by the Senate of the United States by the time Grover Cleveland became president a few days later. A friend of Liliuokalani, Cleveland had received a letter from her about the coup d'état. After his inauguration, he withdrew the treaty from the Senate's consideration and launched a lengthy investigation into the matter. Meanwhile, the provisional government remained in power.

When it became clear that annexation was not imminent, a constitutional convention in 1894 set up what was to be the Republic of Hawaii. Liliuokalani protested to both the United States and Great Britain, but to no avail. An attempt to restore the monarchy was quickly squelched, leading to Liliuokalani's arrest and conviction on charges of treason. She was imprisoned in the Iolani Palace and forced to sign abdication papers. Hawaii was officially annexed to the United States on August 12, 1898, but the republic continued to govern the islands under the authority of the president of the United States.

Liliuokalani was pardoned in 1896, and in that year she traveled to the United States to visit her late husband's relatives, trying to forget her sorrows over recent events. She returned in August of 1898, her enthusiastic welcome home showing how much support she still retained among both native-born and foreign-born Hawaiians.

While in the United States, she wrote her autobiography, *Hawaii's Story by Hawaii's Queen* (1898), as well as translating an ancient Hawaiian poem. Liliuokalani died on November 11, 1917, in Honolulu, Hawaii.

SIGNIFICANCE

Although Liliuokalani's reign was Hawaii's last as an independent nation, her impact on Hawaii's history cannot be denied. Because she was part of a tradition in which women played important roles, she never questioned her right to rule. Although she believed in a strong monarchy, Liliuokalani organized institutions for the improvement of the health, education, and welfare of her native Hawaiian compatriots. She was an educated woman who valued learning, and she was both an author and a composer. A native Hawaiian, she was also an enthusiastic participant in the Victorian-inspired society of her times. Her downfall was her accession to the throne at a time when her tiny kingdom, influenced as it was by both European and American values and politics, could no longer remain independent. Although she resigned herself to Hawaii's annexation to the United States, she never agreed with the idea, always remaining convinced of the value of national autonomy for her islands.

Liliuokalani is something of a tragic figure. Trained and educated as a potential ruler, passionate about her country and her people, a woman of cosmopolitan learning and taste, she nevertheless came to power at a time when her method of rule came into conflict with the movement of history.

—*Eleanor B. Amico*

FURTHER READING

Kuykendall, Ralph S., and A. Grove Day. *Hawaii: A History, from Polynesian Kingdom to American State*. Englewood Cliffs, N.J.: Prentice-Hall, 1948. The parts of this book labeled books 3 and 4 (chapters 11 and 12) give a helpful chronicle of the events of the latter years of the Hawaiian kingdom. They help the reader understand the background to the situation that Liliuokalani inherited, as well as the outcome of her own reign.

Liliuokalani. *Hawaii's Story by Hawaii's Queen*. Rutland, Vt.: Tuttle, 1964. The queen's autobiography is the best source for learning about her early life. Although it is somewhat rambling, it is invaluable because it gives Liliuokalani's perspective on events in her own words. It ends with her return from the United States in 1898.

Loomis, Albertine. *For Whom Are the Stars?* Honolulu: University of Hawai'i Press, 1976. A highly readable and sympathetic account of the end of the Hawaiian monarchy, discussing the revolution and events leading up to it, the first failure to annex Hawaii to the United States, the founding of the republic, the rebellion of 1895, and the queen's arrest and trial.

"Native Hawaiians Seek Redress for U.S. Role in Ousting Queen." *The New York Times*, December 11, 1999, p. A20. A report about a group of Hawaiians seeking redress for the U.S. involvement in Liliuokalani's overthrow. Discusses the apology of then-president Bill Clinton for the incident.

Russ, William Adam, Jr. *The Hawaiian Republic, 1894-98, and Its Struggle to Win Annexation*. Selinsgrove, Pa.: Susquehanna University Press, 1961. This book follows up on Russ's earlier book (below). This volume analyzes the years of the Hawaiian Republic, between the time of Liliuokalani's abdication and Hawaii's annexation by the United States.

———. *The Hawaiian Revolution, 1893-94*. Selinsgrove, Pa.: Susquehanna University Press, 1959. Analyzes in readable detail the events of the revolution that deposed Queen Liliuokalani. It also examines the involvement of the United States and American interests in the overthrow of Hawaiian autonomy.

Tate, Merze. *The United States and the Hawaiian Kingdom: A Political History*. New Haven, Conn.: Yale University Press, 1965. This book focuses on the period of Hawaiian history that included Liliuokalani's life and work: 1864 to 1898. Chapters 4 through 7 deal specifically with various events of her reign: her attempt to change the constitution, the revolution of 1893, and annexation by the United States.

Lincoln, Abraham

Young, Lucien. *The Real Hawaii: Its History and Present Condition.* New York: Doubleday & McClure, 1899. An eyewitness account of the revolution of 1893 and the events that followed. The author was on a ship stationed at Honolulu at the time. Written to discount the reports of James H. Blount, the envoy of Liliuokalani to President Cleveland, the book gives an account of Hawaiian culture, history, and economy as well as of the revolution and its aftermath.

ABRAHAM LINCOLN

❝ *It is for us the living . . . to be here dedicated to the great task remaining before us . . . that this nation, under God, shall have a new birth of freedom—and that government of the people, by the people, for the people, shall not perish from the earth.* ❞

President of the United States (1861-1865)

A towering figure in American history, Lincoln played a leading role in the abolition of slavery and is generally credited with primary responsibility for preserving the Union through the unprecedented challenges of the Civil War.

Born: February 12, 1809; near Hodgenville, Kentucky
Died: April 15, 1865; Washington, D.C.
Also known as: Honest Abe; the Rail-Splitter
Areas of achievement: Government and politics; civil rights; oratory

EARLY LIFE

Abraham Lincoln was born on the same date that the great British naturalist Charles Darwin was born. The place of his birth, Sinking Spring Place, was a farm three miles south of Hodgenville, Kentucky. Lincoln's mother was the former Nancy Hanks, and his father was Thomas Lincoln, both natives of Virginia whose parents had taken them into the Kentucky wilderness at an early age. Thomas Lincoln was a farmer and a carpenter. In the spring of 1811, they moved to the nearby Knob Creek Farm.

The future president had a brother, Thomas, who died in infancy. His sister, Sarah (called Sally), was two years older than he. Much has been made in literature of his log-cabin birth and the poverty and degradation of Lincoln's childhood, but his father—a skilled carpenter—was never abjectly poor. The boy, however, did not aspire to become either a farmer or a carpenter. A highly intelligent and inquisitive youth, he considered many vocations before he decided upon the practice of law.

In Kentucky during his first seven years, and in Indiana until he became an adult, Lincoln received only the rudiments of a formal education, about a year in total. Nevertheless, he was able to read, write, and speak effectively, largely through self-education and regular practice. He grew to be approximately six feet four inches tall and 185 pounds in weight. He was angular and dark-complected, with features that became familiar to later generations.

Lincoln, Abraham

Moving with his family to Spencer County, Indiana, in December, 1816, Lincoln learned to use the American long ax efficiently on the Pigeon Creek Farm, where his father constructed another simple log cabin. He grew strong physically, and, largely through books he was able to borrow from neighbors, he grew strong mentally as well. The death of his mother from "the milk sick" in the summer of 1818 left both the boy and his sister emotionally depressed until the arrival of their stepmother, Sarah Bush Johnston Lincoln, from Elizabethtown, Kentucky. This strong and resourceful widow brought love and direction back to Lincoln's life and introduced him to her lively children, Elizabeth, Matilda, and John D. Johnston, then aged twelve, eight, and five, respectively.

While in Indiana, Lincoln was employed in 1827 as a ferryman on Anderson Creek and on the Ohio River into which it flowed. Then, in cooperation with Allen Gentry and at the behest of Gentry's father, he took a flatboat full of goods down the Mississippi River to New Orleans in 1828. Another childhood companion of this time was Lincoln's cousin, Dennis Hanks, who, in his later years, would relate many colorful stories about the future president's boyhood.

In March, 1830, the family moved to central Illinois, where Thomas Lincoln had heard that the farming was superior. They situated their cabin on a stretch of prairie in Macon County, some ten miles west of Decatur. There Lincoln split many rails for fences, although not as many as would later be accredited to the Rail-Splitter. Another nickname he earned in Illinois that would serve him well in his later political career was Honest Abe. His honesty in business dealings became legendary.

Again, in the spring of 1831, Lincoln took a flatboat laden with supplies down the Mississippi River to New Orleans, this time commissioned by Denton Offutt and in the company of John Hanks and John D. Johnston. Hanks would later claim that the sight of a slave auction on this visit to the busy southern city stirred in Lincoln his famous opposition to slavery, but historians now discredit this legend. Upon his return, Lincoln, having reached maturity, struck out on his own for the village of New Salem, Illinois.

Life's Work

Lincoln had been promised a store clerk's position in New Salem by Offutt and worked at this task for almost a year before the store "winked out." Then, in the spring of 1832, he served as a captain of volunteers in the Black Hawk War for thirty days. This service was followed by twenty days under Captain Elijah Iles and thirty days under Captain Jacob M. Early as a mounted private seeking to discover the whereabouts of the Indian leader for whom the war was named. While he saw no action, the war soon ended, and Lincoln returned home something less than a war hero.

Immediately upon returning to New Salem, Lincoln threw himself into an election for the lower house of the Illinois state legislature but, having no reputation, failed to win the seat. He was a loyal supporter of Henry Clay for president and therefore a Whig, but Clay also failed. In desperation, Lincoln became a partner in a store with William Berry, but its failure left him with an eleven-hundred-dollar "national debt." In 1834, however, and in 1836, 1838, and 1840 as well, Lincoln won consecutive terms in the state house of representatives. He also served as postmaster of his village

Lincoln, Abraham

from 1833 to 1836 and as deputy county surveyor from 1833 to 1835. Effective in these roles and being groomed for a leadership position in the legislature by Whigs such as John Todd Stuart, Lincoln studied law and passed the state bar examination in 1836.

New Salem was too small a village to sustain a lawyer, and Lincoln moved to the new capital city of Springfield in April, 1837, to join the law firm of Stuart and Lincoln. This firm was successful, and Lincoln won more cases than he lost, but Stuart wanted to devote more time to his political career. In 1841, the partnership was dissolved, and Lincoln joined, again as junior partner, with the master lawyer Stephen T. Logan. Finally, in 1844, he formed his last partnership, taking on young William H. Herndon as his junior partner.

In 1839, Lincoln met his future wife, Mary Todd, at the home of her sister, Mrs. Ninian Edwards. Lincoln and Edwards were already Whig leaders and members of the influential Long Nine. Lincoln and Todd intended to marry in 1841, but on January of that year, he suffered a nervous breakdown, broke the engagement, and then cemented it again. Their marriage took place at the Edwards home on November 4, 1842. From this union would be born four children: Robert Todd (1843), Edward Baker (1846), William Wallace (1850), and Thomas, called Tad (1853). Lincoln was always a kind and caring husband and father. Their home, purchased in 1844, was located at Eighth and Jackson streets.

When Clay again ran for president in 1844, Lincoln campaigned energetically on his behalf, but Clay was defeated once again. Two years later, Lincoln canvassed the district on his own behalf and won his sole term in the U.S. House of Representatives over the Democrat Peter Cartwright. During this term, which ran from 1847 to 1849, the Mexican War was still in progress, and Lincoln followed the Whig leadership in opposing it. For this decision, he suffered among the voters at home and had to content himself with the single term. Before leaving Washington, however, he patented a device for lifting riverboats over the shoals.

During the early 1850's, Lincoln concentrated upon his legal practice, but perhaps his most famous legal case came much later, in 1858, when he defended Duff Armstrong successfully against a charge of murder. Lincoln was a friend of Duff's parents, Jack and Hannah, and took the case without charging a fee. His use of an almanac in this case to indicate the brightness of the moon on the night of the purported murder is justly celebrated in the annals of courtroom strategy.

The passage of the Kansas-Nebraska Act in 1854 and the Supreme Court decision in the *Dred Scott* case in 1856 aroused Lincoln's antislavery fervor and brought him back into active politics. In 1855, he campaigned as an Anti-Nebraska (later Republican) candidate for the U.S. Senate but was compelled to stand aside in favor of his friend Lyman Trumbull, the eventual victor. A year later, Lincoln campaigned on behalf of presidential candidate John C. Frémont. Then, in 1858, he contended with his archrival, Stephen A. Douglas, for another Senate seat.

Before engaging in the famous debates with Douglas, Lincoln gave his most famous speech to date at Springfield, in which he proclaimed, "A house divided against itself cannot stand . . . this government cannot endure permanently half slave and half free." This House Divided speech set the tone for his antislavery attacks in the debates

Abraham Lincoln.
(Library of Congress)

that followed. Lincoln was a Free-Soiler and was truly outraged by Douglas's amoral stance on slavery. Many observers thought that Lincoln had won the debates, but largely because of a pro-Democratic apportionment, Douglas won reelection. Nevertheless, the fame Lincoln achieved through these debates assured his consideration for a presidential nomination in 1860.

The Republican Convention of that year was held in Chicago, where Lincoln was especially popular. Then, too, the original leading candidates, William Seward and Salmon Chase, detested each other; accordingly, their delegates turned to Lincoln as a "dark horse" when their favorites destroyed each other's chances. The Democrats then split their support with the dual nominations of Stephen A. Douglas and John C. Breckinridge. What was left of the old Whig Party split the South further by nominating as the Constitutional Union nominee John Bell of Tennessee.

Lincoln grew the dark beard associated with him during his campaign. He did not campaign actively but was elected over his divided opposition with 173 electoral votes, while Breckinridge amassed 72, Bell 39, and Douglas merely 12. Lincoln had the necessary majority of the electoral college but did not have a majority of the popular votes—no one did. The division in the country at large was made even more coldly clear when seven southern states seceded over his election.

Inaugurated March 4, 1861, Lincoln took a strong stand against secession; when

Lincoln, Abraham

newly armed Confederate troops fired upon and captured Fort Sumter on April 12-13, 1861, he announced the start of the Civil War by calling for seventy-five thousand volunteers and a naval blockade of the southern coast. Four more states then seceded, and the War Between the States began in earnest, lasting four years.

During the war, President Lincoln often visited the fighting front, intercepted telegraphic messages at the War Department, and advised his generals as to strategy. He was a remarkably able wartime leader, but Lincoln was deeply dissatisfied with his highest-ranking generals in the field until he "found his general" in Ulysses S. Grant.

In the midst of the struggle, Lincoln drafted his Emancipation Proclamation, calling for the freedom of the slaves. A few months later, in 1863, he wrote and delivered his most famous speech, the Gettysburg Address. This speech summed up the principles for which the federal government still fought to preserve the Union. Upon being reelected in 1864, over Democratic nominee General George B. McClellan, the president gave another stirring speech in his Second Inaugural Address. Final victory was only achieved after the defeat of Confederate general Robert E. Lee's Army of Northern Virginia at Appomattox Court House on April 9, 1865. Less than a week later, on April 14, Lincoln was assassinated by the southern partisan actor John Wilkes Booth at Ford's Theatre in Washington, expiring the following morning. Secretary of War Edwin Stanton then was heard to say: "Now he belongs to the ages."

Significance

More books have been written about Lincoln and more legends have been told about him than about any other individual in American history. This sixteenth president often is regarded as the greatest leader the United States has yet produced or is likely to produce, yet he came from humble stock and little was given him that he had not earned.

Lincoln was the first Republican president, was twice elected, and had to fight a cruel war yet remained sensitive, humble, and magnanimous to the end. It was his intention, had he lived, to "bind up the nation's wounds" with a speedy and liberal method of reconstruction. His death assured the opposite, or Radical Reconstruction.

Lincoln's greatest achievements were the preservation of the federal Union and the liberation of the slaves. The former was achieved with the cessation of fighting in the South, which came only days after his death. The latter was brought about at last by the Thirteenth Amendment to the Constitution a few months later. However, the nobility and simple dignity that he brought to the nation's highest office are also a part of his legacy.

—*Joseph E. Suppiger*

Further Reading

Donald, David Herbert. *Lincoln.* New York: Simon & Schuster, 1995. A definitive, best-selling biography. Donald portrays Lincoln as ambitious, often defeated, and tormented by a difficult marriage yet having a remarkable capacity for growth and the ability to hold the nation together during the Civil War.

Gienapp, William E. *Abraham Lincoln and Civil War America: A Biography.* New York: Oxford University Press, 2002. All but seventy pages of this biography deal with Lincoln's public and private life during his years in the White House. The book describes his handling of the Civil War, depicting him as a shrewd politician and an extraordinary military commander.

Guelzo, Allen C. *Lincoln's Emancipation Proclamation: The End of Slavery in America*. New York: Simon & Schuster, 2004. Examines how and why Lincoln persuaded himself to issue the proclamation, portraying him as a man with an inordinate understanding of his fellow citizens and the needs of the nation.

Herndon, William H. *Herndon's Lincoln: The True Story of a Great Life*. 3 vols. Chicago: Belford, Clarke, 1889. The color and dash of Lincoln's law partner almost make up for his lack of objectivity. Herndon is strongest when he speaks from experience, weakest when he deals with Lincoln's early years and personal relationships.

Kunhardt, Philip B., Jr. A *New Birth of Freedom*. Boston: Little, Brown, 1983. A concentrated examination of the background and circumstances of Lincoln's greatest speech, the Gettysburg Address. Vivid in the memory of a nation, this speech was considered a failure at the time by the president himself. Well written and beautifully illustrated, the book itself is one of the more important works dealing with a segment of Lincoln's life.

Lamon, Ward Hill. *The Life of Abraham Lincoln*. Boston: J. R. Osgood, 1872. Lincoln's longtime friend, fellow attorney, and marshal of the District of Columbia knew him well but was not particular about his sources. Certainly he relied too heavily upon Herndon's fulminations about the Ann Rutledge love affair (a myth) and Lincoln's stormy marriage to the former Mary Todd.

Nicolay, John G., and John Hay. *Abraham Lincoln: A History*. 10 vols. New York: Century, 1890. This major production is based on Lincoln's personal papers but is rather laudatory. There is, perhaps, too much detail and too little insight in these volumes.

Oates, Stephen B. *With Malice Toward None*. New York: Harper & Row, 1977. An excellent scholarly biography, reflecting much new research. It is well written and well documented.

Sandburg, Carl. *Abraham Lincoln: The Prairie Years*. 2 vols. New York: Harcourt, Brace & World, 1926.

———. *Abraham Lincoln: The War Years*. 4 vols. New York: Harcourt, Brace & World, 1939. These two sets are beautifully poetic but lacking in historical accuracy at times. Many readers have started with Sandburg, gained a sense for the subject, and gone on to develop a profound love of Lincolniana.

Thomas, Benjamin. *Abraham Lincoln*. New York: Alfred A. Knopf, 1952. One of the finest biographies of Lincoln available, combining a balanced scholarly-popular work in one volume. It is a must for any shelf of Lincoln books.

Vidal, Gore. *Lincoln*. New York: Random House, 1984. The most celebrated novel yet written about Lincoln's presidential years. Well worth reading by those who would gain an understanding of his actions. Without psychoanalysis or unfettered pathos, Vidal has portrayed Lincoln and his wartime contemporaries with exceptional accuracy, taking only a few liberties with history.

Lindbergh, Charles A.

CHARLES A. LINDBERGH

" *God made life simple. It is man who complicates it.* **"**

Aviator

Lindbergh's historic New York-to-Paris solo flight in 1927 was a turning point in aviation history, and he continued to play a major role in both civil and military aviation, as well as environmental conservation, throughout his life.

Born: February 4, 1902; Detroit, Michigan
Died: August 26, 1974; Hana, Maui, Hawaii
Also known as: Charles Augustus Lindbergh (full name)
Areas of achievement: Aviation; military

EARLY LIFE

Charles A. Lindbergh (LIHND-burg) was the only son of Swedish-born Charles August Lindbergh (not Augustus as sometimes incorrectly cited), a Minnesota congressman, and Evangeline Lodge Land Lindbergh, a Michigan native and chemistry teacher of English-Scotch ancestry. The elder Lindbergh, a Little Falls, Minnesota, lawyer and businessman, served as a Progressive Republican in the United States House of Representatives from 1907 to 1917, where his reform interests included such issues as banking and currency, the midwestern farmer, and the European war. Charles August and Evangeline Lindbergh were estranged early in their marriage, but young Lindbergh regularly spent time with both parents, thus living primarily in Minnesota and Washington, D.C. The elder Lindbergh had remarried after his first wife's death and young Lindbergh had two half sisters, Lillian and Eva. In his early years, Lindbergh showed his mechanical and scientific bent when, for example, he visited the laboratory of his grandfather Charles Land (a dentist and researcher) in Michigan, and when he drove the car in his father's 1916 campaign for the United States Senate. He was graduated from Little Falls High School in 1918, and, early in the same year, began working the home farm, where he remained until the fall of 1920.

After three semesters at the University of Wisconsin, where he enrolled in the mechanical engineering program and was a member of the rifle team, Lindbergh quit school in early 1922 and became a flying student at the Nebraska Aircraft Corporation in Lincoln, Nebraska. During this period, "Slim" Lindbergh (he was six feet three and one half inches tall) gained a reputation as an expert mechanic, parachute jumper, wing-walker, and pilot. He made several swings on the barnstorming circuit in the Midwest and Great Plains with other flying buddies, and, in 1923, he purchased his first airplane, a surplus World War I Curtiss Jenny. In 1924 and 1925, he completed U.S. Army Air Cadet programs at Brooks and Kelly fields in Texas and was graduated at the top of his class with the rank of second lieutenant.

Lindbergh then moved to St. Louis, Missouri, where he was head pilot for Robertson Aircraft Company and joined the Missouri National Guard unit. In April, 1926, he became one of the early pilots to carry United States mail when he began flying routes to Peoria and Chicago, Illinois, for Robertson. To compete for the twenty-five-thousand-dollar Orteig Prize for the first New York-to-Paris flight, Lindbergh then secured financial backing from St. Louis supporters; with engineer Donald Hall, he helped to design the specially built monoplane, *The Spirit of St. Louis*, at Ryan Airlines in San Diego, California. In early May, 1927, he set a transcontinental speed record when he flew from San Diego to New York via St. Louis.

Even at this point in his life, certain characteristics about Lindbergh had emerged: a constantly inquiring mind, a total sincerity, a meticulous attention to detail and accuracy, and a sense of humor. Like his father, the reform-minded congressman and scholar, he also had a stubborn independence, a sense of courage, and a quiet personal nature.

Life's Work

Lindbergh established a milestone in aviation history, when, on May 20-21, 1927, he flew *The Spirit of St. Louis* nonstop from New York to Paris. His historic flight of 3,610 miles in thirty-three hours and thirty minutes was the first one-person crossing of the Atlantic Ocean by air. The flight was followed by an unprecedented and prolonged public response, and, overnight, Lindbergh became a world figure. After receptions in Europe, Lindbergh returned to the United States aboard the cruiser USS *Memphis*, a trip arranged by President Calvin Coolidge, and was honored in many cities. He received numerous honors and awards, including the Congressional Medal of Honor and a promotion to colonel. Lindbergh also made trips to Latin America and to Mexico, where he met Anne Spencer Morrow, the daughter of United States Ambassador Dwight W. Morrow. Lindbergh and Morrow (now Anne Morrow Lindbergh) were married in 1929.

During the period of rapidly expanding aviation activity after the famous flight and through the 1930's, Lindbergh served as technical adviser to Transcontinental Air Transport (TAT, later Trans World Airways, or TWA) and Pan American World Airways (Pan Am). In this capacity, he played a major role in the testing of new aircraft, in planning the first transcontinental route for TAT (he flew the last leg in a Ford Tri-Motor), and in developing regular transoceanic routes for Pan Am. It was Lindbergh, representing TWA, for example, who demanded that the Douglas DC-1 airplane be able to take off and land safely with one engine. Ultimately, the design resulted in the legendary DC-3. The pioneer aviator was among the first to recommend the use of land planes crossing the oceans, a practice now accepted after the early use of Clipper flying boats. On international route development and mapping, Charles and Anne Lindbergh made several long test flights about the world in his Lockheed Sirius monoplane, the *Tingmissartog*, one of which Anne described in her book *North to the Orient* (1935). Lindbergh also served as a consultant to the Guggenheim Fund and the United States Bureau of Aeronautics, and, when the airmail crisis occurred in 1934, he took a stand in opposition to President Franklin D. Roosevelt's decision to allow the U.S. Army to fly the mail.

The 1930's also brought tragedy to the Lindberghs. In 1932, their first child, Charles Augustus, Jr., was kidnapped and murdered. The extensive publicity that continued during the trial, conviction, and execution of Bruno Richard Hauptmann for the crime was so distasteful to the Lindberghs that they sought refuge in Europe in 1935.

Lindbergh, Charles A.

They lived in England and on an island off the coast of France, seeking privacy in rearing their family, which came to include five other children: Jon, Anne, Land, Scott, and Reeve. At this point in his life, Lindbergh's interest turned to scientific research; he worked closely with surgeon Alexis Carrel in developing a perfusion pump (frequently referred to as a mechanical heart) that was able to sustain life in animal organs outside the body, and with Robert Goddard, the founder of modern rocketry, for whom Lindbergh secured important financial support.

While in Europe, Lindbergh studied European military aviation and made three major inspection trips to Germany between 1936 and 1938. After these visits, convinced of German air superiority, he warned against the growing airpower of the Nazi regime. In 1939, Lindbergh returned to the United States and, at the request of General Henry Arnold, assessed United States air preparations.

With the outbreak of war in Europe, Lindbergh began his antiwar crusade. Fearing possible U.S. involvement, he took a public stand for neutrality and later joined the isolationist America First Committee. Because of this controversy, the Lindbergh image was tarnished as political charges were made over his disagreement on U.S. foreign policy with the Roosevelt administration. Bolstered by his father's adamant stand against Wilsonian policies before American entry into World War I, Lindbergh remained firm in his views.

Charles A. Lindbergh.
(Library of Congress)

Lindbergh, Charles A.

Following the Japanese attack on Pearl Harbor, however, Lindbergh supported his country fully when it entered the war. Only later was it known that the famous aviator, who resigned his military commission in 1941 under political pressure, had personally tested every type of fighter aircraft used by the United States in the South Pacific. Although a civilian, Lindbergh flew some fifty combat missions, passing on technical knowledge that enabled American pilots to save on fuel consumption and shooting down an enemy plane. During the war, he was also a consultant to the Ford Motor Company at the Willow Run plant and made high-altitude chamber tests at the Mayo Clinic in Rochester, Minnesota.

After World War II, Lindbergh continued to be active in commercial and military aviation, but, increasingly, his time was devoted to two other concerns, conservation and writing. The pioneer aviator, continuing his association with Pan Am and with his friend Juan Trippe (his TWA affiliation had ended in the 1930's), early advised the introduction of jets and jumbo jets, which opened a new era in air travel. During the postwar years, he served in an advisory capacity on such matters as the Berlin airlift and selection of the U.S. Air Force Academy site. On a long-term appointment, Lindbergh was a consultant to the U.S. Department of Defense, and he was awarded the rank of brigadier general in the Air Force Reserve in 1954 by President Dwight D. Eisenhower. In this role, one of his most important contributions was his involvement with the structuring and implementation of the Strategic Air Command.

Devoted to the idea of world ecology and the preservation of natural resources, Lindbergh came to the conclusion that modern technology endangered the natural environment of the world—a conflict he described as civilization versus the primitive. Thus, his interests moved from science to mysticism and the study of primitive peoples. Lindbergh valued simplicity in life—the earth and sky—perhaps harking back to the roots of the Minnesota farm boy with his exposure to woods and water. Indeed, Lindbergh felt strongly about his Minnesota and Scandinavian background, and he participated in several projects concerning the Minnesota Historical Society; the biography of his father, Charles August; and the proposed Voyageurs National Park in the state.

When Lindbergh became involved with conservation, especially in his work as director with the World Wildlife Fund, he relaxed somewhat his strong aversion to the press. As early as 1948, he had warned, in his brief study *Of Flight and Life* (1948), that the human race could become a victim of its own technology. Further, according to Lindbergh, the overall quality of life should be the paramount goal of humankind. He put it simply when he wrote in 1964, "If I had to choose, I would rather have birds than airplanes." Lindbergh, aviator and technician, thus was complemented by Lindbergh, conservationist and defender of wildlife. While he encouraged the use of the Boeing 747 as an efficient aircraft, for example, he questioned the economic efficiency and environmental impact of the supersonic transport and spoke out against it during the debate in 1970. His struggle with changing values is also seen by his support of American retaliatory power during the Cold War, which was set against his worry that aviation and technology had made all people vulnerable to atomic annihilation.

Lindbergh also spent considerable time in many successful writing efforts. *We* (1927) is a brief account of the famous flight; *The Culture of Organs* (1938), written with

Lindbergh, Charles A.

Alexis Carrel, is a record of the research on which the two collaborated. Among his many publications in the post-World War II era are his firsthand and thorough account of the 1927 flight, *The Spirit of St. Louis* (1953), which won a Pulitzer Prize; his *Wartime Journals* (1970), drawn from extensive handwritten diaries; *Boyhood on the Upper Mississippi* (1972), an account of boyhood experiences in Minnesota; and, posthumously, *Autobiography of Values* (1977), a reflective statement on his life and concerns.

After World War II, Lindbergh lived with his family in Connecticut and then, later, in Hawaii. He continued in his duties as consultant to Pan Am and to the Department of Defense and served on a number of aeronautical boards. Lindbergh died in Hana, Maui, Hawaii, on August 26, 1974.

SIGNIFICANCE

Lindbergh is remembered first for his long and significant contributions to aviation history. From the barnstormers of the 1920's to the jumbo jets of the 1970's, Lindbergh was at the center of the immense changes that characterized aviation and aerospace technology in the twentieth century. Evidence of Lindbergh's superb technical knowledge and substantial leadership is clear, as he participated in numerous crucial decisions affecting its development. It was the 1927 flight that propelled Lindbergh to prominence, and the effects were immediate. For aviation, the historic flight launched a modern era in aviation history. More than any single event, it made the American people aware of the potential of commercial aviation, and there followed a Lindbergh "boom," with a rapid acceleration in the number of airports, pilot licenses, airlines, and airplanes in 1928-1929. While the crush of publicity was overwhelmingly favorable in 1927, Lindbergh soon came to realize that demands on his time and privacy had irreversibly changed his life. He struggled to maintain his privacy for much of the remainder of his life. From an early dislike of expressions such as Lucky Lindy and the Flying Fool, his distrust for the media deepened after the 1932 kidnapping tragedy. However, the demanding response to Lindbergh was, in part, the history of the 1920's, an age of expanding print and broadcast journalism. Amid the sensationalism and the Prohibition experiment of the Jazz Age, Lindbergh emerged as an authentic hero to many Americans. People responded enthusiastically to the youthful Lindbergh's individualism and modest character as well as to the new technology of the airplane.

Lindbergh's influence, however, includes more than the 1927 flight, significant as it may have been. He was not simply another flyer who set a record. Indeed, his contributions to American life in the forty-seven years between the flight and his death in 1974 included substantial activity in civil and military aviation, scientific research, and conservation. Ultimately, Lindbergh was a man both of science and of philosophical thought. His broad legacy is represented not only in aviation but also in his insistence that, if the planet is to survive, there must be an understanding between the world of science and the world of nature.

—*Bruce L. Larson*

FURTHER READING

Bilstein, Roger E. *Flight in America, 1900-1983: From the Wrights to the Astronauts.* Baltimore: Johns Hopkins University Press, 1984. The best general scholarly treatment of American aviation. Although Lindbergh is mentioned only briefly, historian Bilstein provides the necessary framework to understand total aviation and aerospace development. Good twenty-page bibliographical note section.

Cole, Wayne S. *Charles A. Lindbergh and the Battle Against American Intervention in World War II*. New York: Harcourt Brace Jovanovich, 1974. Well-researched, scholarly study of Lindbergh's involvement in the noninterventionist movement prior to World War II. Cole, who also authored a book on the America First Committee, utilized Lindbergh interviews and the Lindbergh Papers in his work.

Davis, Kenneth S. *The Hero: Charles A. Lindbergh and the American Dream*. Garden City, N.Y.: Doubleday, 1959. Popular account of Lindbergh's life by a well-known journalist. As in many such accounts, there are factual inaccuracies regarding Lindbergh history, yet Davis provides a good overview and some insights into Lindbergh's life. Includes an eighty-two-page bibliographical essay.

Gardner, Lloyd C. *The Case That Never Dies: The Lindbergh Kidnapping*. New Brunswick, N.J.: Rutgers University Press, 2004. Gardner delves into the questionable aspects of the Lindbergh kidnapping case and subsequent trial.

Hardesty, Von. *Lindbergh: Flight's Enigmatic Hero*. New York: Harcourt, 2002. Hardesty, a curator at the Smithsonian National Air and Space Museum, provides a thorough and insightful biography, enlivened with hundreds of color illustrations.

Lindbergh, Charles A. *Autobiography of Values*. Edited by William Jovanovich and Judith A. Schiff. New York: Harcourt Brace Jovanovich, 1977. Published posthumously, this study was drawn from extensive manuscript material and notes written over a forty-year period. It touches on virtually all aspects of Lindbergh's varied life and career but strongly emphasizes his growing concern for the natural environment and his plea for a balance between science and nature. An essential work.

_____. *Boyhood on the Upper Mississippi: A Reminiscent Letter*. St. Paul: Minnesota Historical Society, 1972. Lindbergh responded to Minnesota Historical Society director Russell W. Fridley's request for Lindbergh data with this long letter, which recounts his boyhood years.

_____. *The Spirit of St. Louis*. New York: Charles Scribner's Sons, 1953. Lindbergh's thorough account of the New York-to-Paris flight in 1927. This literary effort won for him the 1953 Pulitzer Prize for autobiography and biography in 1954. He writes a compelling narrative of the flight and also uses the flashback technique to touch briefly on earlier parts of his life. Lindbergh's book was the basis for the film *The Spirit of St. Louis* (1957).

_____. *The Wartime Journals of Charles A. Lindbergh*. New York: Harcourt Brace Jovanovich, 1970. Selected portions from lengthy handwritten diaries Lindbergh kept during the wartime era between 1938 and 1945. Helpful in clarifying his involvement with the nonintervention movement, relations with the Roosevelt administration, and his wartime activities after Pearl Harbor.

Ross, Walter S. *The Last Hero: Charles A. Lindbergh*. Rev. ed. New York: Harper & Row, 1976. Popular account of Lindbergh's life. Contains some factual inaccuracies. Book went through several editions from first publication in 1964. Broad overview for the lay reader, mostly drawn from secondary sources, with an eighteen-page note section on research.

Lockwood, Belva A.

BELVA A. LOCKWOOD

❝ *The glory of each generation is to make its own precedents.* **❞**

Lawyer and social reformer

Lockwood obtained passage of federal legislation giving women equal pay for equal work in government service in the United States. She also was the first woman granted the right to plead cases before the U.S. Supreme Court and was a committed activist for women's rights.

Born: October 24, 1830; Royalton, New York
Died: May 19, 1917; Washington, D.C.
Also known as: Belva Ann Bennett (birth name); Belva McNall
Areas of achievement: Law and jurisprudence; women's rights

EARLY LIFE
Belva Ann Bennett (BEHN-neht) was the second of the five children of Lewis Bennett and Hannah Green Bennett. She attended country schools and completed her education by the age of fifteen. Her father's opposition to her educational ambitions, as well as a lack of funds, led her to begin a career in teaching. She taught school for four years before marrying Uriah McNall, a local farmer. The young couple moved to the country near Gasport, where Belva gave birth to a daughter, Lura. When her husband died in a sawmill accident in 1853, Belva returned to school to further her education in order to support herself and her child.

Belva sold the farm and entered Gasport Academy. She also continued to teach school. As a teacher, she experienced at firsthand inequities toward women when she was offered half the salary paid to male teachers. Angry and upset, she left her daughter with her parents and entered Genessee College, where she studied law, political economy, and the U.S. Constitution. On June 27, 1857, she received a bachelor of science degree from the college that was to become Syracuse University.

In 1857, Belva became headmistress of Lockport Union School, where her daughter studied. For the next four years, she supervised the staff, taught courses, and, despite conservative disapproval, encouraged gymnastics, public speaking, nature walks, and skating for young women. She also taught at the Gainesville Female Seminary and later became proprietor of the Female Seminary in Oswego, New York. In 1866, while in her mid-thirties, Belva, with her daughter Lura, left for Washington, D.C. Her profession was still teaching, but she had political ambitions that would eventually take her far beyond the classroom.

In 1867, Belva opened a school of her own. On March 11, 1868, she married Ezekiel Lockwood, a dentist and former Baptist minister. Their only child, Jessie, died in infancy. Ezekiel Lockwood assumed the administrative duties of his wife's school so that she could pursue a law degree. Denied admission to Columbia, Georgetown, and Harvard because she was not only a woman but also a married one, Lockwood was finally accepted at the National University Law School. She completed her studies in

Lockwood, Belva A.

1873 but was awarded her diploma only after she petitioned President Ulysses S. Grant, the school's ex officio president, to intervene on her behalf. Her husband, who had continued to supervise her school in Washington, was finally forced to close it because of his ill health. He died in 1877.

Life's Work

After judicial rules were changed and women were allowed to practice law in the District of Columbia, Belva Lockwood was admitted to the bar on September 24, 1873. At the age of forty, she embarked on a distinguished career in law. When one of her cases came before the Federal Court of Claims that winter, Lockwood was refused, because she was a woman, the right to plead a case. Her petition for admission to the Supreme Court of the United States (1876) was denied on the basis of custom, but Lockwood would not admit defeat. She petitioned Congress to pass a declaratory act or joint resolution "that no woman otherwise qualified, shall be debarred from practice before any United States Court on account of sex."

Reasoning that if women had the right to practice law they were entitled to pursue legal matters through the highest courts in the country, Lockwood pushed enabling legislation through Congress. By means of energetic lobbying, and with the support of such pro-suffrage senators as Aaron A. Sargent of California and George F. Hoar of Massachusetts, Lockwood secured the passage of the Lockwood Bill, which permitted women to practice before the Supreme Court. On March 3, 1879, she became the first woman to be admitted to the Bar of the U.S. Supreme Court. Three days later, she was admitted to the U.S. Court of Claims.

A year later, on February 2, 1880, in a striking demonstration of her commitment to racial equality, Lockwood appeared before the Supreme Court of the United States and made a motion that Samuel R. Lowery, an African American, be allowed to practice before the Supreme Court. Lowery, who was the principal of the Huntsville Industrial University in Alabama, became the first black Southerner to practice law before the Supreme Court of the United States.

Lockwood became a familiar sight in Washington as she pedaled throughout the city on "Challenge No. 2," an English tricycle that she introduced to the nation's capital. She rode the vehicle to the Capitol, the courts—wherever her work led her. By 1890, Belva was well established in her law career, specializing in pension and claims cases against the U.S. government. It was this specialty that led her to one of the greatest legal triumphs of her career. The Cherokee Indian Nation secured Lockwood to represent it in claims against the U.S. government related to an 1891 treaty involving the sale and purchase of more than eight million acres of land known as the Cherokee Outlet. Lockwood was entrusted with defending nearly fifteen thousand Cherokee clients. After reviewing the numerous treaties and statutes that governed the history of the Cherokees, she filed a petition to uphold the claim of her Indian clients.

On March 20, 1905, the case of the Eastern and Emigrant Cherokees against the United States was decided before the Court of Claims. Following an impassioned argument by Lockwood, the chief justice agreed that the United States had broken and evaded the letter and spirit of its agreement with the Cherokees. Nevertheless, although he decreed that the Cherokees recover certain amounts due in the account rendered by the government, he could not bring himself to allow the full interest on those amounts. The case was appealed to the Supreme Court, where, on April 30, 1906, Lockwood again argued for the Indians and their rights. The Court agreed and awarded the Cherokees five million dollars.

As a feminist, Lockwood did much to further women's rights. In 1867, she was one of the founders of Washington's first suffrage group, the Universal Franchise Association. During the 1870's and early 1880's, she was active in the Washington conventions of the National Woman Suffrage Association (NWSA). In January, 1871, Belva Lockwood presented a memorial to the U.S. Senate on "The Right of Women to Vote."

Lockwood addressed congressional committees and drew up innumerable resolutions and bills that would help bring equality to women in the United States. She circulated a petition at the meetings of the National and American Woman Suffrage Associations in New York that hastened the passage, in 1872, of legislation giving women government employees equal pay for equal work. In 1873, she represented a woman in a divorce case, charging the defendant with drunkenness, cruel treatment, desertion, and refusal to support. She won the case for her client, obtaining the decree of divorce and alimony with costs. Later, in 1896, as a member of a committee of the District Federation of Women's Clubs, she helped Ellen Spencer Mussey and others secure passage of a law liberalizing the property rights of married women and equal guardianship of their children in the District of Columbia. In 1903, she proposed the inclusion of woman suffrage clauses in the statehood bills for Oklahoma, Arizona, and New Mexico, which were then under consideration.

In 1872, Lockwood spoke at Cooper Union in New York on behalf of Victoria Woodhull's candidacy for president of the United States. Lockwood herself was nominated for president in 1884 by women representing the National Equal Rights Party. Her platform reflected her commitment to civil rights, temperance, and feminism. She encompassed equal rights for all, including African Americans, Indians, and immigrants. She advocated curtailment of the liquor traffic, reform in marriage and divorce laws, and universal peace. She flourished a banner inscribed on one side with the words "Women's Rights" and on the other with the word "Peace."

Although Lockwood's campaign alienated many members of the organized suffrage movement, including Susan B. Anthony, it generated much public interest. Astonishingly, she won the electoral vote of Indiana, half that of Oregon, nearly captured New Hampshire, and made a respectable showing in New York. A second campaign four years later was less successful. Her political aptitude was recognized by President Grover Cleveland, who sent her as the U.S. delegate to the Congress of Charities and Correction in Geneva, Switzerland.

Increasingly committed to the cause of world peace, Lockwood put much of her energy into peace organizations after the 1880's. One of the earliest members of the Universal Peace Union, Lockwood served at various times during the 1880's and 1890's on the union's executive committee and the editorial board of its paper, the *Peacemaker*, as a corresponding secretary and vice president, and as one of the union's chief lobbyists. She was the union's delegate to the International Peace Congress of 1889 and its successors; served as the American secretary of the International Bureau of Peace, founded in Berne in 1891; and served on the nominating committee for the Nobel Peace Prize. In all these organizations, she agitated for the arbitration principle as a means of settling world problems.

Lockwood remained politically active into her later years. She continued lecturing well into her eighties, and at the age of eighty-seven she campaigned for Woodrow Wilson. In 1909, she was awarded an honorary LL.D. degree by Syracuse University, and in 1913 she was presented with an oil portrait of herself by the women of Washington, D.C. The portrait now hangs in the Art Gallery of the National Museum.

Following the death of her daughter Lura in 1894, Lockwood's financial fortunes collapsed, and her last years were spent in ill health and relative poverty. She died at George Washington University Hospital in 1917 and was buried in the Congressional Cemetery in Washington. The funeral service held in the Wesley Chapel of the Methodist Episcopalian Church recalled the triumphs of her life, and the newspapers recorded her history. A scholarship was established in Lockwood's name, and a bust of Lockwood was unveiled by the Women's Bar Association of the District of Columbia to commemorate the seventy-fifth anniversary of her admission to the Supreme Court.

SIGNIFICANCE

Legally and socially, Belva Lockwood scored important victories for women. Marriage, she concluded, should be a civil contract in which property rights were equal. She rebelled against the law in the District of Columbia that could compel a man to support his illegitimate child but could not compel him to support his wife and his legitimate children. She worked for the reform of probate law and recognition of the rights of widows and orphans. Single-handedly, Lockwood moved the U.S. Congress to open the highest court to women lawyers. She fought for civil rights for all Americans. Up to the day she died, she worked for world peace.

Over the years of her practice, Lockwood gave aid, advice, and encouragement to women from all parts of the country who were attempting to become attorneys-at-law. Lockwood's hard-won battles, confidence, and fortitude are an inspiration to women throughout the world.

—*Diane C. Vecchio*

FURTHER READING

Curti, Merle. *Peace or War*. New York: Garland, 1972. Curti discusses Lockwood's pacifism and her efforts to advance peace on the national and international scenes.

Fox, Mary Virginia. *Lady for the Defense: A Biography of Belva Lockwood*. New York: Harcourt Brace Jovanovich, 1975. A useful treatment of Lockwood's life and work.

Klebanow, Diana, and Franklin L. Jonas. *People's Lawyers: Crusaders for Justice in American History*. Armonk, N.Y.: M. E. Sharpe, 2003. Contains short biographical chapters on ten civil rights attorneys, including Lockwood. Features a biography of her life and career, a chronology of key events in her life, a review of her major cases, and an annotated bibliography.

Norgren, Jill. "Lockwood in '84." *Wilson Quarterly* 26, no. 4 (Autumn, 2002): 12. Examines Lockwood's 1884 presidential campaign, describing her personal life and career and her opinions of women's suffrage.

Stanton, Elizabeth Cady, et al., eds. *History of Woman Suffrage*. New York: Arno Press, 1969. Contains informative accounts of the NWSA's Washington conventions, 1870 to 1874, in volumes 2 through 4 (1882-1902) and useful chapters on the District of Columbia in volumes 3 and 4.

Stern, Madeleine. *We the Women*. New York: Schulte, 1963. This work contains the most complete account available of Belva Lockwood's life. Stern discusses, at length, Lockwood's most celebrated court cases, including her own quest to practice before the Supreme Court. This is the best source to consult regarding Lockwood's commitment to women's rights, civil rights, and pacifism.

Whitman, Alden, ed. *American Reformers*. New York: H. W. Wilson, 1985. A brief but fairly thorough account of Lockwood's life, highlighting her women's rights and peace activism.

HENRY CABOT LODGE

" *Animosity is not a policy.* **"**

U.S. congressman (1887-1893) and senator (1893-1924)

Combining integrity, acumen, and strong Republican partisanship, Lodge helped shape U.S. political history throughout his thirty-seven-year tenure as a congressman and senator.

Born: May 12, 1850; Boston, Massachusetts
Died: November 9, 1924; Cambridge, Massachusetts
Area of achievement: Government and politics

EARLY LIFE

Henry Cabot Lodge was born into an environment dominated by wealth and prestige. Often called Cabot or Cabot Lodge by contemporaries, the future senator could claim several noteworthy ancestors. His most famous progenitor, George Cabot, served in the United States Senate and acted as confidant to such notables as George Washington and John Adams. His mother, Anna Cabot Lodge, could trace her lineage through many generations of a distinguished colonial family. John Ellerton Lodge, Henry's father, continued his family's tradition of success in shipping and other mercantile concerns. Though not as steeped in the nation's past as the Cabots (the Lodges had come to the United States from Santo Domingo in 1781), the Lodges could also count themselves among Boston's finest families at the time of Henry's arrival.

Cabot Lodge matured and received his formal education in the city's blue-blood milieu. Prominent men of the time, Charles Sumner and George Bancroft among others, frequently visited his childhood home. Yet Lodge described his youth as that of a normal boy. He learned to swim and sail in the waters off Nahant on the Atlantic coast of Massachusetts. Later in life, he would make his home in this area, which he came to love above all others. Lodge was a proper although sometimes mischievous child, taking part in the usual juvenile pranks. He maintained an especially close relationship with his mother, and this bond grew even stronger after his father's death in 1862 and continued until Anna's death in 1900. The family—Henry's mother, his sister, her husband, and he—made a grand tour of Europe in 1866. The following fall, he entered Harvard College. His matriculation coincided with the start of Charles W. Eliot's tenure as the institution's president, an exciting period of change and growth. Though never more than an average student, Lodge benefited from his years at Harvard. Specifically, he began a lifelong friendship with one of his mentors, Henry Adams.

Lodge ascended slowly to national prominence. He married Anna Cabot Mills Davis, or Nannie as she was called, a cousin of his mother and member of an equally prominent family, the day after his college graduation in 1871. Lodge's social stratum had felt the impact of the rapid change that occurred after the Civil War, and Lodge, like many others in his social class, wondered about his place in the new order. He first did literary work for the *North American Review* under the tutelage of Henry Adams. Under Adams's prodding, Lodge began to take an active interest in politics. Adams urged him to work for reform. In the 1870's, this meant attempting to elect honest men to office. Political independents first attracted Lodge's attention, but he soon drifted into the Republican Party. He absorbed what happened around him and learned the nuances of the political world. At the same time, he furthered his literary reputation and did graduate study at Harvard. Lodge worked under his close friend Adams, and in 1876 he received his Ph.D. in history—one of the first Americans to gain this degree. He thereafter lectured at his alma mater and published *The Life and Letters of George Cabot* in 1877. Four years later, he published *A Short History of the English Colonies in America* (1881). These major works, supplemented by numerous shorter pieces, established him as a literary scholar of some note. He continued to write and publish throughout his life.

Politics, however, became Lodge's principal concern. In 1879, he secured the Republican nomination to represent Nahant, by then his place of residence, in the state legislature. The candidate showed a marked determination to achieve his goals, a quality he would exhibit throughout his public career. Lodge served two one-year terms and accumulated a respectable record. In 1880, he went as a delegate to his party's national convention. The next year, he lost in his bid for a state senate seat and for a United States congressional nomination. He failed again to secure the latter two years later but distinguished himself through party service. He remained loyal to Republican presidential candidate James G. Blaine, even though he lost several close personal friends because of it. At the same time, he began a friendship with Theodore Roosevelt; like Henry Adams, Roosevelt would remain a lifelong intimate. In 1886, Lodge's fortunes improved. He won election to the United States House of Representatives and took his seat on December 5, 1887. He would remain in an elected national office until his death in 1924.

Life's Work

Lodge began his congressional tenure by watching, waiting, and learning. He quickly came to understand that a lawmaker must be practical as well as principled. He and

Lodge, Henry Cabot

Nannie immersed themselves in Washington society. Lodge continued his close association with Roosevelt and Adams, and he developed new friendships, such as that with the British diplomat Spring Rice. In the House, the nascent legislator proved to be an honest, hardworking, and vain combatant. Though an open-minded person, he was a single-minded politician. He established himself as a principled partisan, one who would support the party but who maintained a strong sense of right and wrong. Lodge did not fail to support President Grover Cleveland, a Democrat, when he thought the chief executive had acted properly. Lodge chaired the House Committee on Elections. He devoted considerable energy to the cause of civil service reform and efforts to pass the Force Bill, a forerunner to the voting rights acts of the 1960's. In 1891, the congressman turned his attention to capturing a United States Senate seat. He succeeded when the Massachusetts legislature elected him to the position in 1892.

Lodge held his Senate seat for thirty-two years. The specifics of such a lengthy term are too numerous for individual coverage, but two issues, immigration policy and foreign affairs, deserve special attention. Lodge witnessed the changes in the United States brought on by industrialization and urbanization. One of these was the marked increase in the number of foreign immigrants arriving annually. Their presence was made even more apparent by their propensity to crowd into the slums of the nation's largest cities. There, they seemed to contribute disproportionately to numerous social ills: squalor, labor unrest, crime, pauperism, and disease. In addition, an ever-increasing percentage of the new arrivals came from nontraditional sources of immigrants. Lodge, along with many other Americans, viewed their influx as a threat to the nation's social and political fabric and tried to bring about their exclusion. In the Senate, and earlier in the House, he made numerous speeches on behalf of the literacy test, the most widely advocated means of general restriction. Lodge worked with the provision's other supporters to secure its ultimate passage in 1917. He also served for a time as the chair of the Senate Committee on Immigration and as a Senate appointee on the United States Immigration Commission from 1907 to 1910.

Lodge earned his greatest reputation in the area of foreign policy. His father's association with shipping influenced him in this field. As a child, he had considered a nautical career. The years of his Senate tenure provided numerous opportunities for him to exercise his knowledge and pursue his interest in world affairs. After 1890, American involvement in foreign events dramatically increased. Lodge was one of many public figures who advocated preparedness for international conflict, a large navy, and an aggressive global policy. He believed, simply, in imperialism and expansion. As senator, he contended that the United States should establish naval superiority over its rivals. Naval supremacy, he believed, would be followed by American dominance of the international marketplace. Yet Lodge balked at entanglement in European alliances.

A number of events from 1892 to 1924 allowed the senator to refine his theories and ideas and put them into use. In 1893, he supported American annexation of Hawaii. Two years later, he stood behind President Cleveland's attempts to enforce the Monroe Doctrine in regard to the Venezuela boundary crisis. Lodge, in this instance, claimed party politics should stop at the water's edge. His active participation in the affair and the strong sense of nationalism that he displayed won for him a place on the Senate Foreign Relations Committee. When the Cuban insurrection of 1895 escalated into war between the United States and Spain, Lodge applauded American involvement. The senator reveled in the subsequent American victory, though he realized it saddled the nation with global responsibility. He saw the acquisition of new territory as expansion, not imperialism. In his mind, the new lands were dependencies, not colonies. The senator used strategic and economic arguments to defend his position, and he worked diligently to solve the myriad problems related to the takeover of former Spanish possessions. Lodge also helped work out an acceptable Isthmanian Canal treaty. In 1902 and 1903, he won acclaim for his service on the Alaskan Boundary Tribunal, which successfully negotiated a settlement of the border's long-disputed location. His praiseworthy effort, however, failed to earn for him the chairmanship of the Foreign Relations Committee.

New foreign policy concerns, as well as many domestic issues, came to the forefront following Woodrow Wilson's election to the presidency in 1912. During the period prior to his victory, Lodge had had to watch his party divide into two camps, one of which broke away to support the candidacy of his close personal friend Theodore Roosevelt. Now the senator found much to dislike about the new chief executive. He

Henry Cabot Lodge.
(Library of Congress)

believed Wilson had deserted his true convictions for political expediency. This is not to say Lodge never supported the president, but the two men were often at odds. Differing opinions about the conduct of foreign affairs produced the most serious confrontations.

Lodge disapproved of the choice of William Jennings Bryan as secretary of state. He also found fault with Wilson's Mexican policies and his attitudes toward the growing conflict in Europe. While the president tried to adhere to a policy of neutrality in regard to the latter, Lodge and Congressman Gardner championed preparedness. As hostilities in Europe increased and actions by both sides pulled the United States into the conflict, Wilson began to formulate plans for a moderate peace. Lodge thought Germany should be totally defeated and believed the Allies should impose a harsh settlement. He sharply criticized the president's Fourteen Points, and he refused to support the treaty that Wilson helped draft at the Paris Conference in 1919. Lodge thought Congress should have been consulted during the peacemaking process, believed the League of Nations would compromise American sovereignty, and contended that certain treaty provisions would infringe on the Senate's foreign policy prerogatives. For these reasons, he led the fight to defeat Wilson's peace plan. When a compromise could not be worked out, the Senate refused to ratify the treaty. Right or wrong, Lodge, by then Foreign Relations Committee chair, used his power and position to ensure defeat of the president's measure. The senator felt so strongly about his actions that he wrote *The Senate and the League of Nations* (1925) to explain and justify his behavior.

SIGNIFICANCE

Friends and associates lauded Lodge's numerous accomplishments following his death in 1924. He was remembered for community service, scholarship, public service, and friendship. Many of those who had known him talked or wrote of his industry and tenacity of purpose. One who paid tribute quoted the senator's campaign speech made at Symphony Hall in Boston in January, 1911: "The record is there for the world to see. There is not a page on which the people of Massachusetts are not welcome to look. There is not a line that I am afraid or ashamed to have my children or grandchildren read when I am gone." Such is a fitting epitaph. Lodge, statesman, author, lawmaker, and Republican politician, who once wondered about his place in a nation in transition, found it in honestly serving his country for thirty-seven years.

—*Robert F. Zeidel*

FURTHER READING

Cooper, John Milton, Jr. *Breaking the Heart of the World: Woodrow Wilson and the Fight for the League of Nations*. New York: Cambridge University Press, 2001. A history of the League of Nations focusing on President Woodrow Wilson's efforts to create the organization and his failure to win Senate ratification for America's participation in the league. Describes the role of Lodge and other isolationists in defeating ratification.

Garraty, John A. *Henry Cabot Lodge: A Biography*. New York: Alfred A. Knopf, 1953. A most complete treatment of Lodge, though Garraty emphasized the senator's foreign policy activities in the coverage of his career after 1900. The work also contains commentary by Lodge's grandson, Henry Cabot Lodge, Jr. The author is generally sympathetic to the subject of his study.

Lawrence, William. *Henry Cabot Lodge: A Biographical Sketch*. Boston: Houghton Mifflin, 1925. Written by the bishop of Boston, who was a close personal friend of the senator. More of a testimonial than a legitimate history. Still, a useful source.

Link, Arthur S. *Wilson*. 5 vols. Princeton, N.J.: Princeton University Press, 1947-1965. The most complete biography of Lodge's major opponent in foreign policy and other areas. It offers another perspective on some of Lodge's most important legislative struggles.

Lodge, Henry Cabot. *Early Memories*. New York: Charles Scribner's Sons, 1913. An autobiographical account of Lodge's early life. Written many years after the events that it describes, it is very impressionistic. It nevertheless provides insight into aspects of the senator's early life that is not obtainable elsewhere.

_____. *Selections from the Correspondence of Theodore Roosevelt and Henry Cabot Lodge, 1884-1918*. 2 vols. New York: Charles Scribner's Sons, 1925. Not complete, judicious, or objective, yet the two volumes provide access to the workings of the very close friendship that existed between the two men. Also details both men's thoughts on many issues.

Schriftgiesser, Karl. *The Gentleman from Massachusetts: Henry Cabot Lodge*. Boston: Little, Brown, 1944. A good sketch of the senator that covers most of the important events of his life. Written in the immediate post-New Deal era, it tends to be critical of Lodge.

Widenor, William C. *Henry Cabot Lodge and the Search for American Policy*. Berkeley: University of California Press, 1980. Deals primarily with foreign policy matters and foreign affairs. Widenor stresses the importance of understanding the senator's ideas to comprehend more fully his actions; he also argues that the senator was every bit as much an idealist as his bitterest foe, Woodrow Wilson.

Zimmerman, Warren. *First Great Triumph: How Five Americans Made Their Country a World Power*. New York: Farrar, Straus, and Giroux, 2002. Describes how Lodge, Theodore Roosevelt, Elihu Root, John Hay, and Alfred T. Mahan articulated American imperialism and made the United States a world power during the early years of the twentieth century.

HUEY LONG

" The time has come for all good men to rise above principle. "

Governor of Louisiana (1928-1932) and U.S. senator (1932-1935)

As a governor and a senator, Long joined a sincere concern for the economic plight of the common people with an overwhelming desire to realize his ideas and plans to fashion a political career of great accomplishment for both good and ill.

Born: August 30, 1893; near Winnfield, Louisiana
Died: September 10, 1935; Baton Rouge, Louisiana
Also known as: Huey Pierce Long (full name); the Kingfish
Area of achievement: Government and politics

EARLY LIFE

Huey Pierce Long was the second son of seven children born to Huey Long, Sr., and Caledonia Tison Long. All the children would receive at least part of a secondary education, an achievement insisted on by their mother. The Long family was not poor, as later stories would claim, chief among them told by Huey Long himself. The elder Long was actually a moderately prosperous farmer whose wealth consisted of land, crops, and animals rather than actual cash.

From his earliest days, Huey Long was restless and energetic; he would undertake any prank to be the center of attention. He read widely, chiefly in history, the works of William Shakespeare, and the Bible, but his favorite book was Alexandre Dumas, père's *The Count of Monte Cristo* (1844-1845); he was impressed by the hero's tenacious quest for power and revenge.

In school, Huey was able and demonstrated early his remarkable memory. He often gained his wishes through sheer boldness and manipulation, as when he convinced the faculty to promote him a grade on his own recommendation. In 1910, Huey left school without graduating. He worked for a while as a salesman, and he met his future wife, Rose McConnell, at a cake-baking contest. They were married in 1913 and had three sons and one daughter. In 1914, Huey entered Tulane Law School in New Orleans as a special student; he did not pursue a formal degree but instead concentrated on the courses needed for the bar exam, which he passed in 1915.

As a lawyer, Long took cases protecting the economic rights of the common folk, such as workers' compensation claims. He became convinced of the need to redistribute wealth and found precedence for this particularly in the Bible, which enjoined the periodic remission of debts and readjustment of riches.

Early in his twenties, Long looked much as he would for the remainder of his life. He was not quite six feet tall and generally weighed around 160 pounds; as he grew older, he had a tendency to become heavier. His face was full, even fleshy, with a round and prominent nose, dark eyes, a wide mouth, and a dimpled chin. Depending on his mood, his appearance could be comical or impressive. His reddish-brown hair was unruly, and he often ran his fingers through it while speaking; one strand usually drooped over his forehead. His most notable characteristic was his unbounded energy: Constantly in motion, he ran rather than walked and spoke with an intensity that kept his listeners spellbound.

Long delighted in his courtroom battles, but early in life he had already settled on the path he intended to follow: state office, the governorship, the Senate, the presidency. In 1918, he decided that he was ready to begin.

Life's Work

In 1918, Louisiana was a state ruled by a few, powerful interests: a handful of large corporations, chief among them Standard Oil; the banks and railroads; and the remnants of the old plantation aristocracy. The average citizen earned little, received few services, traveled on wretched dirt roads, and sent his or her children to ill-funded schools. This was the situation that Long was determined to change.

He ran for a position on the State Railroad Commission, a regulatory body much like modern public service commissions. A tireless campaigner, Long spoke widely and also began the use of circulars—short, vividly written handbills stating his views and attacking his opponent. He would make brilliant use of this technique throughout his career, always writing the copy himself, using a pithy style that appealed to the voters.

Elected to the Railroad Commission, Long vigorously attacked the dominant force in Louisiana political and economic life, the giant Standard Oil Company. In speeches, commission hearings, and circulars, he detailed the improper influence the company had on Louisiana state government, and, in 1921, Long was found "technically guilty" of libeling the state's governor. His fine was nominal, but his position as champion of the common folk of Louisiana was firmly established. In 1923, he ran for governor.

He had none of the traditional supporters a candidate of that time was careful to recruit: no banks, no sugar barons, no railroads, no corporations, no political machine. The small, elite group that had dominated Louisiana politics for a century was against Long, and Long was fundamentally hostile to their rule. He was opposed by the only large corporation then in the South—Standard Oil—and by the region's only true big city machine—the Old Regulars in New Orleans.

With such a combination against him, it is not surprising that Long lost in 1923, but the size of his vote revealed that Huey Long and his ideas of economic and political reforms had substantial approval across the state. This fact was evident in 1924, when he was reelected to the Public Service Commission (the new name of the Railroad Commission) by an 80 percent majority. When he ran again for governor in 1928, he won decisively, and his victory signaled a new day for Louisiana.

As governor, Long moved to implement programs that would benefit the majority of Louisiana residents: paved roads and highways, public bridges, free textbooks to students (not schools, thus bypassing the church-state controversy in largely Roman Catholic Louisiana), and increased taxes on corporations and business to pay for these programs. Remarkably, most of his agenda was enacted during his first year in office, a tribute to his own personal magnetism, his brilliant political skills, and his immense popular support. His enemies were repulsed, rather than convinced, by this support. When Long asked the legislature for a tax on the huge profits of Standard Oil, the result was an effort to impeach him in April, 1929. The charges, many of them absurd, were all rejected. After the impeachment fight, Huey Long was stronger than ever; he secured a tax on Standard Oil and expanded the reach of his programs.

It was during this time that his political strength and the efforts of his enemies combined to undermine much of the idealist nature of Long. Realizing that his opponents would use any tactics to destroy him and wreck his programs, he came to believe that he must crush his adversaries, leaving them no option but to join him or face extinction. It was also at this time that the fabled Long machine came into being: a powerful institution that reached into every parish in Louisiana, able to dispense jobs, help friends, harm foes, and, most important, get out the vote. One by one, the existing political factions were absorbed; the last to submit was the once-mighty Old Regular machine in New Orleans, which finally yielded to Long in the mid-1930's.

Long became known as the Kingfish, a name adopted from the popular "Amos and Andy" radio program. It perfectly suited his style of leadership: a combination of low comedy and high political acumen. His opponents sneered at him as a buffoon, only to realize too late that they had underestimated the Kingfish.

In 1930, Long's term as governor ended with an impressive list of accomplishments: paved roads and public bridges, better hospital facilities, the expansion of Louisiana State University into a nationally recognized educational institution, more and better public education, free schoolbooks, improved port facilities and an airport for New Orleans, and, symbolic of it all, a new state capitol building. Typically, the construction was a modern, up-to-date skyscraper, visually demonstrating how Huey Long had brought Louisiana into the twentieth century.

Unable to serve a second term as governor, Long was elected to the United States Senate in 1930, but for the remainder of his life, Long remained the effective, if not official, chief executive of Louisiana, commanding special sessions of the legislature whenever he pleased and ordering passage of the laws he desired. This heavy-handed, unmasked expression of power was the most unpleasant aspect of Long's career; apparently he had reached the conclusion—probably confirmed by the impeachment battle—that his enemies had forced him to employ any means, however questionable or undemocratic, to achieve his high-minded and progressive ideals.

Long used the Senate to espouse with fervent intensity his plans to redistribute wealth in the United States. Pointing out that a minority of the population owned the majority of the riches, Long urged taxes that would limit both earned and inherited wealth and spread the wealth among everyone. "Every man a King" was his slogan, and he used it as the title of his 1933 autobiography. Spread the Wealth clubs were organized throughout the country to support the Long program.

Long supported Franklin D. Roosevelt for president in 1932, but the honeymoon with Roosevelt soon ended. The president moved too slowly for Long, and Long was often an annoyance, sometimes a threat to the president, who was trying to hold a Depression-shaken country together. Long made some positive efforts—increasing federal banking insurance, for example—but was generally opposed to Roosevelt's plans as being too timid and too superficial. He grew more open in his plans to defeat Roosevelt in 1936 by supporting a Republican or third-party candidate, then sweeping into office himself in 1940 as the only man who could save the country.

While involved in national affairs, Long remained closely connected with events in

Louisiana. He had his selected governor summon sessions of the state legislature to pass bills that Long wrote, rushed through committee, and shepherded through the final vote. His efforts were increasingly aimed at overawing his opponents; during the 1934 mayoral elections in New Orleans, he ordered out the state militia to control the balloting. Such high-handed techniques, combined with his vitriolic attacks on the popular Roosevelt, began to erode his support. Undeterred, he pressed onward. In 1934, he had a series of radical measures introduced into the Louisiana legislature, which were a preview of what he soon hoped to attempt on a national level. His consistent theme had not changed: He urged economic opportunity for all, but his reliance on brute power had greatly increased.

There had always been strong, indeed violent, opposition to Long in Louisiana. He had fought too many entrenched interests and helped too many of the poor and oppressed for it to be otherwise. Now this opposition began to organize and become dangerous. The Square Deal League raised an armed force that seized control of the Baton Rouge jail in early 1935; it dispersed only after a siege by the state militia. Later that year, the Minute Men of Louisiana formed, claiming to have ten thousand members, all ready to end the rule of the Kingfish, by murder if necessary.

It was in such a climate of violence that Huey Long's life and career ended. On the evening of September 8, 1935, Long was confronted in the state capitol by a young doctor, Carl Austin Weiss, who apparently hated Long for both personal and political reasons; there is no evidence that he was part of any organized plot. Weiss fired two shots at Long and was immediately gunned down himself by Long's bodyguards. The wounded Long was rushed to the hospital. An operation to save him failed, and on September 10, 1935, Huey Long died. His last words were, "God, don't let me die. I have so much to do."

SIGNIFICANCE

In his 1928 race for governor, Long gave a speech that so well expressed his political philosophy that he reprinted it later in his biography, *Every Man a King* (1933). He began by referring to Henry Wadsworth Longfellow's poem "Evangeline," and then continued:

> But Evangeline is not the only one who has waited here in disappointment. Where are the schools that you have waited for your children to have, that have never come? Where are the roads and highways that you send your money to build, that are no nearer now than ever before? Where are the institutions to care for the sick and disabled? Evangeline wept bitter tears in her disappointment, but it lasted through only one lifetime. Your tears in this country, around this oak, have lasted for generations. Give me the chance to dry the eyes of those who still weep here!

The bright side of Huey Long's career and legacy was that he answered the needs of the people of Louisiana for the schools, roads, institutions, and services that they so desperately needed. He broke a century-old tradition of rule by the few and wealthy, and he made the government benefit all the people.

On the dark side, however, he turned the state legislature into his personal tool and the state government into an extension of the Long machine. His supporters have insisted that he was driven to these tactics by the implacable opposition of his foes. There is truth to this: Huey Long was intensely despised and feared by many in Louisiana, often for the good that he had done. Long, however, was not the first popular leader to use questionable methods to obtain worthwhile ends.

During his career, Huey Long was passionately loved and hated; he was called both a fascist and a friend of the common man. His enemies admitted his political brilliance; his friends acknowledged his irregular methods. His many accomplishments have never resolved some basic questions: Was he the best leader to arise in Louisiana, or its worst political disaster? Had he lived, would he have proven to be a national figure of genius, or the architect of a homegrown fascist state? These puzzles have no answer—or too many answers—and the life and career of Huey Long remain an American enigma.

—*Michael Witkoski*

Further Reading

Brinkley, Alan. *Voices of Protest: Huey Long, Father Coughlin, and the Great Depression*. New York: Alfred A. Knopf, 1982. Helps to place Long in the context of the economic and social situation of the 1930's, when the country was wracked by depression and a number of theories competed with Share the Wealth and Roosevelt's New Deal as solutions to the United States' economic problems.

Cortner, Richard C. *The Kingfish and the Constitution: Huey Long, the First Amendment, and the Emergence of Modern Press Freedom in America*. Westport, Conn.: Greenwood Press, 1996. Examines Long in relation to freedom of the press.

Davis, Forrest. *Huey Long: A Candid Biography*. New York: Dodge, 1935. Reprint. Ann Arbor, Mich.: University Microfilms, 1969. A contemporary portrait of Long, this biography is more balanced than most produced at the time. Davis used his extensive interviews with Long.

Dethloft, Henry, ed. *Huey P. Long: Southern Demagogue or American Democrat?* Lexington, Mass.: D. C. Heath, 1967. Part of the Problems in American Civilization series and contains essays and articles by a variety of authors, including Huey Long and historians such as T. Harry Williams and V. O. Key, Jr. A good source for sampling the intense emotions that Long and his program could arouse.

Deutsch, Hermann. *The Huey Long Murder Case*. New York: Doubleday, 1963. While this work concentrates on Long's assassination, it does provide some helpful background on his political career, especially in relationship to the Louisiana legislature.

Hair, William Ivy. *The Kingfish and His Realm: The Life and Times of Huey P. Long*. Baton Rouge: Louisiana State University Press, 1991. A biography of Long that looks at the range of his power.

Long, Huey. *Every Man a King*. New Orleans, La.: National Books, 1933. Reprint. Chicago: Quadrangle Books, 1964. This reprint of Long's 1933 autobiography was edited with an excellent introduction by T. Harry Williams. The autobiographical section can be lean on facts and naturally stops with Long in midcareer, but it offers a fascinating glimpse of his energetic personality.

Opotowsky, Stan. *The Longs of Louisiana*. New York: E. P. Dutton, 1960. A general biography of the Long family and their roles in state, regional, and national politics. It clearly shows that, while Huey Long was the most brilliant politician of his family, others shared some of his gifts.

White, Richard D., Jr. *Kingfish: The Reign of Huey P. Long*. New York: Random House, 2006. Well-researched and readable biography recounting the details of Long's life and political career.

Williams, T. Harry. *Huey Long*. New York: Alfred A. Knopf, 1969. This is the definitive biography of Long, unlikely to be surpassed. Williams worked extensively with contemporaries of Long, including many members of the Long organization, who spoke remarkably freely. The book is excellently researched and extremely well written; it is a classic of modern American biography.

JOE LOUIS

" Once that bell rings you're on your own. It's just you and the other guy. "

Boxer

World heavyweight boxing champion from 1937 to 1949, Louis was a hero to black Americans of all backgrounds. Although some maintained that a boxer should not have been so celebrated, Louis was perhaps more widely recognized and applauded by the black community than any other individual prior to the modern Civil Rights movement.

Born: May 13, 1914; near Lafayette, Alabama
Died: April 12, 1981; Las Vegas, Nevada
Also known as: Joseph Louis Barrow (birth name); the Brown Bomber (nickname); the Dark Destroyer (nickname)
Area of achievement: Sports

EARLY LIFE

Born in a sharecropper's shack in the Buckalew Mountain region of east-central Alabama, Joseph Louis Barrow was the seventh of eight children of Lillie Reese Barrow and Munroe Barrow. In 1916, Joe's father was committed to a hospital for the insane. Believing that her husband had died (in fact, he lived, institutionalized, for twenty more years), Mrs. Barrow married widower Pat Brooks, who had five children of his own. The couple had several more children. The combined families lived in Brooks's small wooden house in tiny Mt. Sinai, Alabama.

In 1926, Pat Brooks got a job with the Ford Motor Company in Detroit, and the family moved north to an ethnically mixed Detroit slum. Joe, already behind in his education because of inadequate schooling in Alabama, was placed in a class with younger children. He developed a stammer and became a loner. Officials assigned him to a vocational school, mistaking his difficulties for lack of mental ability.

Louis, Joe

Joe Louis. (Library of Congress)

Brooks lost his employment during the Depression, and Joe had to do odd jobs to help support the large family. At that time Joe began boxing at the Brewster Recreation Center, where he used the ring name Joe Louis for fear that his mother would find out he was boxing and insist that he stop. Instead, his new interest won her approval. When he quit school to get a job at an auto body plant, however, he had neither time nor energy to train properly. He temporarily gave up the sport after suffering a bad beating at the hands of a member of the 1932 Olympic team, but, with his mother's backing, he soon quit his job to concentrate on the ring.

Life's Work

As an amateur light-heavyweight, Louis won fifty of fifty-four fights in the next year and was becoming known in boxing circles by early 1934. In April, he won the National Amateur Athletic Union title. Under the guidance of a man from Detroit's black community, he then turned professional, using part of his earnings to provide for his family. Louis's color might have delayed his chance to break into the big time; an earlier black heavyweight, Jack Johnson, had provoked the wrath of the white public prior to World War I through his enormous success as a fighter and his lifestyle outside the ring. According to Louis's best informed biographer, Johnson's controversial actions "confirmed the worst stereotypes of black behavior."

Louis's break came in early 1935 when New York ticket-broker and promoter Mike

Louis, Joe

Jacobs took an interest in him. Unlike other promoters of the time, recalled Louis, Jacobs "had no prejudice about a man's color so long as he could make a green buck for him." Although Jacobs himself was not knowledgeable about boxing, he sought good advice about Louis and was impressed with what he saw and was told. *The New York Times* described Louis in 1935 thus:

> He has sloping shoulders, powerful arms with sinews as tough as whipcords and dynamite in his fists. A slim perfectly modeled body, tapering legs, an inscrutable, serious face that reveals no plan of his battle, gives no sign whether he is stung or unhurt—these are his characteristics.... Louis has about the most savage, two-fisted attack of any fighter of modern times. He doesn't punch alone with one hand. He destroys with either or both.

Jacobs had as silent partners several Hearst sportswriters; therefore, favorable publicity began to grow not only in the influential Hearst press but also in other papers. Remembering the follies of Johnson, Louis's managers were careful to cultivate the image of Louis as a model of middle-class propriety. He did not smoke or drink, he read the Bible, he was modest, and he was generous. He was indeed many of these things; in areas where his behavior was not exemplary—for example, his profligacy with money and his pursuit of women—he was discreet, and the image his managers sought to develop remained substantially intact. It was probably not true that John Roxborough, the man who first sponsored Louis's professional career, intended all along for Louis to become a racial ambassador, but as Louis's fame grew, he did become one.

After his well-publicized fifth-round knockout of former heavyweight champion Primo Carnera on June 25, 1935, Louis was being ballyhooed as the greatest gate attraction in boxing since Jack Dempsey. Less than three months later, Louis whipped another former champ and gained widespread recognition as the world's best heavyweight, if not yet champion. Also in 1935, he married Marva Trotter, a young Chicago secretary; they had two children.

Louis's march to the title received an unexpected setback on July 10, 1936, when he met the prominent German boxer Max Schmeling, a former titleholder yet a big underdog to Louis. In the fourth round, Louis was knocked down for the first time in his professional career. Schmeling won by a knockout in the fourteenth round.

Much of the white press seemed to be waiting for this chance to rejoice in Louis's defeat. Racism, especially in the South, came through clearly in columnists' analyses of the match, and Louis was now being called just another fighter. In Germany, the Nazi press was ecstatic. Louis's managers scheduled Louis for other fights to keep him from brooding over his defeat. He kept on winning, and Jacobs got Louis a title bout with James Braddock in June, 1937. A journeyman who had held the title since 1935, the underdog Braddock fought gamely in their Chicago match but was clearly weakening by the middle rounds. Louis's corner spotted this, and he was able to knock Braddock out in the eighth. Louis had become only the second black man to hold the heavyweight title and at twenty-three was the youngest champion in his division.

Louis had still to win recognition as a great champion. Erasing the stigma of his loss to Schmeling would help Louis gain this status. The two men met again on June 22, 1938. Since their first battle, Americans had come to understand much more about Na-

Louis, Joe

zism, and although Schmeling was not a Nazi himself, he was now seen as the representative of Hitler's Germany. Louis, in contrast, had grown in stature and was perceived as a symbol of freedom. Now the crowd's favorite, Louis at six feet two inches, was in superb condition, weighing barely less than two hundred pounds.

Louis, the aggressor from the opening moments, pummeled Schmeling thoroughly and was proclaimed the winner by a technical knockout scarcely two minutes into round one. Louis was now acclaimed virtually everywhere, even in the Deep South. He was an unusually active champion, fighting so often that one writer called his schedule the "Bum-of-the-Month Club." Whether his opponents were "bums" in the ring or among the best of a poor lot of heavyweight contenders, as Louis believed, he met no serious challenger until his eighteenth title defense, when he fought the recent light-heavyweight champion Billy Conn in June, 1941. Nearly thirty pounds lighter than Louis, Conn had public sentiment on his side. He used his superior quickness to outbox Louis through twelve rounds. Rather than fight cautiously (as his handlers were advising in the belief that Conn was winning on points), Conn continued to fight aggressively. Louis staggered Conn with several punches and knocked out the challenger with two seconds to go in round thirteen of what is still remembered as one of the classic heavyweight bouts. The Brown Bomber or the Dark Destroyer, the nicknames by which Louis was most often known, remained heavyweight champion.

World War II came when Louis's skills were at their height. Although he could have claimed deferment from military service as the sole support of his mother and his wife Marva, Louis believed that it was his duty to join. In addition, to seek a deferment in the aftermath of Pearl Harbor might have been disastrous for Louis's image. Jacobs further improved Louis's public standing when he arranged a January 9, 1942, title defense against Buddy Baer, the bulk of the proceeds to go to the Navy Relief Fund. Louis won and promptly enlisted in the U.S. Army. Praise for Louis was never higher; the white press now viewed him not only as a credit to his race and a great champion but also as a good American. His public statement that the United States would inevitably win because "we are on God's side" became one of the most quoted patriotic phrases of the war.

Louis's role in the army, like that of many other celebrities, was to boost morale. He made goodwill visits to various bases and military hospitals and appeared in a few films, most notably *This Is the Army* (1943), starring Ronald Reagan. He also defended his title in 1942 for the benefit of Army Emergency Relief. From late 1943 to the end of the war, Louis was the star of a touring troupe of boxers that included the young Sugar Ray Robinson and other black fighters. Louis fought ninety-six exhibitions while in the service. In some ways his army experience brought Louis added maturity; away from his managers, Louis had to confront Jim Crow on his own. His approach was that when off-post he would accept local conditions concerning segregation, but when on a military base he would insist on fair treatment for himself and for other black soldiers present.

In other ways, however, Louis remained much the person he had been. He continued his free spending habits, borrowing money from Jacobs and others while a federal tax bill in excess of $100,000 still hung over him. Jacobs's bad advice and Louis's divorce in 1945 compounded his financial problems. Although Joe and Marva Louis were soon remarried, the birth of a son in 1947 (the couple had previously had one daughter) gave Louis added financial responsibility.

By this time Louis's ring skills had begun to erode, and after two title defenses in 1946, the first a much-anticipated but disappointing rematch with Billy Conn in which neither man recaptured his 1941 form, Louis found himself without a challenger who could help draw a profitable gate. After two victorious matches with Jersey Joe Walcott, another aging boxer, Louis, now fighting at about 215 pounds, found his reflexes slowing and announced his retirement early in 1949.

Continued financial problems drew him back into the ring. In September, 1950, he lost to the new heavyweight champion, Ezzard Charles, by a unanimous decision, beat several mediocre opponents, and on October 26, 1951, fought Rocky Marciano, ten years Louis's junior and the most promising heavyweight contender. The clearly lethargic Louis suffered his first knockout since his first match with Schmeling fifteen years before. The Marciano fight was Louis's last, save for a few exhibitions. His financial difficulties remained unsolved. He had outspent his income during his prime years and after the war as well, made poor investments, and by the mid-1950's owed more than one million dollars in back taxes and interest. He made a brief, unfortunate effort to become a professional wrestler, earned some money from promotional appearances, and finally settled with the Internal Revenue Service to pay twenty thousand dollars a year on his back taxes. He never did succeed in paying them, and the IRS, while not forgiving Louis's tax obligation, eventually quit trying to collect.

Louis had other troubles. He and Marva Louis were divorced again in 1949; in 1955, he married Rose Morgan, the prosperous proprietor of a Harlem beauty salon. They separated in 1957, and by mutual consent the marriage was annulled. As before, Louis simply could not settle down but traveled extensively, played golf during the day when at home, and stayed out many nights. In 1959, Louis married Martha Malone Jefferson, the first black woman to be admitted to the California bar. She was bright and compassionate, sacrificing her own career to help Louis through some of his most difficult years. He had affairs with other women, became a cocaine user, and began to suffer paranoid delusions severe enough for him to be confined at the Colorado Psychiatric Hospital for several months in 1970. Martha Louis and Joe Louis Barrow, Jr., his son by his first marriage, agreed on treatment for Louis.

Although he was never completely rid of his delusions, Louis was able to drop his use of cocaine and lived a reasonably normal life in Las Vegas with Martha Louis and several children she convinced him to adopt. Employed at Caesar's Palace casino as a greeter, he was provided with a luxurious house and a handsome salary. According to Joe Louis Barrow, Jr., Louis was happy with his job, which consisted largely of being seen, shaking hands, and giving autographs. In 1977, Louis suffered a major heart attack followed shortly by a stroke. He was confined to a wheelchair for the rest of his life but was still able to make appearances at some Caesar's Palace functions. He died at his home on April 12, 1981.

Significance

Joe Louis held the heavyweight boxing championship for twelve years, longer than any other boxer in his division. At his prime as a boxer, before World War II, he won

Louis, Joe

acclaim that endured for decades. His skills were such that he was, arguably, the greatest heavyweight ever. During the 1960's he was perceived by some blacks as an Uncle Tom, but he was recognized even by many civil rights activists as having done much for the cause of blacks in the United States in an earlier day. Boxing in the 1930's had not been totally segregated as major-league baseball then was; the mores of white society, however, certainly influenced the way the few prominent black boxers were perceived and made it more difficult for others to become successful professionals. In the white community, Louis won widespread acceptance as an American champion and a man of dignity. To his black contemporaries, who knew little but racism and financial deprivation, he was a symbol of hope and pride. "We all feel bigger today because Joe came this way" stated the Reverend Jesse Jackson in his eulogy.

—*Lloyd J. Graybar*

FURTHER READING

Astor, Gerald. *". . . And a Credit to His Race": The Hard Life and Times of Joseph Louis Barrow, a.k.a. Joe Louis.* New York: E. P. Dutton Saturday Review Press, 1974. A well-written book, published when Louis's mental illness made him more newsworthy than he had been in years.

Erenberg, Lewis A. *The Greatest Fight of Our Generation: Louis Versus Schmeling.* New York: Oxford University Press, 2006. Recounts the boxing match between Louis and Max Schmeling held on June 22, 1938, describing the significance of the event and of Louis's victory in the ring.

Hietala, Thomas R. *Fight of the Century: Jack Johnson, Joe Louis, and the Struggle for Racial Equality.* Armonk, N.Y.: M. E. Sharpe, 2002. Examines how the two boxing champions, Johnson and Louis, affected and reflected American racial attitudes during the first half of the twentieth century.

Louis, Joe, with Edna Rust and Art Rust, Jr. *Joe Louis: My Life.* New York: Harcourt Brace Jovanovich, 1978. Written in the first person, this book is especially useful for its abundant photographs and supplement listing each bout in Louis's professional boxing career.

Margolick, David. *Beyond Glory: Joe Louis Versus Max Schmeling and a World on the Brink.* New York: A. A. Knopf, 2005. Tells the story of two fights between Louis and Schmeling, the first in 1936 and a rematch in 1938, where Louis emerged the victor, describing the political and social implications of the two sporting events.

Mead, Chris. *Champion: Joe Louis, Black Hero in White America.* New York: Charles Scribner's Sons, 1985. Perhaps the best biography of Louis. Mead views Louis within the framework of American popular culture and places much emphasis on Louis as symbol. Also contains a helpful bibliography.

Monninger, Joseph. *Two Ton, One Fight, One Night: Tony Galento Versus Joe Louis.* Hanover, N.H.: Steerforth Press, 2006. A narrative of a boxing match held in June, 1939, in which Galento defeated Louis, the long-reigning champion.

Nagler, Barney. *The Brown Bomber: The Pilgrimage of Joe Louis.* New York: World, 1972. This is another book published when Louis's mental illness returned the former champion to the headlines. Written by a longtime boxing writer, it is useful for many phases of Louis's career.

Roberts, Randy. *Papa Jack: Jack Johnson and the Era of White Hopes*. New York: Free Press, 1983. A study of the great black heavyweight champion whose controversial career burdened Louis's own. Johnson lived long enough to know and resent Louis.

Van Deusen, John. *"Brown Bomber": The Story of Joe Louis*. Philadelphia: Dorrance, 1940. Written at the height of Louis's career, this book is a study in hero worship. Van Deusen accepts the press agents' portrayal of Louis without question, but his book is useful for its rather detailed descriptions of Louis's fights.

JULIETTE GORDON LOW

" The work of today is the history of tomorrow, and we are its makers. "

Girl Scouts founder

The principal founder of the Girl Scouts of the United States of America, Low spent the last fifteen years of her life working for an organization that would be similar to, but independent of, the Boy Scouts of America.

Born: October 31, 1860; Savannah, Georgia
Died: January 18, 1927; Savannah, Georgia
Also known as: Juliette Magill Kinzie Gordon (birth name)
Area of achievement: Education

EARLY LIFE

Juliette Magill Kinzie Gordon, the second of six children and the second of four daughters, was born in the middle of the secession crisis of 1860. Juliette's mother, Eleanor Lytle Kinzie Gordon, a Chicago native, had learned about the frontier experience from her father, who was a government agent to the Indians. Juliette's father, William Washington Gordon II, was a cotton broker who served during the Civil War as an officer in the Confederate army and later served as a general and peace negotiator for the United States in the Spanish-American War.

Full of energy, quick of wit, and blessed with an artistic nature, Juliette Gordon displayed much of the wit and charm attributed to her mother. She early exhibited the strong will and organizational abilities of her father, often taking charge of the childhood activities that she, her sisters, and more than a dozen cousins engaged in every summer at the Cliffs, the home of her aunt in northern Georgia. The Gordon girls and their cousins swam, camped, and sometimes hunted, and they often acted in and wrote several plays. Daisy, as Juliette was called by her family, usually acted several parts in each play.

Juliette attended private schools in Georgia, Virginia, and New York. The private school in New York City, nicknamed the Charbs by its students, was a finishing school run by the Charbonnier sisters, two extremely circumspect Frenchwomen who had immigrated to the United States following the Franco-Prussian War. While in New York City, Juliette wrote additional plays, acted in amateur productions, and studied painting. Once her formal education was finished, Juliette Gordon began dividing her time between living in the United States and visiting Britain and Europe, a pattern she would continue until her death.

While on one of her visits to Britain, Juliette fell in love with William Mackay Low, the son of a wealthy Englishman with Savannah connections. After a four-year courtship, which she attempted to conceal from a doting and protective father who viewed William Low as a social playboy, Juliette and William were married in Savannah, Georgia, in December of 1886. Juliette became part of the social elite in Britain, where her multimillionaire husband owned substantial property and was a close friend of the Prince of Wales and his entourage. The Lows hunted at their own estate in Scotland and entertained extensively in England and the United States. In addition, Juliette was presented at Court to Queen Victoria.

Beneath the surface, however, all was not well. Increasingly Low was left alone as her husband went throughout the world on game-hunting expeditions and engaged in other gentlemanly pursuits. Kept even from her favorite pursuit of horseback riding by an injury, Low took up sculpting and oil painting to fill the lonely hours. She also carved a mantlepiece for the smoking room at her Warwickshire estate, forged a pair of iron gates for the entrance to the Wellesbourne property, and often traveled without her husband (but always properly with a female companion). When the Spanish-American War began in 1898, Juliette helped her mother operate a hospital for soldiers in Miami, Florida.

Meanwhile, her marriage continued to disintegrate. In 1902, she consented to a separation and, after her husband's affair with an attractive widow became common knowledge to English society, agreed to begin proceedings for a divorce. William Low died before the divorce was concluded, leaving his estate to his lover. After several months of tense negotiations with estate lawyers, Juliette was granted a settlement of approximately $500,000, making her financially secure for the remainder of her life. Low resumed her active social life, alternating her time between London and Scotland while wintering in Savannah, Georgia, and other parts of the United States.

Life's Work

A turning point in Juliette Gordon Low's life came in 1911, when she met Sir Robert Baden-Powell, the hero of the defense of Mafeking in the Boer War and the founder of the Boy Scouts. She admitted later that she had disliked Baden-Powell before she met him, believing that he had received public acclaim at the expense of some of her friends who had participated in the rescue of Mafeking during the Boer War, but she and Baden-Powell soon became close friends and quickly discovered they had much in common. She shared with him a book that her mother had written about the frontier experiences of Juliette's maternal grandfather; he introduced her to his sister, who had founded the Girl Guides in England.

Low had found the rewarding service she had been seeking throughout her life. She organized a troop of Girl Guides in Scotland and two troops of Girl Guides in London

Low, Juliette Gordon

Juliette Gordon Low.
(AP/Wide World Photos)

before deciding to expand the movement to include girls in her native country. On her return to the United States, Low established a Girl Guide unit on March 12, 1912, consisting of sixteen young girls in two troops that met in the carriage house in the rear of the garden of her house in Savannah, Georgia. The first Girl Guide was her niece, Margaret Eleanor ("Daisy") Gordon. The young girls, dressed in middy blouses, dark blue skirts, light blue ties, and dark cotton stockings, wearing large black ribbons in their hair, engaged in camping and other sports and were soon the envy of the young girls of Savannah. Juliette Low rapidly moved to make the Girl Guides a national organization.

William Gordon's death, although a serious blow to his worshipful daughter, caused only a slight delay in Low's plans. After a year abroad in England with her mother, Low returned to the United States and resumed her efforts to make the Girl Guides a national organization. At first, she hoped to merge the existing Campfire Girls organization, founded in 1910, with her Girl Guides organization and call the new organization the Girl Scouts, but the merger fell through. Undaunted, Low continued her dream of a national organization. She began organizational efforts in various states, created a national headquarters, and enlisted prominent Americans to serve on the national board. In 1915, the Girl Scouts of the United States of America was incorporated, with Low serving as its first president. By early 1916, more than 7,000 young women in the United States had registered as Girl Scouts.

Although World War I did not appear to affect Low's travels between the United States and Britain, it did take its toll on her finances. She had been the major financial supporter of the Girl Scouts before the outbreak of the war; with the increasing success of the organization, however, she discovered that even her substantial finances were insufficient to keep pace with the growth of the organization. She adopted little economies to save money for her Girl Scouts. Her famous teas began to feature cakes that were recycled until either they were eaten or ingeniously disposed of by her guests. She refused to permit the electric lights to be turned on in her home until half past five, regardless of how dark the day might be. Her friends and relatives claimed that she was saving pennies while spending hundreds of dollars on the Girl Scouts. Others suspected that her "economies" were a ruse to encourage donors to give more generously to the cause of Girl Scouting.

With the advent of their nation's entry into World War I, the Girl Scouts performed valuable services for their country, donations increased, and the organization soon grew too large to be staffed by volunteers alone. Juliette Low, recognizing that her responsibilities could be handled by a new generation of leaders, resigned as the president of the Girl Scouts in 1920 but remained active in her support and was granted the title "The Founder."

Diagnosed with cancer in 1923, Juliette Low continued to demonstrate the energy and will she had exhibited throughout her life. She attended the World Camp of the Girl Scouts in England the following year and soon became involved in plans to hold the World Camp of 1926 in New York State. When told by a friend to wait until 1928 to bring the World Camp to the United States, Juliette Low responded that she would not be around in 1928.

Although she found it difficult to conceal the increasing pain of her illness, Juliette Low summoned the energy to engage in the weeklong meeting of the World Camp in New York State in 1926. Following the World Camp's closing, she sailed for England, bidding her farewells to friends who were unaware of her condition, and returned to her beloved Savannah, where she died on January 18, 1927.

Significance

Juliette Gordon Low would not be surprised by the size and importance of the Girl Scouts movement today. She had faith in her abilities and the abilities of the young women she attracted to the Girl Scouts. Her indomitable will, boundless energy, and belief that physical challenges, such as her own increasing hearing impairment, only slowed advances, never stopped them, proved to be an inspiration both to the young girls fortunate enough to know her personally and the young women who would follow in their footsteps. The last message that she received from the national headquarters of the Girl Scouts shortly before her death adequately sums up her life: She was, the telegram read, "not only the first Girl Scout," she was "the best Scout of them all."

—Robert L. Patterson

FURTHER READING

Choate, Anne Hyde, and Helen Ferris, eds. *Juliette Low and the Girl Scouts: The Story of an American Woman, 1860-1927*. Garden City, N.Y.: Doubleday, 1928. Rev. ed. New York: Girl Scouts of America, 1960. First published for the Girl Scout organization shortly after Juliette Low's death, this collection of reminiscences by friends and family members is filled with anecdotal information about the eccentricities of the Girl Scouts founder. The revised edition, prepared by Ely List, who was the assistant to the director of the public relations department of the Girl Scouts, is an updated and shortened version of the Choate collection.

Degenhardt, Mary, and Judith Kirsch. *Girl Scout Collector's Guide: A History of Uniforms, Insignia, Publications, and Memorabilia*. 2d ed. Lubbock: Texas Tech University Press, 2005. This guide to Girl Scout uniforms and other collectibles includes several chapters chronicling the organization's history, including information on Low.

Kludinski, Kathleen. *Juliette Gordon Low: America's First Girl Scout*. New York: Viking Children's Books, 1988. Designed for juveniles, this brief book provides a useful introduction to the life of Juliette Low.

Saxton, Martha. "The Best Girl Scout of Them All." *American Heritage* 33 (June/July, 1982): 38-47. Although brief, this article could be used as an introduction to an examination of Juliette Low's life.

Schultz, Gladys D., and Daisy Gordon Lawrence. *Lady from Savannah: The Life of Juliette Low*. New York: J. B. Lippincott, 1958. Although it does not have either a bibliography or an index and nearly half of it concentrates on the Kinzie and Gordon family histories, this book continues to be useful as the most thorough treatment of the life of Juliette Gordon Low.

Strickland, Charles E. "Juliette Low, The Girl Scouts, and the Role of American Women." In *Women's Being, Women's Place: Female Identity and Vocation in American History*, edited by Mary Kelley. Boston: G. K. Hall, 1979. Strickland uses Erik Erikson's life-cycle model to analyze the reasons why Juliette Low became the founder of the Girl Scouts of the United States. Although designed for specialists in gender and child development studies, this essay can be read with benefit by the nonspecialist. Contains useful bibliographical references.

Lucid, Shannon W.

Shannon W. Lucid

> " ... all my life I'd been told you can't do that because you're female. . . . I just went ahead and did what I could and then, when the stars aligned, I was ready. "

Astronaut

Chosen by NASA as one of the first American female astronauts, Lucid was a mission specialist on five shuttle flights and lived for six months on Russia's Mir space station. Her time on Mir led to the U.S. record for the most flight hours in orbit by a non-Russian and the international record for the most flight hours of any woman, a record held for more than a decade.

Born: January 14, 1943; Shanghai, China
Also known as: Shannon Matilda Wells Lucid (full name)
Area of achievement: Aviation and space exploration

Early Life

Shannon W. Lucid (LEW-sihd) was born Shannon Matilda Wells in Shanghai, China, where her parents, Oscar and Myrtle Wells, were serving as Baptist missionaries. During the Japanese occupation, Lucid, her parents, and other members of her family were interned by the Japanese in the Chapei Civil Assembly Center prison camp. Early in 1944 they were evacuated aboard the Swedish ship *Gripsholm* in an exchange of noncombatant citizens of the warring nations. Lucid learned to walk onboard ship and received her first pair of shoes when the ship was docked in the port of Johannesburg on its way to the United States. The family spent the remaining years of the war in Fort Worth, Texas, where Lucid's younger sister, Ann, and brother, Joe, were born. The family later returned to China, where Lucid was enrolled in a Chinese-speaking school.

When the Communist Party took over China in 1949, Lucid and her family returned to the United States and settled in Bethany, Oklahoma, near Oklahoma City. As a young girl she was fascinated with airplanes and was influenced by a book about Robert H. Goddard, the founder of modern rocketry. After graduating from Bethany High School in 1960, she began college in Illinois at Wheaton, where she spent two years completing basic science and mathematics courses along with German, literature, and biblical studies. In 1962, she transferred to the University of Oklahoma after taking summer courses there, and along with her work in chemistry she learned to fly and earned a pilot's license. She completed a bachelor of science degree in chemistry in 1963 and remained for another year as a teaching assistant in the Chemistry Department.

Life's Work

During the next few years after graduation, Lucid held several positions in chemistry and obtained commercial, instrument, and multiengine ratings as a pilot. From 1963 to 1964 she served as a teaching assistant at Oklahoma, was a senior laboratory technician at the Oklahoma Medical Research Foundation from 1964 to 1966, and was a research chemist at Kerr-McGee in Oklahoma City from 1966 to 1968. While at Kerr-McGee, she met and married Michael F. Lucid of Indianapolis, Indiana, and they had two daughters, Kawai Dawn and Shandra Michelle, and one son, Michael Kermit. Lucid returned to the University of Oklahoma in 1969 as a graduate assistant in the university's Health Science Center, earning a master of science degree in biochemistry in 1970 and a doctor of philosophy degree in biochemistry in 1973. From 1974 to 1978, Lucid returned to the Oklahoma Medical Research Foundation as a research associate and began the application process for the space program as soon as women were recruited for the astronaut corps.

On January 16, 1978, Lucid was selected by the National Aeronautical and Space Administration (NASA) as one of thirty-five astronauts from a pool of more than two hundred finalists. She was one of six women in the first astronaut class that accepted women, a class that included Sally Ride, Judith Resnik, Anna Fisher, Margaret Seddon, and Kathryn Sullivan. After a period of intense training and rigorous physical and psychological testing, Lucid became an astronaut in August, 1979, qualifying as a mission specialist on space shuttle flight crews. Although Lucid was not the first American woman in space, she is America's most experienced female astronaut.

Lucid's technical assignments included work with the Shuttle Avionics Integration Laboratory; the Flight Software Laboratory in Downey, California; and the Astronaut Office interface at Kennedy Space Center, Florida, on shuttle testing and launch countdowns. She also was a spacecraft capsule communicator at the Johnson Space Center, Mission Control, Houston, during many space shuttle missions. She was chief of Mission Support, chief of Astronaut Appearances, and chief scientist of NASA from 2002 to 2003.

Lucid was part of the crew of five spaceflights and logged 223 days in space, more than any other woman until surpassed by U.S. astronaut Sunita Williams on June 16, 2007. Lucid's maiden space voyage was a seven-day mission on the space shuttle *Discovery* (STS-51-G) from June 17 to 24, 1985. On this mission the crew deployed three communication satellites and used the Remote Manipulator System to deploy and retrieve the *Spartan* satellite after its seventeen hours of X-ray astronomy observations. The crew also conducted biomedical experiments during *Discovery*'s 112 orbits of Earth, covering a distance of 2.5 million miles.

Lucid's next two orbital flights were both on space shuttle *Atlantis*. Her second shuttle flight was a five-day mission (STS-34) from October 18 to 23, 1989. On this flight she deployed the *Galileo* spacecraft to explore Jupiter and its moons, mapped atmospheric ozone using ultraviolet solar back-scattering, and conducted research on lightning, microgravity effects on plants, ice crystal growth in space, and many other secondary experiments during seventy-nine orbits. Her third shuttle flight was a nine-day mission (STS-43) from August 2 to 11, 1991. On this mission the crew deployed a tracking and data relay satellite (TDRS-E) and conducted during 142 orbits thirty-two science experiments related to extended spaceflights.

Lucid's fourth spaceflight was a fourteen-day mission on the shuttle *Columbia* (STS-58) from October 18 to November 1, 1993. This record-duration shuttle flight was considered the most successful Spacelab-related mission flown by NASA. The

Lucid, Shannon W.

crew conducted sixteen engineering tests and twenty extended-duration medical experiments on themselves and on forty-eight rats during 225 orbits. Even before her record-breaking Mir flight, Lucid had logged 838 hours and 54 minutes in space, more than any other American woman.

On her last and most famous spaceflight, Lucid gained the U.S. single-mission space-endurance record of 188 days while aboard Mir. After a year of training in Star City, Russia, she began her journey from Kennedy Space Center on March 22, 1996, aboard *Atlantis* (STS-76) and was transferred to Mir, where she served as board engineer 2 with Russian cosmonauts Yuri Onufrienko and Yuri Usachev. She conducted many science experiments during her six months in space and became the first American to participate in extravehicular activity, or space walking, while stationed on Mir. Her return was scheduled for July 31 but was delayed nearly two months because of mechanical and weather problems with shuttle launches. She returned to Kennedy Space Center aboard *Atlantis* on September 26 after traveling more than 75 million miles in space.

Significance

Lucid's space career reaffirmed that female astronauts could equal or surpass their male counterparts. When no other astronaut seemed interested in an extended trip on the sparse Mir space station, she was the one who volunteered, and by doing so she established several space records. Given her six months of weightlessness on Mir, doctors thought that she would have to be carried off the shuttle upon her return to Earth. She surprised the experts, however, by walking on her own to the medical transporter. She became NASA's most important source for data on the effects of space on the human body and was monitored and tested for three years after her trip.

In addition to her many scientific experiments in space, Lucid helped to facilitate space exploration. She launched several satellites, contributed to the exploration of Jupiter by launching the *Galileo* spacecraft, and assisted with many aspects of the space program on the ground. In December of 1996, she became the tenth astronaut to receive the Congressional Space Medal of Honor, and, in February of 1997, she won the Free Spirit Award from the Freedom Forum.

—*Joseph L. Spradley*

Further Reading

Atkins, Jeannine. *Wings and Rockets: The Story of Women in Air and Space*. New York: Farrar, Straus and Giroux, 2003. A children's book about pioneers in air and space travel that includes a chapter on Lucid.

Lucid, Shannon W. "Six Months on Mir." *Scientific American*, May, 1998, 46-55. A personal account of Lucid's life on Mir, including information on weightlessness, safety in space, and her experiments and other activities.

Shayler, David, and Ian Moule. *Women in Space—Following Valentina*. New York: Springer, 2005. A history of women in space, from balloonists to astronauts, with updated accounts based on interviews with women, including Lucid, with careers in flight.

DOUGLAS MACARTHUR

> **❝** *As a rule, they who preach by word or deed 'peace at any price' are not possessed of anything worth having. . . .* **❞**

Military leader

MacArthur, Supreme Commander of the Allied Powers from 1945 through 1951, had a greater impact on American military history than virtually any other officer in the twentieth century. Variously gifted, he was a hero to much of the American public but a center of controversy on several occasions.

Born: January 26, 1880; Little Rock, Arkansas
Died: April 5, 1964; Washington, D.C.
Area of achievement: Military

EARLY LIFE

Douglas MacArthur (ma-KAR-thur), the son of Captain Arthur MacArthur and Mary Pinckney "Pinky" Hardy, was born at an Army post in Little Rock, Arkansas. MacArthur and his older brother (another had died early) led gangs of young Army brats, growing up in a succession of forts scattered throughout the United States as his father, a Civil War veteran of distinction, climbed to the highest ranks of the Army before running afoul of civilian authorities and ending his career in bitterness in 1909.

In 1899, Douglas MacArthur entered the United States Military Academy in West Point, New York. Nearly six feet tall, he was slender—as a plebe he weighed less than 140 pounds—but gave the impression of Western ruggedness. Pushed to excel by his devoted mother, who resided in the West Point area during his four years there, MacArthur finished first in his class academically, rivaling the record compiled by Robert E. Lee more than half a century before. Also like Lee, MacArthur achieved the signal honor of being chosen cadet first captain in recognition of his leadership and military bearing.

However, MacArthur also exhibited some of the character traits that were to make his later years so controversial. One cadet found that it was impossible to be neutral about MacArthur. If one knew him at all well, another cadet concluded, one ended up either admiring him to the point of adulation or hating him. So extreme was MacArthur's sense of honor that he threatened to resign over an interpretation of the rules in a mathematics class. He won the confrontation with his professor, a lieutenant colonel, but jeopardized his career in doing so.

LIFE'S WORK

The Army in which MacArthur was commissioned as a second lieutenant in June, 1903, had outgrown its post-Civil War doldrums, but it was still a small force by European standards. Promotion was accordingly slow, and he did not gain the rank of captain until 1911. As an engineer officer, the branch to which the top-ranking graduates of West Point were usually assigned, he saw service in Wisconsin, Kansas, Michigan, Texas, Panama, and the Philippines. On detached duty, he accompanied his father on a lengthy tour of Asia in 1906, and in 1914 he undertook a risky intelligence mission in Mexico during the American occupation of Veracruz.

635

MacArthur, Douglas

Douglas MacArthur.
(Library of Congress)

Before and after his assignment in Mexico, MacArthur had staff duty in Washington and proved of great value in public relations. MacArthur, who could be as genial as he could be arrogant and supercilious, excelled in this role and also performed important work in setting up and selling to Congress and the public the selective service law when it was enacted after the United States entry into World War I. Unlike some career Army officers who disliked relying on the National Guard in wartime, MacArthur believed in it and in its public relations value and suggested that National Guard units from several states be combined into a division for duty in France. MacArthur, who requested a transfer to the infantry, was promoted to colonel and designated by the secretary of war to be chief of staff of this new division.

MacArthur remained with the Forty-second "Rainbow" Division from its arrival in France in October, 1917, until the end of the war. He showed himself to have both the administrative talent required of a capable staff officer and an unusual flair for leadership. Although his duties did not require it, he paid frequent visits to the trenches and accompanied troops on several raids. His unconventional dress, highlighted by sweaters and scarves, also won for him much attention. Promoted to brigadier general in the summer of 1918, MacArthur received command of a brigade. Twice wounded in combat, he led his brigade throughout the Meuse-Argonne campaign, moving up to acting

MacArthur, Douglas

divisional commander shortly before the armistice. For his exploits, he received a Distinguished Service Medal, two Purple Hearts, several other decorations from his own government, and many more from Allied nations, emerging from the war as one of the Army's brightest young officers.

The postwar demobilization, however, would cause many other officers of equal merit to wait years between promotions. Good luck and good timing enabled him to retain his brigadier's rank, and, after service with the American contingent stationed in the Rhineland, he became superintendent of West Point in June, 1919. He went there at a time when West Point's image had been tarnished by excessive hazing and an outdated curriculum. Although in politics he would be identified with conservative Republicans, MacArthur (as he proved over twenty-five years later when commander of the occupation of Japan) could also be a champion of progressive ideas, and he brought about some liberalization of cadet life and improvement in the curriculum.

Between 1922 when he left West Point and 1930 when he became chief of staff, MacArthur served two tours of duty in the Philippines and was twice assigned corps commands in the United States. In 1922, he married Henrietta Louise Cromwell Brooks, a wealthy divorcée. They had no children and were divorced in 1929. He married Jean Marie Faircloth in 1937; they had one son.

Promoted to major general in 1925, the youngest man to hold the rank at that time, MacArthur was named chief of staff by President Herbert Hoover in 1930. The position carried with it the rank of general. His five years in the post were not easy. The Depression made it difficult to accomplish much in the way of the modernization the Army required; his outspoken advocacy of preparedness at a time of financial austerity and antiwar sentiment earned for him much criticism, as did his linking of pacifism with communism as a threat to American security. His identification with the dispersal of the Bonus Army of unemployed veterans, who had come to Washington in 1932 to seek financial relief, also was controversial. Despite the understanding he frequently showed in public relations and his oft-demonstrated ability to use the media to his own advantage, in this case MacArthur misjudged the situation. He disregarded the advice of his assistant, Dwight D. Eisenhower, that he remain in the background and instead dressed in full uniform and, wearing his decorations, proceeded personally to lead the troops sent to evict the veterans from the old federal building they had been occupying. Ignoring the instructions sent from the secretary of war by messenger, MacArthur ordered the marchers to be forced back to their encampment, which went up in flames. Exactly who was responsible for setting the fires was not ascertained, but the affair proved to be a public relations disaster both for the Hoover administration and for MacArthur personally, and it helped attach an authoritarian image to him.

MacArthur continued to serve as chief of staff during the first two years of the New Deal, making a genuine contribution to its domestic program. Instructed to do so, he effectively utilized Army personnel to organize the camps of the Civilian Conservation Corps, one of the New Deal's most popular and productive agencies.

At the request of the new Philippine Commonwealth government, MacArthur was named military adviser to the Philippines in 1935 with the duty of developing its armed forces. It was then anticipated that the Philippines would become an independent na-

MacArthur, Douglas

tion in 1944, at which time it would have to provide for its own security. MacArthur performed essentially the same role for about six years, first as adviser to the Philippine Commonwealth, then, from 1937 on, when he retired from the Army, as a field marshal in Philippine service.

In the summer of 1941, with war between the United States and Japan becoming more and more likely, President Franklin D. Roosevelt recalled MacArthur to active service. Given the command of United States Army Forces Far East, he was quickly promoted to lieutenant general and led both the Filipino troops, whose training he had directed, and a small but slowly growing contingent of American forces.

When war struck the Philippines in December, 1941, neither the training of Filipino forces nor the buildup of American troops had advanced far enough to avert disaster. MacArthur's initial troop dispositions only compounded the difficulties—defending the beachheads with inexperienced personnel, failing to move adequate supplies to the strategic Bataan Peninsula, where MacArthur soon ordered a delaying action, allowing his air power to be caught on the ground and largely destroyed even though he had ample warning of the strike on Pearl Harbor. Perhaps because of his command's forward position, however, he ironically emerged from the debacle as a hero and was promoted to full general in late December.

The gallant though doomed defense of Bataan and Corregidor increased MacArthur's heroic stature, which his staff at headquarters was careful to enhance with laudatory press communiqués then and throughout the war. As the campaign on Bataan ground along, estrangement grew between MacArthur and his superiors in Washington, who were unable to send the reinforcements for which he kept pleading and which he kept promising his increasingly embittered troops. In March, 1942, MacArthur and his family left their Corregidor quarters under orders to proceed to Australia. In April, he was named commander of the Southwest Pacific Area, a newly formed theater of war. On his arrival in Australia, he had made the dramatic statement, "I shall return," fostering the image of resolute leadership that would characterize his strategy throughout the war.

Eventually, MacArthur's forces did return to the Philippines, but first it was necessary to augment his troop strength, halt the Japanese advance in his theater in late 1942, and then begin the laborious process of advancing northward along the coast of New Guinea and nearby islands. Relying on a strategy of using the superior air and sea power that he had begun to achieve by mid-1943, MacArthur was able to bypass enemy strong points. In cooperation with Admiral William F. Halsey's forces operating in the Solomon Islands, troops under MacArthur and his able air, naval, and ground commanders moved throughout 1943 from the Papuan region of New Guinea to Salamaua, Lae, and Finschhafen in the Huon Gulf area. In 1944, his forces advanced more than one thousand miles, into and beyond Hollandia in New Guinea to Morotai in the Molucca Islands. In doing so, his ground forces suffered fewer than two thousand combat casualties.

While operations were still being conducted by other troops on Leyte, in the central Philippines, which had been invaded in October, 1944, General Walter Krueger's Sixth Army landed at Lingayen Gulf on Luzon in January, 1945, initiating the largest American ground campaign of the entire war in the Pacific. With the campaign on this strategic northern island progressing satisfactorily, units from the Eighth Army made numerous amphibious landings to liberate islands in the central and southern Philippines. Many of these operations were conducted without explicit approval from the Joint Chiefs of Staff, continuing MacArthur's long-standing habit of ignoring instructions he did not like and undertaking campaigns in advance of firm directives.

By the spring of 1945, American forces were converging on Japan itself, and the division of the Pacific into Southwest Pacific and Pacific Ocean areas had become meaningless. Admiral Chester W. Nimitz, previously the commander of the Pacific Ocean area, would henceforth command all United States naval forces. As the newly appointed head of all U.S. Army forces in the Pacific, MacArthur, who now held the five-star rank of general of the Army, would have overall command of the ground phases of Operations Olympic and Coronet, the planned invasions of the Japanese home islands of Kyūshū and Honshū scheduled to take place in November, 1945, and early 1946, respectively.

The announcement of Japan's surrender in August, 1945, following the dropping of the atomic bombs on Hiroshima and Nagasaki and the Soviet declaration of war on Japan, abrogated these plans, and President Harry S. Truman designated MacArthur Supreme Commander, Allied Powers (SCAP). As such, he conducted the surrender ceremonies on board the battleship *Missouri* on September 2, 1945, and commanded the Allied occupation of Japan itself.

MacArthur's years as SCAP have often been regarded as his finest and most enduring accomplishment. The Japanese armed forces were demobilized with little difficulty. Democratic advances were made in land ownership, education, labor relations, and the structure of government, and antitrust legislation directed against the prewar holding companies, the *zaibatsu* (financial clique), was promulgated. The actual story was more complicated, for some of the reforms were more cosmetic than real and many could not be credited solely to MacArthur but to a complex interplay between Japanese elites and various American authorities. MacArthur's most conspicuous failure was his attempt to promote evangelical Christianity in Japan: The people simply did not want it.

Some of MacArthur's actions were undoubtedly carried out with his own presidential ambitions in mind—he would gladly have accepted the Republican nomination in 1944, 1948, or 1952, had it been forthcoming—but, for whatever motives, MacArthur's tenure as SCAP was in general a success. In his final years, he seems to have recognized that it was his most lasting contribution to world peace.

The war that broke out in divided Korea in June, 1950, brought MacArthur new military laurels followed by an abrupt end to his long career. After initial retreats, the forces under MacArthur's command recovered following the Inchon landings that reprised the best of his World War II operations for audacity and success, and by October, victory seemed at hand. Tensions instead mounted between the general and President Truman following the Communist Chinese entry into a war that settled down into one of attrition. In April, 1951, MacArthur was relieved of all his military responsibilities following the publication of a letter the general had sent to an influential Republican politician making clear his disagreement with the president's policies of limiting the warfare in Korea until a negotiated peace could be had. In a way, the very

MacArthur, Douglas

success of Inchon could be blamed for his unceremonious relief, for it made the aging general more certain than ever of the correctness of his own judgments and by the same token made it more difficult for President Truman and the Joint Chiefs of Staff to question his recommendations and to make clear that he was insubordinate when he issued policy statements, as he had in a letter to the Veterans of Foreign Wars in August, 1950.

Within a week after his dismissal, MacArthur was being greeted as a hero in the several stops he made en route to Washington, D.C., where he spoke to a joint session of Congress. His remarks critical of Truman's policies were applauded, but in the Senate hearings held about his dismissal, the enthusiasm of many for MacArthur's views on the Korean conflict cooled.

MacArthur still had political aspirations and gave the keynote address at the 1952 Republican National Convention. It was a poor speech and helped neither the cause of Senator Robert A. Taft, whom MacArthur supported, nor his own chances for a draft should Taft falter and the convention delegates look elsewhere for a nominee. Eisenhower received the nomination.

MacArthur lived twelve more years, residing in New York City, discharging his nominal duties as chair of the board of Remington Rand and making only infrequent public appearances, one of them a visit to the Philippines in 1961. He died at Walter Reed Army Hospital in Washington, D.C., on April 5, 1964, only a few months after he had completed writing his memoirs.

Significance

MacArthur served in the U.S. Army for almost fifty years, achieving his country's highest honors. He led his forces to memorable victories after appalling defeat, only to have his career end amid controversy. Throughout, he was an actor almost as much as a soldier, a characteristic that was recognized by many who observed him closely. His use of distinctive attire, his often brilliant if theatrical speeches, his seeking of the headlines, all added to the aura of a larger-than-life personality. Was it because of his flamboyance that he never achieved the presidency, a position he would have liked but preferred not to seek openly? Unlike Eisenhower, whose unassuming mannerisms made him the perfect citizen-soldier, MacArthur always seemed too removed from the people of the United States to become their president. Perhaps he was indeed, as one of his biographers has put it, the "American Caesar."

—*Lloyd J. Graybar*

Further Reading

Harvey, Robert. *American Shogun: General MacArthur, Emperor Hirohito, and the Drama of Modern Japan.* Woodstock, N.Y.: Overlook Press, 2006. Describes how American-Japanese relations were shaped by MacArthur and Hirohito both during and after World War II.

James, D. Clayton. *The Years of MacArthur.* 3 vols. Boston: Houghton Mifflin, 1970-1985. Magnificent study of MacArthur. Critical of the general's weaknesses but also shrewd in appreciating and evaluating his many strengths. Not likely to be surpassed as the definitive work.

Kenney, George C. *General Kenney Reports: A Personal History of the Pacific War.* New York: Duell, Sloan and Pearce, 1949. An example of a memoir written by one of the able field commanders who joined MacArthur in Australia. Kenney built and led a superb air arm for MacArthur to use on the road back.

Leary, William M., ed. *MacArthur and the American Century: A Reader.* Lincoln: University of Nebraska Press, 2001. Collection of essays about MacArthur's life and career written by MacArthur and others, including Dwight D. Eisenhower and D. Clayton James.

MacArthur, Douglas. *Reminiscences.* New York: McGraw-Hill, 1964. A memoir that is a fine example of selective memory in writing. Better for MacArthur's perception of himself than as historical record.

Manchester, William. *American Caesar: Douglas MacArthur, 1880-1964.* Boston: Little, Brown, 1978. Not very well received as history, certainly not in a class with James's study, but readable and a good one-volume biography.

Petillo, Carole M. *Douglas MacArthur: The Philippine Years.* Bloomington: Indiana University Press, 1981. Reveals one of the more questionable episodes in MacArthur's life, his acceptance of a large cash payment from the Philippine Commonwealth early in 1942. The author speculates: Was it a bribe to ensure that MacArthur would see that Philippine leaders were evacuated to safety, or was it in the Filipino tradition of gift giving? Mainly concerned with establishing the psychological impact on MacArthur of the many years he spent in the Philippines at various intervals in his career, this work belongs to the genre of psychobiography, the controversial but sometimes rewarding use of psychoanalytic theory in the writing of biography.

Schaller, Michael. *The American Occupation of Japan: The Origins of the Cold War in Asia.* New York: Oxford University Press, 1985. A study of American occupation policy in Japan, revisionist in nature and laudable in its effort to place the occupation in the context of the Cold War.

Smith, Robert Ross. *Triumph in the Philippines.* Washington, D.C.: Office of the Chief of Military History, 1963. One of several detailed books in the official series The United States Army in World War II, that together provide a comprehensive view of MacArthur's campaigns from Bataan to the triumphant return to Luzon. Indispensable on the subject of MacArthur's campaigns. A similar series is available for the Korean conflict.

Weintraub, Stanley. *MacArthur's War: Korea and the Undoing of an American Hero.* New York: Free Press, 2000. Chronicles MacArthur's key actions during the Korean War. Weintraub maintains that MacArthur's character and methods led him to make serious errors of judgment.

Madison, Dolley

DOLLEY MADISON

> " *It is one of my sources of happiness never to desire a knowledge of other people's business.* "

First Lady of the United States (1809-1817)

First Lady Dolley Madison's popularity and social acumen made her a political asset to President James Madison. The leading social figure in the capital city for years, she was arguably the most beloved and important American woman of her times, and she served as a role model for future First Ladies.

Born: May 20, 1768; Guilford County, North Carolina
Died: July 12, 1849; Washington, D.C.
Also known as: Dorothea Dandridge Payne (birth name); Dolley Payne Todd (first married name)
Area of achievement: Government and politics

EARLY LIFE

Dolley Madison (MA-dih-suhn) was the daughter of John and Mary Coles Payne, who moved to Piedmont, North Carolina, from Virginia. It was there that Dolley was born in 1768. The following year, the Payne family moved back to their native Virginia. In 1783, after freeing his slaves, John again moved his family, this time to Philadelphia, Pennsylvania, where the Paynes raised their eight children in the strict disciplinary tradition of the Quaker Society of Friends. Dolley was also raised modestly, as her father had failed in business.

In 1790 Dolley married John Todd, Jr., a successful lawyer and Quaker. Dolley and John had two sons: John Payne in 1790 and William Temple in 1792. Tragedy struck when the yellow fever epidemic hit Philadelphia in 1793 and claimed the lives of Dolley's husband, both of his parents, and Dolley's son William, leaving her a young widow with an infant child. The strong-willed Dolley was determined to persevere and make something of herself. Among her many courters at this time was the "Father of the Constitution" and author of the Bill of Rights, Representative James Madison of Virginia. They seemed to make an unlikely couple, as the longtime bachelor James was seventeen years Dolley's senior. He was also unlike most of the dashing gentlemen of his time, because he had not been a soldier, did not dance, and did not ride horses. However, Dolley eventually fell for the intelligent but dour James. They were married on September 15, 1794, and enjoyed a happy but childless marriage. After abandoning her Quaker roots for James's Episcopalianism, she was disowned by the Quakers.

LIFE'S WORK

Dolley appears to have completely shed her conservative Quaker upbringing after her second marriage and developed a love of music, gardens, and socializing. She also acquired a taste for fashion that could not have been further from the social standards of the day that included bright colors, scandalously low-cut dresses, and a bold hairstyle of large curls. Incredibly, for much of the early nineteenth century she was at the center of social life in Washington, D.C. During this time, Dolley was quite possibly the most widely known and beloved woman in the country. A highly capable woman, Dolley managed the Madison family plantation when James was away in Washington, D.C. Admired for her outgoing, pleasant personality, she is widely considered to have been the most talented social hostess in the history of the White House. In this endeavor she was aided by what appears to have been a deep, selfless, and genuine love of people and a knack for remembering everyone's name.

In 1801, newly elected President Thomas Jefferson appointed James as his secretary of state. As a widower, Jefferson asked James's wife Dolley to help serve as the White House's social hostess. For eight years she presided over the social affairs of the Jefferson White House. This was followed by another eight years during which her husband was president of the United States from 1809 to 1817. It was Dolley who presided over the nation's first inaugural ball in 1809.

Among the Washington social crowd and much of the nation, Dolley was hailed as "Queen Dolley," "Lady Presidentress," or the "Queen of Washington City." Her socials were the events of the social season, and all of Washington awaited an invitation. Breaking with tradition, she served American dishes for dinner (even contacting people all over the country for recipes), rearranged rooms to better accommodate her guests, and defied convention by sitting at the head of the table at dinners.

Dolley Madison.
(Library of Congress)

Madison, Dolley

Dolley set a precedent for future First Ladies when she renovated and redecorated the White House. Strategically, she invited members of Congress to the White House so they could see the poor condition of the building; after securing congressional funding for the renovation project, she even worked with the supervising architect. She successfully blended European flair with American homespun simplicity in her entertaining and invited a wide array of guests to the White House. Although the historical record is far from complete, she seems to have made a positive impression on almost every visitor to the White House. She also emerged as a fashion trendsetter as the nation took a keen interest in her taste for European attire, jewels, bird plumes, and even what became known as "the Dolley Madison turban." Details of her social events and attire were reported in newspapers.

Along with her successful social role, she was the perfect political partner for James. In comparison with his subdued seriousness, she was funny, talkative, and engaging. As was the norm for women of the eighteenth and nineteenth centuries, Dolley had little formal education and was not as well read or intellectual as her predecessor, Abigail Adams. She had been tutored at her childhood plantation home in Virginia and had received some education at a Quaker school in Pennsylvania. Yet, in an era during which women rarely spoke publicly and took no interest in politics, Dolley functioned as an adviser to her husband on both social and political matters. She traveled with him, campaigned with him, and appeared in public with him. James was proud of his wife's accomplishments. He appears to have recognized her social abilities and his limited interpersonal skills. He often sought and took her advice, appreciating her political astuteness, warm personal touch, and legendary tact.

Even though James had been the secretary of state, it was Dolley who was the diplomat. She took no formal or public role in politics and claimed disinterest in political affairs. However, her actions revealed her many political contributions to James's presidency. Many historical accounts exist of Dolley disarming her husband's political opponents, charming his potential supporters, and captivating statesmen, dignitaries, and other White House guests. Dolley made sure she invited every member of Congress to dinner at least once during legislative sessions. In doing so, she was a century ahead of her time as the first presidential spouse to blend White House social events with political agendas. She also held socials in honor of U.S. accomplishments, including the capture of British ships during the War of 1812.

When the British sacked the capital city and set the White House ablaze during the War of 1812, Dolley was among the last Americans to leave. The president and cabinet had already evacuated the city. Refusing pleas to abandon the capital city, Dolley watched the approach of the British through a spy glass. Unconcerned about her own safety, she thought to load as many White House archives as possible (including official papers, china, and silver, as well as such artifacts as the famous Gilbert Stuart portrait of George Washington) onto a wagon while the British army literally marched into the city. With a wagon full of priceless items, she fled to Virginia at the last possible moment. Her courageous act inspired a nation stung by the defeat and the August 24, 1814, burning of the White House. After the war an unfazed but heroic Dolley continued entertaining in her temporary quarters in a private home on Penn Avenue in Washington, D.C. She proclaimed to a cheering city, "We shall rebuild Washington!"

Madison, Dolley

SIGNIFICANCE

After James's second term as president ended in 1817, he and Dolley returned to Montpelier, their plantation home in Virginia, where they enjoyed a comfortable retirement highlighted by the many visitors and guests who attended Dolley's parties. Dolley continued to support her husband's political work by taking dictation for him through his failing health during the last years of his life. James Madison died in 1836, and in the autumn of 1837, Dolley returned to the capital city to live. She moved into a small home that James had built some years earlier. Back in Washington, Dolley returned to the social and political life, enjoying an honorary seat on the Senate floor, attending social events, and receiving lifetime franking privileges from Congress. She wisely sold James's official papers to the government for $30,000 to both assure their preservation and provide for herself financially. She remained a central figure until her death in 1849.

Dolley Madison loved living in the White House and was perhaps the first presidential spouse as well as one of the few women prior to the twentieth century to develop an identity of her own beyond that of her husband. She fashioned the social side of the office of First Lady and consequently became a role model for many future First Ladies. On her death, President Zachary Taylor aptly described her as "Our First Lady for a half-century."

—*Robert P. Watson*

FURTHER READING

Anthony, Carl Sferrazza. *First Ladies: The Saga of the Presidents' Wives and Their Power, 1789-1961.* New York: William Morrow, 1990. Contains a chapter on each First Lady, including Dolley. Anthony provides both personal and political details of Dolley's life.

Arnett, Ethel Stephens. *Mrs. James Madison: The Incomparable Dolley.* Greensboro, N.C.: Piedmont Press, 1972. A source for Dolley's life before meeting James Madison and later in the White House. Examines her personality and character.

Cote, Richard N. *Strength and Honor: The Life of Dolley Madison.* Mount Pleasant, S.C.: Corinthian Books, 2004. A well-researched, comprehensive biography of the woman Cote describes as the "best-loved first lady of the nineteenth century."

Gould, Lewis L., ed. *American First Ladies: Their Lives and Their Legacy.* New York: Garland, 1996. Contains a chapter on each First Lady that includes an examination of their contributions to the presidency. Includes a helpful bibliography.

Hunt-Jones, Conover. *Dolley and the "Great Little Madison."* Washington, D.C.: American Institute of Architects Foundation, 1977. Hunt-Jones explores the Madisons' marriage, their long life together, and Dolley's influence on her "Great Little Madison."

Ketcham, Ralph. *James Madison: A Biography.* Charlottesville: University Press of Virginia, 1990. Insights on the life and presidency of the fourth president. Dolley is discussed periodically, but it also benefits one studying Dolley to know James Madison, his times, and life in the Madison White House.

Madison, Dolley. *The Selected Letters of Dolley Payne Madison.* Edited by David B. Mattern and Holly C. Shulman. Charlottesville: University Press of Virginia, 2003.

Contains a carefully edited selection of letters to and from Madison. Also features short, factual essays placing Madison's letters within the context of her life and times and biographies of the people mentioned in the letters.

Truman, Margaret. *First Ladies: An Intimate Group Portrait of White House Wives.* New York: Random House, 1995. Contains numerous discussions of Dolley's sense of style, famous social events, renovation of the White House, and heroism during the War of 1812. The book is written in a conversational, nonacademic style and is very readable.

JAMES MADISON

> *Each generation should be made to bear the burden of its own wars, instead of carrying them on, at the expense of other generations.*

President of the United States (1809-1817)

Madison was the primary architect of the U.S. Constitution and the fourth U.S. president. His lasting reputation is based less on his conduct as president or as secretary of state than on his contribution to the writing of the Constitution and securing its ratification. He also is remembered for helping to establish the new government and political parties, and for being a superior legislator and nation builder.

Born: March 16, 1751; Port Conway, Prince George County, Virginia
Died: June 28, 1836; Montpelier, Orange County, Virginia
Also known as: Father of the Constitution
Area of achievement: Government and politics

EARLY LIFE

James Madison (MA-dih-suhn) was the son of James Madison, Sr., and Nelly Conway Madison. James, Jr., was the eldest of twelve children. The family was not wealthy but lived in comfortable circumstances. Young Madison was enrolled at the age of eleven in the boarding school of Donald Robertson, and he studied under him for five years. He studied two additional years at home under the tutelage of Thomas Martin, an Anglican minister. In 1769, Madison entered Princeton. Because of his previous training, he was able to complete the four-year course in two years, graduating in September, 1771. This effort took a toll on his health. He appears to have suffered from depression and epileptiform hysteria.

In May, 1776, Madison began his political career as a member of the convention that drew up the Virginia constitution. He was then elected to the Virginia Assembly. There, Madison joined with Thomas Jefferson in an effort to disestablish the Church of England. They eventually became lifelong friends and close political associates. Madison was not reelected, but he was chosen by the legislature in 1778 to the governor's council. Despite his unimposing five-foot, six-inch stature and a slender frame and boyish features, Madison obviously made an impression upon the legislature with his intelligence and diligence. He was never a great orator, but he was an agreeable, persuasive speaker. He possessed great political skill and generally was a dominating figure in legislative bodies throughout his career.

In December, 1779, Madison was chosen a delegate to the Continental Congress. He took his seat in March, 1780, and quickly established himself as one of the most effective and valuable members of that body. For most of the next forty years, he would play an important, and at times major, role in the critical years of the early republic.

Life's Work

In the Continental Congress, James Madison took a nationalist position. He often collaborated with Alexander Hamilton. He labored hard to strengthen the government and amend the Articles of Confederation to give it the power to levy duties. Madison wrote an earnest address to the states, pleading for national unity, but it was to no avail, and the amendment failed.

In 1784, Madison was elected to the Virginia legislature, where he worked to defend religious freedom. His famous "Memorial and Remonstrance Against Religious Assessments" helped defeat a scheme by Patrick Henry to impose a general assessment for the support of religion. Madison then pushed Jefferson's "Bill for Religious Liberty" to passage, completing the disestablishment of the Anglican Church begun in 1779. Madison's "Memorial and Remonstrance" foreshadowed the clause on religious liberty in the First Amendment to the U.S. Constitution.

Madison was a delegate to the Annapolis Convention of 1786, and he was named to the Virginia delegation to attend the federal convention at Philadelphia in 1787. When the convention opened in May, Madison had prepared an extensive proposal to revise the Articles of Confederation. The Virginia Plan, presented by Edmund Randolph but based on Madison's ideas, became the basis of discussion throughout the summer months. Madison led the movement to grant the federal government greater authority over national affairs. While he did not always carry his point of view, he clearly was the dominating figure in the convention, so that he is often called the "Father of the Constitution." The journal that he kept on the convention is the most complete record of the proceedings available.

Madison also played a prominent role in securing the ratification of the Constitution in Virginia. His influence was crucial in overcoming the opposition of Patrick Henry and George Mason. In retrospect, perhaps his most important work was in cooperating with Alexander Hamilton and John Jay in writing a series of essays for New York newspapers that were later collected and published in 1788 as *The Federalist*, also known as the *Federalist* papers. Madison wrote nearly thirty of the eighty-five essays, which are justly celebrated today as still the most authoritative commentary on the U.S. Constitution and a major contribution to political science. His most notable contributions were his reflections on the plural society in numbers ten and fifty-one; the dual nature of the new government, federal in extent of powers and national in operation, in number thirty-nine; and the interrelationship of checks and balances in number forty-eight.

Madison, James

Madison was elected to the House of Representatives, and within a week of entering the House in April, 1789, he began the work of establishing a strong and effective central government. He led the movement to establish revenues for the new government by imposing import duties; he presented a motion to create the Departments of State, Treasury, and War and gave the executive broad powers over these offices; and he proposed a set of constitutional amendments that eventually became the Bill of Rights.

Madison served in the first five congresses. His inherent conservatism manifested itself in his growing opposition to Hamilton's fiscal policies and the government's pro-British tendency. After 1790, Madison organized the congressional alliances that became the basis for the first national political parties. More than Jefferson, Madison deserves to be called the founder of the modern-day Democratic Party.

On September 15, 1794, at the age of forty-three, Madison married a young widow, Dolley Payne Todd. It proved to be a long and happy marriage, and the young wife, Dolley Madison, gained a reputation as a famous hostess during her husband's presidential years.

Madison retired from Congress in 1797. Federalists, taking advantage of the hysteria generated by the XYZ affair and the quasi-war with France, passed the Alien and Sedition Acts to curb foreign- and native-born critics of the administration. Madison and Jefferson drafted resolutions adopted by the Kentucky and Virginia legislatures in 1798. These resolutions not only criticized the Alien and Sedition Acts but also laid down the doctrine of nullification for states' rights. In later years, Madison argued that these statements were protests intended primarily to secure the cooperation of the states, but they also expressed positions dangerous to the unity of the new republic. Nevertheless, these resolutions contributed to the overthrow of the Federalists and secured the election of Jefferson in 1800. Jefferson brought his longtime friend into the government as his secretary of state.

Later, in 1807, Madison became president, primarily a result of support from Jefferson, but his presidency was beset by many problems in the early years of the nineteenth century. In the closing years of his presidency, Madison signed bills establishing a standing army and enlarging the naval establishment, the Bank of the United States, and a protective tariff. He did, however, veto an internal improvement bill as unconstitutional. He left office on March 4, 1817, and except for participation in the Virginia Constitutional Convention in 1829, his political career was over. He lived his remaining years quietly at Montpelier. Occasionally, he offered advice to his successor, James Monroe, and he wrote defending his actions over his long career. He also devoted time to arranging his notes on the Constitutional Convention for publication. They were not published until 1840, four years after his death on June 28, 1836.

SIGNIFICANCE

James Madison was truly a nation builder. Perhaps the most outstanding political theorist and political writer in a generation that produced many first-rate thinkers, Madison often carried his position by sheer brilliance and cool, dispassionate reasoning. He lacked the dramatic style often useful in public life. He advanced because of his abilities and not because of his personality. He was a first-rate legislator, one of the most effective this country has produced. He was, on the other hand, only an average administrator. He failed to provide dynamic leadership during his presidency, especially during the War of 1812.

There are certain consistent themes throughout his career. First, there were his efforts to secure freedom of conscience and other personal rights and liberties. Second, he consistently supported and advanced the republican form of government based broadly on the popular will. Finally, throughout his life his devotion to the Union was paramount. One of the last actions of his life was to write a document entitled "Advice to My Country." It concluded with the advice that the Union "be cherished and perpetuated."

—*C. Edward Skeen*

FURTHER READING

Brant, Irving. *The Fourth President: A Life of James Madison*. Indianapolis, Ind.: Bobbs-Merrill, 1970. A distillation of Brant's standard six-volume biography of Madison. Valuable especially because of the author's extensive knowledge of his subject. For a complete study of Madison's life, consult Brant's six-volume study.

Cooke, Jacob E., ed. *The Federalist*. Middletown, Conn.: Wesleyan University Press, 1961. There are many editions of the *Federalist* papers, but this collection is especially useful because of Cooke's extensive and valuable notes.

Ketcham, Ralph. *James Madison: A Biography*. Charlottesville: University Press of Virginia, 1990. The best one-volume biography. Ketcham's work is well researched, well documented, and well written. Although based heavily on Irving Brant's six-volume study, it is more balanced than Brant's biography.

Koch, Adrienne. *Jefferson and Madison: The Great Collaboration*. New York: Alfred A. Knopf, 1950. An excellent study of the collaboration of the two men but weighted heavily to the years before Jefferson's presidency. Koch is superb at analyzing political philosophies, describing how Madison was more cautious and often exerted a calming influence on Jefferson.

Matthews, Richard K. *If Men Were Angels: James Madison and the Heartless Empire of Reason*. Lawrence: University Press of Kansas, 1995. A revisionist, negative interpretation of Madison, portraying him as a consistent liberal who highly valued personal liberties. Matthews argues that Madison's views produced a vulgar, materialistic, and anti-intellectual nation.

Meyers, Marvin, ed. *The Mind of the Founder: Sources of the Political Thought of James Madison*. Indianapolis, Ind.: Bobbs-Merrill, 1973. A collection of Madison's letters and writings oriented toward his political thought. Includes an informative introduction by the editor.

Moore, Virginia. *The Madisons: A Biography*. New York: McGraw-Hill, 1979. A combined biography written in a breezy, journalistic style, concentrating on the Madisons' private lives. It is well researched and illuminates early nineteenth century society.

Rutland, Robert Allen. *James Madison: The Founding Father*. Columbia: University of Missouri Press, 1997. A biography by a noted Madison scholar and the editor of Madison's papers. Rutland brings a human dimension to his subject, recounting Madison's goals, frustrations, victories, and defeats.

Malcolm X

Stagg, J. C. A. *Mr. Madison's War: Politics, Diplomacy, and Warfare in the Early American Republic, 1783-1830.* Princeton, N.J.: Princeton University Press, 1983. An extremely well-researched and well-written work. Madison's political and economic views are extensively covered.

Wills, Garry. *James Madison.* New York: Times Books, 2002. One in a series of books providing brief overviews of American presidents' lives and accomplishments. Despite his many achievements before becoming president, Madison, the author argues, lacked executive ability and his presidency was a near disaster.

MALCOLM X

❝ *If you don't stand for something you will fall for anything.* ❞

Religious and political leader

Malcolm X rose from life as a criminal hustler to become the national minister of the Nation of Islam and a popularizer of black nationalism, which emphasized self-defense for African Americans and independence from white America. Malcolm X's separatism served as a political alternative to Martin Luther King, Jr.'s advocacy of nonviolence and desegregation.

Born: May 19, 1925; Omaha, Nebraska
Died: February 21, 1965; New York, New York
Also known as: Malcolm Little (birth name); El-Hajj Malik el-Shabazz
Areas of achievement: Civil rights; oratory; religion and theology

EARLY LIFE

In his best seller *The Autobiography of Malcolm X* (1964), Malcolm X (MAL-kuhm ehks), who was born Malcolm Little, described his father, Baptist preacher Earl Little, and his mother, Granada native M. Louise Norton, as dedicated followers of Marcus Garvey. Garvey, founder of the United Negro Improvement Association, argued that black people in the Western Hemisphere could achieve political freedom only by returning to the African homeland and could win economic independence by developing black-owned businesses. According to the autobiography, Louise was pregnant with Malcolm when Ku Klux Klan night riders, angered at Earl's preaching, appeared at the Little home and warned them to move out of Omaha.

Nineteen months after Malcolm was born, the family left Omaha, eventually settling in Lansing, Michigan. According to the autobiography, a local white hate group called the Black Legion became alarmed about the "uppity" Earl Little, suspecting him of spreading unrest in the African American community. In late 1929, a deliberately set fire broke out at the Little home. The family escaped unharmed, but Earl was forced to build a new home outside East Lansing. On September 28, 1931, Earl died after being struck by a streetcar. Malcolm later claimed that the Black Legion murdered his father.

Alone, Louise had eight children to raise. Worried about her family and embarrassed by having to accept welfare, she suffered a nervous breakdown eight years after her husband's death. The courts divided the Little children among several foster families. Often hungry as he grew up during the Great Depression, Malcolm still did well in school through the eighth grade. He made the highest grades among his peers and became class president in the seventh grade even while enduring condescending, racist comments from teachers and his peers. A previously supportive white English teacher asked Malcolm what he wanted to do for a living. When Malcolm said he wanted to become a lawyer, the teacher told him, "that's no realistic goal for a nigger," and advised him to become a carpenter. Disillusioned, Malcolm withdrew from white society and committed petty thefts before spending time in a detention home. Malcolm's problems prompted his move in 1941 to Boston, where he lived with his half sister Ella.

Malcolm accepted several low-paying jobs, including work as a busboy, dishwasher, and shoe shiner. He also drifted to the fringes of Boston's underworld and spent his years in Boston and New York as "Detroit Red"—a zoot-suit-wearing dope dealer, con artist, and pimp who organized a burglary ring. In February, 1946, when Malcolm was picking up a stolen watch he left at a Boston jewelry store for repairs, police arrested him for several felony charges, including illegal breaking and entering. The court sentenced him to serve seven years in prison.

Life's Work

While in Charleston Prison, Malcolm began an intense self-education program, copying a dictionary word for word and voraciously reading at the prison library. By the time he was transferred to a prison in Concord, Massachusetts, his brothers Philbert and Reginald had exposed him to the teachings of the Nation of Islam religious sect led by Elijah Muhammad. The Nation of Islam (NOI), founded in Detroit around 1930, taught that white people were an inherently evil race created in ancient times by a dissident black scientist named Yacub. The slave trade destroyed the great African civilizations, stripped black men and women of their culture, and deceived them with a Christian religion that left them vice ridden and subservient. The NOI taught that political reform was futile in an innately evil world. Only the final judgment of the NOI deity, Allah, against the white race could bring justice. Until then, black people should redeem themselves by surrendering vices such as alcohol, avoiding impure foods such as pork, and rediscovering past achievements of the black race. Rather than integration into a white society poisoned with racism, black people needed separation from the white world and the creation of a financially independent black homeland.

Muhammad's teachings explained for Malcolm his past experiences with racial injustice. Released from prison in 1952, Malcolm replaced his last name with "X," which represented the African family name lost under slavery. After working briefly in Michigan as a furniture salesperson and auto assembly worker, he soon devoted himself full-time to the Muslim ministry and became Muhammad's most effective recruiter and spokesperson.

An imposing figure, Malcolm stood about six feet five inches tall with a lanky physique, light skin, closely cropped reddish hair, and grayish eyes that peered intensely through horn-rimmed glasses. Despite his intense appearance, he often surprised audi-

Malcolm X

Malcolm X.
(Library of Congress)

ences and visitors with his politeness and charm. He rose quickly through the NOI ranks, becoming an assistant minister at Detroit Temple Number 1 in late 1953, then holding minister's posts in Boston, Philadelphia, and, in June, 1954, at New York Temple Number 7. It was there that he met his future wife, Betty Saunders. Malcolm and Betty married in January, 1958, and eventually had six daughters.

Malcolm acquired high visibility when New York City police beat and jailed NOI member Hinton Johnson in April, 1957. Malcolm led a contingent of fifty Muslims who gathered outside the Harlem police station where Johnson was being held. Malcolm insisted that Johnson be transferred to a hospital for medical treatment. When police complied, the incident prompted front-page coverage by the black-owned *Amsterdam News* and inspired closer police surveillance of the Muslims and their charismatic minister.

Malcolm gained national exposure with the July, 1959, New York broadcast of "The Hate That Hate Produced," a television report by journalist Mike Wallace. Malcolm boldly denounced not only white people but also middle-class black leaders, who he dismissed as Uncle Toms. Malcolm called Martin Luther King, Jr., a "chump" for advocating integration and insisted that "an integrated cup of coffee was insufficient pay for 400 years of slave labor." Malcolm rejected the vision of brotherhood in King's "I Have a Dream" speech during the 1963 March on Washington as a nightmare. At times straying from NOI's doctrine, Malcolm called for a global "black revolution" aiming at independence, not the integration sought by King's "Negro revolution."

By 1964, Malcolm's flamboyant rhetoric had made him the second most sought after speaker on college campuses, after Republican presidential candidate Barry Goldwater. Many within the NOI considered him Muhammad's heir apparent. Under Malcolm, the NOI grew from a few hundred adherents to 100,000 or more members during the early 1960's. Malcolm's successes sparked jealousy within the NOI even as Malcolm found himself frustrated with the NOI's apolitical approach. For all its rhetoric of self-defense and autonomy, the NOI stood on the sidelines while the Civil Rights campaign directly challenged white authority.

Reports that the married Muhammad had affairs with several secretaries and fathered six illegitimate children further alienated Malcolm. Corrupt NOI officials may have also feared that Malcolm, if he succeeded Muhammad, would crack down on financial improprieties. When Malcolm described the recent assassination of President John F. Kennedy as a case of "chickens coming home to roost" at a New York rally in December, 1963, Muhammad feared a backlash and suspended Malcolm from his ministry for ninety days. The breach, however, proved permanent.

On March 8, 1964, Malcolm announced a formal break with the Nation of Islam. He sought closer ties with the mainstream Civil Rights movement, saying that he and King both sought black freedom. Malcolm urged black people to make their voting rights a reality. He hoped to link the struggle of African Americans with the liberation struggles fought by people of color around the globe. He soon formed Muslim Mosque Inc. and the Organization of Afro-American Unity, which aimed to make the rights of African Americans an international issue. Malcolm completed his transformation that April when he undertook the journey to Mecca, Saudi Arabia, required of traditional Muslims. There he encountered Muslims of all colors who were experiencing spiritual brotherhood. He no longer saw all white people as devils but would judge white individuals by their actions. Concluding that the racist theology of the NOI conflicted with traditional Islam, he converted to the Sunni branch of Islam and took the name el-Hajj Malik el-Shabazz.

Malcolm sought a United Nations hearing on the suppression of black human rights in the United States, a goal never realized. His New York home, rewarded to him for his ministerial work, was firebombed on February 14, 1965, four days before the NOI evicted him. On February 21, at the start of a speech at the Audubon Ballroom in New York, Malcolm was shot repeatedly by Talmadge Hayer. A grand jury later indicted Hayer, Norman 3X Butler, and Thomas 15X Johnson for Malcolm's murder. All three had ties with the Nation of Islam and were convicted the next year. One day after the murder, Muhammad denied involvement with the assassination.

Significance

Malcolm X's influence increased after his death with the publication of his autobiography. As racism and black poverty persisted even with the signing of major civil rights legislation by Lyndon B. Johnson in 1964 and 1965, Malcolm's rage rang true for increasingly radicalized youth in organizations such as the Student Nonviolent Coordinating Committee (SNCC). The "black is beautiful" slogans of the 1960's and the development of black studies programs at universities and public schools echo Malcolm's emphasis on black pride and knowledge of the African past. The Black

Malcolm X

Panther Party, founded in Oakland, California, in 1966, acknowledged their ideological debt to Malcolm X and his emphasis on self-defense and the economic roots of racism. Transformed into a merchandising franchise by director Spike Lee's 1992 film biography *Malcolm X*, Malcolm's image haunts rap music videos, while rap recordings sample his speeches. In popular culture, Malcolm X now serves as both antihero and hero in the guise of the street-smart hustler and the self-educated minister who redeemed himself from an intellectual ghetto.

—Michael Phillips

FURTHER READING

Bassey, Magnus O. *Malcolm X and African-American Self-Consciousness*. Lewiston, N.Y.: Edwin Mellen Press, 2005. Explores Malcolm X's life within the context of his times, describing how he transformed black Americans' self-consciousness through the ideas of Islam and humanism.

Dyson, Michael Eric. *Making Malcolm: The Myth and Meaning of Malcolm X*. New York: Oxford University Press, 1995. At 215 pages, this work explores the political uses (and abuses) to which Malcolm's memory is subjected. The book includes analysis of previous biographers and provides a helpful overview of the scholarly literature on Malcolm X, summarizing academic disagreements about the man, his life, and his cultural impact.

Gallen, David. *Malcolm X as They Knew Him*. New York: Carroll & Graf, 1992. Gallen's book includes vivid reminiscences of Malcolm from friends and associates, a Playboy interview of Malcolm by Alex Haley before they worked together on the autobiography, and lively essays from writers as diverse as Black Panther Eldridge Cleaver and southern novelist and poet Robert Penn Warren.

Malcolm X. *The Autobiography of Malcolm X*. 1964. Reprint. New York: Ballantine, 1992. This autobiography contains both the eloquent oration that actor Ossie Davis delivered at Malcolm's funeral and Haley's illuminating epilogue, which captures the pressures, fears, and hopes of Malcolm's last months. Compellingly written, this remains the definitive text on Malcolm's life.

Natambu, Kofi. *The Life and Work of Malcolm X*. Indianapolis, Ind.: Alpha, 2002. Concise biography recounting Malcolm X's childhood, years as a street hustler, conversion to and work for the Nation of Islam, and assassination.

Perry, Bruce. *Malcolm: The Life of a Man Who Changed Black America*. Barrytown, N.Y.: Station Hill Press, 1991. Aggressively revisionist, Perry suggests that a childhood of physical abuse and guilt over an ambiguous sexual orientation partly drove Malcolm's rage and the sudden shifts in his identity. Critics complain that Perry carelessly evaluates the quality of his evidence.

Sales, William W., Jr. *From Civil Rights to Black Liberation: Malcolm X and the Organization of Afro-American Unity*. Boston: South End Press, 1994. Sales seeks to shift attention from Malcolm the emotionally powerful icon to Malcolm the political and economic thinker. He sees the post-NOI Malcolm as an almost Marxist revolutionary who clearly articulated the relationship of capitalism and colonialism to the oppression of black people.

WILMA MANKILLER

> " ... I believe in the old Cherokee injunction to 'be of a good mind.' Today it's called positive thinking. "

Principal chief of the Cherokee Nation (1985-1995)

As the first woman principal chief of the Cherokee Nation of Oklahoma, or of any major American Indian tribe, Mankiller renewed a long tradition of female leadership in Cherokee affairs. She coupled feminist ideas with Cherokee tradition to form a strong tribe with a renewed spirit of independence.

Born: November 18, 1945; Tahlequah, Oklahoma
Also known as: Wilma Pearl Mankiller (full name)
Areas of achievement: Native American affairs; women's rights

EARLY LIFE

Wilma Mankiller was born in the W. W. Hastings Indian Hospital in Tahlequah, Oklahoma. Her mother was Clara Irene Sitton, who was of Dutch-Irish descent, and her father was Charley Mankiller, a full Cherokee; they had married in 1937. Mankiller was the sixth of eleven children. The family lived on Mankiller Flats in Adair County, northeastern Oklahoma. Mankiller Flats was an allotment of 160 acres that had been given to John Mankiller, Charley's father, in 1907, when Oklahoma became a state.

The name "Mankiller" was a Cherokee military title that had to be earned, like that of the armed forces ranks of major or captain. Mankiller's great-great-great grandfather, Mankiller of Tellico, earned the title in the eighteenth century and then established it as a family surname. (During her days as chief, Mankiller often told white males that she had earned the name herself.) Tellico is in eastern Tennessee and was part of the original Cherokee Nation. The Mankillers and most other Cherokee were forcibly moved to the Indian Territory, later the State of Oklahoma, along the infamous Trail of Tears in 1838-1839.

The first eleven years of Wilma's life were spent on Mankiller Flats and within traditional Cherokee culture. In 1956, however, the Mankiller family moved to San Francisco, California, as part of a government relocation plan to move American Indians to large cities and into mainstream American life. Life in San Francisco was shocking to the family, especially for the Mankiller children, but they soon adjusted.

On November 13, 1963, Mankiller married Hugo Olaya, a member of a wealthy Ecuadoran family, who was then a student in San Francisco. Two daughters, Felicia and Gina, were born to the couple before differences in lifestyles led to a divorce in 1974. During these years, Wilma had earned a degree from San Francisco State College (now university).

Mankiller was poignantly reminded of her Cherokee background again when, in 1969, a group of American Indians occupied Alcatraz Island in San Francisco Bay to gain support for American Indian rights. Alcatraz was considered indigenous territory, and Mankiller and many others in her family participated in that occupation, in which Mankiller's life of political activism began.

Mankiller, Wilma

Mankiller's father, who had become a longshoreman and a union organizer in California, died in 1971. Charley always had encouraged his children, especially Wilma, to read books, which were always in abundance in their home. His body was returned to his native Adair County for burial. Wilma heard older Cherokee men say that her father had "come back" home. The emotions of the day of her father's burial seemed to be a signal for family members to return, one by one, to Oklahoma. Mankiller returned in 1975, a year after her divorce. Only two older brothers remained in California.

Living in two worlds, Mankiller's life mirrored that of Nancy Ward, an eighteenth century Cherokee who had earned the title Beloved Woman and who also had lived in the white world as well as the Cherokee. Like Ward, Wilma was able to combine the best of Cherokee tradition with the best of European-American civilization. Mankiller's balanced philosophy led her to contribute greatly to the welfare of the Cherokee Nation.

Life's Work

Mankiller began her work to improve American Indian life before she left California. In 1974, with Bill Wahpapah, she cofounded the American Indian Community School in Oakland. However, her return to Oklahoma marked the beginning of her full-time service to her people.

The Cherokee Nation of Oklahoma, with 55,000 acres of northeastern Oklahoma and a federally recognized "enrollment," or population, of about 250,000 people, was ranked second only to the Navajo in size among American Indian tribes in the United States. When Oklahoma became a state in 1907, the traditional tribal government of the Cherokee was dissolved. This created a unique political organization, neither a reservation nor an autonomous government, with unique political and social problems and concerns. Mankiller now began directing her energy toward solving those problems.

Mankiller's first regular job with the Cherokee Nation began in 1977 as an economic-stimulus coordinator. Her job was to guide as many people as possible toward university training in fields such as environmental science and health and then to integrate them back into their communities. She soon became frustrated with the slow-moving male-dominated bureaucracy of the Cherokee Nation, a bureaucracy she believed had been imposed on them by whites and which was supported by the insecurity of Cherokee men forced to live in a white-dominated society.

Before Europeans came to North America, Cherokee women such as Ward occupied leadership roles in tribal affairs. The original Cherokee Nation was matrilineal, and the name Beloved Woman was given to those who performed extraordinary service. Women had a major voice in choosing chiefs and in other tribal affairs. The first Europeans to contact the Cherokee accused them of having a "petticoat government." After this contact, the influence of Cherokee women began to decrease. In her autobiography *Mankiller: A Chief and Her People* (1993), Mankiller declared her belief that the Trail of Tears, combined with the tremendous strain of relocation in the West, was the final step in the forced development of a more subservient position for women.

A significant development in 1971 helped to open the way for a return to more female participation in Cherokee affairs. A revision of the tribal constitution provided that, for the first time since Oklahoma statehood in 1907, the principal chief would be elected by the people of the tribe rather than appointed by the president of the United States. An entirely new constitution in 1976 solidified that change and provided for the election of a new fifteen-member tribal council.

In 1979, after working for two years as an economic-stimulus coordinator, Mankiller was made a program-development specialist and grant writer. Her immediate success in this position, especially in writing grant proposals, brought her to the attention of the tribal council and Principal Chief Ross Swimmer. This phase of her work was soon interrupted by tragedy. On November 9 she was seriously injured in a head-on collision on a country road. The driver of the other car was Sherry Morris, a white woman who was a very close friend of Mankiller. Morris was killed. Within a year of the accident, Mankiller developed a rare form of muscular dystrophy.

These back-to-back experiences caused Mankiller to reach more deeply into her Cherokee background and led to a change in her philosophy of life. In 1981, although still undergoing physical therapy, she was able to return to her work with the Cherokee Nation, and she did so with her old energy. In that year she helped establish the Cherokee Nation Community Development Department and became its first director.

The next step in Mankiller's career came in 1983, when Chief Swimmer asked her to join his reelection ticket as his deputy chief. This request was unusual for two reasons: Mankiller was a woman, and she was a liberal Democrat; Swimmer was a conservative Republican. After first declining, Mankiller accepted the offer as a way to help her people.

One of Mankiller's opponents for deputy chief was Agnes Cowan, the first woman to serve on the tribal council. Mankiller was surprised when gender became an immediate issue in the campaign. The hostility she faced included the slashing of her car tires and death threats. She fought the negative campaigning by conducting a positive and cheerful campaign based primarily on her past service to the Cherokee people. The victory for the Swimmer-Mankiller ticket meant that, on August 14, 1983, Mankiller became the first female deputy chief in Cherokee history.

In 1984, Deputy Chief Mankiller participated in a significant meeting—a reunion between the Cherokee Nation of Oklahoma and the Eastern Band of the Cherokee from North Carolina. The Eastern Band had descended from those who escaped the Trail of Tears by hiding in the mountains. This meeting, the first full tribal council since 1838, was held at Red Clay in Tennessee, on the Georgia state line. Red Clay was the last capital of the original Cherokee Nation. At that reunion, an eternal flame was lit and still burns at Red Clay. In her autobiography, Mankiller emphasized the tremendous historical and emotional impact that this event had on the Cherokee people.

A major career surprise for Mankiller came in 1985, when U.S. president Ronald Reagan nominated Chief Swimmer as assistant secretary for the Interior Department's Bureau of Indian Affairs. As a result, on December 14, Mankiller became the first woman principal chief of the Cherokee Nation. Without hesitation she declared that economic growth would be the primary goal of her administration. She described her guiding theory as bubble-up economics, in which the people themselves would plan and implement projects that would benefit the tribe in future years. In a famous quotation, she reminded her people that, in traditional Iroquois society, from which the

Cherokee descended, leaders considered seven generations past and seven generations future when making major decisions.

Until the next scheduled election in 1987, Chief Mankiller, governing without a mandate from the people, faced strong opposition that limited her real power. In October of 1986, while considering whether to run for a full term, Mankiller had married Charlie Soap, a full Cherokee who she had met in 1977. She described her new husband as the most well-adjusted male she had ever known. It was Soap who persuaded her to run in the 1987 election, which she won in a runoff. Because the Cherokee Nation had now returned to the strong female leadership of its past, Chief Mankiller described her election as a step forward and a step backward at the same time.

Although Mankiller's first full term was successful in terms of economic progress, her level of personal involvement was curtailed by a resurgence of kidney disease from which she had suffered for many years. This led to a kidney transplant in June, 1990. The donor was Mankiller's older brother, Don. By 1991, only a year after her transplant, Chief Mankiller had sufficiently recovered to run for a second full term. She won that election by an overwhelming 82 percent of the vote. The same election put six women on the fifteen-member tribal council. With a resounding voice, the Cherokee had returned to their ancient tradition of shared gender leadership. Mankiller's work of improving the everyday lives of her people continued during her second term of office. During her ten years as chief, the population of the Cherokee Nation of Oklahoma increased from 55,000 to 156,000 people.

Mankiller's impact reached far beyond the borders of the Cherokee Nation. In 1988, she was named Alumnus of the Year by San Francisco State University. This was followed, in 1990, by an honorary doctorate from Yale University. In 1993, Mankiller gave a well-known speech at Sweetbriar College, "Rebuilding the Cherokee Nation," in which she reviewed the progress made by the tribe and expressed her hopes for its future. Poor health forced Mankiller to retire from her position in 1995. A fitting tribute to her wide-ranging influence was the election of Joyce Dugan as the first female chief of the Eastern Band of the Cherokee in North Carolina.

In her years after retirement, Mankiller continued her work, including much literary output, as a political, cultural, and social leader of the Cherokee and as a spokesperson for the rights of all women. The honors bestowed upon her, in addition to her 1993 induction into the National Women's Hall of Fame, are proof of her lasting influence. Other honors include Woman of the Year from *Ms.* magazine (1987); the John W. Gardner Leadership Award, Independent Sector (1988); the Indian Health Service Award, U.S. Public Health Service (1989); and the Oklahoma State University Henry G. Bennett Distinguished Service Award (1990). The Presidential Medal of Freedom, the nation's highest civilian honor, was bestowed on her by President Bill Clinton in 1998.

Significance

Mankiller's leadership led to both tangible and intangible changes for the Cherokee Nation. The most significant tangible changes were the benefits for the Cherokee that came from the development of the U.S. Department of Commerce, which was created soon after Mankiller's 1987 victory. The Commerce Department helps to coordinate the business enterprises of the Cherokee tribe and is mandated to balance tribal income with the needs of tribal members; this, in turn, creates jobs and profits. The intangible results include a renewed spirit of independence for all Cherokee and a renewed confidence that Cherokee women once again can influence the destiny of the tribe.

In 1990, Mankiller signed a historic self-governance agreement that authorized the Cherokee Nation to administer federal funds that previously had been administered by the Bureau of Indian Affairs in Washington, D.C. The same year saw a revitalizing of tribal courts and tribal police as well as the establishment of a Cherokee Nation tax commission.

—*Glenn L. Swygart*

Further Reading

Edmunds, R. David., ed. *The New Warriors: Native American Leaders Since 1900.* Lincoln: University of Nebraska Press, 2001. Features a variety of American Indian leaders, including Mankiller, as part of a generation who rose to the challenges of the twentieth century.

Janda, Sarah Eppler. *Beloved Women: The Political Lives of Ladonna Harris and Wilma Mankiller.* DeKalb: Northern Illinois University Press, 2007. A fascinating look at the two American Indian activists—Mankiller and Harris—who were at the forefront of American Indian relations with the U.S. government and in tribal development. Focuses on how feminism coupled with a sense of "Indianness" shaped the political lives of the two leaders.

Mankiller, Wilma. *Every Day Is a Good Day: Reflections by Contemporary Indigenous Women.* New York: Fulcrum, 2004. Mankiller and eighteen other indigenous women of the Americas discuss their lives and those of their people, living in a Eurocentric world.

———. *Mankiller: A Chief and Her People.* New York: St. Martin's Press, 1993. This autobiography is by far the best source for Mankiller's life, career, and philosophy. Includes many excellent photographs of the Mankiller family, other key individuals, and major events in Mankiller's life.

Mankiller, Wilma, et al., eds. *The Reader's Companion to U.S. Women's History.* New York: Houghton Mifflin, 1998. Among the five editors of this volume, Mankiller is listed first. In addition to several references to her in other essays, she contributed two essays: on the Iroquois Confederacy and on feminism.

Van Viema, David. "Activist Wilma Mankiller Is Set to Become the First Female Chief of the Cherokee Nation." *People Weekly*, December 2, 1985. Based on an interview with Mankiller by Michael Wallis, this article conveys the initial impression she had of her new job as chief. Reveals Mankiller's identification with her Cherokee roots.

Wallace, Michele. "Wilma Mankiller." *Ms.*, January, 1988. Wallace emphasizes the role of women in Cherokee history. Also covered is Mankiller's philosophy of leadership and her influence on women's rights in general. Includes her plans for Cherokee progress.

ROCKY MARCIANO

> *I have always adhered to two principles. The first one is to train hard and get in the best possible physical condition. The second is to forget all about the other fellow until you face him in the ring and the bell sounds for the fight.*

Boxer

Marciano retired as the only undefeated heavyweight champion in boxing history. The son of poor Italian immigrants, he dignified the legendary belt and brought great pride to the Italian American community.

Born: September 1, 1923; Brockton, Massachusetts
Died: August 31, 1969; near Newton, Iowa
Also known as: Rocco Francis Marchegiano (birth name)
Area of achievement: Sports

EARLY LIFE

The first born of Pierino Marchegiano and Pasqualena Marchegiano, Rocco Francis Marchegiano, later Rocky Marciano (mahr-see-AN-noh), survived a life-threatening bout with pneumonia in March, 1925. The experience presaged the determination that he would later show in the ring. The doctor who was attending eighteen-month-old Marciano advised his mother that if the youngster had the spirit to survive, he would be a strong boy. The crisis passed, and the doctor's prediction came true.

First, however, Marciano had to overcome the temper of the times and the circumstances of his family's poverty. When Marciano was born, the shadow of the Red Scare hung over the Italian American community. United States Attorney General A. Mitchell Palmer directed raids against immigrant groups and deported many. Based on what many felt was circumstantial evidence, two Italian anarchists, Nicola Sacco and Bartolomeo Vanzetti, were tried, convicted, and executed for allegedly murdering a payroll guard in Braintree, Massachusetts. Marciano's father, a frail, hardworking laborer in a shoe factory, resented the anti-Italian sentiment. He had been gassed while serving in the U.S. Army on the western front during World War I and was proud of his service to his country. Marciano's mother, a homemaker, set a good table of mostly simple fare of pasta, soup, and vegetables. She was further kept busy by the births of five more children between 1925 and 1939. With the onset of the Great Depression, factory pay remained low, and the Marchegianos, like many families, struggled to survive.

Marciano's first love was baseball. Growing up in the shadow of James Edgar Playground, he and his buddies dreamed that they would one day make the major leagues. As a catcher for the Saint Patrick's Church baseball team, he helped them to an archdiocese championship. At fifteen he was also the starting linebacker on the Brockton High School football team. Never a serious student, he quit school at sixteen to work while continuing to pursue his dream of playing professional baseball.

What marked Marciano from his earliest sports endeavors through the end of his fighting career was his intense dedication to training to make himself a better athlete.

He was self-conscious about his small and short arms, so he began lifting homemade weights and doing development exercises. He lacked a strong throwing arm, so every evening he practiced for hours just throwing from home plate to second base. He was clumsy and slow, so every evening after throwing he ran hills and did wind sprints in the park. He developed into a powerful hitter, but his other limitations denied him a professional baseball career.

Marciano took various jobs, but the one he hated most was a stint in a shoe factory. He swore he would not do factory work for a living. Much later he commented, "I couldn't stand the smell of wet leather—it nauseated me—but I had to have a job. Whenever a boxing match isn't going my way, I can smell my sweat on my opponent's leather gloves. . . . I then give the fight that extra effort and I win." In March, 1943, he was drafted into the U.S. Army and sent to Wales to ferry supplies across the English Channel. After the end of World War II, he was sent back to Fort Lewis, Washington, where he found the path leading to the world's heavyweight championship.

Life's Work

At Fort Lewis, Marciano fought to avoid having to work undesirable details and also played on the baseball team. While home on leave in April, 1946, Marciano impressed his uncle, Mike Piccento, with stories about his fighting prowess in the Army. Through a local booking agent, Generosa "Gene" Caggiano (who later sued Marciano for breach of a management contract), Piccento arranged Marciano's first local bout on April 15, 1946, against a former New England Golden Gloves heavyweight champ named Henry Lester. Overweight and out of shape from rich home cooking, Marciano was through by the second round. Sensing defeat, he kneed his opponent in the groin and was disqualified. It would be the only disqualification of his career.

He returned to Fort Lewis and began serious training for the Amateur Athletic Union (AAU) championships in Portland, Oregon. Needing to win three fights, he took the first two with dramatic first-round knockouts. He had, however, painfully dislocated a knuckle in the second fight. Fighting one-handed, the five foot ten inch Marciano lost to six foot three inch Joe De Angelis of Chelsea, Massachusetts, in the decisive bout.

Honorably discharged, Marciano returned to Brockton in the summer of 1946. He also returned to his first love, baseball. He played for a regionally famous semipro team, Taunton Lumber Company. He also took a quick fling at professional boxing. Trained and managed by his boyhood friend Allie Colombo, Marciano agreed to fight a four-rounder in Holyoke, Massachusetts, against a local favorite named Lee Epperson. To protect his amateur status, Marciano fought under the pseudonym Rocky Mack. It was March 17, 1947 (St. Patrick's Day). He began his professional career with a third-round knockout. The purse was thirty-five dollars. Then he accepted an invitation from a baseball scout from the Chicago Cubs to a tryout in Fayetteville, North Carolina. After a three-week trial, he was rejected because of his weak throwing arm.

His throwing arm would, however, never affect his punching power. He returned home and, despite his mother's misgivings, embarked on a training regimen to become a professional boxer. He worked the bags, sparred, and ran eight miles per day in specially weighted training boots. In January of 1948, Marciano entered the Golden

Marciano, Rocky

Gloves tournament in Lowell, Massachusetts, and quickly recorded three straight knockouts. Hurting from a bad knuckle, he lost to Bob Girard but went on to win the New England championship before losing to Coley Wallace in the Eastern championships. It would be his last loss inside a ring. He completed his amateur career of twelve fights with a record of eight wins and four losses.

Marciano was twenty-five, engaged to be married, and smallish for a heavyweight when a New York manager named Al Weill came calling. Weill introduced him to the famous trainer Charley Goldman, and Marciano's professional career began in earnest. On July 12, 1948, in Providence, Rhode Island, Marciano faced twenty-one-year-old Haroutune "Harry" Bilazarian of Bolyston, Massachusetts, who had been the Army light-heavyweight champ in Sapporo, Japan, in 1947. Marciano knocked him out during the first round. It was Weill who turned Rocky Marchegiano to Rocky Marciano and booked the rest of his pro career.

After wading through a series of lesser opponents, Marciano's big break came when Weill matched him against unbeaten Roland LaStarza at Madison Square Garden on March 24, 1950. The crafty LaStarza countered the powerful Marciano until, after ten rounds, it was up to the judges to award a split decision to Marciano. One year later, Marciano knocked out the legendary Joe Louis, who was attempting a comeback at age thirty-seven.

Meanwhile, Marciano had married his longtime sweetheart, Barbara Cousins, on December 31, 1950, at St. Coleman's Church in Brockton. She was a tall, athletic, dark-haired Irish girl of twenty-two. The marriage produced a daughter, Mary Anne, born in Brockton on December 6, 1952. The couple also adopted an infant, Rocky Kevin, who was only seventeen months old when Marciano died in 1969.

Marciano's career was now in its ascendancy. The Louis bout led to a title fight in Philadelphia on September 23, 1952, against thirty-eight-year-old champion "Jersey Joe" Walcott. Overcoming a first round knockdown, Marciano came back to claim the title with a thirteenth-round knockout. The following May in Chicago, Marciano took Walcott out in the first round.

Marciano would successfully defend his crown once against Roland LaStarza, twice against former champ Ezzard Charles, and once against Don Cockell. In his final fight, against light-heavyweight champion Archie Moore, Marciano recovered from an early knockdown to knock down Moore three times en route to a ninth-round knockout.

As a fighter, Marciano was known for his crowding style and aggressiveness, complemented by a good left hook and a devastating overhand right. He could take a hard punch but had a penchant for bleeding. He almost lost the second Ezzard Charles fight because his corner was unable to staunch the bleeding from a split nose. Rocky had to summon his reserves to knock out Charles in the eighth round before the referee could stop the fight.

On April 28, 1956, Marciano retired from the ring with a record of forty-nine wins (forty-three of which were knockouts) and no losses. He cited the need to spend more time with his family. Other reasons may have been more compelling. He distrusted Weill, whom he thought shorted him on purses. He also had a bad back from years of almost fanatical training. He had made more than four million dollars during his professional career and had spent very little of it. After his retirement, Marciano settled in

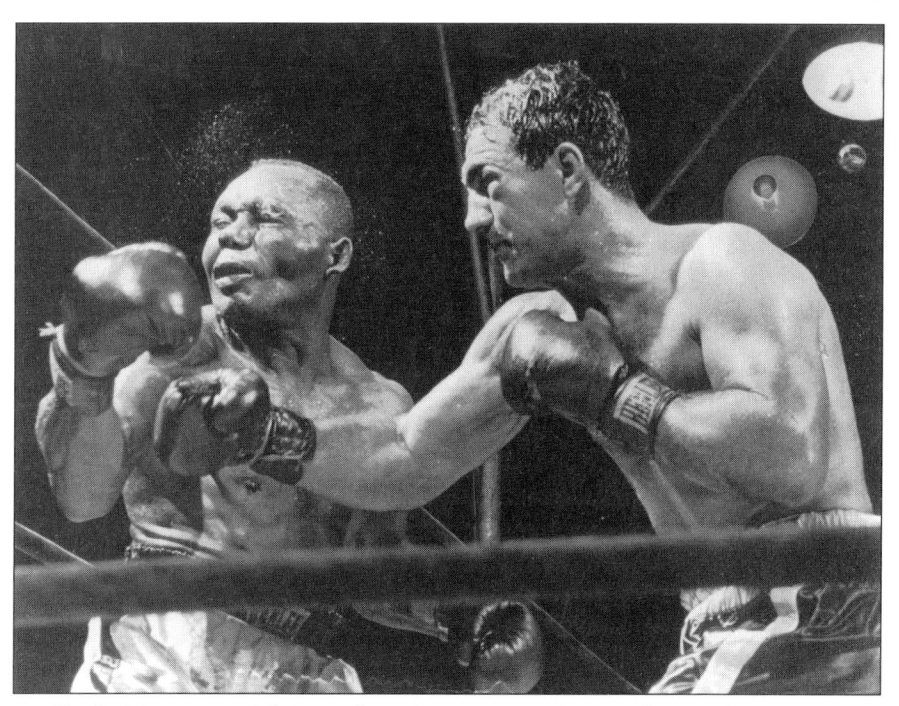

Rocky Marciano (right) punching Jersey Joe Walcott. (Library of Congress)

Fort Lauderdale, Florida, but never spent much time with his family. He bounced around the country making public appearances and hanging out with celebrities. He could be generous to friends (especially former pugilists) but was secretive and miserly with his money. He usually let hangers-on pick up the tabs for the parties.

In 1957, in conjunction with Charley Goldman, Marciano lent his name to a book, *Rocky Marciano's Book of Boxing and Bodybuilding.* He did a couple of bit parts in motion pictures and, in the summer of 1969, agreed to a simulated match with Muhammad Ali in which they sparred over several days while a computer picked the winner. Marciano shed fifty pounds and actually got himself into some semblance of fighting shape. Marciano won the ersatz bout.

On Sunday, August 31, 1969, Marciano was a passenger with one other man on a flight in a small plane from Chicago to Des Moines. He was to attend a birthday party as a favor to a friend. Stormy weather and an inexperienced pilot contributed to the plane crashing near Newton, Iowa. The three men aboard were killed on impact. It was the day before Rocky's forty-sixth birthday.

SIGNIFICANCE

As a heavyweight boxer, Rocky Marciano was a transitional figure between the greats of the Depression era, led by Joe Louis, and the greats of the 1960's, led by Muhammad Ali. He is the only heavyweight champion to retire undefeated, but some claim he was aided by weak competition. However, no one can doubt his punching power.

Marshall, George C.

As a public figure, Marciano was idolized for his ethnic background and also as something of a "Great White Hope." At his zenith, at the same time that the modern Civil Rights movement began to break down Jim Crow laws, he was lauded in some circles for his victories over black boxers. His fame was also abetted by being the first heavyweight champion to benefit from television exposure. His brawling, bleeding, bombastic style played well to the camera.

—Brian G. Tobin

FURTHER READING

Marciano, Rocky, with Charley Goldman. *Rocky Marciano's Book of Boxing and Bodybuilding.* Englewood Cliffs, N.J.: Prentice-Hall, 1957. Includes photographs of Marciano training.

Nelson, Allan. "The Scent of Failure." *American Heritage* (February-March, 1997): 56. A personal anecdote about Marciano's aversion to leather work.

Skehan, Everett. *Undefeated Rocky Marciano: The Fighter Who Refused to Lose.* Cambridge, Mass.: Rounder Books, 2005. Assisted by two of Marciano's brothers and his daughter, Skehan produces a definitive account of the boxer's life and career. Contains many photographs.

Sullivan, Russell. *Rocky Marciano: The Rock of His Times.* Urbana: University of Illinois Press, 2002. Solid biography, recounting the events of Marciano's life and career and providing detailed descriptions of his fights.

Varveris, Michael N. *Rocky Marciano: The Thirteenth Candle—The True Story of an American Legend.* Youngstown, Ohio: Ariana, 2000. This biography of Marciano describes his life, including a contemplated comeback bout against Ingemar Johansson.

GEORGE C. MARSHALL

" *Don't fight the problem, decide it.* **"**

U.S. secretary of state (1947-1949)

General Marshall created the U.S. Army of World War II, picked the commanders who led it to victory, and exemplified the best in the American military tradition: civilian control, integrity, and competence.

Born: December 31, 1880; Uniontown, Pennsylvania
Died: October 16, 1959; Washington, D.C.
Also known as: George Catlett Marshall, Jr. (full name); Wizard (nickname)
Areas of achievement: Military; diplomacy

EARLY LIFE

George Catlett Marshall, Jr. (KAYT-leht MAR-shuhl), was born the second son of George C. Marshall, a businessman, and Laura Bradford Marshall. He was an enterprising boy who enjoyed history and who, possibly because of his reading, became in-

Marshall, George C.

terested in a military career. After attending Uniontown's public schools, he went to the Virginia Military Academy at Lexington. By this time, young Marshall had grown to just under six feet in height and was tough; despite weighing only 145 pounds, he starred in football. His bearing became very military, and he gained self-confidence along with military skills; as first captain, he made his voice heard across the length of the parade ground. Marshall's manner grew austere, and his "cold blue and seldom smiling eyes" were piercing to those who did less than their best. Despite his bony face, under a thatch of sandy hair, he was becoming a formidable person.

On his graduation, Marshall married the beauty of Lexington, Elizabeth "Lily" Coles, on February 11, 1902. Three years after her death, in 1927, he married Katherine Tupper Brown.

LIFE'S WORK

Marshall was commissioned a second lieutenant of infantry in the U.S. Army in January, 1902, with date of rank from 1901. He was immediately assigned to the newly conquered Philippine Islands, where he was often on his own with troops and where he revealed the abilities to learn rapidly and to discover and put to best use his subordinates' talents. He served in Oklahoma and Texas before being assigned, in 1906, to the Infantry and Cavalry School at Fort Leavenworth, Kansas. Promoted to first lieutenant that year, he stood first in his class and came to the notice of General J. Franklin Bell, the commandant, who kept Marshall on as an instructor. Displaying unusual talent in that capacity, Marshall also learned to watch several maneuvers at once in war games. Returned to the Philippines in 1913, he was made chief of staff for one side in maneuvers, despite his junior rank, effectively commanding five thousand troops. He also visited Japan and Manchuria to learn how the Japanese had won the Russo-Japanese War (1904-1905).

Reassigned as aide to General Bell, Marshall was promoted to captain in August, 1916. As the United States entered World War I, in April, 1917, Bell became commander of the Eastern Department. Marshall virtually ran the office during Bell's illness, learning how to cut red tape in the hasty mobilization. Because of his now-great reputation as both a thinker and a doer, Marshall was sent to France with the First Division, becoming its chief of operations. He became a major in November, 1917, and a lieutenant colonel in December. By July, 1918, he was an acting colonel at General John J. Pershing's headquarters, already famous for his gifts of organization and improvisation and nicknamed Wizard. There, and as chief of operations for the First Army, Marshall learned how to maneuver large bodies of troops and how to solve the many problems that arise in war.

At the end of World War I, reduced to the rank of major, Marshall became Pershing's aide. Because of Pershing's trust in him, Marshall's duties were broad; he took part in inspections of many Army posts and in Pershing's dealings with Congress, coming to know intimately the army he would command after 1939. Also serving in China, the Pacific Northwest, the Midwest, at the Army War College, and as assistant commandant of the Infantry School, he came to know well some 150 future generals of World War II. A colonel again by 1933, he became a brigadier general in 1936. In 1938, he was assigned to Washington, D.C., first as chief of war plans and then as deputy chief of staff of the Army.

Marshall, George C.

George C. Marshall.
(Library of Congress)

On September 1, 1939, as World War II began in Europe, Marshall became chief of staff of the Army, with the temporary rank of four-star general. President Franklin D. Roosevelt named him to the post because of his breadth of experience, his ability to organize and to train troops, and his ability even to be unorthodox, qualities desperately needed in the building of the Army.

Marshall took command of an army that was small, poorly equipped, and poorly trained. He built a reputation for truth with both the president and Congress, won their respect and support, and slowly obtained the money to build a modern army. He was aided by a new secretary of war, Henry L. Stimson, who, after 1940, used his own considerable influence on Marshall's behalf. The task was formidable, for World War II brought with it the Blitzkrieg, the "lightning war" of tanks and mobility. Marshall had not only to argue for money but also to find commanders who would use resources effectively. He promoted Dwight D. Eisenhower, Omar N. Bradley, Henry H. Arnold, Mark W. Clark, George S. Patton, and Matthew Ridgway. Marshall was also tireless in supervising the development of new weapons and equipment and of training and maneuvers.

When the United States entered the war after the Pearl Harbor attack of December 7, 1941, Marshall also had to work with Allies, especially the British, but also the Russians, Free French, and Nationalist Chinese. He had to deal with British prime minister Winston Churchill, who saw himself as a military genius, and British reluctance to at-

Marshall, George C.

tack Adolf Hitler's strong fortifications in Western Europe. Britons were afraid of such trench warfare as had decimated the armies of World War I. Marshall agreed with reasonable British ideas, such as clearing North Africa of Axis forces, but kept the focus on plans for the invasion of France and the defeat of Nazi Germany. He personally chose Eisenhower to command the North African invasion, worked with Roosevelt and Stimson to limit later Mediterranean operations to Italy, and built an ever larger American Army for invading Europe. From less than 200,000 men in 1939, the Army and its air force grew to some 8,300,000 by early 1945, Marshall also building an air force that was capable of destroying German industry. While accomplishing all this, he never forgot that soldiers are human beings and constantly guarded their welfare, from making sure that they received needed medical treatment and their mail, to explaining the reasons for the war to Americans who had to fight thousands of miles from home.

Marshall wanted to command the invasion of France in 1944 but revealed no disappointment when Roosevelt insisted that he remain as chief of staff, saying that he could not sleep well with Marshall out of the country. Marshall then gave Eisenhower the command, supporting him in every possible way. Marshall's own job became one of keeping supplies flowing and mediating between General Douglas MacArthur and the Navy's commanders in the Pacific. Marshall supported the Navy's strategy of a direct attack on Japan itself, via the Pacific Islands, rather than MacArthur's longer route through Southeast Asia.

Named a five-star general of the Army on December 15, 1944, Marshall retired as chief of staff on November 26, 1945. President Harry S. Truman soon asked him to try to bring peace to China, then torn by civil war. Marshall spent almost a year seeking some agreement between Nationalists and Communists but ultimately failed. Truman then appointed him secretary of state on January 21, 1947, and he served until January, 1949, when ill health forced his retirement. As secretary of state, he helped devise the Marshall Plan, massive economic aid to Western Europe that literally rebuilt that region, and helped Truman find ways to deal with the Cold War. He was awarded the Nobel Peace Prize in 1953 because of the Marshall Plan. He served as head of the American Red Cross from 1949 to 1950 and as secretary of defense from September, 1950, to September, 1951. His task was again organizing mobilization, this time for the Korean War, and finding a new commander for Korea and Japan when Truman fired the insubordinate MacArthur. He chose Matthew Ridgway, whose World War II record was superb. Marshall last served his country as its representative at the coronation of Queen Elizabeth II of Great Britain in June, 1953.

SIGNIFICANCE

Marshall represented the best in the American military tradition: belief in civilian control, uncompromising integrity, and quiet competence. Able to learn from the broad experience of a long career, he put what he had learned to work in the United States' most significant and dangerous war, that against the Axis powers. A superb organizer, he created the Army of World War II, saw that it was competently commanded, kept it well supplied, and never forgot the welfare and morale of the troops in the field. He was able to deal with foreign politicians and military officers with both tact and force,

Marshall, George C.

ultimately putting his own stamp on the winning strategies. Indeed, Winston Churchill described Marshall as "the true organizer of victory."

Marshall's devotion to his country permitted President Truman to call on him repeatedly for further service, despite the general's advancing age and worsening health. Marshall attempted an impossible mission in China, led the State Department for two years with an impressive record of realism regarding the Soviet Union, helped rebuild Western Europe, and, as secretary of defense, turned the chaos of sudden remobilization into order.

—*Robert W. Sellen*

FURTHER READING

Ferrell, Robert H. *George C. Marshall*. In *The American Secretaries of State and Their Diplomacy*. Vol. 15. New York: Cooper Square Press, 1966. The only major work on Marshall as secretary of state, it was written before many documents were declassified. Gracefully written and well balanced.

Marshall, George Catlett. *"The Soldierly Spirit," December, 1880-June, 1939*. Vol. 1 in *The Papers of George Catlett Marshall*, edited by Larry I. Bland and Fred L. Hadsel. Baltimore: Johns Hopkins University Press, 1981. This is the first in a series of volumes containing letters, speeches, and other revealing documents.

Marshall, Katherine T. *Together: Annals of an Army Wife*. Atlanta, Ga.: Tupper and Love, 1946. An affectionate but useful memoir.

Mosley, Leonard. *Marshall: Hero for Our Times*. New York: Hearst Books, 1982. The best full biography, covering Marshall's Army career and postwar civilian appointments. Especially good on the controversies surrounding Pearl Harbor, Marshall and MacArthur, and the World War II summit meetings.

Perry, Mark. *Partners in Command: George Marshall and Dwight Eisenhower in War and Peace*. New York: Penguin Books, 2007. Dual biography tracing the friendship and collaboration of the two men, including their military leadership during World War II and their postwar efforts to implement the Marshall Plan and the work of the North Atlantic Treaty Organization (NATO).

Pogue, Forrest C. *George C. Marshall*. 3 vols. New York: Viking Press, 1963-1972. A three-volume definitive biography, based on exhaustive research. The first volume covers Marshall's boyhood, education, and Army career to his appointment as chief of staff (1880-1939). The second tells of Marshall's creation of the United States Army of World War II, his search for new leadership, and the early war years (1939-1942). The third volume carries the tale to victory in Europe in May, 1945, including summit conferences and the invasion of France in June, 1944.

Stoler, Mark A. *George C. Marshall: Soldier-Statesman of the American Century*. Boston: Twayne, 1989. Biography emphasizing 1939-1951, when Marshall served in World War II, was a special representative to China, and served as secretary of state and defense.

John Marshall

> *" We must never forget that it is a constitution we are expounding. "*

Chief justice of the United States (1801-1835)

During his long tenure as chief justice of the U.S. Supreme Court, Marshall used his considerable intelligence, personal charm, and political skills to make the Court the chief arbiter of constitutional doctrine, firmly establishing what had been the weakest branch of the national government as an equal with Congress and the executive.

Born: September 24, 1755; Germantown (now Midland), Virginia
Died: July 6, 1835; Philadelphia, Pennsylvania
Area of achievement: Law and jurisprudence

Early Life

John Marshall was the eldest of fifteen children. His father was a planter of moderate means who in time became a wealthy leading citizen of Virginia and later of Kentucky, serving in numerous official capacities in both states. Through Mary, the Marshall family was connected to most of the important families of Virginia. Growing to manhood among the landed gentry molded John Marshall's character, yet his too casual and occasionally sloppy appearance was at odds with his background. Marshall's education was a typical blend, for the sons of southern colonial gentry, of intermittent and limited formal instruction by tutors in the classics and informal instruction by his parents in reading, writing, and elementary mathematics. The few books in the family library included several on law and served as Marshall's introduction to the subject; from his family's participation in state and local government, he learned about politics.

Only nineteen years old in 1774, when the chain of events beginning with the Boston Tea Party led to the American War of Independence, Marshall followed his father's example and enthusiastically took the patriots' side in the quarrel with England. He was a popular first lieutenant in the local militia when the fighting started but followed his father into the Continental army as soon as it was formed. He served with distinction until independence was nearly won, rising to the rank of captain and becoming something of a hero. He fought in several battles, was wounded, and was with George Washington at Valley Forge.

During a lull, while stationed in Virginia, Marshall studied law and other subjects for three months at the College of William and Mary in Williamsburg. His law teacher was George Wythe, one of the most respected colonial lawyers, with whom Thomas Jefferson, Marshall's cousin, had also studied. Although short, Marshall's legal education was better than most, because there were no law schools in America. The College of William and Mary was one of the few to offer any law classes as part of the undergraduate curriculum. Most lawyers learned only by self-study while working as clerks in practicing attorneys' offices. During these months of study, Marshall also met and began courting Mary Willis Ambler, known all of her life as Polly.

Marshall had passed the bar examination and received his license to practice from Governor Thomas Jefferson in August of 1780. He returned to Oak Hill in Fauquier County, the family estate, to begin his career. In April of 1782, Marshall was elected to represent his county in the House of Delegates. In the state capital, Richmond, Marshall was introduced to a world beyond that of the country lawyer and landed gentry, and his ambition to be part of it was fired. Marshall renewed his courtship of Polly Ambler, whose family now lived in Richmond, and they were married on January 3, 1783, when he was twenty-seven and she was nearly seventeen. Marshall decided to move to Richmond to practice and became a leading member of the bar within three years.

LIFE'S WORK

The man who had joined the mainstream of Virginia's affairs was a commanding, lean figure, six feet in height, black-haired, with a nearly round face and strong, penetrating black eyes, complemented by a smile that seemed to disarm everyone. Honest, capable of sustained hard work, and possessed of a probing intellect, Marshall was also a gregarious man who loved games and athletic activity and who radiated a captivating friendliness. By nature, he was a gracious person, although he did not have a polished manner. As happened with so many patriots who actively participated in the military and political events of the War of Independence, Marshall had acquired a deep sense of nationalism from his travels through the former colonies and the comradeship of men from all parts of the emerging nation. The fact that this new nation should survive and prosper became a concern of Marshall for the remainder of his life.

Marshall worked hard to build his Richmond practice. He held various official positions with the state and local governments but refused any that would seriously interfere with his private law work. A major reason was Polly's poor health after 1786. Their second child died shortly after birth, and then Polly miscarried a few months later. The shock of these two tragedies brought on a nervous breakdown from which Polly never totally recovered. For the remainder of their long married life and through the eight children yet to come, Polly could not abide crowds or noise. It was necessary to have servants to perform the routine household duties, and Marshall personally did the family marketing.

The condition of the nation worried Marshall throughout the 1780's. He thought the national government was too weak to protect the new nation from foreign threats or to restrain state governments from abuses of power. For this reason, he wholeheartedly supported the work of the Constitutional Convention of 1787 to create a "more perfect union." Elected as delegate to Virginia's special convention to decide whether to adopt the new national constitution, he spoke strongly for it. Once the issue was favorably resolved, however, and the new national government was instituted under the leadership of his idol, George Washington, Marshall's attention returned to the practice of law.

Marshall refused all offers of appointment to national office, including the cabinet, until 1797, when he accepted what he thought would be a short-term diplomatic appointment from President John Adams. When Marshall returned to the United States in July of 1798, he was feted as a national hero for his part in what had become known as the XYZ affair. George Washington persuaded him to capitalize on his public recognition and run for a seat in the House of Representatives. Washington had persuaded him to agree to leave his lucrative private practice by convincing him that the republic was in danger from the development of political factionalism.

In the conventional wisdom of his day, Marshall believed that political factions were a threat to the smooth and stable operation of a republican government. Factionalism stirred up the masses to interfere in the affairs of government, best left to the better-educated and propertied gentry, who alone could be expected to function from motives of civic virtue and on the basis of practical common sense. Although willing to fight for fundamental principle, Marshall was a man who otherwise believed in moderation and compromise on matters of policy; he saw that political polarization, if unchecked, would eventually destroy the nation. In Congress, he became the leading House spokesperson for President Adams's moderate Federalist administration. In recognition of his service he was promoted to secretary of state in 1800, and, when the Federalists lost the election that year, to chief justice of the U.S. Supreme Court in 1801. He would remain chief justice until 1835, the year he died.

The Supreme Court in 1801 had serious problems with low public esteem, low pay, poor morale, and rapid turnover of justices. The Court had developed no corporate sense of identity. Marshall's first innovation was to persuade the justices not to give their written opinions *seriatim*—that is, "in a series," each justice writing his own. Instead, in most cases Marshall persuaded the justices to confer until they reached a consensus so that a single opinion could be issued for the majority. Marshall correctly reasoned that the Court's decisions would be much more authoritative if the majority spoke with one voice. The institution of this practice was the single most important reason for the rise of the Supreme Court to equality with the other branches of government. To facilitate the development of collegiality, he also encouraged the justices to lodge at the same Washington, D.C., inn during the one- to two-month yearly sessions.

A distinctive feature of the American system of government is the power of its courts to declare actions by other parts of the government unconstitutional. This power, called judicial review, had not yet been exercised except by some state courts (with mixed results) when Marshall became chief justice. The first instance of the power's use arose out of the fury of President Jefferson and his party over the famous Midnight Appointments of President Adams in 1801, in the case of *Marbury v. Madison* (1803). The case involved a request that the Supreme Court issue a writ of *mandamus* (a court order) to Secretary of State James Madison. The Court's decision, written by Marshall, first lectured Jefferson and his party on their failing in the practice of principles of good government and then announced that the writ of *mandamus* requested in this case could not be issued because section 13 of the Judiciary Act of 1789, which gave the Court the power to issue the writ, was unconstitutional.

This self-denial by the Court was a shrewd political maneuver. In its first big constitutional case under Marshall, the Court had exercised judicial review and declared an act of Congress unconstitutional, and there was nothing anyone could do about it. It was also a brave act in the face of the enormous antijudiciary bias of the Jeffersonians. Although the Court did not declare another act of Congress or the president unconstitutional during Marshall's tenure, it did so for state laws on a number of occasions. Thus, the practice as well as the principle of judicial review was established.

After 1805, the political pressure on the Court decreased, partly because the government's attention was increasingly focused on foreign affairs and partly because, under Marshall, the Court had acquired greater respect and, therefore, greater independence. The work of the Court now centered more on two objectives: the supremacy of the national government and the preservation and protection of rights. The two were directly related in Marshall's view.

The point in establishing the supremacy of the federal Constitution, statutes, and treaties over the states was to counter the threat to inalienable rights from abuses of power by the states. Marshall perceived this as the most serious threat of all. For example, the Constitution prohibited the states from interfering with the obligations of the parties to a contract, yet many states were doing just that in numerous ways. In a long line of cases interpreting the "contract clause," Marshall's court fashioned from it a powerful defense of the private citizens' right to whatever property they had come by honestly. In the famous trial of Aaron Burr for treason, Marshall interpreted the Constitution to prevent the charge of treason from becoming an instrument to punish political enemies.

In *Gibbons v. Ogden* (1824), Marshall's court struck down a law creating a steamboat monopoly, not only because it infringed on federal power to regulate interstate commerce but also because the Constitution's Framers had given the commerce power to Congress in order to establish the whole of the United States as a free trade area, and the steamboat monopoly violated freedom of commerce. The issue of slavery presented a serious problem for Marshall; on the one hand, the slave owner's property right had to be protected, like any other property right, but on the other hand, Marshall thought that black slaves had the same rights as white people. It seemed to him that the only solution to this dilemma was the American Colonization Society. This organization hoped to remove all black slaves from the United States to Liberia, Africa.

The Jackson years disheartened Marshall. He hated the viciously partisan character assassinations of the Jackson campaign, and he feared that universal manhood suffrage, a major Jacksonian goal, could only result in politicians pandering to the prejudices of the common people. He also believed the states' rights orientation of the Jackson appointees to the Court threatened all of his work to establish the supremacy of the Constitution, guarantees of rights, and restraint of state uses of power.

As Marshall increasingly saw himself as a relic of the past, he found it necessary to compromise on some issues to save at least something of his work. When Polly died in 1831, he was desolate and felt very much alone. There were, however, some positive moments. When Jackson stood up for the supremacy of the national government in 1832 against South Carolina's attempt to nullify a national tariff, Marshall relented somewhat in his dislike of the old general. Although unable to stop Georgia from brutally removing the Cherokee Indians from the state and humiliated at seeing the state of Georgia flout the Supreme Court's decision forbidding the removal—the Court had no means of enforcing it and the president would not—a remedy was provided. President Jackson's Force Bill, passed by Congress in connection with the Nullification Crisis, provided the Court with its own officials to enforce future decisions.

In 1835, Marshall was seventy-nine when he suffered a spinal injury in a stagecoach accident from which he never fully recovered. He also suffered from serious liver trouble. When told that his time was short, he put his affairs in order and, on July 6, 1835, he died.

SIGNIFICANCE

Marshall built better than he knew. He was mistaken in his beliefs about political parties and the superior governing abilities of the gentry, but practices he established for the Court and many of his judicial doctrines are still important. Supreme Court majorities continued after Marshall generally to speak with one voice. His example of collegial leadership remains the standard for chief justices. The defense of property rights based on the contract clause and his interpretation of the commerce clause contributed significantly to the legal environment necessary for the free enterprise economic system to flourish. Treason remains only a crime and not a weapon against the enemies of whatever politicians are in power.

In raising the visibility and authority of the Supreme Court to a position of equality with the other branches, Marshall created a potent force for political stability within the American system of government. This was his most important achievement. The government's ability to correct its mistakes through the Supreme Court's exercise of the power of judicial review inspires confidence and trust in all levels of the system. The Supreme Court became the guardian and final arbiter of the Constitution, establishing the primacy of the constitutional principles of the nation's Founders. In 1801, when John Marshall became chief justice, none of this was certain to evolve, but the fundamentals were all in place when he left, thirty-four years later. During that time, he wrote 519 of the Court's 1,106 opinions, including 36 of the 62 involving major constitutional questions. John Marshall had a major hand in creating the most balanced and equable judicial system in the world.

—*Richard L. Hillard*

FURTHER READING

Baker, Leonard. *John Marshall: A Life in Law*. New York: Macmillan, 1974. A good biography of Marshall's professional life; includes some private matters as well. Explains many details about how Marshall and the legal system in his time worked. Also explains his reasoning in his Supreme Court decisions.

Baxter, Maurice G. *Daniel Webster and the Supreme Court*. Amherst: University of Massachusetts Press, 1966. A superb and scholarly examination of the relationship between Daniel Webster, one of the leading constitutional lawyers of his day and a Marshall supporter, and the development of judicial doctrine by the Supreme Court during much of Marshall's tenure as chief justice.

Beveridge, Albert J. *The Life of John Marshall*. 4 vols. Boston: Houghton Mifflin, 1916-1919. Detailed and wonderfully told story yet sadly lacking in balance, making Marshall seem a heroic savior of his nation against arch-villains. Even so, these four volumes are still the starting point for Marshall scholarship.

Faulkner, Robert K. *The Jurisprudence of John Marshall*. Princeton, N.J.: Princeton University Press, 1968. Definitive examination of the political philosophy of Mar-

Marshall, John

shall. Traces the origins to a mix of the theories of John Locke, American nationalism, and the respect for landed gentry typical of the classical Romans, especially Cicero.

Horwitz, Morton J. *The Transformation of American Law: 1780-1860*. Cambridge, Mass.: Harvard University Press, 1977. Mentions Marshall only briefly. Probably the best one-volume legal history of the era to date. Emphasis is on the transformation of English law in the colonies into a modern national legal system and how this transformation aided economic development.

Newmyer, R. Kent. *John Marshall and the Heroic Age of the Supreme Court*. Baton Rouge: Louisiana State University Press, 2001. Focuses on Marshall's legal philosophies, analyzing some of his Supreme Court decisions and placing his beliefs in historical context. Describes how Marshall's experiences as a soldier in the Revolutionary War, his legal career, and his childhood in Virginia influenced his constitutional thinking.

———. *The Supreme Court Under Marshall and Taney*. New York: Thomas Y. Crowell, 1968. A succinct but thorough and perceptive study of the Marshall court in the context of the people and events of the times. The Marshall chapters concentrate on Marshall as chief justice, and little of his personal life is included.

Robarge, David. *A Chief Justice's Progress: John Marshall from Revolutionary Virginia to the Supreme Court*. Westport, Conn.: Greenwood Press, 2000. Focuses on the formative influences in Marshall's life before he joined the U.S. Supreme Court, including his upbringing in Virginia, military service, legal career, and experiences as a federalist and diplomat.

Simon, James F. *What Kind of Nation: Thomas Jefferson, John Marshall, and the Epic Struggle to Create a United States*. New York: Simon & Schuster, 2002. Describes how Marshall, a proponent of federalism, and Jefferson, an advocate of states rights, engaged in a lengthy competition to determine the direction of the newly created United States.

Stites, Francis N. *John Marshall: Defender of the Constitution*. Boston: Little, Brown, 1981. This is an excellent short biography of Marshall. Well researched and carefully written, it brings together in a reasonable synthesis the voluminous scholarship available on Marshall.

THURGOOD MARSHALL

> *In recognizing the humanity of our fellow beings, we pay ourselves the highest tribute.*

Associate justice of the United States (1967-1991)

Marshall, a brilliant litigator, was the first African American member of the U.S. Supreme Court. As an advocate and jurist, he had a sustained commitment to equal justice under the law.

Born: July 2, 1908; Baltimore, Maryland
Died: January 24, 1993; Bethesda, Maryland
Also known as: Thoroughgood Marshall (birth name)
Areas of achievement: Law and jurisprudence; civil rights

EARLY LIFE

Thurgood Marshall (THUHR-good MAR-shuhl) was the son of William Canfield Marshall, a waiter who became head steward at the affluent Gibson Island Club on the Chesapeake Bay by the time Marshall reached school age, and Norma Arica (née Williams) Marshall, a teacher in the Baltimore schools for more than thirty years. Both of their families had resided in Maryland for some time. The Marshall family enjoyed a comfortable, stable, middle-class existence. The achievement of this status by a black family less than forty years after the abolition of slavery in the United States is remarkable. Although Maryland, in general, and Baltimore, in particular, were quite well known for their relatively large, free black populations, even modest financial legacies were the exception rather than the rule for most blacks in those decades following the Civil War.

One of Marshall's great-grandfathers had been a slave, and little is known about him. Marshall's paternal grandfather, Thoroughgood Marshall (after whom he was named), served in the United States merchant marine for many years, and his maternal grandfather, Isaiah Olive Branch Williams, also spent a number of years traveling abroad. Both gave up a life at sea to settle in the Baltimore area; also, both owned and operated grocery stores.

Marshall grew up in a world of books, opera, and tales of adventure. He came into contact with black men who were important and influential in their own communities, and, consequently, he lived in a world of conversation, debate, curiosity, and political and racial awareness. He enjoyed a supportive, extended family network that protected and encouraged in him the growth and development of an independent, well-adjusted, and assertive personality.

Two ambitious, disciplined, and playful young men grew up in the Marshall household. Both sons earned undergraduate degrees at Lincoln University in Oxford, Pennsylvania. Opened in 1856, the historically black university offered the two Marshall youths unique educational and social opportunities. In addition to employing an all-white, essentially Princeton-trained faculty, the college attracted a variety of individuals from throughout the black community. Marshall's classmates included, for example, Kwame Nkrumah, president of Ghana between 1960 and 1966, and Nnamdi Azikiwe, who served as president of Nigeria between 1963 and 1966. Marshall's older brother, William Aubrey, chose medicine as his profession and became a surgeon. Only a quarter of a century before Marshall's graduation, there were only 1,734 black doctors in the United States and even fewer black lawyers—only 728.

Before he was graduated from Lincoln, the gregarious Marshall married Vivian Burey and became more focused in his academic interests. He was graduated at the top of his class and chose to attend Howard University Law School in Washington, D.C.

Marshall's school years do not, at first glance, seem to have anticipated his participation in a more equal, more fully integrated society. He grew up in an essentially segregated community, attending segregated public schools, a black university, and a predominantly black professional school. Clearly, this environment reflected the legacy of racism, yet Marshall's experiences during this period helped him to secure his racial identity, his long-standing principles, and his tendency to work and to fight for those things in which he believed. During this period, too, he came into contact with faculty members of vision who recognized his talent, challenging and directing the lanky, brash, and assertive young man in his preparations for a highly competitive profession. Particularly important was Marshall's association with Charles H. Houston, a Phi Beta Kappa at Amherst and a Harvard Law School graduate. Under Houston's tutelage, Marshall excelled as a law student; later, when Houston became counsel to the National Association for the Advancement of Colored People (NAACP), he hired Marshall as assistant counsel.

Life's Work

Marshall began his law career when he was graduated from the Howard University Law School at the head of his class in 1933. His career began inauspiciously in Baltimore, Maryland, as the Great Depression hung over the nation. Marshall was not immune to the hardships most Americans were experiencing and found it necessary to supplement the meager income he earned in his law practice with money he earned by acting as counsel to the local NAACP branch. The young lawyer unknowingly took the first step in an association through which he would reach the top of his profession.

In 1936, Marshall's former law professor and mentor, Charles H. Houston, invited him to accept the position of assistant special counsel to the NAACP in New York. The regularity of the small salary attached to the position was attractive to Marshall, and he was happy to renew his association with Houston, one of the top black attorneys in the United States.

Significantly, Marshall moved from being a practicing attorney to being a politician-lawyer, from counselor to advocate. In 1940, he became director-counsel of the NAACP Legal Defense Fund. In this capacity, he came to be known as a "pioneer civil rights lawyer" and the "legal champion of black Americans." He was, from his earliest involvement with the NAACP, an important figure in what was emerging as a remarkable alteration of the legal position of blacks in the United States.

Although the NAACP's legal team enjoyed a number of successes and victories under Marshall's leadership, his greatest legal triumph was in 1954, when he successfully argued before the Supreme Court in *Brown v. Board of Education of Topeka*, and the Court decided unanimously that school segregation violated the equal protection provision of the Fourteenth Amendment to the Constitution. Thereafter, in addition to enjoying greater prominence in his profession, Marshall, as President Lyndon B. Johnson would remark at a later date, had "already earned his place in history."

Marshall's nomination, in 1961, to a federal judgeship on the United States Court of Appeals by President John F. Kennedy was almost anticlimactic given Marshall's earlier victory. He agreed to serve, however, and after lengthy debate by the United States Senate, he won confirmation.

Citing competence, wisdom, and courage, President Johnson selected Marshall to become solicitor general of the United States. He was speedily confirmed by the Senate and became the government's chief legal spokesperson. At the same time, Marshall became the first black person to hold that position. Marshall, thanks to the interest of Presidents Kennedy and Johnson, was becoming more broadly engaged in the legal profession and less narrowly identified with the Civil Rights movement. In 1967, only two years after Marshall was appointed solicitor general, President Johnson, in perhaps the most dramatic appointment of his administration, named Marshall as his candidate to fill the vacancy created on the United States Supreme Court by the retirement of Justice Tom Clark.

Thurgood Marshall.
(Library of Congress)

Johnson's political instincts were never better or his moral leadership more pronounced. As the nation anguished over urban unrest and the Civil Rights movement began to crest, Johnson chose Marshall and others—Robert Weaver, the first black to hold a cabinet post; Andrew Brimmer, Federal Reserve Board governor; Patricia Harris, ambassador to Luxembourg; Walter Washington, mayor of Washington, D.C.—to assume significant public offices. In his autobiography, *The Vantage Point* (1971), Johnson said that he had not chosen these leaders for the color of their skin, but he "also deeply believed that with these appointments Negro mothers could look at their children and hope with good reason that someday their sons and daughters might reach the highest offices their government could offer." Johnson personally announced the appointment of Marshall on June 14, 1967. The American Bar Association (ABA) found the president's nominee "highly acceptable," and the Senate voted sixty-nine to eleven for confirmation on August 30, 1967.

Marshall's credentials were extraordinary, but when an old friend of the new justice was asked to account for his success, he observed that Marshall was a tolerant person who could relax in his interpersonal relationships, had an unusual ability to put people at ease, and was earnest about finding solutions to human problems.

On the Supreme Court, Marshall proved to be a skilled and practical jurist who had special concern for the plight of the poor and disadvantaged. Ramsey Clark, former attorney general of the United States and son of Justice Tom Clark, has argued that Marshall's full power as a jurist and his concern for humanity were most clearly demonstrated in his application of the principles of the Constitution to the death penalty. In poor health, Marshall retired from the bench in 1991. He died eighteen months later, of heart failure.

Significance

Marshall had a far-reaching, direct, and dramatic impact on American life. He was a pioneer in the Civil Rights movement, successfully argued the case of *Brown v. Board of Education* and numerous other cases before the Supreme Court, served on the United States Court of Appeals for the Second Circuit, served as solicitor general of the United States, and was appointed to the Supreme Court.

Born black early in the twentieth century, he overcame the restrictions of a segregated society and worked to advance the cause of blacks in the United States. Marshall has become both a symbol of equal opportunity under the law and of the commitment to the rule of law. Marshall urged African Americans to use the courts to secure their legal rights, successfully arguing their cases before the Supreme Court. These cases established milestones in the areas of voting rights, fair housing, and integration. As an attorney, he worked tirelessly to obtain factual data to help lessen the existence of racism and its negative impact on the lives of the powerless. Marshall brought to the Supreme Court an understanding of the consequences of unequal justice under the law, and he extended this understanding to the elderly, the poor, women, and those on death row.

—*Michael J. Clark*

FURTHER READING

Bland, Randall Walton. *Justice Thurgood Marshall: Crusader for Liberalism, His Biography, 1908-1993*. Bethesda, Md.: Academic Press, 2001. A study of Marshall's legal and philosophical beliefs.

_____. *Private Pressure on Public Law: The Legal Career of Justice Thurgood Marshall*. Port Washington, N.Y.: Kennikat Press, 1973. An examination of the judicial behavior of Marshall before his appointment to the Supreme Court. Emphasizes Marshall's conservatism in interpreting the law.

Friedman, Leon, ed. *The Justices of the United States Supreme Court: Their Lives and Major Opinions*. Vol. 5. New York: Chelsea House, 1978. Contains an excellent essay by Ramsey Clark that focuses on questions regarding Marshall's confirmation and his role on the Court.

Johnson, Lyndon Baines. *The Vantage Point: Perspectives of the Presidency: 1963-1969*. New York: Holt, Rinehart and Winston, 1971. Very few references to Marshall but useful for background information and a presidential perspective of the Civil Rights movement.

Kluger, Richard. *Simple Justice: The History of Brown v. Board of Education and Black America's Struggle for Equality*. New York: Vintage Books, 1975. An excellent history of *Brown v. Board of Education*, including an invaluable account of Marshall's role in that landmark decision. One full chapter is devoted to Marshall.

Sitkoff, Harvard. *A New Deal for Blacks: The Emergence of Civil Rights as a National Issue*. New York: Oxford University Press, 1978. A comprehensive account of the emergence of the Civil Rights movement. Only mentions Marshall but excellent for understanding the forces that operated on those who were early leaders in the civil rights field.

Tushnet, Mark V., ed. *Thurgood Marshall: His Speeches, Writings, Arguments, Opinions, and Reminiscences*. Chicago: Lawrence Hill Books, 2001. Includes some of Marshall's legal briefs and oral arguments, selected writings, and the transcript of a lengthy interview with Marshall conducted in 1977.

Williams, Juan. "Poetic Justice." *The New York Times*, January 18, 2004, Education Life Supplement, p. 25. A history of Marshall's campaign to end racial segregation in American schools and colleges.

Witt, Elder. *A Different Justice: Reagan and the Supreme Court*. Washington, D.C.: Congressional Quarterly, 1986. A portrait of the contemporary Court. Questions how the Court may change in the future. Contains a short discussion of Marshall's role on the Court.

Woodward, Bob, and Scott Armstrong. *The Brethren: Inside the Supreme Court*. New York: Simon & Schuster, 1979. A resourceful account of the contemporary Court. Contains useful and interesting information regarding Marshall's relationship with other members of the bench.

GOLDA MEIR

> *One cannot and must not try to erase the past merely because it does not fit the present.*

Prime minister of Israel (1969-1974)

Meir was a leading Zionist and inspirational figure for world Jewry who rejected life in the United States to immigrate to Palestine in 1920. She became a major role player in Zionist organizations there, eventually rising to become Israel's first ambassador to the Soviet Union (1948), minister of labor (1949), foreign minister (1956), and prime minister (1969).

Born: May 3, 1898; Kiev, Ukraine, Russian Empire
Died: December 8, 1978; Jerusalem, Israel
Also known as: Goldie Mabovitch (birth name); Goldie Meyerson
Area of achievement: Government and politics

EARLY LIFE

Golda Meir (GOHL-dah mah-YEER) was born to Moshe Yitzhak Mabovitch, a carpenter by training. Moshe and his wife had two other children: Sheyna and Zipke. The family moved from Kiev to their ancestral town of Pinsk after Golda's birth but ultimately sought to leave Russia because of the violent attacks that threatened Jewish life there. In 1906, the family immigrated to Milwaukee, Wisconsin. Golda worked with her sisters in the family's grocery store. Sheyna became involved in 1915 in the Poale Zion movement, a labor- and socialist-oriented branch of the Zionist movement, which in turn became an inspiration for Golda. Poale Zion aspired to national and social equality of the Jewish people in their own homeland through labor.

Golda fled home in 1912 at age fourteen and moved to Denver to live with Sheyna, who had gone there earlier for treatment of tuberculosis. Four years later (1916), she returned to Milwaukee under extreme parental pressure. While in Denver, she met Morris Meyerson (the name was Hebraized to "Meir" in 1956), whom she married in 1917. For a short time after her return to Wisconsin, Golda was enrolled in Milwaukee Normal School for Teachers. The idea of living and working in the United States did not have much appeal for Golda, who was more attracted to the Poale Zion leaders A. D. Gorden, Nachman Syrkin, and Shmaryahu Levin. She was instrumental in organizing the first Midwest marches in Milwaukee to protest the 1919 pogroms against the Jews in the Ukraine. On May 23, 1921, the Meyersons departed for Palestine on the SS *Pocahontas*. They arrived in Egypt and then transferred by train to Tel Aviv. During the fall of 1921, the Meyersons joined Kibbutz Merhavia (a collective farm based on egalitarian principles). The kibbutz placed Golda face-to-face with issues relating to feminism and female emancipation. Golda, however, never considered herself a feminist. She worked in the fields picking almonds, planting trees, and taking care of chickens. On kitchen duty, she became known for introducing oatmeal and glasses into an otherwise Spartan environment.

In 1922, the Meyersons left Merhavia because of Morris's health and because of his unwillingness to have a child reared by the collective methods of the kibbutz. Their first child, Menachem, was born in November, 1923. The Meyersons moved to Jerusalem to work for Solel Boneh, a government-owned company that was at that time in poor financial standing. A second child, Sarah, was born during the spring of 1926. Meir later lamented that if she could do things over again, she would have remained on the kibbutz. In this period, Meir believed that the application of Jewish labor to Palestine would also improve the quality of life for the Arabs. She always believed that had been the case, justified by the rise in the Arab population during the period of the British mandate over Palestine.

LIFE'S WORK

During 1928, Meir became secretary of Moezet ha-Poalot, the Women's Labor Council of the Histadrut (Jewish labor union of Palestine/Israel) and supervised training of immigrant girls. In 1932, she was sent back to the United States as a representative to the Pioneer Women's Organization, where she would remain until 1934. Around this time her marriage broke up, but there was never a divorce. Morris continued to live in Israel and died there in 1951.

In 1934, Meir became a member of the executive committee of the Histadrut and head of the political department, which allowed her advancement into higher circles. In 1938, she was a Jewish observer to the Evian Conference, which failed to solve the problem of Jewish emigration from Europe in the face of Nazi brutality. During World War II, Meir was a member of the War Economic Advisory Council set up by the mandatory government in Palestine. In 1946, Meir was made acting head of the Jewish Agency after the British mandatory authorities arrested the leaders of the Jewish community following outbreaks of violence in the country. She later commented that her failure to be arrested was a minor insult of sorts because the British apparently believed she was unimportant. In fact, she was one of the most important negotiators for the Jewish community of Palestine during the last two years of the mandate. Meir remained as head of the Political Department until statehood.

During the last years of the mandate, Meir was an active opponent of Ernst Bevin, British foreign secretary, who favored the position of the Palestinian Arabs. Meir was indignant over powerlessness imposed on Jews by the white paper of 1939. She also expressed regret with the boundaries for a Jewish state proposed by the United Nations Special Committee on Palestine (UNSCOP) in 1947, which excluded Jerusalem and parts of Galilee from the Jewish zone. In November, 1947, the United Nations proclaimed the partition of Palestine. In January, 1948, Meir visited the United States in the hope of raising between $25 and $30 million from American Jews for the State of Israel's survival. In fact, she raised more than $50 million.

Meir visited King Abdullah of Transjordan twice in an attempt to avert war between Jews and Arabs. The first time was November, 1947, when Meir, head of the Jewish Agency, met the king in a house at Naharayim, near the Jordan River. At this meeting, Abdullah indicated his desire for peace and that the two shared a common enemy, Hajj-Amin al Husseini, the mufti of Jerusalem and leader of the Palestinian community. On May 10, 1948, the two again met in Amman after Meir crossed into Transjordan in disguise, hoping to avert a Jordanian invasion of Palestine. Abdullah asked her not to hurry in proclaiming a state. She responded that Jews had been waiting for two thousand years. Abdullah requested that the Jews drop their plans for free immigration. Later, rumor had it that Abdullah blamed the war on Meir, as she was perceived as being too proud to accept his offer.

Meir was one of the twenty-five signators of the Declaration of Independence on May 14, 1948. Shortly thereafter, she was again dispatched to the United States for additional fund-raising. She again raised millions of dollars that helped the state survive. Meir, however, did not have time to savor the fruits of statehood and was immediately dispatched to Moscow in 1948 as Israel's first ambassador to the Soviet Union. She arrived in Moscow on September 3, 1948, and established the Israeli mission there. She became the center of a famous demonstration outside the Moscow synagogue on Rosh Hashanah, 1948, which was one of the first indications that Zionist aspirations still existed among Soviet Jews. More than fifty thousand Soviet Jews came to see the first Israeli delegation in Moscow, which provided the first hint of the potential of a large exodus of Jews to Israel and the West.

After departing Moscow in 1949, Meir served in the Israeli Knesset (parliament) until 1974 and rose to many top governmental positions. As a member of the Mapai (labor) Party, she was elected to the First Knesset in 1949 and was appointed minister

Golda Meir.
(Library of Congress)

of labor. In charge of the large-scale emigration of Jews from Arab lands, particularly Iraq and Morocco, she was responsible for settling newcomers in tents and later in permanent housing. More than 680,000 Jews from Arab lands arrived in Israel during the period of her ministry. She had running battles with Minister of Finance Levi Eshkol about financial allocation for housing. All newcomers, however, were placed under shelter when they arrived in Israel, although conditions were very poor from 1950 to 1952. Meir's theory was that all new immigrants had to be employed and get paid for their work. This employment came through huge public works projects, focusing on road building.

Meir herself believed that the most significant thing she did in politics was the work connected with the ministry of labor, because it symbolized social equality and justice. She was instrumental in the presentation of Israel's first National Insurance Bill in 1952, which came into effect in 1954; the establishment of vocational training for adults and youngsters by allying the ministry of labor with older voluntary Jewish organizations such as the Histadrut (labor union), Organization for Rehabilitation Through Training (ORT), Hadassah (women's organization), and Women's International Zionist Organization (WIZO); and the development town projects, which were of only modest success.

In 1955, Meir attempted to become mayor of Tel Aviv but was defeated when the religious bloc in the Israeli Knesset refused to vote for a woman. In 1956, Meir became foreign minister, succeeding Moshe Sharett. She flew to France in 1956 with Shimon Peres and Moshe Dayan to plan a joint attack on Egypt as an ally of Great Britain and France. She gave a speech at the United Nations General Assembly in March, 1957, in which she announced the Israeli military withdrawal from the Sinai Peninsula and Sharm-el-Sheik, which had been occupied by Israel in October, 1956, as a response to Gamal Abdel Nasser's blockade of the Gulf of Aqaba, and in which she called for all states of the Middle East to join in peaceful endeavors.

As foreign minister, Meir developed an energetic development program with emerging African nations. Part of this strategy was to obtain votes at the United Nations, but the bottom line on Israeli-African policy was the common history of suffering. Oppression against the Jews, in Meir's mind, was similar to African slavery and European imperialism. During the late 1950's, Meir traveled to Ghana, Cameroon, Togo, Liberia, Sierra Leone, Gambia, Guinea, the Ivory Coast, and other states. African leaders often found her honest in her appraisals of the possibilities of development and the problems of instant solutions. The African policy, however, collapsed during and after the 1973 Arab-Israeli War, when most African states bowed to Arab oil pressure and severed relations.

In 1965, Meir retired as foreign minister and became secretary-general of the Mapai Party. This was a critical period in the development of the center-left Israeli political parties, as part of the Mapai Party had split with David Ben-Gurion to establish Rafi, while Achdut Ha Avodah represented another position of labor. Meir believed that unification was necessary to ensure the future of the Mapai Party. During the crisis before the Six-Day War, Meir was brought into the government and supported a hesitant Eshkol. After the war, she participated in the unification in 1968 of the three labor parties into the new Israeli Labor Party.

Meir, Golda

When Prime Minister Eshkol died on February 16, 1969, Meir was chosen as prime minister (March 7, 1969) as a means to avoid an open struggle between Dayan and Yigal Allon. On matters involving peace with the Arabs, Meir was often said to possess hard-line bargaining positions. She believed that the only alternative to war was peace and that the only way to peace was negotiations. She indicated her willingness to go anywhere to talk peace and to negotiate anything except national suicide. She was never willing to talk with the Palestine Liberation Organization (PLO), however, which she viewed as a terrorist organization.

Late in 1969, Meir went to the United States to meet with President Richard M. Nixon and to fill a shopping list for weapons, especially a specific request for twenty-five Phantom and eighty Skyhawk jet aircraft. It was a warm meeting with the American president, and Meir stayed on for an extended speaking tour. In January, 1973, Meir met with Pope Paul VI, the first Jewish head of state to do so.

The October, 1973, Yom Kippur War was a watershed in Israeli history and a horrible period in Meir's life. She became aware of plans for an Egyptian and Syrian attack against Israel but held off mobilization of reserves. Israel won the war but with substantial casualties. Meir also had a rift with General Ariel Sharon over disposition of the Egyptian Third Army, which had been surrounded by Israeli forces in Sinai. Meir, to save Sadat's position as possible negotiator, ordered Sharon not to move against the Third Army. Meir also had ambivalent feelings about United States secretary of state Henry Kissinger, who threatened economic retaliation against Israel during cease-fire and disengagement negotiations. In the end, Meir believed that she had been correct in rejecting a preemptive strike against the Arab states, as the Arab attack ensured American aid, which, she believed, saved lives.

The Labor Party again prevailed in elections held on December 31, 1973, but Meir resigned less than four months later, on April 11, 1974. She became a casualty of the Yom Kippur War, so to speak, after the Agranat Commission's report indicted the general staff, the military intelligence, the Sinai field commanders, and David Eleazar, who was the commander in chief, but not the minister of defense, Dayan. Meir left office on June 4 at age seventy-six. She continued as a spokesperson for Israel in academic and public circles. On December 8, 1978, she died of leukemia, which she had lived with since the early 1970's but managed to hide from public view.

SIGNIFICANCE

Meir was one of the most beloved of Israel's leaders but unfortunately left office after what became a national disaster—the Yom Kippur War. Still, she was highly regarded, even by her former enemies. In November, 1977, when President Anwar el-Sadat of Egypt went on a peace mission to Israel, Meir was at the airport to greet him; Sadat regarded her as "the tough old lady." Meir was generally considered a tough and often stubborn politician, holding on to views that had a foundation deep in her Zionist ideology, which was influenced by memories of atrocities against the Jews in Eastern Europe during her childhood and the Holocaust of World War II. This quality was useful for Israel as a nation of embattled people but became problematic once peace initiatives appeared, for Meir often believed such initiatives were insincere.

Meir helped create certain problems in the peace process that continued beyond her

Meir, Golda

tenure as prime minister. She failed to establish any specific position about the occupied territories—the West Bank and Gaza Strip. She insisted on direct negotiations with the enemy and opposed any form of mediation by outsiders. She refused, perhaps correctly, any interim withdrawal before a peace treaty was signed. Her most serious misjudgment was probably the failure to take up Sadat's explorations for peace in 1971. Yet she was an exponent of peace and held a consistent view.

—*Stephen C. Feinstein*

FURTHER READING

Bar-Joseph, Uri. *The Watchman Fell Asleep: The Surprise of Yom Kippur and Its Sources*. Albany: State University of New York Press, 2005. A history of the Yom Kippur War, focusing on the failure of Israeli intelligence before the 1973 Arab attack.

Gorenberg, Gershom. *The Accidental Empire: Israel and the Birth of the Settlements, 1967-1977*. New York: Times Books, 2006. Chronicles the birth of the settler movement in the Gaza Strip after the Six-Day War, including information about Meir's administration.

Martin, Ralph. *Golda Meir: The Romantic Years*. New York: Charles Scribner's Sons, 1988. An examination of Meir's personal life, with less emphasis on the politics of the Middle East.

Meir, Golda. *My Life*. New York: G. P. Putnam's Sons, 1975. The most valuable work for understanding the life of Meir. This is not a diary but rather an exposition of what Meir believed were her most important accomplishments. Includes some texts of her more important speeches.

Rafael, Gideon. *Destination Peace: Three Decades of Israeli Foreign Policy*. New York: Stein & Day, 1981. An examination of Israeli foreign policy from the perspective of an individual who served as Israeli ambassador to London, permanent representative to the United Nations, and director-general of the Israeli Foreign Ministry. Contains many insightful references to the career of Golda Meir.

Sachar, Howard M. *A History of Israel*. 2 vols. New York: Oxford University Press, 1974. A comprehensive history of Zionism and the state of Israel, with particular references to Meir's prime ministry.

Shenker, Israel. "Golda Meir: Peace and Arab Acceptance Were Goals of Her Years as Premier." *The New York Times*, December 9, 1978, p. 7. This is an article that appeared as part of an extensive obituary of Meir, summarizing her main approaches to the peace process.

Syrkin, Marie. *Golda Meir: Israel's Leader*. New York: Putnam, 1969. An early and sympathetic portrait by a fellow American Zionist. Syrkin's father, Nachman Syrkin, was a leading labor Zionist and strong influence on Meir during the 1930's. Because they were completed before Meir's tenure as prime minister was completed, neither this work nor Syrkin's earlier on provides a full picture of Meir's life.

_____. *Golda Meir: Woman with a Cause*. New York: Putnam, 1963. This portrait, like Syrkin's later work, is based on a very close friendship between Meir and Syrkin.

THOMAS MERTON

> *Your life is shaped by the end you live for. You are made in the image of what you desire.*

Monk and philosopher

Merton is best known for his spiritual autobiography The Seven Storey Mountain, *in which he explores how one might become a spiritual person in a nonspiritual age. His later works continued the search for spirituality through his experiences as a monk, and though for a time he seemed to be renouncing the world, he became a sort of prophet seeking to reform it.*

Born: January 31, 1915; Prades, France
Died: December 10, 1968; Bangkok, Thailand
Also known as: Tom Merton (birth name); Brother Louis; Father M. Louis; Father Louis
Areas of achievement: Religion and theology; philosophy

EARLY LIFE

Thomas Merton (MUR-tuhn) spent the early years of his life being shuttled between France, England, and the United States. His parents, artists Owen Merton and Ruth Jenkins Merton, were from New Zealand and the United States respectively, but had met and married in Europe and had settled in the small town of Prades in the French Pyrenees, where Thomas (actually registered at birth as Tom) was born.

The family did not stay long in Prades, however, leaving in 1916 to escape from World War I. They lived on Long Island, New York, with Ruth's parents. Five years later, when Thomas was only six, his mother died of cancer. After that, he lived variously with his father, his mother's parents, other relatives, and family friends. In 1925 his father took him to the south of France to live, where he spent two unhappy years at a French school. Young Merton was happier in England, where he and his father moved in 1928. He attended Oakham School, wrote for the school paper, and eventually became its editor.

In 1931 his father died of a brain tumor. After graduating from Oakham in 1933, Merton had a disastrous year at Clare College, Cambridge, where he spent most of his time partying; he also might have fathered an illegitimate child. In 1934 he withdrew from Cambridge, returned to New York, and enrolled at Columbia University.

Merton did well at Columbia, completing bachelor's and master's degrees and writing a thesis on the mystical poetry of William Blake. He continued to live a bohemian life but also began to become interested in religion, especially Roman Catholicism, although he had been raised in the Anglican Church. He converted to Catholicism in 1938 and expressed an interest in becoming a priest or a monk. He also was interested in a writing career. He produced several novels that no one would publish but succeeded in publishing some poems and book reviews. He also took a position teaching English at St. Bonaventure College (now University) in New York.

Still seeking to become a monk, Merton applied to the Franciscans but was turned down by them. He then went on a retreat at the Abbey of Our Lady of Gethsemani in rural Kentucky and knew immediately it was the place for him. He entered the monastery permanently on December 10, 1941.

LIFE'S WORK

Except for a few trips to conferences in his later years, Merton spent the rest of his life at the monastery or in Louisville, Kentucky, on brief outings. The monastery Merton chose was a strict one that belonged to the Cistercian Order of the Strict Observance, also known as the Trappists. He took vows of poverty, chastity, and obedience and found himself in an institution in which he and his fellow monks were expected to spend most of their time in communal prayers and manual labor while eating a meager diet and wearing simple robes. They also were to be silent most of the time and use sign language instead of speaking.

Merton discusses his decision to subject himself to this strict discipline in his bestselling autobiography *The Seven Storey Mountain* (1948). His idea was to free himself from the dissipated, undisciplined life he had led before entering the monastery. His original view was that he had to reject the world entirely, but he slowly gave up this idea. In the last ten years of his life especially, he saw his mission as one of reaching out to humanity while still maintaining his distance from the world.

Thomas Merton.
(Library of Congress)

For a while Merton even thought that, in order to purify himself and devote himself to God, he would have to give up his writing, but writing was too strong a drive in him. To his surprise, he found that his superiors in the monastery encouraged him to write, though they did also censor what he produced. Merton thus found himself in the paradoxical situation of having joined a monastery dedicated to the rule of silence and yet being able to speak, through his writings, to the world outside the monastery. Furthermore, he was quite candid about this paradox and about his struggles over his writings. He also struggled over his desire for greater solitude.

The Trappists were a communal order, and the monks at Gethsemani spent most of their time together. Merton soon decided that a hermit's life would be ideal, like that practiced at some other, more contemplative monasteries. However, his superiors told him it was God's will that he remain a Trappist, and he did, though he eventually won concessions, including a little hut that he used as a private hermitage on the monastery's grounds.

Merton wrote about his struggles with his monastic life in several journals he published, notably *The Sign of Jonas* (1953) and *Conjectures of a Guilty Bystander* (1966). He also wrote books on contemplation, such as *New Seeds of Contemplation* (1961), in which he connected contemplation and prayer with community, wrote that contemplation was not just for monks, and argued that it must be accompanied by compassion for others.

Acting on his conviction that the truly spiritual person, even a solitary monk like himself, must connect to the world, Merton in his last years began writing about political issues. He opposed the Vietnam War, called for racial harmony, denounced nuclear weapons, and supported nonviolence. Also in these years he began to explore other spiritual traditions, such as Zen Buddhism, Daoism, and Sufi mysticism.

Exploring these traditions led him to Asia in late 1968, where he met the Dalai Lama and attended a religious conference in Bangkok, Thailand. He died there on December 10, 1968, after he was accidentally electrocuted.

Significance

Merton became instantly famous with the publication of *The Seven Storey Mountain*, a spiritual autobiography depicting his search for meaning in an apparently meaningless world. The book struck a chord in the postwar world of 1948, as did some of his later works in which he tried to explain prayer and contemplation through his personal experiences. Paradoxically, even though *The Seven Storey Mountain* ended by renouncing the world, it nevertheless appealed to that world as it spoke to all who were eager to follow him in his search for spirituality in a secular era.

Merton became a prophet for his era, trying to lead people away from mindless conformity and faith in technology. He tried to show them a path of contemplation through which they might connect with the deepest, most interior part of their being, and by doing so connect with God.

—*Sheldon Goldfarb*

FURTHER READING

Cunningham, Lawrence. *Thomas Merton and the Monastic Vision*. Grand Rapids, Mich.: William B. Eerdmans, 1999. Clear and informative account of Merton's life after he joined the monastery and of the works he composed there. Discusses Merton's views on prayer. Includes a useful annotated bibliography.

Elie, Paul. *The Life You Save May Be Your Own: An American Pilgrimage*. New York: Farrar, Straus and Giroux, 2003. An examination of Merton alongside Catholics Dorothy Day, Flannery O'Connor, and Walker Percy. These writers, taken together, paint a vivid portrait of the "Catholic moment" of the mid-twentieth century.

Furlong, Monica. *Merton: A Biography*. San Francisco, Calif.: Harper & Row, 1980. Overview of Merton's life, with useful discussion of his work as a teacher of novice monks. At times seems unsympathetic, presenting him as suffering from neuroses.

Kramer, Victor A. *Thomas Merton*. Boston: Twayne, 1984. Includes a biographical sketch and a discussion of Merton's major works. Also includes a useful chronology, a bibliography, and an index.

Labrie, Ross. *The Art of Thomas Merton*. Fort Worth: Texas Christian University Press, 1979. Literary analysis of Merton's writings. Discusses his struggle over whether he could be both a monk and a writer. Index, bibliography.

Mott, Michael. *The Seven Mountains of Thomas Merton*. Boston: Houghton Mifflin, 1984. The authorized biography. Focuses on the details of Merton's everyday life rather than on the nature of his achievements. Illustrations, bibliography, index.

Padovano, Anthony. *The Human Journey: Thomas Merton, Symbol of a Century*. Garden City, N.Y.: Doubleday, 1982. Focuses on Merton's significance as a symbol of his age. Places him in the American context.

Shannon, William H. *Thomas Merton: An Introduction*. Cincinnati, Ohio: St. Anthony Messenger Press, 2005. Revised edition of *Something of a Rebel*. Includes a clear and informative biographical sketch, an insightful examination of Merton's continuing significance, a discussion of his most important writings, and an explanation of his notion of contemplation. Index.

Shannon, William H., Christine M. Bochen, and Patrick F. O'Connell. *The Thomas Merton Encyclopedia*. Maryknoll, N.Y.: Orbis Books, 2002. A good resource that outlines Merton's life and writings in an easy-to-read encyclopedic format. Includes name and subject indexes and a bibliography.

JOHN R. MOTT

> *We have nothing less to do than to get inside of whole peoples and change their motives and dispositions.*

Ecumenical movement leader

The central figure in at least four worldwide Christian movements, Mott combined missionary zeal and personal piety with administrative efficiency. Cowinner of the Nobel Peace Prize in 1946, he is widely regarded as the founder of the ecumenical movement, the most significant religious movement of the twentieth century.

Born: May 25, 1865; Livingston Manor, New York
Died: January 31, 1955; Orlando, Florida
Also known as: John Mott (birth name); John Raleigh Mott (full name)
Area of achievement: Religion and theology

Early Life

John R. Mott was the third of four children and the only son of John Stitt Mott and Elmira Dodge Mott. When he was only four months old, his father, a farmer, moved the family to Postville, Iowa, where he entered the lumber business and soon became the leading lumber and hardware dealer in town. While working in his father's lumberyard, Mott learned to keep meticulously accurate and detailed records, which he continued to do throughout his life. John Mott expressed his individuality early when, at age eleven, on his own initiative he added the initial "R" (for "Raleigh") to his name.

Mott acquired from his mother much of his personal piety, together with an almost insatiable desire for knowledge. Elmira was an earnest Methodist and subscribed regularly to such magazines as *Harper's Weekly*, *The Youth's Companion*, *The Christian Advocate*, and *The Guide to Holiness*, all of which were eagerly devoured by young Mott. The family also had a relatively large library, and his mother told him much about European history and public affairs, both absorbing interests of his in later years. At the age of thirteen, Mott came under the influence of an Iowa Quaker evangelist, J. W. Dean. Shortly thereafter, a young circuit-riding Methodist pastor, the Reverend Horace E. Warner, not only instilled in him the desire and purpose to obtain a college education but also convinced his parents to make it possible for him to do so.

In the fall of 1881, Mott, at age sixteen, enrolled in Upper Iowa University, a small Methodist preparatory college at nearby Fayette. His primary interests in his years there were English literature, history, and philosophy, with special emphasis on politics, constitutional law, and logic. He joined the Philomathean Society, a debating club, and won prizes in historical and political oration and debate. Mott's debates and orations, in preparation for a political career, were to prove highly useful to him in later years, as did his nearly complete mastery of *Robert's Rules of Order* (1876).

During his years at Upper Iowa, Mott was not particularly religious, although he did become a charter member of the local Young Men's Christian Association (YMCA). His decision to transfer to Cornell University in Ithaca, New York, seems to have been motivated primarily by a need for wider horizons in his preparation for a career in politics and law but also by a desire to attend a large secular institution in hopes of escaping religious influences. Such was not to be. On Friday evening, January 15, 1886, Mott attended a lecture by J. E. K. Studd, a famous English cricketer from Cambridge (later to be knighted and become lord mayor of London), and heard Studd utter three sentences that changed his life. As Mott took his seat, having arrived late, Studd announced his text: "Seekest thou great things for thyself? Seek them not. Seek ye first the kingdom of God." Mott later wrote, "These words went straight to the springs of my motive life. I have forgotten all else that the speaker said, but on these few words hinged my life-investment decision. I went back to my room not to study but to fight." Following an interview with Studd the next day, Mott wrote his parents of his decision "to devote my whole life and talents to the service of Jesus."

Mott immediately began a period of intensive Bible study and prayer, along with holding religious services in the local jail. He was elected vice president of the Cornell YMCA, whose membership rapidly grew from 40 to 150. In the summer of 1886, he was selected to represent Cornell at the first international and ecumenical Christian Student Conference, a gathering of 251 young men from eighty-nine colleges and universities in the United States and Canada, at Mount Hermon, Massachusetts, under the leadership of the evangelist Dwight L. Moody. Mott returned to Cornell from Mount Hermon determined to complete his education and to devote his life to missionary work. He was elected president of the Cornell YMCA, and its membership rapidly grew to 290. He also was instrumental in raising the money for a building for the Cornell YMCA. In 1888, he was graduated with degrees in philosophy, history, and political science, along with membership in Phi Beta Kappa.

Life's Work

Rejecting several opportunities for further study and travel, Mott agreed to a trial period of one year as student secretary of the International Committee of the YMCA. This involved extensive traveling to college campuses and coordination of campus Christian activities. Mott was to remain in this position not one year but for the next twenty-seven years until 1915, at which time he became the committee's general secretary until 1931. Only four months into his new job, however, Mott also accepted the additional responsibility of chair of the newly organized Student Volunteer Movement for Foreign Missions, the missionary branch of the YMCA, the YWCA, the American Inter-Seminary Missionary Alliance, and the Canadian Intercollegiate Missionary Alliance. This post Mott would hold until 1920, and he continued to solicit funds for it most of his life. Its slogan, The Evangelization of the World in This Generation, was the title of one of his most important books (1900). Mott had an almost uncanny ability to seek out other capable leaders and to inspire them by his own contagious enthusiasm and zeal. In addition to Mott's extensive travels, he sent out others to work with student Christian groups on various campuses. By 1925, his efforts had resulted in the recruitment of more than ten thousand American and Canadian student volunteers for various mission boards.

In November of 1891, Mott married Leila Ada White, an English teacher and graduate of Wooster College, at her family home in Wooster, Ohio. Leila accompanied him in much of his travel and was a devoted wife and partner for nearly sixty-one years, un-

Mott, John R.

til her death in 1952. The Motts had four children: John Livingstone, Irene, Frederick Dodge, and Eleanor, all of whom grew up in Montclair, New Jersey, while their father commuted to offices in New York City when not traveling elsewhere. Mott is described by his biographers as six feet tall, with handsome features and an impressive bearing. His reddish-brown hair, gray in later years, topped a large, finely molded head. Photographs indicate his most impressive facial feature to have been his thick, shaggy eyebrows. His entire physique suggested strength: square shoulders and square head, firm mouth, and dark brown, piercing eyes. Small wonder that at least one student is said to have emerged from a conference with Mott and commented, "It was like being in to see God!"

Mott defined his life's work as one of weaving together Christian movements—particularly among students—all over the world. In 1893, he organized the Foreign Missions Conference of North America in an effort to unite missionary work on that continent. He was repeatedly elected to its executive committee and was made an honorary life member in 1942. Mott also was one of the leaders in founding the World's Student Christian Federation (WSCF) in Badstena, Sweden, in 1895, and he became its first general secretary. In this role, he organized student movements in China, Japan, India, New Zealand, and Australia, as well as in Europe and the Near East. International meetings were held in such unlikely places as Tokyo, Constantinople, Jerusalem, Beijing, and Madras. By 1925, the WSCF claimed the membership of more than 300,000 young men and women in more than three thousand colleges and universities in twenty-seven different nations. Mott served as chair of its executive committee from its inception until 1920, then as general chair until 1928.

A high point in Mott's career came in June of 1910, when he was elected chair of the World Missionary Conference, attended by more than twelve hundred delegates, in Edinburgh, Scotland, which Mott himself called "the most notable gathering in the interest of the worldwide expansion of Christianity ever held, not only in missionary annals, but in all Christian annals." Mott was also made chair of a "continuation committee" to carry on the work of the Edinburgh conference until the next one. He toured the Far East in this role and organized regional missionary councils in various nations, including India, Japan, Korea, and China. Mott spent his days organizing these councils and his evenings addressing huge throngs of students. Although he spoke through interpreters, his impassioned words were interrupted time and again by applause. Mott deserves much of the credit for the leading role assumed by the "younger churches" in later missionary conferences throughout the world. Against strong opposition, he recruited Roman Catholic and Eastern Orthodox Christians into ecumenical groups. The "continuation committee" was succeeded by the International Missionary Council in 1921, with Mott as its chair. In 1942, when he retired from that position, he was named its "honorary chairman."

Mott's travels on behalf of various Christian causes were prodigious. Following extensive trips throughout the United States and Canada, he made his first visit to Europe in 1891. For the next sixty years, he crossed the Atlantic both ways almost annually, occasionally twice or three times, and the Pacific at least fourteen times, in all logging well over two million miles and visiting eighty-three countries. One indication that these travels were far from pleasure junkets is that Mott was often afflicted by motion

John R. Mott.
(© The Nobel Foundation)

sickness—not only on sea travels but on trains as well. When he accepted the Nobel Peace Prize in 1946 (after his first intercontinental flight), this "world citizen" received congratulatory messages from seven chiefs of state and numerous other world leaders. He died January 31, 1955, a few months before his ninetieth birthday, and was buried in the Washington Cathedral. Among his last recorded words were these: "While life lasts I am an evangelist."

SIGNIFICANCE

For many years, Mott was the central figure in at least four major world Christian movements: president of the World's Alliance of YMCAs, general secretary and later chair of the WSCF, chair of the International Missionary Council, and the first honorary president of the World Council of Churches. As an American Methodist layman, he was awarded an honorary doctor of divinity degree by the (Russian) Orthodox Theological Institute of St. Sergius, in 1940. He declined many prestigious opportunities during his career, including President Woodrow Wilson's offer to become United States Ambassador to China and offers of the presidencies of Princeton University, Oberlin College, and Yale Divinity School. At President Wilson's request, he served on the Mexican Commission in 1916 and the Special Diplomatic Mission to Russia

Mott, John R.

(the "Root Mission") in 1917, utilizing the latter as an opportunity to bring the Russian Orthodox Church into the ecumenical network. Mott was awarded the Distinguished Service Medal for his fund-raising work and other service during World War I, at the conclusion of which he also made significant contributions to the peace conferences at Versailles. In addition to the Nobel Peace Prize, which he shared with the pacifist Emily Greene Balch in 1946, he was the recipient of eight honorary degrees—the Imperial Order of Meija from Japan, the Order of the Saviour from Greece, the Order of the Holy Sepulchre from Jerusalem, the Prince Carl Medal from Sweden, the Order of the White Rose from Finland, the Second Order of the Crown from Siam, the Order of Polonia Restituta from Poland, the Order of the Italian Crown—and he was made a chevalier, and later an officer, of the French Legion of Honor. He raised more than $300 million for his various Christian causes, most of it for World War I relief work.

Although a brilliant organizer and fund-raiser, Mott also had deep spiritual strength. "Organize as though there were no such thing as prayer," he said, "and pray as though there were no such thing as organization." President Wilson once called him "the world's most useful man."

Mott was typical of much of early twentieth century American religious thought. An evangelical liberal, he eagerly embraced the "social gospel" and applied it to missions and other burning issues of his day. Mott was probably influenced as well by the social Darwinism of the period; there was unbounded optimism in the popular slogan The Evangelization of the World in This Generation. This slogan did not originate with Mott, although he made it his own. Yet it is also clear that he knew the difference between the "evangelization" of the world and its "conversion." He simply wanted the Christian Gospel to be preached to the entire world and sincerely believed it could be done in a single generation. Perhaps in part because of his lack of a seminary education, Mott was not deterred by theological niceties in urging ecumenical cooperation. He made the words of Jesus, "that they all may be one," into an ecumenical rallying cry.

In his speech responding to the 1946 Nobel Peace Prize, Mott characterized his career: "My life might be summed up as an earnest and undiscourageable effort to weave together all nations, all races, and all religious communions in friendliness, in fellowship, and in cooperation." In its 1965 tribute to him, on the one hundredth anniversary of his birthday, the General Board of the National Council of Churches called Mott "the greatest missionary statesman since the Apostle Paul." If anyone ever deserved the title of founder of one of the most important religious movements of the twentieth century, the ecumenical movement, it was John R. Mott.

—C. Fitzhugh Spragins

FURTHER READING

Fisher, Galen M. *John R. Mott: Architect of Cooperation and Unity.* New York: Association Press, 1952. Written shortly before his death, this volume is very positive throughout in its analysis of Mott's many contributions. The book contains many quotations from distinguished churchmen in praise of Mott's work. The concluding chapter compares Mott's service with that of Saint Paul.

Hopkins, Charles Howard. *John R. Mott, 1865-1955: A Biography*. Grand Rapids, Mich.: William B. Eerdmans, 1979. The definitive biography of Mott by an emeritus professor of history at Rider College, Philadelphia, this is a detailed, straightforward, and well-documented account of Mott's career and influence. The result of fifteen years of research, this volume tends to emphasize Mott's social concern and the details of his travels, perhaps to the neglect of his evangelicalism and churchmanship.

Howe, W. Tracy, and Nancy Reece, eds. *Strengthening the Organizational Heart: Fifteen Timeless Lessons from Legendary YMCA Leader, John R. Mott*. Franklin, Tenn.: Providence House, 2006. Mott summarized what he had learned in fifteen basic principles. YMCA leaders examine his precepts to describe how they can be applied to contemporary issues.

Mackie, Robert C. *Layman Extraordinary: John R. Mott, 1865-1955*. New York: Association Press, 1965. A brief monograph of nearly unbridled praise and enthusiasm on behalf of Mott and his accomplishments.

Mathews, Basil. *John R. Mott: World Citizen*. New York: Harper and Brothers, 1934. This book was authorized by Mott to describe the principles and experiences of his life as examples for young people. An excellent portrayal of his personality and character written some twenty years before his death, this volume portrays Mott as one who applied the principles of business to the work of Christian missions.

Mott, John R. *Addresses and Papers*. 6 vols. New York: Association Press, 1946-1947. Mott wrote at least sixteen books himself, as well as many shorter works, which are included in these volumes. His personal papers and his comprehensive archives of the World's Student Christian Federation are in the Mott Collection of the Yale Divinity School Library, New Haven, Connecticut.

Rouse, Ruth. *John R. Mott: An Appreciation*. Geneva: World's Student Christian Federation Press, 1930. A well-balanced portrayal of Mott in midcareer by an admirer and historian of the ecumenical movement.

———. *The World's Student Christian Federation: A History of the First Thirty Years*. London: S.C.M. Press, 1948. Mott wrote the foreword to this volume, which traces the WSCF from its origins prior to Vadstena, Sweden, in 1895, to High Leigh, England, in 1924, with appropriate attention to Mott's contributions.

Woolverton, John F. *Robert Gardiner and the Reunification of Worldwide Christianity in the Progressive Era*. Columbia: University of Missouri Press, 2005. This biography of Gardiner, a leader in the Christian ecumenical movement, includes a discussion of Mott.

John Muir

❝ *Climb the mountains and get their good tidings.* **❞**

Naturalist and conservationist

Combining his skills as a scientist, explorer, and writer, Muir played a significant role in the conservation movement and in the development of the United States National Park system and left a legacy that has kept his name honored in the twenty-first century.

Born: April 21, 1838; Dunbar, Scotland
Died: December 24, 1914; Los Angeles, California
Areas of achievement: Exploration; environmentalism

Early Life

John Muir (mewr) was the eldest of three sons and the third of eight children of Ann Gilrye Muir and Daniel Muir. His father grew up under the harshest poverty imaginable but eventually gained stature as a middle-class grain merchant and became a Presbyterian of severe fundamentalist religious beliefs. He worshiped a God of wrath who found evil in almost every childish activity. Typically, John and his playmates would leave the yard, and his tyrannical father would fly into a rage and punish the innocent lad. When his father did not have the total devotion of his entire family, he would punish them with the greatest severity.

In 1849, at the age of eleven, John and his family immigrated to the United States in search of greater economic opportunity. The Muirs moved to Portage, Wisconsin, an area that had a fine reputation for wheat growing, where they purchased farmland. John marveled at the beauty of the countryside. He kept busy with farm chores and read at night when he was thought to be asleep. He also developed an early love of machinery and began the practice of waking at one in the morning to go to his cellar workshop to build things out of scraps of wood and iron. His father considered his inventions a waste of time, but John built a sawmill, weather instruments, waterwheels, and clocks. In 1860, at the age of twenty-two, he displayed his inventions at the state fair in Madison. His gadgets were well received, but his dour father only lectured him on the sin of vanity.

At this juncture in his life, John decided to leave home to make his own way. First, he moved to nearby Madison and attended the University of Wisconsin. He followed no particular course of study; he took classes that interested him. He seemed more concerned with learning than with earning a degree. Muir excelled in the sciences and also enjoyed the outdoor laboratory of nature. A tall, disheveled, bearded man with penetrating, glacial-blue eyes, Muir eventually grew tired of the regimentation of college. He liked books, but he loved experience more. Some men from the university were leaving to fight in the Civil War. Muir was twenty-five years old and in his junior year of school, but he also decided to leave.

From Madison, he journeyed into Canada to take odd jobs and to study the botany of the area. Later, he turned up in Indianapolis, Indiana, working in a carriage shop.

With his inventive mind, he proved a success in the factory environment until one day he suffered an eye injury while working on a machine. The puncture wound affected both eyes, and soon he lost his eyesight. After a month of convalescence in a darkened room, his vision slowly returned. With a new lease on life and his eyesight fully restored, Muir decided to abandon the factory world and enjoy nature.

LIFE'S WORK

In September of 1867, Muir began a walking tour that would take him from Louisville, Kentucky, to the Gulf Coast of Florida. He found the wildlife and plants of the South fascinating. His travels took him through Kentucky, Tennessee, Georgia, and Florida, until he reached the Gulf at Cedar Key. He had no particular route planned, other than to head south. He was not disappointed in what he found on his four-month trek and decided to continue his journey. He had often read the exciting travel accounts of Alexander von Humboldt, who had explored widely in South America. Such exploration was Muir's dream also, but it was interrupted by a three-month bout with malaria. When he was almost recovered, he set off for Cuba, but, upon reaching that tropical island and after waiting for a southbound ship for a month, he settled on a new destination.

Muir believed that California offered the best climate for his malarial disorder and also afforded an environment of substantial botanical interest. He made the long journey to the West and settled in beautiful Yosemite Valley, which was snuggled in the Sierra Nevada. At times, he worked as a sheepherder and at a lumber mill, but he spent most of the time exploring the beautiful countryside, taking notes of his findings, and looking for one more glorious site of the wondrous Sierra. In 1869, Muir and a friend built a one-room cabin of pine logs near Yosemite Falls, and this became his home. He had famous visitors such as Asa Gray, the Harvard botanist; the novelist Therese Yelverton; and the renowned Transcendentalist, Ralph Waldo Emerson. With all, he shared the exhilarating scenes of the high country.

After four years in Yosemite Valley, Muir moved to San Francisco and dreamed of other trips. He traveled up the coast to Oregon and Washington and climbed Mount Shasta and Mount Rainier. He also made six excursions to Alaska, where he climbed mountains and studied glaciers. His favorite area was Glacier Bay in southern Alaska, but he loved any place where he could find a mountain to climb. During his stay in Alaska, he also studied the customs of the Tlingit Indians.

Muir also found time for romance. A friend introduced him to Louisa Strentzel, daughter of horticulturalist Dr. John Strentzel and owner of a large fruit ranch east of San Francisco, near the town of Martinez. Louisa and John were married on April 14, 1880. At the same time, he became the overseer of the Strentzel ranch and introduced changes that brought production to peak efficiency. Muir grafted one hundred varieties of pears and grapes onto the best strains. His effective management of the ranch provided him with economic security. For the next ten years, he neglected his writing and mountain climbing, but he and his wife grew reasonably prosperous and reared their two daughters, Wanda and Helen.

Nine years after his marriage, Muir took an important trip back to Yosemite. With him was Robert Underwood Johnson, an old friend and editor of the influential *The Century*. The two were dumbfounded by the changes that had taken place in the Sierra during such a short time. Sheep and lumberjacks had created great devastation in the valley and high country. Forest land was bare, and grass root structures were severely damaged by the sharp hoofs of the sheep. Johnson was moved to action. He promised to lobby influential congressmen, and he encouraged Muir to convince the American public of their conservationist cause and the need to take action before it was too late. Muir accepted the challenge, and, in two well-argued articles published in *The Century*, he convinced many readers of the desperate need to preserve some of the natural wonders of the California highlands.

In 1890, the federal government rewarded the efforts of Muir, Johnson, and other conservationists by creating Yosemite National Park. Other victories followed when Congress established Mount Rainier, the Grand Canyon, the Petrified Forest, and parts of the Sierra as national preserves. The following year, Muir worked for the passage of legislation that eventually allowed President Benjamin Harrison to set aside thirteen million acres of forest land and President Grover Cleveland, twenty-one million acres more. Muir continued the conservationist cause by helping to create the Sierra Club in 1892. He became the club's first president, and the members vowed to preserve the natural features of the California mountains.

John Muir.
(Courtesy, The Bancroft Library, University of California, Berkeley)

With the total support of his wife, Muir decided to abandon the ranch work and concentrate on furthering his writing career. In 1894, he published *The Mountains of California* and followed it with *Our National Parks* (1901), *Stickeen* (1909), *My First Summer in the Sierra* (1911), *The Yosemite* (1912), and *The Story of My Boyhood and Youth* (1913). In these works, he richly illustrated the growth of a conservationist mind and presented forceful arguments for preservation and ecological protection.

In his last years, Muir traveled to Europe, South America, and Africa, always learning and experiencing what he could. Seventy-six years of life and accomplishment came to an end in December of 1914, when Muir died in Los Angeles on Christmas Eve, a victim of pneumonia.

SIGNIFICANCE

For John Muir, it had been a full life. Forced to make a decision at an early age between machines and inventions on the one hand and nature and conservation on the other, he chose the path of mountains, flowers, and preservation. In nature, he found his cathedral, and there he preached the gospel of conservation, preservation, and ecology. He walked the wilderness paths with Ralph Waldo Emerson and Theodore Roosevelt; in the end, he convinced many of his contemporaries of the rightness of his ideas.

Muir lived at a time when the United States was becoming a great industrial leader in the world. Nevertheless, he was able to point to the wisdom of preserving many natural wonders of the American West. Although an earlier generation had plundered the East, his efforts and those of others helped to save significant portions of the West, to create large national parks and forest preserves, and to protect the ecological systems so necessary for the survival of nature.

—*John W. Bailey*

FURTHER READING

Badè, William Frederic. *The Life and Letters of John Muir*. 2 vols. New York: Houghton Mifflin, 1924. The best collection of Muir's letters.

Ehrlich, Gretel. *John Muir: Nature's Visionary*. Washington, D.C.: National Geographic Society, 2000. Insightful biography, containing many quotes from Muir's unpublished journals and his other writings. Well illustrated with landscape photographs.

Fox, Stephen R. *John Muir and His Legacy: The American Conservation Movement*. Boston: Little, Brown, 1981. This is a biography of Muir, a chronological history of the conservation movement from 1890 to 1975, and an analysis of what conservation means in historical terms.

Melham, Tom. *John Muir's Wild America*. Washington, D.C.: National Geographic Society, 1976. A good place to begin the study of Muir. Beautiful illustrations and sound background history.

Nash, Roderick. *Wilderness and the American Mind*. New Haven, Conn.: Yale University Press, 1967. This work traces the idea of wilderness from an early view as a moral and physical wasteland to its present acceptance as a place to preserve. John Muir emerges as one of many significant figures in this intellectual transformation.

Smith, Herbert F. *John Muir*. New York: Twayne, 1964. Approaches Muir through his writings as literary works and places him in the context of Transcendentalist literature.

Turner, Frederick. *Rediscovering America: John Muir in His Time and Ours*. New York: Viking Press, 1985. A good, sound coverage of Muir's life in the context of his times and the development of the United States.

Williams, Dennis C. *God's Wilds: John Muir's Vision of Nature*. College Station: Texas A&M University Press, 2002. Examines Muir's views of nature, morality, and conservation, locating their source in his nineteen century Calvinist upbringing.

Wolfe, Linnie Marsh. *Son of the Wilderness: The Life of John Muir*. New York: Alfred A. Knopf, 1945. Reprint. Madison: University of Wisconsin Press, 2003. A well-written biography based on solid research that shows the many-faceted dimensions of Muir's personality.

EDWARD R. MURROW

" *To be persuasive we must be believable; to be believable we must be credible; to be credible we must be truthful.* **"**

Broadcast journalist

Murrow, the pioneer of news broadcasting, set the standard for objective reporting while warning against the potential for manipulation by electronic journalism.

Born: April 25, 1908; Greensboro, North Carolina
Died: April 27, 1965; Pawling, New York
Also known as: Egbert Roscoe Murrow (birth name); Edward Egbert Roscoe Murrow (full name)
Area of achievement: Journalism

EARLY LIFE

Egbert Roscoe Murrow (EHG-burt RAWS-koh MUHR-roh), called "Egg" by family and friends, changed his name to the more common "Edward" as a young man. When he was still a child, his family moved to the Pacific Northwest, where Murrow spent summers working in the logging camps. In high school, he was a superachiever on several levels: a successful athlete, valedictorian of his class, student body officer, and, prophetically, star of the debate team. Following his graduation, the rangy, six-foot two-inch young man returned to the logging camps. In 1926, after one year of this hard labor, he had saved sufficiently to enroll at Washington State University.

His popularity continued in college, enhanced by his dark, handsome looks—a physical appearance that would prove useful in his final career choice. In college, he majored in speech, honing his communication skills; he also added acting to his list of credits and began to cultivate the taste for elegant, expensive clothes for which he would later be known.

As the president of the student government, Murrow was a delegate to the annual convention of the National Student Federation of America (NSFA), of which he was elected president. Immediately following his graduation with a B.A. in speech, he moved to New York City to undertake his new, unpaid responsibilities. His tenure with the NSFA afforded him travel throughout Europe, where he began to establish a network of friends and acquaintances that would eventually encompass the most influential people of the time. During these early Depression years, he also traveled frequently within the United States; these experiences were to affect his developing social and political conscience. Murrow resigned from the NFSA in his second year as president (1931) to take a salaried position with the Institute of International Education.

In this position, he was assistant to Stephen Pierce Duggan, director of the institute, a reformer who believed in the betterment of humankind and in the principle of noblesse oblige. Duggan and the Eastern Establishment, to whom he introduced his young protégé, further contributed to Murrow's political development as well as adding to his list of valuable contacts.

In 1934, Murrow married Janet Brewster. He was earning five thousand dollars a year, a comfortable sum by Depression standards, when he accepted a position at Columbia Broadcasting System (CBS) Radio. Eventually, he was made European director for CBS in London. This posting marked the beginning of the CBS wartime news team and Murrow's own beginning as the major influence in broadcast journalism.

LIFE'S WORK

For an energetic, talented, and idealistic young reporter, there could have been no better vantage point from which to view the ensuing struggle than prewar London. By 1939, Murrow had established a crew that included Eric Sevareid, Bill Henry, William Shirer, and Cecil Brown, among others. Murrow charged them to report the human side of the news, not only the facts but also how the average person reacted to the facts. He also urged them to speak naturally, to be honest, and to be neutral. One of his greatest achievements was the training of this impressive group of reporters, who could communicate over the air a sense of the drama unfolding around them. For the first time, broadcast journalism eclipsed print in popularity. Without endless rewrites, copy editors, layouts, and printings, it was demonstrated that the electronic medium could accurately report the news and do so faster.

As radio's most recognizable personality, Murrow himself did not realize the extent of his influence or his huge listenership until a 1941 trip to the United States. At a banquet in his honor, the poet Archibald MacLeish, commenting on Murrow's reports on the attack on London, acknowledged his achievement.

> You burned the city of London at our doors and we knew that the dead were our dead... were mankind's dead... without rhetoric, without dramatics, without more emotion than need be... you have destroyed... the superstition that what is done beyond 3,000 miles is not done at all.

Never content to sit back and be the London bureau chief, Murrow needed to face danger, to be present to absorb the flavor of the events he reported. He stood on a rooftop

Murrow, Edward R.

Edward R. Murrow.
(Library of Congress)

and watched the bombing of London. He flew twenty-five bombing missions, refusing even the president of CBS's plea that he cease such a dangerous practice. He was in Vienna when the city was occupied by the Nazis and saw at first hand the atrocities of which they were capable. He walked among the half-dead inmates of the concentration camp at Buchenwald soon after it was liberated. His harrowing broadcast describing this experience was reprinted in the media and replayed over and over on the air.

Many years previously, Murrow had begun smoking. As early as 1942, this pleasure had become an addiction; he was smoking up to three packs of unfiltered cigarettes a day. He was already exhibiting a "weak chest" and other pulmonary problems. His restless nature, probing mind, need for experience, and inability to relax all led him to periodic exhaustion, requiring hospitalization.

On November 6, 1945, Janet Murrow, at age thirty-five, gave birth to a son, Charles Casey Murrow. With the war over, it was time for the family to return to New York. Murrow took the position of vice president and director of public affairs for CBS.

This was a difficult period of adjustment. Postwar New York was brash and wealthy, in stark contrast to war-torn London; Murrow missed his old friends and colleagues and the excitement of covering the war. After eighteen months in the position,

Murrow, Edward R.

Murrow resigned to return to broadcasting the news. He settled into a comfortable life, doing what he knew and loved best at a salary of $125,000 a year, an amount necessary for a man who enjoyed fine clothes, a good address, fast cars, and the best restaurants.

Augmenting this income were royalties from the *Hear It Now* recordings. This record was the brainchild of Fred Friendly, a colleague whose partnership would span the remainder of Murrow's broadcast career. Released in 1948, the record brought together the actual recorded speeches of such personalities as Winston Churchill, Franklin D. Roosevelt, Adolf Hitler, Huey Long, Will Rogers, and Edward VIII, with Murrow narrating. A quarter of a million copies were sold in the first year.

See It Now, the documentary program that established Murrow's reputation as a television journalist, debuted on November 18, 1951, the result of another partnership with Fred Friendly. A precursor to the present-day documentary, the program was improvised and rife with technical problems: blackouts, loss of picture, and so on. The show explored contemporary issues, from what it was like underground with coal miners in West Virginia to the experience of riding a school bus following desegregation in the South. A particularly moving segment was on Korea at Christmas. Rather than focus on military strategies, Murrow interviewed average soldiers and their reactions to the war. Before being canceled, his show won three Peabodys, four Emmys, and various other awards from *Look*, *Saturday Review*, the New York Newspaper Guild, and others.

Along with *See It Now*, Murrow's other venture into television was *Person to Person*, a program that took cameras into the homes of the rich and famous while Murrow interviewed them by remote from the studio. *Person to Person* was an enormous commercial success, widening his audience to include millions of viewers who would never have watched *See It Now*. Through *Person to Person*, Murrow became as familiar as the celebrities he interviewed, vastly increasing his credibility. The show also served to document an era, featuring interviews of such diverse subjects as Marilyn Monroe, Fred Astaire, Fidel Castro, and John F. Kennedy and his wife, Jacqueline.

In early 1953, Murrow was targeted by the House Committee on Un-American Activities. He had been too consistently critical of Joseph McCarthy; he was prominent and, through his activities in the 1930's, he was vulnerable. Murrow fought back with a segment of *See It Now* entitled "A Report on Senator Joseph R. McCarthy." His strategy was to catch McCarthy in his own contradictions by splicing together his various speeches with Murrow's voice-over narration. Murrow ended with a speech spoken directly to the camera, not read as was his normal practice.

> He [McCarthy] didn't create this situation of fear, he merely exploited it; and rather successfully. Cassius was right. "The fault, Dear Brutus, is not in our stars, but in ourselves."

By the following morning, CBS had received one thousand telegrams applauding the telecast. Murrow, returning from lunch the next day, was mobbed on Fifth Avenue. *Variety* labeled him "practically a hero." McCarthy's power was beginning to wane.

In 1961, exhausted from his years in broadcasting and disillusioned with CBS, Murrow accepted the directorship of the United States Information Agency in the Kennedy administration. His tenure ended after three years, after surgery for cancer of

Murrow, Edward R.

the lung. Awarded the Presidential Medal of Freedom in 1964, Murrow died at his farm in New York on April 27, 1965, at the age of fifty-seven.

SIGNIFICANCE

Murrow spent his life following the dictates of his conscience: struggling with the top executives at CBS, with Kennedy, with McCarthy, and even with his adoring public. With a profound commitment to fair reporting, Murrow set the standard for broadcast journalism.

He became a dedicated antifascist in the early 1930's, working with the Emergency Committee to bring out of Europe ninety-one scholars whose lives and works were endangered. These activities would figure prominently in smear tactics made against him by the House Committee on Un-American Activities. Although his head-on collision with McCarthy was considered by many to be television's "finest hour," Murrow himself agonized over its production. His objectivity and his dedication to balanced presentation were lacking. He called it a "half hour editorial."

In a career-long relationship, flawed at times with serious bitterness, CBS found the perfect vehicle in Murrow. Not only had nature bequeathed him a mellifluous baritone voice and dark good looks, but he was also a trained and skillful debater. His speaking ability, his passionate social conscience, and his dedication to providing the truth infused his broadcasting with a rare vitality. Yet Murrow was taxed by television in a way that his audiences would never guess: He was incredibly camera shy. He had been nervous on the radio, but television added the dimension of the camera. His hands trembled, the heat of the lights made him perspire and squirm; under the table, his nervous leg jumped.

Murrow's most enduring battle was with broadcasting itself, to see that it upheld its integrity. Repeatedly—to colleagues, in speeches, and in articles—he warned of the potential of broadcasting to manipulate the news and the public. At the same time, he believed that broadcasting had the potential to be "a real aid in keeping the light of Western Civilization burning." In his lifetime, he saw that light burn dangerously low.

—*Terrill Brooks*

FURTHER READING

Edwards, Bob. *Edward R. Murrow and the Birth of Broadcast Journalism*. Hoboken, N.J.: Wiley, 2004. Edwards chronicles Murrow's career, describing how his broadcasting innovations affected radio and television newscasts.

Friendly, Fred W. *Due to Circumstances Beyond Our Control*. New York: Random House, 1967. In this occupational memoir of his sixteen years at CBS, Friendly presents a critical, disturbing picture of commercial television. He also discusses *See It Now* from a production point of view.

Kendrick, Alexander. *Prime Time: The Life of Edward R. Murrow*. Boston: Little, Brown, 1969. Kendrick was one of the so-called Murrow Boys, trained in his tradition. This training gives him an insider's view in this profusely illustrated and anecdote-rich biography. Often insightful, he captures Murrow's involvement and his conscience but stops short of any criticism. Good for an overview of the sins of commercial television.

Murrow, Edward R. *In Search of Light: The Broadcasts of Edward R. Murrow, 1938-1961*. Edited by Edward Bliss, Jr. New York: Alfred A. Knopf, 1967. These selections were made from five thousand broadcasts, which spanned Hitler's seizure of Austria to Kennedy's inaugural address. Bliss, a longtime CBS staffer, has chosen broadcasts that add dimension to history or show Murrow's perspective on the development of his style.

_____. *This Is London*. New York: Simon & Schuster, 1941. Texts of his London radio broadcasts from August, 1939, to December, 1940, when he was chief of the European bureau for CBS. The broadcasts read well because Murrow was not only a good speaker but also a sensitive writer with a good grasp of the language. An excellent source for a historical perspective.

Paley, William S. *As It Happened: A Memoir*. New York: Doubleday, 1979. This autobiography by the founder and president of CBS describes the heyday of radio and television programming, including controversies with Murrow, Daniel Schorr, and the CIA. Often pretentious, he presents a one-sided view without attempting to be analytical. Important for the corporate view of broadcasting.

Seib, Philip. *Broadcasts from the Blitz: How Edward R. Murrow Helped Lead America into War*. Washington, D.C.: Potomac Books, 2006. Describes how Murrow covered events in Britain during World War II and how his reporting rallied Americans to support the British by entering the war.

Sperba, A. M. *Murrow: His Life and Times*. New York: Freudlich Books, 1968. Exhaustive biography. Almost obsessive in its documentation of each detail of Murrow's life, this well-balanced, critical presentation, penetrates the reasons for Murrow's actions and the sources of his beliefs while communicating Murrow's passion for proper news reportage. The definitive biography.

RALPH NADER

> " *A society that has more justice is a society that needs less charity.* "

Attorney, consumer advocate, and politician

As a pioneer of the American consumer movement and a third-party political candidate, Nader played a key role in the creation of dozens of regulatory agencies and watchdog groups, in the passage of landmark consumer-rights legislation, and in the controversial outcome of the U.S. presidential election of 2000.

Born: February 27, 1934; Winsted, Connecticut
Areas of achievement: Consumer rights; government and politics; environmentalism

EARLY LIFE

The son of Lebanese immigrants, Ralph Nader (NAY-dur) was introduced to politics at an early age. His father, Nathra, often engaged his customers in political discussions at the restaurant that the family owned and operated, and young Nader became attuned to the problems and concerns of ordinary citizens through these discussions. After graduating magna cum laude from Princeton University in 1955, Nader entered Harvard Law School, where he began his lengthy career as a consumer advocate by writing articles on consumer product safety for the *Harvard Law Journal*. Nader received his law degree from Harvard in 1958, and, after spending six months in the U.S. Army, he began work as an attorney in Hartford, Connecticut, in 1959.

Nader expanded upon his interest in consumer safety as an attorney and law professor in the early 1960's, exposing deficiencies in the safety of American-made automobiles. His early research into the topic led to the publication of a 1959 article in the magazine *The Nation*, "The Safe Car You Can't Buy," which revealed the development of an automobile at the Cornell Aeronautical Laboratory that had been proven to protect its occupants from serious injury in crashes occurring at speeds of up to fifty miles per hour. Nader cited this information as evidence that many deaths and serious injuries in automobile accidents were the result of poor design rather than excessive speed. He rapidly developed a reputation as an expert in automobile safety and was called to testify before state legislative committees in Massachusetts and Connecticut.

LIFE'S WORK

Nader rose to national prominence with his book *Unsafe at Any Speed: The Designed-in Dangers of the American Automobile* (1965), a study of unsafe design and manufacturing practices in the American automobile industry. The book, a seminal work of consumer activism, was instrumental in the enactment of the Traffic Safety Act of 1966, which provided for the establishment of uniform governmental safety standards for automobiles sold in the United States.

Unsafe at Any Speed was particularly critical of the Chevrolet Corvair, a popular compact sports car of the early 1960's. Nader alleged that the Corvair contained many safety flaws of which its manufacturers should have been aware. These flaws included, most notably, a suspension system that caused the car to handle poorly, making it particularly susceptible to accidents if a driver lost control of steering.

According to Nader, automobile designers often ignored or overlooked such safety issues in an effort to emphasize speed and aesthetic appeal. General Motors, the manufacturer of the Corvair, responded by launching a campaign to discredit Nader by hiring detectives to investigate his personal life and allegedly hiring prostitutes to lure him into incriminating behavior. Their efforts were unsuccessful, prompting Nader to file a lawsuit against the company. General Motors was forced to apologize publicly to Nader and, ultimately, to settle the lawsuit for a sum reportedly exceeding $400,000.

Using the proceeds of his out-of-court settlement from General Motors, Nader expanded his consumer advocacy work in 1969, assembling a team of students and volunteers to assist him in exposing consumer abuses and government corruption. By then, Nader had established himself as a leader of a nascent consumer movement, exposing unsanitary practices in the meat-packing industry, unsafe conditions in coal mines, and the potential dangers of the insecticide dichloro-diphenyl-trichloroethane, or DDT. His work inspired the passage of numerous legislative measures, such as the Wholesome Meat Act of 1967, the Natural Gas Pipeline Safety Act of 1968, and the

Federal Coal Mine Health and Safety Act of 1969. With his army of activists, who came to be known as Nader's Raiders, Nader expanded his efforts to expose corporate and governmental abuses.

At the height of their strength and influence, Nader's Raiders numbered in the hundreds, and their work was unprecedented in its breadth and zeal. As a result of their investigation of the Federal Trade Commission (FTC), the FTC was forced to reorganize. Their exposure of corruption in the Food and Drug Administration and the Interstate Commerce Commission led to similar reforms. The safety of consumer products and services from railroads to color television sets were called into question. Several government regulatory agencies, including the Environmental Protection Agency and the Consumer Product Safety Commission, owe their existence to Nader and his team, who were officially organized in 1971 into a nongovernmental organization known as Public Citizen. In 1970, Nader had created the Public Interest Research Group (PIRG), a student-run organization that encouraged college and university students to advocate for consumer causes.

The success of Public Citizen further catapulted Nader to national prominence, as his well-established reputation for austerity and incorruptibility grew. Although known as a consumer advocate, he vehemently opposed excessive material consumption both in his personal life and in the public sphere. Nader did not own an automobile, and he was said to possess only two suits, both of them gray. Simple wooden planks supported by cinder blocks served as bookshelves in his office. He rejected grants from foundations and other organized interests, preferring contributions from individual citizens. His organizations conducted their investigations with very limited budgets and very little waste. Much of his activism, however, concerned issues not related to consumerism. The dozens of nonprofit organization that Nader founded following his resignation from Public Citizen in 1980 were devoted to a variety of issues, including the rights of women, environmental conservation, and legal representation for the poor.

Although the political empowerment of citizens was a primary focus of his activism, Nader himself avoided involvement in elective politics until the early 1990's, preferring instead to effect policy changes through his various nongovernmental organizations. A movement to draft Nader onto the ballot for U.S. president in 1972 had failed. (Nader had never authorized this attempt to place his name in the race.) Although he considered organizing a third party devoted to consumer rights and governmental reform in the early 1990's, his participation in the election of 1992 was limited to a write-in candidacy in the New Hampshire primary.

In 1996 the Green Party, a minor political party in the United States but popular in Europe, whose platform emphasized environmental issues, drafted Nader as its presidential candidate and placed him on a number of state ballots. Although he received less than 1 percent of the popular vote, his campaign raised the national profile of the Green Party and called attention to his agenda of citizen empowerment and increased governmental control over multinational corporations.

Nader again ran on the Green Party ticket in the 2000 presidential election. Claiming that few differences existed between the major-party candidates for president, Nader received more than 2.8 million votes, including 97,421 votes in the state of

Nader, Ralph

Florida, far exceeding the 647-vote margin between Republican front-runner George W. Bush and Democratic candidate Al Gore. After a contentious recount, the U.S. Supreme Court certified the election results in Florida, and Bush was declared the winner of the national election. As a result, many Americans subsequently attributed the Bush victory to the candidacy of Nader.

Nader again announced his candidacy for president as an independent in 2004, despite the efforts of some Democrats to dissuade him from running. Advocating a familiar platform of governmental reform and citizen empowerment, Nader received less than half a million votes. Campaign donation records indicate that a large number of donations to the Nader campaign came from donors who gave comparable amounts to the Bush campaign. In 2007, Nader raised the possibility of launching another presidential campaign in 2008, and he continued to insist that few differences existed between the candidates of the two major American political parties.

Significance

Nader virtually single-handedly founded the American consumer movement, setting a precedent for organized activism through nongovernmental organizations and the use of investigatory journalism. His work, a reaction to the consumerism and conformity of the 1950's, is both a reflection of the spirit of activism of the 1960's and a blueprint for the proliferation of grassroots efforts to effect political and societal change during the 1960's and 1970's. The efforts of Nader and his associates to expose abuse and negligence both in the public and private sectors resulted in an increased emphasis upon safety and accountability in American business and government during the late twentieth century.

However, Nader has often been the subject of criticism from opponents as well as former associates for his alleged egotism, vindictiveness, and harsh management style. In addition, Nader has often been criticized for alleged superficial research and slanted arguments. Some detractors have suggested that his conclusions regarding safety flaws in the Corvair were biased and erroneous, although many industry insiders have supported his claims. The controversy surrounding his personal and professional conduct combined with his persistent and equally controversial quests for political office ensured that Nader would remain an influential and controversial figure well into the twenty-first century.

—*Michael H. Burchett*

Further Reading

Marcello, Patricia Cronin. *Ralph Nader: A Biography*. Westport, Conn.: Greenwood Press, 2004. One of the few extant biographies of Nader. Presents a detailed account of his life and work despite heavy reliance upon Nader and his family for source material.

Martin, Justin. *Nader: Crusader, Spoiler, Icon*. New York: Basic Books, 2003. Balanced and detailed biography of Nader that includes extensive and unprecedented interviews with friends and family.

Nader, Ralph. *In Pursuit of Justice: Collected Writings, 2000-2003*. New York: Seven Stories Press, 2004. In this collection of more than five hundred pages, Nader addresses consumer safety, corporate abuse, environmental issues, and more. Includes an index.

_____. *The Ralph Nader Reader*. New York: Seven Stories Press, 2000. This collection of Nader's writings illustrates his views of activism, consumer safety, and citizen empowerment.

_____. *The Seventeen Traditions*. New York: Harper, 2007. A personal account of the childhood influences that shaped Nader's political and social philosophy.

Carry Nation

> *God was certainly standing by me. I smashed five saloons with rocks before I ever took a hatchet.*

Social reformer

An activist in the temperance and women's rights movements, Nation gained international notoriety by smashing saloons and is remembered as the most outstanding nineteenth century icon of the temperance movement. She also demonstrated the strength and place of women in temperance reform.

Born: November 25, 1846; Garrard County, Kentucky
Died: June 9, 1911; Leavenworth, Kansas
Also known as: Carry Amelia Moore (birth name); Mother Nation
Area of achievement: Social reform

Early Life

The daughter of George Moore and Mary Campbell Moore, Carry Nation (NAY-shuhn) was born Carry Amelia Moore. (The name "Carry" was written in her illiterate father's hand in the family Bible with that spelling.) She grew up amid the slave culture of Kentucky. Her father was a prosperous planter and stock trader; her mother suffered from a delusionary mental illness and assumed she was Queen Victoria, demanding the appropriate degree of respect from those around her.

At the age of ten, Carry was converted at a Campbellite revival, an event that had a profound effect on her spiritual development. Her early secular education was limited because her family moved at least a dozen times between Kentucky, Missouri, and Texas before she was sixteen. She did manage, however, to attend a teacher's college in Missouri, where she earned a teaching certificate.

Carry's father lost his slaves and land as a result of the Civil War and took his family back to Missouri, settling in Belton. Carry met and fell in love there with a young army physician, Charles Gloyd. They were married on November 21, 1867; however, because of Gloyd's alcoholism and fierce devotion to the Masonic Lodge, the marriage deteriorated soon after the nuptials. Despite her love for Charles, she never persuaded him to stop drinking, which he did in the company of his fellow Masons, and within two years of their marriage he was dead, leaving Carry with an infant daughter,

Nation, Carry

Charlien, who may have grown up insane, an elderly mother-in-law, and an intense dislike for both alcohol and secret societies.

For several years, Carry supported herself, her daughter, and her mother-in-law by teaching in a primary school in Holden, Missouri. In 1877, she married David Nation, an attorney, minister, and editor who was nineteen years her senior. They had little in common, and for Carry it proved to be an unhappy match. They lived for several years in Texas, where Carry supported the family by running a hotel. In 1890, they moved to Medicine Lodge, Kansas, where David became a minister and then left the pulpit to practice law. His practice grew large enough to free Carry from the necessity of supporting the family, and as a result she became active in the temperance movement as well as in religious and civic reform. Because of her interest in charitable activities, the residents of Medicine Lodge called her Mother Nation. Her second marriage also deteriorated, however, and in 1901 Carry's husband divorced her.

LIFE'S WORK

Before David and Carry Nation moved to Kansas, a constitutional amendment adopted in 1880 had made it a dry state. This occurred nearly half a century before the passage of the Eighteenth Amendment and fifty years after the beginning of the temperance movement in the United States. In Kansas, a legal technicality allowed liquor in its original container to be served. Carry, believing that she had a divine mission to stop the drinking of alcoholic beverages, organized a chapter of the Woman's Christian Temperance Union (WCTU) with the intention of driving out the "wets" (those who drank).

Carry's first major confrontation took place in 1899, when, in the company of several other WCTU members, she managed through nonviolent means to shut down seven liquor distributors. During the following year, she changed her tactics when she traveled twenty miles by buggy to smash three "joints," or saloons, using rocks and brickbats, in Kiowa, Kansas. Carry rationalized that because those establishments were illegal, they had no protection under the law; therefore, she had the right to destroy them. From Kiowa she went to Wichita, where she used a hatchet to destroy the bar in the Hotel Carey. This venture resulted in several thousand dollars of property damage for the saloon owner and seven weeks in jail for Nation. From there it was on to Enterprise and then the state capital, Topeka, for several days of bar chopping. Each incident earned for her more time in the local jail, usually for disturbing the peace.

Prior to her appearance in Topeka, Nation's activities had been of the hit-and-run variety. She would typically break up a few saloons and then either leave town or go to jail. Realizing that she could not single-handedly close down all the offending liquor establishments in Kansas, she intended to use Topeka as a focal point for an organization that, she hoped, would achieve her goal.

After holding an unsuccessful meeting with the governor of Kansas, Carry Nation set about to organize her mostly feminine supporters into an army of Home Defenders. Led by General Nation, who was ably supported by assistant generals, the force numbered several hundred. Nation accepted numerous speaking engagements to spread her message that the only way to close the joints was to increase the agitation against them. In keeping with her message, she took her Home Defenders on the offensive,

Carry Nation.
(Library of Congress)

smashing the ritzy Senate Saloon. In the melee, Nation, who was often in physical danger, received a nasty cut on the head. Despite the destruction, the bar reopened within hours, selling beer, whiskey, and souvenirs from the wreckage.

Carry Nation's actions exacerbated the split in the temperance movement: on one hand, between the sexes, and on the other hand, between those who supported such violence as necessary and those who took a more passive and traditional approach to the liquor-control issue. Nation helped to focus the issue of prohibition in Kansas. Generally, the Prohibitionists, who represented the more radical fringe, supported her tactics, while the Woman's Christian Temperance Union leadership, made up mostly of Republicans or Populists, opposed them. Those who opposed Nation disliked her taking the law into her own hands, and they rejected her argument that the joint owners, being lawbreakers themselves, deserved to be put out of business violently.

Nation supported herself and paid her fines by means of lecturing, stage appearances, and the sale of souvenir miniature silver hatchets. For a time, she earned as much as $300 a week. To help with her finances, she employed a management firm, and she later hired her own manager, Harry C. Turner. However, Nation had little business sense, giving away most of her money to the poor and to temperance groups, not all of which were legitimate.

Nation also took on a few publishing ventures to spread the word. At varying times, *The Smasher's Mail*, *The Hatchet*, and *The Home Defender* appeared. While in Topeka, she wrote her autobiography, *The Use and Need of the Life of Carry A. Nation, Written by Herself* (1905).

Although she spent the majority of her time in the temperance crusade in Kansas, she did venture to the East Coast, where she visited both Yale and Harvard. However, on both occasions she allowed herself to be portrayed as a buffoon, thus adding to the negative image surrounding her. She later toured England, where again her welcome was less than expansive.

Physically, Carry Nation was a large woman. Nearly six feet tall, she weighed approximately 175 pounds and was extremely strong. When she and her minions broke up the Senate Saloon, she lifted the heavy cash register, raised it above her head, and smashed it to the ground.

After less than a decade in the public spotlight, however, her health failed, and she retired to a farm in the Ozark Mountains of Arkansas. She spent the last several months of her life in a Leavenworth, Kansas, hospital and died there on June 9, 1911. After her death, friends erected a monument at her gravesite with the inscription "She hath done what she could."

Significance

Carry Nation's impact is both real and symbolic. She did show the nation that direct action can help to focus attention on a moral issue. When, in 1901, Nation went to speak to the Kansas legislature, she told them that since she was denied the vote, she would have to use a stone, and use the stone (or hatchet, to be more specific) she did. The joints she smashed were not significant in terms of her impact on temperance and prohibition. In fact, at least a few of them reopened within hours or days of her visit. Her impact had to do with her ability to rally support to her cause. She focused attention on the issue of alcohol consumption. Representing the views of a majority of Kansans, she showed them that one individual could make a difference.

Nation also had a significant impact on women's rights. She certainly broke with the traditional roles of woman as wife and mother, although she did fulfill both roles. At a time when few women engaged in public protest, Nation was at the cutting edge of that activity. She opened a home in Kansas City for women who had suffered at the hands of male alcoholics. She determined that her activity had been made necessary by a male-dominated world—as a woman, she did not have access to political power. As time went on, however, Nation appeared to be moving toward nonviolent direct action and away from saloon smashing. The masthead of her newspaper *The Hatchet* (1905) encouraged women to seek the vote instead of resorting to the hatchet.

Carry Nation has been badly treated by most of her biographers. In part, she was responsible for her own bad reputation. In her autobiography, she perhaps revealed too much of her personal and religious life, thus exposing herself to criticism. She played into the hands of her critics when she made outrageous statements or visited college campuses where she should have expected to be placed in a bad light. Her methods appeared unfeminine in a decade when feminine virtue was extolled. She also became the victim of the eastern press, which delighted in poking fun at the crude ways of westerners by mocking Nation as a social misfit and a religious freak.

Carry Nation died almost a decade before the passage of the Eighteenth Amendment, which outlawed the manufacture, distribution, sale, and consumption of alcoholic beverages. Whether people remembered her in 1919 is not of great importance; the amendment passed in part at least because she focused the attention of many Americans on the issue of prohibition. Whether one was for or against temperance, it would have been difficult in the first decade of the twentieth century to ignore the issue, especially when Carry Nation went storming into bars with hatchet in hand. She also died a decade before the passage of the Nineteenth Amendment, which granted women the right to vote. Her statements to the Kansas legislature, as well as her newspaper's masthead, indicates that Carry Nation well knew the power of the ballot and the importance of working for the right of women to vote.

—*Duncan R. Jamieson*

FURTHER READING

Asbury, Herbert. *Carry Nation*. New York: Alfred A. Knopf, 1929. This older biography paints Nation as a social misfit.

Bader, Robert Smith. *Prohibition in Kansas*. Lawrence: University Press of Kansas, 1986. This general history of prohibition in Kansas contains a positive chapter on Carry Nation and her contribution to the temperance movement.

Flexner, Eleanor. *Century of Struggle: The Woman's Rights Movement in the United States*. Rev. ed. Cambridge, Mass.: Belknap Press of Harvard University Press, 1975. Provides an excellent starting point for anyone interested in the women's rights movement.

Grace, Fran. *Carry A. Nation: Retelling the Life*. Bloomington: Indiana University Press, 2001. Grace contradicts earlier biographers who portrayed Nation as crazy, fanatical, and either over- or undersexed. She presents a more complicated portrait of Nation, tracing the roots of her religious piety and social activism and describing how contemporaries admired Nation's riveting speeches and political courage.

Gusfield, Joseph. *Symbolic Crusade: Status Politics and the American Temperance Movement*. Urbana: University of Illinois Press, 1963. An interesting and useful history of the temperance movement from its nineteenth century roots to the passage of the Eighteenth Amendment.

Mattingly, Carol. *Well-tempered Women: Nineteenth Century Temperance Rhetoric*. Carbondale: Southern Illinois University Press, 1998. Recounts the techniques and rhetoric women used to create the Woman's Christian Temperance Union and campaign for prohibition.

Nation, Carry. *The Use and Need of the Life of Carry A. Nation, Written by Herself*. Topeka, Kans.: F. M. Steves & Sons, 1905. Nation's autobiography sets the negative tone for her biographers.

Schwarz, Frederic D. "1900." *American Heritage* 51, no. 3 (May/June, 2000): 107. Describes Nation's campaign to close bars in Kiowa, Kansas that served liquor to customers in 1900.

MARTINA NAVRATILOVA

❝ *Disability is a matter of perception. If you can do just one thing well, you're needed by someone.* **❞**

Tennis player

As a leading figure in women's tennis from the mid-1970's into the twenty-first century, Navratilova was instrumental in demonstrating the professionalism of women's sports and proving that women athletes deserved comparable financial rewards. She followed Billie Jean King in coming out as lesbian at a time when being an openly lesbian or gay athlete was considered impossible.

Born: October 18, 1956; Prague, Czechoslovakia (now in Czech Republic)
Also known as: Martina Subertova (birth name)
Area of achievement: Sports

EARLY LIFE

Martina Navratilova (mahr-TEE-nah nah-vrah-tih-LOH-vah) was born in Prague, Czechoslovakia (now in Czech Republic). Her parents divorced when she was three years old, and her mother then married Mirek Navratil. Navratilova lived a robust outdoor life in the Krknoše Mountains until the age of five, when her family moved to Revnice near the capital city of Prague. She started skiing before she was three years old and within a couple of years became an excellent skier. She preferred playing rough games such as soccer with boys rather than playing with girls. From earliest childhood she exhibited exceptional strength and athletic ability. Her mother and stepfather were concerned about her "unfeminine" behavior but were impressed by her physical gifts; they believed she would become a champion if she could find the right sport on which to focus her energies.

In the densely populated urban environment near Prague, Navratilova found that opportunities for vigorous physical activity were limited. Nevertheless, the city offered ample facilities for playing tennis. Her whole family played the game. Her maternal grandmother, Agnes Semanska, had been a national champion before World War II. Both of Navratilova's parents competed in amateur tournaments and served as tennis administrators for the Czech government. They were on the courts practically every day and brought Navratilova with them. Her stepfather cut down an old racket for Navratilova to use, and he became her first tennis instructor. She immediately became enthusiastic about tennis and was competing in junior tournaments by the age of eight. Soon she was beating players five and six years older than herself. All the while she had to attend school full-time and watch over her younger sister.

By age sixteen, Navratilova had won three national women's championships with her aggressive play. She was ecstatic when selected by the Czechoslovakian Tennis Association to tour the United States in 1973 with a team of the best men and women players. She was enchanted by the freedom she found in the United States, which was so different from the repressed spirit of her Communist-dominated homeland. Fascinated by American music, fashions, and food, she returned home twenty pounds heavier. Her first trip to the United States made an impression that changed her life. She realized that many of the negative things she had heard about the United States were merely Communist propaganda.

Navratilova became pregnant when she was seventeen and had an abortion. She later said that she regretted the whole affair because she had not truly been in love. She eventually acknowledged that she felt a strong sexual attraction to women. Indeed, after she gained U.S. citizenship, she became candid about her sexuality, which would have been impossible to acknowledge in ultraconservative Czechoslovakia.

While still a teenager, Navratilova asked the U.S. government for political asylum and applied for citizenship. For years she lived in fear of being kidnapped by her government's secret police because she was creating negative publicity for the whole Communist system. In defecting to the United States, Navratilova knew she was cutting herself off from home and family, because she would not be allowed to visit her homeland after becoming an American citizen. She bravely faced the future in a strange new land with a limited knowledge of the English language.

Navratilova has been universally called Martina. In her autobiography *Martina* (1985), she explains her preference for being called by her first name because Americans, including sports announcers, have so much trouble pronouncing her surname. She wrote that her last name should be pronounced with emphasis on the second and last syllables.

Life's Work

Once Navratilova discovered tennis, she devoted her life to it with the intensity that was her outstanding characteristic. Women's tennis had been a game of finesse until Navratilova burst on the scene. She turned it into a game of speed and power—one that was less "ladylike" than it had been in the past but far more interesting to spectators. Navratilova brought to professional tennis a cannonball serve that was clocked at a higher speed than the serves of some of the better professional male players. She was left-handed, which is considered an asset in tennis, and was noted for her powerful forehand as well as her aggressive charges to the net.

Navratilova's rivalry with Chris Evert became legendary. For years, the two battled for first place at the world's most important tournaments: the Australian Open, the U.S. Open, the French Open, and Wimbledon in England. Navratilova won so many titles on the grass courts of the historic All English Lawn Tennis and Croquet Club (Wimbledon) that people said she owned the tournament there. Despite their rivalry, Evert and Navratilova became good friends and often played as partners in doubles matches. Navratilova's record at doubles became almost as impressive as her singles record.

Navratilova was not a popular player when she entered professional tennis. Because she possessed a steely determination and demeanor unmatched since Helen Wills Moody was champion, spectators thought of Navratilova as an iceberg. Her limited knowledge of English made it difficult for her to communicate with the press, and she had a subtle sense of humor that did not translate easily into English. Because of her size and strength, she gave the impression that she beat other women players simply by overpowering them. This was not true, although she could hardly be blamed for making the most of her physical assets. At five feet eight inches tall and about 145 pounds, she was tall enough to serve and volley well yet small enough not to strain her joints excessively. This matter of strain was crucial, because an extremely high level of conditioning powered her performance.

Navratilova quickly became wealthy from prize money and endorsements. She brought her parents to the United States and gave them a beautiful house near her own home in Texas. She continued to pursue an active professional schedule into the 1990's, one that included travel, public appearances, and all sorts of athletic activities. Navratilova also began exploring other interests, and she signed a contract with a New York publisher to write mystery novels; she co-wrote three during the 1990's. Her leisure time remained intensely active, as she enjoyed ice hockey, mountain biking, scuba diving, skiing, snow boarding, basketball, golf, and horseback riding. She also earned a pilot's license and took up photography, shooting in Africa and exhibiting her work in Prague.

Navratilova established an example for women who are not considered feminine in the conventional sense. She proved that there are as many different types of women as there are different types of men and that each woman has the option to develop to her fullest potential.

In the midpoint of her professional tennis career, Navratilova had become one of the most popular personalities in the game. She was the number-one-ranked female player in the world for seven years, and in 1984 she secured a record for the longest consecutive string of match wins (seventy-four). It was a tearful crowd that saw her play her tennis matches at Wimbledon in 1993. She made it to the semifinals but had to bow to talented younger players, such as Monica Seles and Steffi Graf, who were only half her age and had learned to play her aggressive style of tennis. In 2003, however, she tied Billie Jean King's record of twenty Wimbledon titles when she won the mixed doubles crown with Leander Paes. The same year she captured the only Grand Slam victory that had escaped her: She won the mixed doubles title and was the oldest player ever to win a Grand Slam competition.

Success had made Navratilova feel more relaxed and amiable, while at the same time the public had come to understand that her impassive exterior concealed a sensitive temperament. Like Jimmy Connors and John McEnroe, two of the greatest male tennis players of all time, she was disliked at the beginning of her career but came to be adored for courage and her dedication to excellence.

As an international superstar, Navratilova's personal life has been a subject of great media interest. She soon realized that it was impossible to conceal her sexuality or her intimate relationships with women. One of the biggest news stories had to do with the so-called palimony suit involving Judy Nelson, who sued Navratilova for half of the money Navratilova earned during the years they had lived together. The suit was finally settled out of court, with Nelson receiving a house in Aspen, Colorado, and an undisclosed amount of cash. Navratilova later brought suit to oppose antilesbian and antigay legislation in Colorado, spoke out against scientific research trying to show that homosexuality can be treated as a disease, and donated money in support of the search for a cure for acquired immunodeficiency syndrome (AIDS).

In 1994, shortly before Navratilova announced her retirement from professional

Navratilova, Martina

tennis, she had won her 167th singles title by defeating Julie Halard of France in the Paris Women's Open (with a prize of $400,000). This set an all-time record for career singles championships for women as well as men. Navratilova had also earned more money in prizes than any other male or female tennis player in history. In addition to more than $21.4 million in prize money, she had received a huge amount of funds for sponsoring various products. This was a fantastic achievement, considering that when she entered professional tennis the lion's share of the big prizes as well as the lucrative advertising fees went to men.

In 2004, Navratilova returned to singles play for two years. By the time she retired completely in 2006 she had won 1,442 games and lost 219. This record includes 167 singles titles and 177 doubles titles, of which 18 of the singles and 41 of the doubles were Grand Slam titles. Her last Grand Slam title came in 2006 when she took the mixed doubles title at the U.S. Open with Bob Bryan.

Navratilova was placed nineteenth on the list of the 100 Greatest Athletes of the Century by sports television network ESPN and second among the 40 Greatest Players of the Tennis Era listed by *Tennis* magazine. In 2000 she was inducted into the International Tennis Hall of Fame. Still, the greatest testimony to her athletic prowess came from the many fellow professionals who consider her abilities unmatched. King stated it simply when she said that Navratilova was "the greatest singles, doubles, and mixed doubles player who's ever lived."

Significance

Navratilova contributed greatly to women's tennis and to women's sports in general by demonstrating that women could compete just as fiercely as men and could play with as high a degree of technical excellence. Many sportswriters suggested that she was sufficiently strong and aggressive to compete with the best male players. Shrugging off such speculations, she helped to popularize women's tennis as a spectator sport, thereby attracting larger crowds as well as broader television coverage.

Navratilova also had a tremendous impact in the area of lesbian and gay rights because she was one of the few public figures who was out as lesbian or gay and who was politically active. She called for greater public understanding and tolerance. Her charities have included the Rainbow Endowment, which supports lesbian and gay causes and research on AIDS; the Laureus World Sports Academy; the Sierra Club; Save the Rhino, a retirement home for horses; and People for the Ethical Treatment of Animals. Her efforts on behalf of gay and lesbian rights and for children brought her the 2000 National Equality Award from the Human Rights Campaign.

The publicity generated by Navratilova on and off the tennis court increased as well the use of professional women athletes as product endorsers (and increased their salaries), but she also led the charge for professional women athletes to be compensated at the same level as men in their respective sports.

—Bill Delaney

Further Reading

Blue, Adrianne. *Martina: The Lives and Times of Martina Navratilova.* New York: Crown, 1995. This biography covers Navratilova's life until her first retirement, focusing on the obstacles she faced in becoming a professional tennis player and living as an out lesbian. Blue argues that no other sports champion was so involved with the sexual politics of the times. Includes photographs.

Faulkner, Sandra, with Judy Nelson. *Love Match: Nelson Versus Navratilova*. New York: Carol, 1993. A full-length book about the notorious palimony suit brought against Navratilova by her former partner, Judy Nelson. Brings out much information about Navratilova's character away from public view.

Henry, William A., III. "The Lioness in Winter." *Time*, November 30, 1992. A brief retrospective article on Navratilova's career and her feelings about professional sports, lesbian and gay rights, and life in general as she was approaching the end of her illustrious tennis career.

Howard, Johnette. *The Rivals: Chris Evert Versus Martina Navratilova: Their Epic Duels and Extraordinary Friendship*. New York: Broadway Books, 2005. The eighty tennis matches between Navratilova and rival Evert were among the most popular sports spectacles of tennis's golden age, but, despite their fierce competition, the two remained friends. Howard discusses their intertwined careers and their combined effect on tennis. Includes photographs.

Kort, Michele. "Ms. Conversation." *Ms.*, February, 1988. An interesting interview with both Navratilova and another great tennis player, Billie Jean King, who discuss their views on women's tennis, their personal lives, and other subjects.

Navratilova, Martina. *Shape Your Self: My Six-Step Diet and Fitness Plan to Achieve the Best Shape of Your Life*. Emmaus, Pa.: Rodale Books, 2006. Navratilova relates personal stories to illustrate her program that small changes in habits (such as eating natural foods), fun exercise, and greater mental focus lead to health and fitness. Affords a glimpse into how she prepared herself during her career.

Navratilova, Martina, with George Vecsey. *Martina*. New York: Alfred A. Knopf, 1985. A frank and revealing autobiography in which Navratilova describes her unhappy childhood and conflicts about her sexuality. Displays her sympathetic and human personality in dramatic contrast to the cold, aggressive image she projected on the tennis courts.

Vecsey, George. "Martina's Last Bow? 1993 Wimbledon." *Tennis*, July, 1993. Discusses Navratilova's anticipated appearance in the 1993 Wimbledon tennis tournament and the unsurpassed record she established at this prestigious event, beginning in 1974. Paints a word picture of the historical Wimbledon as well. Includes photographs.

LRC - Batavia HS
Batavia, IL 60510